DUQUESNE STUDIES

Philological Series

2

A Critical Edition of John Lydgate's

LIFE OF OUR LADY

The whiche childe spake to hem anoon
Above the hill wittie wyse and there benyng
And had hem hyȝe that they shulde gone
Into Juda right as any lyne
And folowe all waye the sterre for a sygne
That stille bryng to that kyngdom
Where at the knyȝt most worthy of renoun

Was born that tyme to have the regals
Of Jewes lande of sterren hwo rightt
Whom the sterre dyd specifie
When he was born to his clere light
And ther anoon whan passed was the nyghtt
The next morne no lenger lust abyde
But toward hym cast hem for to ryde

With mete away and full apperayle
As was pytyng to her worthynesse
They shove hem putte and for they nolde fayle
To done honor unto his nobleness
With hem they toke golde and moch ricchesse
To spende and yeve and also for they ment
With yeftes grete the childe to present

And furthe they gone no lenger wolde they tarye
Thorugh many a lande and many dyvers yle
Ryche of hem on a dromondarye
Whiche weren so swyfte that full many a myle
They passed hem not in a shortt while
That in the space of dayes but nyne
By condit only of the sterre shene

They entrede hem into Therutm
That of Juda was the chiefe cyte
Conveyed euer by the bryght beme
Of this sterre that was so fayre to see
And whan that they amydde the cyte be
Not astonyed, aspede in audience
Where is the kyng greatest of reverence

How the kyng came to
Therutm and asked
wher cristo war
borne ffo · ·xij· ·A·

DUQUESNE STUDIES
Philological Series
2

A Critical Edition of
John Lydgate's
LIFE OF OUR LADY

by

JOSEPH A. LAURITIS, C.S.SP., PH.D.,
general editor

RALPH A. KLINEFELTER, PH.D.
VERNON F. GALLAGHER, C.S.SP., PH.D.

Frontispiece: facsimile of Durham University ms. Cosin V. ii. 16, folio 75b.

DUQUESNE UNIVERSITY, Pittsburgh, Pa.
EDITIONS E. NAUWELAERTS, LOUVAIN
1961

DUQUESNE STUDIES

Philological Series

Volume One—John Milton: A Bibliographical Supplement 1929-1957, by Calvin Huckabay, Ph.D., xi and 211 pages. Price: $6.25 bound.

Volume Two—A Critical Edition of John Lydgate's Life of Our Lady, by Joseph A. Lauritis, C.S.Sp., Ph.D., Ralph A. Klinefelter, Ph.D., and Vernon F. Gallagher, C.S.Sp., Ph.D., ix and 742 pages. Price $12.50 bound.

At present, Duquesne Studies comprises three series:

Philosophical Series. Eleven volumes published thus far.

Spiritan Series. Three volumes to date.

Philological Series. Two volumes published to date.

Catalog will be sent upon request. Twenty percent discount on standing or continuation orders for each series.

Library of Congress Catalog Card Number: 60-11950

PREFACE

As long ago as 1866, Georg Fiedler announced that he was editing Lydgate's *Life of Our Lady* for the Early English Text Society.[1] Though the announcement appeared repeatedly in the list of works in preparation for the Early English Text Society, the edition was never prepared.

Professor Albert C. Baugh proposed this work to the editors in 1949 and guided them through separate dissertations at the University of Pennsylvania in 1951, 1952 and 1958. We owe to him whatever scholarly merit it possesses. The general editor of this edition has in preparation for separate publication, studies of the language, further observations on the style and metre, and contemporary analogues to themes in the poem.

The editors wish to thank Miss Eleanor McCann and her staff at Duquesne University Library, whose gracious and unstinting efforts were both beneficial and inspiring. Dr. Henry N. MacCracken, formerly President of Vassar College, gave us many helpful suggestions, besides presenting us with his own Lydgate photostats and notes. The Most Reverend Geoffrey Francis Fisher, His Grace, the Lord Archbishop of Canterbury, and The Most Honorable Henry Frederick Thynne, the Marquis of Bath, were kind enough to allow us to have microfilms made of manuscripts in their private libraries.

It is a pleasure to record indebtedness to many libraries and librarians, especially to Mr. C. Seymour Thompson, Mr. Walter W. Wright, and the staff of the Library of the University of Pennsylvania; to Mr. R. W. Hunt, Keeper of Western MSS., Bodleian Library, Oxford; to Mr. C. H. Minns and Mr. R. C. Davis, of the British Museum; to Mr. David Ramage, University Library, Durham; to Doctor W. R. Cunningham, University of Glasgow; to Mr. Frederick R. Goff, Library of Congress.

For their kindness in allowing us to have microfilms made of manuscripts in their keeping, we are grateful also to the librarians of Jesus College, Oxford; Corpus Christi College, Oxford; Trinity College, Cambridge; Gonville and Caius College, Cambridge; Corpus Christi College, Cambridge; University Library, Cambridge; University of Edinburgh; St. John's College, Oxford; Trinity College, Dublin; the Chetham Library, Manchester; the Society of Antiquaries, London; the University of Chicago; and the Henry E. Huntington Library, San Marino, California. Our thanks also are due to Messrs. C. A. Stonehill, Bernard Quaritch, Paul Langeard, Professors George B. Parks, Rossell Hope Robbins and Father H. E. G. Rope, who aided in tracing the present whereabouts of the manuscripts.

---

[1] See *Anglia*, XV (1893), 395, where Prof. Fiedler reaffirmed his intention.

TABLE OF CONTENTS

———

1. INTRODUCTION

PRELIMINARY REMARKS

If we may judge by the number of extant manuscripts, the *Life of Our Lady*[1] enjoyed great popularity during the fifteenth century. There are in all forty-two extant manuscripts; thirty-seven are complete or nearly so, and five are fragments.[2] Caxton printed the poem in 1484,[3] and probably in a second edition.[4] Robert Redman reprinted the Caxton text in 1531. More recently in 1872, Charles E. Tame published the first twenty-three chapters of the *Life of Our Lady,* collated from the manuscripts in the British Museum, as Volume II of the *Early English Religious Literature* series.[5] Books IV, V, and VI of the *Life of Our Lady,* the verses relating to the Circumcision, the Epiphany, and the Purification, were included in a volume, *The Visions of Tundale,* published in 1843.[6] The Magnificat (*Life of Our Lady,* II, 981-1060) is included in two publications of the Bannatyne Manuscript.[7]

---

[1]In all probability Caxton gave the title *Lyf of Our Lady* to Lydgate's poem when he added the colophon, "Here endeth the book of the lyf of our lady made by dan John Lydgate monke of bury at thynstannce of the moste crysten kynge kyng Harry the fyfth" to the 1484 imprinting. Manuscripts give the title as the "Byrthe" or the "Natiuitye" of the Mother of God.

[2]Only the *Fall of Princes* with thirty-one complete MSS and twenty-four extracts, surpasses the *Life of Our Lady. The Siege of Thebes* survives in twenty-seven MSS; the *Troy Book* in twenty-one; the *Temple of Glas* in nine.

[3]The imprint carries no date, but most Caxton scholars agree on a 1484 dating.

[4]This is a subject of much discussion. There are extant four fragments of the Caxton print consisting of four leaves each (leaves 2, 3, 6, and 7 of quire a). E. Gordon Duff, *Fifteenth Century English Books* (Oxford, 1917), p. 75; Eustace F. Bosanquet, *Library,* XVII (1937), 362-363; and Seymour de Ricci, *A Census of Caxtons* (Oxford, 1909), pp. 76-78, agree that the fragments are cancelled sheets or waste copy. Curt F. Bühler, *Library,* Series 4, XVII (1937), 155-156, and *Library,* Series 4, XX (1940), 266-271, thinks the fragments represent leaves from a missing Caxton edition because of differences in spellings in these leaves and in the original 1484 print.

[5]There is no data on the book, but Georg Fiedler, *Anglia,* XV (1893), 394, notes that he had a copy, a gift from Tame's father-confessor, with a publisher's note and a date of Nov. 15/72. The book is very scarce since most of the copies were burned in a fire at the publisher, R. Washbourne, London.

[6]W. B. Turnbull, *The Visions of Tundale* (Edinburgh, 1843). This is a printing of the MS Advocates 19. 3. 1. (Adv[2]).

[7]See *The Bannatyne Manuscript,* Hunterian Club (3v, Glasgow, 1873), "Song of the Virgin Mary", I. 64-67. See also *The Bannatyne Manuscript,* ed. by N. Tod Ritchie (Edinburgh and London, 1928), pp. 60-63. The Bannatyne Manuscript is now MS Advocates 1. 1. 6. (Adv[1]).

There has never been doubt as to Lydgate's authorship of the poem. The *Life of Our Lady* is listed as one of Lydgate's works by Stephen Hawes in *The Pastime of Pleasure, lines* 1338-43:

"And after hym [Chaucer] my mayster Lydgate
The monke of Bury dyde hym well apply
Bothe to contryve and eke to translate
And of vertue ever in especyally
For he dyde compyle than full nyally   (almost)
Of our blyssed lady the conversacyon"[8]

Eugen Burkart claims that "conversacyon" in line 1343 is a mistake for "commendation" and implies that Hawes refers to Lydgate's "Ballade in commendation of our Ladye."[9] Burkart seems to disregard the fact that "conversacyon" here has its common meaning of mode or course of life, the action of living or having one's being in a place or among persons.[10]

Bale (1548) records: "Joannes Lydgate, monachus Buriensis, scripsit . . . De vita S. Marie, ad regem Henricum quintum. li. 1. 'Dolorosum cor merore consopitum.' "[11] Again, "Joannes Lydgate, monachus, Buriensis, poeta scripsit . . . Vitam dive Marie, li. 1, 'Dolorosum cor discrimine tactum.' "[12]

In Speght's edition of Chaucer, 1598, are listed: "31. Magnificat (Life of Our Lady, c. XXII) . . . 34. Life of Our Lady."[13] This is a listing of MS B. M. Additional 29729, and MS Trinity College, Cambridge R. 3. 21.

Pits (1619) merely repeats Bale's entries.[14] Tanner (1748) lists the *Life of Our Lady* among Lydgate's work.[15] Ritson (1802) includes: "The lyf of our lady: printed by W. Caxton, without date, and by R. Redman, 1531, 4to" as numbers 5 and 187 in his list of Lydgate's works.[16]

---

[8]*The Pastime of Pleasure,* ed. W. E. Mead (*EETSES,* 173), p. 55.

[9]*The Pastime of Pleasure* (London, 1899), p. 24. This error is repeated by Mead, *op. cit.,* p. 231.

[10]*NED, s. v.* conversation, II, 1-2.

[11]John Bale, *Index Britanniae Scriptorum* (Oxford, 1902), p. 229.

[12]*Ibid.,* p. 230.

[13]Thomas Speght, *The Workes of Our Antient and Learned English Poet, Geffrey Chaucer, newly Printed* (London, 1598), f. 394.

[14]John Pits, *Relationum Historicarum de Rebus Anglicis* (Paris, 1619), I, 632-634.

[15]Thomas Tanner, *Bibliotheca Britannico-Hibernica* (London, 1748), pp. 489-490.

[16]Joseph Ritson, *Bibliographia Poetica* (London, 1802), p. 67.

Warton[17] praises Lydgate's style in the *Life of Our Lady,* quoting copiously from the text and comparing Lydgate to Cicero, Petrarch, and Chaucer.[18]   Warton concludes:

> We are surprised to find verses of so modern a cast at such an early period; which in this sagacious age we should judge to be a forgery, was not their genuineness authenticated, and their antiquity confirmed by the venerable types of Caxton and a multitude of unquestionable manuscripts.[19]

---

[17]Thomas Warton, *The History of English Poetry* (London, 1871), III, 58-60.

[18]*Ibid.,* III, 58.

[19]*Ibid.,* III, 59.

THE DATE

The date of the *Life of Our Lady* is an unsettled question. Professor Schick, in his excellent account of Lydgate's life and the chronology of his work, gives 1409-11 as the date.

> I have little doubt that this was the last important work of Lydgate's first period, before he began the translation of the *Troy Book* in 1412. For we know that it was undertaken at the command of Henry V. Now we have seen that Lydgate, from 1412-1422 was occupied with *Troy Book* and *Story of Thebes*. Therefore, it seems most natural that the *Life of Our Lady* should have been written before these works. Moreover, we have an astronomical datum in the work. On folio 4b,[1] we hear that our monk made a certain prayer when "Lucina was passed late from Phebus" and the statement seems to refer to the first of January. There was a new moon, in 1410, on the 26th of December, which agrees very well with that statement. I should think that the *Life of Our Lady* was written about 1409-11. The poem, with its comparative freshness—at least in some parts—still belongs to Lydgate's better works.[2]

On the other hand, Sidney Lee records, without evidence or documentation, that Lydgate secured an introduction to Henry IV's court and "at the request of the Prince of Wales he began his *Troy Book* or *Destruction of Troy*. When it was completed in 1420, Lydgate presented it to the prince, then Henry V, who showed his appreciation by inviting him to undertake a *Life of Our Lady*."[3]

This same order of Henry's commissions to Lydgate is cited by G. M. Towle. He notes that Henry first commissioned Lydgate to translate the *Destruction of Troy* out of his love for "books of chivalric histories and those traditions which preserved tales of knightly prowess and the memorable battles of the Crusades."[4] In like manner

---

[1]"Whan Ianus Byfrons in colde Ianuarie
With frosty berde entreth in the yere
And phebus chare neyeth to aquarye
His watry beameʒ to fore feverer
Whan that his light was pale and no thyng clere
And from hym late was partyd lucyne
The same nyght as I sawe her shyne
Ournede newe *with* beameʒ glad and merye
On the heven and caste his stremes adovne
I gan Remembre of the high ferye
That callede is the Circumcisyon" (Book IV, 1-11)
[2]J. Schick, *Temple of Glas* (1891; *EETSES*, 60), p. cviii.
[3]*DNB*, XII, 307.
[4]*The History of Henry the Fifth* (New York, 1866), p. 232.

J. Endell Tyler comments: "He [Henry] was so much enamoured of the 'Tale of Troy divine' that he directed John Lydgate, Monk of Bury St. Edmund's, to translate two poems, 'The Death of Hector' and 'The Fall of Troy' into English verse, that his own countrymen might not be behind the rest of Europe in their knowledge of the works of antiquity."[5]

This is merely a paraphrase and amplification of Lydgate's lines in the Prologue to the *Troy Book*:

> "Whiche [Henry] hath desire, sothly for to seyn,
> Of verray knighthood to remembre ageyn
> The worthynes, ʒif I schal not lye
> And the prowesse of olde chivalrie,
> By-cause he hath joye and gret deynte
> To rede in bokys of antiquite
> To fyn only, vertu for to swe
> Be example of hem, and also for to eschewe
> The cursyd vice of slouth and ydelnesse." (lines 75-83)[6]

Lydgate adds that Prince Henry commanded him to write the *Troy Book*,

> "By-cause he wolde that to hyʒe and lowe
> The noble story openly wer knowe
> In our tonge, aboute in every age,
> And y-writen as wel in oure langage
> As in latyn and in frensche it is" (Prologue, 111-115)[7]

Henry N. MacCracken comments:

> It is probably safest to date the *Life of Our Lady* within the reign of Henry V, because the rubric of every manuscript that I have seen,[8] as well as Caxton's print, states that the poem was written 'at the stiring and excitacion of King Henry the Vte' and there is nothing in the character of the King's attitude toward religion to make against the assertion. There is no evidence whatever aside from the rubrics.[9]

In attempting to establish a date for the *Life of Our Lady* I would like to point out that Jean Galopes, dean of the collegiate church of St.

---

[5]*Henry of Monmouth* (2v, London, 1838), I, 328.
[6]Henry Bergen, *Lydgate's Troy Book* (1906-35; *EETSES*, 97, 103, 106, 126), I, 3.
[7]*Ibid.*, I, 4.
[8]This is true of only MSS B⁴, C⁵, H³, H⁴, H⁶, Ad², D, L, Ash¹, Ash², and Lg. The other MSS omit this introductory rubric and its accompanying list of chapter headings, or have lost this portion of the poem.
[9]*Studies in the Life and Writings of John Lydgate, the Monk of Bury* (Harvard diss., 1907), p. 52.

Louis of Salsoye, in Normandy, translated the pseudo-Bonaventure *Meditationes Vitae Christi*[10] from Latin into French and presented his work to Henry V while the latter was in France.[11] There is a prologue to the book in which Galopes names Henry, "a tres hault, tres fort, et tres victorieux prince Henri quint de ce nom, par la grace de dieu roy d'Angleterre heretier et regent de France et duc d'Irlande."[12] A picture in the front of the book shows Henry seated on a throne, with two ecclesiastics at his right hand and Thomas Beaufort, Duke of Exeter, also mentioned in the prologue of the work, on his left. Before the king, in a kind of doctor's robe of light purple, kneels Jean Galopes, the translator, offering his book covered with crimson velvet.[13] On the first page of this book some letters seem to have been erased, which might have been the king's name, for underneath is the following usual prayer for his soul: "diu par sa grace ait mercy de son ame. Amen." At the end of the book in a round hand of the time of Henry VIII or Elizabeth, is written this entry: "This wasse sumtyme Kinge Henri the fifeth his booke."

The popularity of the pseudo-Bonaventure *Meditationes Vitae Christi* and its relationship to Lydgate's *Life of Our Lady* will be discussed at length in the section dealing with sources.[14] The first part of the *Meditationes,* those meditations devoted to Monday, relates the life of the Virgin Mary from her birth to the Purification, the exact extent of Lydgate's *Life of Our Lady*. Margaret Deanesley points out that this was a popular tradition in medieval lives of Mary.[15]

Naming Henry "heretier et regent de France" dates the book as after the Treaty of Troyes in May, 1420. At this time these two

[10]The *Meditationes Vitae Christi* was one of the most widespread Gospel Harmonies in the Middle Ages. It was popular over the whole of Europe and was rendered into the vernacular of most continental countries. The authorship of the *Meditationes* is a matter of controversy. Scholars have proposed Bonaventure of Padua, Joannes de Caulibus of Santo Geminiano and an unknown Friar Minor. For the latest discussion of the matter and a bibliography see Sister M. Immaculate, "The Four Daughters of God in the Gesta Romanorum and the Court of Sapience", *PMLA,* LVII (1942), 963n.

[11]See Margaret Deanesley, "The Gospel Harmony of John de Caulibus," *Collectanea Franciscana,* X (1922), 11.

[12]Corpus Christi College, Cambridge MS 213.

[13]For a description of the picture see the Rev. Mr. Tyson, *Archaelogia,* II, 194.

[14]Cf. page 91 for Lydgate's references to the *Meditationes.* In this same light, Nicholas Love's translation of the *Meditationes* in 1410 was presented to Archbishop Arundel as a weapon against Lollardry.

[15]"The Gospel Harmony of John de Caulibus," *Collectanea Franciscana,* X (1922), 17.

titles were bestowed on Henry, while Charles VI retained the title
of King of France. Henry was at Troyes, May 21-26, 1420. He
remained in France until January, 1421. At that time he returned
to England, where he spent six months touring the country, introducing his new queen, Katherine.[16]

Lydgate finished the Troy Book in the middle of December,
1420.[17] No doubt he presented the finished work to Henry at the
time of this triumphal tour.[18] I suggest that gratitude to the Virgin
Mary for the success of his campaign in France and the recent
presentation by Jean Galopes of the *Meditationes Vitae Christi*
inspired Henry to commission Lydgate to write the *Life of Our
Lady*,[19] and that Lydgate fulfilled this commission some time during
1421 and 1422.

Certainly if we may judge Henry's character, 1421-22 seems
a more likely date for his thinking along religious lines than does
1409-11. Historians of his own time record that Henry's conduct as
prince was marked by levity and that a sharp change took place on
his accession to the throne. So great was this change in Henry's
character that some people doubted that he was the same man they
had known as prince.[20]

Henry's devotion to the Mother of God[21] is noted especially in
his will made prior to leaving England for France in 1415.[22] In the
will Henry hoped that he would be received into Abraham's bosom,
not through any merit of his own, but "through the prayers of Mary,
the High Mother of God"; he directed that he be buried at West-
minster, and that an altar be erected at his tomb in honor of the
Annunciation of Our Lady. He desired that all extravagance be
avoided at his funeral but that thirty poor men be fed and clothed for
a year on condition that they say every day the Office of the Virgin
Mary and add at its conclusion: "Mother of God, remember thy
servant Henry who placed his whole trust in thee." According to the
will three masses were to be said every day for Henry's soul, one of

---

[16]R. B. Mowat, *Henry V* (Boston, 1919), p. 324, gives Henry's itinerary
at this time.

[17]Bergen, *op. cit.,* IV, 2.

[18]See MacCracken, *op. cit.,* p. 54.

[19]Lydgate's beginning of the *Life of Our Lady* in the winter (Book I, 2)
is in keeping with this theory.

[20]Cf. C. L. Kingsford, *Henry V* (New York, 1923), pp. 86-90, who cites
Elmham, *Vita,* p. 12; Walsingham, *Hist. Angl,* II. 290; and Hardyng, *Chronicle,*
p. 372.

[21]James H. Wylie, *The Reign of Henry V* (Cambridge, 1914), I, 539.

[22]Thomas Rymer, *Foedera* (London, 1709), IX, 289-293.

which was to commemorate a mystery of Our Lady's life; to wit, her Assumption, Annunciation, Nativity, Immaculate Conception, and Purification. In addition, five thousand masses were to be said for Henry, "in honorem Quinque Gaudiorum beatae Virginis." This will was signed in Henry's hand: "R. H. Jesu Mercy and Gremercy. Ladie Marie Help."

On August 14, 1416, the king (Henry V) sent his brother, the Duke of Bedford, to break a siege at Harfleur. He achieved the victory:

> "Whanne this was don, the said duke with his prizes and prisoners returned into Engelond agayne: and forasmoche as this was don on the Vigil of the Assumpcioun of Our Lady, the kyng commaunded that his chapelaynes sholde say every day while he lived, an anthem with the versicle and collect in remembrance of our lady."[23]

A dating for the *Life of Our Lady* in 1421-2 seems consistent with other facts. Professor Schick's conclusions allow a 1421-2 dating. There was time for Lydgate to write both the *Life of Our Lady* and the *Siege of Thebes* between 1421-2. We know that Lydgate could write about 5000 lines a year.[24] He finished the Troy book in December 1420. He could have written the *Life of Our Lady* (5932 lines) and the *Siege of Thebes* (4716 lines) before the death of Henry, on August 31, 1422. *Guy of Warwick,* assigned by both Zupitza[25] and Schick[26] to 1420, has been definitely dated by Dr. F. N. Robinson as not earlier than 1442[27] and thus removed from this period of Lydgate's career.

Prof. Schick offers the "freshness" of the *Life of Our Lady* as evidence for an early date. Although "freshness" is a very relative term, I presume Prof. Schick refers to the rather vivid imagery and the personal feeling in some portions of the *Life of Our Lady*. This "freshness", however, is present only in passages praising the Virgin Mary. The same quality is found frequently in Lydgate's minor works of devotional expression to the Mother of God.[28] Much of the rest of the poem is in Lydgate's unrelieved and repetitious style.[29]

---

[23]*An English Chronicle of the Reigns of Richard II, Henry IV, Henry V and Henry VI*. Edited by J. S. Davies (Camden Society, No. 64, 1856), p. 43.
[24]See Schick, *op. cit.,* p. cv.
[25]"Zur Literaturgeschichte des Guy von Warwick," *Sitzungsberichte der Kais. Wiener Akad. der Wissenschaft, Ph.-Hist. Klasse, LXXIV* (1873), 623.
[26]*Op. cit.,* p. civ. Page cxii gives "1423(?)".
[27]*Studies and Notes in Philology and Literature,* V (8196), 177-220.
[28]Cf. H. N. MacCracken, *Minor Poems of Lydgate* (*EETSES,* 107), pp. 260-323.
[29]Bernhard Ten Brink, *History of English Literature* (New York, 1892), II, 232.

The astronomical allusion cited by Prof. Schick does point to a new moon around January first.[30] However, that there was a new moon on December 26, 1410 does not compel us to date the *Life of Our Lady* 1409-11.[31] Dr. Nicholas E. Wagman, of the Allegheny Observatory of the University of Pittsburgh, informs me that there was a new moon on December 24, 1421. A date 1421-22 would fit the astronomical allusion equally well.

There is very little internal evidence for a date in the entire poem. Only in Lydgate's frequent condemnation of heretics do we find a reference to contemporary events. No doubt he had in mind the Lollards, but the entire reign of Henry V, 1413-22, was a period in which Lollardy was vigorously condemned.

Lydgate mentions specific dates and seasons throughout the poem. In the Prologue (I, 2) he tells us that he was awakened out of a "slombre of slouthe this long wynters nyght." In Book II, 1612, he hopes to describe the feast of the Incarnation before "the kalendes of apryll or of may." In Book II, 1617-18 he comments that before "phebus enters in the signe, Wythe his carte, of the ariete"[32] he will write of this same feast. In Book III, 10, he is writing "or maies dai the ferthe." Later in Book III, 1766-71, the poet prays to Our Lady and notes that it is "mydwynter" in the month of December. As Prof. Schick points out, Lydgate makes a direct reference to his writing of the Circumcision around January first (Book IV, 1-11). Finally, in Book VI, 450-452, Lydgate prays, "Graunt vs lorde while that we ben here, in februarye—phebus dothe retourne." Such references, though not actually dating the *Life of Our Lady,* indicate a beginning in one winter and a completion in, possibly, the following February. The composition of the poem would thus have extended over about a year, possibly a month or two more.

The evidence indicates that Henry's love of chivalry prompted him to commission Lydgate to write the *Troy Book* in 1412. The presentation by Jean Galopes of his French translation of the *Meditationes*

---

[30]*Life of Our Lady,* Book IV, 1-11.

[31]See Schick, *op. cit.,* p. cxiv, where he lists all the new moons from 1410 until 1420.

[32]This statement implies the first day of spring, since Phœbus is the sun god and Aries, the constellation which the sun enters on the first day of spring. This is March 20 or 21 nowadays. On the Julian calendar of Lydgate's time it would have been about March 12.

Vitae Christi in May, 1420, and its relationship to the *Life of Our Lady;* the matured, more religious character of Henry by 1421; his possible gratitude to Our Lady for the success in France; and the astronomical allusions point towards 1421-22 as the date of the *Life of Our Lady.*

THE MANUSCRIPTS

Lydgate's *Life of Our Lady* is extant in forty-two manuscripts.[1] These comprise: Bodleian MS 120 or 27643 (B^1); Bodleian 596 or 2376 (B^2); Hatton 73 or Bodleian 4119 (B^3); Rawlinson poet 140 or Bodleian 14634 (B^4); Bodleian 75 or 2253 (B^5); Bodleian 6919, known as Ashmole 39 (Ash^1); Bodleian 6943, known as Ashmole (Ash^2); Harleian MSS 3862 (H^1); 2382 (H^2); 629 (H^3); 1304 (H^4); 3952 (H^5); 4011 (H^6); 4260 (H^7); 5272 (H^8); Corpus Christi College, Oxford MS 237 (CC); St. John's College, Oxford MS 56 (J); Cambridge University MS Kk. 1. 3. (C^1); Cambridge University MS Mm. 6. 5. (C^2); Trinity College, Cambridge, MS 601, R. 3. 21 (C^3); Gonville and Caius College, Cambridge, MS 230 (C^4); Trinity College, Cambridge, MS 602, R. 3. 22 (C^5); Arundel MS 168 (Ar); Sloane MS 1785 (S); British Museum Additional MSS 29729 (Ad^1); 19452 (Ad^2); 19252 (Ad^3); Advocates Library, Edinburgh, MSS 1. 1. 6 (Adv^1) and 19. 3. 1. (Adv^2); Chetham Library, Manchester, MS 6709 (Ct); Durham University MS Cosin V. ii. 16 (D); Hunterian Museum, Glasgow, MS 232 (Hu); Lambeth Palace MS 344 (L); Society of Antiquaries MS 134 (An); Longleat MS (Lg); Chicago University MS 566 (Ch); Huntington Library MSS HM 115 (Hn^1) and HM 144 (Hn^2); Cotton Appendix MS VIII (Co); Venerable English College, Rome, MS 1306 (V); and Mostyn Hall MSS 85 and 257.

MSS C^4, Ad^1, and Adv^1 are fragmentary, consisting only of the poetic paraphrase of the Magnificat (II, 981-1060). They offer very little ground for comparison, since all the MSS are complete and peculiarly identical in this portion of the poem. They are omitted from the stemma. MS Adv^2 is also a fragment, containing only Books IV, V and VI. MS Ct is obviously a copy of Caxton's print.[2]

The whereabouts of the Mostyn Hall MSS is unknown. They were both sold at auction July 13, 1920, at Sotheby's, London. MS Mostyn Hall 257 was sold as Lot 75 to Bernard Quaritch, Ltd., London, who bought the manuscript for the late Sir Leicester Harmsworth. After Sir Leicester Harmsworth's death, the manuscript was again sold by Messrs. Sotheby as Lot 2019 in the Harmsworth sale

---

[1]The listing is found in Carleton Brown and R. H. Robbins, *The Index of Middle English Verse* (New York, 1943), p. 404. The Venerable English College MS was discovered during the editing of the poem.

[2]This is corroborated by John M. Manly and Edith Rickert, *The Text of the Canterbury Tales* (8v, Chicago, 1940), I, 82-84.

of October 16, 1945. It was then bought by Mr. C. A. Stonehill of Great Bookham, Surrey, and New Haven, Connecticut. Mr. Stonehill in turn sold the manuscript to an unidentified buyer, from whom Mr. Stonehill has been unable to obtain information about its present whereabouts. MS Mostyn Hall 85 was sold at the same auction, July 13, 1920, to a buyer identified as "Mr. Abbott." Inquiries addressed to Messrs. Quaritch, Sotheby, C. A. Stonehill, Rosenbach, and to the present Lord Mostyn, have thrown no light on the identity of the buyer or the whereabouts of the manuscript.

THE RELATIONSHIP OF THE MANUSCRIPTS

The manuscripts fall into two groups, between which the most noticeable distinction is the treatment of the stanza composed of lines II, 1397-1403. In one group (group *b*) this stanza reads:

"For in myself [Abiathar] perfightly I knowe
She is a maide but yf it be fore the
Quod Joseph thanne with hed inclined lowe
The sothfast lord that every thynge may se
My trust is fully he wole excuse me
Of rightwisnesse and shelde me from shame
Of alle that ever ye put me in blame."

Group *b* comprises MSS D, C^1, C^3, B^1, H^7, H^8, Ar, Ash^2, Hn^1, H^2, B^5, Co, Ad^3, J, Hu, S, and Hn^2.[3]

In the second group (group *c*) this stanza reads:

"Quod Joseph than with head inclined lowe
Sires speake I will if it your will be
Of this thynge I am not a knowe
The sothefast lord that everything may see
My trust is fully he woll excuse me
Of rightwisnesse and shelde me from shame
Of all that ever ye put me in blame."

Group c includes MSS B^2, Ch, B^4, H^1, C^2, Ash^1, H^3, H^4, H^5 H^6, Ad^2, Lg, An, L, B^3, CC, and C^5.[4]

---

[3]Though MSS Hn^1 and S lack this passage, other identities place them in group *b*.

[4]This division of the manuscripts into groups *b* and *c* is supported by a number of major variants in the first four books.

In group *b,* MS D stands by itself because of singular errors, the omission of line III 1426 and V 532, and the transposition of stanzas IV 162-168 and IV 169-175.[5] All the other MSS have these stanzas in the order of our text.

MSS Ad³, B¹, H⁷, and Ar form a related group (sub-group *p*) within group *b.* These MSS omit stanza III 680-686 and invert VI 97-98. Again, MSS B¹ and H⁷ are closely related it seems, because they alone include a lengthy rubric marking the end of Book I : "Here endith the first book the wheche telleth of the natiuite of our lady ande now suet the secunde book the wiche tellet of the redempcioun of man kynde how that thorowȝ ryȝtwisnesse trowthe merci and pes redemcioun was ordeined by the holi trinite to deliver manes soule that lay in peinful derknesse. How rygthwysnesse trowthe merci and pes disputede for the redempcioun of man." MS Ar omits this rubric; MS Ad³ lacks this portion of the poem. MS S, a badly mutilated MS, is close to MSS Ar, B¹, and H⁷ in variant readings, and is included in this group. MS Hu omits line II 735, places line II 236 after II 238 and garbles Books III and IV badly. MS Hu also has very poor readings in lines I 270, 290, 410, 416, 788, 807, 877, etc. Since these readings are not shared by any other MS, Hu must be responsible for them. However, a study of the major variants in the first four books shows MS Hu to be affiliated with MSS Ad³, B¹, H⁷, Ar and S in group *p,* though the influence of group *m* is seen in a good many agreements. MS H² seems affiliated with group *p.* The evidence of the major variants is stronger for group *p,* in Books III and IV than in Books I and II. Most frequently MS H² agrees with MS B¹ in single variant readings.

MSS B⁵ and Co both omit lines II 1404-1459 at the proper point, adding these lines after II 1515. A similar error occurs again in MS Co when lines II 1628-1669 and III 1-14 are omitted in the proper place and added after III 70. These misplacements of lines occur in the middle of the page in MSS B⁵ and Co. These errors would occur if MSS B⁵ and Co derive from MSS with wrongly folded sheets. MS B⁵ is a copy of a manuscript *g* in which a sheet containing lines II 1404-1515 had been folded incorrectly, giving four pages with lines II 1460-1487, 1488-1515, 1404-1431, 1432-1459. MS Co includes this error and adds the misplacement comprising lines II 1628-

---

[5]For this study of the relationship of the MSS, I have had access to Fr. V. F. Gallagher's notes on the readings of the MSS for Books III and IV, and Fr. J. A. Lauritis' readings of Books V and VI.

1669 and III 1-14. Obviously, MS Co is a copy of a manuscript *l* which, besides copying the lines II 1404-1515 incorrectly from the wrongly folded sheet of MS *g,* itself contained a wrongly folded sheet containing II 1628-III 70. This wrongly folded sheet in MS *l* would have the line sequence III 15-42, III 43-70, II 1628-1669 and III 1-14. MS Co also omits II 229, 733 and III 1094-5 independently of B⁵.

MSS J, Hn¹, H⁸ and C³ transpose lines I 468-9. MS C³ transposes also lines I 601-602; MS C¹ transposes only lines I 601-602. In all probability MSS J, Hn¹, H⁸, and C³ are copies of MS *m,* which contained the transposition of lines I 468-9. MS C¹ is copied from MS *n,* having the transposition of lines I 601-602; MS C³ may have this transposition by contamination with MS *n.* MSS J and H⁸ are alike in the frequent use of "whilom" for "some tyme"; and they both insert "Explicit liber primus" after I 875, immediately before Lydgate's prayer to the Virgin at the end of Book I. MS J omits lines III 63-67. Though MS Hn² contains only lines II 1-504, many major variant readings place it in this group. On the basis of major variants MS Ash² belongs with MSS H⁸-J for Books I and II (thirteen agreements with MS H⁸ and twenty-one with MS J). For these two books MS Ash² agrees with no other manuscript more than six times (MSS Ar, Hn¹, Hn²). For Books III and IV there is only one agreement with MSS H⁸-J; eight agreements with MS H², and nineteen agreements with MS H¹.[6] The omission in MS Ash² of some 1200 lines in Books III and IV might account for lack of variant evidence in these two books.

Within group *c,* MSS B² and CC are closely related, both omitting stanza I 771-777, lines III 63-67, 69-70, and sharing many common readings.

As a further subdivision of group *c,* MSS Ch, H³, C², H⁴, Ash¹, An, H⁶, Ad², C⁵, B⁴, and Lg contain a common error. These MSS omit a stanza comprising lines III 610-616, insert in its place stanza III 666-672, then repeat stanza III 666-672 at its proper place in the poem. Since line III 666 occurs fifty-six lines after line III 610, or two pages later (with twenty-eight lines to the page), it appears that the scribe of MS *d,* or of a related MS, turned two leaves instead of one and wrote stanza III 666-672 instead of stanza III 610-616. Then discovering his error and not wishing to disturb the later pagination, he deliberately omitted III 610-616 to save the space of one stanza.

---

[6]It will be shown below that MS J changes affiliation in Books III and IV. It will be shown also that for Books III and IV MS H¹ is affiliated with a MS in group *b,* in all probability MS Ash², or one closely related to it.

Possibly the copying had been parceled out among two or more scribes, who were reproducing their exemplar page by page or quire by quire. If line III 609 came at the end of the next to the last leaf of a quire and line III 666 began a new quire (already copied by another scribe) the saving of space would have been necessary rather promptly. MSS Ash¹, H³, H⁴, C¹, Ad², An, all transpose V 586-587.

Within group *d*, MSS Ash¹ and H⁶ are obviously related (sub-group *j*) since they both omit lines III 141-168 and share many peculiar line readings. MSS An and H⁴ are related (sub-group *k*). They both omit lines II 1092, III 1032, and IV 327-328 and share many singular major variant readings. MSS C² and Lg are related (subgroup *i*); they both transpose lines III 664-665 and share, with MS H¹, many major variants, especially in Books III and IV.

MS H⁵ is the most difficult of the MSS to classify. On the basis of the reading of stanza II 1397-1403, MS H⁵ belongs to group *c*. Since it omits line II 175, as does also MS H³, MS H⁵ may belong with H³ in sub-group *d* for this part of the poem. On the other hand MS H⁵ does not have the error at stanzas III 610-616 and III 666-672, common to all MSS in group *d*. In addition, with regard to major variant readings, MS H⁵ agrees most often with group *p*, often with group *m*, and quite frequently with *c* and *d*. It is possible that MS H⁵ may be related to MS H³ in group *d* for Books I and II (see sub-group *r*), because of the mutual omission of line II 175. However, in Books III and IV, MS H⁵ had as an exemplar a manuscript in either *p, m,* or *c*.

CHANGE OF AFFILIATION

MS J, definitely a member of group *b* in Books I and II, changes affiliation and joins group *c* for Books III and IV. This is shown by its omission of lines III 63-67, linking it with MSS B² and CC, and an unusually large number of major variants in which it consistently joins group c in readings; especially does it agree with MSS B² and CC in many major variant readings.

According to major variants, somewhere around III 863, MS C¹ becomes a *c* manuscript, since it shares numerous *c* readings from that point on. As noted above, MS H⁵, in group *c* and probably linked with MS H³ in sub-group *d* for Books I and II, seems to change affiliation to sub-group *p* for Books III and IV. MS Ash², affiliated with MSS H⁸ and J in sub-group *o* for Books I and II, seems to change affiliation to sub-group *p* for Books III and IV. MS H², affiliated with sub-group *m* for Books I and II shows an affiliation with sub-group *p* for Books III and IV.

CONTAMINATION

MSS B³ and L (sub-group *q*) are obviously related since they have common errors in lines I 331, 334, 645, II 80, etc. In addition they both transpose lines IV 284-285.[7]

For the variant reading of stanza II 1397-1403, MSS B³ and L have the reading of group *c*. However, judging from many major variants in Books I and II, MSS B³ and L seem to derive from an exemplar which in Books I and II has been corrected in a good many readings by comparison with a *b* manuscript. For Books III and IV MSS B³ and L share many major variants with the MSS of group *c*.

MS H¹ is related to MS Lg for Books I and II (sub-group *i*). They both omit lines I 721 and II 651; they both garble lines I 653-4 and I 796-7. For Books III and IV, however, MS H¹ shows evidence of frequent comparison with group *b*.[8] This contamination is seen in its numerous *b* readings for major variants in Books III and IV and in its inclusion of stanza III 610-616. As explained above, all MSS of group *d* omit this stanza and substitute in its place stanza III 666-672, repeating stanza III 666-672 in its proper place later. MS H¹ has III 666-672 before III 610-616, then repeats III 666-672 later. This restoration of III 610-616, in the face of the repetition of III 666-672, seems to show a comparison with some other exemplar.

Judging from major variant readings in Books II, III, and IV, MS H² is strongly contaminated with group *c* readings. Since MS H⁶ transposes lines IV 162 and IV 169 and MS D transposes stanzas IV 162-168 and IV 169-175, one must assume that MS H⁶ has been partially contaminated by comparison with a manuscript related to MS D. In Books II and III MS Hn¹ is partially contaminated with group *c* readings. Even in groups of the stemma which are closely affiliated by reason of mutual omissions or major errors, there is sometimes from the nature of the variants evidence of contamination.

---

[7]This same relationship of MSS B³ and L is noted by F. N. Robinson in his "Textual Notes" for Chaucer's minor poems, "Truth" and "Lak of Stedfastnesse." See *The Poetical Works of Geoffrey Chaucer* (Cambridge, 1933), pp. 1037-1038.

[8]From a study of major variants in Books III and IV, MS H¹ seems closely related to MS Ash² for these two books.

THE STEMMA[9]

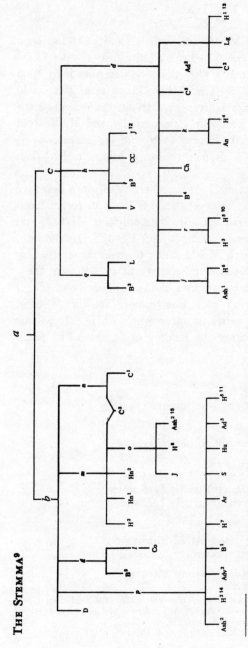

[9]MSS C⁴, Ad¹, Adv¹, Adv², and Ct are omitted from the stemma. MSS C⁴, Ad¹, and Adv¹ are fragmentary, consisting only of the *Magnificat* paraphrase (II, 981-1060). MS Adv² contains only Books IV, V, and VI. MS Ct is a copy of Caxton's print.

[10]MS H⁵ is in group *c* for Books I and II and may be related to MS H³ in sub-group *d*, since they both omit line II 175.

[11]In Books III and IV MS H⁵ omits the error at stanza III 610-616 and III 666-672, common to all *d* MSS. On the basis of variants MS H⁵ is in group *b* for these two books, with some agreement with groups *m* and *c*.

[12]As explained above, MS J, definitely a member of group *b* in Books I and II, changes affiliation and joins group *c* from Book III through Book IV.

[13]MS H¹, related to MS Lg for Books I and II, shows evidence of frequent comparison with group *b* in Books III and IV. Readings in major variants show a close relationship with MS Ash² in Books III and IV.

[14]On the basis of variant readings MS H² seems affiliated with group *b*. This affiliation is stronger in Books III and IV. In Books I and II the evidence of the major variants points to an affiliation of MS H² with group *m*. For Books III and IV the evidence of major variants shows an affiliation with MS H² in group *b*.

[15]MS Ash² belongs with group *o* for Books I and II.

The Text

The Durham University MS Cosin V. ii. 16 (MS D) has been chosen as the text for this critical edition of the *Life of Our Lady*. The manuscript is an early one. The catalogue describes it as "non multo post ipsum Auctorem."[16] Through the kindness of Mr. David Ramage, Librarian at Durham University, MS D was examined for me by Mr. Conway Davies, Reader in Palaeography, and Mr. Harold Johnson, of the Public Record Office. They date the manuscript as "circa 1450, with perhaps a preference for a minus rather than a plus."

Many of the manuscripts of the *Life of Our Lady* are defective with large lacunae.[17] MS D, however, besides being an early manuscript, is fairly complete and correct. It omits only line III 1426 and V 532 and transposes stanzas IV 162-168 and 169-175. In addition, there are several lines in which MS D seems to make better reading than the other MSS, both in sense and construction. I present these by way of showing particular instances of the superiority of the D text. In the parentheses after each line number are the MSS in which this same reading is found in agreement with D. It will be noticed that these MSS, sharing the reading of D, are all in group *b* in the stemma.

1) I 309 (C³, Hn¹, J)

   "Ester was meke but not lyke hir mekenesse"

   is better than:

   "Hester was meke but not to her mekenesse"

2) I 388-9 (C¹, C³, Hn¹, J)

   "That some tyme were *with* gostly fyre so clere
   Thorough light of vertu inwardely Iocounde"

   is better than:

   "That sumtyme were *with* gostly lyght so clere
   Thorugh lyght of vertu inwardely jocounde"

   since the repetition of *lyght* seems incorrect.

---

[16]See the *Catalogues of the Library of Durham Cathedral Including Catalogues of Library of Abbey of Hulne and of MSS Preserved in the Library of Bishop Cosin at Durham* (London, 1838), p. 157.

[17]See "2. Descriptions of the Manuscripts and Prints", p. 21.

3) I 398-9 (Co)

"That vp to god hottest Ran the fyre
With hete of clennes to all by desyre"

is better than:

"That up to god hotteste ran the fyre
With herte of clennesse to all by desyre"

4) II 554-5 (Co)

"And right as the rayne in Apryll or in may
Causyth the vertu to renne oute of the rote"

is better than:

"Ne as the reyne in April or in May
Causeth the vertu to renne out of the rote"[18]

5) II 1324 (C³, Ash², J)

"Of this light by revelacion"   (truth, knowledge)

is better than:

"Of this night by revelacion"[19]

6) II 1471 (C¹, C³, J)

"But whan that trouthe settyth abroche his tonne"
is more exact than:

"But when the trouthe settith abroche his tyme"[20]

7) II 244 (C³, Hn¹, Hn², Ash², H⁸, J)

"Thoroughe oute the worlde to serche all mankynde"

is better than:

"Thorought the world to reherse all mankynde"[21]

---

[18]Here Lydgate is using the rain as a symbol of the Virgin, a source of God's grace to man. The negative "Ne" seems incorrect here.

[19]Joseph complains in this line that he could not have come to the knowledge of Christ's Incarnation except by divine revelation.

[20]The phrase "set abroche his tonne" means to break the cask, or tun, and let the contents (here, the truth), run free. It is a frequent phrase in Lydgate. The word "tyme" not only spoils the sense but also breaks the rhyme.

[21]Here the line means that God will search the world in vain to find a man without sin.

8) II 1100 (C^1, C^3, Co, H^2, Ash^2)

"In Caphernam w*ith* his full entent"

is more exact than:

"In carpentrye with al his full entent"[22]

In the light of the early date of MS D, of its comparative completeness and correctness, and of the lines in which its seems superior, I have chosen it as our text. No other manuscript is better than MS D for any reason.

It will be noticed that in many instances the reading of MS D is singular. In some of these, the variant of MS D is as good as the readings of the other MSS; in other cases, the MS D reading is better, as shown above. There are, however, several instances in the text of MS D in which the reading of MS D is clearly erratic. The last-named conclusion is apparent in those lines in which many MSS in both groups *b* and *c* have the same variant reading. In such cases the variant common to both branches of the tradition (*b* and *c*) must have been reading of the archetype. Where this occurs I have substituted in the text the reading of MS B^1 for the variant shared by the MSS in groups *b* and *c* and I have noted the MS D variant and all other manuscript variants in the textual footnotes.[23]

It is regrettable that the spelling of MS D shows a slight northern coloring, undoubtedly that of the scribe. This fact, however, has not seemed sufficient to outweigh the other considerations which have led to the adoption of MS D as the base manuscript.

In transcribing the text from MS D, I have used commas where the manuscript has small diagonal strokes within the line.

---

[22]The line means that Joseph was in Capharnaum in Galilee while the Annunciation was taking place. The line in D is in agreement with the source, the Gospel of Pseudo-Matthew. Joseph was working in carpentry at the time, but this fact is mentioned in the poem two lines later, II 1102. The "carpentrye" of the other MSS in line II 1100 is a misreading of Capharnaum or an error caused by anticipation of "carpentrye" in line II 1102.

[23]In those cases in which MS B^1 has a lacuna or has a peculiar reading, the reading in MSS H^7 or Ad^3 has been chosen.

2. DESCRIPTIONS OF
THE MANUSCRIPTS AND PRINTS

Present records show forty-two extant manuscripts of the *Life of Our Lady*.[1] Fourteen are in the British Museum; seven in the Bodleian Library at Oxford; three in the University of Cambridge Library; two in Trinity College Library, Cambridge; two in the Advocates Library, Edinburgh; two in the Henry E. Huntington Library, San Marino, California; and one each in the Chetham Library, Manchester; the Hunterian Museum, Glasgow; Corpus Christi College Library, Oxford; St. John's College Library, Oxford; Lambeth Palace Library, London; Society of Antiquaries Library, London; the University of Chicago Library; Durham University Library; the Venerable English College Library, Rome; and the private library of the Marquis of Bath, Longleat, Wilts. The exact location of two others, Mostyn Hall MS. 85 and MS. 257, could not be determined. Neither Lord Mostyn, son of the former owner, nor Messrs. Quaritch, Sotheby, Abbott and Stonehill, through whose hands they passed since their sale in 1920, were able to give any assistance in tracing them.[2]

A list of the manuscripts and the symbols used in this edition is appended herewith:[3]

D	—Durham University MS. Cosin V. ii. 16
B[1]	—Bodleian MS. 120 or 27643
B[2]	—Bodleian MS. 596 or 2367
B[3]	—Bodleian MS. 4119 or Hatton 73
B[4]	—Bodleian MS. 14635 or Rawlinson poet 140
B[5]	—Bodleian MS. 75 or 2253
H[1]	—Harleian MS. 3862
H[2]	—Harleian MS. 2382
H[3]	—Harleian MS. 629
H[4]	—Harleian MS. 1304
H[5]	—Harleian MS. 3952
H[6]	—Harleian MS. 4011

---

[1]MS. 1306 of the Venerable English College in Rome is not included by Carleton Brown and R. H. Robbins, *The Index of Middle English Verse* (New York, 1943), p. 404. Otherwise their list is complete.

[2]Cf. "1. Introduction. The Manuscripts", pp. 11-12.

[3]Microfilms of all MSS used in this edition were obtained through the courtesy of the various librarians and owners.

H[7]	—Harleian MS. 4260
H[8]	—Harleian MS. 5272
C[1]	—Cambridge University MS. Kk. 1. 3.
C[2]	—Cambridge University MS. Mm. 6. 5.
C[3]	—Trinity College Cambridge MS. 601,R.3.21.
C[4]	—Gonville and Caius College, Cambridge MS. 230
C[5]	—Trinity College Cambridge MS. 602,R.3.22.
Ad[1]	—British Museum Additional MS. 29729
Ad[2]	—British Museum Additional MS. 19452
Ad[3]	—British Museum Additional MS. 19252
Ash[1]	—Bodleian MS. 6919, known as Ashmole 39
Ash[2]	—Bodleian MS. 6943, known as Ashmole 59
Adv[1]	—Advocates Library Edinburgh MS. 1.1.6.
Adv[2]	—Advocates Library Edinburgh MS. 19.3.1.
Hn[1]	—Huntington Library MS. HM 115
Hn[2]	—Huntington Library MS. HM 144
Ch	—Chicago University MS. 566
Co	—Cotton Appendix MS. VIII
Lg	—Longleat MS.
An	—Society of Antiquaries MS. 134
L	—Lambeth Palace MS. 344
Hu	—Hunterian Museum MS. 232
Ct	—Chetham Library MS. 6709
S	—Sloane MS. 1785
Ar	—Arundel MS. 168
J	—Saint John's College MS. 56
CC	—Corpus Christi College MS. 237
V	—Venerable English College MS. 1306

Caxton attested to the contemporary popularity of the poem by printing it in or near 1484.[4] After that, it did not come to press again until Robert Redman brought it forward in 1531, and C. E. Tame edited it from "manuscripts in the British Museum" in 1872. These will be discussed more at length in the individual descriptions of manuscripts that follow.

D—Durham University MS. Cosin V. ii. 16.

Library of Durham University, Durham, England. See the *Catalogues of the Library of Durham Cathedral Including Catalogues*

---

[4]cf. "1. Introduction. Preliminary Remarks", p. 1.

of Library of Abbey of Hulne and of MSS Preserved in the Library of Bishop Cosin at Durham (London, Surtees Society, 1838), pp. 156-157. See also Carleton Brown and R. H. Robbins, *The Index of Middle English Verse* (Index Society, New York, 1943), p. 404 and Carleton Brown, *A Register of Middle English Religious and Didactic Verse* (2v, Oxford, 1920), II, 234.

Vellum, measuring 285 x 185 mm., single columns, 35 lines to the page, dated as 1450 or earlier.[5] The binding is mid-nineteenth century, dark brown full polished morocco with seven bands and two clasps, in poor condition, lettered, "Lidgate / Life of the / Virgin Mary // V. / II. 16. /." The contents index (ff. 3a-4b) has the initial letters touched up with red and the chapter references in red. The marginal headings corresponding are also in red throughout, as are the chapter numbers at the tops of the pages, which have frequently been altered in black ink. The large initials are in blue with red decorations spreading down the margins.

There are three preliminary vellum leaves. These contain some writing, including three ownership inscriptions on (iib), "Jhesu marcy. / thys boke ys Janes Fyz loy wys" (*sic,* i.e., Fitzlewis), in a late 15th century hand. There is also on this page, "Geo. Davenport / 1664." This refers to the collector (d. 1677) of most of this group of MSS, who passed them on to Bishop Cosin's Library, of which he had charge. There is also a coat of arms (crudely executed in ink), a chevron and three trefoils, with a name or phrase which may be "Mary reward." The arms of the Fitzlewis family were Argent, a chevron between three trefoils sable.

On a preliminary leaf (iiib) is written in a 17th century hand, "Pitsæus anno / 1440 / Johannes Lidgatus scripsit Vitam S. Mariæ ad Henricum Quintum. Moe ro — / re ac vario contactum. MS Oxonij in bibliotheca publica," a quotation from Pitsæus: *De Rebus Anglicis* (1619), p. 632. On the first leaf of the book itself (f. 3a), there is a note in the hand of Thomas Rud and another owner's name "W. Browne", found in other Davenport-Cosin MSS.

Through the courtesy of Mr. David Ramage, Librarian at Durham University Library, the manuscript was examined by Mr. Harold Johnson, of the Public Record Office, and Mr. Conway Davies, Reader in Palaeography at Durham University. They date the manuscript as "circa 1450, with perhaps a preference for a minus rather than a plus."

---

[5] See "1. Introduction. The Text", p. 18.

There is a table of contents on ff. 3a-4b; the poem begins with the Prologue on f. 5a. The poem ends on f. 90b. A "Calendar" follows our poem, beginning on f. 90b. A later editor has altered chapter numberings in all books after Book I. He has also reduced the number of Books in the poem from six to four. These alterations are noted in the text.

MS. D omits line III 1426 and V 532. Stanzas IV 162-168 and IV 169-175 are inverted. There are many scribal insertions within the line. For the reasons given by Prof. Klinefelter in his discussion of the "Relationship of Manuscripts," MS. D has been chosen as the basic manuscript for this edition.[6]

B¹—BODLEIAN MS. 120 (OR BODLEIAN 27643).

Bodleian Library, Oxford. See F. Madan and H. H. E. Craster, *A Summary Catalogue of Western MSS in the Bodleian Library at Oxford* (Oxford, 1895-1924), V, 318; C. Brown and Robbins, *Index,* p. 404; C. Brown, *Register,* II, 234; H. N. MacCracken, *Minor Poems of John Lydgate* (1911-34; *EETSES,* 107 and *EETS,* 192), I,xx.

On parchment, second half of 15th century. $11 \times 7\text{-}\frac{5}{8}$ inches, V + 106 leaves. It is written in single columns; the number of lines is 28 for ff. 1a-8b and 33a-end, 38 on ff. 8b-32b. The poem begins on f. 1a and ends on 94a. The capitals for chapter beginnings are illuminated for ff. 1a-8b, and 33a-94a; they are plain for ff. 8b-32b. The poem is written in two hands. Hand number one is seen in ff. 1a-8b, and ff. 33a-94a (end of poem); hand number two is found in ff. 9a-32b.

A rubric on page V reads: "A Poem of þe V. Mary. May 7° MDCCIV Bibliotheca Bodlejana dono dedit Vir pereruditus Guilielmus Brewster, de Herefordia, M. D." On f. 100a, there is a note "Really 106 leaves as 21, 31, 54, 72, and 75 are double." On f. 1a is the library catalogue number: "NE F. 9. 16, N 120." Owned in 1687 (?) by "Theo: Myll*er*," an erased and uncertain name on f. 1a. The poem is divided into six books, at ff. 14b, 36, 68b, 75a, 86b.

Lines omitted are I 453, 612; II 527-8. Line II 295 is inserted but only half of it appears. Line II 1134 is garbled, with half of II 1134 and half of II 1135. Lines II 1363-1367 are obscure. Lines III 680-686 are omitted; lines III 40-41, III 270-271, III 411-412,

---

[6]See "1. Introduction. The Text", p. 18 ff.

III 921-922, III 1320-1321, III 1495-1496, III 1588-1589, V 690-692, V 561-562 and VI 97-98 are transposed. The poem ends imperfectly on f. 94a at line V 454.

B² — BODLEIAN MS. 596 (OR BODLEIAN 2376).

Bodleian Library, Oxford. See Madan and Craster, II, Part 1, 335-336; C. Brown and R. H. Robbins, *Index,* p. 404; C. Brown, *Register,* II, 233.

Parchment; eleventh to fifteenth century; 9-⅞ by 7 inches; a composite volume consisting of four separate pieces bound together in 1605. The *Life of Our Lady* is section B of the volume; it is fifteenth century, with a few miniatures and illuminated capitals. There are forty-two lines to the page, single columns.

Our poem begins with the Prologue on folio 86a. There are illuminations before chapter beginnings on ff. 86a, 87a, 89a, 96a, 98a, 104b. The chapters are numbered by book. On folio 174b occurs the colophon: "Compiled by John Lydgate monke of bury on whos soull god have mercy. Amen. Explicit vitam beate Marie virgine."

Lines I 768-774, folio 90a; II 120-126, folio 101b; II 141-147, folio 101b; III 1314-1320, folio 119a and V 141-147 are omitted. One line is added between I 89-90, folio 87b: "They ought not presume nor be so bolde." On folio 118a, line II 1248 is repeated in a later hand. The rubrics include the names of writers mentioned in the text, the petitions, the virtues in dispute, the Latin "Magnificat" and "Ave Maria."

The poem is divided into four books.

B³ — HATTON MS. 73 (OR BODLEIAN 4119).

Bodleian Library, Oxford. See Madan and Craster, II, Part 2, 850-851; C. Brown and R. H. Robbins, *Index,* p. 404; C. Brown, *Register* II, 233; H. N. MacCracken, *Minor Poems,* I, xx.

Parchment; middle of fifteenth century; 12⅛ by 8⅜ in.; i + 125 leaves, twenty-eight lines to the page, single columns.

The poem begins on folio 10a without title, but Lydgate's name is given in the colophon on f. 117a: "This book was compiled by John Lydgate Monke of Bury at the excitacioun of Kyng Harry the

V[th] in honour of our lady. Divided and chaptred after this table."
Then on ff. 117a, 117b, 118a, 118b follows a table of contents in four
books; the chapters are numbered according to book.

The beginning of each book is highly illuminated. Chapter
capitals are illuminated. There are no chapter headings; the only
rubrics are those in Latin, paraphrasing the "Magnificat." Lines
IV 284-285 are transposed.

On folio 1a we find: "Domina Margareta More" and "Domina
Elizabeth Wyndesor"; on folio 9b, "Mary Gertrude". On folio 121b,
is written, "Thys is my lady More boke and sumtym it was Quene
Margarete boke"; on 122a, "Thys ys my lady Dame Elizabeth
Wyndesor boke the XIIIIth day of December in the IIIIth yer of the
reyngn of King Harry the VIIIth"; on 123a, "Thys boke was late
my lady dame Elizabeth Windesore, who departed owte of thys
woruld the XVIIth day of January in the yere of our lorde god
MVXXXI and the yere of the reygn of kyng Henry the VIIIth the
XXIIth On whos soull Jhu have mercy. Amen. Quod Clarke."
This writing is all early 16th century.

Other contents of the volume are: minor poems by Lydgate,
ff. 116, 119b and two ballades by Chaucer, written in a slightly later
hand on ff. 118b, 119a.

Doubtless the volume was acquired by Lord Hatton from Thomas
Windsor, sixth Lord Windsor of Stanwell (d. 1641), who was
fourth in descent from Dame Elizabeth Windsor. The Hatton collection was bought by the Bodleian from Robert Scot, who purchased
part of the library of Christopher, first lord Hatton (d. July 4, 1670).
The collection was acquired by the Bodleian Library in September,
1671.

B⁴—RAWLINSON POET MS. 140 (OR BODLEIAN 14634).

Bodleian Library, Oxford. See Madan and Craster, III, 312;
C. Brown and R. H. Robbins, *Index,* p. 404; C. Brown, *Register,* II,
234; H. N. MacCracken, *Minor Poems,* I, xx.

Parchment; fifteenth century; 9⅜ by 6⅞ in.; iii + 110 leaves,
with colored initials; 28 lines to the page, single columns.

Between f. 23b and 24a, lines II 232-II 287 are missing. Other
lines missing are II 987 (f. 36a), II 992 (36b), II 1003 (36b), I
1011 (36b), II 1027 (37a), II 1035 (37a), II 1042 (37a), and
II 1057 (37b).

The inside cover has Rawlinson's bookplate. On page ia; "Part of This MS. was printed by Will. Caxton but without Date and only 82 of the first Chapters, which make [sic] this more valuable. On iib: "N. Mawnsell (15th cent.); 'C'est l[i]vre apelle la Nativite de notre Dame et apartiente a cest armes,' scil party per pale on the dexter side an eagle displayed, on the sinister lozengy, with T. M." (15th cent.): (iiia) "Tho. Wilsons purchased out of the Library of the Reverend Mr. Jo. Briggs M. A. Later Vicar of Kirkburton in York- shire." Then follows a description of Lydgate's life and work, ex- tending to page iiib. On iiib is an engraving of the Virgin Mary with "Marie conceived without original sinne."

The poem begins on f. 1a with: "This boke was compiled by ʒon Lidgate monk of Bury at the excitacion and steringe of oure wor- shipful Prince Kyng Henry the fifthe in the worshipe honour and glorie of the birthe of the moste glorious mayde wif and modur of oure lorde Jhu Crist Chapitred and marked after this table;" then follows a table of a prologue and 87 chapters.

The poem ends on f. 109a with:

> "Pees maketh plente
> Plente maketh pride
> Pride maketh plee } and therefore
> Plee maketh povert
> Povert maketh pees

Grace growth aftyr gou*er*naunce[7]

B⁵—BODLEIAN MS. 75 (OR BODLEIAN 2253).

Bodleian Library, Oxford. See Madan and Craster, II, Part 1, p. 280; C. Brown and R. H. Robbins, *Index,* p. 404; C. Brown, *Register,* II, 233; H. N. MacCracken, *Minor Poems,* I, xx.

On paper; third quarter of the fifteenth century; 7⅝ by 5½ in.; v + 87 leaves; with a few illuminated capitals. The first and last

---

[7]This formula is found frequently in literature of the period. Lydgate him- self expounded it into three 7-line stanzas in *Horse, Goose and Sheep,* ed. M. Degenhart (Munich and Leipzig, 1900), pp. 70-71. It is found in French and Latin versions and in later English writing. See C. Brown and R. H. Robbins *Index,* p. 432; Henry Bergen, *Lydgate's Troy Book* (1906-35; *EETSES,* 97, 103, 106, 126), IV, 26.

leaves of the first quire (after v) are lost, so no contemporary title or author is now in the volume. On folio 1a "Vox Clamantis" is lined through at the top of the page. There are thirty-five lines to the page, single column.

The poem begins on folio 1a with line I, 71, "The which flour preserved mann fro dethe." It ends on 83b with: "Here endith the poem entitled the Life of Our Lady by John Lydgate there wants a leafe in the beginning which may be supplyed out of MS. NE F. 3.9."

Between folio 6b and 7a one leaf is missing (seventy lines). There is a note: "Amissum est fol. unicum inter VI^m et VII^m 1881." On folio 31b there is an omission of fifty-six lines; these lines are included on folio 32b (Note this same error in MS. Co.). Folios 85, 86, 87 are blank. Line III 810 is missing, for which line III 798 is repeated; lines III 830-831 and VI 383-384 are transposed.

There is much scribbling through the manuscript. The following names are written in the volume in sixteenth century hands: "sir George Winter" (ff. 29, 76), "Thomas and Henry Boynton" (ff. 7, 50b, 66, 84), "John Robson" (f. 75b), "Richard Horff . . ." (f. 75b), "John Clarkson in Rychmond" (f. 84). On folio 7 is written: "My lady boynton god to her yeve ever."

There are many Latin rubrics written beside the text, usually expressions concerning the text. The scribe uses the word "force" instead of "strength" or "strong". This manuscript probably reached the Bodleian Library in 1603 or 1604.

H¹—HARLEY MS. 3862.

British Museum. See *Catalogue of the Harleian Manuscripts in the British Museum* (London, 1808), III, 88; C. Brown and R. H. Robbins, *Index,* p. 404; C. Brown, *Index,* II. 234; *DNB,* s.v. "Lydgate"; H. N. MacCracken, *Minor Poems,* I, xx (listed as "3362") ; William Blades, *The Life and Typography of William Caxton* (2v, London, 1863), II, 172.

Vellum, ii + 107 folios; fifteenth century, written for someone of importance whose arms are emblazoned on the first page. Within the cover is written by T. Hearne, "Pervolutavi, mihi accommodante amico egregio Thoma Rawlinsono, armigero. Tho. Hearne, Oct. 21, 1719."

The poem begins on f. 1a which is highly illuminated in a complete border. Page 1b is blank, has markings at top of family coat of arms.

Inside the cover are many names "Robert Mignior, Simon M. Wilson, Giles Gamson, M. William Gibonur." Also: "Edwardus sextus dei gra Angli Franc (?) *and* visu Wey fidei defensor in terra enlic Anglicani visane supur caput"; again, "Edwardus sextus dei grat."

Errors in the text: folio 3b, I 144 and 145 are transposed; f. 3b, line I 150 is merely a repetition of I 143; f. 3b has a recent note at bottom, "The 2 following leaves are transposed," this is true; f. 4b (should be 5b) lines I 207, 208, 209, 210 are garbled, they read 208, 209, 207, 210; f. 5a, has "her" for "herte" in line I 226 ("herte" is written in right margin); f. 7a, line I 338 ends "terment", in the right margin is "of mine"; f. 10a line I 500 has "to" written twice, the second one crossed out; f. 10a, lines I 514 and I 515 are transposed; f. 12b, line I 654 placed after line I 657, line I 653 is garbled, with half of line I 654; f. 14a, a line is added between I 719-720; f. 14a, line I 721 is omitted; f. 15a, lines I 769 and 797 are joined, a new line is added between I 798-799; folio 19b, lines II 153 and 154 are transposed; f. 27a, lines II 565 and 566 transposed; f. 28b, line II 651 missing; after f. 29b, lines II 722-757 are missing (2 pages); f. 30b returns to line II 750; this continues to end of page and line II 777 inclusive; f. 31a lines II 778-805 are repeated as on f. 30a (differences in spelling and letter formations prove this a manuscript repetition); on f. 35a after line II 1004 follow lines II 1013-1028 inclusive, then after II 1028 follow lines II 1005-1012, then line II 1029 follows; f. 39a, lines II 1260 and 1261 are joined, thus giving the stanza only six lines; f. 42b, lines II 1442-1443 are transposed. Line III 378 is missing; lines III 12-13, III 748-749, III 774-775, III 1594-1595-1596, IV 206-207 are transposed; stanza III 344-350 is inserted between lines III 364-365. Lines V 247, V 532, VI 26 are missing; lines V 228-229, V 362-363 and V 502-503 are transposed.

Catchwords: f. 16b, "and thorough her"; f. 24b, "For of my selfe"; f. 40b, "touchyng this"; f. 32b, "And as the snow"; f. 48b, "The sinogogue"; f. 56b, "Affter the comyng"; f. 64b, "Where the fest"; f. 80b, "The third tyme"; f. 88b, "And of the prophet"; f. 96b, "For in sothfastnesse."

There are many textual corrections made by some scribal editor. There are chapter headings, unnumbered. On f. 2a there is a large picture of the "Tree of Jesse". The tree grows out of the sleeping Jesse. Our Lady, holding the Infant, sits in the branches. There are about twenty crowns scattered among the branches. Jesse's left hand holds up the branches; his right hand is under his head.

According to the catalogue, tnis MS was bought at Mr. Rawlinson's Sale in 1734.

H²—HARLEY MS. 2382.

British Museum. See the *Catalogue of Harleian Manuscripts,* II, 675; J. M. Manly and E. Rickert, *Canterbury Tales,* I, 245-248; H. N. MacCracken, *Minor Poems,* I,xx; C. Brown, *Register,* p. 234; C. Brown and R. H. Robbins, *Index,* p. 404; W. Blades, *Caxton,* II, 172.

Paper, quarto, dated 1470-1500, 128 folios, in single columns normally 36 lines, varying 33-37. The MS contains also the "Testament of Lydgate," the "Prioress's Tale," "The Second Nun's Tale," "The Child of Bristow," and a poem on the Assumption of Our Lady (not by Lydgate).

Our poem begins on f. 1a (the page is torn) imperfectly at line I 427, although portions of lines I 422-426 are legible. On folio 1b lines I 455-458 are missing, and lines I 459-461 are partially lost. The poem ends on f. 74b. Missing lines include II 372-579 and II 1142. Line II 987 is omitted in the text, but added in the right margin in the scribal hand. Lines II 1042-1044 are transposed, as are lines II 1050-1051. Lines III 81, III 117, III 196-202, and III 883-889 are missing. Lines III 52-53, III 232-233, and III 1439-1440 are transposed. Lines V 620-627, VI 249 and VI 397 are missing; lines VI 111-112 are transposed.

The writing is a loose, careless, ugly cursive script. There are the usual Latin glosses.

H²ᵃ—SLOANE MS. 297.

British Museum. See C. Brown and R. H. Robbins, *Index,* p. 404; C. Brown, *Register,* II, 234; H. N. MacCracken, *Minor Poems,* I,xx.

This is a single, torn leaf, from Harley MS. 2382 (H²), containing lines III 1671-1741. There is a note in the upper left-hand corner of the page, "This leaf belong to Harley ms. 2382 in which it came between ff. 51 and 52. 18 Oct. 1917. I. P. G." (Israel P. Gollancz?).

H³—HARLEY MS. 629.

British Museum. See *Catalogue of Harleian Manuscripts,* I, 392; C. Brown and R. H. Robbins, *Index,* p. 404; C. Brown, *Register,* II, 234; H. N. MacCracken, *Minor Poems,* I, xx; W. Blades, *Caxton,* II, 172.

Parchment, folio, 32 lines to the page, single column. The poem begins on f. 2a with a table of contents; the Prologue begins on f. 4b.

Folio 2a is highly illuminated with a complete border of lilies. On f. 1b is a picture of the Blessed Virgin lying in bed, with Anna, the prophetess, holding the Christ Child in her arms. Joseph is standing by, while the star shines over the Virgin. All chapter beginnings are illuminated.

Line II 175 is missing; line I 64 is repeated, as are also line II 1669 and V 418. Lines V 586-587 and V 546-547 are transposed. There are eleven catchwords and the usual rubrics in the margin. The poem ends on f. 97a with the colophon "Pees maketh plente / Plente maketh pride / Pride maketh plee / Plee maketh pou*er*te / Pou*er*te maketh pees / and therefore Grace growith after gou*er*naunce."[8]

On f. 97b: "In the yere of þe lorde god M"V xxxi the iiii daye of Dece*m*bre was master Rysse beheaded at the towre hyll in london and one wyllm Howlle [Howsse?] beyng his frand was drawne throwe london to Tyborn and there hanged for tresson."

H⁴—HARLEY MS. 1304.

British Museum. See *Catalog of Harleian Manuscripts,* I. 654-655; C. Brown and R. H. Robbins, *Index,* p. 404; C. Brown, *Register,* II, 234; H. N. MacCracken, *Minor Poems,* I, xx; W. Blades, *Caxton,* II, 172.

Paper, folio, fifteenth century. Other items in the manuscript are: "Questiones bytwene the Maister of Oxenforde and his Clerke"; "The A b c e of Aristotille; or proverbial Verses beginning alphabetically according to the Letters of the Alphabet; each Verse also having other Words with the same letter according to the manner of Piers Plowman and others;" "Other proverbial Sentences, Cautious or Negative Advices according to the letters of the Alphabet."

The poem begins with the table of contents on f. 1a, there are 31 lines to the page, single column. The poem ends on f. 99a with "Explicit vita beate marie."

Between ff. 19b and 20a, four leaves are lost, since lines II 91—II 340 are missing. Line II 1092 is missing. Lines V 586-587 are transposed. There are numerous marginal corrections in the hand of the scribe. Spaces have been left vacant for the illumination of chapter initials, but the initials are lacking. There are seven catchwords and the usual Latin rubrics spread interlinearily through the text.

---

[8]See note for MS. B⁴, p. 27.

"Liber Johanne Hall" is written on the inside cover with the drawing of an ax. The name "Thomas" occurs on f. 82a.

H⁵—HARLEY MS. 3952.

British Museum. See *The Catalogue of the Harleian Manuscripts,* III, 98; C. Brown and R. H. Robbins, *Index,* p. 404; C. Brown, *Register,* II, 234; H. N. MacCracken, *Minor Poems,* I,xx; *DNB,* s.v. "Lydgate"; W. Blades, *Caxton,* II, 172. There is no date in the catalogue. On f. 1a is the title, "Lydgate's Life of the Virgin Mary," in a modern hand.

The poem begins on f. 1a with "Ca° XXXVIII" of the table of contents. The Prologue begins on f. 2a. The poem ends on f. 105a. There are 28 lines to the page, single column.

Line II 175 is omitted; a leaf has been lost between ff. 10b and 11a. This comprises lines I 491—I 546. A note on f. 11a reads, "1 leaf missing here consisting of the end of capitulo V and the commencement of cap VI. March, 1871. C. Tame." Lines transposed are II 767-768, II 885-886, I 794-795, I 858-859, I 223-224, I 410-411; lines garbled are II 756, II 1100, I 814, I 243. Line II 661 is omitted, but added at the bottom of the page. Lines III 219-220, III 949-950 are transposed; lines III 743-770 omitted, added between lines III 798-799. Lines V 291 and V 407-518 are missing; line VI 2 is written after VI 7 and VI 401 after VI 403.

The poem has the usual rubrics and has been corrected in a later hand. There are marginal corrections for errors in the text. On the inside back cover is written, "folio 105 Ed in May 1883."

H⁶—HARLEY MS. 4011.

British Museum. See *Catalogue of Harleian Manuscripts,* III, 103; C. Brown and R. H. Robbins, *Index,* p. 404; C. Brown, *Register,* II, 234; *DNB,* s.v. "Lydgate"; H. N. MacCracken, *Minor Poems,* I,xx; W. Blades, *Caxton,* II, 172.

The manuscript is of paper. Other items in the manuscript: 1. a short poem by Lydgate, preceded by a fragment of another. 2. His translation of "Stans puer ad mensam." 3. Lenvoye to Humfray late Duke of Glowceter. 4. Desolation of Rome. 5. A devout Oryson to the holy sacrament. 6. Art of Dying. "For as myche as the passage of deth." 7. John Lydate's Life of the Virgin Mary. 8. A

Poem entitled the Libelle of English policy; "exhorting all Englande to keepe the See envyron, and mainly the narrow See. Shewyng what profite cometh thereof, and also what worship and salvation to England." 9. John Lydgate's Calendar, from March to December. 10. Rules for health, in verse. 11. Mappula Anglie. "For as muche as in the English boke the which y have complied of *Legenda aurea."* 12. An Almanack. 13. A Copy of Verses beginning, "Miseremini mei ye that ben my fryndys." 14. Domestic Precepts for K. Edward 3. "In nomine Patris, God kepe me." Written in verse.

The poem has been corrected by a later hand. There are many erasures. On f. 56a lines II 1203-1207 are omitted in the text; added in the aforementioned later hand at the bottom of the page. Lines III 141-168, III 1623, IV 393-399 are missing; lines IV 162 and IV 169 are transposed. Lines V 451 and VI 262-318 are missing.

The first letter on each page is highly illuminated with floral designs and pictures. There is much scribbling throughout the manuscript. On f. 76b, "Wyllyam Wyllyam Don;" on 78b, the alphabet is scribbled on the side of the page; on 82a, "God save kyng hedward syxe"; on 95a, "Thomas Misruncibus (?) ;" on 98a, "Wyllyam Potter of the hoye"; on 99b, John Francis Vyeccord (?)"; on 111b, "hary lambe"; 115b, "This is Magod feschares bok"; on 119a, "Explicit John lydgate monke of Bury Bood W. Granell"; and on 119a, "Etto Gobeth." There are also the usual rubrics referring to the text.

H⁷—HARLEY MS. 4260.

British Museum. See *Catalogue of the Harleian Manuscripts,* III, 130; C. Brown and R. H. Robbins, *Index,* p. 404; C. Brown, *Register,* II, 234; H. N. MacCracken, *Minor Poems,* I,xx.

On paper, fifteenth century. The poem begins with the Prologue on f. 2a; it ends on f. 108a. Folio 99b is blank. There are spaces for illuminated capitals in the beginning of each book, but the illuminations were never made. Only the small guide letters are present. The pages are lined, with 28 lines to the page. There is much correction throughout the MS in the same hand as the text. The text is divided into six books, with 61 chapters.

One leaf is missing between ff. 8b and 9a, comprising lines I 393-448. Line I 628, omitted in the text, is added at the bottom of the page. Lines III 680-686 are missing; line III 774 is written in the margin, omitted in text. Line VI 449 is missing; lines VI 97-98 are transposed; line V 464 is written after V 467. There are ten catchwords and numerous rubrics, the latter alluding to sources for scriptural material.

On f. 108a, at the end of the poem there is added, "Grace grewith after gou*er*naunce."[9] Then follows much scribbling and:

PROTEGE X° [Christie?] Rosam / flo*s* floru*m* nu*n*c speciosam

Ut regat ip*s*a gregem / Rectu*m* statuat quoque legem

Domine saluu*m* fac Regem / Regem honorificate

A Domino factum est istud / Rex v*er*o laetabitur in deo.

The first three lines of the above appear, then under them, and clearer, the four lines as written here.

H⁸ — HARLEY MS. 5272.

British Museum. See *Catalogue of Harleian Manuscripts,* III, 257; H. N. MacCracken, *Minor Poems* I,xx; C. Brown and R. H. Robbins, *Index,* p. 404; *DNB,* s.v. "Lydgate"; C. Brown, *Register,* II, 233; W. Blades, *Caxton,* II, 772.

Vellum, 28 lines to the page, single column, fifteenth century. Other items are a life of St. Dorothy and the prose work, the Abbey of the Holy Ghost.

Our poem begins imperfectly on f. 1a with line I 419. Lines I 468-469 are transposed; lines I 792 and II 649, omitted in the text are added in the margin. Lines III 536-591 are omitted; lines III 882-883 are transposed. The poem ends on f. 98b with the colophon, "here endith the life of oure lady. Quod Johes Forster."

There is much scribbling throughout the MS. Some names are noted Thomas (ff. 1b, 42b, 50a, 54a), John Cradocke (32a, 74a, 98a), John Mallon (18b, 33a), and Elizabeth (42a).

C¹—Cambridge University MS. Kk.1.3.

Library of Cambridge University. See *A Catalogue of the Manuscripts, The Library of University of Cambridge* (Cambridge,

[9]See note for MS. B⁴, p. 27.

1861), III, 554; J. M. Manly and E. Rickert, *Canterbury Tales,* I. 302-303; C. Brown and R. H. Robbins, *Index,* p. 404; *DNB,* s.v., "Lydgate"; C. Brown, *Register,* II, 234; H. N. MacCracken, *Minor Poems,* I,xx.

Paper, 11¼" x 8½", single columns, 35 lines to the page, dated 1420-1450. Other items in this manuscript are Hoccleve's *Regiment of Princes,* the prose treatise, *Three Kings of Cologne,* a *Chronicle of England* and Chaucer's *Prioress's Tale.*

Our poem is item number 10 in the book, beginning on folio 2a. The tops of ff. 2a, 2b, 3a, 3b, 4a, and 4b are completely lost; all other pages are water-stained, some (ff. 5a-10b) to a point of illegibility.

The first full line of the *Life of Our Lady* is line I 75. The poem ends on f. 94a with, "Here endith the boke of the Nativite of our lady and of the birth of our lord Jh*esu* Criste".

Lines II 427-430 are omitted. Lines I 601-602, I 846-847, II 55-56, and III 1680-1681 are transposed. Lines III 900-901 are omitted and lines III 895-896 are substituted; lines III 1779-1780 are repeated between lines III 1781-1782; line IV 195 is omitted, line IV 191 is repeated in its place. Lines III 1-3 are repeated; line II 508 is garbled. Lines V 34, 35, 147, 181, 182, 233, 234, 363, 364, 602, 609, 623, 682, 683, 698, VI 230, 295-301, 373, 418 are missing. Lines V 611-612 and V 586-587 are transposed.

On f. 80a is written "Lanselat Welles son of Wyllm Welles." The poem has ten catchwords, many Latin glosses.

C²—Cambridge University MS. Mm.6.5.

Cambridge University Library. See *A Catalogue of the Manuscripts, The Library of University of Cambridge* (Cambridge, 1861), IV, 383; C. Brown and R. H. Robbins, *Index,* p. 404; C. Brown, *Register,* II, 234; H. N. MacCracken, *Minor Poems,* I, xx (incorrectly labeled "Mm. 6. 15").

Parchment, octavo, containing 145 folios, 21 lines to a page, well-written in a hand of the former half of the fifteenth century. It has illuminated capitals.

Inside the cover: "From the library of Richard Holdsworth, D. D., Master of Emmanuel College. 1664." On page ia; "Holdsworth 150." The poem begins on f. la, which is highly illuminated in a complete border of flowers.

On folio 60a line II 1589 *than* is written twice; the second word is underscored with three dots. Lines V 694-VI 1 are missing. Lines VI 216-222 are repeated. Lines III 664-665 and VI 310-311 are transposed. Catchwords occur on: 16b, "A dove"; 24b, "Ys not thy Mercy"; 32b, "and when the angel"; 40b, "And he that "; 48b, "What shall"; 56b, "For no thyng"; 64b, "the sinagoge"; 72b, "Amyd the"; 79b, "And soth"; 87b, "And evyn"; 95b, "Unto"; 103b, "Whan Janus"; 111b, "For of our"; 119b, "In franke"; 127b, "Now C'este"; 135b, "That his lif." Line V 313 is written after V 315; two halves of V 587-588 are reversed.

Folios 26b, 27a, 32b, 106a, 108a, 110a are obscure in places. On back inside cover there is the name, "John Pinalt" in script (for his identity see Manly-Rickert, *The Text of Canterbury Tales,* I, 214-215). There is a folio number missing between ff. 73 and 74.

Spelling peculiarities are "sche" for "she"; "hit" for "it"; "trewly" for "pleynly"; "sikirly" for "pleynly". Beginning with folio 17a there is a change in the writing. Occasionally when lines run over, the omitted word at the end of the line is added to another line. Proper names, virtues, etc., are underlined in the text.

The poem ends on 141a with: "Explicit vita beate Marie virginis et matris dei."

C³—TRINITY CAMBRIDGE MS. 601 (R.3.21).

Library of Trinity College, Cambridge. See M. R. James, *The Western MSS in the Library of Trinity College,* Cambridge (4v, Cambridge, 1900-1904), II, 83-95; C. Brown and R. H. Robbins, *Index,* p. 404; C. Brown, *Register,* II, 234; H. N. MacCracken, *Minor Poems,* I, xx.

Paper, 10⅞ x 7⅞, 320 folios, varying numbers of lines to the page. Fifteenth century, time of Edward IV (1461-1483), the manuscript is very neatly written. It was given to the library by George Wilmer (B.A., Trinity College, 1622). It once belonged to John Stowe, whose name is on ff. 1 and 320. At the bottom of f. 1b is, "Tho. Griffith 1650." The volume includes many Lydgate items, mostly minor poems.

Our poem begins on 85a and ends on f. 156b. There are spaces for illuminated capitals throughout the poem, but the capitals are missing. Line II 523 is missing. Lines I 468-469, I 601-602, III

1259-1260, III 1439-1440, and IV 405-406 are transposed. There are three catchwords and many Latin glosses. The poem is in the six-book divisions, ending on f. 156b with, "Explicit purificacio *and* finis libri compilati *per* Johen Lydgate monach*um* de Bury."

C⁴—GONVILLE AND CAIUS, CAMBRIDGE MS. 230 (*Magnificat* only).

Gonville and Caius Library, Cambridge. See M. R. James, *Catalogue of MSS. in Gonville and Caius College Library* (2v, Cambridge, 1907), I. 268-276; MacCracken, *Minor Poems,* I, xx; C. Brown and R. H. Robbins, *Index,* p. 404.

Vellum, folio, 5½ by 4, leaves 164 plus 8; 23 lines to a page, fifteenth century.

There is an old foliation (XV cent.) running to f. 182 and a modern pagination, which includes the flyleaves and makes 350 pages. Original binding is of skin over pads of leather. The volume is from St. Alban's Abbey, as appears by many of the verses contained in the volume. It is closely connected with Abbot John Whetham.

Our poem is item 26 in the volume: *Magnificat* in English verse (stanzas of eight lines by Lydgate; f. 54a-55b, pp. 113-116).

On folio 54a is the title "Magnificat;" after the selection on 55b is written, "j. lytgate." The text is lines II 981-1060 of the *Life of Our Lady.* The stanzas are separated by the Latin text of the *Magnificat.*

C⁵—TRINITY CAMBRIDGE MS. 602 (R.3.22).

Trinity College Library, Cambridge. See M. R. James, *The Western Manuscripts in the Library of Trinity College, Cambridge* (4v, Cambridge, 1900-1904), III, 95; C. Brown and R. H. Robbins, *Index,* p. 404; C. Brown, *Register,* II, 234; H. N. MacCracken, *Minor Poems,* I, xx.

Vellum, 9½ x 6½, 210 folios, 28 lines to the page. Fifteenth century, early. Given to library by George Wilmer (B.A., Trinity College, 1622). The manuscript contains also Hoccleve's *Regiment of Princes,* beginning on f. 111a.

Our poem begins on f. 1a with the Table of Contents. It ends on f. 109b with the aphorism, "Pees maketh plente," etc.[10]

---

[10]See footnote for MS. B⁴, p. 27.

Line III 1097 is written after III 1099; line III 1405, omitted in the text, is written in the margin. Lines V 197, 198, 199 are repeated.

AD[1]—B. M. ADDITIONAL MS. 29729 (*Magnificat* only).

British Museum. See the *Catalogue of Additions to Manuscripts in the British Museum, in years 1854-1875* (London, 1877), II, 696-701. See also E. Sieper, *Reson and Sensuallyte* (1901-3; *EETSES,* 84, 89), I,xiii-xviii; C. Brown and R. H. Robbins, *Index,* p. 404.

Quarto, 1558, written in a cursive script. This is a large collection (52 items) in the hand of John Stowe, the historian. On the last page is the note: "This boke perteynethe to John Stowe and was by hym wryten in the yere of owr lord MDLVIII."

Item 15 is the paraphrase of the *Magnificat* (II 981-1060). It begins on f. 122a and ends of f. 123a with "Amen lidgate, Finis: John Stowe." The *Magnificat* in Latin is written interlinearily between stanzas.

Other important items in the manuscript are: *The Court of Sapience, The Siege of Thebes, Reason and Sensuality,* and *The Life of Saint Margaret.*

AD[2]—B. M. ADDITIONAL MS. 19452.

British Museum. See *Catalogue of Additions to the Manuscripts in the British Museum in the years* 1848-1853 (London, 1868), p. 242; C. Brown and R. H. Robbins, *Index,* p. 404; C. Brown, *Register,* II, 234; H. N. MacCracken, *Minor Poems,* I,xx (listed as "Addit. 19432"); W. Blades, *Caxton,* II, 172.

Vellum; quarto; dated by catalogue as the earlier half of the fifteenth century. There are thirty lines to the page, single columns. A table of contents begins on f. la, ending at "Ca° XXV" at the bottom of f. 1b.

The poem proper begins imperfectly at line I 31. Between ff. 6b and 7a lines I 328-799 are missing. The leaf containing ff. 7a and 7b is torn; parts of lines I 829-836 are missing. Between ff. 11b and 12a there is a leaf lost, losing lines II 207-266. Lines V 691-VI 51 are missing; lines V 586-587 are transposed. The manuscript ends imperfectly on f. 89b with line VI 277, "Of dethe to eschewethe *pr*eservacion." There are the usual rubrics. All chapter initials are illuminated.

Ad³—B. M. Additional MS. 19252.

British Museum. See the *Catalogue of Additions to the Manuscripts in the British Museum, in the years 1848-1853* (London, 1868), p. 208; H. N. MacCracken, *Minor Poems,* I,xx; C. Brown and R. H. Robbins, *Index,* p. 404; C. Brown, *Register,* II, 234.

Vellum, folio, early part of fifteenth century. The poem begins imperfectly on f. 4a with line I 113. On f. 16b a note "one leaf gone" refers to the lack of lines I-841-I 889 inclusive. Again the loss in Book II of lines II 1631-II 1669 is referred to by a note on f. 45b, "A leaf wanting." Lines III 1-15, III 680-686, III 1206-IV 57 and V 1-28 are missing. Lines VI 97-98 are transposed.

The manuscript is highly illuminated. Chapter initials and the beginning of each book are adorned. The manuscript has been emended with personal readings.

Ash¹—Ashmole MS. 39 (Bodleian 6919).

Bodleian Library, Oxford. See W. H. Black, *A Descriptive Analytical and Critical Catalogue of the Manuscripts Bequeathed Unto the University of Oxford by Elias Ashmole, Esq., M.D., F.R.S.* (Oxford, 1845), pp. 61-62; C. Brown and R. H. Robbins, *Index,* p. 404; *DNB,* s.v., "Lydgate"; C. Brown, *Register,* II, 233; H. N. MacCracken, *Minor Poems,* I,xx.

Paper, folio, 109 leaves, written in the latter part of the fifteenth century. The poem begins on f. 1a with the table of contents and ends on f. 109a; there are 28 lines to a page. All chapters begin with an illuminated capital, a marginal number and an interlinear title.

Line II 987 is missing; the leaf, with ff. 41a and 41b is torn, losing parts of lines II 1224-1228 and II 1247-1257. A note reports, "In this torn state 1 June 1831." Lines I 354-355 and II 1246-1247 are transposed. Lines III 141-168 are missing; lines III 1514-1515 are transposed. Lines VI 210-216 are missing; lines V 586-587 are transposed. There are four catchwords and the usual Latin marginal glosses.

On the parchment which lines the wooden covers of the volume, are many vestiges of its former possessors; among which are the names (probably the autographs) of Sir T. Bourchier, Anne Bourgchier, and Sir William Rous knight, at the beginning; and at the end, Isabell Bourchier, and the following stanza:

> O ye women wyche be enclyned
> be the enflewens off *your* nature
> To be as pure as fold reffyned
> In yowre trowth tendure
> Arme *your* sselffe in strong armure
> lest men assaye yowr sekernesse
> sset uppon *your* brest *your* sselffe to assure
> A myghtty scheld of dowbelnesse."

There is also a large decorative "T" and:

> "What shuld I say sithe faith is ded
> And truth is exiled in womanhed."

Beneath this is: "Bourscher Richard Daniel —

> My harte ys yours ye may be sure
> And so shall it be while lyff shall indure."

Ash²—Ashmole MS. 59 (Bodleian 6943).

Bodleian Library, Oxford. See W. H. Black, *Catalogue of Manuscripts in the Ashmole Collection* (Oxford, 1845), pp. 95-104; C. Brown and R. H. Robbins, *Index,* p. 404; C. Brown, *Register,* II, 233, H. N. MacCracken, *Minor Poems,* I,xx; *DNB,* s.v., "Lydgate."

A paper, folio volume, the manuscript contains two major works. The first, of 134 numbered leaves, dated as fifteenth century, consists of sixty-six minor works of Chaucer, Gower, and Lydgate. The second part (beginning on f. 135a), written in a secretary-hand of the time of Queen Elizabeth, contains the *Life of Our Lady* and part of Lydgate's *Troy Book.*

Our poem begins imperfectly; the Prologue is missing, Lines I 68, I 451, II 1020, II 1561, II 1637, III 643, III 897-IV 225 are lacking.

Lines transposed are I 208-209, II 927-928, II 1076-1078; lines II 855-868 are placed after line II 875; line III 660 is placed after III 642; lines III 769-770 are garbled. Lines VI 210-216 are missing. The poem ends imperfectly with line VI 301.

The manuscript has numerous marginal Latin glosses. There is a change of hand beginning with f. 144a. On folios 181b-182a are the epilogue verses of Caxton, written in an entirely different hand.[11] On f. 182a there is, "Here endith the Life off our Lady."

Adv[1]—ADVOCATES MS. 1.1.6 (*Magnificat* only).

See C. Brown and R. H. Robbins, *Index,* p. 404; C. Brown, *Register,* II, 234; *The Bannatyne Manuscript,* ed., N. Tod Ritchie (Edinburgh and London, 1928), II, 60-63; *The Bannatyne Manuscript* (Hunterian Club Publications, 3v, Glasgow, 1873), I, 64-67.

This fragment of the *Life of Our Lady* contains only the paraphrase of the *Magnificat* (II 980-1061). In the manuscript, our poem begins on f. 25b with, "The Song of the Virgin Mary." It ends on f. 26b with "Finis, Followis ballatis of the nativitie of chryste."

There are Latin glosses interlinearily between stanzas. Lines II 1003, 1011 and II 1027 are missing. In line 1060, "have" is written incorrectly, then lined through.

Adv[2]—ADVOCATES MS. 19. 3. 1.

Advocates' Library, Edinburgh, Scotland. See W. Turnbull, *Visio Tundalis* (Edinburgh, 1843); C. Brown and R. H. Robbins, *Index,* p. 404. C. Brown, *Register,* II, 234; H. N. MacCracken, *Minor Poems,* I,xx (listed with former catalogue number, "Jac. V. 7").

Quarto, fifteenth century, single columns, 22 lines to the page, 216 folios. This manuscript contains also "The Visions of Tundale", "The Trentalle of Saint Gregory", and various hymns and prayers.

Our poem begins on f. 176a with Book IV, line 1, "Whan Ianus bifrons in cold Ienuare", and ends on f. 210a. Thus, only Books IV, V, and VI of the *Life of Our Lady* are in this MS. On f. 75b is found, "Johannes Houghtton me fecit." The admonition, "Take gude hede", occurs on f. 193b and f. 195a. Lines VI 302-462 are missing. Lines IV 271-272 are transposed. The poem ends imperfectly at line VI 301.

---

[11]See the description of Caxton's first edition, below in "The Prints", p. 51ff.

Hn¹—Huntington MS. HM 115.

Henry E. Huntington Library, San Marino, California. See Seymour de Ricci and W. J. Wilson, *Census of Medieval and Renaissance MSS in the United States and Canada* (3v, New York, 1935-40), I, 52; C. Brown and R. H. Robbins, *Index,* p. 404; C. Brown, *Register,* II, 234.

Vellum, early XVth century, 113 ff. (22 x 15 cm.), ff. 110-112 supplied on modern vellum by a XIXth century hand. The binding is blue morocco by Kalthoeber. The poem begins on f. 1a with a Table of Contents and ends on 112a. The number of lines to the page varies between 23 and 28. Someone has recently collated the chapter divisions in this MS with those of Caxton's print and reported the comparison with marginal notes.

There are six catchwords and numerous rubrics referring to scriptural identities in the text. There are many marginal corrections in the hand of the scribe.

Lines I 469-470 are transposed; lines II 423-4 and II 361-362 are garbled, thus omitting II 424 and II 362. Lines III 1439-1440 are transposed.

According to S. de Ricci and W. J. Wilson, *op. cit.,* the recent history of this MS has been the John Towneley sale (London 1814, I, n.880, rather than n.881); William Bragge sale (London, 1876, n.287) to Ellis and White; Robert Hoe collection (Cat. 1908, p. 126); his sale (New York, 1911, I. n.2148) to G. D. Smith.

Hn²—Huntington MS. HM 144.

Henry E. Huntington Library, San Marino, California. See Seymour de Ricci and W. J. Wilson, *Census of Medieval and Renaissance MSS in the United States and Canada* (3v, New York, 1935-40), I, 58. See also John M. Manly and Edith Rickert, *The Text of the Canterbury Tales* (8v, Chicago, 1940), I, 289-294 and 642; C. Brown and Robbins, *Index,* p. 404.

Paper, 151 folios, single columns, 28 lines to the page, dated 1480-1500. The manuscript contains sixteen items, mostly of religious nature. Interesting inclusions are Chaucer's *Monk's Tale* and the *Tale of Melibeus,* and Lydgate's *The Churl and the Bird* and *Horse, Goose, and Sheep.*

Our poem is item 2: "How Merci and Pees Ryghtwisnes and Trouthe disputyd for the Redempciun of Mankynde", ff. 11a-20a. This is only Book II, lines 1-504 of the *Life of Our Lady* and comprises only the Four Daughters of God allegory. There is an error on f. 17a, an insertion of lines II 615-620 between lines II 347 and 348. On f. 17b, lines II 369 and 370 are joined, thus omitting a line. On f. 18b line II 433, written incorrectly as a last line of one stanza, is crossed through and added as the first line of the following stanza. MS. Hn² was formerly in the Huth Library.

Ch—CHICAGO UNIVERSITY MS. 566.

University of Chicago Library. See Seymour de Ricci and W. J. Wilson, *Census of Medieval and Renaissance MSS in the United States and Canada* (3v, New York, 1935-40), I, 592; C. Brown and R. H. Robbins, *Index,* p. 404; C. Brown, *Register,* II, 234; N. H. MacCracken, *Minor Poems,* I,xx.

Vellum, 108 folios, 26 x 16 cm., fifteenth century, modern red-brown morocco binding. Twenty-eight lines to the page, single column.

The poem begins imperfectly on f. 2a with Chapter XXXI of the table of contents, completes this table then skips to line I 113. Lines II 1613, III 24-52, III 331, III 462, III 840 and III 1143 and V 291 are omitted. Lines III 906-907-908 are transposed; line IV 149 is repeated.

There are 13 catchwords and the usual Latin glosses for references in the text.

On the inside front cover and fly-leaf, Sydney C. Cockerell, a former owner, has written a description of the MS, naming other MSS of our poem. He adds a brief history of MS. Ch; "Bought from the Chaucer Book Co. 37 St. Martin's Court, London. Cat. no. 7, p. 5. (bought by them at Puttick's Dec. 21, 1904 lot 179, 18). Rebound for me in red seal skin by *Miss* Adams of Broadway, 1905. $\begin{bmatrix} \text{Mr.} \\ \text{Mc} \end{bmatrix}$. The seller at Puttick's was Colonel Taylor, as it came from a library which had been for many years at Newnton Priory, Gloucestershire—". According to de Ricci and Wilson, MS. Ch was given to the University of Chicago in 1931 by an anonymous donor.

The names of earlier owners are found in the MS: "E. B. 1578" (f. 23a), "W. Battis" (f. 23b), "Humphrey Carrew" (ff. 69b, 76b, 90a). The poem ends with the aphorism, "Pees maketh plente/ Plente maketh pryde/ Pryde maketh plee/ Plee maketh pouert/ Pouert maketh pees/Grace growth after gouernaunce."[12]

Co—Cottonian MS. Appendix VIII.

British Museum. See *A Catalogue of the Manuscripts in the Cottonian Library Deposited in the British Museum,* Printed by Command of King George III, 1802, page 615; C. Brown and R. H. Robbins, *Index,* p. 404; C. Brown, *Register,* II, 234; H. N. Mac-Cracken, *Minor Poems,* I,xx; W. Blades, *Caxton,* II, 172.

Velum, quarto, fifteenth century; IV + 108 leaves. Also in the volume is "Memoranda for the use of travellers in the East," beginning on f. 108b. Twenty-eight lines to the page, single column.

Folio 1a has, "Johens Lydgate ad Edmundi sanct Bursenis Camoby monachus omnium suis temporis in Anglia Poetarum admirabia dicto, facile primus floruit, sexagenarius A. D. 1440 sub Rege Henrico VI°. Scripsit Vitam Sanctae Mariae ad Henricum V° et alia multa Balae, p. 980." Below is added: "John Lydyat monk of Bury St. Edmunds On the Praise of the Virgin Mary."

The manuscript is obscure in many places, notably ff. 2a, 2g, 3a, 15a, 17a, 58a, 60a, 61b, 62a, 64a, 67a, 94a. On folio 22a, line II 229 is omitted and in its place line II 226 is repeated in error. On folio 31a, line II 735 is omitted. Folio 43a, fifty-six lines are omitted, but they are inserted on folio 44a fifty-six lines later. (This same error occurs in MS. B[5]). On folio 47a the poem breaks off after line II 1628 and omits lines II 1628 to II 1669 inclusive; line II 1628 begins on folio 48a after line III 14 in Book III.

The only rubrics are interlinear, the seven gifts of the Holy Ghost in Latin on folio 8b, the seven petitions of Our Lady on folios 10a, 10b, 11a, 11b.

Catchwords are 17b, "and thourgh"; 25b, "For of myself"; 41b, "and they echone"; 49b, "ayenst"; 57b, "The wondrest"; 65b, "Betwene his sone"; 73b, "The tyme of tymes"; 81b, "The fyve tymes."

---

[12]See note for MS. B[4], p. 27.

The scribe uses "force" for "strength"; "also" for "eke"; "scheo" for "she." At the bottom of 40a is written "Anne". On 40b at the bottom is written "Balgud(?) Coldwall 55." On 36a, line II 1026, "adown" is written for "aside", then crossed out and "aside" is added.

Lg—Longleat MS.

Library of Marquis of Bath, Wiltshire, England. See *Historical MSS Commission Report III* (London, 1872), p. 180; C. Brown and R. H. Robbins, *Index,* p. 404; C. Brown, *Register,* II, 234; *DNB,* s.v. "Lydgate."

Quarto, vellum, 15th century. The poem begins on f. 2a with a table of contents; it ends imperfectly on f. 104b with line VI 128. The description in the *Historical MSS Commission Report III,* identifies the last line as "the 30th line of cap. 73." This is an error, the last line is line 30 of chapter 83, or line VI 128, as mentioned above.

Omissions include lines I 259-336, I 362, I 541, I 667, I 671, I 721, I 796, II 651, II 756, II 1661, V 168, V 291, V 329, V 424 and VI 68, Lines I 653-654 are garbled, as are lines I 755-756, I 796-797, II 270-271 and II 300-301. Lines I 345-356, II 361-362, II 569-570 and V 526-532 are transposed. Line II 447 is omitted and the phrase "To seke or write" is inserted in its place. Lines III 664-665, III 677-678, and III 1173-1174 are transposed.

There are no illuminations, although spaces are left for them. On f. 2a the first page of the table of contents is highly decorated. There are catchwords and rubrics. On the inside back cover there is scribbling and the name, "James Whys." On f. 5a is found "Liber Joannus Thynne", Jon Thynne", "I have me commaund", "So muche", "Jon Commaunde hankennt cokenolde". The inside cover leaf, "This boke was compylyde be John Ludgate", "In celas aungel wrot After this sonne a [mist?]."

An—Society of Antiquaries MS. 134.

Library of the Society of Antiquaries, London. See *A Catalogue of Manuscripts in the Library of the Society of Antiquaries of London* (London, 1816), pp. 45-46; MacCracken, *Minor Poems,* I,xx; C. Brown and R. H. Robbins, *Index,* p. 404; C. Brown, *Register,* II, 234.

Vellum, folio, fifteenth century. Contains also Gower's *The Confessio Amantis, The Poems of Thomas Occlef* (sic), and *A Metrical Version of Boethius de Consolatione Philosophiae.* The catalogue adds that the manuscript appears formerly to have belonged to the Priory of Hales Owen in Shropshire.

The poem begins imperfectly on f. 1a with line II, 222 and ends on f. 30a with "explicit vita beate marie" and the aphorism, "Pees maketh plente", etc.[13]

The manuscript omits lines II 1092, II 1114, and II 674-II 990 inclusive. Lines V 586-587 are transposed. There is some scribbling in the volume. On f. 1b there is a space left for a picture, but no picture. Line III 766, omitted in the text, is added at the bottom of the page.

L—LAMBETH MS. 344.

Library of the Archbishop of Canterbury, Lambeth Palace, London. See Henry J. Todd, *A Catalogue of the Archiepiscopal Manuscripts in the Library at Lambeth Palace* (London, 1812), p. 45; H. N. MacCracken, *Minor Poems,* I,xx; C. Brown and R. H. Robbins, *Index,* p. 404; C. Brown, *Register,* II, 234.

Parchment, quarto, 99 leaves, fifteenth century. There are six items in the manuscript besides the *Life of Our Lady;* all are minor poems of Lydgate.

Our poem begins on f. 13a with the Table of Contents. Lines I 71-77, II 280, II 1618, V 252, VI 145 and VI 383 are omitted. Lines I 12-13, I 285-286 and IV 284-285 are transposed. Lines I 133, I 175, I 737, omitted in the text, are added in the margin. Line I 744, written after I 736, is repeated in its proper place; line II 441 is repeated after line II 447, then crossed through.

Hu—HUNTERIAN MS. 232.

Hunterian Museum, University of Glasgow Library. See *A Catalogue of the Manuscripts in the Library of the Hunterian Museum in the University of Glasgow* (Glasgow, 1908), pp. 183-185; C. Brown and R. H. Robbins, *Index,* p. 404; C. Brown, *Register,* II, 234.

---

[13]See footnote for MS. B⁴, p. 27.

Vellum, 11⅜ x 7⅝, 104 folios, in single columns of 28 lines each. Fifteenth century. Binding is of millboards, covered brown (faded crimson) grained Russia, gilt-tooled sides and edges, recently re-backed, old dark and light green morocco shields, with the title (gilt) replaced: Sacred/Poems/M.S.

The poem begins on folio 1a and ends imperfectly with line VI 308. There is much scribbling throughout the volume, doggerel verse, and names of former owners.

Ct—Chetham MS. 6709.

Chetham Library, Manchester. See J. M. Manly and Edith Rickert, *The Text of the Canterbury Tales* (8v, Chicago, 1940), I, 82-84; the *Catalog of MSS in the Chetham Library* (2v, Manchester, 1849), II, 621; C. Brown, *Register,* II, 234; C. Brown and R. H. Robbins, *Index,* p. 404.

Vellum and paper, 282 folios, 21 lines to the page, single columns, dated March, 1490 (f. 170a). Written in a small cursive hand by "William Cotson, cannonicus" (ff. 5a, 170a, 282b). Other items in this MS are the "Second Nun's Tale," the "Prioress's Tale," Lydgate's lives of Sts. Margaret, George, Edmund and Fremund.

Our poem begins on f. 6b and ends on f. 156a with a colophon identical with that of Caxton's print of 1484.

Lines II 1313 and II 1646 and VI 210-216 are missing. Lines I 375-376, II 508-509, and II 720-721 are transposed.

J. M. Manly and Edith Rickert (*op. cit.,* I, 84), believe this MS is a copy of Caxton's second printing of the "Second Nun's Tale" and the "Prioress's Tale." Many major variant readings and the transposition and garbling of lines II 720-721 show that the MS. Ct version of the *Life of Our Lady* must also be a copy of Caxton's print of 1484.[14]

S—Sloane MS. 1785

British Museum. See E. J. L. Scott, *Index to Sloane Manuscripts in the British Museum,* (Clowes; London, 1904), p. 327; C. Brown and R. H. Robbins, *Index,* p. 404; C. Brown, *Register,* II. 234; H. N. MacCracken, *Minor Poems,* I,xx.

---

[14]See R. A. Klinefelter, "Lydgate's 'Life of Our Lady' and the Chetham MS. 6709," *Papers of the Bibliographical Society of America,* XLVI (1952).

Fifteenth century, imperfect; 28 lines to page, sometimes 21.

Poem begins on f. 14a (old 13 crossed out) with line I 434; the poem ends on f. 29b, with line I 795. There are spaces left for illuminated capitals, but only the small guide letters are present.

There are many errors in the manuscript: f. 15a has only 21 lines, and between 14b and 15a, lines I 482-797 are missing. Folio 16a begins with line II 442. Missing between ff. 15b-16a are lines I 848-II 441 inclusive. Between 16b-17a lines II 498-707 inclusive are missing; f. 17b ends with II 762; f. 18a begins with line II 8. On f. 18b, line II 49 is missing, is added at the bottom of the page, and marked. On f. 21a, lines II 190-196 are missing; f. 21b, line II 208 is missing; f. 23b ends with line II 343, but f. 24a begins with line I 482, goes on to f. 29b and ends at line I 797.

Poem ends at f. 29b with line I 797. It is easily seen that the manuscript is quite garbled.

Ar—ARUNDEL MS. 168.

British Museum. See the *Catalogue of Manuscripts in the British Museum* (London, 1834), I, 46; C. Brown and Robbins, *Index,* p. 404; C. Brown, *Register,* II, 234; W. Blades, *Caxton,* II, 172; H. N. MacCracken, *Minor Poems,* I,xx (listed as "Arundel 66").

Paper and vellum, folio, fifteenth century. The manuscript contains eleven items, of which the most important are: *The Legend of St. Dorothe, The Legend of St. Kataryne* by Capgrave, and the *Life of Our Lady.*

Our poem begins imperfectly on f. 66a with line I 414. The manuscript is in double columns, 70 lines to the page. Lines II 164, II 185 and II 583 are omitted in the text but added in the margin. Lines II 593, III 680-686, and III 1020 are missing entirely. The manuscript ends imperfectly on f. 85a with line III 1208. There are no chapter headings.

J—ST. JOHN'S, OXFORD MS. 56.

Library of St. John's College, Oxford. See H. O. Coxe, *Catalogue Codicum MSS Qui in Collegiis Aulisque Oxoniensibus Hodie Asservantur* (2 Parts, Oxford, 1852), II, 16; C. Brown and R. H. Robbins, *Index,* p. 404. C. Brown, *Register,* II, 234; *DNB,* s.v., "Lydgate"; H. N. MacCracken, *Minor Poems,* I,xx.

Paper, folio, 88 folios, fifteenth century, 42 lines to the page. A note on f. 1a attests, "Ex dono venerabilis viri Richardi Tilesly, SS. Theol. doctoris, archidiac. Roffensis et quondam socii." The manuscript contains also Lydgate's poem beginning, "Quis dabit capiti meo fontem lacrimarum" (f. 74b), and his poem on the interpretation of the Mass (f. 76b). At the end of the book are two letters by Thomas Elmes, to Mr. Bachous, dean of Oundhill, and to Robert Andrew, of Peterborough.

Folios 9 and 24 are mutilated; lines I 673-697, I 698-739, II 1053-1137, are thus lost. Lines III 63-67 are omitted; lines I 468-469 and II 1511-1512 and V 116-117 are transposed.

CC—CORPUS CHRISTI, OXFORD MS. 237.

Corpus Christi College Library, Oxford University. See Henricus Coxe, *Catalogue Codicum MSS Qui in Collegiis Aulisque Oxoniensibus Hodie Adservantur* (Oxford, 1852), II, 98-99; MacCracken, *Minor Poems,* I, xx; C. Brown and R. H. Robbins, *Index,* p. 404; C. Brown, *Register,* II, 234.

Paper, quarto, fifteenth century, 237 folios. This MS contains fifteen items. Some of the other works are: "Life of St. Katherine translated from that of Athanasius"; "Life of St. Margaret, in verse"; "A vision of the pilgrimage of the soul after its separation from the body translated from the French, in five books, 'with somwhat of addissiouns.'" At the end of the MS is written: "By me Jamys Benyt, partynt therto liber, here endit the boke off lyffes off the seintes-by me Jamys Benyt."

Our poem begins on f. 158a with "Be Gyns þe prologue of þe lyfe of oure lady." There are 32 lines to the page, single column. Line I 245 is omitted, with line I 246 repeated in its place. Lines I 684, I 771-777, I 876-889 V 524-536 and VI 138 are omitted; lines I 471-472, II 156-157, II 528-529 are garbled; lines II 186-187 and II 524-525 are transposed; lines I 576-579 are repeated, then crossed through. Lines III 63-67, III 69-70, III 649-715, IV 3, and IV 124 are missing; lines III 859-860, III 933-934 and III 1707-1708 are transposed. The poem ends on f. 240a with "Explicit vite Marie."

V—VENERABLE ENGLISH COLLEGE ROME MS. 1306.

Library of the Venerable English College, Rome. Paper, 159 unnumbered folios, measuring 26 by 19 centimeters, with an average of 35 lines to the page. The book is bound in boards covered with parchment. A few of the titles and page headings have been trimmed off by the binder. The text is in sepia-colored ink; capitals and headings are in blue and red ink. Judging from the watermarks the manuscript is dated 1436-1456.[14]

The poem begins imperfectly on f. la with line II 365; it ends on f. 65b. Lines II 925-1074 are omitted.

Other items in the volume include: Lydgate's "Dietary", his "The Daunce of Machabre", and other of his minor poems; a prose treatise, *The Master of Game;* and Benedict Burgh's *Parvus Cato* and *Cato Major.*

There are many scribblings in a 16th century hand throughout the book, mostly those of an inferior writer trying his pen over various letters, repeating parts of the text, adding lists of figures, etc. On f. 121b is written: "This is Richard Turbyll is bocke Recorde of Sir Thomas Carne and many more of the hospitale in Rome wrytin the first of marche"; and on f. 159a: "This is Rychard Turbyll is bocke recorde of wyllam baker and many more in Rome." At the end of the book on f. 159a is written: "J. Preston", apparently the name of the scribe. At the bottom of f. 121b is found: "Jankyn Turbyll" and on f. 159a: "henry pezevy".

The "Sir Thomas Carne" referred to on f. 121b may have been Sir Edward Carne (or a kinsman), England's ambassador to the Holy See in Queen Mary Tudor's reign. Upon Elizabeth's accession to the throne in 1558 Carne remained in Rome and was appointed governor of the English hospice there until his death in 1561. The "Turbylls" (or Turbervilles?) seem to have been using "Sir Thomas Carne" and "wyllam baker" as witnesses to protect the book against theft and resale. According to the Rev. Henry E. G. Rope, Librarian of the Venerable English College Library, there is no record of the *provenance* of the book.

---

[14]In ff. 1-73, and perhaps ff. 90-121, the watermark is an anchor, corresponding to Briquet 376, assigned to Lille 1438, Pont à Mousson, 1445. Interspersed through ff. 76-89, and ff. 122-159, is a stag's head, not Briquet, but in the first classification, subgroup of A.D. 1436-1456; the closest identification is Briquet 14228, assigned to Rouen, 1447. See R. A. Klinefelter's description of this manuscript in *Modern Language Quarterly* (March, 1953), XIV, 3-6 and Rossell Hope Robbins, "A Middle English Diatribe Against Philip of Burgundy", *Neophilologus* (Groningen, 1955), pp. 131-132.

THE PRINTS

CAXTON'S EDITION (N.D., 1484?)[15]

See Seymour de Ricci, *A Census of Caxtons* (Oxford, 1909), pp. 76-78; E. Gordon Duff, *Fifteenth Century English Books* (Oxford, 1917), pp. 263-264; Joseph Ames, et al., *Typographical Antiquities* (4v, London, 1810-1819), I, 336-341; W. Blades, *Caxton,* II, 171-174; C. Brown and R. H. Robbins, *Index,* p. 404; C. Brown, *Register,* II, 234; L. Hain, *Repertorium Bibliographicum* (2v, Stuttgart, 1826-1838), II, 304; *The British Museum Catalogue of Printed Books* (35v, Ann Arbor, 1946), XXXIII, 58.

Folio, 96 leaves, the last blank; two folios lack signature. The collation is a-1⁸, m⁶. There are thirty-five lines to the page, 195 × 125 mm. According to S. de Ricci (*op. cit.,* 76), there are eleven known extant copies of this edition of Caxton. I examined a microfilm of the British Museum copy, King's Library, C. 10, b. 18. The copy is perfect. The binding is old blue morocco with the royal arms on the front cover. The cover is 276 × 198 mm.

The Caxton print has no title page, catchwords, or marginal glosses. Spaces are left for the insertion of initials one to three lines deep. The text begins, with space for a three-line initial on the recto of the first leaf,

> "This book was compyled by dan John lydgate monke of burye / at the excitacion and styryng of the noble and victoryous prynce / Kyng harry the fyfthe / in thonoure glorye *and* reuerence of the byrthe of our moste blessyd lady / mayde wyf / and moder of our lord Jhesu cryst / chapytred as foloweth by this table"

The table follows immediately, finishing with nine lines on the verso of the second leaf.

The poem begins on signature A¹ recto. It ends on signature M⁴ verso with a colophon, and some original verses by Caxton:[16]

---

[15]The date of Caxton's print is uncertain; however, 1484 is accepted by most scholars. W. Loftus Hare (*A Newly Discovered Volume Printed by William Caxton,* London, n.d., p. 11), records the mistaken inclusion of sixteen pages of *Life of Our Lady* in Caxton's edition of Lydgate's translation of Guillaume de Deguilleville's *Le Pelerinage de l'Ame.* According to the colophon, the latter work was finished on June 6, 1483.

[16]See W. Blades, *Caxton,* II, 172, for Caxton's authorship of these verses.

"Here endeth the book of the lyf of our lady
made by dan John lydgate monke of bury /
at thynstaunce of the moste crysten kynge /
King harry the fyfth

Goo lityl book and submytte the
Unto al them / that the shal rede
Or here / prayeng hem for charite
To pardon me of the rudehede
Of myn enpryntyng / not takyng hede
And yf ought be doon to theyr plesyng
Say they thyse balades folowyng

Sancte *et* Indiuidue trinitati, Jhesu cristi
crucifixi humanitate gloriose beate marie
virgini, sit sempiterna gloria, ab omni
creatura, per Infinita seculorum secula.
Amen.[17]

Unto the holy and undeuyded trynyte
Thre persones in one veray godhede
To Jhesu crist crucefyed humanyte
And to our blessyd ladyes maydenhede
Be geuyn laude and glorye in veray dede
Of euery creature, what someuer he be
World withouten ende. Amen say al we.

Benedictum sit dulcissime nomen Jhesu
crysti, *et* gloriosissime marie matris eius
ineternum *et* vltra Nos cum prole
pia benedicat virgo maria. Amen

Blessid be the swettest name of our lord
Jhesu crist / and most glorious marie
His blessyd moder / with eternal accord
More than euer / tendure in glorye
And with hir meke sone for memorye
Blesse vs marie / the most holy virgyne
That we regne in heuen with the ordres nyne.

Enpryntyd by Wyllyam Caxton"

A blank leaf completes the volume.

Line II 1313 is missing; lines I 375-376, II 508-509, II 720-721
are transposed. Line II 720 is garbled and a line is added between
II 1317-1318. Stanzas III 610-616 and VI 210-216 omitted, and

---

[17]From the Breviary. This is the final prayer of the Office every day.

stanza III 666-672, inserted in place of stanza III 610-616, is repeated in its proper place. This error places the Caxton print in sub-group *d* in the Stemma. An examination of major variant readings shows that the Caxton print is close to MS. C⁵ in that same sub-group *d*.

ROBERT REDMAN'S EDITION (1531).

See Joseph Ames, et al., *Typographical Antiquities,* III, 221 (entitled, "Lydgate's Lyf of Christe") ; *The British Museum Catalogue of Printed Books,* XXXIII, 58; C. Brown and R. H. Robbins, *Index,* p. 404; C. Brown, *Register,* II, 234; S.T.C. 17025.

Quarto, 119 leaves, the pages are 4⅞" by 6⅞"; the signatures are A⁴ - H⁴, J⁴ - X⁴, Aa⁴ - Jj⁴. The title page reads:

> This boke is compyled by Dan John // Lydgate monke of Burye / at the excitacion & sty // rynge of the noble and victorious prynce / kynge // Henry the fyfthe / *in* the honoure glorie & reue // rence of the byrthe of our moste blessed // Lady / mayde / wyfe / & mother of our // lorde Jesu Christe / Chapitred // as foloweth by this Table. //

A Table of Contents follows (pp. 3-8). The poem ends on p. 235 with "Here endith the boke of the Lyf of our Lady // made by Dan John Lydgate mo*n*ke of Bury // at thyn*stau*nce of þe most criste*n* kynge // Kynge Henry the fyfth. // Then follow the verses of Caxton[18] and on page 236 is the colophon:

> Here endeth the lyfe of our Lady // Imprynted at London in the Flete // strete by me Robert Redman dwellynge in // saynt Dunstones parysshe next þe chur // che. In the yere of our lorde god // MCCCCCXXXI. The firste daye of the moneth // of Nouembre.

There are four woodcuts in the print: a woodcut of the Annunciation (p. 1) ; one of the birth of Christ (p. 2) ; another of the Flight into Egypt (p. 237) ; and a fourth of the Virgin holding the Infant (p. 238).

Redman's print is an identical copy of Caxton's edition. This is shown by numerous major variants and by mutual errors and omissions in the text.

---

[18]See the description of Caxton's print, p. 51.

TAME'S EDITION (1872).[19]

See *The British Museum Catalogue of Printed Books,* XXXIII, 58; C. Brown and R. H. Robbins, *Index,* p. 404; C. Brown, *Register,* II, 234.

On p. i:

The Life of Our Lady / Part I / Edited from MSS. in the British Museum / by Charles Edward Tame / Author of "The Supremacy of the Holy See," / "The Church's Law," etc. / With Glossary and a Biographical Notice of the Author / London: R. Washbourne, 18, Paternoster Row.

On p. ii:

Sancte et Individue Trinitati / Jesu Cristi crucifixi humanitati gloriosse beate Marie Virgini / sit sempiterna gloria / ab omnia creatura / per infinita seculorum secula. Amen.

Octavo, 68 pages, contains a biographical account of Lydgate (pp. iii-xi), a table of contents in 86 chapters of the *Life of Our Lady* (xiii-xvii), beginning: "This book was compiled by dan John Lidgate // monke of Burye, at the excitation and // steryng / of oure worshipful prynce Kyng Harry // the Fifthe, in thonoure, glorie, and reverence // of the birthe of our most blessyd Lady, maide, // wife, and moder of oure Lord Jh*e*su Criste, // chapitred and markyd after this table." The text of the *Life of Our Lady* covers pages 1-64 and comprises all of Book I and Book II up to and including line II 1095. There are 35 lines to the page; the stanzas are numbered in the right margin, 1-282. There is a glossary on pp. 65-68.

As the title page informs us, this edition of C. E. Tame was based only on the manuscripts in the British Museum. An examination of the text, especially in regard to major variant readings, shows a strong leaning to MS. H³.

Only a few copies of this edition are available today. There is a copy in the British Museum (3605. a a a), G. Fiedler owned a copy,[20] and my dissertation supervisor, Dr. A. C. Baugh, owns a copy, which he kindly allowed me to examine. This scarcity exists because a fire at the publishers' destroyed most of the copies.

---

[19]There is no date on the book. However, G. Fiedler (*Anglia,* XV (1893), 394), reports that he had a copy, a gift of Tame's father-confessor, Rev. Father Mooney. This copy was dated, in the hand of the publisher, "Nov 15/72."

[20]See *Anglia,* XV (1893), 394.

ADDITIONS TO THE STEMMA

Prof. Klinefelter has already presented the stemma of manuscripts in his introductory study.[1] It is our purpose now to add these two manuscripts to the stemma (they have been inserted in the stemma on page 17).

MS. V.

There are no omissions and only one instance of inverted lines in this manuscript throughout Books III and IV. The inversion occurs at III 458-459, and in this it is followed by none of our other manuscripts. MS. V definitely belongs to the *c* group of Dr. Klinefelter's stemma, since it almost invariably goes along with MSS. Ch, H[3], H[4], H[5], H[6], B[2], B[3], B[4], C[5], Ash[1], An, J, and Lg in all significant readings.[2] There are occasional instances in which it stands alone. These latter cases are limited to words and phrases which do not substantially change the sense of the line but do preclude the possibility (together with the inversion mentioned above) of any of our manuscripts being a copy of MS. V.

Although clearly falling into the *c* group, it cannot be placed in subdivision *d,* because it does not make the scribal error of omitting and later inserting the stanza which begins at III 610. It must, therefore, be added to *q* or *h.* A sampling of variant readings shows that MS. V is closer to B[2] and J than it is to B[3].[3] MS. V must accordingly be placed under sub-group *h,* bearing a horizontal relation to B[2], CC and J.

MS. Adv[2].

This manuscript lacks Books I, II, and III. Its place in the stemma must, then, be determined from approximately fifty per cent of the text. No lines are omitted or inverted in Books V and VI. In Book IV there is only one instance of inversion (lines IV 271-272) and again there are no omissions. The manuscript represents, therefore, a complete copy of the poem as far as it goes.

---

[1] The stemma appears on p. 17.
[2] It will be remembered that MS. J transfers to the *d* group after Book II.
[3] MS. V is not at all close to MS. L.

Since none of the other manuscripts agrees with Adv^2 in the inversion of lines IV 271-272, this textual flaw is of no service in determining relationships beyond indicating that, unless contamination has occurred, there can be no vertical line of descent between Adv^2 and any of the manuscripts with which we have dealt. Moreover, the probability of contamination is effectively reduced by the substantial number of readings in which Adv^2 stands alone. It must be presumed, then, to have been copied from a hypothetical manuscript.

A comparative analysis of the text shows clearly that this hypothetical archetype must be *b* or an equally hypothetical descendant. There are consistent agreements in the variant readings with sub-group *p*. Out of thirty-seven typical variants, Adv^2 was found to agree twenty-seven times with Hu, twenty-four times with B^1 and H^7, twenty-one times with C^3 and B^5, and twenty times with Co, H^8, and Ad^3. The number of agreements with Ad^3 would have been considerably higher if that manuscript were not so defective. In fact, wherever Adv^2 and Ad^3 are both represented, the concurrence of readings is especially high. On this account, and because of the evidence presented above, Adv^2 has been inserted in the stemma between Hu and Ad^3.

3. SOURCES

BOOKS I AND II

The ultimate source for the major portion of Books I and II of the *Life of Our Lady* is the Apocryphal Gospel of Pseudo-Matthew.[1] Although much of the material for Lydgate's early life of the Virgin is legendary and can be found in other accounts,[2] the Gospel of Pseudo-Matthew offers not only a complete source for the narrative in Books I and II of the *Life of Our Lady* but is identical in numerous details.

The Gospel of Pseudo-Matthew provides the ultimate source for such narrative portions of Books I and II of the *Life of Our Lady* as the birth of the Virgin Mary (I, 113-133), her presentation in the Temple (I, 183-224), the daily life of Mary in the Temple (I, 239-294), her marriage to Joseph (I, 553-819), the chagrin of Joseph when he found Mary with child (II, 1096-1345), and the trial of Joseph and Mary (II, 1346-1592). Particular details in which both the Gospel of Pseudo-Matthew and the *Life of Our Lady* agree in these passages are numerous as the following study indicates. In this study it will be noticed that the account in the Gospel of Pseudo-Matthew is a continuous narrative. The section from the *Life of Our Lady* omits those portions in which Lydgate included long, unnecessary ramblings.

1) The birth of Our Lady:

Life of Our Lady (I, 113-133)
And from the stooke, of Ioachym and
    Anne
This holy floure hadde hir orygynall
To hem afforne, by synge Ishewede
    whanne
The Angell tolde hem playnely þat
    ther shall
Of hem be borne, a mayde in speciall
Chosyn of godde most chefe of hir alye

Pseudo-Matthaei Evangelium, Cap. III-IV Cumque triginta dies ambularent et essent jam prope, apparuit Annae in oratione stanti angelus domini dicens ei : Vade ad portam quae aurea vocatur et occurre viro tuo, quoniam veniet ad te hodie. At illa festinanter perrexit cum puellis suis, et coepit in ipsa porta stans orare. Et cum diutius exspectaret et longa exspectatione deficeret,

---

[1] The full title is the *Liber de Ortu Beatae Mariae et Infantia Salvatoris A Beato Matthaeo*. The best edition is that of Constantinus Tischendorf, *Evangelia Apocrypha* (Leipzig, 1876), pp. 51-112.

[2] Cf. the *Legenda Aurea,* ed. Th. Graesse (2 ed., Leipzig, 1881) ; the *Protevangelium of James,* Tischendorf, *op. cit.,* pp. 1-50; the *Gospel of the Nativity of Mary,* Tischendorf, *op. cit.,* pp. 113-121; the *History of Joseph the Carpenter,* Tischendorf, *op. cit.,* pp. 122-139; and R. Reinsch, *Die Pseudo-evangelien von Jesu und Maria's Kindheit in der romanischen und germanischen Literatur* (Halle, 1879).

For hir mekenesse and hatte shall
  Marye
And whanne the Angell, at the gate of
  golde
Had of this mayde hir birthe prophecied
And all the man*e*re to bothe hem tolde
In bok*es* olde, as it is specifiede
Home to her houses a noon thay haue
  hem hyed
And she concevyed, this faythfull trwe
  wyf
By Ioachym, the holy frute of lyfe
Oute of the which gan growe all our
  grace
Our olde sorowes, fully forto fyne
The bitter gall, playnely to enchace
Of the venym, callet serpentyne
For when that Anne, hade monethes
  nyne
Borne this frute so holy and entere
Thorough *g*race of god, a noon it dyd
  appere

elevans oculos suos vidit Joachim ven-
ientem cum pecoribus suis, occurrens-
que Anna suspendit se in collo ejus,
gratias agens deo et dicens: Vidua
eram, et ecce jam non sum; sterilis
eram, et ecce jam concepi. Et factum
est gaudium magnum vicinis omnibus
et notis ejus, ita ut universa terra
Israel de ista fama gratularetur. Post
haec autem expletis mensibus novem
peperit Anna filiam, et vocavit nomen
ejus Mariam. C. Tischendorf (*Evangelia Apocrypha,* Leipsig, 1876, pp.
60-61).

2) The presentation of Mary in the Temple:

Life of Our Lady, (I, 183-217)
Ande aftir iii yere, as was the vsage
Hir modir pappis, she left as in
  soukyng
And thanne anoon, in hir tendre age
Vnto the Temple, deuoutely they hir
  bryng
And unto god they made offryng
Of this mayde, for to abyde there
W*ith* othir maydens, that in the temple
  were
And not w*ith*stondyng hir passyng
  tendirnesse
Hir grene youthe, but of yeres thre
Thorough godd*es* helpe, this braunche
  of holynesse

Pseudo-Matthaei Evangelium, Cap.
IV-V Cum autem tertio anno per-
lactasset eam, abierunt simul Joachim
et Anna uxor ejus ad templum domini,
et offerentes hostias domino tradide-
runt infantulam suam Mariam in con-
tubernium virginum, quae die noctuque
in dei laudibus permanebant. Quae
cum posita esset ante templum domini,
quindecim gradus ita cursim ascendit
ut penitus non aspiceret retrorsum,
neque, ut solitum est infantiae,
parentes requireret. In quo facto
omnes stupore attoniti tenebantur, ita
ut et ipsi pontifices templi mirarentur.
Tunc Anna repleta spiritu sancto in

W*ith* outyn helpe went vp, gre by gre
Fyftene on lofte, that wondir was to see
Tofore the auter, of so grete an hight
Thenne whanne hir modir, ther of had
    a syght
For verrey Ioye, a noon she fell a
    dovne
And seide thus, that all myghten here
God frome above, hath herde myne
    orysoune
Of his godenesse, and graunted my
    prayer
And Recomfortede, myn oppressede
    chier
In sight of hem, that lowghen at my
    payne
And of malice, gan at me disdeigne
Now hathe he been, my synguler refute
To my tristesse, consolac*i*on

For he hath made the bareyn to bere
    frute
Thorough his myghty vesitacion
And made eke clere, my confuc*i*on
And all my woo, for to overgone
Only by grace, a myddys all my foon
And thurgh his myght, þe hertes hath
    ybowed
Of hem that gan, to chace at me by
    pryde
Wherfore she hath, vnto god avowed
That hir dought*er*, shall in the Temple
    abyde
The holy gost, for to be hir guyde
For eu*er*more, by godd*es* purviaunce
Thurgh her mekenesse, hym to do
    plesaunce

conspectu omnium dixit: Dominus deus exercituum memor factus est verbi sui et visitavit plebem suam visitatione sancta sua, ut gentes quae insurgebant in nos humiliet et convertat ad se corda eorum: aperuit aures suas precibus nostris, et exclusit a nobis insulationes inimicorum nostrorum.

Sterilis facta est mater, et genuit exultationem et laetitiam in Israel. Ecce potero offerre munera domino, et non poterunt a me prohibere inimici mei. Dominus convertat corda eorum ad me, et det mihi gaudium sempiternum. (C.Tischendorf, *Evangelia Apocrypha*, pp. 61-62).

Although the presentation of Mary in the Temple is found in both the *Protevangelium* and the *Gospel of the Nativity of Mary,* there is nothing in either of these versions of the prayer and rejoicing of Anna (I, 197-217).

3) The life of Our Lady in the Temple:

Life of Our Lady (I, 239-259)	*Pseudo-Matthaei Evangelium,* Cap. VI
And whan þat she • V • yere dyd atteyne	Quae cum V esset annorum, ita maturo gressu ambulabat et perfectissime loque-
She was as sadde in conuersacyon	batur et in dei laudibus studebat, ut
And also demure, sothely forto seyne	non infantula esse putatur sed magna,
From all childehode and dissolucion	et quasi triginta annorum jam esset ita
In gouernaunce and in discrecion	orationibus insistebat.
And in talkyng alse wise and alse sage	
As any mayde of xxxᵗ¹ yere of Age	
And of hir Rull, this was hir vsaunce	Hanc autem regulam sibi statuerat, ut
Fro day to day, this holy mayde enter	a mane usque ad horam tertiam oration-
Fro prime at morowe, by continuaunce	ibus insisteret; a tertia autem usque ad
To thre at bell to be in hir prayer	nonam textrino opere se occuparet; a
And till the sonne was at mydday spere	nona vero hora iterum ab oratione non
On golde and silke and on wolleȝ softe	recedebat usque dum illi angelus domini
With hir handys, she wolde wyrke ofte	appareret, de cujus manu escam ac-
And even at none to brynge hir her fode	ciperet, et melius atque melius in dei
Fro god above, ther was an Angell sent	laudibus proficiebat.
Wiche that she tooke, as for hir lifelode	
Thankyng hym aye, with hir hole entente	
And aftir mete, a noon this mayde is went	
Agayne to praye, tyll phebus went to west	
And Evyn at eve, with hym she tooke hir Rest[3]	

There is no mention whatever in any other apocryphal account of this daily life of Our Lady in the Temple. Interesting parallel identities in the Gospel of Pseudo-Matthew and the *Life of Our Lady* are the maturity given to Mary at the age of five (I, 239-245), and her daily schedule in the Temple (I, 246-259).

Lines I, 262-275

And neuer man sawe, this mayde wrothe	Hanc nemo irascentem vidit, hanc maledicentem nunquam ullus audivit.

---

[3]Omissions or breaks in the text represent lines in which Lydgate simply expanded the idea of the source. I omit such unnecessary ramifications for reasons of ecouomy of space.

But ever meke, and full of paciens
Of hert clenne and pure in concience
This lif she ledde, *and* as bokes teche
Of wordes fewe *and* wondir softe of
  speche
The mete also that was to hir brought
Out of þe temple, for her sustenaunce
With hert gladde, and with a perfyte
  thought
To pore and nedy, that leven in
  penaunce
To giffe it frely, was all hir pleasaunce
And who that euere, of hir hadde a
  sight
Of all disese, was made glad and light
And euery wyght, grevyde with
  sekenesse
A touche of hir, made hem hoole a noon

Omnis autem sermo ejus ita erat gratia
plenus, ut cognosceretur in lingua ejus
esse deus.

Cotidie esca quam de manu angeli
accipiebat ipsa tantum reficiebatur;
escam vero quam a pontificibus con-
sequebatur pauperibus dividebat.

Si quis autem de infirmantibus tetigisset eam, salvus ad domum suam
eadam hora remeabat.

Lines I, 281-283
And of this mayde eke, as it is tolde
Hir godely face, was so full of light
That no man myght, susteyne to be
  holde

Et resplendebat facies ejus sicut nix,
ita ut vis possent in ejus vultum in-
tendere. (C. Tischendorf, *Evangelia
Apocrypha,* pp. 62-64).

    With reference to the virtues of Mary in the Temple, the *Protevangelium*
mentions only that she dwelt in the Temple as if she were a dove, and that she
received food from an angel. The *Gospel of the Nativity of Mary* records that
Mary advanced in age and virtue, that she was daily visited by an angel, and
that she daily enjoyed a divine vision, which preserved her from evil. Only in
the Gospel of Pseudo-Matthew do we find the same detailed listing of the virtues
of Mary as in the *Life of Our Lady,* her giving the food of the Temple to the
poor, the healing qualities of the sight and touch of her, and the resplendent
beauty of her face.

    4) The desire of the high priest, Abiathar, to marry Mary to his son and
Mary's commendation of chastity:

Life of Our Lady (I, 542-589)
Of whiche a Bisshoppe callet Abiathar
Cast hym fully, forto sette asyde
Hir purpoys playnly, and so forth to
  provyde

Pseudo-Matthaei Evangelium, Cap.
VII Tunc Abiathar sacerdos obtulit
munera infinita pontificibus, ut accip-
erat eam filio suo tradendam uxorem.
Prohibebat autem eos Maria dicens:

That hir avowe, made of chastite
Shall not holde but outrely that she
Sholde be weddyde, sothely if he myght
Vnto his sonne, of his affection
For that she was, in euery whyght*es*
   syght
So passyng gode of condicion
And to fulfill his entencion
Abyathar behotyth, golde and Rente
To the Bisshoppys, to make hir to
   assente

To his purpose, and to hir thay gone
And what thay may, thay gan hir excite
And afferme, to hir euerychone
With sugrede tonge, of many wordeȝ
   whyte
That god above, dothe hym more
   delyte
In birthe of chyldren then in virginite
Or any suche, avowede chastite
And more in children, is he honourde
   certyn
And more in hem, hathe he his
   pleasaunce
Than in suche, as be not but baren
Without frute, thorough
   misgouernaunce
And holy writte, makyth
   Remembraunce
That no man, was sothely forto tell
Withoutyn seede, blesset in Israell

To whome anone, with loke don caste
   and chere
Right benyngly, and in full humble
   wyse
This holy mayde, sayde as ye shall here
Certes quod she, yf ye yov wele aduise
Whiche in your self, so prudent ben
   and wyse
And woll aduerte in youre discrecion

Non potest fieri ut ego virum cognoscam aut me vir cognoscat.

Pontifices autem et omnes ejus affines dicebant ei: Deus in filiis colitur et in posteris adoratur, sicut semper fuit in Israel.

Respondens autem Maria dixit illis: Deus in castitate primo omnium colitur, ut comprobatur. Nam ante Abel nullus fuit justus inter homines, et iste pro

That abell hadde, some tyme a double
   crowne
One for his faythfull and trwe sacrifyce
Offred to god, of humble hert free
And an othir, as I shall yov devyse
For he his body, kept in chastite
And hely eke, as ye may rede and see
For he in hert, was a mayde clene
He was Ravysshede above the sterreȝ
   seven*e*
Body and all Right in a chare of fyre
For he hym kept from all corrupcyon
Therfore in vayne is playnly *your*
   desyre
To speke to me, of this opynnyon
For god wele knawithe, myne entenc*i*on
Howe I have vowede, as it to hym is
   couthe
To ben a mayde, fro my tendir youthe
All my life, so forthe to *p*erceuer

oblatione placuit deo, et ab eo qui
displicuit inclementer occisus est. Duas
tamen coronas accepit, oblationis et
virginitatis, quia in carne sua nunquam
pollutionem admisit. Denique et Helias
cum esset in carne assumptus est, quia
carnem suam virginem custodivit. Haec
ego didici in templo dei ab infantia mea,
quod deo cara esse possit virgo. Ideo
hoc statui in corde meo ut virum penitus non cognoscam. (C. Tischendorf,
Evangelia Apocrypha, p. 65).

Only the Gospel of Pseudo-Matthew recounts Abiathar's desire to have Mary
as a wife for his son; Abiathar's sending gifts to the bishops to solicit their aid in
accomplishing his plan; the visit of the bishops to Mary and their citing Holy
Scripture in attempting to persuade her; the reply of Mary and her recalling the
rewards of the virginity of Abel and Elias as testimony for divine blessing on her
chastity; and Mary's steadfast adherence to her vow.

5) The Marriage of Mary and Joseph:

Life of Our Lady (I, 596-790)
And whan thay sawe hir hert not
   mutable
But ay stedfaste, of oon affection
And euere Ilyche, as any centr*e* stable
Thay haue made, a conuocacion
Of all the kynrede as in conclusion
The viii day forto come in fere
By one assent, to trete of this matier
This is to say, þat the olde vsage
Of Custome kept, for a memoriall

Pseudo-Matthaei Evangelium, Cap.
VIII Factum est autem cum XIIII
annos aetatis haberet, et esset occasio
quae Pharisaeos faceret dicere, jam
consuetudinem adesse feminam in
templo dei non posse morari, inventum
est tale consilium ut mitteretur praeco
per omnes tribus Israel, ut omnes
octavo die in templum domini con-
venirent.

That eu*er*y mayde, xiiii yere of age
Riche and pore, and of the stok Royall
In the Temple, no longer dwell shall
But by statute, shall be take and maried
By the lawe, and no lenger tariede
And whan thay were, assembled all in
    oon
I3acar, in open audience
Gan to p*r*onounce to forne hem
    eu*er*ycheone
Full prudently, the Som*m*e of his
    sentence
And sayde syrrys wi*th* you*r* pacience3
So þat youre eres, offende not ne
    greve
Declare I shall, my menyng with your
    leve
If ye Remmembre, sith Salamon the
    kyng
In Isaraell, Septer bare and crovne
In this Temple, so Royall in bildyng
Haue yong maydens, by deuocion
Of custome hadde here conu*er*sacion
Bothe kyng*es* doughtirs, and p*r*ophete3
    eke
As ye may fynde, yf ye liste to seke
Vnto the age of xiiii yere
Abydyng here, and no lenger space
As ye wele knawe, wi*th*outyn any wer
And anne be remeved fro*m* here place
And in hir stede, othir did pace
As custome was, and eke in hir lynage
Delyuerde was, vnto theyre mariage
And as a lawe, it hathe be kept full
    trwe
Vnto this tyme, to high and lawe estate
But now Marie, hath founde an ordre
    newe
To kepe hir clene and inviolate
Agaynst which, ther helpith ne debate

Cum autem universus populus convenisset, surrexit Isachar pontifex et ascendit in altioribus gradibus, ut ab omni populo audiri posset et videri; et facto magno silentio dixit:
Audite me, filii Israel, et auribus percipite verba mea. Ex quo aedificatum est templum hoc a Salomone,

fuerunt in eo filiae regum virgines et prophetarum et summorum sacerdotum et pontificum; et magnae ac mirabiles exstiterunt. Tamen venientes ad legitimam aetatem, viros in conjugio sunt adeptae, et secutae sunt priorum suarum ordinem et deo placuerunt.

A sola vero Maria novus ordo placendi deo inventus est, quae promittit deo se virginem permanere.

But of free choys, and hertly volunte
She hath to god, avowede chastite
Wherefore me semyth it were Right
    wele fyttyng
To this purpoos, by good discrecion
First how we myght fully haue
    knawyng
Of godys will, in this opynyon
For than it were, of more perfeccion
Hir clene entent as semyth vnto me
And eke the strenger of Auctorite
Firste þat we might knawe verily
To whose kepyng she shall comitted be
And thay assentide, herto vttirly
Withoute more of high and lawe degre
And of one accorde and of oon vnyte
The prestes alle, gonnen to procede
To coste lotte, down by Iche kynrede
The which lotte, on Iuda fell a none
As I suppose thorough goddes
    purviaunce
And Iȝacar, among hem euerychone
Purposed hath a newe ordynaunce
That euery wyght, of that aliaunce
That wyfeles were, withoutyn more
    delay
Sholde brynge a yerde, a gaynst the
    next day
And to the Bisshop, highest of Ichoon
Eueryche of hem did his yerde bryng
Among whiche Iosephe hath brought
    oon
Though he were olde passit his lykyng
And he anon made his offryng
To god above, and eke a sacrifice
In the olde lawe suche as was the gyse
And god to hym did anoon apere
And with the yerde, badde than þat he
    shulde goon
And putten hem, euerychone in fere

Unde mihi videtur ut per interrogationem nostram et responsionem dei possimus agnoscere cui debeat custodienda committi.

Tunc placuit sermo iste omni synagogae. Et missa sors sacerdotibus super duodecim tribus Israel, et cecidit sors super tribum Juda. Dixitque sacerdos: In sequenti die quicumque sine uxore est veniat et deferat virgam in manu sua.

Unde factum est ut Joseph cum juvenibus virgam deferret. Cumque tradidissent summo pontifici virgas suas, obtulit sacrificium deo, et interrogavit dominum. Et dixit dominus ad eum: Intromitte omnium virgas intra sancta sanctorum, et ibi maneant virgae. Et praecipe ais ut mane veniant

In *Sancta* Sanc*torum* lyggng oone by
oon*e*
And on the morowe, to come a gayne
Ichone
Eu*er*yche his yerde, for to Receyve a
gayne
Vppon which, ther opynly was sayne
A dove apere and vp to hevyn flee
He that shall haue wi*th*outyn more
obstacle
Marie in kepyng so fayre vpon to see
As it is Right, for the high myracle
And than thay come vnto the tabernacle
As ye have herde, the Bisshopp
deuoutly
Eu*er*yche his yerde, delyuerde by and
by
But vttirly vppon noon of all
At his tyme, was there noo thyng seyne
For goddys heste, was not yet fall
Of hir desyre, to putt hem in certeyne
Wherefore the Bisshopp, wi*th* newe
fyre agayne
Entride is into þe seintwarye
And whiles þ*at* he, a while there gan
tarie
Goddis Aungell aperyth to hy*m* newe
Downe from hevyn, by myracle sent
And tolde playnly the heste of god was
trwe
But how hym self, was som*e* what
negligent
For to delyuere, by commaundement
Bu*ery* man his yerde, as he aughte
And whan the Bisshopp, a Right hym
bethought
He gan Remembre, playnly in his
mynde
That of disdayne, and wilfull
necgligence

ad te ad recipiendas virgas suas, et ex
cacumine unius virgae columba egredietur et volabit ad caelos; in cujus manu
virga reddita hoc signum dederit, ipsi
tradatur Maria custodienda. Factum
est autem ut altero die maturius venirent universi, et facta oblatione incensi
ingressus pontifex intra sancta sanctorum protulit virgas. Cumque erogas-
set singulas et ex nulla exisset columba,
induit se Abiathar pontifex duodecim
tintinnabulis et veste sacerdotali, et
ingressus in sancta sanctorum incendit
sacrificium. Et fundente illo orationem
apparuit ei angelus dicens: Est hic
virgula brevissima, quam pro nihilo
computasti, illamque simul cum ceteris
posuisti: hanc cum tu protuleris et
dederis, in ipsa apparebit signum quod
locutus sum tibi.

The yerde of Iosephe was lefte by
   hynde
Wherby he knewe, he had doon offence
And gan anoon, to bryng it in presense
And toke it Iosephe devoutly in his
   hands
Among hem all, there he dyd stonde
Alle by hynde, dyseuerede fro the prees
With humble chere, in the lawest place
And of his yerde, in maner Rekeles
Full styll of porte, with a dredefull face
And whan he dyd, with his hande
   enbrace
His yerde a gayne, full debonayre of
   loke
By Innocens of humble fere, he quoke
And sodenly, thorough grace, above
   devyne
All opynly in euery weyghteȝ sight
Vppon the yerde, of Ioseph full benyng
Was sene a dove, of fetheres lylly white
That towardes, hevyn, evenshe toke hir
   flyght
And with oo voys, the people thoo
   obreyde
And vnot Ioseph, all at onys thay sayde
Blesside art thow, and blisside is thy
   chaunce
Thy fate is blesset, and thyne aventure
And blissed is thyne, humble
   attendaunce
And thow art blisset, so long to endure
For to possede, so fayre a creature
So goode so holy, nowe in thy passed
   age
So clene a mayde, to haue in mariage
And she a noon, by prestes of the lawe
Assigned was, vnto his gouernaunce
But sely Iosephe, gan hym to
   withdrawe

Erat autem haec virga Joseph, eratque ipse abjectus habitus, quoniam senex erat, et ne forte cogeretur accipere eam, requirere noluit virgam suam. Cumque staret humilis et ultimus, voce magna clamavit ad eum Abiathar pontifex dicens: Veni et accipe virgam tuam, quoniam tu expectaris. Et accessit Joseph expavescens quod summus pontifex cum clamore nimio vocaret eum.

Mox autem extendens manum ut suam virgam acciperet, statim de cacumine ejus egressa est columba nive candidior, speciosa nimis; et volans diu per templum fastigia petivit caelos.

Tunc universus populus congratulabatur seni dicentes: Beatus factus es tu in senectute tua, ut idoneum te deus ostenderet ad accipiendam Mariam.

Cum autem sacerdotes dicerent ei: Accipe eam, quia ex omni tribu Juda tu solus electus es a deo, coepit adorare et rogare eos atque cum vericundia

With humble chere, and shamefaste
  contenau*n*ce

And sayde certis, there is noon
  accordaunce

By twyxe hir yought, flouryng in
  fayrenesse

And me whome age, w*ith* vn lust doth
  oppresse

For she is fayre, and fresshe as Rose in
  may

And well Iwote, also mayden clene

And I am olde, w*ith* white lockes graye

Passed full ferre, my tendre yeres grene

Wherfore I pray yov, to considre and
  sene

Tacorde discordant, and speke to me
  noo more

By twene hir beaute, and my lockes hore

And whan the bisshope sawe the humble
  entent

Of this Iosephe, and eke the Innocence

And how that he, to take hir nolde
  assent

To hym he sayde, in opyn audience

Ioseph quod he, take hede to my
  sentence

And be welware þat thou the not excuse

Ageynst the will of god, forto Refuce

This holy mayde, assignet vnto the

By opyn signe, whiche all the people
  seye

Thorough godd*es* grace, and myghty
  volunte

Agaynst whiche, be warr to disobeye

And þenke how he su*m*tyme made to
  deye

Dathan Abyron • only for offence

Done vnto hym, of Inobedyence

Quod Iosephe thanne, I woll not for
  no thyng

dicere: Senex sum et filios habeo, ut
quid mihi infantulam istam traditis?

Tunc Abiathar summus pontifex dixit:
Memor esto, Joseph, quemadmodum
Dathan et Abiron et Core perierunt,
quia voluntatem domini contempserunt.
Ita tibi eveniet si hoc quod a deo
jubetur tibi contempseris.

Et dixit ei Joseph: Ego quidem non
contemno voluntatem dei, sed custos

To godd*es* will or byddyng be contrar
But hir accept vnto my kepyng
For whom god hath shewed signe so
    fayre
Whiche is so goode, benyngne and
    debonayre
That I to hir seruaunt woll be and gyde
Tyll god for hir, lust bett*er* to provyde
And as the custume, of the lawe theym
    bonde
So made was tho, the confirma*ci*on
By hest of wedlok, by twene theym
    hande by hande
And he hir toke, to his possession
W*ith* hert clene and meke affeccion
But while he went to Bedlem the Cite
Mary abode styll in Galile
At Naȝareth in hir faders house
Like hir avowe, of hert all way oon
And fyve maydens the most vertuose
Of the Temple, were chosyn oute a
    noon
Of the Bisshop w*ith* hir for to goon
To wayte on hir, by humble
    attendaunce
In what þey can, to s*er*ve and do
    pleasaunce
Of whiche the first, was callet Rayca
And Sephera, the secund as I fynde
Susanna ȝabel, and Abygea
The othir thre, as bokes makyn mynde
Which neu*er* wolde, for slouthe be
    byhynde
But ay in oon, as it is specified
In werke and prayer, weren occupyed
And vnto hem, as made is mencion
That of levyng, so faythfull weren and
    trwe
And diligent in occupa*ci*on
Delyu*er*ede was silke, of sondry hewe

ejus ero, quousque hoc de voluntate dei
cognosci possit, quis eam possit habere
ex filiis meis conjugem. Dentur aliquae
ex sodalibus ejus virgines, cum quibus
interim degat.

Et respondens Abiathar pontifex dixit:
Virgines quidem ad solatium ejus da-
buntur, quousque dies statutus veniat
in quo tu eam accipias; non enim pot-
erit alii in matrimonio copulari. Tunc
Joseph

accepit Mariam cum aliis quinque virginibus, quae essent cum ea in domo
Joseph. Erant autem istae virgines
Rebecca, Sephora, Susanna, Abigea et
Zahel: quibus datum est a pontificibus
sericum et jacinthum et byssus et coccus
et purpura et linum.

For to make, of dyu*e*rse werk*es* newe
In the Temple of entencion
Onely to be, in mynystracion
And as it is put in Remembraunce
Eu*e*ryche hir silke, toke by aventure
Lyke as hir hande, fell ther on by
 chaunce
But Marye, as god tho schope hir vre
The purpyll silke, she toke in cure
By graciouse happe, of sort wi*th*outen
 sight

Miserunt autem sortes inter se quid
unaquaeque virgo faceret; contigit
autem ut Maria purpuram acciperet ad
velum templi domini. (C. Tischendorf,
Evangelia Apocrypha, pp. 66-70).

. . .

Lines I, 813-819
And of this purpill that I of spake to
 forne
I fynde playnely, how that Marye
 wrought
Thylke vayle that was in tweyn torne
The same houre whan he so dere vs
 bought
Loo howe þat godd in his et*er*nall
 thought
Provydede hathe, by Iust purveyaunce
The p*u*rpull silke, vnto his moders
 chaunce

  Both the *Protevangelium* and the *Gospel of the Nativity of Mary* relate the story of the dove emerging from Joseph's rod and the subsequent betrothal of Mary to Joseph. In neither account is there the detail found in the *Life of Our Lady* and the Gospel of Pseudo-Matthew. Those details in which these two accounts are singularly parallel are: the convocation held on the eighth day; the address of Izachar to the crowd (almost word for word); the falling of the lot on Juda; the detailed actions of the Bishop and his two visits to the Sancta Sanctorum; the appearance of the angel, chiding the Bishop for his neglect of Joseph; Joseph's humility in taking the rod; and the appearance of the dove with white feathers. The Gospel of Pseudo-Matthew alone notes Joseph's promise to watch over Mary as a servant until the will of God should be made known, and only the Gospel of Pseudo-Matthew names the five maidens given to Mary as companions. The *Protevangelium* omits the maidens altogether; the *Gospel of the Nativity of Mary* refers to them only as seven maidens of Mary's age.

6) The chagrin of Joseph at seeing Mary with child:

Life of Our Lady (II, 1096-1104)

This meane while, Iosephe ay
 soyo*ur*nede
In Galile god wote full Innocent
Of al this thyng, and why he nat
 Reto*ur*nede
Was for that, þat he was so diligent
In Caphernam w*ith* his full entent
Sondry werk*es*, of mervylous enp*ri*se
By Carpentrye, to forgen and devyse
For in that Crafte, passyng excellence
He had in sothe, and high discrecion

. . .

Lines II, 1110-1132

And whan he had, all his werke
 achevede
He is Repayred, to Naʒareth agayne
But lorde howe he was, in his hert a
 meovede
Whan that Marye, he hath w*ith* childe
 sayne
That for astonyde, he noot what he
 myght sayne
And at his hert, it satte so Inwardely
Tyl at the laste, he abrayde sodenly
And sayde alas, howe, is it falle of newe
In myne absence, or what thyng may
 this be
Sythen this mayde, so faythfull and
 trwe
Is with chylde, and god wot not with
 me
That some tyme had, avouede chastyte
And to my kepyng, eke delyuered was
What shall I say nowe of this soden
 case
What shall I answer, my self to excuse
Vnto the Bisshopp, if he me apose
For eythyir moste I, playnely hir acuse

Pseudo-Matthaei Evangelium, Cap. X

Cum haec agerentur, Joseph in Capharnaum maritima erat in opere occupatus, erat enim faber ligni: ubi moratur est mensibus novem.

Reversusque in domum suam invenit Mariam praegnantem. Et totus contremuit et positus in angustia exclamavit et dixit: Domine deus, accipe spiritum meum, quoniam melius est mihi mori quam vivere.

Or ellys my self, with this gilte enoyse
This thyng is opyn, I may it nat enclose
O blissefull god, so do me nowe this
    grace
Oute of my breste, my woofull gooste
    to Race
For certis lorde, and it were thy wille
I had leuere vtterly to dey

      .   .   .

Lines II, 1166-1207

And whan the maydens, that weren aye
    present
And euere in one, abydyng on Marye
Vndirstondyng what that Iosephe ment
Al at onys, they be gan to crye
And sayde Iosephe, leve this fantasye
And thyne erroure, for it is folye
Withoutyn avyse, to deme sodenlye
Fro certenly, with all our hert entyer
Of knowledyng, in verrey sykernesse
We will Recorden, euerycheone in fere
All opynly, touchying hir clennesse
And ther vpon, beren opynly witnesse
For we in sothe thourgh bysy diligence
Haue been with hir, bothe day and
    nyght
And neuere partyde, oute of hir
    presence
But euer in oon, of hir had a sight
And late and erly, with all our full
    myght
On hir awayted, withoutyn wordes
    moo
That fro our sight, she neuere dydde
    goo
And euere houre, bothe tyde and tyme
Of vs ther was, no dyvysion
And all the day, fro the self prime
She neuere stynte, of high deuocion
To be in prayer, and in oryson
And iche a day, be continuaunce

Cui dixerunt virgines quae cum Maria
erant: Quid ais, domine Joseph? Nos
scimus quoniam vir non tetigit eam;
nos scimus quoniam integritas et virginitas in ea immaculata perseverat.

Nam custodita est a deo, semper in
oratione nobiscum permansit; cotidie
cum ea angelus domini loquitur, cotidie
de manu angeli

A certeyne houre, she hadde daliaunce
With holy Angels, that with hir kneyld
   or stode
And at oo tyme, thorough goddes
   purvyaunce
Of his hande, she tooke hir holy foode
As nedefull was, vnto hir sustinaunce
And this in sothe, hath ben hir
   gouernaunce
As we ycheone, of hir can Recorde
Wherefore Iosephe, this lyfe dothe not
   accorde
In sothefastnesse, to thyne opynyon
That so mysdemys, of this mayde fre
Of fantasye, or false suspecion
For to acuse, hir virgynyte
Of whiche thyng, we dar assure the
That no wyght made, sothely to devyse
But the holy goste, hir wombe to aryse

.   .   .

Lyke as we knowe, vnto this same daye
Though all the worlde, at ones wolde
   saye naye

II, Lines 1219-1256
Certys quod he, I may not voyde oute
My fantasye, to assent in any wyse
It shulde be, liche as ye devyse
For by an Angell, it were impossible
Hir to conceyve, lyke as ye expresse
But if it so were, if it be credible
Som wyght by sleyght, takying the
   lyknesse
Of an angell, thorow fraudulent
   falsnesse
Thorough Innocence, shortly to
   conclude
By engyne of fraude, hir yougth to
   delude
And efte agayne, for his Inwarde
   payne

escam accipit. Quomodo fieri potest
ut sit aliquod peccatum in ea?

Non sit in te aliqua suspicio de ipsa,
quia non nisi spiritus sanctus gravidam
eam fecit

Joseph autem dixit: Ut quid me sedu-
citis ut credam vobis quia angelus
domini impraegnavit eam? Potest
enim fieri ut quisquam se finxerit an-
gelum domini et deceperit eam.

He gan to chaunge, bothe face and
    huwe
And from his eyne, the salt tereȝ Reyne
Lyke as he wolde, drowne hym self of
    newe
So sore he gan, in hert for to rewe
For this matier, that for his mortall
    woo
He can noo Rede, ne wote what he
    may doo
And in his hert, he caste many a waye
To have founden Refute with all his
    full mynde
And thought all waye, he wolde hir not
    be traye
For he was Rightfull, playnely as I
    fynde
And thus he gan, in sondry thoughteȝ
    wynde
As in balaunce, purposede uppe and
    downe
Tyll at the last, in conclusion
He fully purposeth, and caste hym
    vtterly
To gone his waye, shortly if he myght
And thought he wolde, forsake hir
    prively
And neuere more to come in hir sight
Till an Angell, on the same nyght
Sent downe from god, to Ioseph dyd
    apere
Whyle þat he slepte, and sayde as ye
    shall here
O thou Ioseph, ne drede the not blyve
Thou son of Dauid, of lyne by discent
For to take marye, vnto thy wyve
Whiche is a Mayde, with all hir full
    entent
With whome is ay, the holy goste
    present

Et haec dicens flebat at dicebat: Qua
fronte ad templum dei iturus sum?
Qua facie visurus sum sacerdotes dei?
Quid

facturus sum? Et haec dicens cogita-
bat occultare se et dimittere eam. Cumque ordinasset in nocte exsurgere ut
fugiens habitaret in occultis, ecce in
ipsa

nocte apparuit ei in somnis angelus
domini dicens: Joseph fili David, noli
timere accipere Mariam conjugem
tuam, quoniam quod in utero ejus est,
de spiritu sancto est. Pariet autem
filium, qui vocabitur Jesus: ipse enim
salvum faciet populum suum a pecca-
tis eorum.

Of whome is all, I tel it the be forne
In verrey sothe, that shall of hir be
  borne

. . .

And whan þat Iosephe, abrayde oute of
  his slepe
And in his hert, by Reuelucion
Gan for to cast, and to take kepe
Ayenst the morowe, of his avysyon
And caught comfort, and consolacion
Of all that euere he was to forne
  dispayrede
And to Marye, he agayne repayrede
And thanketh god, with all his hole
  hert
That he to hym, so graciously
In Recomfort of his Inwarde smerte
His grete myght hathe, declared opynly
And of marye, full benyngly
He axed mercy, of humble affection
That euere he had, to hir suspecion

Exsurgens autem Joseph a somno gratias egit deo suo, et locutus est Mariae
et virginibus quae erant cum ea

et narravit visum suum. Et consolatus
est super Maria, dicens: Peccavi,
quoniam suspicionem aliquam habui
in te. (C. Tischendorf, *Evangelia Apocrypha,* pp. 71-3).

The chagrin of Joseph upon finding Mary with child is found also in the
Protevangelium. However, there is no mention in the *Protevangelium* of numerous
details found in both the *Life of Our Lady* and the Gospel of Pseudo-Matthew.
Among these are: Joseph's being in Capharnaum at the time of Mary's conceiving;
the testimony of the five maidens in regard to Mary's innocence; their mentioning
the daily visits of the angel; the belief of the maidens that the Holy Ghost had
caused Mary's pregnancy; Joseph's suspicion that a man dressed like an angel
had seduced Mary; and Joseph's apologies to Mary, after the nocturnal visit of the
angel had dissolved his doubt.

7) The trial of Joseph and Mary:

Life of Our Lady (II, 1346-1386)
And thus in Ioye, a while I late hem
  dwell
And of this Bisshop, furthe I will yov
  telle

Pseudo-Matthaei Evangelium, Cap.
XII: Factum est autem post haec et
exiit rumor quod Maria esset gravida.
Et comprehensus a ministris templi
Joseph ductus est ad pontificem, qui

Touchyng this thyng, playnely if I
   conne
Howe worde by worde, sothely in
   sentence
Of all this thyng, the Romour is Ronne
And Reportede that thorough necli-
   gence
Of this Ioseph, or by violence
How this Marye, gothe with chylde
   grete
Wherefore thay haue in a soden hete
Cyted hym, aforn hem to apere
And he cam furthe, with sobre
   contenaunce
Of whom a noon, the Bisshop gan
   enquyre
Abiathir, of his gouernaunce
Fro poynt to poynte with euery
   circumstaunce
Touchyng this thyng, what it myght
   amounte
Or howe that Ioseph, wolde giffe a
   compte
That Marye, debonaire and so mylde
Whiche som tyme, was of such opynyon
In the temple, is nowe grete with childe
Agayne the lawe, of hir professyon
By some engyne, or by collusion
In preiudice, of hir virgynyte

Nought with standyng vtterly that she
A vowede hadde, of holy affection
Al hir lyfe, to have kepet hir
   maydynhede
And was that tyme, of suche perfection
That sothefastly withoute any drede
Of suche a nothir, couthe I neuere
   Rede
Hir vertueȝ all, to Reken hem by and
   by
Fro day to day, all that tyme vtterly

una cum sacerdotibus coepit exprobrare
ei et dicere: Ut quid fraudatus es nup-
tias tantae ac talis virginis, quam
angeli

dei sicut columbam in templo nutri-
erunt, quae virum numquam nec videre
voluit, quae in lege dei eruditionem
optimam habuit? Tu autem si ei vio-
lentiam non fecisses, illa hodie virgo
perseverasset.

She neuere stynte, for to wirke or
  praye
But lyke a myrrour, of all holynesse
The wille of god, holyche dyd obeye
With all hir hert, and all hir bysynesse
And with all this fulfilled of mekenesse
She was ensample, to every maner
  wight
That there abode or of hir had a sight
And every day withoute wordes moo
Stound mele fro the hevyn doune
Goddys Angell, cam to and froo
Where as she laye, in contemplacion

* * *

II, Lines 1399-1418

Quod Ioseph than, with heed enclyned
  lowe
The sothefaste lorde, that euery thyng
  may see
My trust is fully, he will excuse me
Of Rightwysnes and shelde me from
  shame
Of all that euere, ye put me in blame
For I haue kepet hir, in the same
  poynt
Of maydenhed, that she was me by
  take
Of whiche as yet, she stant in noo
  disioynt
I dar afferme, and swere it for hir sake
And for my part, what preve ye lust
  I make
I will be Redy, and let it not be spared
Tyll verrely, the sothe be declared
Than quod the Bisshop all suspecion
For to voyde, all ambiguyte
That god may make, demonstracion
Of yov tweyne, how the trouthe be
Ye shall ataste, bothe thou and she

Joseph autem devotabat se jurans
quod numquam tetigisset eam.

Cui Abiathar pontifex dixit: Vivit
deus quoniam modo te faciam potare
aquam potationis domini, et statim
apparebit peccatum tuum.

Of thylke wat*er* to speke in word*es*
  fewe
By god ordenyde, trouthe forto shewe
To exclude playnely, eu*ery* conceyte
  newe

* * *

II, Lines 1446-1448

And she a noon, was of hir frende꙯
  brought
Knowyng Right nought, what all this
  wolde mene
Devoyde of drede, bothe in hert and
  thought

* * *

II, Lines 1502-1592

And so marye stondyng, in the place
And all hir frendes, aboute environ
Wher men may see, vpon many a face
Of frendely Routhe, and compassion
The salt teres, fall, and Renne dovne
For drede and love, thay had for to sene
So hard assay made, on hir age grene
But she all way constant, as a wall
In thought ne chere, abaschede neu*er*
  a dele
Ne in hir hert, dredyth not at all
But vpon god, trustyth all waye wele
That he of trouthe, shall trye oute the
  stele
Al be that she, speke but wordes fewe
Withoutyn speche, shall the dede
  shewe
And whan the wat*er*, fully was
  confecte
Lyke the statute, of the Rites olde
The Bisshopp hathe the cuppe, furst
  directe

Tunc congregata est omnis multitudo
Israel, quae dinumerari non poterat,
et adducta est etiam Maria ad templum
domini. Sacerdotes vero et affines ac
parentes ejus flentes dicebant ad
Mariam: Confitere sacerdotibus peccatum tuum, quae eras sicut columba
in templo dei et accipiebas cibum de
manu angeli.

Vocatus est autem et Joseph ad altare,
et data est ei aqua potationis domini:
quam si gustasset homo mentiens et
septies circuisset altare, dabat deus
signum aliquod in facie ejus. Cum

Vunto Ioseph, and the parell tolde
And manfully, he gan it holde
And dranke it vp, and chaunged not
  his chere
And vii tymes, about the Autere
He went thanne, by custome as he
  aught
Of face and colo*ur*, alway elyche newe
And to Marye, also the Bisshopp
  brought
A cuppe of water, and she w*ith* hert
  trewe
Acceptyth it, this goodly fresshe of
  hewe
And or she dranke, this perfyte holy
  mayde
All opynly to god, thus she sayde
Sothefast lorde, that haste the
  knowlegyng
Of eu*er*y thyng, thorowe thy grete
  myght
And art so trewe, and so Iuste a kyng
To lowe and high, that thou wilt do
  right
And no thyng may, be shadwede fro
  thy sight
Thorough noon engyne, ne fro thy
  face astert
But sothefastly, thou knowest eu*er*y
  hert
So that no wyght, fage may ne fayne
To for the eye, of thy sapyence
Nowe late thy grace, downe fro hevyn
  Rayne
Clerly in dede, and nought be aparence
To shewe in me, if ther be offence
Or any gilt, myn avowe to a peche
To the I pray, so thy light to Reche
That it be couthe, here all playnely
To wit in sothe, whether I in chastyte

ergo bibisset securus Joseph at giras-
set altare, nullum signum peccati
apparuit in eo. Tunc sanctificaverunt
eum sacerdotes omnes et ministri et
populi dicentes: Beatus es tu, quoniam
non est inventus reatus in te.

Et vocantes Mariam dixerunt ei: Tu
quam excusationem poteris habere?
aut quod signum majus apparebit in
te quam hoc quod prodit te conceptus
ventris tui? Hoc solummodo a te
requirimus, ut quia Joseph mundus est
a te, confitearis quis est qui te decepit.
Melius est enim ut te tua confessio
prodat, quam ira dei dans signum in
facie tua in medio populi te manifestet.
Tunc Maria constanter et intrepida
dixit: Si est in me aliqua pollutio aut
aliquod peccatum, aut fuit in me aliqua
concupiscentia vel impudicitia, detegat
me dominum in conspectu omnium
populorum, ut sim omnibus emenda-
tionis exemplum.

Haue led my lyfe, of hert faythefully
Lyche as thou knoweste, for the love
   of the
And if I haue, myne virgynyte
Conservede hoole, this is my oryson
Make opynly a demonstracion
And with that worde, the drynke she
   dyd a taste
And went hir cours, aboute the Autere
And all the people, be gan to gasen
   faste
If any signe, did in hir apere
Outhir in colour, in contenaunce or
   chere
But all for nought, playnely as I tolde
The more on hir, they loken and
   byholde
The more she was, to her sight fayre
And lyche as phebus, in Ioly grene
   maye
Whan he hathe chasede, the derke
   mysty eyre
Shyneth more bright, the clere somers
   daye
Whan þikke vapours, ben dreven clene
   awaye
Right so Ioseph, and also Marye
So fresshe werne, in euery wightez eye
That to beholde, they thought it dyd
   hem goode
The longe day, in hir opynnyon
For in her face, al waye was the blode
Withoutyn palyng, or any drawyng
   dovne
Al way more fayre, of inspeccion
Of whiche thyng, the people gan
   mervayle
And for astonede, thought hir wittes
   fayle
And in party gretely werne dismayed

Et accessit ad altare domini confidenter et bibit aquam potationis et septies circuivit altare, et non est inventa in ea ulla macula. Et cum omnis populus stuperet et haesitaret, videntes conceptum ventris at nullum signum in facie ejus apparuisse, coeperunt inter se varia populi loquacitate turbari. Alii dicebant sanctitatem, alii vero per malam conscientiam accusabant eam.

Tunc omnes osculabantur eam rogantes ut malis suspicionibus eorum daret indulgentiam et omnes coeperunt osculari pedes ejus et genua ejus amplecti. Et deduxerunt eam omnes populi et sacerdotes et omnes virgines cum exultatione et gaudio usque ad domum suam, clamantes et dicentes: Sit nomen

Leste that of theym, take were
    vengeaunce
For thay so ferre, haue goddes myght
    assayede
Of errour blynde and verrey
    ignoraunce
And Right furthe with, of hertly
    Repentaunce
They bonche ther brestez, with fistez
    wondir sore
And al at onys, fell dovne afore
This holy mayde, with humble
    Reuerence
And wold hir fete, have kyssed ther
    anone
Axyng mercy, of thayre grete offence
And she forgaf it, to hem euerycheone
And all the Bisshoppez, and the people
    goon
Benyngly, to brynge hir awaye
And to hir paleys, fully hir conveye
Of whome the noyse, to the hevyn rong
With hert and speche, as thay
    magnyfye
The lorde above, and euery wightys
    tunge
For Ioye and myrthe, gan hym
    gloryfie
And all the day, thus in melodye
Thay led furthe, tyl it drewe to eve
And gudely thanne, of hir thay toke her
    leve

domini benedictum qui manifestavit sanctitatem tuam universae plebi Israel. (C. Tischendorf, *Evangelia Apocrypha,* pp. 73-75).

The trial of Joseph and Mary is narrated sketchily in the *Protevangelium.* The Gospel of Pseudo-Matthew alone mentions the rumor circulating about Mary's pregnancy; the summoning of Joseph and the High Priest's recalling Mary's virtuous life in the Temple; Joseph's avowal of innocence; the bringing of Mary to the Temple; the exact details of the ordeal of drink, including the walking about the altar seven times; the prayer of Mary, asking God to show her virginity; the desire of the people to kiss Mary's feet; and the loud rejoicing of the people as they led Mary to her home after she had successfully survived the trial.

That the Latin text of the Gospel of Pseudo-Matthew is the immediate source of the *Life of Our Lady* is an open question. There are certain details in which the two accounts differ. With regard to the birth of the Virgin the Gospel of Pseudo-Matthew relates how the angel in a vision told Anna to go to the Golden Gate to meet Joachim. Upon their meeting, Anna tells Joachim that she has already conceived. In the *Life of Our Lady* the angel appears to both Joachim and Anna at the Golden Gate and prophesies Mary's birth. Anna and Joachim then return home and Mary is conceived.[4]

During the Virgin's life in the Temple, the Gospel of Pseudo-Matthew recalls that she began the pious custom of greeting everyone with "Deo Gratias," that she outshone her companions in virtue, that angels spoke with her and obeyed her, that her speech was so full of grace God was acknowledged to be in her tongue. There is no mention of these details in the *Life of Our Lady*. The *Life of Our Lady* adds to the Pseudo-Matthew version by noting that no one was tempted to sin by looking at Mary. There is a minor variant; the *Life of Our Lady* records that an angel brought Mary food at noon, while the Gospel of Pseudo-Matthew states that Mary prayed until evening when the angel brought her food.

In the marriage of Joseph and Mary there are certain differences in the two versions. The *Life of Our Lady* makes no mention of Joseph's having sons, or Joseph's promise to the high priest that he will keep Mary until God reveals which of his sons is to have her.[5] The *Life of Our Lady* omits Core in the high priest's warning to Joseph that Core, Dathan, and Abiron disobeyed God and were punished. Lydgate also omits mention of the jealousy of the other maidens when Mary chose purple silk and wove the veil of the temple, and the visit of the angel to the maidens, prophesying Mary's future status. The *Life of Our Lady* adds to the Gospel of Pseudo-Matthew in saying that Mary returned to her father's house at Nazareth and Joseph went to Bethlehem after their betrothal. Lydgate also adds that the veil which Mary wove was the one later torn asunder at Christ's death on Calvary.

In describing the trial by drink the Gospel of Pseudo-Matthew differs from the *Life of Our Lady* in noting that the people, the priests, and Mary's parents begged her to confess her sin, and adds that even after Mary successfully survived the drink ordeal, the people doubted her innocence. The *Life of Our Lady* adds that Abiathar referred to the Book of Numbers in ordering the trial by drink and that the

---

[4]In the Gospel of the Nativity of Mary, Anna conceives after the Golden Gate incident.

[5]Brother C. Philip Deasy, F.S.C., *St. Joseph in the English Mystery Plays* (Washington, 1937), pp. 32-33, points out that in the Mystery Plays no mention is made of any previous marriage of Joseph, despite the fact that the conception of Joseph as widower was prevalent in medieval literature. Lydgate seems to be leaning toward the pious belief in the perpetual virginity of Joseph.

people and the bishops were afraid after the trial that God might punish them for doubting Mary.

These variations in the two versions are, for the most part, minor ones. Yet we are at a loss to account for Lydgate's omissions and additions with regard to the Gospel of Pseudo-Matthew. One explanation might lie in Lydgate's having used an intermediary text, possibly a French translation of the Gospel of Pseudo-Matthew, or a French life of the Virgin[6] with the Gospel of Pseudo-Matthew as its source.[7] That there may be a single source, possibly French, becomes even more probable when we note the various other sources for large portions of Books III-VI of the poem. It seems unlikely that Lydgate would have used so many different sources in writing the *Life of Our Lady*. Such a procedure was not the practice in medieval composition. All search for such a single text, English or French, has thus far been in vain.

It is important to consider here that although there are extant lives of the Virgin based on the Gospel of Pseudo-Matthew such as "Joachim and Anne,"[8] "La Nativite Nostre Dame,"[9] "La Nativite Nostre Seignur et Ses Enfances,"[10] "The Life of Mary and of Christ,"[11] "Les Anfances Nostre Dame et de Jhesu,"[12] these versions differ from the *Life of Our Lady* in various details. The *Life of Our Lady* mentions that when Mary was *five* years old she was as wise as a woman of thirty. The other versions give her this maturity at *three* years of age. The *Life of Our Lady* records that the people gathered to choose a husband for Mary on the *eighth* day after the proclamation was dispatched; the other versions place this gathering on the *third* day. The *Life of Our Lady* names *Iȝachar* as the priest who arose to address the crowd at the convocation; the other versions say *Abiathar* made this address. In the *Life of Our Lady* the five maidens, attempting to prove Mary's virginity, express a belief that Mary conceived of the Holy Ghost. The other versions have the maidens ascribing her conception to an angel of the lord. The *Life of Our Lady* adds that the people would have fallen on their knees and kissed Mary's feet after she successfully survived the trial by drink. The other versions, which include the trial, omit this comment. Upon comparing the *Life of Our Lady* with C. Tischendorf's edition of the Gospel of Pseudo-Matthew we discover that these variations of Lydgate are found in the manuscripts B, D, and E

---

[6]Lydgate's major works, excepting only the *Troy Book,* are translations of French works.

[7]M. R. James, *The Apocryphal New Testament* (Oxford, 1924), p. 79, discusses the popularity of the Gospel of Pseudo-Matthew in the later Middle Ages.

[8]Cf. W. B. Turnbull, *Legendae Catholicae* (Edinburgh, 1840), pp. 125-164.

[9]Cf. R. Reinsch, *op. cit.,* pp. 31-37.

[10]*Ibid.,* pp. 37-40.

[11]Trinity College, Dublin MS 423. See Thomas K. Abbott, *Catalogue of the MSS in the Library of Trinity College, Dublin* (London, 1900), p. 65.

[12]MS B.N. 1553, described in R. Reinsch, *op. cit.,* p. 91.

with which Tischendorf collated his text.[13] In all probability, therefore, Lydgate's source was a manuscript similar to one of these three or a text based on such a manuscript.

The opening chapters of Book II, lines 1-350 comprise Lydgate's version of the Four Daughters of God, an allegory very popular in medieval and Renaissance literature. This theme, otherwise known as "The Reconciliation of the Heavenly Virtues" or "The Parliament of Heaven", is an extension of Psalm 84;11· "Misericordia et veritas obviaverunt sibi; justitia et pax osculatae sunt." After Adam's fall, four virtues, Justice, Mercy, Peace and Truth, quarreled concerning the ultimate destiny of sinful Man. God's Justice and Truth demanded satisfaction; His Mercy and Peace urged forgiveness. The reconciliation of these opposing principles was accomplished when the Son of God offered Himself as a redeeming Sacrifice.

The best discussion of the theme in its many versions is that of Miss Hope Traver.[14] Miss Traver traces the early development of the allegory in the Jewish *Midrash,* in a commentary of Hugo of St. Victor (1097-1141),[15] and in a sermon of St. Bernard of Clairvaux (1091-1153).[16] She surveys its later appearance in such works as Robert Grosseteste's *Le Château d'Amour,* the *Gesta Romanorum,* the *Cursor Mundi,* the pseudo-Bonaventure *Meditationes Vitae Christi,* Guillaume de Deguilleville's *Pèlerinage de l'Ame,* and the *Court of Sapience.*[17]

Miss Traver believes that Lydgate's version of the allegory is modelled on the work of St. Bernard. She observes:

> Lydgate's dependence upon Bernard is unmistakable. Especially noteworthy borrowings, because nowhere else adopted, are the statements that man had lost the protection and guidance of each of the four Virtues, and the comparison of his wretched state to that of the traveller toward Jericho. Less striking coincidences are also to be seen; for example, the Father's answer to Mercy and Peace that their sisters must also be summoned to present their wishes before He pronounce judgment,[18] and His direction that Trouthe and Mercy go before Christ and prepare His way.

> Besides the general dependence upon Bernard, one observes in Lydgate's poem a number of touches which reveal the influence of later versions of our allegory. The speech of Pees before God's throne suggests Grosseteste in its insistence

---

[13]*Op. cit.,* see especially pp. 62n., 66n., 72n. and 75n.
[14]*The Four Daughters of God* (Philadelphia, 1907).
[15]See Migne, *Patrologia Latina,* CLXXVII, 621-625.
[16]"In Festo Annuntiationis Beatae Mariae Virginis," Sermo I, Ps. 84; 10, 11. (A. D. 1140). See *Sancti Bernardi Opera Omnia,* ed. J. Mabillon (4 ed., 5v in 3, Paris, 1839), III, 2093-2102, esp. 2096-2102.
[17]Samuel C. Chew, in *The Virtues Reconciled* (Toronto, 1947), shows the popularity of the Four Daughters of God allegory in medieval and Renaissance art. The inclusion of eighteen plates enhances the value of this monograph and makes it an excellent companion volume to Miss Traver's study.
[18]This decision of the Father is found also in the pseudo-Bonaventure *Meditationes Vitae Christi,* as will be shown below.

upon the exalted position and dignity of herself and Mercy, and the conse-
quent necessity of granting their joint request, though in Grosseteste it is
only her own position which she rates so highly.[19] Again, in the passage
where Riȝt declares that by just doom man must die "thouȝ he were my
brother", one is reminded of *Piers Plowman*.[20] But these are minor points;
the important source is Bernard.[21]

Besides the parallel passages in Bernard and Lydgate noted by Miss Traver,
there are identities also in Truth's charge that Mercy (or Peace) was moved
by a misguided zeal in defending man, thus destroying Truth and Justice; and
in God's sending Gabriel to tell Mary, the daughter of Sion, to prepare for the
coming of her King.

There are a few verbal similarities in the two versions:

a) Describing the state of man after his fall from grace:

> "And [he] was of vertu nakede made and bare" (*Life of Our Lady*, II, 32)

> "An non despoliatus, qui Domino veniente nudum se esse conqueritur." (*Sancti Bernardi Opera Omnia*, III, 2097).

b) Discussing man's loss of the Virtues:

> "For when he gave credence to the snake
> He made his quarrel even against Right" (*Life of Our Lady*, II, 64-65)

> "Perdidit homo justitiam, cum Eva serpentis, Adam mulieris voci obedivit
> potius quam divinae." (*Sancti Bernardi Opera Omnia*. III, 2098).

c) Describing God's plan to call Justice and Truth before making a decision
   in the plea of Mercy and Peace:

> "And whan he [the Juge] had longe kepet sylence
> For all the skylleȝ to hym that they layde
> Yet at the laste to hem thus he sayde
> Myne awne doughtirs next of alye
> Though youre request come of tendre hert
> Ye must consydre with a prudent eye
> Of rightwysnesse it may nat me astert
> Lyke your askyng by favour to adverte
> Unto the cause that is represent
> But right and trouth fully will assent

---

[19]But this long speech of Peace is very similar to that of Mercy in the *Meditationes*.
[20]This expression was a common one. See Chaucer's *Canterbury Tales* (Prologue, 735)
in which Chaucer protests that an author must record the exact words of his character,
"although he were his brother." See also *Parliament of Fowls*, line 566, and *Troilus and
Criseyde*, I, 51; III, 252.
[21]Hope Traver, *op. cit.*, p. 25.

With outyn whome I may not procede
To execute any judgment
Wherefore lette call hem in this gret nede" (*Life of Our Lady*,
II, 180-192)

"Et quamvis diu multumque visus sit dissimulare
Pater miserationum, ut interim satisfaceret zelo justitiae
et veritatis; non tamen infructuosa fuit supplicantium
importunitas, sed exaudita est in tempore opportuno. Forte
enim interpellantibus tale dicatur dedisse responsum:
Usquequo preces vestrae? Debitor sum et sororibus vestris,
quas accinctas videtis ad faciendum vindictam in nationibus,
justitiae et veritati. Vocentur, veniant, et super hoc verbo
pariter conferamus." (*Sancti Bernardi Opera Omnia*, III, 2099).

Despite these identities, however, it is difficult to establish the sermon of St. Bernard as the source of the allegory in the *Life of Our Lady*. There are too many points of divergence. For example, in discussing man's lot after his fall, St. Bernard launches into a long digression on the difference in man between the image and the likeness of God. There is nothing of this in Lydgate. The sermon of St. Bernard recounts that in the midst of the dispute, God wrote with His finger in the earth, describing His dilemma in attempting to satisfy the sisters. He then suggested that an innocent victim die for man's sin. The incident of the writing is omitted in the *Life of Our Lady;* and Mercy, not God, makes the suggestion of an innocent substitute for man. In St. Bernard Truth searches the earth for a sinless volunteer; Mercy searches the heavens, both in vain. Then Peace suggests that God solve the problem. God agrees to undergo the punishment for man whom He created. There is no mention of this actual search in Lydgate (Mercy merely mentions the impossibility of finding such a sinless person) and God offers His Son voluntarily.

In the *Life of Our Lady,* lines II, 1-37, Lydgate describes at great length the misery and anguish of man, lying in the prison of hell. This has no counterpart in St. Bernard. The long speech of Peace, extolling the greatness of God's mercy (lines II, 106-175), has no source in St. Bernard. There is nothing in St. Bernard connecting the allegory of the Four Daughters of God with the power of a virgin over a unicorn (lines II, 339-347).[22] Regarding sequence of ideas and method of treatment the two versions have very little in common. There is a narrative continuity and pattern in the *Life of Our Lady* not found in the sermon of St. Bernard. The latter work is sketchy in relation to the allegory itself, lengthy in discussing moral and theological allusions in the allegory.

---

[22]For a discussion of this legend see the note for lines II, 339-347, p. 679.

On the other hand, the lines in the *Life of Our Lady,* II, 1-37, describing man's wretched state in hell, could have been suggested by Nicholas Love's *The Mirrour of the Blessed Lyf of Jesu Christ,* an English translation of the pseudo-Bonaventure *Meditationes Vitae Christi.* In the introduction of the Council of Heaven in the *Mirrour,* man is described as lying wretchedly in prison and in bonds, exiled by sin.[23]

> After the tyme that man was exiled oute of the hiȝe Citee of heuene by the riȝtwis dome of all myȝty god / souereyne kyng therof / for his trespas and his synne: and so wrecchedly lay in presoun / and was holden in the bondes of that tyraunt the deuel of helle / that none myȝte come aȝen to that blessed citee the space of fyue thowsand ȝere and more: alle the blessid spirites of heuene desirynge the restorynge of her companye / that was fallen doun with lucifer / hadden grete compassioun of so longe meschief of man that was made to here restorynge / and preiden often for his restorynge / but specially and with more instaunce whan the tyme of grace was comen.[24]

Lydgate's lines seem an echo of this passage. Love's translation is even closer to Lydgate than is the original Latin version of the *Meditationes.*[25] That Lydgate may have known Love's *Mirrour* is highly probable. Nicholas Love, a Carthusian monk, wrote the *Mirrour* before 1410 and presented it in that year to Archbishop Arundel as a weapon against Lollardry. The work is extant in twenty-three manuscripts and four prints, one by Caxton, one by Pynson, and two by Wynkyn de Worde. This is ample evidence of its popularity.

This same condition of man, mentioned again by Lydgate in the speech of Peace (*Life of Our Lady,* II, 145-147), is described by the angel Gabriel in the *Mirrour.*

> But loo / good lorde / now alle thei perisshen and none is saued: and in so manye thowsand ȝere passed / we seie none of hem alle here. Oure enemyes hauen the victorie and of hem oure party is noȝt restored / but the prisoun of helle continuelliche filled.[26]

---

[23]This description of the wretched prisoner is found also in Grosseteste's *Le Château d'Amour,* the *Cursor Mundi,* and the *Gesta Romanorum,* as will be seen below.

[24]*The Mirrour of the Blessed Lyf of Jesu Christ,* ed. by Lawrence F. Powell (Oxford, 1908), pp. 13-14.

[25]See *Sancti Bonaventurae Opera* (13v, Venice, 1756), XII, 381-382: "Cur per longissima tempora ultra spatium quinque millium annorum miserabiliter jaceret genus humanum, & nullus propter peccatum primi hominis ascendere posset ad patriam, beatissimi Angelici spiritus, compatientes tantae ruinae, & de sua restauratione soliciti, licet etiam pluries, primo tamen adveniente plenitudine temporis, devotius, & instantius taliter supplicaverunt Domino procidentes in facies suas ante thronum ejus simul omnes congregati . . ."

[26]*The Mirrour,* p. 14. Cf. *Sancti Bonaventurae Opera,* XII, 382: "Sed Ecce pereunt omnes, & nemo salvatur, & in tot annorum curriculis hoc videmus, quod de omnibus hostes nostri **triumphant,** & de ipsis non nostri triumphant, & de ipsis non nostrae ruinae, sed tartarae speluncae replentur."

The accentuation of man's suffering by remembering his former destiny in heaven (*Life of Our Lady,* II, 25), lacking in St. Bernard, is mentioned in the *Mirrour* in this same plea of Gabriel.[27]

> Almyȝty lord / it liked in ȝoure hiȝe maieste / of ȝoure endeles goodnesse / to make of nouȝt that noble and resonable creature / man / for oure conforte and oure goodnesse: that of hym schulde be made the restorynge of oure false com-panye / lucifer and his felawes / that fellen doun fro vs by apostacie: so that he schulde dwelle here in this blessed place with vs / louynge and worschippynge ȝow with outen ende.[28]

The long speeches of the sisters in the *Mirrour* and the *Meditationes* alluding to scriptural praises of God's virtues seem closer to Lydgate's treatment than do the short, terse speeches in St. Bernard. Common parallels in St. Bernard, Lydgate, the *Mirrour,* and the *Meditationes* versions are: the decision of God to call Justice and Truth before He judged the plea of Mercy and Peace, and the accusation by Justice (or Truth) that Mercy (or Peace) is moved by the false zeal of pity to free man and thus destroy the sisters. Otherwise, the version in the *Mirrour* and the *Meditationes* is close to that of St. Bernard; indeed, the author of the *Meditationes* mentions his dependence on the sermon of Bernard, and Nicholas Love includes this reference in his translation.

Two differences between St. Bernard and the *Mirrour* and *Meditationes* ver-sion are: the omission in the latter version of God's sending Mercy and Truth before His face and the addition in the same version of a long discourse by Reason proving why the Second Person of the Trinity should suffer for man's sake, rather than the Father or the Holy Ghost.

This comparative study inclines me to disagree with Miss Traver in her view of Lydgate's dependence on Bernard. Most likely Lydgate used an intermediary source, combining features of the St. Bernard sermon, the *Mirrour* and the *Medita-tiones*; or he may have used the *Mirrour* alone, and other treatments of the popular allegory; or Lydgate's version is his own, composed of elements from these treat-ments. As Curt Bühler points out, it is difficult to determine the source of an al-legory so popular as that of the Four Daughters of God, since this story belongs properly to the store of all medieval tradition.[29] He adds, quoting Miss Frances Foster: "This store [tradition] was common property then as it could not be now; for in those days of few books, reading was nearly synonymous with committing to

---

[27]There is a suggestion of this also in *Piers Plowman,* Text B, Passus XVII, lines 201-227; Text C, Passus XXI, lines 209-235.

[28]*The Mirrour,* p. 14. Cf. *Sancti Bonaventurae Opera,* XII, 382: "Domine placuit majestati vestrae, & rationalem creaturam, scilicet hominem creare propter vestram bonitatem, ut ipse esset hic nobiscum, & ut nobis ex ipso nostrarum contingeret restauratio ruinarum."

[29]*The Sources of the Court of Sapience* (Leipzig, 1932; *Beiträge zur engl. Phil.,* XXIII), p. 18.

memory, and a poem read was likely to influence plays or poems afterwards written."[30]

Save for general resemblances the *Life of Our Lady* has nothing in common with the accounts in Robert Grosseteste's *Le Château d'Amour*,[31] the *Cursor Mundi*,[32] or the *Gesta Romanorum*.[33] These three versions of the allegory are almost identical, the latter two probably modelled on the first, in placing the story in a feudal setting and giving a great king four daughters (the four virtues) and a son.[34] The king has, besides, a faithless servant, who is imprisoned for a misdeed. Mercy seeing the captive in his torment, pleads with the king for his release. Then the usual dispute follows. To settle the dispute the king's son volunteers to take upon himself the clothing of the servant and suffer in his stead. General resemblances in the *Life of Our Lady* and these three versions are: the unhappy lot of the faithless servant in prison, the lengthy speeches of the sisters, Peace's reminder to the king that he is prince of peace, and Mercy's claim to sovereignty over all the king's works.

There is an interesting verbal parallel in both the *Life of Our Lady* and the English translation of the *Gesta Romanorum*. In describing the dispute, the author of the *Gesta Romanorum* notes: "Then seide sothefastnes, with a Sterne countenans."[35] This is very close to Lydgate's "Cam trowth forthe, with a sterne face."[36]

The version of the allegory in *Piers Plowman*,[37] as a prelude to the Harrowing of Hell, bears little or no resemblance to the *Life of Our Lady*. The *Piers Plowman* version is a very sketchy discussion about the manner in which Christ shall redeem man. At first only Truth and Mercy are depicted as disputing the efficacy of Christ's death in freeing man from hell. Then Peace and Righteousness join in the fray. General resemblances are Peace's promise to free man who has known sorrow all the more, having once known happiness;[38] and Mercy's statement

---

[30]Frances Foster, *The Northern Passion* (1913; *EETS,* 145), p. 101.
[31]Edited by J. Murray (Paris, 1918).
[32]Edited by R. Morris (1874-8; *EETS,* 57, 59, 62, 66, 68).
[33]Edited by Thomas Wright (2v, London, 1871). See also *The Early English Versions of the Gesta Romanorum,* ed. by S. J. H. Herrtage (1889; *EETSES* 33).
[34]For a discussion of the dependence of *Le Château d'Amour* upon a Latin version of the allegory, *Rex et Famulus,* see Sister M. Immaculate, C. S. C., "The Four Daughters of God in the Gesta Romanorum and the Court of Sapience", *PMLA,* LVII (1942), 951-965.
[35]*The Early English Versions of the Gesta Romanorum,* ed. by S. J. H. Herrtage (1889; *EETSES,* 33), p. 133.
[36]*Life of Our Lady,* II, 41.
[37]See W. W. Skeat's edition of the three Texts (1867-84; *EETS,* texts in Vols. 28, 38, 54, notes and glossary in Vols. 67, 81). The Four Daughters of God allegory occurs in Passus XVIII of text B, Passus XXI of text C.
[38]Text B, Passus XVIII, lines 201-227; Text C, Passus XXI, lines 209-235; *Life of Our Lady,* II, 25.

that by the death of Christ, "venim shall destroy venim" and "death shall destroy death."[39]

Since Spindler, on rather conclusive evidence, has removed the *Court of Sapience* from the Lydgate canon and dated it as after 1450 and most probably 1475,[40] there is no need to consider this work as a source for Lydgate's version of the allegory in the *Life of Our Lady*. We might, however, note Curt Bühler's comment of relationship between the two versions by virtue of their mutual expression of the great role of Mercy in Man's salvation and the exaltation of Mercy by Peace in the heavenly court.[41] In all probability these two ideas were taken originally from both the *Meditationes* and *Le Château d'Amour,* upon which the *Court of Sapience* leans heavily for its version of the allegory.[42]

Guillaume de Deguilleville's version of the allegory in the *Pèlerinage de l'Ame*[43] has nothing in common with the version in the *Life of Our Lady*. Only in the pleading of the good angel that man had been committed to certain guardians on earth is there a reminder of Lydgate's comment that man had lost the protection of each of the four virtues. But, as we have seen, Lydgate here seems close to St. Bernard in enumerating the virtues and the manner of man's losing each. In Deguilleville there is only the general statement of the loss.

In Book I, lines 435-532 of the *Life of Our Lady* we learn that during her youth in the temple Mary made a daily prayer of seven petitions. Lydgate cites as his source, "And in the boke of Eliȝabethe / That tytlede is in hir avysions."[44] The "Eliȝabethe" to whom Lydgate refers in all probability is St. Elizabeth of Schönau, O.S.B. (1129-1165).[45] Revelations made to her by the Mother of God occurred during the years 1152-1165. The seven petitions mentioned by Lydgate were revealed to St. Elizabeth in the fourth revelation. These seven petitions of Our Lady in the temple were very popular in medieval religious writings.[46] Though they occur in

---

[39]Text B, Passus XVIII, lines 150-160; Text C, Passus XXI, lines 154-166; *Life of Our Lady,* II, 342-347.

[40]See *The Court of Sapience,* ed. by Robert Spindler (Leipzig, 1927; *Beiträge zur engl. Phil.,* VI), pp. 80-83.

[41]*Op. cit.,* pp. 20 and 31.

[42]For the dependence of the *Court of Sapience* on these two works see C. F. Bühler, *op. cit.,* pp. 18-25.

[43]See the editions of Deguilleville's three poems, *Le Pèlerinage de la Vie Humaine, Le Pèlerinage de l'Ame,* and *Le Pèlerinage de Jesucrist,* by J. J. Stürzinger for the Roxburghe Club, London (1893-1897).

[44]*Life of Our Lady,* I, 435-436.

[45]L. Oliger, "Revelationes B. Elizabeth," *Antonianum,* I (1926), 24-83, discusses the identity of the Elizabeth to whom these revelations were made. He presents rather conclusive evidence in favor of St. Elizabeth of Schönau, thus contradicting Count C. F. de Montalembert who, in his *Histoire de Sainte Elisabeth de Hongrie, Duchesse de Thuringe* (Paris, 1861), ascribed them to St. Elizabeth of Hungary (1207-1231). For an account of the life and visions of St. Elizabeth of Schönau see Migne, *PL,* CXCV, 114-194 and the *Acta Sanctorum,* ed. J. Carnandet, XXIV, 499-532.

[46]A listing of the occurrence of the seven petitions is given in the note for lines I, 435-532.

the pseudo-Bonaventure *Meditationes Vitae Christi*,[47] already mentioned in reference to its relationship with the *Life of Our Lady,* and from which Lydgate quotes two passages,[48] I think that here Lydgate is using St. Elizabeth's revelations at first hand. For in a later reference to the revelations of St. Elizabeth[49] Lydgate notes that Our Lady "was of age who so wyl take hede sixtene yere" at the time of Our Lord's birth. The *Meditationes* gives Our Lady's age at that time as fifteen.[50]

A comparative study of the lines in Lydgate and of the listing of the petitions in the revelations of St. Elizabeth show their mutual identities clearly.

Life of Our Lady (I, 435-532)

And in the boke, of Eliȝabethe
That tytlede is, of hir avisions
I fynde how this mayde of Naȝareth
Sayde euery day seven orysions
Whiche clepyde ben, hir petycions

Withe humble hert, this yong blisfull mayde

Ful lowely knelynge, evyn thus she sayde

O Blisfull lorde, that knawest the entent

Of euery hert, In thyne eternal sight

Yeffe me grace, the firste commaundement

To fulfille as it is skyll *and* right

And grant also, w*ith* herte will and myght

And all my savle, and all my full knawyng

The for to love, aboven all othir thyng

And gyffe me myght, playnely to fulfille

The next byddyng, lyke to thy pleasaunce

And for to loue, withe hert and all my will

("Quarta Revelatio," see L. Oliger, *op. cit.,* p. 54-56. This text is from MS 442. Bibl. municip. Assisi, f. 190v.)

Primo petebam gratiam per quam possem implere dilectionis preceptum, se ipsum diligere ex toto corde, etc.

Secundo petebam gratiam qua possem diligere proximum secundum voluntatem et beneplacitum suum et ut faceret me amare omnia que ipse amat et diligit.

---

[47]See *Sancti Bonaventurae Opera* (13v. Venice, 1756), XII. 384; and *The Mirrour of the Blessed Lyf of Jesu Christ,* ed. Lawrence F. Powell (Oxford, 1908), p. 21.
[48]Book III, 539-548 and Book IV, 30-63.
[49]Book III, 564-568.
[50]*Sancti Bonaventurae Opera,* XII, 390; *The Mirrour,* p. 46.

My neghbore in dede, and contenaunce
Right as my self, *with* eu*er*y
   circu*m*staunce
And her withall, for Ioye woo or
   smerte
That thou lovest, to love with all myn
   hert
The thride precepte graunte eke that
   I may
Fulfille also, bo*þ*e erly and late
In such maner, as is most to thy pay
Benigne lorde, and make me for to hate
Mankyndes foo, for he made furst
   debate
In kynde of man, and made hym to
   trespace
Agayns the and to lese his grace

And lorde graunte me, for thy mercy
   dygne
Above al thyng, for to haue mekenesse
And make me sufferaunte, humble and
   benigne
W*ith* paciens and inwarde myldenesse
Of all vertues, gyf me eke largesse
To be accepte, the to queme and s*er*ue
To fynde only thy grace I may dis*er*ue

And lorde also, *with* quakyng herte
   and drede
Mekely I pray vnto thy deite
Me forto graunte of thy godelyhede
The gracious hour, forto abyde and see
In whiche, the holy chosyn mayden
   free
Into this worlde here aftir shall be
   borne
Lyche as prophete꙾, have wryten here
   to forne
Howe *þat* she shall by thyne eleccion
Be maide and modur, to *þi* sone dere
Now goode lorde, here myn orisoun

Tertio petebam ut faceret me odire et
fugere omnia que odit.

Quarto petebam humilitatem, patien-
tiam, benignitatem, et mansuetudinem,
et omnes virtutes per quas efficerer
gratiosa ante conspectum suum.

Quinto petebam ut faceret me videre
tempus, in quo esset nata illa sanctis-
sima

virgo que debebat Dei Filium parere
et ut conservaret oculos meos, ut possem ipsam videre, aures, ut possem
ipsam audire, linguam ut possem ipsam laudare, manus, ut possem ipsi

To kepe my eyne, and my sight entier
That I may see, hir holy halowed chier
Hir sacrede beawtee, and hevynly
   contenaunce
If thou of grace liste me, so moche
   avaunce
And kepe myne eren þat I may also
Here hir speche, and hir daliaunce
And with my tonge, speke that maiden
   to
Paciently thorough hir sufferaunce
Of worldly Ioye, this were my
   suffisaunce
And hir to love, lyke as I desyre
Benygne lorde, thou set myne herte
   afyre
And also lord, on me safe þou vouche
Though I therto, have nowe noo
   worthynesse
That holy mayde, forto handyll and
   touche
Myn owne ladi, and myn maystresse
And that I maye, with humble
   buxumnesse
Uppon my feet, in all my best wyse
Go vnto hir, for to do servise
And to that floure, of virginitee
Graunte also lorde, þat I may haue
   space
Mekely to bowe, and knele vppon my
   kne
Vndir supporte only, of hir grace
And to honour the godely yong face
Of hir sonne, as she dothe hym wrappe
In clothis softe lyggyng in hir lappe
And luffe hym best playnly to my laste
With all myne herte, and myne hole
   servise
Withoutyn chaunge, while my lyve
   may laste

servire, pedes ut possem ire ad servitium suum, genua, ut possem adorare Dei Filium in gremio suo.

Right as thy self lorde canst best
  devyse
So that I may, in faythfull humble
  wyse
In all this worlde, no more grace
  atteyne
Then love hym beste, with all my
  might and peyne
And to thy grace, also lorde I pray
Thou graunte it me to fulfyll in dede
Hooly thy statutes and mekely to
  obeye
Within the Temple, as I here hem
  Redde
For but thou helpe, I may no thyng
  spede
As of myself, therfore vnto the
All I committe, Right as thou luste
  it be
The observaunceȝ and the precepteȝ
  all
That to thy Temple, oo lorde by
  pertynent
So latte thy grace, by mercy on me fall
That I may done hem, with all my
  hole entente
And euery byddyng, and
  commaundement
That thy mynystreȝ, assignede vnto me
Make me fulfill, with all humillite
And thy Temple, and thyne holy house
Benygne lorde, kepe frome all damage
And make thy people, to be vertuouse
To thy pleasaunce of euery manere age
The forto serve, with herte and hoole
  corage
And where they erre, o lorde on any
  syde
Or thou do Right, latte mercy be hir
  gyde

Sexto petebam gratiam obediendi man-
datis et ordinationibus pontificis templi.

Septimo petebam ut templum et uni-
versum populum suum ad suum servitium conservaret.

For his narration of the Annunciation to Mary by the Angel Gabriel (*Life of Our Lady,* II, 351-371, 442-497) Lydgate follows exactly the Gospel of St. Luke, I, 26-38. The story of the angel's visit is treated fully in the Bible and in Lydgate. The version of the Annunciation in the Gospel of Pseudo-Matthew is both sketchy and incomplete.[51]

The Visit of Our Lady to her cousin Saint Elizabeth (*Life of Our Lady,* II, 944-1067) is from the Gospel of St. Luke, I, 39-56. There is no mention whatever of this visit in the Gospel of Pseudo-Matthew. In two lines Lydgate refers to the "gospell" as his source for this episode in the *Life of Our Lady.*[52] Included in this portion of the *Life of Our Lady* (II, 981-1060) is a beautiful paraphrase in eight-line stanzas of the *Magnificat* of the Virgin Mary. These lines are from the Gospel of St. Luke, I, 46-55.

In the *Life of Our Lady,* II, 652-931, Lydgate presents forty-two examples of phenomena in nature to prove the Virgin Birth. Such a practice was common in medieval times. G. R. Owst treats this subject at great length.[53] An example of collections of this nature is the *Defensiorum inviolatae perpetuaeque virginitatis castissimae Dei genetricis Mariae,* Franciscus de Retza, 1470. This work consists of sixteen folios, with fifty-four pictures and accompanying texts, presenting arguments from the Fathers to prove that Mary retained her virginity even in giving birth to Christ. There are examples from St. Ambrose, St. Jerome, St. Gregory, St. Augustine, and others. Other enlarged editions of this work were published in 1471, 1480, and 1490.[54] I have found no exact source for this portion of the *Life of Our Lady,* though many of these same examples occur in other works, as the notes point out.

In recounting the visit of the angel to Joseph, Lydgate gives three reasons why Joseph should reject his plan to leave Mary (*Life of Our Lady,* II, 1257-1277). Lydgate cites as his source "Crysostomus." The lines are a close paraphrase of a passage from St. Chrysostom's homily, "Eruditi Commentarii in Evangelium Matthaei Incerto Auctore":

Propter tres ergo causas apparuit ei. Primum ne justus homo ignorans faceret rem injustam ex proposito justo; deinde propter honorem matris ipsius. Nam si dismissa fuisset, etsi non apud fideles, tamen apud infideles turpi suspicione carere non poterat. Tertio, ut intelligens Joseph sanctam conceptionem diligentius se in futurum custodiret ab illa, quam prius."[55]

---

[51]Cf. Tischendorf, *op. cit.,* pp. 70-71. The Gospel of Pseudo-Matthew mentions two visits of the angel, the first of these at a fountain.

[52]See lines II, 956: "Reioysyde hym the gospell sayet expresse;" and II, 1065: "Thre monethez the gospell may not ley."

[53]*Literature and Pulpit in Medieval England* (Cambridge, 1933), pp. 149-209.

[54]See the *Catalogue of Printed Books in the British Museum* (Ann Arbor, 1946), XXXV, 18.

[55]Migne, *PG,* LVI, col. 683.

Chapter XVII of the *Life of Our Lady* (II, 379-406), "A Lamentacion of Saint Barnarde," is a paraphrase of a passage from St. Bernard's homily, "De Laudibus Virginis Matris."[56] The praises of St. Ambrose concerning Mary's virginity (*Life of Our Lady,* I, 407-413), are found in his sermon, "De Virginibus."[57] I have included these passages in the Notes.

_____

[56]*Sancti Bernardi Opera,* edd. Horstium and Mabillon (4v, Paris, 1719), I, 75.
[57]*Sancti Ambrosii Mediolanensis Episcopi Opera* (Paris, 1690), II, 165-166.

BOOKS III AND IV

This section of the *Life of Our Lady* has for its basic sources the *Apocryphal Gospel of Pseudo-Matthew,*[1] the *Legenda Aurea,*[2] the *Meditationes Vitae Christi* attributed to Saint Bonaventure,[3] and the Vulgate Bible. Less extensive use is made of the works of Saint Augustine, Saint Bernard, Alcuin, Innocent III, John of Salisbury, and Robert Grosseteste.

While it is true that certain factors point to a single French source for the entire composition,[4] all search for it has thus far proved fruitless. For the present, then, we are constrained to indicate in the order of their occurrence such varied materials as Lydgate seems to have used in fashioning his poem. We shall put off drawing any conclusions on the question of source until the reader has had an opportunity to view certain parallel texts at first hand.

Book III begins with the beautiful Biblical excerpt that constitutes one of the motifs of the Christmas Office :[5]

Whanne al was hust *and* al was in silence	Cum enim quietum silentium contineret omnia, et nox in suo cursu medium iter haberet,
And in his course the longe starry nyght	
Was passed half and fresche of aperaunce,	
Lucyne shone on hevyn fayre and bryght;	
Thy worde, oo lorde, that is moste of myght,	Omnipotens sermo tuus de coelo a regalibus sedibus,
Whiche ay abydythe and partyth not from the,	
Sent and discendid from thy Royall see,	

---

[1]*Evangelia Apocrypha,* ed. Constantinus Tischendorf (Leipzig, 1876), pp. 51-112.

[2]*Legenda Aurea,* ed. Th. Graesse (2 ed., Leipzig, 1876).

[3]*Sancti Bonaventurae Opera Omnia* (13v, Paris, 1868), XII, 509-630. Chapters VII and VIII deal with the material of Books III and IV of the *Life of Our Lady.*

[4]R. Klinefelter remarks in his edition of Books I and II of the *Life of Our Lady,* p. 83, that all of Lydgate's major works except the *Troy Book* had a single French source. It will be noted too that in the *LOL* (*Life of Our Lady*) proper names are usually in the French form.

[5]*Wisdom,* XVIII, 14-15. This text was frequently accommodated to the Nativity theme. It is to be found in Christmas sermons such as those of Peter Comestor, *Sermo VI In Nat. Dni.,* Migne, *PL,* CXCVIII, 1758; and Petrus Cellensis, *Sermo In Nat. Dni.,* Migne, *PL,* CCII, 658; in the *Historia Scholastica,* Migne, *PL,* CXCVIII, 1539; and as the Antiphon for the Magnificat at Vespers on the Sunday within the Octave of Christmas.

Hath sodenly upon all the erthe   durus debellator in mediam terram pro-
Shed his light for our saluacion.[6]   silivit.

From this prelude, Lydgate proceeds immediately to a discussion of the circumstances that attended the birth of Christ. He begins by stating that the Nativity
occurred in the forty-second year of Augustus' reign, five thousand one hundred
and ninety-nine years after the beginning of the world, "as Beda liste to diffyne",
and in the hundred ninety-third Olympiad.[7] Bede, however, states it this way:
"*Hujus (i.e., Octaviani) anno xlii Dominus nascitur, completis ab Adam
annis 3952. Juxta alios 5199 . . .*"[8] And in another place: "*Anno Caesaris Augusti
xiii . . . Olympiadis cxciv anno tertio.*"[9] In giving the hundred ninety-third
Olympiad, Lydgate is closer to Peter Comestor than to Bede.[10] It may very well
be, of course, that he was merely quoting from memory the Martyrology of the day.

The next section,[11] dealing with Augustus' command that all the world should
be enrolled, treats information that is stated fully, but in differing sequence, by the
Historia Scholastica.[12] Lydgate's familiarity with the Gospel story and its embellish-
ments in apocryphal and legendary literature may have given him a certain freedom
here in using Peter Comestor's data. It is remarkable, though, that no other version
contains all the facts.

Equally remarkable, too, is the fact that Lydgate soon seems to depart from
Comestor and swing to the Apocrypha for his material.[13] In the description of
Joseph's and Mary's trip to Bethlehem, the Gospel of Pseudo-Matthew closely
parallels our poem.[14] We are told

    . . . that Joseph must gone   Necesse autem fuerat ut Ioseph cum
To Bedeleem for conclusion,   Maria proficisceretur in Bethlehem,
To pay his tribute in his owne towne,   quia exinde erat,
As the statute afore doth specifye;
Because that he and also eke Marye

Werne of the householde and of the   et Maria de tribu Iuda et de domo ac
  trybe borne   patria David.
Called Iuda, and of the kynrede

---

[6]*LOL* III, 1-9.
[7]*LOL* III, 12-20.
[8]Migne, *PL,* XC, 290.
[9]Migne, *PL,* XC, 545.
[10]Migne, *PL,* CXCVIII, 1285.
[11]*LOL* III, 22-87.
[12]Migne, *PL,* CXCVIII, 1539.
[13]*LOL* III, 88-149.
[14]Tischendorf, pp. 76-80. Also found in *Legenda Aurea,* ed. Graesse, p. 41, but lacking
the angel's reprimand to Joseph.

Of worthy Dauid, as I haue sayde
  to-forne.
And on her Iournay, as thay gan
  thayme spede,
And holy Ioseph dyd hir brydill lede,
Sodenly marye full sone she abrayede,
And unto Ioseph evyn thus she sayde:

Cum ergo Ioseph et Maria irent per
viam quae ducit Bethlehem, dixit
Maria ad Ioseph:

"I wys," quod she, "me thynkyth þat
  I see
Two folkys gretly discordyng,
Upon the waye aperen vnto mey.
The tone Reioysyng, that othir
  compleynyng."
To whome Ioseph benyngly lokyng,
Ansewerde agayne and bad hir Ryde
  in pees;
And prayed hir also nat to be reccles,

Duos populos video ante me, unum
flentem et alium gaudentem.

Cui respondit Ioseph: Sede et tene te
in iumento tuo et noli

Any wordys for to speke in vayne,
But holde hir way and in hir Iournay
  Right.[15]

superflua verba loqui.

And vnwarly, aforne hem in the
  playne,
Apered as Angell w*ith* face sterne and
  bryght
Of whome the beaute yaf a plesant
  lyght,
The place envyron and a sote odoure.
And his clothyng like the lely floure

Tunc apparuit puer speciosus ante
eos, indutus veste splendida,

Was whit in sothe as snowe that
  fallith newe;
Whiche gan a-noon chere and loke to
  meve,
And ther-w*ith*-al with a chaunged
  hewe,

---

[15]If Lydgate intended to translate *iumentum* as "iourney" it does not speak well for his Latinity.

By-gan also Ioseph to repreve.
And shortly bad his wordes that he
　leve,
And sayde, in sothe, that he was to
　blame
For to be bolde any wordes to atame

Ayens Marye; thorugh his necligence,
To saye that she spak any worde in
　vayne.
For that she sawe was non apperance,
But verrey sothe as she hath it seyne.
"For truste me well and be right
　certeyne,
Of this folke of whiche she spake to the,
In sothefastenesse, lyche as thou shalt
　see,

Ben the peoples and the folkeȝ tweyne,
That ben disceuerde in full large space:
The ton of Ieues, that wepe shull and
　pleyne,
With many atere distyllyng on his
　face,
That wilfully shall refuse his grace,
Of frowarde hert for to be benyng,
To devoyde and playnely to Resygne

The Sinagoge, with hir Riteȝ olde,
Which in shorte tyme shall drawe to
　declyne,
And hir phares quenche and waxen
　colde
With sacrede light, that were wonte to
　shyne.
For tyme is come þat they must fyne,
Ande the weylinge of her derked chere
Vncloos shall and shewe al bryght and
　clere,

et dixit ad Ioseph: Quare dixisti

verba superflua esse de duobus populis
de quibus locuta est Maria?

Populum enim Iudeorum flentem vidit
quia recessit a deo suo

As phebus dothe at mydday in the
    sowthe,
When eu*er*y Rakke and eu*er*y cloudy
    skye
Is voyde clene, so hir face vncouthe
Shall shewe in opyn and fully ben
    vnwry.
And the peple which that marye   et populum gentium gaudentem
Reioysyng say for yoye and gladnesse,
Ben paynymes þat mekely shall hem
    dresse,

This tyme of grace fully to obey,
With hert and will, and full humble
    chere.
For goddes words that no man maye   quia accessit et prope factus est ad
    *with*saye   Dominum secundum quod promisit
Hath hastyd it gon ful many a ȝere   patribus nostris Abraham, Isaac, et
To Abraham and Isaak in-fere   Iacob;
And to Iacob, that in hir holy seede,
Full hastely, who so luste take hede,

shall all peples pleynly blissede be,   tempus enim advenit ut in semine
Thorugh-oute the worlde in eu*er*y   Abrahae benedictio omnibus gentibus
    londe and Realme."   tribuatur.
And with that worde, as Ioseph myght
    see,
The Angell sty above the sonne beame.

Curiously, after this close parallelism Lydgate seems to depart from the *Evangelium Pseudo-Matthaei* when the time comes to describe the entry into Bethlehem. He speaks of a stable rather than a cave as does the apocryphal gospel, and he completely omits the angel's command to Joseph and Mary that they alight at the cave's mouth. Instead, Luke's New Testament account of the overcrowded city takes precedence.[16] Immediately thereafter, however, the narrative of Pseudo-Matthew is taken up again.[17]

---

[16]*LOL* III, 152-167; *Luke* ii. 6-7.
[17]*LOL* III, 168-177; Tischendorf, p. 77.

And as she entrede a newe soden light
Gan the place enlumen envyron,
That shone as bright as eny someres
  day,
So that this lityll humble mancion
Was fresche of light as phebus is in
  may;
Whiche gan to waxen and encrece aye
While she was there, all-be þat it was
  nyght.
And ryght anoon, the sothefaste sonne
  of myght,

Of all our Ioye, caste hym to aryse
And shed his light to glad all man
  kynde.

Ad ingressum vero Mariae tota spelun-
ca coepit splendorem habere, et quasi
sol ibi esset ita tota fulgorem lucis
ostendere; et quasi esset ibi hora diei
sexta, ita speluncam lux divina illus-
travit; nec in die nec in nocte lux ibi
divina defuit quamdiu ibi Maria fuit.

Our author now enters into a laudatory disquisition on the Virgin Birth and
its attendant prerogatives. Pseudo-Matthew says nothing of this, but the *Legenda
Aurea*[18] remarks on the extraordinary character of Mary's motherhood and brings
forward abundant Scriptural testimony to support its contention. It may be, therefore that Lydgate derived his inspiration for these lines (178-200) from the
Legenda.

Be that as it may, the midwives' episode which follows immediately[19] can be
traced back with close textual similarity to the *Pseudo-Matthew Gospel*.[20] The
only departure from this source occurs shortly after the subject is introduced, and
it can be found in Bonaventure.[21] The Pseudo-Matthew lines, together with the
interruption by Bonaventure, are given here as they occur:

And, as I fynde, at hir delyueryng
Ther was no wight, but hir self aloon.
For þylke tyme Ioseph was out goone,

In full gret hast, to enquere and seke
Some Mydwyfe, to helpe in this nede.

Iam enim dudum Ioseph perrexerat

ad quaerendas obstetrices. Qui cum
reversus esset ad speluncam, Maria

---

[18]Graesse, p. 41.
[19]*LOL* III, 201-440.
[20]Tischendorf, pp. 77-79.
[21]*Meditationes Vitae Christi*, XII, 518. The incorrect attribution of this work to the
Seraphic Doctor is discussed by A. C. Peltier in the above-mentioned edition, XII. xlii-xliii, and
by R. Klinefelter, p. 6, note 10.

And in this while, with hir eyne meke,

She childed hath, this floure of
  maydenhede.
And home agayne as Ioseph gan hym
  spede
And to the place the mydwyfeȝ
  brought;
Evyn at the dore, abasshede **in theyr**
  thought,

Stoden styll astonyed of that **light,**
Ande the bryȝghtnesse þat shon in þat
  place,
Aȝen kynde, that tyme of the nyȝght,
That they ne myght susteyne in her
  face.

         *   *   *

And knelyng downe [she] **began to**
  enbrace
His tendre lymmes in hir Armes
  tweyne,
And wrappede hym in clothes
  tendrely,
And toke hi*m* up and sooftly gan **him**
  leyne
In hir lappe; and full humbly
She be-helde his feturs by and by,
So fayre shapen in party and in all.
And w*ith* hir mylke, verrey celestiall,

And hevenly licour of hir pappes
  small,
His tendre lymmes she sprede in
  eu*er*y coste,—
The white bavme to make it avale,
Fette fro the condyth of the holy goste,
Vpon the thyng that she loved most;

iam infantem genuerat. Et dixit
Ioseph ad Mariam: Ego tibi Zelomi et
Salomen obstetrices adduxi quae foris
ante speluncam stant et prae splendore
nimis huc introire non audent. . .

Et mater incontinenti se inclinans, re-
colligens eum et dulciter amplexans,
posuit in gremio suo et ubere de coelo
pleno, et Spiritu sancto edocta, coepit
lavare sive linire ipsum per totum cum
lacte suo; quo facto involvit eum in
velo capitis sui, et posuit eum in praesepio.

Lydgate now follows Bonaventure through a loving description of Mary's welcome of the Child, and then considers her kneeling at the manger and praying to her Son in a way that far surpasses the text of the *Meditationes*. After this first adoration, in which Joseph subsequently joins, we are reminded that the midwives, blinded by the light, are still waiting at the door. This is, as it were, a signal to take up the *Pseudo-Matthew Gospel* once more:

And aftir that, she [Mary] mekely vp
   Rose,
And to the dore, wondre womanly
She went apas, and when she dyd se
The mydwyfes, full benygnely
She brought hem in with all
   humylite,—
Scephora and also Solomee,—   Tunc iussit unam ex eis intrare ad se.
And hem welcomyth in full lawe   Cumque ingressa esset Zelomi,
   man*ere*.
And when that thay these signes sawe
   in-fere,

Of the sterre and the beste3 knele
Tawarde the childe to do hym
   Reu*er*ence,
And gan also by othir tokens fele   ad Mariam dixit: Dimitte me ut tan-
Of maydynhede ther was none offence,   gem te. Cum permisisset se Maria
But that she stode hole in the   tangi, exclamavit voce magna obstet-
   excellence   rix et dixit:
Of *per*fyte clennesse and hool
   virgynyte,
Mothir to be, and floure in chastite,

W*ith*outyn wem on eny party founde,   Domine, domine magne miserere.
For all the preves that thay make
   coude;
And whan thay sawe hir pappes so
   abounde
W*ith* hevenly mylk*e* sent from above
   the cloude,
Scephora began to cry lowde
That a mayde hath a chylde borne,—

The wiche thyng was not seen afforne

In all this worlde, who so luste take
  hede.
For it, in sothe, the right of all nature
Passeth playnely, and also doth excede
The witte of man, I do yov well assure.
But I se well thorughe the myghty
  cure
Of goddys honde this thyng is brought
  aboute;
Wher of plattely I am no-thyng in
  doute,

But assented *with* hert and hole
  credence,
Ther-of havyng noon ambiguyte.
And then a-noon for the grete offence
And for wantruste, hir felowe Solomee
Opynly, that all myght it see,
Waxe in that Arme dede and colde
  as stone,
Withe the whiche she was hardy for
  to gone

The childe to touche of presumpcion;
And his mothir, *with*-outen Reuerence,
Devoyded of drede or devocion,
Or eny faythefull, humble adu*er*tence,
Done as hir aughte to his
  magnyfycence.
Where-fore a-noon, for hir high
  trespace,
All opynly in the same place,

She pun[i]shede was, that all myghten
  se;
And gan to sorowe, wepe, and
  complayne,
And sayd: "O lorde, haue pyte vpon
  me,

Nunquam hoc auditum est nec in suspicione habitum ut mamillae plenae
sint lacte et natus masculus matrem
suam virginem ostendat. Nulla pollutio sanguinis facta est in nascente,
nullus dolor in parturiente. Virgo concepit, virgo peperit, virgo permansit.
Audiens hanc vocem alia obstetrix
nomine Salome dixit: Quod ego audio
non credam nisi forte ipsa probavero.
Et ingressa Salome ad Mariam dixit:

Permitte me ut palpem te et probem
utrum verum dixerit Zelomi. Cumque
permisisset Maria ut eam palparet,
misit manum suam Salome. Et cum
misisset et tangeret, statim aruit manus
ejus, et prae dolore coepit flere vehe-
mentissime et angustari et clamando
dicere:

And of mercy Rewe vpon my payne,
And of myne offence þat thou not
  disdeyne,
Ne to thy highnesse be no displesaunce,
That I a wreche, blynde of ignorance,

Offendyde haue gretly in thy sight,
Of moche vnconnyng and of
  discrecion."
Ande sodenly in her alther syght,
Evyn a-myddes of that mansion,
An Angel bright, sent from hevyn
  dovne,
Dyde appere; byddyng hir a-noon,
With deuoute herte þat she sholde goon

Full humbly in hir best entente,
Vnto the chylde for to haue socoure,
And touche the hem of his vestement
Reuerently, *and with* gret honoure.
For he, in sothe, is the Savyoure
Of all the worlde and of all mankynde,
And power hathe playnly to vnbynde

All tho that pleyne hem and ben in
  distresse,
Whan thay to hym mekely wolle call.
And Salomee deuoutly gan hir dresse
Towarde the childe, and on hir knees
  felle,
And sayd: "O lorde, that power haste
  of all,
So latte thy mercy goo[d]ly on me
  sprede,
Me for to socoure now in this grete
  nede;

Me wrecchede wight, pun[i]schede
  Rightfully,
And loste for eu*ere*, saue only thy
  grace.

Domine tu nosti quia semper te timui
et omnes pauperes sine retributione
acceptionis curavi, de vidua et orphano
nihil accepi et inopem vacuum a me
ire nunquam dimisi. Et ecce misera
facta sum propter incredulitatem
meam, quia ausa fui temptare virginem
tuam. Cumque haec diceret, apparuit
iuxta illam iuvenis quidam valde
splendidus dicens ei: Accede ad infantem et adora eum et continge de
manu tua, et ipse salvabit te quia ipse
est salvator saeculi et omnium speran-
tium in se.

Quae confestim ad infantem accessit
et adorans eum tetigit fimbrias pan-
norum in quibus infans erat involutus,

For in sothe, lorde, excepte thy mercy,
I haue loste myne Arme, alas, for my
    trespasse."
And w*ith* that worde, as she dyd
    enbrace
To touche the clothe that he lay in
    bounde,
With-oute more this Solome hath
    fou*n*de

Remedye and was made hole agayne   et statim sanata est manus eius. Et
Sodenly or she coude it asspye.   exiens foras clamare coepit et dicere
And vp she Roos and may no longer
    fayne,
But in the strete opynly gan crye,
Howe the lorde that all the worlde may
    gye,
Discendyd is and become man.   magnalia virtutum
And whileʒ that she thus in the strete
    ran,

Tellyng the byrthe, and of the sterre   quae viderat et quae fuerat et quem-
    also,   admodum curata fuerat, ita ut ad
And of hir Arme, and of hir soden   praedicationem eius multi crederent.
    cure,
The peple gan to drawen faste hir to,
To herken more of this aventure;
And in her speche som gan hem assure,
And thought hir wordes myght be
    credible.

    This episode of the midwives has been quoted somewhat extensively for a two-fold purpose: it shows Lydgate's indebtedness to the *Evangelium Pseudo-Matthaei*, and at the same time provides an excellent example of his (or his author's) handling of source material. Our English text has Mary admitting both midwives at the same time, while the Latin version brings them in singly; it gives the name Sephora to the first,[22] although she is known as Zelomi in the apocryphal gospel; it suppresses the mode of direct address in reporting the midwives' startling request, and

---

[22]For a discussion of the use of this name, see note to III, 355, p. 692.

couches Salome's penitent outburst in entirely different terms from those of Pseudo-Matthew. In general it might be said that, while our poem bases itself at this point rather completely on the Latin text just quoted, it vivifies and dignifies the original narrative considerably.

Despite the close dependence on the apocryphal gospel, there are two items in the next section of the *Life of Our Lady* that cannot be traced to it: the setting of these events on a Sunday, and the determination of Mary's age at the time of the Nativity. As the poet continues, we are told that

> . . . al this thyng, fel vpon the nyght
> On a sonday, my auctor will not varye,
> As ye may fynde, yf ye luste to Rede
> The viij kalendes, for sothe, of Ianuarie;
> Whan marye, example of maydynhede,
> Was of age, who so wil take hede,
> Sixtene yere, this floure of Naȝareth,
> As the vision of Eliȝabeth
> Playnely recordyth, loke and ye may see.[23]

The *Legenda Aurea*,[24] Peter Comestor,[25] and Bonaventure[26] all contain the reference to a Sunday midnight, but the Pseudo-Matthew is curiously lacking it. None of these except the *Meditationes*[27] gives Mary's age, and even there it is stated as fifteen, not sixteen. The *Vision of Elizabeth* (whether of Hungary or of Schonau)[28] is likewise in disagreement with Lydgate. One might infer therefore that the poet abandoned his books at this juncture and called upon a fictitious "auctor" to support a failing memory.

This conjecture is strengthened by the fact that Lydgate is about to take up the Gospel account of St. Luke,[29] in order to introduce the shepherds and the

---

[23]*LOL* III, 448-449.
[24]Graesse, p. 41.
[25]In *Scholastica*, Migne, *PL*, CXCVIII, 1540.
[26]*Meditationes*, p. 518.
[27]*Ibid.*
[28]*Visio Elizabeth Schonaugiensis*, Migne, *PL*. CXCV, 114-194. The visions of Saint Brigid would be much more applicable here. It incorporates much of the Pseudo-Matthew, the *Legenda* and the *Meditationes* and achieved great popularity throughout Europe just at this time due to her preliminary canonization by Boniface IX in 1390 and her formal canonization at the time of the Council of Constance in 1415. See Reinhard Frauenfelder, *Die Geburt des Herrn, Entwicklung und Wandlung des Weihnachtsbildes vom Christlichen Altertum bis zum Ausgang des Mittelalters.* (Leipzig, 1939), pp. 48-49.
[29]*LOL* III, 457 sqq. He might, of course, have kept to the *Legenda,* where the text has: "*Gloria in Altissimis etc.,*" —the "etc." being literally interpreted by Lydgate!

angelic chorus. The song of the heavenly host goes beyond the Scriptural verse to include the entire *Gloria* as it appears in the Ordinary of the Mass:[30]

"Glory and hono*u*r in the hevynly see
Be vnto God ete*r*nally duryng,
And in earthe pees and reste be
To all the men, that of one vnyte
This high feste honour and magnyfye.
And we ichone, with oo melodye,

Gloria in excelsis Deo et in terra pax hominibus bonae voluntatis.

O myghty lorde, we preyse and blisse the,
And worship eke w*ith* humble Reue*r*ence,
And gloryfye thy high mageste,
And thankynge yef to thyn magnyficence
For thy glory and thyn excellence.
O thou lorde god, O kyng celestiall,
O god the fadir, moste myghty founde at all,

Laudamus te, benedicimus te, Adoramus te, glorificamus te, gratias agimus tibi propter magnam gloriam tuam. Domine Deus, Rex celestis, Deus Pater Omnipotens.

And god the sonne, his childe alone ete*r*ne,
Christe Ihe*s*u, borne of thys hevynly qwene,
Of god also the chose lambe so derne,
Sonne of the fadir w*ith*-oute spotte all clene,
That doste away this worldes synne and tene,
Haue mercy on vs of thy high godenesse,
Sythe thou thy-self in p*er*fyte holynesse,

Domine Fili Unigenite, Jesu Christe, Domine Deus, Agnus Dei, Filius Patris, Qui tollis peccata mundi, miserere nobis[31] Quoniam

Alone art holy, sothely, and no moo;
Ande lorde aloone, ou*er* all other thynge,

Tu solus sanctus, Tu solus Dominus, Tu solus altissimus, Jesu Christe, Cum Sancto Spiritu in gloria Dei Patris.

---

[30]*LOL* III, 485-511. For the Latin, see any Roman Missal.
[31]For some reason these lines are omitted by Lydgate: *"Qui tollis peccata mundi, suscipe deprecationem nostram. Qui sedes ad dexteram Patris, miserere nobis."*

And worthyest and higheste eke also;
O Ih*e*su criste, of hevyn and erthe
     kyng,
With the hooly goost in glorie
     reynynge,
Ay *with* the fadre by eternyte,
Thre knytte in oon thorughe p*er*fyte
     vnyte."

    After this apparently original insertion of the liturgical *Gloria,* Lydgate resumes
the Gospel narrative according to St. Luke and then falls back on the *Meditationes.*[32]
He tells us that Bonaventure describes the new-born Christ as a spouse proceeding
from his bridal chamber—an obvious reference to David's *Sicut sponsus procedens*
and not remarkably original with Bonaventure, but the sequence of material at this
point makes it clear that another source book has been opened.[33]

Whiche on this day, as saythe Bona-
     venture,
Lyche a spouse fro his chaumbre is
     gone,
His chosyn chyldren thrugh his benyg-
     nyte,
In his chirche to Ioye hem of Syon
By p*er*fyte pees and sothefaste vnyte.
And he this day hathe shewede the
     beaute
Of his face of excellent fayrenesse;
In whose honoure this day of high
     gladnesse

Was made the ympne, the gospell
     saythe also,
Our althir myrthe and yoye to
     encrece;
Gloria in excelsis deo.
And in erthe this day a p*er*fyte pees

Hodie Spiritus Sanctus, Ecclesiae elec-
torum caput, processit de thalamo suo.
Hodie desideratam faciem ostendit,
forma speciosus prae filiis hominum.
Hodie factus est ille hymnus angelicus:
Gloria in excelsis Deo. Hodie pax
hominibus est annuntiata, ut in eodem
hymno continetur. Hodie, etiam can-
tat Ecclesia, per totum mundum melli-
flui sunt coeli, et in terra canunt
Angeli. Hodie primitus apparuit ben-
ignitas et humanitas Salvatoris Dei
nostri. Hodie adoratus est Deus in
similitudine carnis peccati. Hodie illa
duo miraculi contigerunt,

------

[32]*LOL* III, 539-574.
[33]*Meditationes,* p. 520.

To man was shewed, withoutyn eny
   lees.
And as saythe poule, goddys benygnyte
This day aperyd in his humanyte

And more ouer as he eke telle can,
God was this day in simylytude,
In erthe honourede in likenesse of man.
And he this day his godhede did
   Include
In our manhode; and shortely to
   conclude,
This day also, yf I shall not feyne,
Byfel also othir thynges tweyne,—

The wondreste *and* the moste
   merueilous
That eu*e*re yet were sene to-forne,
Wher-of no witte, by kinde is
   capciouse.
Firste howe that god, to save that was
   for-lore,
Lowly in erthe luste to be bore;
And howe a mayde in hir virgynyte,
Might also childe and mothir be.

quae superant ominem intellectum, et sola fides apprehendere potest, scilicet quod Deus nascitur, et Virgo parit. Hodie aliorum miraculorum claruit multitudo.

Lydgate then enters the field of Old Testament prophecy, although not, as one might expect, according to the accepted pseudo-Augustinian approach.[34] The series of prophecies in the *Life of Our Lady* seems to follow no easily explicable order. Moreover, the situation is further complicated by the fact that there are two lists of prophecies in the work, and neither seems to bear any relation to the other.[35] In fact, certain repetitions in the second sequence would prompt the reader to feel that Lydgate forgot his earlier treatment of prophetic utterances by the time he reached the later one.

Between line III, 579 and 679, nine Old Testament witnesses are called forth in the following order :[36]

---

[34]See Karl Young, *The Drama of the Medieval Church,* (2 v, Oxford, 1933), II, 126 sqq., for a discussion of this tradition.

[35]*LOL* III, 527 sqq. and III, 614 sqq.

[36]Isaias is summoned twice.

LOL	*Q. T. (Vulgate)*
III, 578-583	*Psalm* lxxix, 20[37]
III, 584-595	*Isaias* xvi, 1
III, 596-609	*Ecclus,* xxxvi, 1-18[38]
III, 613-623	*Zacharias,* ix, 9-10
III, 624-629	*Baruch,* iv, 36
III, 630-637	*Isaias,* xlv, 8
III, 638-655	*Jeremias,* xxxiii, 15-18
III, 656-662	*Malachias,* iv, 2
III, 663-667	*Micheas,* v, 2
III, 668-679	*Daniel,* ii, 34-45

After developing these prophetic quotations from the Old Testament, Lydgate proceeds to apply other Scriptural figures to Mary and her Child: the dew of heaven, the cloud seen by the servant of Elias, the sweet-smelling field blessed by Isaac, the beloved of the *Canticle,* the wholesome pomegranate, the fruitful olive tree, the multi-colored coat of Joseph, the sheaf adored by the other sheaves, the seven prosperous years of harvest. Since the references are of passing nature and follow no particular order, it is conceivable that this part of the work was based on leisurely recollection. However, such "emotion recollected in tranquility" would hardly account for Jacob's prophecy in regard to Juda:[39]

"O Iuda, Iuda, thy bretherne
euerychone
Shall prese and worship the high
renoun
Of thyne estate, which shall of all thy
fone
The pryde opresse and make hem loute
dovne;
That shal be cleped the whelpe of the
lioun,

Juda, te laudabunt fratres tui: manus tua in cervicibus inimicorum tuorum, adorabunt te filii patris tui. Catulus leonis Juda: ad praedam fili mi ascendisti:

---

[37]See also *Matt.* iv, 16 and *Isaias* ix, 2.

[38]Although Lydgate speaks here of "David in the sauter," I have been unable to locate a psalm that expresses exactly the idea contained in these lines. Nor does the later mention of Solomon provide any clue. Despite their attribution to David and Solomon, these thoughts can be found in the *Ecclesiasticus* verses. Canticles such as this were (and are) included in the Psalter of the Breviary and thus could very readily have passed as psalms of David or Solomon. This particular one occurs as the fourth psalm of Lauds on Saturday.

[39]*LOL* III, 869-909. For the source, see *Genesis* xlix, 8-12.

The Royall beste whiche, maugre who
  saythe nay,
Shall myghty be to cache and take his
  pray

And proudely bere it home vnto his   requiescens accubuisti ut leo, et quasi
  cave,—   leaena,
My sonne Iuda, in they dredfull tene,
For thorugh they myght thou shalt
  victory haue,
Maugre echone that the reuers mene.
For who shall mowe *with*stonden or   Quia suscitabit eum?
  susteyne
Thy kyngly power, to make resistence
A-gayne thy manhode and thy
  magnyficence,

That shall in the so clerly showe and
  shyne,
*With*outyn clipsyng or any man*ere*
  clowde;
The septre of whome, in sothe, shall   Non auferetur sceptrum de Juda,
  neu*ere* fyne,
To be famous by Reporte lowe and
  lowede,
Nor neu*ere* sese in couerte ne in
  shrowde,
Till a duke aryse of thy kynrede,   et dux de femore ejus, donec veniat
Whom all the world shall obey and   qui mittendus est,
  drede.

The whiche, in sothe, is for to be sente
Ou3t of thi sed by dwe successioun,
Liche a kyng to holde his parleamente,
With his legees a-mydde his region,
And he shall be to eu*ery* nacion   et ipse erit expectatio gentium.
Sothefaste abydng and socour in her
  nede.
And he shall bynde his myghty sterne   Ligans ad vineam pullum suum,
  stede,

Of verrey fors, at the holesome vyne;   et ad vitem, O fili mi, asinam suam.
And tye his asse vnder the grapes
    Rede.
Ande he is stole þat lyke to golde doth
    shine,
And his palle, by myght of his   Lavabit in vino stolam suam, et in
    manhede,   sanguine uvae pallium suum.
He shall wasshe in grapes that shull
    blede
The Rede blode, depper than skarlet
    hewe.
And thus arrayede in his vesture newe,

Of loke he shall be sterner to
    by-holde,
Than the stremes of the light sterre;
And of eyne fayrer many folde,   Pulchriores sunt oculi ejus vino, et
Thanne wyn fined shynynge thorowe a   dentes ejus lacte candidiores.
    verre
And like yuory that comes fro so fer,
His tethe shall be evyn, smothe and
    white."[40]

At the end of Jacob's prophecy concerning Juda, the apocryphal dream of the
patriarch Joseph is ushered in.[41] Lydgate tells us in the text that his information
has been gleaned from Robert Grosseteste's version,[42] and the closeness of his
redaction leaves little doubt that this is the case. One can easily detect the parallelism
between the two accounts:

---

[40]I have regarded these lines as taken from *Genesis* rather than from the *Liber de Testamentis XII Patriarcharum* although a marginal gloss in the MS indicates this as the source.
The Scriptural account is much closer to Lydgate, as can be seen from the following text of
the *Liber:* "Juda, thy hand shall bee on the necke of thine enemies. Thy brethren shall stoope
unto thee: as a Lyons whelpe shalt thou com up from the spoile: thou shalt couch as a Lyon,
and as a Lyonesse. Who shall stirre thee up? The scepter shall not depart from thee, nor a
law-giver from betweene thy feete, untill Shilo come, all Nations shall seeke after him. Thou
shalt binde the asse fole to the Vine; thou shalt wash thy garment in wine, and thy cloke in
the bloud of grapes: thy eyes shall bee red with wine, and thy teeth white with Milke." *The
Testaments of the Twelve Patriarchs* (London: Stationers Company, 1619), pp. B₂b—B₃a.
The English version has been quoted here because the Latin text does not contain the prophecy
concerning Juda. It begins with Reuben.

[41]*LOL* III, 910-937.

[42]*The Testaments of the Twelve Patriarches, the sonnes of Jacob: translated out of
Greek into Latin by Robert Grosthead, sometime Bishop of Lincolne; and out of his copie,
into French and Dutch by others: and now Englished* (London; The Stationers Co. 1619),
p. K₄b. See also the Latin version: *Testamenta Duodecim Patriarcharum Haganae,* 1532).
Samuel Pegge, in his biography of Grosseteste, assigns this work to the year 1242. See the
Life of Robert Grosseteste (London, 1793), p. 289.

How that he sawe twelfe hertes white,
Full lustely goon in her pasture.
And after that, as Lincolne liste to
    wryte,
He sawe of Iuda borne a creatur*e*,
Of thought and dede, a verrey mayden
    pure.
And in his dreme, hym thought he
    dyd sene
Of hir brought furthe, wi*th*outyn spote
    all clene,

And what dreames I have seen, my
children now heare. There were XII
Harts feeding . . . also I saw that of
Juda was a Virgine borne having a
white silken robe, and of her came
forth an immaculate Lambe.

A lambe moste fayre to his inspection,
That eu*ere* he sawe vnto his plesaunce;
On whose lefte hande stode a fyers
    lyon,
And best*es* many by one alyaunce,
That were in erthe thorugh cruell
    resemblau*n*ce
Aforsyng hem by sheltroun in batayle,
By felle malice the fayre lambe to
    assayle.

And on the left hand of the saide
Lambe was as it were a Lyon, and
all Beasts made against him, and the

But or that thay avayle myght in
    fyght,
The lambes power made hem for to
    dye;
And hem venquyschede thorugh his
    humble myght,
That man and Angell when thay this
    conqueste seye,
Thay fell downe streght and the lambe
    obeye,
That was sent of god, this meke
    werryour.

Lambe overcame them, and trode them
under his feete, and in him joyed the
Angels, the men and all the earth.

After a brief excursion into the genealogical background of the new-born Christ, and a demonstration that kingship and priesthood were here joined together because the blood of Juda and Levi met in the Saviour, our author enters into a discussion of the marvels that attended this tremendous event. Tradition has it that all creation joined in the praise of the Incarnate Word, and Lydgate prepares to enumerate some of the ways in which that praise was given. For this section, therefore, he seems to return to the *Legenda Aurea* and its stories of the Roman temple and its statue, the brilliant night sky, the well that ran oil, the three suns that converged into one, the Ara Coeli vision of Sibyl, the vines of Engaddi that shed balm in midwinter, and finally, the fall of the Egyptian statue.[43] He departs from the *Legenda's* sequence of events, however, and in one place inserts the story of the statue of Romulus, although only passing mention is given to the destruction of an image in both the *Legenda* and the *Meditationes*. The episode introduced here obviously anticipates the *Policraticus* material which Lydgate takes up in the next section.[44] In general, then, it may be said that he is here leaning rather heavily on the *Legenda Aurea*,[45] but is in no way slavishly following it.

For on this nyght, by euery creature
Was sothely shewed his Natyuyte
In Bedleme : how that of a mayden pure
A childe was borne, moste souerayne of
   degre.
And firste of all, in Rome the Cyte,
His birthe was shewede by myracle.
For well and Roof, toure and pynacle

Of the Temple moste famous in the
   towne,
To god of pees that was consecrate,
The same nyght to grovnde fel adovne
Pleyne with the erthe, wast and
   desolate ;
In whiche temple, moste Riall of estate,
The statue stode of myghty Romulous,
And at the byldyng, the story tellyth
   thus,

Of this temple, thay of Rome wente
To appollo with humble sacryfice,
To haue answeer in hir beste entent,
How long this fane Riall of asyse,

Notandum autem quod nativitas Christi fuit mirabiliter facta...

Romae enim, ut testatur Innocentius papa tertius, duodecim annis pax fuit,

igitur Romani templum pacis pulcherrimum construxerunt et ibi statuam Romuli posuerunt.

Consulentes autem Apollinem, quantum duraret,

[43]*LOL* III, 1065-1316.
[44]*LOL* III, 1317 sqq.
[45]Ed. Graesse, pp. 41-45.

So strong bilt, and in so thrifty wyse,
That it shulde lasten, and so to endure
Ayeyne a-sault of **any aventure,**

Or p*er*turbyng on any maner syde.
And he yaf answewer vnto one and all,
Howe this temple w*ith* his walle3 wyde,   acceperunt responsum
W*ith* his creste3 and batelyng Riall,
Shall eu*er*e stonde sure w*ith*outyn fall,
Vnto the tyme that a mayde childe.   quousque virgo pareret.
And thay a none that first made it bilde,

Of this answer glade and full credible   Hoc autem audientes dixerunt: ergo
That this temple eu*er*e shulde stande.   in aeternum durabit. Impossibile enim
For hem thought it was impossible,   crediderunt quod unquam pareret
A mayde eu*er*e, othir on see or lande,   virgo.
To haue a childe and so thay
    vndirstonde.
And thay a-noon yaf the temple a name,
By one assente, for the grete fame,

And called it, as I can discerne,   unde in foribus templi titulum hunc
The Temple of pees w*ith* his wallys   scripserunt: templum pacis aeternum.
    white;
And ther w*ith* all namede it et*er*ne,
And at the entre so thay dyd write.
But on the nyght, the trouthe to   Sed in ipsa nocte qua virgo peperit,
    endite,   templum funditus corruit
Whan criste was borne of a mayden
    clene,
This temple fel dou*n* endelong the
    grene,

To fulfill the trwe p*ro*phecye
Of appollo that tolde hem all this
    thyng.
Ande in that place in wurship of marie   et ibi est modo ecclesia Sanctae Mariae
And of hir sone of heuene and erth   Novae . . .
    kynge,
Stant a cherche full ryall of byldyng.
And even like the self same tyme,
The grete statue, long or it were p*ri*me,

Of Romulus that was deifyede,[46]
Fell to erthe and braste on peces small;
And thogh Ramaynes made hym
    stellifiede,
His grete hede for all that dyd avale;
Of whome also, the werkeman made a
    tale
That forget it many day affore,
And sayde, in sothe, till a childe be bore

Of a mayde, it shulde stonde vp-Right,
Þis grete ymage, *and* neu*er*e his hede
    encline;
But he aloute vpon the same nyght,
Whan crist was borne of a pure
    virgyne,
Like as the werkemen dyd afore
    devyne,
Ayene that conseyte and the entencion
Of that he ment in his opynyon.

I fynde also, that the skyes donne,
Whiche of custome corteyne so the
    nyght,
The same tyme w*ith* a sodeyn sonne
Enchasede were, that it wex as light,
As at mydday, whan phebus is moste
    bright,
To shewe sothely that the sonne of lyfe
Was borne that nyght, to stynte all our
    stryfe.

Nam in ipsa nocte nativitatis domini-
cae obscuritas noctis in claritatem diei
versa est.

And even than, also as bokes telle,
In verrey sothe, withoutyn any werre,
The selfe tyme in Rome was a well,
Of his stremes passyngely entiere.
To loke vpon as any cristall clere
From his vaynes as it dyd boyle;
Of whiche the water chaunged into
    oyle

Romae etiam (ut attestatur
Orosius et Innocentius papa tertius)
fons aquae in liquorem olei versus est

---

[46]See note on John of Salisbury's version below, p. 126.

The same nyght, and to Tybre Ran
So large plentee that all myght it see.
Of whiche well longe before or than,
Al opynly, in Rome the Cytee,
Sybelle the wyse, that had
    souereygnete
Of *pr*ophecye, playnely wrote and tolde,
That the water of this well shulde

et erumpens usque in Tibrim profluxit
et toto die illo largissime emanavit.
Prophetaverat enim Sibylla

The same nyght chaunge his lycour
Into oyle, and so a day endure,
Whan of this worlde was borne the
    savyour,
In Bedlem of a mayde pure.
And as I fynde also in scripture,
The same day, high in the firmament,
Towarde the partye of the oryent,

quod quando erumperet fons olei, nasceretur Salvator.

In ipsa etiam die tres soles in orientem
apparuerunt,

Wer seyn thre sonnes lustyly apeer,—
*Eu*eryche of hem large Rounde and
    bright;
That caste abrode her fayre beameʒ
    clere,
Thourgh all the worlde in *eu*ery manes
    sight.
The whiche sonnes drowe lyne Right,
Her cours holdyng in hast and that
    a-noon,
Till all thre were Ioynede into oon;

qui paulatim in unum corpus solare
redactae sunt.

To mankynde playnely to declare
That he was bore, in whom were I
    founden thre,
To encrece our Ioye and also our
    welfare,
Flesshe and soule, and eke the deyte,
Knytte all in one by sothefaste vnyte;
Which as a sonne, voydyng schoure
    and shade,
Was borne this day all the worlde to
    glade.

Per quod signabatur quod trini et
unius Dei notitia orbi imminebat, vel
quia natus erat ille in quo tria, scilicet
anima, caro et divinitas in unam personam convenerunt . . .

Also in rome as wrightet innocent,
In his cronycle makyng mencion,
How the Senates all, by one assent,
In concistorye, of affection
Whiche they hadde in her opynyon,
Vnto her noble *and* miȝti Emperour
Octouyan, of worthynesse the flour,

Octavianus insuper imperator (ut ait
Innocentius papa tertius) universo orbe
ditioni Romanae subjugato in tantum
Senatui placuit

Wolden Ichone hym haue deyfyede,
And callede hym by name Immortall.
The whiche thyng when he had
   espyede,
As he that was ful prudent founde at
   all,
To his p*r*esence made a-noon to calle
Sybelle, that was myrrour of sapyence,
Here upon to here, her sentence;

ut eum pro Deo colere vellent. Prudens
autem imperator se mortalem intelligens immortalitatis nomen sibi noluit
usurpare. Ad illorum instantiam

And ther-with-all that she moot
   dyffyne,—
Wi*th*outyn doute of ambyguyte,
As fer in sothe as phebus doth now
   shyne,—
If ther wer any of power more than he
Or p*e*regall vnto his degre,
Fro Est to west, here in erthe lowe,
In all this worlde that she couthe of
   knowe.

Sibyllam prophetissam advocat scire
volens per ejus oracula

an in mundo major eo aliquando
nasceretur.

And this was done vpon the selfe day
Whan criste was borne in Bedlem by
   myracle.
And she full wysely putte hym in
   delaye,
To yef answer makyng a small
   obstacle;
Til at the laste, the fin of hir oracle,
Amydde the chaumbre of the
   Emp*e*rour,
Stondyng envyron many a Senatour,

Cum ergo in die nativitatis domini
consilium super hac re convocasset et
Sibylla sola in camera imperatoris
oraculis insisteret,

Was playnely this, w*ith* chere and face
   bolde,
"O Emp*er*our, lifte vp a-noon thyne
   eyne,
And loke vp yonder and se the cercle
   of golde
A-boute the sonne, whiche easi is to
   asspyen,
And ther by-holde, thou maiste it not
   denyen,
A mayde sitte of beaute moost
   souereyne,
Holdyng a childe in her Armes
   tweyne."

in die media circulus aureus apparuit circa solem et in medio circuli **virgo** pulcherrima, puerum gestans in **gremio.**

And ryght a-noon, as this Octovyan
Sawe the childe by clere inspection,
W*ith*oute abode, a voys he herde than
From a-lofte into the chaumbre doune:
"By-holde and se w*ith* humble
   affection,
This is the auctor of the high heven,
Sette in the sonne, clere as any leven."

Tunc Sibylla hoc Caesari ostendit, cum autem imperator visionem plurimum admiraretur, audivit vocem dicentem sibi: haec est *ara celi,*

Where Sybell all a-brode gan saye
To hym a-none and list not to abyde:
"Thy crovne avale, and the childe
   obeye,
Whos face bright the sonne may not
   hyde.
And lat nowe be thy pompe and all thy
   pryde."
And at oo worde she plattely gan hym
   telle,
The childes myght his power dyd
   excelle.

dixitque ei Sibylla: hic puer major **te** est et ideo ipsum adora.

Whiche thyng whan he gan playnely
   vndirstande,
Of faythefull will and hole herte
   entere,

Intelligens igitur imperator quod **hic** puer major se erat, ei thura obtulit **et** Deus de cetero dici recusavit.

He knelyde dovne and list no longer
  stande;
And with encens cast in the sencere,
He dyd worship vnto the Autere,
And to the childe moste excellent of
  fame,
And liste no more vsurpe on hym the
  name,

To be callede ayenste alle skylle and
  Right,
Wrongfully a god sithen ther is but
  one.
And Right a-noon, this noble worthy
  knyght,
Thorowe ouȝt the worlde his *precept*
  made to gone,
To provynces and contreyes ererychone,
Vpon payne of dethe, that noon of hem
  all
Be hardy more a god hym for to calle.

For well he wiste, by signes opynly
And evydenceȝ, eke in speciall,
Ther was oon borne, of power more
  worthy
Then was hym-self, and therto Immortall
To whome no kyng on erthe is *peragall*,
In all this worlde of high ne lowe estate
And for this skylle, aftir dedicate

Was that chaumbre, by high devocion
To marye playnely, this is noo naye
And called eke for this avysion
Are celi; yet into this daye
The name abyt and slydyth not **awaye**,
Ne lesith not the light of his
  brightnesse

Eadem autem camera in honore Sanctae Mariae dedicata est unde usque hodie dicitur Sancta Maria Ara Celi.

Thourgh noon eclippsyng of
    foretylnesse.

And in Engady, the lusty large vynes,   In hac autem nocte . . . vineae Engadi
That tyme in the yere of her kynde   quae proferunt balsamum floruerunt,
    bare,
Gan floresshe and floure and in-stede
    of wynes,
Withe Riche Bavme her braunches to
    to repayre.
And the vertu that wyntre made bare,
Thourgh constreynyng of colde in the
    Rote,
Nature made with fresshe blossomes
    soote,

To assende vpon same nyght   fructum protulerunt et liquorem dede-
Vnto the croppe, with frute and levys   runt.
    newe;
Makyng the bowes as lusty to the
    sight,—
As fresshe, as fayre of coloure and of
    hewe,
And as plentevous her colour to
    Renewe,—
As in Septembre whan Bachus hathe
    power
To shewe his myght that tyme of the
    yere.

Loo howe the lorde and the myghty
    kyng,
That hathe lordship ouere grape and
    vine,
Vnto whose myght euery manere
    thyng,—
Hevyn and erthe,—lowly muste
    enclyne,
Gan braunches bere with fresche
    floures fyne

Araye newe, though thay be seer and
  olde,
In frosty wynter and in wedir colde,

As in somer whan phebus is a-lofte,
Whan flora Reignyth in may and in
  aprill,
And make blossomes to ben as smothe
  and softe
Amyde Decembre, when men for colde
  so chille.
Wherefore this feste, frely at his
  wille,—
The nyght I mene, of his Natiuyte,—
To shewe his myght in herbe, floure,
  and tre,

He made the vynes, as ye haue herde
  me sayne,
In Engady her bavme for to shede,
When thay were moste nakede and
  barayne
And oute of season, who so can take
  hede.
Of whiche nyght long afore, I rede
That in Egipt the prophete Ieremyee,
Full opynly in his prophecye,

Legitur enim in hystoria scholastica[47]
quod Jeremias propheta in Aegyptum
descendens . . . signum dedit, quod
eorum ydola corruerent, cum virgo
filium parturiret.

To the prestes of that kyngdom tolde
That the Idoles of her temples alle,
With outyn arest, by myracle sholde
Breke her neckeȝ and to grounde falle,
Whan a mayde in an oxe stalle
Hathe borne a childe, this thyng shall
  be-tyde.
Wherefore the prestes in her fanes
  wyde,

Quapropter sacerdotes ydolorum yma-

---

[47]Migne, *PL*, CXCVIII, 1440.

Of verrey faythe and of high credence,
Secrely vpon a lytyll stage,
Vpon his worde *with* humble
   reuerence,
Of a mayde let make an Image;
And in hir Arme, a childe of tendre
   age,

And on this feste, ay fro yere to yere,
Thay were a-waytyng whan it wolde
   be;
Til on a day of happe the kyng cam
   nere,—
The noble, worthy, and wyse
   Tholome,—
Þe whiche þing whanne þat he dide
   see,
A-noon of hem the cause he gan
   enquere,
Why and wherefore the Image was
   sette there.

And thay Ichone, of one entencion
Yaffe answer and lust not for to lye
For it was ordenyde of olde tradicion,
Shewede to-forne by holy prophecye,
In whiche thay dyd faythefully aspye,
Vndispeirid the hest shal not varie
Of the prophete awhile though it tarye.

And sothefastly, in conclusion,
Vpon the tyme of the Natyuyte,
The false Idoleʒ in Egipt fel adovne,
And al to-braste in peceʒ moo than
   thre;
To shewe truly that Iborne was hee,
Of heven and erthe that hath the
   Regalye,
And shall distroye al false mawmetre.

ginem virginis puerum in gremio baju-
lantem secreto loco templi statuerunt.

Sed a Ptolomaeo rege postea interrogati,
quid hoc sibi vellet,

dixerunt paternae traditionis hoc esse
misterium quod a sancto viro et prophete
eorum majores acceperant et sic in rebus
venturis credebant.

From the selection just given, it will be seen that Lydgate was in no way trammeled by his sources. The Latin version is cryptic and direct, but the English rendering embodies considerable quantities of descriptive material. Were it possible to assume that no intermediary existed, our poet might here be commended for having significantly improved the literary form of these stories.

Mention was made above of the destruction of the statue of Romulus. Our text now presents another episode so nearly identical with it that one finds it hard to consider the previous narrative as anything more than a confused anticipation of this one which, Lydgate points out, is to be found in John of Salisbury's *Policraticus*.[48] In fact, Webb calls attention to a rather widespread confusion in regard to these two narratives.[49]

The direct relationship of our text with the Latin of John of Salisbury becomes apparent on inspection:

I fnyde also, as wryteth Carnotence,
In his boke, Policraticon,
That whanne Romanes had excellence
Of high lordship, so many day-a-gone,
And that peples and Regnes
    eu*er*cheone
Stoden vnto hym vndir lowe *ser*uage,
Fro yere to yere makyng a payage

Publici namque imago imperii publici metus et Caesareo nomine prostratae urbis erat indicio. Quod si imperii nullam in veritate, quae sic appareret, credidit quis fuisse imaginem, historiarum fide certiorabitur.

Of a tribute that was customable,
To the Empyre of verrey dewte;
For whiche the Romanes and Senate
    hono*ur*able,
Whan thay flourede in moste felicite,
Devysed haue for a grete Ryalte,
A-myd her towne in moste worthy
    place,
A large statue, femynyne of face,

Cum enim maiestatem urbis principes visibili specie censuerunt honorandam,

That maked was of coper and of bras,
Large and long and wonderfull to se,

---

[48]*LOL* III, 1317-1386. For the source, see Salisbury's *Policraticus* ed. Webb (2 v, Oxford, 1909), I, 430d-431a. Two of the Lydgate MSS have "Pollocronicon"—an indication that the scribe had Higden's work in mind. By strange coincidence, the story is contained there too. See *Polychronicon Ranulphi Higden Monachi Cestiensis,* ed. Churchill Babington (London, 1865) I, 234-236.

[49]In his edition of the *Policraticus*. See the note, I, 430d.

And of entayle devydede the compace.
This gret ymage called sholde be
Goddess of Rome, and like a maieste,
In hir Right hande sholde also holde
A large worlde, full sterne to by-holde;

Which sholde of Rou*n*denesse haue the
    fygure,
To signifie that sche moost glorious,
The cyte hath holy in her cur*e*,
And howe by hir thay were victoriouse.
And here vp-on, moste excellent
    famous,
Thay dyd a werke-man seken vp and
    dovne,
It to p*er*forme, thorugh oute all the
    tovne,

Till at the laste of happe sucheon thay
    fynde,
That passede all to werke in entayle,
And was sotyll both of witte and
    mynde,
To werke in metall, and sayde he wolde
    nat fayle
Of this emprise, that may so moche
    avayle
To the cyte. and shortly in this caas,
Thorugh his engyne, it p*er*formede was

So Ryally, þat in the worlde noo man
Couthe a-mende it in that ilke tyde.
And to by-holde it, many a thousande
    ran,—
So gladde of it the were on eu*er*y syde;
Till at the laste, one of verrey pryde,
Presumptuously gan to cry and call,
Ande sayde shortly, the legges were
    to small

exquisito artificio muliebrem formam
quae orbem dextra contineret, in eris
materia studuerunt. Ea vero perfecta
in forma egregia, venusta quantitate,
apta partium dispositione, membris
quoque condecentibus et sibi invicem
congruentibus universis cum non tam
populi examinationem quam admira-
tionem plena sui commendatione de-
posceret, quidam solas tibias tantae
moli perferendae inhabiles esse causati
sunt.

So grete a werke longe to susteyne,
For lak only of gode *pr*oporcion.
Wher-of a-noon, w*ith* soden lre and
　　tene,
The werke man brent in his opynyon,
Rebukyng hym of his *pr*esompcion.
And sodenly *p*erturbede in his mynde,
Answerde ayene, shortly as I fynde,

As it had been halfendele in socrne,
And sayde: "frende, if thou canst
　　vndirstande,
Til *þat* a childe be of a mayde borne,
I vndirtake *þat* this werke shall stonde.
Thyne hede is dulle on watir and on
　　londe
To lak thyng thou canste not a mende."
And the werkeman, sother then he
　　wende,

Had of this werke sayde and
　　prophecyede.

For on the nyght whan that criste was
　　bore,
In verrey sothe, it may not be denyede,
Of bras the goddes is broken and
　　to-tore,
And all the coste of the werke for-lore.
In signe only that the lorde and syre,
And myghty kyng of the high Empyre,

Was borne that tyme in the lityll
　　towne
Of bedlem of a pure virgyne;
To whose power and dominacion,
Grete Rome mekely shall enclyne.
For erthely lordship nedys muste fyne,
Whan the power of this kyng is knowe.

Quibus faber respondit, eas usque-
quaque sufficere donec virgo pareret,
omnino credens impossibilem virginis
partum.

Quod et Christo nato impletum est, ea
corruente et fracta,

quia humanum contrabitur ubi divinum
imperium dilatatur.

　　One sees here the same type of treatment given to the *Policraticus* story as was
accorded the *Legenda* material above. Of particular significance is the picture of

the irate workman. John of Salisbury merely states that he replied to his critics; Lydgate makes something of a dramatic scene out of the episode and even substitutes direct dialogue for the Latin text's oblique report of the answer.

The next part of the *Life of Our Lady* deals with another prophecy pertaining to the Virgin Birth—this time taken from the Tiburtine Sibyl.[50] In it she tells the Roman Senators of her dream of the nine suns which betokened the nine generations to come before the birth of Christ. The elements of this story are not to be found in the sources which Lydgate regularly used.[51]

With questionable orderliness, our author now returns to the prophets of the Old Testament. This listing is more extensive than the one above,[52] but like it is merely a haphazard sequence of paraphrased Vulgate texts:

LOL	*Q.T.* (Vulgate)
LOL III, 1467-1477.	*Abdias,* I, 17-21.
LOL III, 1478-1484.	*Nahum.* I, 15-11, 1.
LOL III, 1485-1498.	*Habacuc* iii, 4-7.
LOL III, 1499-1505.	*Baruch* iv, 36 and
	Jeremias xxiii, 5.[53]
LOL III, 1506-1519.	*Sophonias* iii, 8-11.
LOL III, 1520-1530.	*Daniel* vii, 13-14.
LOL III, 1531-1545.	*Ezechiel* xxxiv, 23:
	xxxvii, 22-23.
LOL III, 1546-1552.	*Aggeus* ii, 7-8.
LOL III, 1553-1563.	*Zacharias* ix, 9-10.
LOL III, 1564-1574.	*Malachias* i, 11.
LOL III, 1575-1579.	*Amos* ix, 11.
LOL III, 1580-1582.	*Isaias* lii, 15 .

Lydgate runs from this long array of prophetic utterances into an apocryphal Old Testament story. He speaks of it as being found in Esdras, but by that he means the third Book of Esdras. Since only the first two books of this title have been

---

[50]*LOL* III, 1387-1455.
[51]The Tiburtine Sibyl appears frequently in Old French plays. This may be another indication of a French source.
[52]See *LOL* III, 577 sqq.
[53]Lydgate wrongly attributes to Baruch a prophecy of Jeremias.

received into the canon, this episode out of Book Three cannot be regarded as Scriptural.[54]   However, older texts of the Vulgate sometimes included this questionably authentic work, and it can be presumed that Lydgate was using one of these.

The narrative referred to is the one of Zorobabel and his answer to the poser regarding the relative strength of wine, women, and kings.[55]   That such a question captured the medieval fancy is evident from the number of references to it in the literature of the Middle Ages.   John Gower, in his *Confessio Amantis,* deals with the identical story,[56] and Lydgate himself uses it again in his *Siege of Thebes.*[57]

As his treatment of the Nativity draws to a close, Lydgate turns to a prolonged commendation of Our Lady.   In the form of a suppliant's prayer, it would seem to be original in its construction, though replete with Scriptural metaphors. In one part of it, our author specifically refers to a sermon of St. Augustine.   The relevant portion is given here:[58]

And as Austyne the holy doctour, write
In a sermon of the Natyuyte,
We may to the sayne, right as he bitte,
With deuoute hert, knelyng on our
    knee:
"O blissed lady, flour of virgynyte,
We prayen ichone, o welle of our
    welfare,
Like a mothir nat thy mylke to spare.

Yeffe hym plentee that is so plentevouse   Lacta, Maria, Creatorem tuum, lacta
Of fulsomnesse Angels to fede;   panem coeli, pretium mundi.
And yef hym souke the pyment
    graciouse   Praebe lambenti mamillam, ut pro te
Of thy pappes: lat the condyte shede   ipse praebeat percutienti maxillam,
                                                nutriatur infans lacte tuorum uberum,
                                                ut pro te etiam accipiat aceti potum.

---

[54]A. Erdmann appears to be mistaken in giving II Esdras, or the Book of Nehemias as the source of this story.   See his discussion in *The Siege of Thebes* (1930; *EETSES,* 125), pp. 112-113.   Augustin Calmet, *Dissertationes in Vetus et Novum Testamentum,* ed. J. D. Mansi (Wurtzburg, 1789), pp. 591-593, outlines the great confusion that existed over the numbering, sequence, and authenticity of the various books of Esdras.   At all events, in Lydgate's time it would have been III and IV Esdras because "in *veteribus Bibliis Latinis impressis plerumque tres Libri Esdras ordine adscribuntur; ita ut primo Esdras succedat Liber Nehemiae, ac deinde tertius. . . .*" (Calmet, p. 592).
[55]III *Esdras* III, 4-IV, 42.   See also *Historia Scholastica,* Migne *PL,* CXCVIII, 1481. Augustine uses it also in *De Civitate Dei* xviii, 36.
[56]*The English Works of John Gower* ed. G. C. Macauley (1900; *EETSES,* 81).   See the Note on p. lxxxi.
[57]Cf. A. Erdmann above.
[58]*LOL* III, 1653-1656.   For the source, see Migne, *PL* XXXIX, 1984.

The sote mylke all aboute in brede,
And motherly makyng it to avale
Of his fayre tendur lymes smale."

The notable freedom in dealing with the source at this point is typical of Lydgate's treatment of the whole closing section of Book III.[59] Our author appears to be giving free rein to an inspiration which, it must be admitted, is always fresher and more alive when it is turned directly on the theme of Mary.[60] Scriptural and liturgical phraseology is deftly woven into the verse in such a way that one would not be justified in seeking for itemized sources here. Further analysis could demonstrate the origin of Lydgate's ideas, but it would probably be a more accurate appraisal of the lines to say that they flow *ex abundantia cordis*.

Many of the phrases here, as well as others throughout Book III, echo the sentiments contained in a sermon of St. Germanus.[61] While it is obvious that this sermon is not the immediate source for these lines, the community of thought is so general that a major part of the homily is reproduced here. It is a typical patristic outburst such as Lydgate must have met frequently in his reading of the Fathers:

Ave Maria, gratia plena, Sanctis sanctior, et caelis excelsior, et Cherubin gloriosior, et super omnem creaturam venerabilior. Ave, columba, quae nobis et fructum fers olivae, et servatorem a spiritali diluvio ac portum salutis annuntias; cujus pennae deargentatae et posteriora dorsi in pallore auri sanctissimi et illuminantis Spiritus fulgore irradiantur. Ave, amoenissimus et rationalis Dei paradisus, benevolentissima et omnipotenti ejusdem dextra hodie ad Orientem plantatus, et ipsi suave olens lilium, et rosam immarcescibilem germinans in eorum medelam, qui pestiferam animaeque exitialem amaritudinem mortis ad Occidentem ebiberant: paradisus in quo ad veritatis agnitionem lignum vivificum efflorescit, e quo qui gustaverint, immortalitatem consequuntur. Ave, sacrosancte aedificatum, immaculatum, purissimumque Dei summi Regis palatium, ejusdem Dei Regis magnificentia circumornatum, omnesque hospitio recipiens ac mysticis reficiens deliciis; in quo non manufactus et vario decore nitens situs est spiritualis Sponsi thalamus; in quo Verbum errantem humanam stirpem revocare volens, carnem sibi desponsavit, ut eos, qui voluntate propria extorres facti fuerant, Patri reconciliaret. Ave, Dei mons praepinguis et umbrosus, in quo enutritus

---

[59]In all this, it is well to keep in mind Professor Schick's observation that "in his so-called translations, the monk usually renders his original in a paraphrastic manner, and puts in many additions foreign to it. He is fond of quoting authorities for his statements; but often enough, he does so—like his great master Chaucer—quite incorrectly and at random." *The Temple of Glas* (1891; *EETSES*, 60), p. cxvii. This is also the contention of A. Erdmann, *The Siege of Thebes* (1911-20; *EETSES*, 108, 125), p. 10, and O. Glauning, *The Two Nightingale Poems* (1900; *EETSES*, 80), p. xli.

[60]Cf. R. Klinefelter's discussion, p. 8.

[61]*Sancti Germani Homilia in Praesentationem Deiparae* II, Migne, *PL*, XCVIII, 307-310.

Agnus rationalis peccata atque infirmitates nostras portavit; mons, e quo devolutus ille nulla manu praecisus lapis, contrivit aras idolorum, et factus est in caput anguli, mirabilis in oculis nostris. Ave, sanctus Dei thronus, divinum donarium, domus gloriae, perpulchrum ornamentum, cimelium electum, et totius orbis propitiatorium, caelumque Dei gloriam enarrans. Ave, urna ex puro auro conflata, et suavissimam animarum nostrarum dulcedinem, Christum scilicet qui manna est, continens. O purissima et omni laude et obsequio dignissima Virgo, Deo dicatum donarium omni creaturarum conditioni praecellens, terra non secta, inaratus ager, vitis floridissima, fons aquas effundens, virgo generans, et mater viri nescia, innocentiae thesaurus absconditus, et sanctimoniae decus; acceptissimis tuis ac materna auctoritate validis precibus ad Dominum ac Deum omnium Conditorem, Filium tuum ex te sine patre genitum, ecclesiastici ordinis gubernacula fac dirigas, et ad portum tranquillum perducas. Sacerdotes justitia, et probatae, immaculatae ac sincerae fidei exsultatione splendidissime induito. Orthodoxis principibus, qui prae omni purpurae aut auri splendore, et prae margaritis ac lapidibus pretiosis, te nacti sunt diadema et indumentum ac firmissimum regni sui ornamentum, in tranquillo ac prospere statu sceptra dirige. Male fidas nationes in te ac Deum ex te genitum blasphemantes, eorum pedibus sternens subjicito; subjectumque populum, ut secundum Dei praeceptum in suavi obedientiae obsequio perseveret, confirmato . . . laudatores tuos ab omni discrimine et animi angore exime; captivis redemptionem tribuito; peregrinis tecto et quovis praesidio destitutis, solamen te exhibe. Universo auxiliatricem manum tuam porrige, ut in laetitia et exsultatione solemnitates tuas simul cum ista, quam modo celebramus, festivitate splendidissimo exitu transigamus, in Christo Jesu universorum Rege ac vero Deo nostro, qui gloria et fortitudo una cum sancto vitaeque principio Patre, et coaeterno et consubstantiali et conregnante Spiritu, nunc et semper et in saecula saeculorum. Amen.

Book IV of the Life of Our Lady has to do with the Circumcision of Christ. It begins with the Gospel story of St. Luke[62] after a brief introductory reference to the god Janus and the month of the year that bears his name.[63] The *Meditationes* attributed to St. Bonaventure now becomes Lydgate's source for the next thirty-five lines.[64]

And he ther-to mekely dyd obeye.	Fuit enim caro ipsius cum cultello
And withe a knyf made full sharpe of stone,	lapideo incisa. Nonne ergo compatiendum est ei? Ita: sic certe et matri.

[62]*LOL* IV, 17-28. See *Luke* ii, 21.

[63]*LOL* IV, 1-11. This passage is cited by J. Schick, *Temple of Glas* (1891; *EETSES*, 60), p. cviii, as proof for dating this composition as 1409-11. For a discussion of this, see R. Klinefelter's, "The Date", p. 4. It will be noted that these opening lines of Book IV are reminiscent of the *Troy Book*, IV, 6974.

[64]*LOL* IV, 29-63. For the Latin text, see *Sancti Bonaventurae Opera* (13v, Paris, 1868), XII, 521.

His mothir lokyng *with* a pytous eye,
The childe was corve ther-*with* al
   a-non,
That all a-boute the rede blode gan gon
*With*oute a boode, as saythe Bona-
   venture,
That for the payne that he dyd endure,

And for sharpnes of the soden smerte,
The childe gan wepe þat pyte was to
   here.
Wherefore his mothir, of verrey tendre
   herte,
Oute brast on teres and myght her-self
   not stere,
That all bydewede were her eyne clere,
Whan she sawe hym that she louede
   soo,
So yonge, so fayre, wepyng so for woo.

But he a-noon in all his passion,
For all that was so yong of age,
In man*ere* he had pyte and compassion,
To se his modyr so wepe in her rage;
And put his hande vnto hir visage,
On mouthe and eyne, passyngly
   benyngne,
And as he couthe goodly made a signe

*With*outyn speche, to stynt her wepyng
That came to her of motherly pyte.
And she full well conceyved his
   menyng,
For poynt to poynt, and then a-noon
   gan she
To loke on hym that was so fayre to
   see,

Ploravit ergo puer Jesus hodie, propter dolorem quem sensit in carne sua: nam veram carnem et passibilem habuit sicut ceteri homines. Sed eo plorante, credisne quod mater potuerit lacrymas continere?

Ploravit ergo et ipsa, quam plorantem filius stans in gremio ejus aspiciens, parvulam manum suam ad os et vultum ejus ponebat, quasi nutu rogans eamdem, ne ploraret: quam enim tenerrime diligebat, a ploratu cessare volebat. Similiter et mater, cujus viscera totaliter commovebantur in dolore et lacrymis filii, et nutu et verbis consolabatur eum. Intelligebat enim tamquam prudentissima voluntatem ejus, quamvis nondum loqueretur. Et dicebat: Fili, si vis me a ploratu cessare, cessa et tu. Non enim possum te plorante non plorare. Et tunc ex compassione matris, filius a singultibus desistebat. Mater vero et ipsius, et

And his fetures considret by and by,
And in her Armes, wonder womanly,

Sche toke hym vp *and* preide him be
styll,
As of modris is pleinly the man*ere*,
And he in all obeythe to her wille,
Though he wer yong and gan to
chaunge his chere.
And w*ith* hir kerchefe she made his
eyne clere,
On his chekes, in all that eu*ere* she may,
Ful modurly the ters wpte away.

suos oculos tergebat, et vultum vultui
applicabat, lactabat eum, et omnibus
quibus poterat modis consolabatur.

The reporting of this little domestic scene follows closely on its source. There are significant departures, however, in the mode of expression. This can be accounted for by the varying purposes for which the two works were composed: the pseudo-Bonaventure thought of his composition as a manual of mental prayer, having as its aim the stimulation of spiritual ardor through the contemplation of a vivified Gospel scene; Lydgate, on the other hand, intended to create a poetic narrative that would fulfill the two-fold end of honoring the Mother of God and pleasing his audience, chief among whom was King Henry the Fifth.[65]

As the poem advances, Bonaventure is abruptly abandoned and Alcuin is brought forward as the source of the next section.[66] This deals with the four manners in which Christ was circumcised: by his Father through the poverty of Bethlehem; by the ritual knife in the Temple; by great adversity; and lastly, by the cruel suffering of the crucifixion. Despite Lydgate's avowed use of Alcuin's material for these lines, I have been unable to find these ideas expressed as such anywhere in the works of that author, nor is he quoted by any of the other sources.

Another enumeration, that of the various occasions on which Christ shed his blood for our redemption, follows upon the "Alcuin" passage without special identification.[67] It can be traced to the *Legenda Aurea*[68] where the five effusions of Christ's blood are discussed. Moreover, the allusion to "Longeus" (Longinus) has to do with another story from the same repository.[69]

---

[65]See Klinefelter, "The Date", p. 7.
[66]*LOL* IV, 64-98.
[67]*LOL* IV, 99-119.
[68]Graesse, p. 82.
[69]The *Legenda's* version of this story is quoted in the Notes (l. 113, IV, p. 705).

Eke ·V· tymes criste in his manhede
Shed his blode by effusion.
And alther firste when he dyd blede
Vpon the day of circumcision;
And next in sothe, to-fore his passyon,
Vpon the hyll for anguysche when he
    swette
The rede blode whiche all his body
    wette;

Quinque enim vicibus sanguinem pro
nobis effudit, primo in circumcisione,
et effusio fuit nostrae redemptionis
initium; secundo in oratione, et haec
ostendit nostrae redemptionis de-
siderium;

The thryed tyme, his blode moste
    vertuouse
Gan rynne oute by many a cruell
    wounde,
Whan that he was, this kyng moste
    graciouse,
Of the Iewes, to a pyler bounde;
The fourt tyme eke, as it is founde,
He spent his blode for our alther
    goode,
When he was nayled high vpon the
    rode;

tertio in flagellatione, et haec fuit
nostrae redemptionis meritum, quia li-
vore ejus sanati sumus; quarto in cru-
cifixione, et fuit nostrae redemptionis
pretium, tunc enim, quae non rapuit,
exsolvebat;

And alther laste, whan Longeus
    a-ferre
Thorugh his hert, playnely as I fynde,
On Caluary hym perced with a spere,
That blode and water, as bokes maken
    mynde,
Gan streme dovne to his eyne blynde;
By whose vertu a-noon this paynym
    knyght,
Only of grace, recouerede hath his
    sight.

quinto in lateris aperitione, et haec
fuit nostrae redemptionis sacramen-
tum. Inde enim exivit sanguis et aqua,
quod figuravit nos per aquam baptismi
debere mundari.

The text continues immediately to recount a Carolingian legend and the theological problem it posed. This too can be found fully treated in the *Legenda Aurea*:[70]

---

[70]*LOL* IV, 120-147. See also Graesse, pp. 86 sqq.

And in bokes, eke as it is tolde,
How the pece of his Incision
Was by an Angell, in an vrne of golde
To Charles brought in a vysyon.
And he a-noon, of grete affection
Of this myracle, for the excellence
Made it be kept for grete reuerence

At aquys grene, but yf bokes lye,
Full many yere by revolucion,
In a chirche, sothely, a marye.
But Clerkes han an opynyon
That in þe day of his resurreccion,—
When criste Ihesu roos fro dethe to
    lyfe,—
The same pece retournede as blyfe

To the place where that it cam froo,
Sythen that it was, sothely as I fynde,
Of his manhede pertenyng therto,
And a partye longyng to his kynde;
Though it so be that bokeȝ maken
    mynde
That it in Rome is as yet reservede,
And yere by yere, whan this fest is
    seruede,

In a chirche, whiche men of custome
    calle
Sancta Santorum of olde fundacion,
The same day ther, the presteȝ all
Solempnyly make a stacion[71]
Whanne alle the peple gon on
    processioun,
Fully in hope the better for to spede,
Fro yere to yere, ther thay syng and
    rede.

De carne autem circumcisionis domini
dicitur, quod angelus eam Carolo
Magno attulit

et ipse eam Aquisgrani in ecclesiam
Sanctae Marie honorifice collocavit,
Carolus vero illam postea fertur
Carosium transtulisse. Nunc autem
dicitur esse Romae in ecclesia quae
dicitur Sancta Sanctorum. Unde et
ibidem scriptum legitur: Circumcisa
caro Christi sandalia clara atque
umbilici viget praecisio cara. Unde
et ea die fit Statio ad Sanctum Sanctorum. Sed si hoc verum valde mirabile est. Cum enim caro ipsa sit de
veritate humanae naturae, credimus
quod resurgente Christo rediit ad locum suum glorificatum. Aliqui dixerunt, quod hoc verum sit juxta opin-
ionem illorum qui dicunt illud solum
esse de veritate humanae naturae quae
ab Adam traducta est, et istam solum
resurgere.

---

[71]Cf. F. J. Furnivall, *The Stacions of Rome,* line 337 (1867; *EETS,* 25), p. 11.

Having discussed the ceremony of the circumcision and vividly described the scene, Lydgate proceeds to exalt the name of Jesus—protesting as usual that his "wittes ben so dull" that he cannot do justice to so sublime a topic. The "rudenesse and ignoraunce" of which he modestly complains, however, do not prevent him from devoting the rest of the work[72] to a protracted disquisition on the Holy Name. Through the remaining two hundred and fifty lines he appears to have made wide but not literal use of the *Legenda Aurea*[73] and St. Bernard.[74] On occasion, the indebtedness is so direct that it merits inclusion here:[75]

It is the well *with* the foure stremes,
Wher-of Bernard wrytyth in sentence,
That thorughe the worlde refressheth
  al Remys,
It is so holsome and of suche
  excellence.
The firste he calleth the streme of
  sapyence,
Of whiche the floode most inly is
  habounde;
And Rightwysnesse he namethe the
  secounde;

And the thryde he calleth holynesse,
For it excellyth in *perfection*;
The fourthe also, as I can well expresse,
Is the floode of our Redempcion.

. . . dicitur fons, unde dicit Bernardus: Jesus est fons vitae signatus, qui in quatuor rivos se diffundit in plateas. Unde qui factus est nobis sapientia, justitia, sanctificatio et redemptio;

By way of illustration, the text is here continued to show Lydgate's freedom in manipulating the materials found in his source:

And of the firste, in conclusion,
Of which the streme₃ bene so fresshe
  and fyne,
Who so loke aright, is holy our
  doctryne.
And of his Right, to make mencion,

sapientia in praedicatione, justitia in peccatorum absolutione,

---

[72]*LOL* IV, 155-406.
[73]Graesse, pp. 80 sqq.
[74]Cf. notes below.
[75]*LOL* IV, 197-224. For the source see Graesse, p. 81.

The holsome welle ay dothe flowe and
    flete,
With mercy medled and remyssion,
Tofore his dome his Ire forto lete.
And of the thryde, the water is so
    swete,

By gode ensample who so can disserne,   sanctificatio in conversatione vel in
In vertu aye how we shull vs gouerne.   conversione, redemptio in passione.
And of the foruthe, to speke in speciall,

Is all our helthe and our saluacion,   Haec Bernardus.[76]
For ther-in is our remedye fynall
Aȝenste dethe and full protection;
Whos floode sprong oute of cristes
    passion.
And who that liste, by water to atame,
He shall it fynde enclosede in this
    name.

The concluding lines of the fourth book of the *Life of Our Lady* constitute a Bernardian rhapsody on the Holy Name and end with a beautiful prayer which, in its manner of expression at least, would seem to be our author's original work. Nowhere, except in the reference to Ignatius the Martyr,[77] is Lydgate too far from the ideas expressed by the *Legenda* under the Feast of the Circumcision, and even the Ignatian story can be found by merely turning forward a few pages in that great collection of medieval narrative.[78] Despite the fact, therefore, that accurate parallelisms cannot be traced in this section, the relevant passage of the *Legenda*[79] is given here in its entirety. It can be compared with Lydgate's text in the body of this edition.

    Secundum est impositio novi et salutiferi nominis, hodie enim impositum est ei nomen novum quod os domini nominavit. Nomen pater, quod non est

---

    [76]*Ipse siquidem fons vitae . . .in quatuor sese rivos diffudit, et derivavit in plateas, ubi videlicet et assignat nobis eum factum a Deo sapientiam, et justitiam, et sanctificationem, et redemptionem . . ."* Sancti Bernardi Opera Omnia, Migne, *PL*, CLXXXIII, 846. It is noteworthy that, although Bernard uses this idea frequently in his sermons, he never seems to develop it as we find it in the *LOL* nor does he here or elsewhere apply it to the name of Jesus. One can safely assume, therefore, that Lydgate did not go directly to Bernard at this point. The *Legenda,* while not identical with our text, is much closer.
    [77]Cf. Note to 1.255.
    [78]Graesse, p. 157.
    [79]Graesse, p. 80-82. This part of the *Legenda,* it will be noted, makes generous use of Bernard's *Sermo XV Super Canticum.* The *Meditationes* quotes it even more accurately and extensively in its final chapter. Cf. *Meditationes,* pp. 629-635.

aliud sub caelo, in quo oportet nos salvos fieri. Nomen quod secundum Bernardum est mel in ore, melos in aure, et jubilus in corde. Nomen, quod, sicut dicit idem Bernardus, instar olei lucet, praedicatum pascit, recogitatum lenit et ungit invocatum. Habuit autem triplex nomen, sicut ex evangelio manifestatur, scilicet filius Dei, Christus et Jesus. Vocatur autem filius Dei, in quantum est de Deo Deus, Christus, in quantum est homo a persona divina in quantum ad humanam naturam assumptus; Jesus, in quantum Deus humanitati unitus. De hoc triplici nomine dicit Bernardus: vos qui in pulvere estis, expergiscimini et laudate. Ecce dominus venit cum salute, venit cum unguento, venit cum gloria neque enim sine salute venit Jesus neque Christus sine unctione, neque sine gloria venit filius Dei, siquidem ipse unctio, ipse gloria. Quantum autem ad hoc triplex nomen, ante passione perfecte notus non erat. Nam quantum ad primum, ab aliquibus cognoscebatur conjecturaliter, sicut a demonibus, qui dicebant ipsum esse filium Dei. Quantum ad secundum particulariter, ab aliquibus enim, licet paucis, cognoscebatur esse Christus. Quantum ad tertium vocaliter, quia quo ad hanc vocem Jesus, licet non quo ad rationem nominis, quod est salutare. Post resurrectionem autem hoc nomen triplex clarificatum est. Primum nomen quo ad certitudinem, secundum quo ad diffusionem, tertium quo ad nominis rationem. Primum igitur nomen filius Dei. Et quod hoc nomen sibi recte conveniat, sic dicit Hylarius in libro de Trinitate: vere Dei filium unigenitum dominum nostrum Jesum Christum esse, multis modis cognitum est. Dum de eo testatur pater, dum de se ipso profitetur, dum apostoli praedicant, dum religiosi credunt, dum demones confitentur, dum Judaei negant, dum gentiles in passione cognoscunt. Idem: Dominum nostrum Jesum Christum his modis cognoscimus, nomine, nativitate, natura, potestate, professione. Secundum nomen est Christus, quod interpretatur unctus. Ipse enim fuit unctus oleo laetitiae prae participibus suis. Per hoc autem quod dicitur unctus, insinuatur, quod ipse fuit propheta, pugil, sacerdos et rex. Istae enim quatuor personae olim consueverunt inungi. Fuit enim propheta in doctrinae eruditione, pugil in dyaboli debellatione, sacerdos in patris reconciliatione, rex in praemiorum retributione. A hoc secundo nomine denominamur, quia a Christo dicimur Christiani. De quo nomine sic dicit Augustinus: christianus justitiae, bonitatis, integritatis, patientiae, castitatis, pudentiae, humanitatis, innocentiae, pietatis es nomen. Et tu istud quomodo tibi defendis et vindicas, cui de tam pluribus rebus nec pauca subsistunt? Christianus est ille, qui non nomine tantum, sed etiam opere est. Haec Augustinus. Tertium nomen est Jesus. Hoc autem nomen Jesus secundum Bernardum dicitur cibus, fons, medicina et lux. His autem cibus multiplicem habet effectum, est enim cibus confortativus, impinguativus, roborativus et vegetativus. De his sic dicit Bernardus: est cibus hoc nomen Jesus. An non toties confortaris, quoties recordaris? Quid aeque mentem cogitantis impinguat? Quid ita exercitatos reparat sensus, virtutes roborat, vegetat bonos mores atque castas fovet affectiones? Secundo dicitur fons, unde dicit idem Bernardus: Jesus est fons vitae signatus, qui in quatuor rivos se diffundit in plateas. Unde qui factus est nobis sapientia, justitia, sanctificatio et redemptio; sapientia in praedicatione, justitia in peccatorum absolutione, sanctificatio in conversatione vel in conversione, redemptio in passione. Haec Bernardus. Alibi quoque sic dicitur: tres rivi fluxerunt a Jesu, verbum doloris, in quo est confessio, sanguis aspersionis, in quo est afflictio, aqua emundationis, in qua est compunctio. Tertio est medicina. Nihil enim ita irae impetum cohibet, superbiae tumorem sedat, sanat livoris vulnus, restringit luxuriae fluxum, extinguit libidinis flammam, sitim temperat, avaritiae et totius dedecoris fugit pruriginem. Quarto est lux, unde ait: unde putas, in toto orbe tanta et tam subita fidei lux, nisi de praedicatione vel praedicato Jesu, hoc est nomen quod Paulus portabat coram gentibus tamquam lucernam super candelabrum. Hoc iterum nomen Jesus est multae suavitatis, unde Bernardus: si scribas, non sapit mihi, nisi legero ibi Jesus. Si disputes ac conferas, non sapit mihi, nisi sonuerit ibi Jesus. Item Richardus de Sancto Victore: Jesus est nomen dulce, nomen delectabile, nomen confortans peccatorem et beatae spei. Ergo Jesu esto mihi Jesus. Secundo est multo virtuositatis, unde Petrus Ravennas: vocabis nomen ejus Jesum, hoc est, nomen quod dedit caecis visum, surdis auditum, claudis gressum, sermonem mutis, vitam mortuis, totamque dyaboli potestatem de obsessis corporibus virtus hujus nominis effugavit. Tertio est multae excellentiae et sublimitatis, unde Bernardus: nomen salvatoris nostri, fratris mei, carnis meae, sanguinis mei, nomen a saeculis absconditum, sed in fine saeculorum revelatum, nomen mirabile, nomen ineffabile, nomen inaestimabile, imo eo mirabilius, quo inaestimabilius, eo magis gratum, quo gratuitum.

By way of summary, it might be said that all the illustrations given above tend to show that Lydgate's material for Books III and IV of the *Life of Our Lady* comes from comparatively few sources. Three of these appear again and again: the *Evangelium Pseudo-Matthaei,* the *Legenda Aurea,* and the *Meditationes Vitae Christi.* These, together with the Vulgate Bible, make up the bulk of the work. With few exceptions, references to other sources (Bernard, Augustine, Innocent, etc.) can be traced to the major repositories.

The general question of Lydgate's method of composition still remains to be taken up. In respect to this matter, two lines of argumentation are possible; either he had at hand a ready-made compilation of the omnibus tradition—perhaps French in origin—or he organized this wealth of material himself out of a few great encyclopedic sources. There is some cause for thinking that the latter alternative has a measure of plausibility. These are the reasons:

1) If a French (or Latin) version of the *Life of Our Lady* had existed in anything near the complete form of Lydgate's text, it would have been a *magnum opus* on the Continent, and could be presumed to have demonstrated its popularity in the usual manner by an early printing and by great numbers of extant manuscripts just as Lydgate's version has, in fact, done.[80] This is definitely not the case.

2) With the exception of the *Meditationes,* the volumes necessary for gathering the information contained in Books III and IV of the *Life of Our Lady* were

[80]Cf. "1. Introduction. The Manuscripts", p. 11.

readily available to Lydgate in his monastic library at Bury as the catalogue clearly shows.[81]

3) The *Meditationes,* source of much of the poem, was just translated out of Latin into French by Jean Galopes, and presented by him to Henry the Fifth at whose bidding the *Life of Our Lady* was written.[82]

4) The unevenness of the style[83] would be hard to explain if Lydgate were doing a mere job of verse translation from a previously existing manuscript.

5) A single source would have obviated such discrepancies as the double listing of the prophecies, the two-fold mention of the *Gloria in excelsis,* and the confused repetition of the story regarding the statue of Romulus all of which are discussed earlier in this chapter and in the notes.

It appears entirely credible, therefore, that Lydgate could have departed once again from his customary use of single French sources. His major materials were close at hand and his Benedictine ear, ringing with the liturgical praises of Mary as they were sung in the Divine Office and in the Mass, could easily have aided his monastic memory, steeped as it must have been in refectory readings and library researches at Bury.

---

[81]M. R. James, *The Abbey of Saint Edmund at Bury* (Cambridge, 1895) pp. 10 sqf.
[82]See R. Klinefelter "1. Introduction. The Date", pp. 4-5.
[83]*Ibid.,* p. 8.

BOOKS V AND VI

The presence in the *Legenda Aurea*[1] of all the principal "story" elements in Books V and VI of *The Life of Our Lady,* in addition to internal references in the *Legenda* itself to its own sources, points strongly to the probability that Lydgate or his possible undiscovered immediate source used the *Legenda* and its sources for the material of Books V and VI.

Book V opens with the account of the origin of the Magi and the description and details of their visit to Jerusalem and to the new king in Bethlehem. The *Legenda* paraphrases the story and refers to "quam Balaam praedixerat" (*Numbers* 24: 17), "Chrysostomos in originali super Matthaeum asserens", "secundum Remigium", "secundum Jeremiam", and twice more to both Chrysostom and Remegius.[2]

The author of the *Legenda* enumerates the existing theories relative to the identity of the Magi and then gives their story:

"Isti reges fuerunt successores Balaam et ad visionem stellae venerunt, propter illam prophetiam patris sui: orietur stella ex Jacob et exsurget homo ex Israel etc. Aliam causam, unde isti moti sunt ad veniendum ponit Chrysostomus in originali super Matthaeum asserens, quosdam dicere, quot quidam secretorum inspectores elegerunt de se ipsis XII, et si quis moriebatur, filius ejus aut aliquis propinquorum in ejus locum substituebatur. Hi ergo per singulos annos post messem ascendebant super montem victorialem et tribus diebus ibidem morantes, se lavabant et orabant Deum, ut iis illam stellam, quam Balaam praedixerat, ostenderet. Quadam autem vice, scilicet montem venit, quae habebat formam pulcherrimi pueri, super cujus capite crux splendebat, quae magos allocuta est dicens: ite velocius in terram Juda et ibidem regem, quem quaeritis, natum invenietis. Tunc illi continuo venire coeperunt."[3]

Except for the reference to the "dromodarye" and the thirteen days required for the Magi to make the journey to Jerusalem, the *Opus Imperfectum*[4] of Chrysostom contains the account of the story as we find it in *The Life of Our Lady.*

The Life of Our Lady (V, 8-112)	*Opus Imperfectum* (637 ff.)
And lat my breste, benygne lorde, be dewede	Legi apud aliquem, magos istos ex libris Balaam divinatoris appariturae

---

[1]*Legenda Aurea,* ed. Th. Graesse (2 ed. Leipzig, 1876).

[2]pp. 89-90.

[3]p. 89.

[4]Joannes Chrysostomus, *Opus Imperfectum,* Migne, *PG,* LVI, 637 ff. Biblical scholars consider this work spurious.

The Life of Our Lady (cont.)

Doun with some drope fro thy
    maieste,
That were this day by a sterre shewede
Oute of the Est to worthy kyngeʒ thre,
Whiche on the nyght of thy Natyuyte,
Gan firste asspye the bright bemes
    clere
Of this sterre on the heven apere—

Of whome the spryng was not causell,
Of fortune ne soden aventure
For many a day or this thyng befelle,
And many a yere by recorde of
    scripture,
With a-waytyng and wondre bysy cure,
In verrey sothe as I Remembre can.
A certeyne kynryde towarde the
    Occian,

Whiche of the stok and the lyne cam—
Who so lust loke, in bokes fro a ferre—
And of the blode of olde Balaam,
That som tyme had with his asse werre,
The whiche sayde ther shulde ryse a
    sterre
Oute of Iacob and from Israell—
Albe ther of no tyme he couthe tell—

Vpon whose words fully in byleve,
Ther shudle aryse such a sterre bright.
Werne xij. chose the trouthe for to
    preve
With-inne mydwynter euer from nyʒt
    to nyght
Whan in aquarye phebus shed his light;
For to awayte in all her best wyse
Whanne þis sterre on heuene wolde
    avise.

Opus Imperfectum (cont.)

hujus stellae scientiam accepisse, cujus divinatio posita est in Veteri Testamento: *Orietur stella ex Jacob et exsurget homo ex Israel, et dominabitur omnium gentium* (*Num.* 24.17). Audivi aliquos referentes de quadam scriptura . . . quoniam erat quaedam gens sita in ipso principio orientis juxta Oceanum, apud quos ferebatur quaedam scriptura, inscripta nomine Seth, de apparitura hac stella, et muneribus ei hujusmodi offerendis, quae per generationes studiosorum hominum, patribus referentibus filiis suis, habebatur deducta. Itaque elegerunt seipsos duodecim quidam ex ipsis studiosiores, et amatores mysteriorum caelestium, et posuerunt seipsos ad expectationem stellae illius. Et si quis moriebatur ex eis, filius ejus, aut aliquis propinquorum, qui ejusdem voluntatis inveniebatur, in loco constituebatur defuncti . . . Hi ergo per singulos annos, post messem trituratoriam, ascendebant in montem aliquem positum ibi, qui vocabatur lingua Victorialis, habens in se quandam speluncam in saxo, fontibus, et electis arboribus amoenissimus; in quem ascendentes, et lavantes se, orabant et laudabant in silentio Deum tribus diebus, et sic faciebant per singulas generationes, expectantes semper, ne forte in generatione sua stella illa beatitudinis oriretur, donec apparuit eis descendens super montem illum Victorialem, habens in se formam quasi pueri parvuli et super se

The Life of Our Lady (cont.)

And these xij. wern of the kynrede
Of balam, as ȝe haue herde me telle,
That yere by yere shulde take hede
Vpon an hill by-syde a lytell well.
And ther in fere a certen space dwelle,
A-noynted *and* bathed *and* in clothes
  whight.
And of custome thay slepen but a lyte,

But in prayer and certeyne ryteȝ vsede,
They muste wake and wayte in
  speciall—
And none of hem plattely excusede—
Vpon this hill namede Victoriall.
And if one dyed, than his sonne shall
By statute olde his place ocupye,
Or elles one that were next of alye.

And this contynuede duryng many
  yere
By custom vsede of antiquyte—
As phebus went by meovyng
  circuler—
So thay kept her tymeȝ by decree,
And iche yere wer certeyne dayes thre
By calkyng cast and computacion,
Sowght *and* chosen ouȝt by good
  eleccioun

For to awayte the vp-rist by the
  morowe,
Of this sterre *with* his bemes glade,
Whiche Balaam sayde sholde avoyde
  her sorrowe.
At his vp-riste whose bemeȝ may not
  fade,
To shede his lyght in eu*er*y shrowde
  and shade
With-oute wrystyng or drawyng to
  declyne.
Til at the last for the same fine—

Opus Imperfectum (cont.)

similitudinem crucis: et loquuta est eis,
et docuit eos, et praecepit eis ut pro-
ficiscerentur in Judeam.

The Life of Our Lady (cont.)

To see his sterre moast famous of
  rennoun
On the heven whan it wold apere—
Be worthi kyngis as made is mencioun,
Vpon this hill to-gydre gon in fere.
For cause thay, who so lust to here,
Werne of the stoke of Balaam dou*n*
  descendyde;
Wher-fore of sort the hylle they ben
  ascendyde,

As fell on hem by custome to succede
At a certeyne yere by reuolucion.
And on this hill estewarde thay toke
  hede,
By gode avyse in her inspeccion,
The same nyght of the Incarnacion,
Whan criste was borne in Bedlem of
  marye.
The same hour the sterre thay aspye

Of newe aryse in the Oryent;
Full lustyly of whome the beme**ʒ** light
Gan enlumyne all the firmament.
Fro Est to West it yafe so clere a
  light,
That of the stremys eu*ery* man*ere*
  wight
Astonyde was thay were so bright and
  shene,
And to the eye so *p*ersaunt for to sene.

The whiche sterre drewe his cours full
  right
Towarde the hill—liche as boke**ʒ** tell—
Where the kyng*es* the long wynters
  nyght
It to awayte solitarye dwelle.
And they anone vpon her knees fell

Opus Imperfectum (cont.)

Proficiscentibus autem eis per bien-
nium praecedebat stella, et neque esca,
neque potus defecit in peris eorum.
Caetera autem quae gesta referuntur
ab eis in evangelio compendiose posita
sunt.

The Life of Our Lady (cont.)

And thanked god w*ith* all her hert*es*
luste
Which hathe not hem defraudyd of her
truste.

And all the nyght to-gydre as thay
woke
Vp on this sterre that shoon so fayre
and clere;
And sodenly vpwarde as they gan loke
They sawe a child above the sterre
apere:
So yong, so fayre, in a golden spere,
Fully ryally stonde, and above his hede
A large crosse that was of blode all
rede.

The wiche childe spake to hem a-noon
Above the hill withe voyse and chere
benyng,
And bad hem faste that thay shulde
gone
Into Iuda right as any lyne,
And falowe all-waye the sterre for a
signe
That shal hem bringe into that
regioun;
Where as the kynge moost worthi of
renooun,

Was borne that tyme to haue the
Regale
Of Iwes lande of verrey dwe right,
Whom the sterre dyd specifie,
Whan he was borne w*ith* his clere
light.
And thay a-noon whan passed was the
nyght,
The next morne no lenger lust a-byde
But towarde hym cast hem for to Ryde.

Cornelius à Lapide, Flemish biblical scholar (1567-1637), acknowledges the existence of the Apocryphal Gospel of Seth and cites many noteworthy Fathers of the Church who seemed familiar with it:

> Ita ex Balaam et Sibylla Magos cognovisse stellam hanc esse indicem Christi, censent S. Basilius, S. Hieronymus, Origines, S. Leo, Eusebius, Prosper, S. Cyprianus, Procopius et alii quos citavi, *Num. 27: 17.*[5]

And in commenting on the interpretation of the child and the cross visible in the star according to the *Opus Imperfectum* version, à Lapide adds:

> Verum hoc gratis dicitur; nulla enim historia id narrat aut testatur, nisi libri Cethianorum haereticorum . . .[6]

I have not been able to discover even the slightest clue to the existence of a manuscript containing the Gospel of Seth but the frequent reference to and quotation from it over the centuries seems to put the fact of its one-time existence beyond all doubt.

The *Opus Imperfectum* alone contains the reference to the trees: "electis arboribus amoenissimus" and the manner in which the Magi travelled: "neque esca, neque potus defecit in peris eorum", and Lydgate omits both.

Peter Comestor in his *Historia Scholastica,* another *Legenda* source, comments on the *Opus Imperfectum* statement that the Magi saw the star two years before the birth of Christ:

> "Chrysostomus dicit stellam multo ante tempore quam Christus nasceretur, apparuisse eis, et ita multo tempore de longinquo venerunt. Patuit autem fieri, ut in tredecim diebus super dromedarios sedentes longa terrarum spatia transmearent".[7]

The *Legenda* paraphrases Remegius in support of the "thirteen days" and cites a prophecy of Jerenias "quod super dromedarios venerunt".[8]

The Life of Our Lady (V, 120-128)	(*Legenda,* p. 89)
And furthe thay gone, no lenger wolde thay tarye,	. . . in tredecim diebus per tanta terrarum spatiis venire potuerunt, . . .

---

[5]Cornelius à Lapide, *Commentaria in Scripturam Sacram* (Paris, 1862), Tomus decimus quintus, p. 75.

[6]*id.*

[7]Petrus Comestor, *Historia Scholastica,* Migne, *PL,* CXCVIII, 1541.

[8]p. 89. The attribution to Jeremias is incorrect. The single Biblical reference to "dromedaries" occurs in *Isaias* 60:8: "The multitude of camels shall cover thee, the dromedaries of Madian and Epha: all they from Saba shall come, bringing gold and frankincense: and showing forth praise to the Lord."

The Life of Our Lady (Cont.)

Thorow mani a londe *and* many a
    diuerse yle,
Eu*er*yche of hem on a dromondarye,
Whiche were so swifte that full many
    a myle
Thay passed han w*ith* in a lytyll while;
That in the space of dayes but xiij ne,
By condit only of the sterre shene,
Thay entred ben into Iher*usalem,*
That of Iuda was the cheffe Cyte;

Legenda (cont.)

secundum Jeremiam, quod super dromedarios venerunt, qui sunt animalia
velocissima, . . .

The sources and Lydgate (V, 153) adhere to the *Matthew* (2: 1-6)[9] version
of the coming of the Magi to Jerusalem:

The Life of Our Lady (V, 127-147)

Thay entrede ben into Iherusalem,
That of Iuda was the cheffe Cyte;
Conveyed eu*ere with* the bright beame
Of the sterre that was so fayre to see.
And whan that they a-mydde the Cyte
    be,
Not astonyed, axede in audience:
Where is the kyng grettest of
    Reuerence,

Matthew (2: 1-5)

. . . there came wise men from the
east to Jerusalem, Saying, Where is
he that is born king of the Jews? For
we have seen his star in the east,

Of Iwes borne for to bere the crowne,
Whose sterre we seen in the Orient
That from hevyn cast his streme3
    downe,
Which all the worlde vndir the
    firmament
Is gladde to see and we on one entent,
Han yftey3 brought oute of our contre,
Hyme to hono*ur* in his ryall see?

and are come to adore him. And king
Herod hearing this, was troubled and
all Jerusalem with him. And assembling together all the chief priests

And whan herode of her comyng
    knewe,

and the scribes of the people, he in-
quired of them where Christ should

[9]*The Holy Bible,* translated from the Latin Vulgate (New York, 1914).

The Life of Our Lady (Cont.)

He troubled was and also all the towne,
And gan a-noon to chaunge chere and
   hewe;
And made in hast, a convocacion
Of all the presteʒ dwellyng environs;
To knowe clerly and be certyfyede,
Of the place that was specifiede

Matthew (cont.)

be born. But they said to him: In
Bethlehem of Juda. For so it is
written by the prophet:

(V, 148-174)

Of prophetis where crist shal be borne.
And thay a-noon the trouthe to hymn
   tolde:
In Bedlem, as thay full long afforne
Founden oute in her bokeʒ olde,
And all the man*ere* to hym thay
   vnfolde,
Fro poynt to poynt, as Mathew
   makyth mynde;
Redyth his gospell and ther ye shall
   it fynde

(2: 7-9)

Then Herod, privately calling the wise
men, learned diligently of them the
time of the star which appeared to
them; And sending them into

And then herde gan the kynges calle,
And of þis mater entretid priueli;
And curiously how that it was falle,
Be-gan enquere and axede bysely.
And of the sterre also by and by,
He axede hem and in wordes few
How and in what wyse it gan firste
   shewe.

Bethlehem said: Go and diligently in-
quire after the child, and when you
have found him, bring me word again,
that I also may

And whan thay had tolde hym eu*ery*
   dele,
Thay dep*ar*tede oute of his pr*e*sence.
But firste he had hem to enquere well
Of the childe w*ith* all her diligence.
And whan thay hade done hym
   Reu*er*ence,
He chargede hem vndir wordes fayre,
Hamwarde by hym algates to repayre,

come and adore him. Who having
heard the king, went their way; and
behold the star which they had seen
in the east, went before them,

The Life of Our Lady (Cont.)	*Matthew* (cont.)
To yeffe hym clerly informacion	until it came and stood over where
Of her exployt and of the childe also;	the child was.
Surely affermyng by fals collusion,	
That he hym-self wold aftir goo	
Vnto the childe and his deuer doo,	
To worship*p* hym— . . .	

In ll. 174-203, Lydgate lashes out at the wickedness of Herod and uses several of his favorite images to color his condemnation: "the worme abit as serpent vnder floures" (l. 175); "fals tygre full of doubleness" (l. 184); "What can sugur vndur galle faine?" (l. 191). We can safely say that these lines and thoughts are original with Lydgate since they do not appear in the sources:

"For I resemble the serpent,
Wych, vnder herbys fressh *and* soote
> (*Pilgrimage of Man,* ll. 15158ff.; see also *Reson and Sensuallyte,*
> ll. 4022-32; *Troy Book,* I,185)

"In porte a lambe, in herte a lyou*n* fel,
Dowble as a tygre sli3ly to compasse
> (*Troy Book,* I,216ff.)

"With sugred wordes vnder hony soote
His galle is hyd lowe by the roote."
> (*Troy Book,* Prolog. 277ff.; *Pilgrimage of Man,* ll. 14286ff.; *Reson and Sensuallyte,* 1.889.)

The *Legenda* seems to be the sole source at this point in reference to the duplicity of Herod. The homilies and glosses speak of it later but not at this point of the narrative:

The Life of Our Lady (V, 204-207)	*Legenda* (p. 90)
And so wi*th* venym in his herte loke	Dixitque iis, invento puero ei renunti-
He yaffe hem leve passe thorough his Reame,	arent, simulans se velle adorare, quem volebat occidere.
In her Repayre hym castyng to be wroke	
If thay reto*ur*ne by Ier*us*ale*m*.	

The source of the lines pertaining to the renewed guidance of the star are also from the *Legenda* (and the *Historia Scholastica* uses almost the identical words[10]).

The Life of Our Lady (V, 208-210)	*Legenda* (p. 90)
And so þe sterre hem brouȝte to bedlem,	. . . stella antecedebat eos, usque dum veniens staret supra, ubi erat puer.
And lyne right the childes hede aboue,	
Where as he lay, stille gan to houe.	

Remegius writes that history lacks reference to the time that elapsed between the visit of the Magi to Herod and the time of their appearance at Bethlehem.[11] *Matthew* says:

> "Who having heard the king, went their way; and behold the star which they had seen in the east, went before them, until it came and stood over where the child was." (2: 9).

There is general agreement among the sources of the joy of the Magi on seeing the new king:

The Life of Our Lady (V, 211-228)	*Matthew* (2: 10-11)
But who the Ioy can tell or endyte,	And seeing the star they rejoiced with exceeding great joy.
Or with his mouthe, who can the myrthe expresse,	
Or who can playnly with his penne wryte,	
The grete blisse or elles the gladnesse	
Which they made in verrey sothefastnesse	
Aftir her iourney and her long waye,	
Above the house whan thay the sterre sey,	
Thatte gan to hem clerly certifie	And entering into the house, they found the child with Mary his mother,
Withoute more the childeȝ dwellyng place?	
And thay a-noon faste gan hem hye	
With lusty hert and gladde of chere and face,	

---

[10]*op. cit.*, c. 1541.
[11]Remegius, *Miscellanea. Homilia VII,* Migne, *PL,* CXXI, 904.

The Life of Our Lady (cont.)   *Matthew* (cont.)

To worthe dou*n* in a lytyll space.
Thay made hem redy and w*ith*
    reverence;
Thay entrede in and cam to his
    p*re*sence,

Wher as the childe, most worthy of
    degre,
Was w*ith* marie in an oxes stalle.
And full humbly the kynge¾ all thre,
To-fore the childen on her knes gan   and falling down,
    falle,   they adored him.

    The *Historia Scholastica* seems to be the source of lines 229-238. The *Legenda* used it: ". . . dicitur in hystoria scholastica, venerunt a finibus Persarum et Chaldaeorum, ubi est flumen Saba, a quo et Sabaea dicitur regio."[12] The "Sabei", writes Peter Comestor a little earlier in the account: "Venerunt enim de finibus Persarum et Chaldaeorum, ubi fluvius est Saba, a quo et Sabaea regio dicitur", col. 1541. Note that Lydgate apparently was reading the *Historia* or the *Legenda* and used "perce and Calde" (1.236) because it suited his metre better than *Saba*.

The Life of Our Lady (V, 229-238)   *Historia Scholastica* (c. 1541)

And brought her tresour and her   . . . obtulerunt puero singuli aurum,
    yeftys alle
As Reuerently as they can devyse.
And hym p*re*sent in all her best wyse,

Lyche her astate¾, eu*e*ryche aftir othir,   thus et myrrham, secundum Sabaeis
Makyng her p*re*sent w*ith* all humylyte,   consuetam oblationem.
Lyche her age as brothir aftir brothir.
Golde, franke and Myrr thay yaffe hym
    all thre,
Aftir the custome of perce and Calde,
For of that lond whanne kyngis
p*re*sent make,
The custome is such yefte¾ for to take.

———
[12]p. 93.

None of the sources refers to the order of dignity followed in the presentation of the gifts. Remegius remarks that "sciendum quia isti non singuli singula, sed singuli tria, id est unusquisque eorum obtulit aurum, thus et myrrham,"[13] which probably accounts for 1.235: "Golde, franke and Myrr thay yaffe hym all thre,". I have not been able to account for the previous line: "Lyche her age as brothir aftir brothir", although, since the Magi were so closely related, it was quite natural for Lydgate to assume some such practice.

The symbolism of the Three Gifts is treated by all the sources and Lydgate seems to have made a selection from among them.

The Life of Our Lady (V, 246-259)

And for that golde is payede for tribute
As it is founde of Antiquyte,
Ther-fore these kynges for a man*ere*
  sewte—
That thay hym aught of verrey duete—
Thay brought hym w*ith*out
  Repentaunce,
Holy of hert for a reconysaunce.

And franke also, as clerke3 can devyse,
Ordenyde is in conclusion,
To God only to make sacryfyce.
W*ith* contryte hert and deuocion,
Therefore to hym for oblacion
Thay broughten frank to signyfye
  thanne,
That he was bothe sothefast god and
  man.

             (V, 260-266)

And for thei wolde in alle thynge obeie
To his highnesse w*ith* all bysy cure,
In token he shulde for mankynde deye
Thay brought hym myrre to his
  sepulture;
For like a man dethe he must endure,
And w*ith* his blode shed in his passion,
Of oure trespas to make redempcioun.

Opus Imperfectum (p. 642)

Regem enim cognoscentes eum, pri-
mitiam mundam, et pretiosam sanctorum, repositum obtulerunt

Divinum autem et caeleste intelligentes
principium ejus, libani obtulerunt
odorem, formam mundae orationis in
odorem suavem. . . .

Remegius (c. 906)

Humanam autem et temporalem sepul-
turam ejus intelligentes, obtulerunt
myrrham.

---

[13]*op. cit.*, c.904.

The Life of Our Lady (V, 267-280)   *Legenda* (p. 93)

In franke also, who þat can discerne,   Per hae tria ergo in Christo intimatur
Is vndirstonde the highe maieste   regia potestas, divina majestas et
Of his power whiche that is et*er*ne;   humana mortalitas.
And eke also his high deite.
And golde betokenyth his high
    dygnyte,
And myrre declareth vnto us at all
Of his manhode that he was mortall.

And golde betokenythe of loue the   . . . quoniam aurum significat dilec-
    fervence   tionem, thus orationem, myrrha carnis
That he to man had of affection.   mortificationem.
And frank betokenethe the sou*er*eygne
    excellence
In holynesse his conu*er*sacion.
And myrre betokenethe the tribulacion
That he suffrede and all the grete
    pen*au*nce,
For vs in erthe by contynaunce.

    For his third symbol of the Three Gifts, Lydgate goes to Venerable Bede,[14]
another *Legenda* source.[15]

The Life of Our Lady (V, 281-288)   *Bede* (p. 12)

In golde he was knowen as a kyng,   In auro regalis dignitas ostenditur
In frank a prest, who so can take hede,   Christi; in thure, ejus verum sacerdo-
Of myrre also this day the offryng   tium, in myrrha mortalitas carnis;
Was longyng only to his manhede.
And thus he was wit*h*outyn any drede,
Bothe kyng and prest as I descerne
    can,
And for our sake in erthe a mortall
    man.

The Life of Our Lady (V, 288-294)   *Legenda* (p. 93)

In golde also, metall most gloryouse,   Per aurum ergo, quod est pretiosius
Fygured was his high deite;   omnibus metallis, intelligitur divinitas

---

[14]Venerabilis Bedae, *Opera Omnia*, Migne, *PL*, XCII.
[15]*op. cit.*, c. 87-88.

The Life of Our Lady (cont.)

In franke also—that is so preciouse—
The soule of criste most perfyte of
  degre;
And Myrre betokeneth thurugh his
  dignyte,
His flesshe the whiche by disposicion,
May neuere suffre noo corrupcion.

Legenda (cont.)

pretiosissima, per thus anima devotis-
sima . . . per myrrham, quae conservat
a corruptione, caro incorrupta.

    Lines 294-336 seem to represent a break in the narrative and portray the poet's reflections on the sentiments of the Magi as they contemplated the child. The fact that they had conversation with Mary about him can easily be presumed without historical evidence but "that he put his Armeʒ right/ Godely to hem makyng a manere signe/ To hem of thankyng," (1.327ff.), has the air of legend although I have not been able to discover the source.

    Lines 337-357 are apparently an original prayer extolling the humility of the queen of heaven and earth and a condemnation of pride.

    Lines 358-427 are a series of rhetorical questions designed to show the proud the modesty of Mary's raiment and residence and an exhortation to all women to imitate her example:

The Life of Our Lady (V, 352-427)

Wer ther of golde any clotheʒ founde,
Of silke damaske or ryche tarteryne?
Or was ther arras a-bouʒte hir heed vp
  boonde,
Or was ther any veluet Crymesyne,
Or was ther any samyte or satyne,
Or wer ther any tappyteʒ large or
  wyde,
The nakyd grounde to keuer or to hide?

Or was her palyce bilt of lyme and
  stone,
Or the pillours sette vp of Marble
  graye,
Or the growne pavede on to gon,
Or fresshe parlours glaʒed bright as
  day,

Opus Imperfectum (c. 641-642)

Numquid viderunt palatium marmori-
bus splendidum? Numquid matrem
ejus diademate coronatam, aut in
lecto aureo recumbentem? numquid
puerum

auro et purpura involutum?

Or were ther any chaumbreȝ of a ray,
Or for estateȝ was ther any hall
Saue a dongon and an oxe stall?

Or of hir bede was the appareyll
Of golde or sylke curteynede large
  a-boute,
Or were ther sheteȝ of longe or wyde
  entayle
Kyt oute of Reynes nay with-outynn
  doute?
Or were there any ladeȝ for to loute
To hir highnesse with bysy obseruance,
Or of maydens any attendaunce?

O as me semythe, of verrey dewe right,
Ye wemen all shulden take hede—
With your perleȝ and your stoneȝ
  bright—
How that your quene, floure of
  womanhede,
Of no devyse enbroyded hath her wede,
Ne furrede withe Ermyne ne with
  tresty graye,
Ne martren ne sable, I trowe in gode
  faye,

Was noon founden in her garment,
And yet she was the fayrest for to see
That euere was vndir the firmament.
Wherfore, me semyth, ye shulde haue
  pite
To se a lady of so high degre,
So semely atyrede, o ye wemen all.
Be-holde howe narowe closed in an oxe
  stalle.

Late be your pryde and your affeccion
Of riche aray, and nothyng yov delite

Sed quid? Pandochium tenebrosum
et sordidum, et magis animalibus quam
hominibus aptum: in quo nemo

contentus erat secedere, nisi itineris
necessitate coactus. Matrem

The Life of Our Lady (Cont.)

In wordely pompe and suche abusion
Of sundri clothis, reede, blake *and*
   white.
And be well ware, or the spere byte
Of cruell dethe and the fell smerte.
My councell is to lyfth vp yowre hert

To that lady and to that worthy quene,
þat ʒou may beest helpe in ʒour nede,
And yov releve in eu*ery* woo and tene,
And delyu*ere* from all myscheve and
   drede.
and þinkeþ pleynly *and* takyth riʒt
   good hede,
þat al schal passe, aray *and* eke
   richesse,
When ye lest wene and all y*our*
   semblynesse.

Lat hem affore be to yov a kalendere:
Isoude, Elyn, and eke polixene,
Hester also and dydo w*ith* her chere,
And Riche Candace, of ethyope
   quene,—
Ligge þei not graue vndre clowris
   grene?
And yet all this may not y*our* pryde
   atame,
Nought withestondyng þat ye shall do
   the same.

Eke after dethe a-bydyth no memorye,
For ay w*ith* dethe comyth foryetylnesse;
And fare well than aray and all
   veyneglorye,
Saue only vertu that stant in
   sikernesse.

Opus Imperfectum (cont.)

ejus vix tunicam unam habentem, non
ad ornamentum

corporis, sed ad tegumentum nuditatis
proficientem, quam habere poterat uxor
carpentarii, et haec in peregre con-
stituta.

The Life of Our Lady (Cont.)

Opus Imperfectum (cont.)

I take recorde of the high mekenesse
Of hir that is of holynesse welle,
Om whome I thinke sothely for to
  telle,

Puerum pannis sordidissimis involutum, et in sordidiore

How that she satte, for all hir
  worthynesse,
Holdyng hir childe full lowly on the
  grounde;
And kyngeʒ knelyng, as ye haue herde
  expresse,
Be-holdyng hir in vertu most
  habounde,
Til at þe laste þay haue a leyser founde
To take her leve, and the same day
Thay gon to Ryde homwarde on her
  waye.

quoque praesepio positum: quia locus
ille sic erat angustus, ut nec ponendi
infantem spatium invenirent.

Lines 428-436 are as "the gospell tellyth vs" (1. 436), except that the Matthew
account makes no mention of "an Angell, a-peryng with grete light" (1.430):

The Life of Our Lady (V, 428-436)

Matthew (2:12)

And sewyng aftir on the next nyght,
While thay slepte at her logyng place,
Came an Angell, a-peryng with grete
  light,
And warnede hem that thay ne trace
By herodeʒ, but bade þat thay shulde
  pace
With-oute a-bood, in all the haste thay
  may
To her kyngedom by another way.

And having received an answer in
sleep that they should not return to
Herod, they went back another way
into their country.

And in shorte tyme, to her Region
Thay ben repayrede, the gospell
  tellyth vs.

The *Legenda* and *Historia Scholastica* both give the names of the Magi but the latter seems to have been Lydgate's model since he follows its spelling more closely. The *Legenda* lists: Appellius, Amerius, Damascus, Galgalat, Melgalat, Sarathim, Caspar, Balthasar, Melchior.[16]

The Life of Our Lady (V, 437-448)	*Historia Scholastica* (c. 1541)
And of her namez, to make mencion,	Nomina trium magorum hae sunt:
The first in Ebrwe was callede	Hebraice Appellus, Amerus, Damasius,
Appellius;	Graece Galgalat, Malgalath, Sarachim;
The next Amerus, the thryde	
Damathus;	
And in greke, the first Galgatha,	
And Serachym, the thryde Malgalatha.	
And in latyn, as bokez maken mynde,	Latine Gasper, Baltassar, Melchior.
The first of hem named was Iasper;	
And the secounde, playnely as I fynde,	
Lyche myne Auctour rehersez as I	
dar,	
Called was and namede Balthasar;	
And the thryde—ye get of me no	
more—	
As I Rede was callede Melchiore.	

Lines 449-452 are precisely the matter of the *Historia* and are then followed by Lydgate's interpretation of verse 8 of Psalm 47:[17]

The Life of Our Lady (V, 437-448)	*Historia Scholastica* (c. 1542-3)
Of whose repayre, as some bokez sayne,	Et venientes Tharsum Ciliciae, con-
That first of all thay went to the see,	ducto navigio, redierunt in regionem
And retournede to her kyngdome	suam . . . Herodes . . . cum iter
agayne.	faceret per Ciliciam, audiens naves
They shipped hem at Tharce the Cyte,	Tharsensium magos traduxisse, in
For whiche heroude, of coursede	spiritu vehementi combussit naves
cruelte,	Tharsis secundum quod David pro-
In Tharce made all the shippez brenne,	phetaverat in quadragesimo septimo
Wher-of wrytheth Dauid, the sauter if	psalmo: "In spiritu vehementi conteres
ye kenne.	naves Tharsis."

---

[16]p. 88.

[17]*The Holy Bible* (Vulgate).

Although the four-part division of the feast of Epiphany is traditional in the Church and mentioned extensively in the writings of the exegetes, the *Legenda* seems to be the sole source of lines 463-539, except for a brief reference to John 2:18[18] and Luke 9:12.[19]

The Life of Our Lady (V, 463-539)

Comyth this worde of Epyphanye.
And this word Epi, by discripcion
Is sayde of heght, as I can signifie;
And of a shewyng by demonstracion
Is phanos sayde, and so by gode reason,
Epi and phanos, both knyt in fere,
Is a shewyng that dothe a-lofte pere.

And for this day, a-lofte was the sterre.
Which christeȝ birthe and Incarnacion
With his stremeȝ gan shew fro so
      ferre,
Fro Est to West in many a Region.
Wherfore this fest, in conclusion,
As ye to-forne haue herde me specifye,
This fest is callede of Epiphanye.

The wheche feste haith a prerogatif
Of myracleȝ notable in special
For thynges foure wrought in cristes
      lyfe
Wern on this day by his power Riall.
The first of all most memoryall
Is of the kyngeȝ, as ye haue herde me
      sayne
Whiche were in ydelle to Reherse
      agayne.

The secounde, is, as it is sothely tolde,
That criste Ihesu, this day of saint
      Iohn,

Legenda (pp. 87-88)

. . . inde dicitur Epiphania ab epi, quod est supra, et phanos, apparitio quia tunc desuper stella apparuit sive ipse Christus

per stellam, quae desuper visa est, magis verus Deus demonstratus est.

Epiphania   domini   quadruplici decoratur miraculo et ideo quadruplici vocabulo nuncupatur. Hodie enim magi Christum adorant,

Johannes Christum baptizat, . . . habebat triginta annos plenos . . . in Jordane

---

[18]*Novum Testamentum.* Vulgatae Editionis (Ratisbonae, 1923). Here Lydgate uses the Latin text for his translation.
[19]*The Holy Bible* (Vulgate).

The Life of Our Lady (cont.)   *Legends* (cont.)

The yere whan he was xxx^ti wynter
olde,
Baptisede was in the flume Iourdan.

At whiche tyme, thre kyngeʒ vnder one,   . . . quia tunc tota trinitas apparuit,
Discendeth this day worthy of memorye.
The firste was that from the high
glorye,

The faders voyce, as clerkeʒ lust   pater in voce,
endyte,
Came dovne to erthe that men myght   spiritus in columba specie,
here;
And like a dove *with* fayre feders white
The holy gost also dyd a-pere;
And criste Ih*e*su, the faders son entere   filius in carne.
This day aperyng in our mortall kynde,
Was of saint Iohn Baptiʒede, as I fynde.

And for as moche as thay all thre
This day were sene by sotherfaste
apparence—
Thay beyng one in p*er*fyte vnyte—
Therfore, this day of moste Reuerence,
Named is truly in sentence,   et ob hoc vocatur Theophania a theos
Theophanos, for god in trible wyse   quod est Deus,
Ther in aperyd, as ye haue herde
devyse.

For theos is as moche for to mene
As god in englisshe, yf ye lust to se;
Phanos a shewyng *with*outen any wene,   et a phanos, quod est apparitio,
As ye haue herde aforne rehersed of me;
And for in erthe, o god in Trynyte,
This day aperede *with*outen any lye,
Ye truly may calle it theophane.

Eke whan crist was passed xxx^ti yere,   cum esset . . . triginta annorum . . .
This day he turnede water in to wyne   aquam in vinum Christus mutavit . . .

The Life of Our Lady (Cont.)

John (2:8)

That passyngly was to the eye clere
And of tarage inly gode and fyne,
The whiche he sent to Archideclyne.
And for this myracle Inly vertuouse,
In galele was shewed in a house.

Dicit eis Jesus: Haurite nunc, et ferte architriclino.

This same day whiche men dyd espye—
As holy chirche maketh mencion—
Therfore it is namede Bethphanye.
For Bethe in Inglisshe by discripcion
Is called an house or a mancion.
Of whiche myracle, renomed of fame,
Bethphanye this day hathe the name.

Ipso iterum die . . .

et ob hoc vocatur Bethania, (*sic*) a beth, quod est domus, quia miraculo facto in domo verus Deus apparuit.

Eke in the yere of his passion,
Fer in desert this day also, I rede,
W*ith* loves fyve, thorough his grete
　　foyson,
Fyve thousande I fynd that he dyde
　　fede.
Of whiche myracle, yf ye take hede,
This day is last namede phagyphanye,
Lyke as it firste was clepid
　　Ephiphanye.

. . . erat autem proximum Pascha per multiplicationem panum in deserto . . . et quinque millia hominum de quinque panibus satiavit, . . . et ob hoc vocetur Phagiphania . . .

For this worde phagi vnto our entent
Is sayde of fedyng or refecction;
For whiche myracle passyng excellent,
That is so famous and of so high
　　renou*n*—
Like as the gospell maketh mencion—
Þerfore þis dai amonge þe oþyr alle,
Ye Iustely may phagyphanye it call.

quod est bucca sive manducare.

(*Luke* 9:12-17)

　　Lines 540-602 are a prayer to Christ for protection through the perils of life in honor of the "worthy kyngeʒ". Lydgate builds his prayer around three sets of gift-symbols: 1) "our gold of p*er*fyte charite" (1.554), "our franke of contempla- tion" (1.558), (a myrrh equivalent is omitted in this set); 2) "golde of trouthe" (1.561), "Our franke also of high p*er*fection" (1.565), "our myrre . . . vs to *pre*serve from all such trecherye" (ypocrysye) (11.577-579) ; 3) "the golde of faythe and stablenesse" (1.585), "the franke of *per*fyte holynesse" (1.586), "such myrre . . . that eu*ery* wight his owne faute₃ knowe" (1.590f.)

The omission of a myrrh equivalent in the first of the above sets points strongly to the probability that Lydgate had a source before him as he worked and simply passed it over inadvertently. The first set resembles the *Opus Imperfectum,* given below.

Furthermore, Venerable Bede indicated the existence of a like symbolism when he wrote:

"aliter, in auro spiritalis sensus, in thure olfactus virtutum, in myrrha mortificatio corporis designatur, quae quotidie omnia ab ista Eccelsia in tribus partibus mundi dispersa Domino offeruntur."[20]

In our lines this interpretation would read thus: *gold:* "perfyte charite", "trouthe", "faythe"-all spiritual qualities; *frankincense:* "contemplation", "high *per*fection", "*per*fyte holynesse"-prayer, devotion and good works; *myrrhe:* omitted in 1), preservation from "ypocrysye", "his owne faute₃ knowe"-mortification and penance for sin.

Remegius writes in similar vein:

"Aliter per aurum designatur coelestis sapientia, unde Solomon ait: Thesaurus desiderabilis requiescit in ore sapientis;" per thus intelligitur oratio munda, ut illud: "Dirigatur, Domine, oratio mea sicut incensum in conspectu tuo; "per myrrham mortificatio carnis; unde Ecclesia in Canticis canticorum de suis fidelibus pro Deo usque ad mortem certantibus dicit: "Manus meae distillaverunt myrrham"; et item: "Messui myrrham meam cum aromatibus", et alibi: "Quae est quae ascendit per desertum sicut virgula fumi ex aromatibus myrrhae et thuris, et universi pulveris pigmentario"? Tunc ergo ei aurum offeruimus cum in conspectu ejus luce coelestis sapientiae resplendemus; tunc thus, cum mundam ad eum orationem dirigimus; tunc tandem myrrham, quando per abstinentiam carnem nostram a vitiis mortificamus."[21]

Looking earlier at another *Legenda* source, St. Gregory the Great, we discover what appears to be the direct source of Remegius' commentary:

"Quamvis in auro, thure, et myrrha intelligi et aliud potest. Auro namque sapientia designatur, Salomone attestante, qui ait: Thesaurus desiderabilis requiescit in ore sapientis. Thure autem quod Deo incenditur, virtus orationis exprimitur, Psalmista testante, qui dicit: Dirigatur oratio mea sicut incensum in conspectu tuo. Per myrrham vero carnis nostrae mortificatio figuratur. Unde Sancta Ecclesia de suis operariis usque ad mortem pro Deo certantibus dicit: Manus meae distillaverunt myrrham."[22]

[20]*op. cit.,* c.20.
[21]*op. cit.,* c.907.
[22]Sancti Gregorii Magni, *Homiliarum in Evangelia,* Migne, *PL,* LXXVI, 1113.

St. Remegius' and St. Gregory's symbols, therefore, would be equivalently:
1) gold:*wisdom;* 2) frankincense:*prayer;* 3) myrrh:*contrition* and *mortification*.
Sedatus, bishop of Biterrenis at the end of the sixth century, writes in the same
tradition: 1) gold:*faith;* 2) frankincense:*piety;* 3) myrrh: a *chaste holocaust*:

> Ac sic Trinitatem oblationis numerus loquitur, unitatem devotio una testatur;
> ac per hoc, vigili intentione cordis coelum studeamus aspicere, si ad Christum
> cupimus pervenire. Dirigat nobis semitas viae perfectas stella justitiae. Ei, qui
> dixit: *Non apparebis in conspectu meo vacuus* (Exod. XXIII) offeramus, et
> nos aurum fidei, pietatis aromata, castitatis holocausta, spiritalem quoque
> myrrham habemus in nobis, quae ita animas nostras condiat, ut illaesas a
> peccati corruptione custodiat. Mutemus viam, si pervenire optamus ad patriam,
> ad patriam utique coelestem. Ac si inter utrumque commercium, ut illius nobis
> proprietatem usu istius comparemus; ita elaboremus, ut illius ista sit pretium.[23]

The *Opus Imperfectum* interprets the gifts as 1) gold: *faith;* 2) frankincense:
prayer; 3) myrrh: *good works*:

> Aurum sunt ergo perfecti fideles et sapientes, dicenti Apostolo: *Si quis aedificat
> aurum, argentum, lapides pretiosos (1. Cor. 3.12)*. Si quis ergo praebet se
> Christo fidei sapientia plenum, obtulit ei aurum. Thus autem est oratio, sicut
> scriptum est: *Dirigatur oratio mea sicut incensum in conspectu tuo (Psal.
> 140.2)*. Si quis ergo Christo mundam offert orationem, obtulit ei thus.
> Myrrham aestimo esse opera bona: quoniam sicut myrrha corpus defunctorum
> insolubile servat, sic bona opera Christum crucifixum in memoria hominis
> perpetuum servant, et hominem servant in Christo. Primum ergo oportet
> Christo offerre fidem rationabilem, deinde orationem mundam, et tertio opera
> sancta. Tu ergo quando venis ad ecclesiam ad orandum Deum, munera tecum
> in manibus tuis porta: da non habentibus, et pete ab illo qui habet, ut oratio tua
> bonis operibus commendetur. Sic et in lege scriptum est: *Ne intres in conspectu
> Domini Dei tui vacuus (Exod. 23.15)*: infirma enim oratio est, quae eleemosy-
> narum virtute non est munita.[24]

Closer to Lydgate's own time is the symbolism of Euthymius (c.1142):
1) gold: *good works;* 2) frankincense: *prayer;* 3) myrrh: *mortification*:

> Sicque offer ipsi pro auro quidem purorum operum splendorem; pro thure
> autem orationem; *Dirigatur* enim *oratio mea,* inquit, *sicut incensum in
> conspectu tuo.* Pro myrrha vero affectionum mortificationem, quae magis
> conservat animae substantiam, et suave implet odore.[25]

Lines 561-588 apparently refer to some contemporary religious disturbance.
Henry V of England, for whom the poem was written, struggled with the heretical
Lollards. John Huss had been condemned and burned in 1415 after the Council
of Constance (1414) had condemned Wycliffism and "Lollardy". The very heart

---

[23]Sedatus, *Homilia de Epiphania,* Migne, *PL,* LXXII, 773.
[24]c.642f.
[25]Euthymius Ziabenus, *Evangelium Secundum Matthaeum,* Migne, *PG,* CXXIX, 146.

of Christendom had been shaken by the struggle of three men for the Papacy in the so-called "Great Western Schism" of 1409.

Lydgate or his source imply that the disturbance continues, because the lines are essentially a prayer for preservation from heresy:

And fayth with fraude is corrupte and affrayed

. . . .

For day of trouthe is turnede vnto night.

. . . .

And þus good feith is rollid up soo doun.

. . . .

Vs to preserve from all such trecherye,

. . . .

There may be little or no significance in the lines:

And trwe meaning darkyd with a skie
That we in English calle flaterye
(11.573f.)

but the suggestion of translation is strong. Lydgate used a like construction in his translation of *The Pilgrimage of the Life of Man:*

Whiche is in englische (for to seyn)
Dethe off the sowle in certeyn.
(1.18909 f.)

He may be translating merely a word or a section, but there seems to be some translation. There is no evidence of anything further unless we examine the whole section, 11.561-588, from the viewpoint of what seems to be an apparently unresolved religious disturbance. This might throw the date of composition of the hypothetical original Lydgate source back into the first decade of the century and place us in the middle of the discussion of the date of *The Life of Our Lady* and out of the limits of this study.

Aside from the above references, I have not been able to uncover Lydgate's proximate source. The similarities among all five quoted sources are quite clear and it appears that Lydgate or his source made a synthesis of all, together with others unknown to me.

The enumeration of the multiple symbolism of the gifts just given is only a small indication of the enormous task required of the author of the *Legenda Aurea* in making his summary and collation. We give it here in full to illustrate both Jacobus

de Voragine's skill in sifting gold from mountains of materials and Lydgate's talent
for purifying his sources through the distillation of poetic genius:

> "Quare autem magi hujusmodi munera obtulerunt, multiplex est ratio. Prima,
> quoniam traditio antiquorum fuit, ut dicit Remigius, ut nullus ad Deum
> vel ad regem vacans introiret, Persae autem et Chaldei talia munera
> consueverant offere. Isti enim, ut dicitur in hystoria scholastica, venerunt
> a finibus Persarum et Chaldaeorum, ubi est flumen Saba, a quo et Sabaea
> dicitur regio. Secunda quae est Bernardi, quoniam beatae virgini aurum
> obtulerunt propter inopiae sublevationem, thus propter stabuli foetorem,
> myrrham propter membrorum pueri consolidationem et malorum vermium
> expulsionem. Tertia, quoniam aurum ad tributum, thus ad sacrificium, myrrha
> ad sepulturam pertinet mortuorum. Per hae tria ergo in Christo intimatur
> regia potestas, divina majestas et humana mortalitas. Quarta, quoniam aurum
> significat dilectionem, thus orationem, myrrha carnis mortificationem. Et haec
> tria debemus Christo offere. Quinta, quoniam per hae tria significantur tria,
> quae erant in Christo, scilicet divinitas pretiosissima, anima devotissima et
> caro integra et incorrupta. Hae tria significabantur per illa tria, quae erant
> in archa. Nam virgo, quae floruit, caro Christi, quae resurrexit, Psalm: et
> refloruit caro mea etc., tabulae ubi erant scripta praecepta, anima, in qua sunt
> omnes thesauri scientiae et sapientiae Dei absconditi, manna deitas, quae habet
> omnem saporem et omnem suavitatem. Per aurum ergo, quod est pretiosius
> omnibus metallis, intelligitur divinitas pretiosissima, per thus anima devotissima,
> quia thus devotissima, quia thus significat devotionem et orationem. Psalm:
> dirigatur oratio mea etc. Per myrrham, quae conservat a corruptione, caro
> incorrupta.[26]

Lines 603-700 are a long prayer that begins with a petition for "The golde of
loue, the franke of Innocence, / And the chast myrre of clene entencion", 1.607f.
This is still another gift-symbol in the Venerable Bede sense discussed above and
from an undiscovered source.

At line 610, the prayer becomes an address to Our Lady in praise of the virtues
she displayed at the Incarnation and Epiphany and petitions for grace to imitate her
example. The prayer is marked by unusual strength, majesty, and tender affection
for Our Lady. It has the pace and clarity of originality and resembles Lydgate's
characteristic summations and prayers as he terminates a section or work.

Book Six begins with three laudatory stanzas to the humility, virginity, meekness and obedience of Mary, "the cheve chaste toure". With line 22 begins the
account of the Purification. The poet reviews the ancient law of Leviticus[27] and
Mary's obedience to it.

---

[26]*op. cit.*, p. 93.
[27]*The Holy Bible* (Vulgate).

The Life of Our Lady (VI, 22-56)

But euer lyke, as it is specifiede,
Leutici, who so can vndirstonde,
To the temple to be puryfyde
Thou mekely came thyn offryng in
    thyne hande,
Al-be þe lawe sette on þee no bonde.
For it is there makede mencion,
Touchyng the lawe of purgacion,

If a woman conceyve by a man
And haue a childe by medelyng hem
    betwene,
Þat be a male, þe lawe techith þan
Fourty dayes that she shulde be
    vnclene,
And kepe her close that no man shulde
    hir seen;
And aftir that she sholde hir offryng,
In lawe expressed, to the temple
    brynge.

But taketh hede in conclusion,
How this lawe like as ye shall fynde,
Ne was not put by condicion
Only to hem that corrupt wer by
    kynde,
Thorugh touche of man, of suche it
    made mynde.
The days noumbrede of her purgacion,
To come and make her oblacion

And bryng a lambe, the whiche in
    sacrifice
Shulde all be brent in the holy place;
And a pygeon, as lawe dothe devyse,
She shuld eke offre as for her trespase.
And than all fylthe fro hir to enchace,
She of the prest, halowede and
    sanctifiede,
Returned hom al fulli purified.

Leviticus (12:2-8)

Speak to the children of Israel, and
thou shalt say to them: If a woman
having received seed shall bear a man
child, she shall be unclean seven days,
according to the days of the separation of her flowers . . . She shall touch
no holy thing, neither shall she enter
into the sanctuary, until the days of
her purification are expired, for a son,
or for a daughter, she shall bring to
the door of the tabernacle of the testimony, a lamb of a year old for a
holocaust, and a young pigeon or a
turtle for sin, and shall deliver them
to the priest: . . . and if her hand find
not sufficiency, and she is not able to
offer a lamb, she shall take two turtles,
or two young pigeons, one for a holocaust, and another for sin; and the
priest shall pray for her, and so she
shall be cleansed.

The Life of Our Lady (cont.)

And if she had in her possession
Redely no lambe only for pou*e*rte,
Then shulde she take for her oblacion
Two turtle doves and ther-w*it*h-all go
    fre;
Or two pegyons, like as ye may se,
Levitici, wher by distynccion,
Or þis offringe is made discripcion.

In lines 57-81 Lydgate outlines the Catholic doctrine that Mary conceived and bore her child without the cooperation of man and was therefore exempt from the law. She remained a virgin before, during and after the conception and birth of the child and suffered no sickness or pain as do other women. Although she was unique for her virginity, she humbly obeyed the law. The poet then proceeds to the account of *Luke* 2:22-39

The Life of Our Lady (VI, 82-95)

And like as lawe ordeynyth by decre,
Aftir all this, of custome as she aught,
To the temple she hir offryng brought,

To yeffe ensample only of mekenesse,
To þe lawe sche mekely wolde obeye

Fro poynt to poynt—the gospell
    saythe expresse—
And on noo syde wold it not with-seye
And þouȝ þat sche bar of golde no
    keye,
To by a lambe for pouert constreynyng,
Yet she full mekely to make hir offryng

Brought two turtleȝ—as it is sayde
    afforne—
That was the offryng of pore folke
    ichone.
Whiche to the temple whan that she
    hath borne,
As custome was, she offrede hem
    a-noon.

Luke (2:22-24)

And after the days of her purification according to the law of Moses, were accomplished, they carried him to Jerusalem, to present him to the Lord . . . And to offer a sacrifice, according as it is written in the law of the Lord, a pair of turtledoves, or two young pigeons:

The description of Simeon seems taken rather from the *Pseudo-Matthaei Evangelium*[28] than from *Luke*:

The Life of Our Lady (VI, 96-113)	*Pseudo-Matthaei* (p. 81)
And aftir that olde Symeon,	Et post haec suscipiens eum in pallio
With humble herte and full bysy payne,	suo adoravit eum iterum
The childe enbrasyng in his Armeȝ twayne,	
Of his modur goodly gan him take.	et osculabatur plantas ejus. . .
Of lovyng hert and grete deuocion,	
And such a ioye of hym gan to make	
Withe-in hym-self of high affection,	
That he ne couthe, neythir by worde ne soun,	
Oute warde declare, neythir with chere ne face,	
The passyng Ioye that gan his hert enbrace.	
And he was rightfull holy and vertuouse,	. . . vir dei perfectus et iustus, nomine
This olde man, this blissede Symeon,	Symeon, annorum centum duodecim
Dredeful also and passyngly famous	
Amonge the preesteȝ to Recken hem euerychone	
That was expectant of full long a-goon,	
On the comfort and consolacion	
Of Iserael in his entencion.	

The poet then returns to the account in *Luke*:

The Life of Our Lady (VI, 113-126)	*Luke* (2:26-27)
For he had answeer of the holy goste	And he had received an answer from
In his prayer that he shoulde see,	the Holy Ghost, that he should not see
The byrthe of cryste that is of power moste	death, before he had seen the Christ of the Lord. And he came by the

---

[28]*Evangelia Apocrypha,* ed. Constantinus Tischendorf (Leipzig, 1876).

The Life of Our Lady (cont.)

And eke fro deeth þat he schal goo free
To the tyme of his Natyvyte;—
And to the day that *with* his eyne olde,
The birthe of hym that he may be-
    holde—

The whiche day is by grace come.
And for þat he bi reuelacioun
The tyme knewe, he hath the waye
    nome
To the temple *with* hygh deuocion,
To se of criste the *presentacion*;
Howe that Marye and Ioseph eke also,
The childe presente *and* her offerynge
    do.

Luke (cont.)

Spirit into the temple. And when his
parents brought in the child Jesus, to
do for him according to the custom
of the law, . . .

The borrowing reverts briefly to the *Legenda*:

The Life of Our Lady (VI, 127-133)

And for that criste was the first born
Aftir the lawe in his tendre age—
Not of levi as ye haue herde to forn,
But of Iuda comyng by lynage—
Therfore his mothir, most holy of
    visage,
Hir offringe made list not for to striue,
For hym ayeyne to pay shillyng*es*
    fyfe—

Legenda (p. 161)

Veniens autem beata virgo ad templum
filium suum obtulit et quinque siclis
redemit.

(VI, 136-203)

And Symeon, beholdyng all this case
Full stilly in his inspeccion,
For love brennyng be affeccion,
Of verrey hert sodenly abrayede,
Holdyng the childe evyn thus he
    sayde:

Luke (2:28-39)

He also took him into his arms and
blessed God, and said:

The Life of Our Lady (cont.)

O blisfull lorde, of thy high grace
If that thou lust now thou maiste me
 lete
Oute of this life in pees and rest pace;
And suffre me to dey in quyete.
For nowe to me dethe is wondir swete;
Nowe haue I seen thy helth and thy
 socour,—
And of mankynde lorde and savyour

Whiche thou hast dight affore the faceȝ
 all,
Of yche peple to make hem glad and
 light—
To lete thy grace so to erthe falle,
Through all the worlde too shew his
 bemeȝ bryght,
That may be callede for comforte of his
 light—
Of foreyne folke the reuelacion,
The glorye also and the savacion

Of Israel thy peple in speciall,
To voyde hem oute of all derkenesse.
And Marye full mekely listenyth all,
And gan merveyle *with* grete
 avysenesse
Of the wordes that he gan expresse;
And Iosephe eke gan to wondir also.
And Symeon he*m* blessynge bothe two,

Spake to Marye and seyde in audience:
By-holde and se in thyn inspection,
How he is put in ruyne and offence
Of many one here in his region;
And to some in resurexion
That shall releve, thorugh his myghty
 grace.
And thorugh thy sawle shall a sharpe
 sworde pace.

Luke (cont.)

Now thou dost dismiss thy servant,
O Lord according to thy word in
peace; Because my eyes have seen thy
salvation, Which thou hast prepared
before the face of all peoples; A light
to the revelation of the Gentiles, and
the story of thy people Israel.

And his father and mother were won-
dering at those things which were
spoken concerning him. And Simeon
blessed them, and said to Mary his
mother: Behold this child is set for
the fall, and for the resurrection of

many in Israel, and for a sign which
shall be contradicted; and thy own
soul a sword shall pierce.

The Life of Our Lady (cont.)

Of hertely woo to see his passion—
That passyngly shall bitt*er* be and
    fell—
To opyn herteʒ by confession
Her synfull thoughteʒ opynly to tell.
And Anna than, the doughter of
    phanuell,—
Born of the trybe and of the kynrede
Called Aser, sothely as I rede,

That was that day Ronne fer in age,—
Whiche in the temple by contynuaunce,
Sole by her self oute of maryage,
Lay niʒt *and* day in fastnyge *and*
    penau*n*ce,
In wyddowe abyte sad of contena*u*nce.
And in prayer was hir bysy cure,
Which in that hour of grace or
    aventure,

Whan criste was ther w*ith* his mother
    dere
In the tyme of his oblacioun—
This Anna cam, demure and sad of
    chere,
And vnto hym w*ith* grete deuocion,
Whan she hym sawe, fel on knees
    dou*n*,
Recomfortede of all her olde smerte,
Hym honouryng w*ith* all hir hole herte.

Sayde opynly that all myghten here:
Bethe m*y*rry and light in yo*ur*
    entencion,
And eu*ery* man be glad and of goode
    chere,
For nowe is borne for our savacion,
He that shall make our Redempcion.
This yonge childe, blissed mot he be,
That me hathe grauntede his face for
    to se.

Luke (cont.)

that out of many hearts thought may
be revealed. And there was one Anna,
a prophetess, the daughter of Phanuel,
of the tribe of Aser; she was far advanced in years and had lived with
her husband seven years from her

virginity, and she was a widow until
four score and four years; who departed not from the temple by fastings
and prayer serving night and day.
Now she, at the same hour, coming
in, confessed to the Lord; and spoke
of him to all that looked for the redemption of Israel.

The Life of Our Lady (cont.)

And then in sothe whan eu*er*y thyng
    was dou*n*
Aftir the lawe wi*th*outen excepcion,
And that Anna and holy Symeon
Had of this childe made declaracion—
As ye haue herde in conclusion—
The childe and Ioseph and this mayde
    free,
Reto*ur*nede home into galelee.

And after they had performed all
things according to the law of the
Lord, they returned into Galilee,

The treatment of the "propretees of the Turtle" is from Venerable Bede, Fulgentius and what is apparently another source I have not been able to trace. The unity and coherence of the whole section seems to indicate a single source with attributions traceable to Bede and Fulgentius. Lydgate uses the narrative and the symbolism of the turtle to exhort his readers to a holy observance of the feast of the Purification. There is a small mistranslation in lines 209-210: "And offre a turtil, firste of Innocence,/ And a dove next for his offence;" from Bede's . . . "ut haec legitime Domino valeant consecrari, ovem necesse est innocentiae, et turturem pariter sive columbam compunctionis offerat."

The Life of Our Lady (VI, 204-210)

Nowe as me semythe in this high ferre
That named is the puryficacioun,
Eu*er*y man aught to be myrry;
And withe gode hert and hole
    entencion,
Deuoutely bryng his oblacion.
And offre a turtil, firste of Innocence,
And a dove next for his offence;

Venerable Bede (p. 342)

. . . ut haec legitime Domine valeant consecrari, ovem necesse est innocentiae, et turturem pariter sive columbam compunctionis offerat.

(VI, 211-224)

For grete mysterye is in bothe
    tweyne:
The tone com*m*endyde for his chastite,
And that other, if I shall not feyne,
Is symple and meke wi*th*oute cruelte;

Fulgentius (p. 667)[29]

In columba enim caritas agnoscitur, in turture castitas invenitur. Turtur namque intemeratam servat uni viro fidem; columba vero aliarum cohabitantium non deserit unitatem.

---

[29]Sancti Fulgentii, *Opera Omnia*, Migne, *PL*, LXV.

The Life of Our Lady (cont.)   *Fulgentius* (cont.)

The turtle prysede of trouthe and
   honeste,
And the dove hathe kyndely excellence
Of mekenesse and hertely pacience.

And who that wol his offrying make
   a-right,
He may not fayle noon of bothe twoo:
Fyrste shyne in clennes with his chaste
   light
As the Turtle, and ther with also,
Liche the dove, bothe in wele and woo,
His hert daunt so by a-temperaunce
To voyde rancour and plant in
   sufferaunce.

Sed nulla potest esse accepta Deo
mortificationis oblatio, in quibus non
fuerit verae caritatis concordia. Pro-
inde non sine causa sacrificium . . .
ex turturibus et columbis fuisse narratur.

          (VI, 225-238)   *Venerable Bede* (p. 345)

And as the Turtle by contemplatyffe
For synne soroweth with
   waymentyng,—
Only for loue of thilke eternall lyfe
That lastythe aye and may haue no
   endyng—
And as the birde sheweth the commyng
Of grene ver with fresshe buddeʒ
   newe,
Ryght so of vertu with floures fayre
   of hewe.

He must ensample of the Turtle take,
And be well ware that he not varye
But life sool whan he hathe lost his
   make;
And in prayer be also solytarye,
And loke all waye that he not ne tarye
On noo caren of no flesshely hede.
And withe all this to take also hede,

Turtur vero qui singularitate gaudet,
adeo ut si conjugem casu perdiderit,
solus exinde permaneat, speculative
vitae culmina denuntiat, quia et pau-
corum est ista virtus, et his singillatim
attributa.

Lines 239-308 could readily be Lydgate's own homily on the Latin stanza of lines 295-301. They have escaped my source-tracing except for two possible Bede borrowings and certainly one from the *Legenda,* the Latin stanza. In the notes, I have listed a number of biblical and natural history analogues.

The Life of Our Lady (VI, 260-273)

And as a dove w*ith* hir eyne meke,—
Of kynde espyeth a-myddes the
    Ryu*ere*
The haukes shadowe when he dothe
    her seke,
And flieth a way or he come eny nere—
Right so must he, w*ith* perfyte eyne
    clere,
A-myd the waters full of woo and
    stryfe,
In the wawes of this mortall lyfe

Venerable Bede (p. 343)

Sicut enim columbae super fluenta residere delectantur, ut accipitris adventum umbrae cursu per aquas praevidere simul et evadere queant; sic profecto, sic animae pauperum spiritu

The dedely shade of the fynde
    eschewe—
That waytyth hym with snares large
    and huge
And to þe deeth eu*ere* doith him
    purswe
To trappe hym here in this deluge—
And like a dove fle to his refuge
By grace only if he may escape,
Or dethe be-tray hym w*ith* his soden
    Rape.

fluctus saeculi mente transcendentes, quo plura in hac Babylone qua suis gemitibus pascuntur, maligni hostis exempla conspiciunt, eo crebriores ad aeterna sui desiderii pennas sustollunt.

(VI, 288-301)

And sothely thanne, ther is no more
    to seyne,
Whan his offryng and oblacion
Is iustely made to god of bothe tweyne,
It is acceptede of more deuocion.
And for to make a shorte discripcion
Of the Turtle and the dove₃ kynde,
Reed here these verses and ye shall it
    fynde:

Legenda (p. 161)

Proprietates turturis habentibus his versibus:

The Life of Our Lady (cont.)

Alta petit Turtur cantando gemit
  veniens ver
Nunciat et caste viuit solus*que* moratur
Pullos nocte fouet morticinium quo*que*
  fugit

Grana legat volitat sociata cadaucra
  vitat
Felle caret plangit socium *que per*
  oscula
Petra dat huic nidu*m* fugit hostem in
  flumine visu*m*
Rostro non ledit geminos pullos bene
  nutrit.[30]

Venerable Bede (cont.)

(the same)

       vivit

fovet que (for quoque)

Proprietates vero columbae his versibus notantur:

       cadavera

(lacks "que")

(the same)

     laedit

Except for two passages from John Beleth[31] the matter of lines 309-434 is directly from the *Legenda*. The author of the *Legenda* paraphrases one of his own sources, Innocent III, which I give here in full:

"Gentiles enim Februarium mensem inferis dedicaverint, eo quod sicut ipsi putabant, sed errabant, in principio ejus mensis Prosperina rapta fuerat a Plutone; quam quia mater ejus Ceres facibus accensis, in Ethan tota nocte per Siciliam quaesisse credebatur, et ipsi ad commemorationem ipsius, facibus accensis, in principio mensis urbem de nocte lustrabant. Unde festum illud appelabatur Amburbale. Cum autem sancti Patres consuetudinem istam non possent penitus exstirpare, constituerunt, ut in honore beatae Virginis Mariae cereos portarent accensos et sic quod prius fiebat ad honorem Cereis, modo fit ad honorem Virginis.[32]

The Life of Our Lady (VI, 309-434)

Some tyme, when Rome thorough his
  high Renou*n*
Was most flouryng in power and in
  myght,
Eu*er*y fifte ʒeere bi reuolucyoun,
In februarie vpon the first nyght,

Legenda (p. 163-165)

Romani enim olim in calendis Februarii ad honorem Februae matris
Martis, qui erat Deus belli, urbem de
quinto in quintum annum cum cereis
et facibus

---

[30]Translation: The singing turtle dove seeks high places, announces the coming of spring; and lives chastely and dwells alone. At night it protects its young and puts to flight harmful things. It picks up grains, flies and avoids corpses banded together. It lacks gall and touches its mate with kisses. It finds its rest in rocks. It flees the enemy seen in the water. It does not harm with its beak; it well protects its kindred offspring.
[31]Jehan Beleth, *Rationale Divinorum Officiorum*, Migne, *PL*, CCII.
[32]Innocentius Papa III, "Sermo XII in Purificatione S. Mariae", Migne, *PL*, CCXVII, 510.

The Life of Our Lady (cont.)

Eche man and childe with a tapre
    light,
Went in the Cyte tweyne and tweyne
    a paas[33]
Vn to a temple which þat sacrid was

To februa of olde fundacion—
Þat modir was to mars omnipotent—
In whose honoure this procession
Ordenede was by grete avysement.
At eche lustre wenyng in her entent,
That hir power and grete worthynesse
Perferryde was, thorough helpe of this
    godesse,

From all assaute of euery aduersarie—
Supposyng fully in her opynyon,
That she fortune made debonayre
For to susteyne the honour of her
    towne,
And thorough her helpe and mediacion,
That myghty mars to encrece her
    glorye,
In all conquest yeff to hem victorye.

For whiche cause thorugh oute the
    cyte,
As ye haue harde of high and lowe
    estate,
Was first ordeynede this solempnyte
In the Temple that was consecrate
To februa, the goddesse fortunate,
Thorough helpe of whome they were
    victoryous.
And so this custum supersticious,

Legenda (cont.)

tota nocte illustrabant, ut filius suus
iis victoriam de inimicis concederet,
cujus matrem tam solemniter honora-
rent, et illud spatium

dicebatur lustrum.

Romani etiam in Februario sacrifica-
bant Februo, id est Plutoni et castris
Diis infernalibus et hoc pro animabus
antecessorum suorum, ut ergo propi-
tiarentur eorum,

---

[33]Beleth, *op. cit.*, c.86: "Erat enim antiquitus Romae consuetudo, ut circa hoc tempus in principio Februarii urbem lustrarent, eam ambiendo cum suis processionibus gestantes singuli candelas ardentes, et vocabatur illud amburbale."

The Life of Our Lady (cont.)

In Rome towne, as my auctour seythe,
Observed was long and many a day.
Yet aftir that they turnede to the
    faythe,
But euere in one this Ryte thay kept
    alway—
For olde custome is harde to putte
    away,
And vsage grevythe folkeȝ full sore
To do a-way that thei haue kepte of
    yore.

But at the laste Pope Sergius,
Of the peple seyng this erroure,
And that the custome was full perilous,
Dyd his devour and also his laboure,
This ryte to chaunge into the honoure
Of our lady, so that this high feste,
Fro the highest doun to the leste,
Euery man and woman in her honde
To the Temple shulde a tapre bryng,
Þoruȝ out þe worlde in euery manere
    londe;
And ther with all make her offryng,
Aftir the gospell the presteȝ hand
    kyssyng,—
With light solempne that all mighten
    sene,—
In honour oonly of þe heuenly quene
That best may be our mediatrice
To hir son that is with-oute fayle,
Bothe lorde and kyng, and she
    Emperatrice
Of londe, of see, of pees *and* of batayle,
Withouten whome no conquest may
    avayle,

Legenda (cont.)

ideo et iis solemnes hostias offerebant
et tota nocte eorum, laudibus insis-
tentes cum cereis et accensis facibus
vigilabant . . . Et quoniam difficile

relinquere, christiani de gentibus ad
fidem conversi difficile poterant relinquere hujusmodi consuetudines pa-
ganorum ideoque Sergius papa hanc
consuetudinem in melius commutavit,
ut scilicet christiani ad honorem sanctae
matris domini omni anno in hac die
totum mundum cum accensis candelis
et benedictis cereis illustrarent, ut
solemnitas quidem staret, sed alia in-
tentione fieret.

The Life of Our Lady (cont.)   *Legenda* (cont.)

For she hath power more in
   sothefastnesse,
Then februa of Rome the goddesse.

And thus this ryte was vtterly
   Refusede
By Sergius, as ye haue herde
   devysse,—
That was afforne of hem of Rome vsede
Full many a day in her paynym wyse
Whom to sue al cristen must dispise—
And of candeles whan this ryte gan
   passe,
Came the name firste of Candelmasse.

This feste also of full long a-gone,   Tertio propter repraesentandam hodi-
The name toke of the procession—   ernam processionem. Nam Maria et
Made of Anna and holy Symeon,   Joseph et Symeon et Anna hodie
When thay hym mette with grete   honorabilem processionem fecerunt[34]
   deuocion,
Brought to the Temple to his oblacion
As was the lawe custom *and* vsaunnce
Of holy chirche for a remembraunce—

Observed furthe yet fro yere to yere   et puerum Jesum in templum praesent-
Of februarye on the first day,   averunt. Sic et nos processionem
Withe sacrede light vpon tapers clere—   facimus et cereum accensum, per quem
Shynyng as bright as phebus dothe in   significatur Jesus, in manibus bajula-
   may,   mus,
Whan the peple in what thay can or
   may,
Full Redy ben of on entencion
To make in fygure a *p*resentacion

Of criste Ih*e*su w*ith* all her full myght,   et usque in ecclesias deferimus. Tria
Sygnyfyede, who so can take hede,   enim sunt in cera:

---

[34]Beleth, *op. cit.*, c.86: Ϋπαντη Domini ideo dicitur hoc festum, quod Simeon atque
Anna prophetissa Christo venerint obviam, cum a suis parentibus afferretur in templum ut
praesentaretur. Ϋπαντη enim oblatio sive praesentatio dicta est."

The Life of Our Lady (cont.)

Withe the tapre that we offre light:
For firste the wax betokenyth his
    manhede,
The weyke his soule, the fyre his
    godhede;
And as the wax is made and wrought
    of newe,—
Thorough small bees of floures freeshe
    of hewe,
Thorughe clennesse only and diligent
    labo*ur*
Of blossomes gedrede and to the hyve
    brought—
So c*r*istes manhode grewe oute of a
    floure,
Whose fresshe beaute of coloure fadyth
    nought;
For of a mayde clene in will and
    thought—
Like as wax of floures soote and glade
Is tried out *and* doith hem not to
    fade—
So criste Ih*es*u, conservyng her
    clennesse,
His manhode toke of a mayden **free,**
She standyng hole flouryng in
    fayrenesse
Withe all the fresshenesse of **virgynte.**
And as a tapre is one to gyder and
    three,
So thilke lorde, that is bothe three and
    one,
Toke flesshe and blode to **save vs**
    eu*e*rycheone,

Of a mayde whiche **this day fro**
    Bedlem,

Legenda (cont.)

lychnus, cera et ignis. Per hae signifi-
cantur tria, quae fuerunt in Christo,
nam tria significant.
Carnem Christi, quae nota est Maria
virgine sine corruptione carnis, sicut
apes ceram gignunt sine alterutrum
commixtione, lychnus in cera latens
significant animam
candidissimam in carne latentem, ignis
vero sine lumen significant divinitatem,
quia Deus noster ignis consumens est.

Quarto, propter instructionem nostram. In hoc enim instruimur, quo si

The Life of Our Lady (cont.)

Mekely went to be puryfyede
To the temple in Iherusalem,—
As here-to-forne it is specifiede,—
In whose hono*ur* this feste is
    magnyfede
Of all cristen w*ith* fresshe tapers shene,
To signyfye, who that will be clene,

Moste offre a tapre to-gyder made of
    thre:
Faythe and werke and trwe entencion;
W*ith* oute partyng or dyvysion,
Neythir his offryng ne oblacion—
How fayre outewarde playnely that it
    seme—
To god above it may neu*ere* cueme.

For þou3 his tapre brene bri3te as day
And environ make his light to shade,
If werke fro faythe proloynede be
    away
And trwe entent followe not the dede,
Fare well his gwerdon, his meryte and
    his mede,
For whan these thre be not knytte in
    one
He is not able to offryng for to gone.

For if these thre to-gyder be not
    meynt—
Faith, werke *and* ho*ol* intencioun
His offryng farythe but as a tapre
    queynt
That yefethe no light ne bryghtnesse
    envyron,
Full derke and dede fro all deuocion.
His offryng is but if these ilke thre
Ben knytte in one thorough p*er*fyte
    vnyte.

Legenda (cont.)

volumus ante Deum esse purificati et
mundi,

tria in nobis habere scilicet fidem
veram, actionem beatam, intentionem
rectam.

Nam candela in manu accensa est fides
cum operatione bona et sicut candela
sine lumine dicitur esse mortua et
lumen per sese sine candela non lucet,

sed mortuum esse videtur, sic et operatio sine fide et fides sine bono opere
mortua esse dicitur. Lychnus autem
intus in cera occultatus est intentio
recta . . .

The closing lines 435-462 are a prayer to Christ for mercy for mankind in honor of Mary whose feast celebrates her meekness in obeying the laws of purification and which end with a supplication to Mary that she to her servants "shelde and socoure be,/ To kepe and save from all aduersyte." (1.461f.).

To sum up, it appears that in Books V and VI Lydgate 1) used the *Legenda Aurea* as his basic source and added several of his own; or 2) had access to a "catena aurea" type source, commonly used in the Middle Ages and still the biblical commentators' standard method of exegesis. In this method the commentator analyzes each verse or part of a verse and then lists outstanding authorities in support of his conclusions.

In the background, of course, is that hypothetical French source[35] which could very well have been a French "catena aurea" still unknown to us. Considering the great volume of writing that Lydgate was commissioned to do nearly all his life, it is not likely that he had the time to research a "catena aurea" of his own for a life of Our Lady. The great number of authorities and sources used both in Books V and VI and in the earlier books of *The Life of Our Lady,* the fact that these authorities appear in the *Legenda Aurea,* the *Historia Scholastica* and in others such as St. Thomas Aquinas' *Catena Aurea,*[36] constrains us to conclude that Lydgate used some single source and did not make an independent selection.

[35]Klinefelter, "That there may be a single source, possibly French, becomes even more probable when we note the various sources for large portions of Books III-IV of the poem", (3. The Sources, Books I and II, p. 83.)

[36]S. Thomas Aquinatis, *Catena Aurea* (Avenna, 1851), 7v.

4. THE METRICAL STRUCTURE

The *Life of Our Lady* is written in rime royal, with the sequence of rhymes ababbcc. The five-stress lines may be scanned according to Professor Schipper's division of sixteen varieties[1] or Dr. Schick's five-type division.[2]

Using the simpler Schick classification, the lines are defined and exemplified as follows:

Type A. "The regular type, presenting five iambics, to which, as to the other types, at the end an extra-syllable may be added. There is usually a well-defined caesura after the second foot, but not always."

According to my scansion, this type is the dominant line in the poem, occurring in more than 50 per cent of the lines: Book I, in 526 out of 889 lines; Book II, in 926 out of 1669 lines; Book III, in 1018 out of 1806 lines; Book IV, in 224 out of 406 lines; Book V, in 403 out of 700 lines; Book VI, in 217 out of 455 lines.

Type B. "Lines with the trochaic caesura, built like the preceding, but with an extra-syllable before the caesura." The occurrence is as follows: Book I, 209 lines; Book II, 475 lines; Book III, 467 lines; Book IV, 116 lines; Book V, 167 lines; Book VI, 118 lines. The incidence is approximately 25 per cent.

Type C. "The peculiarly Lydgatian type, in which the thesis is wanting in the caesura, so that two accented syllables clash together," and the occurrence is as follows: Book I, 84 lines; Book II, 182 lines; Book III, 136 lines; Book IV, 29 lines; Book V, 50 lines; Book VI, 47 lines. The incidence is about 9 per cent.

Type D. "The acephalous or headless line, in which the first syllable has been cut off, thus leaving a monosyllabic first measure," and the occurrence is as follows: Book I, 61 lines; Book II, 82 lines; Book III, 159 lines; Book IV, 22 lines; Book V, 77 lines; Book VI, 67 lines. The incidence is about 8 per cent.

Type E. "Lines with trisyllabic first measure," and the occurrence is as follows: Book I, 9 lines; Book II, 4 lines; Book III, 26 lines; Book IV, 15 lines; Book V, 3 lines; Book VI, 6 lines. The incidence is less than 1 per cent.

The entire poem totals are as follows:

```
Type A lines:  3314
Type B lines:  1552
Type C lines:   528
Type D lines:   468
Type E lines:    63
```

[1]Jacob Schipper, *A History of English Versification* (Oxford, 1910), p. 210.
[2]J. Schick, *Lydgate's Temple of Glas* (1891; EETSES, 60), p. lvii-lx.

Lydgate frequently falls back into the octosyllabic line of four stresses and the occurrences are copious enough to enumerate. The six-stress line, though less frequent, will also be noted:

Four-stress lines:

> Book I, 49 times: 26, 43, 44, 87, 96, 108, 122, 130, 161, 187, 198, 252, 253, 261, 262, 267, 278, 305, 316, 326, 420, 431, 452, 550, 551, 576, 607, 624, 625, 628, 645, 660, 661, 663, 665, 681, 682, 688, 696, 700, 747, 753, 764, 788, 789, 793, 808, 852, 881.

> Book II, 94 times: 47, 48, 53, 114, 119, 169, 183, 220, 221, 225, 254, 276, 277, 289, 292, 383, 385, 405, 498, 505, 548, 585, 591, 627, 647, 655, 656, 668, 669, 711, 724, 728, 738, 740, 754, 761, 782, 793, 803, 805, 819, 821, 828, 830, 835, 839, 847, 853, 854, 856, 904, 921, 955, 972, 1024, 1073, 1095, 1105, 1181, 1189, 1210, 1216, 1246, 1252, 1271, 1286, 1289, 1296, 1311, 1315, 1322, 1325, 1384, 1385, 1414, 1415, 1424, 1447, 1468, 1479, 1506, 1520 1578, 1584, 1591, 1598, 1616, 1620, 1622, 1644, 1663.

> Book III, 150 times: 44, 66, 79, 86, 93, 129, 131, 148, 158, 166, 173, 180, 181, 198, 213, 216, 217, 228, 247, 286, 294, 298, 299, 301, 303, 306, 309, 314, 318, 322, 326, 330, 333, 341, 349, 353, 355, 369, 370, 383, 392, 407, 409, 411, 433, 438, 442, 452, 455, 473, 513, 517, 518, 521, 522, 523, 533, 537, 540, 546, 562, 565, 567, 568, 570, 594, 614, 644, 654, 656, 658, 659, 664, 666, 671, 676, 699, 705, 711, 727, 734, 744, 758, 817, 826, 839, 841, 845, 850, 853, 857, 870, 879, 897, 905, 906, 918, 957, 970, 984, 986, 1012, 1016, 1019, 1070, 1084, 1103, 1106, 1111, 1112, 1140, 1148, 1152, 1163, 1279, 1286, 1300, 1305, 1350, 1371, 1381, 1383, 1388, 1391, 1435, 1446, 1463, 1465, 1470, 1476, 1478, 1531, 1533, 1543, 1567, 1610, 1616, 1624, 1626, 1631, 1634, 1647, 1661, 1666, 1676, 1682, 1717, 1766, 1767.

> Book IV, 8 times: 19, 24, 101, 130, 345, 351, 381, 402.

> Book V, 33 times: 22, 24, 25, 38, 63, 108, 129, 184, 210, 220, 249, 284, 297, 310, 386, 397, 398, 401, 426, 428, 431, 447, 448, 492, 498, 502, 519, 523, 525, 530, 616, 664.

> Book VI, 17 times: 37, 65, 96, 114, 120, 127, 137, 141, 239, 270, 342, 344, 352, 354, 421, 443, 452.

Six-stress lines:

> Book I, 13 times: 27, 28, 68, 97, 176, 222, 234, 581, 804, 859, 867, 868, 883.

> Book II, 27 times: 106, 108, 202, 203, 335, 414, 538, 570, 683, 684, 687, 688, 694, 695, 733, 928, 929, 961, 962, 1194, 1276, 1442, 1495, 1496, 1550, 1612.

Book III, 14 times: 196, 308, 339, 424, 1026, 1043, 1165, 1227, 1396, 1540, 1548, 1585, 1607, 1614.

Book IV, 1 time: 210.

Book V, 16 times: 103, 271, 274, 276, 278, 292, 296, 360, 366, 379, 407, 414, 416, 455, 532, 543.

Book VI, 5 times: 7, 168, 235, 269, 311.

These frequent deviations from the decasyllabic line may be explained by a) carelessness; b) design; c) natural relief from the tension of the five-beat measure. Lichlider's theory seems plausible: "The decasyllabic line, from the standpoint of grouping, is distinctly a-rhythmic and an a-rhythmic series is preserved only with difficulty."[3]

Dr. Bergen issues a further caution:

"The violent prejudice which has occasionally been exhibited against Lydgate's metre seems to have had its origin in poor texts or editions printed from only one text, which, even when good, is no more than human—every copyist like every editor has his personal equation—and Lydgate's own words to the effect that he 'took no heed neither of short nor long'."[4]

To forge his measures and give them continuity, Lydgate made liberal use of elision, syncope, synizesis, diaresis and the double-thesis:

Elision

Book I, 24 times: 10, 44, 77, 104, 122, 124, 135, 169, 301, 308, 351, 380 383, 417, 482, 494, 515, 519, 522, 544, 638, 788, 835, 866.

Book II, 39 times: 10, 14, 48, 107, 150, 151, 177, 216, 265, 420, 429, 590, 704, 736, 796, 909, 926, 979, 1008, 1010, 1039, 1044, 1070, 1089, 1153, 1154, 1167, 1207, 1210, 1220, 1236, 1269, 1290, 1308, 1326, 1369, 1484, 1540, 1599.

Book III, 40 times: 11, 23, 25, 61, 75, 102, 123, 158, 164, 238, 242, 331, 355, 389, 442, 446, 452, 515, 517, 630, 734, 746, 832, 909, 958, 962, 980, 995, 1187, 1197, 1201, 1249, 1354, 1355, 1387, 1402, 1415, 1572, 1620.

Book IV, 2 times: 107, 142.

Book V, 28 times: 14, 17, 18, 41, 75, 121, 141, 171, 202, 308, 338, 346, 347, 348, 352, 391, 404, 473, 478, 489, 517, 530, 610, 611, 612, 658, 666.

---

[3]Albert H. Lichlider, *Chapters on the Metric of the Chaucerian Tradition* (Baltimore, 1910), p. 129.

[4]Henry Bergen, *Lydgate's Troy Book* (1906; EETSES, 97), Part I, p. xvi.

Book VI, 12 times: 1, 134, 137, 191, 231, 277, 323, 338, 340, 368, 396, 436.

Syncope.

Book I, 117 times: 2, 9, 12, 21, 24, 27, 28, 32, 35, 44, 69, 73, 102, 122, 135, 143, 146, 177, 184, 186, 189, 214, 233, 235, 237, 253, 259, 261, 268, 272, 274, 278, 290, 294, 295, 299, 333, 344, 348, 349, 350, 358, 382, 383, 384, 385, 393, 395, 404, 407, 411, 414, 417, 420, 423, 424, 425, 438, 443, 448, 452, 453, 465, 468, 469, 476, 482, 494, 520, 523, 524, 526, 529, 541, 549, 556, 561, 577, 598, 602, 607, 612, 617, 619, 628, 654, 656, 668, 669, 671, 674, 677, 679, 687, 688, 701, 709, 712, 723, 733, 736, 764, 767, 779, 781, 782, 786, 805, 824, 828, 831, 845, 856, 860, 861, 869, 889.

Book II, 209 times: 4, 8, 14, 22, 35, 40, 43, 54, 55, 65, 72, 74, 75, 77, 95, 99, 109, 114, 115, 120, 122, 123, 133, 142, 147, 150, 151, 157, 172, 174, 212, 240, 254, 261, 265, 287, 295, 303, 317, 318, 319, 323, 331, 338, 339, 344, 345, 346, 349, 350, 355, 362, 367, 395, 401, 405, 407, 412, 429, 431, 433, 444, 446, 451, 452, 464, 467, 469, 477, 491, 492, 493, 496, 498, 500, 506, 537, 561, 578, 587, 596, 601, 603, 605, 782, 793, 794, 800, 813, 846, 876, 881, 899, 900, 914, 922, 924, 925, 929, 931, 943, 969, 983, 1002, 1009, 1010, 1017, 1019, 1020, 1024, 1027, 1029, 1031, 1045, 1046, 1053, 1072, 1075, 1077, 1080, 1089, 1096, 1098, 1132, 1139, 1146, 1153, 1157, 1166, 1175, 1177, 1182, 1186, 1187, 1190, 1192, 1195, 1210, 1222, 1226, 1228, 1237, 1257, 1261, 1270, 1283, 1290, 1291, 1297, 1318, 1332, 1333, 1339, 1359, 1370, 1373, 1374, 1376, 1381, 1383, 1394, 1400, 1403, 1416, 1418, 1419, 1436, 1442, 1443, 1461, 1482, 1484, 1501, 1510, 1531, 1536, 1553, 1555, 1562, 1564, 1577, 1582, 1583, 1588, 1593, 1600, 1608, 1620, 1637, 1641, 1642, 1644, 1657.

Book III, 175 times: 27, 44, 48, 54, 66, 75, 95, 129, 158, 159, 170, 173, 189, 191, 193, 209, 217, 218, 230, 233, 264, 281, 305, 306, 309, 326, 349, 368, 422, 445, 449, 451, 467, 473, 534, 540, 541, 560, 615, 617, 636, 640, 656, 666, 671, 675, 686, 705, 727, 729, 741, 743, 744, 746, 753, 758, 774, 775, 787, 788, 792, 793, 832, 839, 841, 853, 856, 860, 869, 879, 884, 885, 887, 894, 902, 909, 912, 926, 935, 953, 955, 961, 970, 983, 984, 990, 991, 992, 1001, 1011, 1014, 1015, 1023, 1025, 1027, 1030, 1031, 1036, 1037, 1040, 1050, 1052, 1061, 1063, 1065, 1068, 1076, 1084, 1090, 1094, 1098, 1106, 1122,

1157, 1159, 1175, 1200, 1209, 1210, 1211, 1227, 1230, 1256, 1262, 1263, 1264, 1270, 1271, 1283, 1295, 1304, 1312, 1315, 1321, 1322, 1326, 1335, 1348, 1372, 1376, 1382, 1392, 1397, 1420, 1439, 1446, 1457, 1465, 1479, 1484, 1490, 1494, 1498, 1508, 1509, 1510, 1512, 1545, 1565, 1569, 1583, 1627, 1631, 1658, 1690, 1692, 1711, 1726, 1733, 1767, 1771, 1782, 1783.

Book IV, 48 times: 20, 28, 45, 55, 66, 67, 79, 83, 87, 90, 97, 116, 135, 140, 145, 150, 158, 160, 178, 180, 193, 217, 222, 238, 245, 246, 248, 252, 259, 262, 270, 274, 276, 279, 282, 285, 294, 295, 301, 313, 314, 347, 372, 374, 381, 394, 395, 398.

Book V, 49 times: 32, 61, 82, 122, 123, 129, 156, 157, 162, 176, 232, 248, 276, 294, 296, 303 305, 315, 318, 328, 331, 333, 337, 345, 346, 355, 377, 384, 385, 386, 388, 402, 428, 430, 438, 546, 549, 553, 556, 571, 591 596, 599, 603, 623, 627, 657, 683, 700.

Book VI, 43 times: 8, 13, 17, 21, 51, 60, 73, 74, 76, 109, 139, 155, 173, 192, 197, 206, 209, 211, 214, 223, 255, 269, 281, 303, 311, 323, 340, 351, 353, 357, 376, 383, 389, 404, 406, 414, 420, 421, 427, 448, 455.

Synizesis

Book I, 5 times: 22, 287, 550, 551, 871.

Book II, 8 times: 136, 168, 375, 376, 542, 954, 1017, 1286.

Book III, 6 times: 58, 68, 231, 954, 1010, 1073.

Book IV, 3 times: 77, 313, 373.

Book V, 2 times: 97, 312.

Book VI, 3 times: 198, 436, 449.

Diaresis: pees II 330; uncloos III 133; knees III 417; cloos III 532; dool III 591; pees III 619, 768, 1101; see III 1651; knees V 89; hie V 584; pees VI 143; knees VI 187.

Double-thesis

Book I, 24 times: 9, 47, 105, 137, 144, 147, 164, 165, 166, 190, 201, 270, 377, 392, 403, 514, 559, 600, 670, 675, 696, 699, 720, 813.

Book II, 53 times: 17, 79, 137, 146, 168, 175, 210, 216, 238, 352, 404, 408, 531, 541, 542, 545, 546, 555, 556, 560, 593, 594, 601, 608, 622, 633, 658, 779, 816, 858, 885, 957, 1019, 1037, 1040, 1114, 1128, 1278, 1281, 1310, 1388, 1426, 1440, 1445, 1469, 1483, 1535, 1559, 1560, 1568, 1648.

Book III, 13 times: 74, 87, 553, 660, 838, 870, 882, 884, 895, 915, 945, 980, 1008.

Book IV, does not occur.

Book V, 22 times: 21, 66, 129, 154, 186, 236, 336, 374, 417, 423, **436,** 466, 482, 504, 507, 510, 536, 545, 549, 578, 624, 636.

Book VI, 17 times: 75, 80, 131, 254, 261, 287, 291, 350, 355, 380, **387,** 393, 394, 399, 425, 430.

The rime scheme is regular throughout in 7-line stanzas ababbcc, **except for** lines 981-1060 of Book II, which rime ababbcbc in 8-line stanzas.

It does not seem useful to enter into the debate on whether the very frequent final -e in the fifth foot should be sounded and hence qualify the line as "waistless" or "double-waistless", or whether it should be considered mute. The latter seems the more plausible on the ground that the sounded -e would multiply the complexity of an already intricate metrical system. Professor Schipper has seven varieties among his basic sixteen types of rime royal.[5]

Professor Skeat may have written the last word about this point when he observed:

"The addition of a weak syllable at the end of a line is easily explained. It is because, at this point, the poet is FREE; that is, the pause that naturally occurs there enables him to insert an additional syllable with ease. Shakespeare did not hesitate even to add *two* syllables there, if he was so minded; as in Rich III, iii 6.9:— 'Untainted, unexamined, free, at liberty.' "[6]

Examples of loose rhyme are found as follows:

Book	I, ll.	155,	157: sprynge	: werkeng
	ll,	260,	262: goyth	: wrothe
	ll.	534,	536: prayers	: desyres
Book	II, ll.	118,	119: requyre	: prayer
	ll.	160,	161: releve	: meove
	ll.	261,	263: blame	: stayne
	ll.	335,	336: clene	: ameyn
	ll.	337,	339: dawngerles	: pees
	ll.	568,	570: breght	: sight
	ll.	687,	689: vultures	: lees
	ll.	694,	696: naturell	: small
	ll.	730,	732: clere	: fyre
	ll.	1022,	1024: knawe	: lowe

[5]*op. cit.,* p. 210.
[6]Walter W. Skeat, *The Complete Works of Geoffrey Chaucer* (Oxford, 1894), VI, **xc.**

Book III, ll.	127,	129: Iherusalem	: beame
	ll. 142,	144: towne	: convocacion
	ll. 170,	172: also	: goo
	ll. 176,	178: couertly	: sodenly
	ll. 193,	194: trayne	: disdeyne
	ll. 205,	207: Reame	: Ierusalem
	ll. 316,	318: delyte	: lyte
	ll. 333,	334: question	: adoune
	ll. 380,	382: hede	: womanhede
	ll. 443,	445: Iasper	: dar
	ll. 485,	487: Iohn	: Iourdan
	ll. 510,	511: lye	: theophane
Book IV, ll.	23,	25: vndirstonde	: hande
	ll. 302,	304: lesse	: candilmasse
	ll. 457,	459: lesse	: asse

Internal rhyme is rare and appears only in the following cases:

Is now fro me chased clene a waye II 1307
So young, so fayre, in a golden spere V 96
Most passyngly vpon hym to see V 317
When criste was ther with his mother dere VI 183
Dyd his devour and also his laboure VI 347

Dr. Ernst Sieper sagely observed that "it is imperative that in each of Lydgate's works the question regarding the final -*e's* should be specially dealt with."[7] The importance of this question, of course, concerns the controversial Lydgatian "C" line with the two accented syllables at the caesura.

Reading Dr. Sieper further, it will be noted that his concern about the final "e" has led him into an astute conclusion:

"Even a cursory glance at the text under consideration will reveal the fact that, however bold the licences the author allows himself in the first foot of a line or at the caesura, he never indulges in any in the second or the fourth foot. Hence, in spite of the variety of ways which some lines admit of scansion, there are a great many verses that can be scanned in one, and only one way. These afford us examples of positive value in the attempt to get at the root of the matter. With their aid we may formulate a law, which even in dubious cases, will help us in deciding how the final -*e* should be sounded.

"Thus we have always a final -*e* in the caesura in order to prevent the clashing of two accented syllables, when such an addition is found to agree with the rules we believe Lydgate to have followed."[8]

[7]Ernst Sieper, *Lydgate's Reson and Sensuallyte* (1903; EETSES, 89), p. 20.
[8]*Ibid.*, p. 21.

This was a well-conceived hypothesis and would have solved a thorny problem in the definition of Lydgate's metrical system except for the existence of too many words before the caesura which simply cannot admit of a final "e". We have selected several of these at random from our poem:

And all my woo, for to overgone I 209
If that hem list of hir that might ler I 224
And say to hir, in al manere thyng II 323
By one assent, and her Rauncour lete II 329
Man yfteyȝ brought oute of our contre V 139
He chargede hem vndir wordes fayre V 167

Professor Schick believed that "type A and C particularly may often seem to have equal claims to a line, according as we read or drop the final -e before caesura."[9] Some of our lines could be reconstructed in that way:

The well of helthe, and of lyfe eterne II 741
And is the prince, and the worthy kyng II 773

Would the poet rather have made the elision or an unmusical separation? Professor Skeat believed that "there is no need to elide a vowel at the caesura; it therefore must be sounded clearly."[10] If this were true, the lines quoted would contain three consecutive weak syllables saved only by the rhythmic accent on the weak medial syllable *and*. Katharine Locock is of the opinion that Lydgate "was accustomed to sound or elide the final *e* according to the requirements of the metre, irrespective of other considerations. When a final *e* preceded the caesura he allowed himself an equal amount of liberty."[11]

Many a type "B" line could be logically scanned as a "C" or vice versa according as we use the final "e".

Doun with some drope fro they maieste V 9
It to awayte solitarye dwelle V 88
That shall releve thorough his myghty grace VI 167

I have leaned perhaps too heavily toward the type "B" line in my scansion because of its greater eminence in the versification of other poets and perhaps because I share the general mystification regarding the type "C".

Professor Schipper may have been closer to the solution of the type C line problem than anyone when he wrote:

───────

[9]*op. cit.*, p. lxiii.
[10]*op. cit.*, p. xc.
[11]Katharine Locock, *The Pilgrimage of the Life of Man* (1904; EETSES, 92), Part III, p. xxxiv.

". . . the varieties (from 16 to 64!) of even-beat metres, especially of the five-foot verse, resulting from these metrical licenses, are much more numerous than those connected with the five main types of the alliterative hemistich. The great diversity of rhythm allowed by this metrical theory has, indeed, been objected to, but evidently without sufficient reason, and, it seems, only because of the unfamiliarity of the idea."[12]

Saintsbury, equally puzzled by the "C" line, dismisses it with an uncharacteristic non sequitur: "The commoner it is, the more fully developed, the more peculiarly Lydgatian, the clearer it is that Lydgate was a bad metrist."[13]

Courthope is even more severe:

". . . in Lydgate's ten-syllable verse, the number of irregularly constructed lines is very large. And though the deviations from the ideal standard can all be classified in distinct groups, the evidence seems to me to show that they are the natural effects of three causes.—a defective ear, ignorance of the grammatical principles on which Chaucer's metrical system was founded, and the gradual disappearance of the final e, representing the old inflections before the tendencies to contraction prevailing in all oral language."[14]

And there are many others who share these unfavorable opinions of Lydgate's metrical talents.

On the other side, Professor Schick lists a formidable array of Lydgate supporters.[15] Courthope also grudgingly concedes that

"it is true that some scholars, who have industriously analyzed the verse of Lydgate, believe it to have been built on a regular principle, and maintain that the numerous metrical licenses it exhibits are the fruits of deliberate purpose."[16]

The ever-fair Saintsbury faithfully reported that

"The fifteenth century, and even a great part of the sixteenth, did not hesitate to rank him with Chaucer and Gower in a trinity of patternhood for English poetry . . . The Elizabethan critics . . . spoke respectfully of him, and in particular assigned him "good verse" . . . He found a singular champion in Gray, who probably transmitted interest in him to Coleridge, and who actually commits himself to the statement that Lydgate 'surpasses Gower in smoothness'."[17]

It is not the province of this study to arrive at a theory of Lydgate's general metrical system but of that of the *Life of Our Lady*. Firm opinions appear in the

---

[12]Schipper, *op. cit.,* p. 212.
[13]George Saintsbury, *A History of English Prosody* (London, 1923), I, 244.
[14]W. J. Courthope, *A History of English Poetry* (London, 1926), I, 328.
[15]*op. cit.,* pp. cxlii-clvii, *passim.*
[16]*op. cit.,* p. 328.
[17]*op. cit.,* p. 219.

judgment of scholars who actually have edited some text of Lydgate's and from the judgment of the readers of the centuries to the present one. Editors seem generally to agree that Lydgate had a definite metrical system and readers seemed to be able to follow and admire it. The non-editing critics seem to form a solid block in disagreement.

My opinion is that Lydgate had a metrical system and it was the one evolved by Professor Schipper and simplified by Professor Schick. What particularly distinguished him from other metrists who used the decasyllabic line was the development of the "C" line beyond what is apparently standard practice, although the nine percent incidence in the *Life Of Our Lady* is hardly extravagant. The acephalous "D" line appears almost as frequently.

Why Lydgate favored the "C" line more than did other poets may never be made known. He certainly used it too often to have it dismissed as simply an eccentricity or inadequacy. The *Life Of Our Lady* scans too consistently to be passed off as the work of a doggerel poet.

Henry Bergen's theory contains a high degree of plausibility: " . . . the tendency he followed. . . was to return from Chaucer's and Gower's syllabic purism to the rougher and readier traditional usage of his countrymen."[18]

Possibly the most balanced statement of the problem of Lydgate's versification came from Professor Erdmann:

> "Lydgate could write good verse, easy-flowing harmonious, regular verse, and there are in his works, not least in *Thebes*, many passages that can be read with real pleasure. His constant occupation as a versifier gave him a great skill in handling the English language metrically, but on the other hand, the strain exercised on his composition by the number of and in some cases the extraordinary length of his poems had an unfavourable influence on his poetic art. Haste in composition led to carelessness. Hence the great number of hard and rugged lines."[19]

A poet whose output approximated 150,000 lines can safely be said to have developed a personal style of mechanics as well as melodies. The exigencies of time alone would necessitate a method and the man and his method would reflect upon each other. If he is the chief exponent of the "C" line, that fact should identify but not necessarily defame him.

The principal objection to the "C" line seems to revolve upon the juxtaposition of two accents. This may be accepted if the meaning of the term "accent" is restricted to the notion of a blow or beat. But is English prosody to be construed and read as a system of light and heavy blows or a system of rises and falls, i.e., arses and theses?

---

[18]*op. cit.*, p. xvii.
[19]Axel Erdman and Eilert Ekwall, *Lydgate's Siege of Thebes* (1930; EETSES, 125), p. 32.

A matter of intensity, strength and weakness, rising and falling? Does it make for more variety and even economy to maintain the voice at a high point for two counts rather than to rise and fall and then rise again? Instead of harsh jarring, it seems to make for a delightful variety and smooth continuity.

Would it be extravagant to theorize that Lydgate, tiring of the regular beat and the regular stop, was more pleased with the idea of sustaining an arsis as a musician would sustain a note for variety? It is a common practice in Gregorian chant which Lydgate probably sang everyday in choir:

> "When in addition to the independence of rhythm and intensity, we consider that the Latin accent is light, lifted up and rounded off like an arch, is not heavy or strongly stressed, is arsic and not thetic, we shall not be surprised to meet frequently in Plainsong accented syllables outside and independent of the ictus or rhythmic step. . ."[20]

> "When, as often happens, a single note is put on the accented syllable and a number of notes is put on the weak penultimate syllable, it is very important to round off and bring out gently the arsic character of the accent. . ."[21]

The acephalous or "D" line could conceivably have originated in the same manner. It is a common practice in Gregorian chant to begin a measure on the "ictus" or accented note. The actual incidence of the "D" line is so frequent in Lydgate that it is somewhat surprising to find that many scholars pass over it. Miss Hammond notes that

> "According to Prosiegel's analysis of the *Secrees,* presumably Lydgate's last piece of work, they (the broken-backed lines) amount there to 10 percent, and the headless lines to about 15 percent of the total; and in the Prologue to the *Fall of Princes* the broken-back verses are much less numerous than are the acephalous."[22]

In the *Life Of Our Lady,* the proportion of "D" to "C" lines is 8 to 9 percent, or only 1 percent difference, so that in a comparison with the *Secrees,* it may be said that Lydgate actually moved a little toward the "D" line because the *Life Of Our Lady* was written in his early period. Miss Hammond cannot account for this except to observe that

> ". . . what Chaucer used as a metrical variant Lydgate erected into a type; Chaucer's 'easements' became Lydgate's 'staples' . . . Lydgate's mass of nine-syllabled lines may have developed thus. I cannot see that they are due, in his work, to the fall of inflexional -e; and neither his association with monastic chanting nor the survival of the alliterative line-cleavage accounts for the appear-

---

[20]*The Liber Usualis.* Edited by the Benedictines of Solesmes (Belgium, 1947), p. xxix.
[21]*id.,* p. xxx.
[22]Eleanor P. Hammond, "The Nine-Syllabled Pentameter Line in Some Post-Chaucerian Manuscripts" (*MP,* Vol. 23), p. 147.

ance in him alone of all these broken-backed verses. Other men in the fifteenth century . . . wrote actual doggerel . . . Their ineptitude is unsystematized; he is systematically inept."[23]

Miss Hammond's dismissal of Lydgate's metrical talent with an epithet containing mutually exclusive terminology is unfortunate. To think of someone as "systematically inept" is to endeavor to evoke a single mental concept that admits of form and regularity together with formlessness and irregularity—an operation of which the mind is incapable simultaneously.

Professor Schick provides what seems to be the most satisfactory though not most conclusive answer to the mystery of Lydgate's versification: ". . . we must at least grant that, if the metre of Lydgate is 'halting', there is, as a rule, method in this halting."[24]

Professor Gummere's theory relative to the evolution of the heroic line is plausible, most attractive and may be relevant to the identification of Lydgate's metrical system:

"The English manner is to make a compromise between native and foreign claims. It lets the foreign form (witness our language itself) assume certain external and regulative functions; it keeps the heart of the thing native. . .

"Is it not probable that the popular native measure and the popular foreign measure should have combined their strength, and so should have produced the favorite modern verse?. . .

"Or is it more likely to be a harmonizing—as Ten Brink puts it—of two great systems, the Germanic and the Romance, the rhythmic and the metric, *on the basis* of *two representative measures?*. . .

"Now, that this swaying between 4-stress and 6-stress should, under pressure of iambic movement compromise with 5-stress, is not unreasonable. And this agrees with my position: that our heroic verse was originally a late form of A.-S. long verse, with a prevailing surplus of light syllables at the pause; to this were applied the iambic movement, the light and shifting pause, and the Romance tendency to count syllables."[25]

Dr. Oscar Triggs likewise looks backwards for a theory of Lydgate's versification:

"The general irregularity of the metre, the intrusion into Chaucer's carefully constructed seven-line stanza of the four- and six-beat lines, and the frequent alliteration, suggest the influence of the older English metrical forms. But it is

---

[23]*op. cit.,* p. 152.
[24]*op. cit.,* p. lxiii.
[25]Francis B. Gummere, "The Translation of Beowulf and the relation of Ancient and Modern English Verse" *The American Journal of Philology* (Baltimore, 1886), V, 54-5, 71.

further obvious that Lydgate used in composition the principle both of metre and of stress."[26]

Lydgate's personal allusions to his metrical deficiencies have been accepted by most of his critic-editors. The evidence, however, seems to support neither. The manner in which, over 150,000 lines, he handles the difficult type "C" and type "D" lines, his deliberate inversions to fit his scansion, his free use of parallelism and alliteration, the total purity of his rendering of the second and fourth foot in the decasyllabic line, his easy handling of elision, syncope, synizesis and diaresis, the competence of his rhyme, the pleasant variety of four- and six-stress lines, reveal the skilled metrist more than they betray the doggerel poet.

Professor Schick cannot be taken seriously when he writes an unscholarly aside such as:

"The greatest wonder to me is how the public of the time of Caxton and his immediate followers could read these things as verses; their ears must surely have been singularly impenetrable to anything like rhythmical harmony."[27]

Certainly the *Life Of Our Lady* does not deserve such condemnation for it not only scans easily (thanks to Professor Schick!) but reads smoothly and contains a great number of colorful and noble lines and images. Perhaps Lydgate was no better than a fair poet. As a metrist, however, he seems to have few equals. He dared to employ a complicated system of versification and emerged with a style which has barked the shins of editors and critics for many years and still eludes definition. This reader will settle for a guess: Lydgate's style was strictly *personal*. He had to write so much so swiftly that the system simply evolved and he found it facile to his purpose. The style was the man and inimitable, for good or ill.

---

[26] Oscar L. Triggs, *The Assembly of Gods* (EETSES, LXIX, 1896), p. XIX.
[27] *op. cit.,* p. lvii.

Scansion

"Type A" lines

Book I

1, 3, 4, 5, 7, 8, 12, 14, 15, 16, 17, 18, 19, 20, 21, 27, 28, 33, 34, 36, 37, 43, 44, 48, 50, 51, 52, 53, 54, 55, 58, 60, 61, 63, 65, 66, 69, 70, 71, 73, 76, 77, 78, 80, 85, 87, 88, 90, 91, 92, 93, 94, 95, 99, 104, 108, 109, 110, 111, 112, 113, 114, 115, 116, 117, 118, 119, 121, 123, 124, 126, 133, 134, 135, 136, 140, 141, 142, 146, 148, 150, 151, 152, 154, 155, 160, 161, 162, 163, 168, 170, 171, 172, 173, 175, 176, 177, 178, 181, 182, 184, 185, 186, 189, 192, 194, 196, 197, 198, 199, 200, 202, 204, 205, 206, 210, 211, 212, 214, 215, 216, 217, 218, 219, 221, 222, 225, 227, 230, 231, 232, 233, 235, 237, 239, 240, 241, 242, 243, 245, 247, 249, 252, 253, 255, 257, 258, 259, 262, 263, 266, 267, 268, 273, 274, 276, 277, 278, 279, 286, 287, 290, 291, 292, 294, 295, 298, 299, 301, 302, 305, 306, 307, 308, 309, 310, 311, 312, 313, 315, 316, 317, 320, 321, 322, 324, 326, 327, 328, 329, 330, 332, 333, 334, 336, 337, 338, 339, 340, 343, 344, 345, 346, 347, 351, 352, 354, 355, 356, 357, 358, 360, 362, 363, 367, 368, 370, 371, 373, 378, 379, 380, 382, 383, 386, 388, 389, 390, 391, 395, 396, 397, 400, 401, 405, 407, 408, 411, 412, 413, 414, 416, 417, 419, 420, 421, 422, 423, 424, 425, 428, 429, 430, 431, 432, 433, 434, 436, 442, 443, 445, 447, 448, 451, 452, 453, 454, 455, 456, 457, 458, 459, 460, 461, 462, 464, 466, 469, 470, 471, 473, 475, 476, 477, 479, 481, 482, 483, 487, 488, 490, 492, 493, 494, 495, 497, 500, 502, 506, 509, 511, 515, 516, 518, 519, 520, 521, 522, 524, 525, 529, 530, 531, 532, 535, 540, 541, 544, 548, 549, 550, 551, 552, 557, 560, 561, 566, 567, 568, 569, 571, 572, 573, 574, 576, 579, 582, 583, 584, 585, 587, 591, 592, 595, 596, 597, 598, 602, 604, 608, 610, 611, 612, 613, 616, 617, 621, 624, 625, 626, 627, 629, 630, 631, 632, 633, 636, 637, 638, 639, 641, 642, 643, 644, 645, 646, 648, 652, 653, 654, 657, 658, 659, 663, 664, 667, 668, 671, 673, 674, 676, 677, 678, 679, 681, 682, 683, 685, 686, 687, 689, 690, 697, 698, 700, 703, 706, 707, 708, 709, 710, 711, 713, 715, 717, 719, 721, 722, 723, 725, 726, 727, 728, 729, 731, 732, 733, 737, 738, 739, 740, 741, 742, 743, 744, 745, 747, 749, 750, 751, 753, 754, 755, 758, 760, 762, 763, 764, 765, 768, 769, 770, 772, 774, 775, 778, 779, 780, 781, 787, 788, 789, 790, 791, 793, 795, 796, 798, 799, 803, 804, 805, 806, 807, 808, 809, 811, 816, 817, 819, 820, 821, 822, 823, 825, 829, 830, 831, 832, 834, 836, 837, 839, 841, 842, 843, 844, 845, 847, 848, 852, 854, 857, 859, 860, 861, 862, 863, 865, 866, 867, 869, 871, 872, 873, 876, 877, 878, 879, 881, 882, 883, 885, 886, 888, 889

Book II

1, 5, 6, 7, 9, 10, 11, 12, 13, 15, 16, 18, 19, 22, 23, 24, 25, 26, 27, 28, 29, 30, 31, 35, 37, 39, 40, 41, 44, 45, 47, 48, 49, 51, 52, 53, 54, 55, 56, 57, 60, 61, 63, 66, 67, 68, 70, 71, 72, 73, 74, 80, 82, 84, 86, 87, 89, 92, 93, 94, 101, 102, 103, 104, 105, 106, 108, 110, 111,

113, 114, 116, 117, 118, 119, 121, 122, 123, 124, 126, 127, 128, 134, 135,
136, 144, 147, 148, 149, 150, 152, 153, 154, 155, 156, 157, 164, 169, 170,
176, 179, 183, 185, 186, 187, 188, 193, 196, 197, 198, 199, 201, 202,
203, 204, 205, 211, 215, 217, 218, 219, 220, 221, 225, 226, 228, 230,
234, 235, 240, 241, 243, 246, 247, 250, 251, 252, 253, 255, 256, 257,
259, 261, 262, 263, 264, 265, 269, 270, 271, 272, 274, 276, 277, 278,
280, 283, 284, 285, 287, 288, 291, 292, 293, 294, 295 299, 301, 303,
305, 306, 309, 311, 316, 317, 318, 319, 320, 322, 326, 331, 335, 342,
343, 344, 345, 350, 351, 356, 358, 359, 362, 363, 365, 366, 368, 369,
370, 371, 372, 373, 375, 376, 377, 379, 380, 381, 382, 383, 385, 386,
388, 390, 391, 392, 393, 395, 397, 399, 405, 407, 409, 410, 411, 412,
413, 414, 415, 417, 418, 422, 424, 425, 426, 432, 433, 434, 436, 438,
443, 447, 449, 452, 455, 458, 460, 461, 462, 463, 465, 467, 469, 470,
472, 473, 475, 476, 479, 483, 484, 486, 487, 488, 490, 491, 492, 493,
494, 495, 496, 497, 498, 500, 502, 505, 507, 508, 509, 511, 512, 513,
514, 515, 518, 525, 526, 527, 529, 530, 532, 536, 538, 543, 544, 547,
548, 551, 552, 554, 558, 559, 561, 563, 564, 565, 566, 567, 569, 570,
571, 574, 575, 576, 577, 578, 580, 585, 587, 589, 591, 592, 595, 596,
597, 599, 600, 602, 603, 605, 612, 613, 614, 615, 621, 623, 624, 625,
627, 636, 639, 641, 644, 645, 646, 651, 652, 653, 655, 656, 659, 662,
663, 666, 668, 669, 671, 672, 673, 675, 676, 677, 679, 681, 682, 683,
685, 688, 690, 692, 693, 697, 699, 703, 705, 706, 707, 708, 709, 713,
714, 715, 721, 722, 726, 728, 729, 730, 734, 737, 738, 740, 742, 743,
744, 748, 749, 750, 751, 752, 754, 755, 757, 758, 759, 760, 761, 762,
763, 765, 766, 768, 769, 771, 775, 776, 777, 778, 781, 782, 783, 784,
785, 788, 789, 790, 791, 793, 794, 795, 799, 801, 802, 803, 805, 807,
808, 809, 810, 811, 812, 814, 815, 816, 817, 818, 819, 821, 822, 824,
825, 827, 828, 830, 833, 834, 835, 837, 839, 840, 841, 843, 844, 846,
847, 848, 850, 851, 852, 853, 854, 855, 859, 860, 861, 862, 863, 864,
867, 868, 870, 871, 873, 875, 876, 879, 880, 881, 882, 883, 884, 886,
888, 890, 891, 898, 899, 900, 904, 906, 908, 909, 910, 913, 916, 917,
919, 921, 922, 923, 925, 926, 927, 929, 930, 931, 933, 935, 938, 940,
943, 944, 946, 947, 949, 951, 952, 953, 954, 955, 956, 960, 962, 964,
965, 966, 967, 968, 969, 970, 971, 972, 973, 974, 975, 977, 978, 979,
981, 983, 984, 985, 987, 988, 989, 990, 991, 992, 993, 994, 995, 966,
999, 1000, 1001, 1002, 1003, 1004, 1005, 1006, 1007, 1008, 1010,
1011, 1012, 1013, 1014, 1016, 1017, 1020, 1021, 1022, 1023, 1024,
1025, 1026, 1027, 1028, 1029, 1031, 1033, 1034, 1035, 1036, 1039,
1041, 1042, 1043, 1044, 1045, 1046, 1049, 1050, 1052, 1053, 1054,
1062, 1064, 1065, 1066, 1068, 1071, 1072, 1073, 1074, 1077, 1079,
1080, 1081, 1082, 1083, 1087, 1088, 1092, 1093, 1095, 1096, 1097,
1098, 1099, 1101, 1102, 1104, 1105, 1106, 1107, 1108, 1109, 1110,
1111, 1113, 1115, 1116, 1117, 1118, 1121, 1122, 1123, 1126, 1127,
1129, 1130, 1135, 1136, 1137, 1138, 1139, 1140, 1141, 1145, 1147,
1148, 1149, 1150, 1154, 1156, 1158, 1159, 1163, 1164, 1167, 1173,
1174, 1177, 1178, 1179, 1180, 1181, 1183, 1186, 1189, 1190, 1195,
1197, 1198, 1200, 1201, 1203, 1205, 1209, 1210, 1213, 1214, 1218,
1220, 1222, 1224, 1234, 1236, 1238, 1240, 1241, 1242, 1245, 1246,

1248, 1249, 1250, 1253, 1254, 1255, 1256, 1257, 1260, 1263, 1264,
1266, 1268, 1269, 1270, 1275, 1277, 1279, 1282, 1283, 1284, 1285,
1286, 1288, 1289, 1290, 1291, 1293, 1295, 1296, 1297, 1298, 1301,
1302, 1303, 1304, 1305, 1306, 1309, 1311, 1312, 1315, 1317, 1319,
1322, 1329, 1331, 1332, 1333, 1336, 1340, 1343, 1344, 1346, 1348,
1356, 1357, 1359, 1363, 1365, 1366, 1367, 1369, 1370, 1371, 1372,
1374, 1375, 1376, 1378, 1379, 1380, 1381, 1382, 1383, 1384, 1385,
1386, 1389, 1391, 1392, 1393, 1394, 1395, 1398, 1399, 1400, 1402,
1406, 1407, 1408, 1409, 1410, 1414, 1415, 1418, 1419, 1421, 1422,
1423, 1424, 1425, 1428, 1429, 1430, 1433, 1439, 1443, 1444, 1446,
1447, 1450, 1451, 1452, 1454, 1456, 1459, 1461, 1462, 1463, 1464,
1465, 1467, 1468, 1469, 1471, 1472, 1475, 1476, 1477, 1478, 1479,
1481, 1482, 1485, 1487, 1491, 1492, 1498, 1499, 1500, 1501, 1506,
1508, 1510, 1518, 1520, 1521, 1525, 1527, 1528, 1531, 1534, 1536,
1542, 1551, 1553, 1557, 1561, 1563, 1564, 1565, 1566, 1570, 1573,
1574, 1575, 1576, 1577, 1579, 1580, 1581, 1582, 1584, 1588, 1591,
1592, 1593, 1594, 1596, 1597, 1598, 1599, 1601, 1603, 1605, 1606,
1609, 1610, 1612, 1615, 1616, 1618, 1619, 1620, 1621, 1623, 1625,
1627, 1630, 1632, 1633, 1636, 1637, 1641, 1644, 1646, 1650, 1651,
1653, 1654, 1655, 1656, 1657, 1658, 1661, 1662, 1663, 1667, 1668,
1669.

Book III

1, 2, 3, 4, 10, 11, 12, 15, 16, 18, 19, 23, 26, 27, 29, 30, 31, 33, 34, 37, 42,
44, 45, 46, 48, 50, 56, 57, 60, 62, 64, 65, 66, 68, 69, 72, 73, 75, 79, 83, 84,
86, 92, 94, 97, 101, 102, 106, 110, 112, 113, 114, 118, 123, 129, 130, 131,
133, 134, 135, 139, 143, 145, 146, 147, 149, 150, 151, 154, 156, 162, 163,
170, 171, 172, 173, 174, 175, 179, 180, 182, 183, 184, 187, 189, 190, 191,
192, 198, 199, 200, 201, 204, 207, 208, 209, 210, 212, 213, 216, 217, 219,
222, 226, 227, 233, 237, 239, 243, 244, 245, 246, 247, 248, 251, 252, 253,
255, 256, 258, 259, 261, 262, 263, 265, 267, 268, 273, 274, 275, 278, 283,
284, 285, 288, 289, 290, 291, 292, 293, 294, 296, 298, 299, 301, 302, 303,
305, 306, 307, 310, 312, 313, 314, 316, 317, 321, 322, 325, 326, 328, 330,
331, 333, 335, 336, 337, 339, 342, 344, 345, 347, 348, 349, 350, 353, 354,
357, 359, 360, 362, 364, 365, 367, 368, 370, 372, 373, 374, 375, 376, 377,
378, 379, 380, 382, 383, 385, 386, 387, 388, 390, 392, 395, 403, 406, 407,
409, 411, 414, 415, 416, 417, 418, 421, 423, 424, 427, 428, 429, 430, 433,
434, 435, 436, 437, 438, 441, 442, 443, 444, 445, 446, 447, 449, 451, 452,
457, 459, 461, 462, 464, 472, 477, 478, 479, 480, 481, 486, 488, 489, 491,
492, 494, 495, 496, 497, 498, 499, 500, 502, 503, 504, 506, 507, 508, 509,
511, 513, 515, 516, 518, 520, 521, 522, 523, 526, 528, 532, 533, 536, 537,
539, 540, 541, 542, 543, 544, 546, 547, 548, 549, 551, 552, 554, 557, 558,
560, 561, 562, 563, 564, 565, 566, 567, 569, 570, 571, 572, 573, 576, 580,
581, 582, 584, 586, 588, 589, 590, 591, 592, 594, 595, 597, 598, 599, 600,
602, 603, 604, 611, 612, 615, 616, 617, 618, 619, 622, 624, 627, 630, 631,
633, 636, 637, 639, 641, 642, 644, 645, 646, 649, 650, 654, 655, 656, 658,
659, 661, 662, 663, 666, 667, 668, 670, 671, 673, 675, 676, 677, 681, 682,

686, 688, 689, 691, 692, 693, 696, 699, 700, 703, 705, 706, 707, 708, 709, 710, 712, 713, 714, 717, 718, 723, 724, 725, 727, 728, 729, 733, 734, 735, 739, 741, 742, 743, 744, 748, 749, 750, 751, 752, 754, 755, 756, 758, 759 762, 764, 765, 766, 767, 772, 773, 775, 776, 779, 782, 783, 785, 786, 787, 788, 790, 792, 793, 795, 797, 798, 802, 805, 806, 808, 809, 810, 811, 813, 815, 816, 818, 824, 825, 827, 828, 829, 830, 835, 839, 840, 841, 844, 845, 850, 851, 852, 854, 856, 857, 871, 872, 873, 874, 875, 876, 878, 879, 880, 883, 885, 886, 887, 891, 893, 894, 896, 897, 898, 899, 904, 905, 907, 909, 910, 912, 913, 914, 916, 917, 918, 920, 922, 924, 925, 926, 929, 931, 932, 935, 938, 941, 944, 946, 947, 948, 952, 954, 955, 958, 960, 961, 963, 964, 965, 968, 969, 970, 972, 973, 976, 977, 981, 982, 984, 986, 987, 990, 991, 994, 995, 996, 998, 1005, 1006, 1007, 1010, 1011, 1012, 1014, 1017, 1018, 1020, 1023, 1025, 1026, 1029, 1030, 1031, 1035, 1036, 1037, 1038, 1040, 1041, 1042, 1043, 1046, 1047, 1048, 1049, 1052, 1054, 1055, 1057, 1059, 1060, 1061, 1062, 1064, 1065, 1067, 1068, 1069, 1070, 1072, 1073, 1074, 1076, 1077, 1080, 1082, 1084, 1085, 1086, 1089, 1091, 1092, 1093, 1097, 1104, 1106, 1108, 1109, 1110, 1112, 1114, 1117, 1118, 1122, 1123, 1127, 1132, 1134, 1135, 1136, 1137, 1139, 1145, 1146, 1148, 1151, 1154, 1158, 1159, 1161, 1164, 1167, 1170, 1175, 1176, 1178, 1180, 1182, 1185, 1186, 1187, 1191, 1192, 1194, 1195, 1198, 1199, 1200, 1201, 1202, 1203, 1205, 1207, 1209, 1213, 1215, 1216, 1217, 1218, 1219, 1220, 1221, 1224, 1225, 1226, 1228, 1229, 1231, 1232, 1233, 1235, 1236, 1237, 1238, 1241, 1242, 1244, 1245, 1250, 1251, 1252, 1255, 1256, 1257, 1260, 1263, 1265, 1266, 1268, 1270, 1271, 1273, 1274, 1275, 1276, 1280, 1284, 1286, 1291, 1292, 1293, 1295, 1298, 1300, 1301, 1302, 1303, 1304, 1308, 1309, 1311, 1312, 1313, 1315, 1316, 1317, 1319, 1320, 1324, 1326, 1327, 1328, 1331, 1333, 1337, 1338, 1339, 1341, 1342, 1344, 1346, 1348, 1349, 1351, 1352, 1355, 1358, 1360, 1361, 1362, 1363, 1364, 1366, 1367, 1369, 1370, 1371, 1372, 1375, 1376, 1381, 1382, 1385, 1388, 1391, 1392, 1394, 1396, 1397, 1398, 1402, 1403, 1404, 1405, 1406, 1407, 1408, 1409, 1410 ,1412, 1413, 1415, 1416, 1417, 1421, 1422, 1423, 1424, 1425, 1427, 1434, 1438, 1439, 1444, 1445, 1446, 1447, 1448, 1449, 1451, 1456, 1457, 1461, 1463, 1464, 1466, 1468, 1470, 1473, 1474, 1481, 1482, 1484, 1486, 1488, 1490, 1492, 1493, 1494, 1496, 1497, 1498, 1507, 1509, 1510, 1514, 1516, 1520, 1523, 1524, 1526, 1527, 1529, 1531, 1533, 1534, 1536, 1538, 1540, 1542, 1543, 1544, 1545, 1546, 1551, 1555, 1561, 1562, 1564, 1567, 1569, 1573, 1577, 1578, 1579, 1582, 1583, 1588, 1590, 1593, 1594, 1598, 1601, 1602, 1603, 1604, 1606, 1608, 1609, 1611, 1615, 1616, 1619, 1620, 1621, 1622, 1623, 1624, 1628, 1635, 1638, 1639, 1640, 1643, 1646, 1647, 1648, 1649, 1652, 1653, 1654, 1658, 1660, 1661, 1662, 1665, 1667, 1669, 1670, 1671, 1674, 1678, 1682, 1684, 1686, 1687, 1690, 1692, 1693, 1694, 1696, 1698, 1700, 1701, 1705, 1706, 1715, 1717, 1718, 1719, 1720, 1721, 1722, 1726, 1727, 1729, 1731, 1732, 1735, 1736, 1737, 1738, 1744, 1745, 1746, 1747, 1748, 1749, 1757, 1760, 1761, 1763, 1764, 1766, 1767, 1770, 1771, 1773, 1776, 1778, 1782, 1783, 1787, 1789, 1795, 1796, 1797, 1798, 1799, 1803, 1804.

Book IV

5, 8, 11, 14, 18, 19, 20, 21, 23, 25, 29, 33, 34, 37, 38, 41, 43, 45, 51, 52,
53, 54, 55, 57, 58, 59, 60, 63, 64, 66, 67, 69, 72, 78, 79, 80, 82, 83, 85,
86, 87, 88, 90, 91, 92, 95, 98, 101, 102, 103, 104, 105, 106, 107, 108,
110, 113, 114, 115, 116, 118, 119, 124, 126, 128, 130, 131, 135, 138, 139,
142, 145, 146, 148, 149, 151, 154, 155, 157, 158, 159, 160, 161, 162, 163,
167, 168, 169, 170, 172, 173, 177, 178, 179, 180, 181, 184, 187, 189, 190,
191, 192, 193, 194, 195, 197, 199, 202, 203, 206, 211, 214, 215, 217, 218,
219, 220, 221, 222, 223, 224, 228, 230, 231, 232, 233, 235, 238, 239, 240,
241, 244, 246, 247, 248, 251, 252, 256, 259, 263, 264, 265, 267, 268, 270,
271, 273, 274, 276, 277, 278, 279, 281, 282, 284, 285, 286, 287, 288, 289,
291, 292, 293, 295, 296, 303, 304, 308, 309, 310, 312, 314, 315, 317, 318,
321, 324, 325, 327, 328, 331, 332, 333, 335, 336, 338, 339, 340, 341, 342,
343, 344, 347, 348, 349, 351, 353, 355, 356, 358, 360, 363, 364, 371, 372,
373, 377, 379, 381, 382, 383, 384, 385, 389, 391, 394, 395, 396, 399, 402,
404, 406,

Book V

1, 5, 6, 7, 8, 11, 12, 15, 18, 20, 22, 23, 24, 25, 28, 31, 37, 38, 39, 40, 41, 42,
43, 44, 46, 47, 48, 49, 51, 52, 54, 55, 57, 60, 61, 63, 64, 67, 69, 70, 71, 73,
74, 75, 76, 77, 79, 81, 83, 84, 89, 90, 91, 92, 93, 94, 95, 98, 100, 101, 103,
104, 105, 106, 107, 109, 110, 111, 112, 113, 115, 117, 118, 119, 120, 121,
122, 124, 125, 126, 127, 131, 133, 135, 137, 138, 142, 143, 144, 148, 149,
153, 155, 156, 157, 158, 164, 168, 170, 172, 174, 175, 176, 177, 180, 188,
189, 192, 199, 200, 206, 209, 211, 212, 214, 217, 219, 220, 221, 224, 225,
237, 238, 239, 240, 242, 243, 246, 249, 251, 252, 253, 255, 258, 260,
262, 265, 266, 268, 274, 275, 276, 277, 278, 279, 281, 282, 285, 286, 287,
288, 290, 291, 292, 293, 298, 299, 300, 303, 304, 306, 307, 308, 309, 310,
311, 314, 315, 318, 319, 321, 323, 324, 325, 327, 328, 331, 332, 333, 334,
335, 337, 339, 341, 347, 349, 350, 352, 353, 354, 355, 356, 357, 359, 364,
377, 380, 383, 385, 387, 388, 393, 394, 395, 397, 398, 399, 400, 401, 402,
405, 406, 408, 409, 410, 412, 413, 414, 416, 418, 419, 421, 422, 424, 425,
426, 428, 431, 432, 433, 438, 439, 441, 442, 443, 445, 449, 450, 451, 452,
453, 454, 455, 456, 457, 458, 459, 460, 461, 462, 463, 465, 467, 469, 470,
471, 472, 473, 475, 477, 478, 480, 484, 486, 487, 488, 489, 490, 491, 492,
493, 495, 497, 498, 499, 500, 501, 503, 505, 508, 509, 511, 512, 514, 516,
518, 519, 523, 524, 527, 528, 529, 531, 532, 538, 539, 544, 546, 547, 550,
551, 552, 553, 554, 555, 556, 557, 558, 560, 561, 563, 565, 569, 570,
571, 572, 576, 580, 582, 583, 584, 585, 586, 588, 590, 591, 592, 593, 594,
595, 596, 598, 599, 601, 602, 603, 604, 605, 606, 607, 608, 609, 610, 611,
612, 613, 614, 616, 617, 618, 621, 623, 625, 627, 628, 629, 630, 634, 638,
639, 640, 642, 643, 644, 645, 646, 647, 649, 651, 652, 657, 658, 659, 660,
662, 663, 664 665, 666, 668, 671, 672, 673, 675, 679, 680, 681, 682,
683, 684, 685, 686, 688, 690, 691, 692, 694, 695, 697, 698, 700.

Book VI

2, 3, 7, 9, 10, 13, 14, 18, 21, 22, 23, 25, 30, 33, 34, 37, 38, 39, 40, 41, 43, 48, 49, 50, 52, 53, 55, 56, 59, 60, 61, 62, 64, 65, 71, 72, 74, 77, 78, 79, 81, 82, 83, 87, 90, 92, 95, 100, 102, 103, 104, 105, 108, 111, 112, 115, 118, 120, 121, 122, 123, 124, 125, 126, 127, 129, 133, 135, 136, 137, 139, 141, 142, 143, 144, 146, 148, 149, 151, 152, 153, 155, 157, 158, 160, 161, 162, 163, 164, 165, 169, 170, 173, 177, 179, 180, 182, 185, 186, 187, 188, 189, 191, 192, 193, 197, 198, 199, 200, 205, 207, 214, 217, 218, 223, 224, 226, 227, 228, 229, 230, 231, 232, 234, 236, 238, 239, 242, 243, 244, 245, 247, 248, 258, 263, 264, 268, 270, 273, 275, 276, 277, 278, 279, 280, 282, 286, 288, 290, 292, 303, 307, 308, 309, 310, 312, 316, 317, 319, 320, 321, 322, 323, 324, 325, 326, 327, 329, 330, 331, 334, 335, 339, 340, 341, 343, 344, 353, 354, 358, 360, 361, 362, 365, 366, 367, 375, 376, 382, 384, 389, 390, 391, 392, 396, 404, 405, 406, 411, 412, 414, 416, 421, 423, 427, 428, 431, 432, 433, 434, 435, 436, 439, 452, 455, 460, 462

"Type B" Lines

Book I

6, 9, 10, 11, 13, 22, 24, 26, 30, 31, 32, 35, 38, 39, 40, 41, 42, 47, 49, 62, 64, 68, 72, 74, 75, 79, 81, 82, 83, 84, 86, 89, 101, 103, 105, 106, 107, 120, 122, 125, 131, 137, 138, 139, 143, 144, 147, 153, 157, 159, 164, 165, 166, 180, 183, 190, 193, 195, 201, 207, 208, 220, 228, 236, 248, 250, 251, 254, 260, 261, 265, 270, 271, 280, 281, 282, 284, 289, 296, 297, 304, 314, 318, 319, 325, 331, 335, 342, 348, 353, 359, 361, 364, 365, 366, 369, 372, 374, 376, 377, 381, 384, 385, 387, 392, 394, 399, 403, 404, 406, 409, 418, 435, 437, 441, 446, 465, 467, 468, 472, 474, 478, 480, 484, 486, 489, 498, 499, 501, 504, 507, 510, 512, 523, 527, 528, 533, 536, 537, 538, 539, 542, 545, 559, 565, 570, 575, 578, 581, 586, 588, 593, 594, 600, 605, 614, 615, 622, 623, 628, 634, 647, 650, 651, 660, 661, 662, 669, 670, 675, 684, 691, 693, 694, 696, 699, 702, 704, 712, 714, 716, 718, 720, 724, 734, 735, 736, 748, 757, 759, 766, 773, 777, 786, 792, 797, 800, 810, 812, 813, 818, 824, 826, 828, 835, 840, 853, 880

Book II

3, 4, 8, 14, 17, 20, 21, 32, 33, 36, 38, 42, 43, 58, 62, 65, 75, 76, 77, 78, 79, 83, 85, 95, 96, 98, 99, 100, 115, 120, 125, 129, 131, 132, 133, 137, 138, 140, 141, 143, 146, 151, 160, 161, 162, 163, 165, 166, 167, 168, 172, 175, 181, 182, 191, 194, 200, 206, 207, 210, 212, 213, 214, 223, 224, 229, 231, 232, 233, 236, 237, 238, 242, 244, 245, 248, 249, 258,

266, 267, 268, 275, 286, 300, 304, 307, 310, 312, 321, 324, 325, 327,
328, 330, 332, 333, 338, 340, 341, 347, 352, 353, 355, 357, 360, 364,
384, 387, 394, 396, 398, 400, 401, 402, 403, 404, 408, 421, 423, 428,
429, 430, 431, 435, 439, 440, 441, 442, 445, 450, 454, 456, 457, 464,
466, 474, 480, 481, 489, 499, 501, 503, 504, 506, 510, 519, 521, 522,
523, 524, 528, 531, 533, 535, 537, 539, 540, 541, 542, 545, 546, 550,
553, 555, 556, 557, 560, 562, 582, 583, 584, 588, 590, 593, 594, 598,
601, 604, 606, 607, 608, 610, 611, 616, 617, 618, 620, 622, 626, 628,
632, 633, 635, 637, 638, 642, 643, 647, 650, 654, 657, 658, 660, 661,
670, 674, 686, 687, 689, 696, 698, 701, 704, 710, 711, 712, 716, 719,
720, 723, 724, 731, 732, 735, 745, 746, 747, 756, 764, 767, 770, 772,
774, 779, 780, 786, 787, 792, 796, 797, 804, 820, 826, 831, 836, 845,
856, 858, 865, 866, 872, 874, 877, 878, 885, 887, 893, 894, 895, 896,
897, 901, 903, 907, 911, 914, 915, 918, 920, 924, 928, 934, 936, 937,
939, 941, 942, 948, 957, 958, 961, 963, 976, 982, 986, 997, 998, 1009,
1015, 1018, 1019, 1030, 1032, 1037, 1040, 1047, 1048, 1057, 1058,
1059, 1060, 1061, 1069, 1070, 1075, 1076, 1085, 1086, 1089, 1094,
1103, 1112, 1114, 1119, 1124, 1125, 1128, 1134, 1142, 1143, 1151,
1153, 1155, 1157, 1161, 1162, 1166, 1170, 1171, 1172, 1175, 1182,
1184, 1185, 1187, 1191, 1193, 1194, 1202, 1204, 1206, 1211, 1212,
1215, 1216, 1223, 1227, 1228, 1229, 1230, 1231, 1232, 1237, 1239,
1244, 1251, 1252, 1261, 1262, 1265, 1267, 1271, 1274, 1278, 1281,
1292, 1294, 1299, 1300, 1308, 1310, 1313, 1314, 1316, 1320, 1321,
1323, 1326, 1327, 1328, 1334, 1337, 1339, 1341, 1347, 1349, 1351,
1352, 1353, 1361, 1362, 1373, 1377, 1388, 1390, 1401, 1403, 1404,
1411, 1413, 1417, 1418, 1420, 1426, 1431, 1434, 1435, 1436, 1440,
1445, 1448, 1449, 1457, 1460, 1470, 1473, 1474, 1480, 1483, 1484,
1490, 1493, 1496, 1502, 1503, 1507, 1513, 1515, 1516, 1522, 1524,
1526, 1535, 1539, 1544, 1545, 1547, 1548, 1549, 1554, 1559, 1560,
1562, 1568, 1571, 1578, 1583, 1585, 1586, 1589, 1600, 1607, 1611,
1614, 1622, 1624, 1628, 1629, 1634, 1635, 1638, 1639, 1640, 1643,
1645, 1648, 1649, 1652, 1659, 1660, 1665, 1666

Book III

5, 6, 7, 21, 24, 25, 32, 35, 36, 38, 43, 47, 49, 51, 54, 55, 59, 61, 63, 67, 70,
71, 74, 76, 77, 78, 80, 81, 82, 85, 87, 88, 89, 91, 93, 95, 98, 100, 103, 104,
111, 115, 117, 119, 121, 122, 127, 128, 136, 137, 140, 141, 148, 152, 159,
160, 165, 166, 176, 178, 186, 188, 193, 197, 203, 206, 221, 223, 224, 225,
230, 231, 232, 234, 235, 238, 240, 241, 242, 250, 257, 264, 269, 270, 271,
272, 276, 277, 279, 280, 281, 282, 286, 297, 304, 309, 318, 319, 329, 341,
343, 346, 351, 355, 356, 361, 363, 366, 369, 384, 389, 393, 394, 397, 398,
399, 400, 401, 408, 413, 419, 420, 422, 425, 426, 431, 439, 440, 456, 460,
463, 471, 473, 474, 475, 482, 483, 490, 493, 501, 505, 510, 512, 514,
517, 519, 524, 527, 529, 531, 553, 556, 568, 574, 575, 577, 578, 579, 583,
585, 587, 593, 596, 601, 605, 607, 608, 609, 610, 614, 620, 621, 623, 626,
628, 629, 632, 635, 638, 640, 643, 647, 651, 652, 657, 660, 664, 665, 669,

672, 678, 679, 680, 683, 684, 687, 690, 694, 697, 701, 702, 704, 711, 716,
720, 721, 722, 731, 732, 737, 745, 746, 747, 757, 760, 761, 768, 769, 770,
771, 777, 778, 781, 789, 791, 794, 796, 799, 800, 804, 807, 812, 814, 819,
832, 836, 837, 838, 843, 846, 847, 848, 849, 853, 855, 858, 860, 861, 862,
867, 868, 869, 870, 877, 881, 882, 884, 890, 895, 902, 903, 906, 908, 911,
915, 921, 923, 927, 928, 930, 933 934, 939, 940, 943, 945, 949, 950, 951,
956, 957, 959, 962, 966, 967, 971, 974, 975, 978, 980, 983, 985, 988, 989,
997, 1003, 1008, 1009, 1013, 1015, 1019, 1021, 1027, 1028, 1032, 1034,
1039, 1044, 1045, 1050, 1053, 1056, 1058, 1066, 1075, 1078, 1081, 1087,
1088, 1090, 1096, 1099, 1101, 1103, 1105, 1116, 1120, 1124, 1125, 1126,
1129, 1130, 1131, 1133, 1141, 1147, 1152, 1153, 1155, 1156, 1160, 1163,
1168, 1171, 1172, 1173, 1177, 1181, 1190, 1193, 1196, 1197, 1204, 1210,
1211, 1212, 1234, 1239, 1240, 1246, 1248, 1259, 1261, 1262, 1267, 1269,
1272, 1277, 1278, 1287, 1288, 1289, 1296, 1297, 1299, 1314, 1322, 1323,
1329, 1330, 1334, 1336, 1340, 1343, 1354, 1356, 1359, 1365, 1368, 1373,
1377, 1378, 1380, 1383, 1384, 1387, 1390, 1393, 1400, 1401, 1411, 1414,
1419, 1420, 1426, 1430, 1431, 1432, 1435, 1440, 1441, 1443, 1450, 1453,
1454, 1455, 1459, 1460, 1462, 1465, 1467, 1469, 1471, 1475, 1476, 1477,
1478, 1479, 1487, 1489, 1491, 1495, 1499, 1501, 1502, 1503, 1508, 1513,
1518, 1519, 1528, 1530, 1532, 1535, 1537, 1539, 1548, 1550, 1552, 1553,
1554, 1556, 1557, 1558, 1560, 1563, 1565, 1568, 1570, 1572, 1574, 1575,
1576, 1580, 1581, 1587, 1589, 1595, 1596, 1597, 1599, 1600, 1612, 1613,
1617, 1618, 1625, 1626, 1627, 1629, 1631, 1632, 1633, 1636, 1637, 1641,
1642, 1645, 1651, 1657, 1664, 1666, 1676, 1677, 1679, 1681, 1685, 1688,
1689, 1691, 1695, 1697, 1702, 1703, 1708, 1709, 1710, 1711, 1712, 1713,
1714, 1723, 1728, 1733, 1734, 1739, 1740, 1741, 1743, 1750, 1751, 1755,
1758, 1759, 1765, 1768, 1769, 1774, 1775, 1777, 1780, 1781, 1784, 1788,
1792, 1801, 1802

Book IV

1, 3, 4, 6, 10, 13, 15, 17, 22, 24, 28, 30, 31, 32, 35, 36, 39, 40, 42, 46,
47, 48, 49, 50, 56, 61, 65, 75, 76, 77, 81, 94, 96, 97, 99, 111, 112, 117,
122, 125, 127, 132, 133, 136, 137, 140, 147, 152, 153, 164, 165, 166,
176, 183, 185, 186, 188, 196, 200, 201, 205, 208, 209, 212, 213, 216,
225, 227, 229, 236, 245, 255, 257, 258, 260, 262, 266, 269, 272, 275,
280, 290, 294, 297, 300, 301, 305, 311, 313, 319, 320, 322, 323, 326,
329, 330, 334, 337, 345, 352, 354, 357, 359, 361, 365, 367, 370, 375,
380, 386, 388, 390, 398, 400, 401, 403

Book V

2, 3, 9, 21, 29, 30, 32, 33, 50, 62, 66, 78, 82, 85, 88, 96, 97, 99, 123,
129, 134, 145, 146, 154, 159, 169, 173, 178, 182, 183, 184, 186, 195,
196, 202, 204, 205, 207, 208, 213, 216, 223, 228, 229, 230, 236, 241,
247, 248, 250, 259, 261, 263, 270, 272, 273, 280, 283, 284, 294, 295,
297, 301, 305, 312, 313, 316, 320, 322, 329, 330, 336, 344, 345, 346,
348, 351, 358, 361, 362, 363, 365, 368, 369, 370, 372, 373, 374, 375,

376, 382, 384, 389, 390, 391, 392, 396, 404, 415, 417, 420, 423, 427, 435, 436, 437, 464, 466, 468, 476, 482, 483, 485, 496, 502, 504, 506, 507, 510, 513, 517, 520, 522, 525, 526, 530, 533, 534, 535, 536, 537, 540, 541, 542, 545, 548, 549, 559, 562, 564, 566, 567, 574, 575, 578, 579, 597, 600, 619, 622, 624, 626, 631, 632, 635, 636, 637, 648, 654, 655, 661, 667, 674, 676, 678, 687, 693

Book VI

8, 11, 12, 16, 17, 19, 31, 35, 36, 42, 46, 47, 68, 70, 75, 76, 80, 85, 88, 91, 93, 94, 98, 101, 106, 109, 110, 113, 131, 138, 140, 147, 154, 156, 167, 171, 172, 174, 194, 195, 196, 204, 209, 211, 212, 215, 219, 220, 225, 233, 240, 241, 246, 249, 252, 253, 254, 257, 259, 260, 261, 262, 265, 267, 271, 272, 274, 281, 283, 284, 285, 287, 291, 294, 305, 306, 313, 314, 315, 332, 336, 337, 342, 346, 348, 355, 356, 357, 363, 370, 373, 378, 379, 380, 385, 393, 394, 395, 399, 400, 401, 402, 403, 410, 417, 418, 419, 425, 430, 437, 438, 441, 442, 449, 451, 454, 456, 458

"Type C" lines

Book I

25, 45, 46, 59, 97, 98, 100, 102, 127, 145, 156, 158, 174, 179, 191, 209, 213, 224, 229, 234, 238, 246, 256, 272, 275, 283, 288, 293, 300, 375, 393, 398, 402, 410, 415, 426, 427, 438, 439, 440, 449, 450, 463, 491, 496, 505, 508, 513, 517, 554, 555, 558, 562, 580, 590, 601, 603, 618, 635, 640, 655, 656, 666, 680, 697, 705, 730, 746, 752, 756, 771, 785, 794, 801, 802, 814, 833, 838, 849, 850, 851, 864, 884

Book II

34, 46, 59, 64, 69, 81, 88, 91, 112, 130, 158, 180, 184, 189, 190, 195, 208, 209, 222, 239, 273, 279, 281, 282, 289, 290, 296, 297, 302, 308, 313, 314, 315, 323, 329, 334, 336, 348, 349, 361, 378, 389, 406, 416, 419, 427, 437, 448, 451, 453, 459, 471, 477, 478, 482, 485, 516, 517, 520, 534, 572, 573, 579, 586, 609, 619, 629, 630, 648, 649, 664, 665, 667, 678, 680, 702, 736, 739, 741, 753, 773, 798, 806, 813, 823, 829, 838, 842, 869, 889, 892, 905, 932, 945, 950, 959, 1051, 1055, 1063, 1067, 1078, 1084, 1090, 1091, 1100, 1131, 1146, 1152, 1160, 1165, 1176, 1188, 1192, 1199, 1208, 1217, 1219, 1221, 1225, 1233, 1258, 1259, 1272, 1280, 1287, 1307, 1335, 1338, 1342, 1350, 1354, 1358, 1360, 1396, 1397, 1405, 1432, 1437, 1438, 1441, 1442, 1455, 1458, 1488, 1489, 1494, 1497, 1504, 1505, 1511, 1512, 1514, 1519, 1529, 1532, 1533, 1537, 1538, 1540, 1541, 1543, 1546, 1550, 1552, 1556, 1558, 1567, 1569, 1572, 1587, 1590, 1602, 1604, 1608, 1613, 1617, 1626, 1631, 1647

Book III

8, 13, 17, 22, 39, 40, 52, 53, 58, 96, 107, 108, 109, 116, 124, 125, 142, 144, 168, 177, 185 194, 195, 196, 202, 214, 218, 236, 249, 254, 260, 320,

323, 334, 352, 371, 381, 391, 396, 402, 404, 414, 448, 450, 458, 465, 466, 467, 468, 470, 476, 484, 559, 613, 648, 698, 726, 738, 763, 801, 822, 834, 863, 864, 865, 889, 919, 936, 942, 992, 993, 999, 1000, 1002, 1022, 1033, 1063, 1071, 1079, 1098, 1100, 1102, 1128, 1142, 1143, 1144, 1149, 1157, 1169, 1179, 1184, 1188, 1189, 1214, 1222, 1223, 1249, 1279, 1281, 1294, 1307, 1310, 1325, 1347, 1357, 1374, 1379, 1418, 1428, 1429, 1433, 1452, 1458, 1480, 1485, 1500, 1504, 1506, 1511, 1515, 1517, 1525, 1547, 1571, 1584, 1644, 1650, 1656, 1704, 1707, 1725, 1752, 1753, 1762, 1779, 1806

Book IV

7, 12, 44, 70, 71, 73, 74, 93, 123, 143, 144, 171, 174, 175, 198, 226, 243, 249, 250, 254, 261, 283, 298, 306, 316, 368, 369, 376, 405

Book V

10, 13, 16, 17, 24, 26, 36, 45, 59, 68, 86, 102, 139, 152, 160, 167, 198, 210, 218, 222, 227, 231, 244, 245, 254, 256, 257, 264, 267, 271, 302, 317, 343, 407, 474, 479, 481, 494, 568, 573, 587, 589, 641, 650, 653, 656, 670, 677, 696, 699

Book VI

26, 27, 28, 44, 58, 63, 89, 96, 97, 116, 119, 128, 132, 145, 150, 168, 176, 178, 183, 201, 202, 203, 208, 250, 255, 256, 269, 302, 328, 338, 364, 368, 372, 377, 381, 386, 397, 408, 413, 420, 422, 424, 426, 440, 445, 453, 459

"Type D" lines

Book I

23, 29, 67, 128, 132, 149, 167, 169, 187, 188, 203, 223, 226, 244, 264, 269, 285, 323, 341, 349, 444, 485, 503, 514, 526, 534, 543, 546, 547, 556, 563, 564, 577, 589, 599, 606, 607, 609, 619, 620, 672, 688, 692, 701, 761, 767, 768, 782, 783, 784, 815, 827, 846, 855, 856, 858, 868, 870, 874, 875, 887

Book II

2, 9, 50, 90, 107, 109, 139, 142, 145, 159, 171, 173, 174, 177, 178, 192, 216, 227, 260, 298, 337, 339, 346, 367, 374, 444, 446, 549, 568, 581, 634, 640, 684, 691, 694, 695, 700, 717, 718, 727, 733, 800, 832, 849, 857, 902, 912, 1038, 1056, 1120, 1132, 1144, 1168, 1169, 1196, 1207, 1226, 1247, 1273, 1276, 1318, 1324, 1325, 1330, 1345, 1355, 1364, 1368, 1387, 1412, 1427, 1453, 1466, 1486, 1495, 1509, 1517, 1523, 1530, 1555, 1595, 1642

Book III

9, 14, 90, 99, 120, 126, 132, 153, 155, 157, 161, 164, 169, 205, 211, 215, 220, 228, 229, 266, 287, 295, 300, 308, 315, 324, 327, 332, 338, 340, 358, 405, 410, 432, 453, 454, 469, 485, 487, 525, 530, 534, 535, 538, 545, 550, 555, 606, 625, 634, 674, 685, 715, 719, 730, 736, 740,

753, 774, 780, 784, 817, 820, 821, 823, 831, 833, 842, 859, 866, 888, 892, 901, 937, 953, 979, 1001, 1004, 1024, 1051, 1083, 1094, 1095, 1107, 1111, 1119, 1121, 1138, 1140, 1150, 1162, 1165, 1166, 1174, 1183, 1206, 1208, 1227, 1243, 1253, 1254, 1264, 1285, 1290, 1305, 1306, 1318, 1321, 1332, 1335, 1345, 1353, 1386, 1389, 1395, 1436, 1437, 1442, 1472, 1483, 1505, 1512, 1521, 1522, 1549, 1559, 1566, 1585, 1586, 1591, 1592, 1605, 1610, 1614, 1630, 1655, 1659, 1663, 1672, 1673, 1675, 1680, 1683, 1699, 1724, 1730, 1742, 1754, 1756, 1772, 1785, 1786, 1790, 1791, 1793, 1794, 1800, 1805

Book IV

68, 84, 100, 120, 121, 129, 182, 210, 234, 237, 253, 299, 302, 307, 346, 350, 362, 366, 374, 387, 392, 397

Book V

4, 14, 19, 27, 35, 53, 56, 58, 65, 72, 80, 87, 108, 114, 116, 128, 130, 132, 136, 140, 141, 147, 150, 151, 161, 162, 163, 165, 166, 171, 179, 181, 185, 187, 190, 191, 193, 194, 198, 201, 203, 215, 226, 232, 233, 234, 235, 269, 289, 296, 326, 338, 340, 342, 360, 366, 367, 371, 378, 379, 381, 386, 411, 429, 430, 434, 440, 444, 515, 521, 577, 581, 615, 620, 633, 669, 689

Book VI

1, 4, 5, 6, 15, 20, 24, 29, 32, 45, 51, 54, 57, 66, 69, 73, 84, 86, 99, 107, 114, 117, 130, 134, 166, 175, 181, 184, 190, 206, 213, 216, 222, 235, 237, 251, 266, 289, 293, 304, 311, 318, 333, 345, 347, 349, 350, 351, 359, 369, 371, 374, 383, 387, 388, 398, 407, 409, 415, 429, 443, 444, 446, 447, 448, 450, 457

"Type E" lines

Book I

56, 57, 96, 130, 303, 350, 553, 649, 665

Book II

254, 468, 980, 1664

Book III

20, 28, 41, 105, 138, 158, 167, 181, 311, 455, 653, 595, 803, 826, 900, 1016, 1247, 1258, 1282, 1283, 1350, 1399, 1541, 1634, 1668, 1716

Book IV

9, 16, 26, 27, 62, 89, 109, 134, 141, 150, 156, 204, 207, 378, 395

Book V

403, 477, 478

Book VI

67, 159, 210, 221, 352, 461

Summary

Book I	A	526	B	209	C	84	D	61	E	9	889
Book II	A	926	B	475	C	182	D	82	E	4	1669
Book III	A	1018	B	467	C	136	D	159	E	26	1806
Book IV	A	224	B	116	C	29	D	22	E	15	406
Book V	A	403	B	167	C	50	D	77	E	3	700
Book VI	A	217	B	118	C	47	D	67	E	6	455
		3314		1552		528		468		63	5932

5. THE STYLE

A first reading of Lydgate's *Life of Our Lady* reveals a metre, style and language entirely in accordance with these features of his other works. What distinguishes it from the general body of his work is an abundance of lyrical description of Our Lady which is of the highest poetical quality.

In the following section, we shall examine the commonest features of the syntax of the *Life of Our Lady*.

Syntactical Style

Anacolutha. Lydgate's involved word-order is often characterized by an abundance of incidental and subordinate clauses, great intervals between dependent clauses and between relatives and antecedents, inverted word-order where adjectives follow nouns, the preposition follows the word it governs, prepositions are thrown forward, verbs precede their auxiliaries, and adverbs and complements are thrown forward.

Incidental and subordinate clauses:

> Wherfor Reioyse, and be right gladde and light
> O Nazareth of name, most flouryng
> For oute of the, a floure mooste fayre of syght
> Moste full of grace, som tyme dydde spryng
> Of the whiche fully Remembryng
> So longe a gon spake hooly Isaye
> When þat he sayde in his prophecye
> That on this flour playnely shulde rest
> The holy gooste, for his chosyn place
> As for the fairest, and also for þe beste
> That euere was and, most full of grace
> Whose passyng beaute, no storme may deface
> But euere yliche contynueth fresshe of hew
> With oute fadyng, the colour is so trwe (I 92-105)

(See also I, 788-819; II, 498-504; II, 557-567)

Great intervals between dependent clauses:

> And to the gospell firste I gan take hede,
> Of this day howe luke luste to endyte;
> Though he thereof spake but a lyte,
> And was full breff and compendious;
> Ʒet of this day, so high and gloryouse,
> He wryte pleynly, and sayth how that a-noon,

Aftir the day of the Natyuyte,
When viii dayes passed were and gone,
The childe was brought with all humylyte
To the Temple, louly for to be,
As the lawe of Iewes had deuised,
The viii day to be circumcisede.

(IV 17-28)

(See also V, 21-35; VI, 127-135)

Intervals between relatives and antecedents:

And who by clennesse with the Turtle fleethe—
As I to forne haue made mencion—
And like the dove, affore his parell seeth,
Of dethe to eschewe the persecucion,
And can be meke in tribulacion,
I dar Recorde and wryte it for a sothe,
Truly to god he his offryng dothe.

(VI 274-280)

(See also I, 337-344; III, 357-372)

Adjectives frequently follow nouns at the end of a line:

For if he haue, his eene hole and clere (II 752)
Apered an Angell, with face sterne and bright (III 102)
Ournede newe, with beameȝ glad and merye (IV 8)

Adjectives are inverted to qualify a noun in the middle of a line:

With hert clene and meke affeccion (I 761)
Thy bilding high shall be brought full lowe (V 343)
For she hath power more in sothefastnesse (VI 363)

Prepositions follow words they govern:

Pure of entent, both in thought and dede (I 158)
Aftir his statute, his tribute for to paye (III 32)
Or elles one that were next of alye (V 49)

Prepositions and prepositional phrases are thrown forward:

And of this purpill, that I of spake to-forne (I 813)
And of mekenesse, haste it not dysdeynede (IV 371)
Wher he of vertu gedre may the greyen (VI 241)

Verbs precede their auxiliaries:

Whiche clepyde ben, hir petycions (I 439)
Ascendyd was vpon that mansion (III 302)
Ordeyned hath a palme of victorie (IV 98)

Adverbs and adverbial phrases are thrown forward:

> Of this feste somewhate forto wryte (IV 16)
> On the heven whan it wold apere (V 65)
> Full Redy ben of on entencion (VI 384)

Objects and complements are thrown forward, especially to the begining of a line:

> Hym honouryng with all hir hole herte (VI 189)
> And Iacob make in plente to habounde (III 815)
> On Caluery hym perced with a spere (IV 115)
> The forto serue, with herte and hoole corage (I 530)

Duplications. The Life of Our Lady abounds in duplicate expressions, and synonymous words and phrases, usually connected by *and* or *or:*

> aswagen and asofte I 12; laude and commendacion I 86; mouthes shette and lippys closed II 1600; halte or lame II 264; ake or smete II 716; to keuer or to hide V 364.

The duplicates are not always synonymous:

> in Rede. . . of purpill hewe I 807f; orysions. . . hir petycions I 438f; ydyll and in veyne IV 353; exile and pylgrymage V 551; sighe and sorowe make V 669.

The duplicates are sometimes a combination of genus and species, universal and particular:

> Estwarde to vs in the orient I 48; houre and tyme I 846; of spotte and fylthe II 255; gylt and transgression II 292; my sonne and myne owne heyre II 326; voys and tunge II 1002; errour and blynde and verrey ignoraunce II 1575; withoutyn synne or vyce III 994.

Some duplicates consist of an affirmative preceding a negative:

> Fresshe of hewe With-oute fadyng I 104f; baren Without frute I 563f; eternally and neuere fyne II 468f; Innocence Devoyde of synne II 1458f; erre and good not lyne Right II 1650; in all the hast . . . withoutyn more delay III 28ff; neuere twynnyth . . . abydyth aye III 264f.

Compound duplicate expressions:

> Incarnate / And wrappe hym-self in the mortall kynde II 313f; thorugh oute the worlde in euery londe and Realme III 149; Gan enlumyne . . . yafe so clere a light V 80f; That lastythe aye and may haue no endyng VI 228.

Many triple synonyms occur in the poem:

> clene pure and innocent II 260; cry and call Ande sayde III 1357f; lawe custom and vsaunce VI 377; þraldom and captiuite . . . preson II 171f; temple and also Receptacle . . . and chosen tabernacle I 349f.

Henry McCracken's observation can well serve us at this point:

> ". . . duplication of terms is an essential quality of English style. It would be dangerous to draw any line between Lydgate's tendency to excessive redundancy and the normal verbiage of monkish poets. There are times when Lydgate is concise, when every line tells; there are times when other poets than Lydgate grow tedious."[1]

Cases of parallelism are found even in lengthy passages.

> For golde of trouthe is falsely nowe alayede
> By feyned loue and Symlacioun,
> And fayth with fraude is corrupte and affrayed
> With double tunges and detraccioun;
> Our franke also of high perfection
> That shulde brenne clere above the skye,
> Is with the Coode medelede of envye. (V 561-567)

> For nought but synne, may engendre shame
> For selde or neuere, be the chekeȝ Rede
> Of hym in sothe, that is devoyde of blame
> For who is clene, takyth lytyll hede

> To wynke or blenke, for any maner drede
> And for thassaut, of eny mysty cloude
> Lyght of vertu, may no while shroude (II 1460-1466)

Miss Locock found "a strong resemblance between Lydgate's parallelisms and those of the Psalmist"[2] and dismisses the theory that Lydgate's style was influenced by Old English poetry. This reader's first impressions immediately suggested the Old English similarity. The frequency of alliteration, the complicated metrical system, the parallelisms and the strong consciousness of the influence of the caesura probably account for the impression.

This trait of Lydgate's style moved Professor Sieper to declare:

> ". . . it must not be thought that we are dealing with a mere chance occurrence. We are dealing with a principle of art consciously employed

---

[1] Henry N. McCracken, *The Minor Poems of John Lydgate* (EETSES, 107; 1911), I, x.
[2] Katharine B. Locock, *The Pilgrimage of the Life of Man* (1904; EETSES, 92), p. xlix.

and systematically carried through. . . . Everywhere we see clearly the results of an effort to find for every sentence, and even for every phrase within the sentence, a corresponding counterpart in a parallel construction . . . Lydgate is, in point of fact, not so far removed from a mere parallelism such as meets us in the poetry of the Hebrews."[3]

Lydgate is prolific in his *variation of terminology.*

Never:

nethir to ne froo II 698; For selde or neuere II 1461; neythir by worde ne soun VI 103.

Always:

boþe erly and late I 457; at morew and eke at eve III 816; firste or laste, al-waye newe and newe III 692; late or elles sone III 1754.

Nowhere, everywhere, throughout:

bothe in lenthe and brede I 75; in lande nor see III 1062; in euery manere londe VI 353.

Under all circumstances:

bothe in thought and dede I 158; bothe in fairenesse and in perfeccion I 317; for lyve or deth I 590.

All, many and various:

bothe face and chere I 808; bothe high and lowe III 31;
bothe god and men III 1566; bothe frende and fame IV 83;
Fro poynt to poynt VI 87.

Aureate terms. Stressing of verbs and adjectives by adverbs especially in the rhyme and pleonasms and tautologies contribute to an impression of tiresome gilding of description throughout the poem.

In gouernaunce and in discrecion (I 243)
Myne awne sonne, with me Incarnate (II 312)
And god the sonne, his childe alone eterne (III 498)
To hem that ben in exile, of outerage, (IV 195)
To his fayrnesse nor peregall (V 310)
God chese thy wombe for his habitacle (VI 12)

Pleonasms:

Now fayre sterre O, sterre of sterres all (I 50)
And lyke as Alquyn wryt, it is devysede (IV 64)
Whanne al was hust and al was in silence (III 1)

---

[3]Ernst, Sieper, *Lydgate's Reson and Sensuallyte* (1903; EETSES, 89) pp. 48, 50.

>It yevethe hym strength, it yeuyth hym sikernesse (IV 238)
>The hole beaute and fayrnesse eke also (V 314)
>That lastythe aye and may haue no endyng (VI 228)

The poet's fondness for tautological exprhesion occurs too frequently to be passed off as syntactical weakness. It seems rather a particular quality of his style and quite deliberate.

>May all the trouble aswagen and a softe (I 12)
>Her welthe affore, to be wepe and wayle (II 20)
>Whan euery Rakke and euery cloudy skye (III 135)
>Of herytykes that falsely disobey (IV 90)
>Whiche of the stok and the lyne cam (V 22)
>And euery man be glad and of goode chere (VI 192)
>He may not fayle noon of bothe twoo (VI 219)

Lydgate's use of "stop-gap" expressions seems to have no other justification than the desire to fill out the measure of his verse. These expressions occur most frequently in the second half of the line.

>Vnto the vertue, who so luste take hede (I 72)
>Sayde vnto hir a noon as ye shall here (II 359)
>And sayde, in sothe, that he was to blame (III 111)
>Also in four manere, who-so can take hede (IV 78)
>In verrey sothe as I remembre can (V 20)
>Called Aser, sothely as I rede (VI 175)

Direct and *indirect discourse.* Sometimes the poet slips from direct into indirect speech and vice versa without apparent cause.

>But lady myne, I put all in thy grace
>This first booke compylede for thy sake
>...................................
>Where as I erre, and put me in her grace. (I 873-4; 882)

>And whan he had, all his werke achevede
>He is Repared, to Naȝareth agayne
>But lorde how he was, in his hert a meovede (II 1110-1112)

>O she that was of hevyn and erthe quene
>And of hell, lady and eke pryncesse
>O what was he, alas, that may susteyne
>To be proude, considryng here mekenesse (V 337-9)

Romance words. A scholarly acquaintance with French and Latin probably led Lydgate to use many romance words in his poem. Following is a list culled by Professor Reismuller:[4]

---

[4]Georg Reismuller, *Romanische Lehnworter* (Ersthelege) *bei Lydgate* (Leipzig, 1911). Muenchner Beitrage zur Romanischen und Englischen Philologie, 48, pp. 18-132, *passim.*

advert, atravers, champolos, chandelabre, concern, condign, crimson, damask, depict, depure, deyner, ennew, ennose, eure, fage, fane, fervence, franc, fraudulent, indurate, interposition, inviolate, maligne, palestre, polimite, possede, proscript, prolong, receptacle, reclinatory, recompense, reedify, secretary, serpentyne, tarage, tempestuous, train, undespaired, victorious.

Romance doublets. In addition to single words are many combinations of Latin and French, Latin or French alone and Latin and/or French with words of Teutonic origin.

> in virginite or chastite I 559; gouerne vs and gye II 636; foyson and plente II 858; By some engyne or by collusion II 1366; sighe and sorowe V 669; his devour and also his laboure VI 347.

The writer's traditional reference to artistic insufficiency is to be found also in the *Life of Our Lady*.

> I am to Rude for to Rehersen, thaym all
> For vnconyng . . . (I 869f.)
> The wrong tracez, of my rude penne (II 1649)
> That I alas, of conyng, am depryvede
> Thorugh lak of witte, on eny manere wyse (IV 159f.)

Lydgate generously acknowledges his sources.

> as saint Ancelme seyth I 337; eke Hildefons tellyth of a tree II 680; as Beda liste to deffyne III 15; how luke luste to endyte IV 18; Wherof wrytheth Dauid V 455; the gospell saythe expresse VI 87.

On the other hand, there seems to be no logical reason for references to unnamed sources, except, perhaps, the exigencies of metrical structure.

> In bokes olde, as it is specifiede (I 123)
> They may ensamples, Right I nowe fynde (II 650)
> And aftir that, I fynde ferthermore (III 56)
> And in bokes, eke as it is tolde (IV 120)
> Who so lust loke, in bokes fro a ferre (V 23)
> In Rome twone, as myn auctour seythe (VI 337)

Poetic Qualities

The study of the many syntactical weaknesses of Lydgate's style has led to an almost universal disparagement of the monk's poetic content. One of Lydgate's most competent and severe editors, Professor J. Schick, cautions the reader on this point:

"There is certainly many a felicitous line and many a poetical sentiment or piece of imagery to be found in his works that would not deface the finest page of a true poet."[5]

Professor Schick further points out a long list of contemporaries who considered Lydgate a great poet[6] and even later luminaries to Elizabeth Barrett-Browning who wrote:

"When he ceased his singing, none sang better; there was silence in the land."[7]

While it is evident that Lydgate often resorts to "stop-gap" expressions to fill out his metre and frequent moralizations suggested by his material, it is equally true that the *Life of Our Lady* is essentially a narrative poem, a medium hardly conducive to the lyric spirit.

Yet within this restrictive frame-work, Lydgate manages to evoke many a singing line and colorful image. In our poem his poetic talents are especially noted in his descriptions of Our Lady. He takes every opportunity the narrative permits him to paint a brilliant picture of some physical or moral quality of his subject. He uses the similes and personifications of the prophets, the sacred writers and other sources and his own insights gleaned principally from nature and astronomy. A selection of the most noteworthy excerpts that exemplify this quality is to be found in Appendix B, p. 227.

Ten Brink's high opinion of Lydgate's poetic talent amazes some scholars.[8] He believed that the poet "possesses great facility of poetic expression and very often hits the proper word. In his poetic work one finds many good, and even excellent things."[9]

This opinion seems aptly verified in the *Life of Our Lady*. Assuming that the personal devotion of the monk to Our Lady may have inspired him to extend himself when writing of her, the supposition does not appear weighty enough to explain away the genuine poetic quality of many other lines of the poem.

That the poem enjoyed great popularity may be judged from the number of extant manuscript copies: thirty-six complete and five fragments. Caxton probably printed two additions circa 1484 and Redman reprinted Caxton in 1531.[10]

---

[5] J. Schick, *Lydgate's Temple of Glas* (1891, EETS, 60), p. clvi.
[6] pp. cxlii-cxliv.
[7] Elizabeth Barrett-Browning, *The Book of the Poets* (New York, 1877), p. 23.
[8] Schick, *op. cit.*, pp. xi-xii.
[9] Bernhard Ten Brink, *History of English Literature* (London, 1893), translated from the German by Wm. Clarke Robinson. II, 223.
[10] See "2. Descriptions of the Manuscripts and Prints", pp. 21 ff.

We have again chosen out of the context lines that bear the unmistakable stamp of the true poet. The list is so long that, together with the excerpts pertaining to Our Lady, they constitute a formidable array of jewels that would grace the crown of any king of song. The total numerical weight of them alone cannot but lead the observer to question the dismissal by some scholars of Lydgate's claim to true poetic stature.

Why so much poetic beauty does not first catch the eye of the beholder, one can only conjecture. Our opinion is that nearly all of it remains hidden behind the metrical system, the silent or pronounced final "e" and the free-wheeling syllabic construction of the Chaucerian and post-Chaucerian eras. The poem unveils after the reader has discovered a systematic scansion and after he has familiarized himself with such things as elision, syncope, synezesis and diaresis.

Appendix *A* (pp. 218 ff.), contains a selection of non-Marian poetic lines.

A third selection of lines has been made to illustrate two points; 1) the heavy dependence of the poet on the alliterative device; 2) the use of this time-honored[11] crutch to fashion many a happy poetic articulation. It simply cannot be gainsaid that a great number of the lines are improved as a result of alliteration. In many cases, it is true that the alliteration is an obvious embellishment of a metrical "filler" but the instances of occurrence are actually numerically less than the superior lines (see appendix *B*) if one must be impressed by statistics. It could be further justly claimed that even in these cases the poet has certainly decorated the crutch.

Miss Locock had like impressions of her study of *The Pilgrimage of the Life of Man.*

> ". . . though alliterative lines are fairly numerous they are employed with considerable self-restraint . . . the alliteration in Lydgate's verse never becomes burdensome, but rather tends to give it a little of the variety it so much needs."[12]

The selection has been made from lines that are unmistakably alliterative and all lines where this reader hesitated about the poet's intention have been omitted (cf. Appendix *C*, pp. 234 ff.).

A final selection of lines has been made to point out Lydgate's use of imagery. The figures of speech are principally simile, metaphor and personification and the poet's use of nature, astronomy and flowers shows a sure hand, a heart fond of big, brilliant and warm pictures, and talent for a neat turning of proverbial and sententious expressions. Because nearly all the lines already appear in the appendices, we give here only the book and line numbers:

---

[11]"As our oldest poetry was alliterative, alliteration has always been considered a permissible, and indeed a favourite, ornament of English verse." Walter W. Skeat, *The Complete Works of Geoffrey Chaucer* (Oxford, 1894), VI, xcvii.

[12]p. xxv.

Nature and astronomy

    Book I 1-7, 22, 35, 143, 159-161, 166, 316-320, 351-352, 824-825; *Book II* 604-606, 626-627, 785-791, 890-893, 941-942, 1303-1304, 1427, 1467-1492, 1558-1562, 1610-1611, 1632-1635; *Book III* 1, 102-106, 123, 129-130, 165, 170-172, 345, 346, 632, 691, 1138-1139, 1253-1260, 1572, 1574, 1755; *Book IV* 209; *Book V* 96, 411, 493, 570-574, 621.

Flowers

    Book I 38-39, 64-65, 94, 99-112, 182, 308, 315, 327-328, 727, 729; *Book II* 551-557, 748-749, 1427, 1442; *Book III* 635-637, 640, 687-688, 702, 730, 786, 947, 1410-1411, 1761, 1768; *Book V* 181-182; *Book VI* 229-231, 391-403.

Proverbial and Sententious Expressions

    Book II 131-133, 246-247, 1483, 1491-1492; *Book III* 1596; *Book IV* 36; *Book V* 181-182, 191, 397-398, 561-564, 594-595; *Book VI* 341-343.

Miscellaneous

    Book I 74, 266, 326, 334-336, 339, 557, 862-863; *Book II* 339-340, 589-590, 735, 741, 900, 922-924, 1509, 1513; *Book III* 655, 686, 906-907, 1018, 1022, 1612; *Book IV* 42, 274-275; *Book V* 96, 387, 663; *Book VI* 145, 168, 425.

Someone has said that the modern approach to Lydgate is to make selections from his works. It has been the experience of this writer, after making the above "anthology" of the *Life of Our Lady,* that that advice is not only correct but also may point to a key that would explain the great popularity of this work in its own day. The imagery is so rich and abundant that it easily colors over whatever the reader may find difficult or dull in other parts of the poem.

We are not familiar with any established numerical norm for the rating of poetical genius but we have a strong conviction that Lydgate should rate a listing of at least average and that we cannot accept opinions such as Professor Courthope's sweeping dismissal of the poet when he writes that "what is really interesting and historically valuable in the art of Lydgate arises from his own incapacity as a poet."[13]

Professor Schick's opinion, at least about our poem, is more acceptable:

    "I should think that the *Life of Our Lady* . . . with its comparative freshness—at least in some parts—still belongs to Lydgate's better works . . . I believe that the scales will be decidedly turned in Lydgate's favour, Ten Brink's comparatively high opinion of the monk still further justified, when certain of his works which lie as yet unpublished in various libraries are made generally accessible. Then it will appear more and more clearly that, in estimating him as a poet, the stress should not so much be laid on the unoriginal and spun-out rhymes of his later age, but rather on the more spontaneous and animated productions of his earlier years."[14]

---

[13]W. J. Courthope, *A History of English Poetry* (London, 1926), I, 320.
[14]*op. cit.,* p. cviii and clvii.

Appendix A

Selected Lines

O thoughtfull herte, plunged in distresse
With slombre of slouthe, this long wynters nyght
Oute of the slepe, of mortall hevynesse
Awake a noon, and loke upon the lyght
Of thelke sterre that with hir bemys bryght
And withe the shynyng, of hir stremys merye
Is wonte to gladde, all our Emysperye [I 1-7]

Amyddeȝ the arke of our merydyne, [I 35]

That she in wepyng dothe on floures flete
In listy Aprill and in fresshe may [I 38-39]

Whose gladde beamys without eclypsyng stonyde [I 47]

So late the golde dewe of thy grace fall
Into my breste, like skales, fayre and white [I 52-53]

A Flour of vertue full longe kepyt in cloose
Full many ver with holsome leves swote [I 64-65]

So fayre som tyme gan to spryng and sprede [I 74]

Wherfor Reioyse and be right gladde and light [I 92]

The nyght is passet, lo the morowen gray [I 143]

Whiche as Aurora, with hir Rawes rede
The nyght avoideth, with his copeȝ donne
Affore the vpryste of the bright sonne [I 159-161]

Whose beaute, fayleth as floure in frosty mede [I 308]

With sugrede tonge, of many wordeȝ whyte [I 557]

And I am olde, with white lockes graye
Passed full fere, my tendre yeres grene [I 731-732]

Whan he of purpill, dyd his baner sprede
On Calvary abrode, vpon the Rode
To save mankynde, whan he schede his bloode [I 810-812]

For in sothenesse the Ioye was not lyche
Of Cresus kyng, for all his riche hurde [I 843-844]

O who can telle, thy holy slepes softe
With god alwaye, full in thy memorye [I 862-863]

Our Lady's life in Nazareth after the wedding to St. Joseph]
[see also Book I. 11.820-868] for lyric description of

For Ioye passet, can hertes more constrayne [II 19]

O who couthe euere, sithe the world by gan
Of more ioye, or of gladdnesse tell
Then some tym couthe, the worthe kynde of man
That shapen was, in paradise to dwell [II 22-25]

And is not mercy of more excellence
Lyke as the Sawter, well reherse can
Upon the herthe, beter than lyfe of man [II 131-133]

And Iob Recordith the holsomest frute
Of all this worlde, spryngyth oute of pees [II 162-163]

For Ruste with Rust, may not scowrede be
Ne foule, with fylthe, may nat be puryfied [II 246-247]

And wrappe hym self, in the mortall kynde
Of man for love, so that he may fynde
A clene grovnde, his paleys onto bylde [II 314-316]

Whileʒ the mayde, that causith al this pees
Hathe the vnycorne, sleeping in hir lappe [II 339-340]

No lytyll sparke, but a flame of fyre [II 396]

O where is al thy transitorye fame
Of pompe and pryde, and Surquydre in feer
Where is your booste, or how dar ye apeer
With your forblowe, blowyng vanyte [II 507-510]

And with a worde, of þe mayden spoke
The holy goste, in her brest Iloke [II 517-518]

And like as dewe, descendeth on the Rose
With siluer dropes, and of the leves fayre
The fresche bewete, ne may not apayre
Ne as the rayne, in Apryll or in May
Causyng the vertu to Renne oute of the Rote
The grete fayrenesse nought apayre may
On violeteʒ, and on arbes soote [II 551-557]

With fyre of love, brynnyng also bryght
. . . .
As done the sterres, in the frosty nyght [II 604-606]

Clad in a sonne, þe wheche brighter shon
Than phebʒ dothe, in his large spere [II 626-627]

She brent in love, hatter than the glede [II 735]

The well of helthe, and of lyfe eterne [II 741]

For he that made bothe leef and lynde
And with oo worde, this waste worlde wilde
Night make a mayde, for to goo with chylde [II 754-756]

For he that dothe, the tendre branches spryng
And fresshe floures, in the grene mede
That werne in wyntir dede, and eke droupyng
Of Bawme voyde, and of all lustyhede
Might he nat make, his greyne to growe and sede
Withe Inne hir brest, that was both mayde and wyfe
Wher of is made the sothefaste brede of lyfe [II 785-791]

And as the snawe, fro Iubiter dothe falle
Thorough the force, of Sagitarrius bowe
And Ʒepherus dothe the flores shale
On white blosomes, whan she dothe blowe [II 890-893]

And þat the claper, of his distouned bell
May cancre sone, I mene his fals tunge
Be dume for euere, and neuere to be Ronge [II 922-924]

Whose fayre stremes, shullen neuer cesse
Withoutyn eclipse, to shyne in clennesse [II 941-942]

And pyte, shall be feffed in his stall
And Ruthe shall, his Right so enbrace
To set mercy, above his werkes all [II 1050-1052]

... in dovble drede
My witte is brought, and wote not whereto turne
For double cause, that I haue to morne [II 1149-1151]

... the mysty blake clowde
Of ignoraunce, is so claryfied
That all the trouthe, to me is verrefyed [II 1303-1305]

My night of errour, is turned in to daye [II 1310]

Tyll the trouth, be Ryped in the Rote [II 1427]

It may a whyle, be derked with askye
As is a monge, the fayre bryght sonne
And with the wyndes, of malice and envye
The shynyng sterres, often wexen donne [II 1467-1470]

As gold in fire is fynde be assay [II 1483]

For light wol oute, it may not be borne dovne
And so will trouthe ... [II 1491-1492]

That he of trouthe, shall trye oute the stele [II 1513]

The more she was, to her sight fayre
And lyche as phebus, in Ioly grene maye
Whan he hathe chasede, the derke mysty eyre
Shyneth more bright, the clere somers daye
Whan þikke vapours, ben dreven clene awaye [II 1558-1562]

And god to forne, yet or the bryddys syng
And or than Flora, dothe the floures spryng [II 1610-1611]

But oo alas, the Retorykes swete
Of petrak Fraunces that couthe so endite
And Tullyus, with all his wordys white
Full longe agone, and full olde of date
Is dede alas and passed into faste [II 1623-1627]

That made firste, to distille and rayne
The golde dewe dropes, of speche and eloquence
Into our tunge, thurgh his excellence
And fonde the floures, first of Retoryke [II 1632-1635]

Whanne al was hust and al was in silence [III 1]

Apered an Angell with face sterne and bryght
Of whome the beaute yaf a pleasant lyght
The place envyron and a sote odoure
And his clothyng like the lely floure
Was whit in sothe, as snowe that fallith newe [III 102-106]

With many stere distyllyng on his face [III 123]

And hir phares quenche and waxen colde
With sacrede light, that were wonte to shyne [III 129-130]

Ful straite and narewe, schadewid with derknesse [III 165]

That shone as bright as eny someres day
. . . .
Was fresche of light as phebus is in may [III 170-172]

Ande alle this worlde myȝght at his wille gouerne
Which in his hands hangeth as a ball [III 345-346]

And whan thay sawe hir pappes so abounde
With henvenly mylke sent from above the cloude [III 367-368]

This myghty lorde for to come adovn,
The high hevens wolde breke entweyne [II 593-594]

From see to see, and all the erthe sprede
Thorugh the worlde bothe in lengthe and brede [III 622-623]

The high hevynes dothe your grace adewe [III 632]

And bad the grovnde, eke in wordes fewe
For to open and thorowe his heuenly showre,
For to buryovne our alther savyour [III 635-637]

A greyn of Dauid, fayrer then floure in may [III 640]

Or that the swerde be whette of vengeaunce [III 655]

Of holsome frute and of herbes soote [III 702]

And of this holy, fayre, fresshe felde,
Sumtyme þe spouse spak in canticis,
When he it sawe so fresshe at his devys,
And habundant of a tempre eyre,
And þat it was so passing Inly fayre [III 731-735]

Amydde the felde that dothe the vertu floure [III 786]

And lete the swetnesse of your notes fall
Doyne to the erthe, wher goddes awne sonne
This day hathe ioye with vs to wonne [III 843-845]

And of eyne fayrer many folde
Thanne wyn fined shynynge thorowe a verre [III 960-907]

As a burgeon oute of a stoke growyng [III 947]

Berne of the blode to be preste and kyng [III 950]

In a closet more clere þan verre or glas [III 1018]

The kyng Dauid entune dyd his harpe
And with the tenoures and the trebles sharpe,
He to heuene gan enhaunce and ryse
This day of dayes, moste worthy and famous [III 1049-1052]

Angelles full low Swiftely dovne a-light,
For the honour this holy sacrede nyght,—
The nyght of nyghtes, highest of ycheone [III 1056-1058]

Of his stremes passyngely entiere
To loke vpon as any cristal clere [III 1138-1139]

Ne lesith not, the light of his brightnesse
Thorught noon eclippsyng, of foryetylnesse [III 1245-1246]

Nature made with fresshe blossomes soote
To assende vpon this same nyght
Vnto the croppe, with frute and levys newe,
Makyng the bowes as lusty to the sight,—
As fresshe as fayre of colour and of hewe
And as plentevous her color to Renewe,—
As in Septembre when Bachus hathe power
To shewe his might that tyme of the yere. [III 1253-1260]

And of beames waxen wonder donne [III 1399]

Oute of the stoke of Iuda, that shall haunte
His myghty hande, her tyranye to daunte [III 1406-1407]

And oute of hem even Ilyke procede
As dothe a floure oute of the rough spyne [III 1410-1411]

The tyme of tymeȝ, the tyme of lyfe and grace
The tyme of Ioye and no-thyng to morne
Sythe he is borne with so fayre a face,
The golden worlde makyng to retourne,
The worlde of pece, the kyngdome of Satourne [III 1457-1461]

And sayde of Dauid a burioun and the spryng
Shall be susteynede and Regne like a kyng [III 1502-1503]

Till Efte ayeyne his charet he bryng
Into the Est, that dothe the larke syng
For Ioye only that his bemes ryse [III 1572-1574]

Fro woman firste trouthe moste aryse [III 1596]

How trouthe and mercy in a mayden mette [III 1612]

. . . for the londe of mede,
Wher the hylles of golde ben, as I rede,
May no tresoure in his maynes Reyse,
Ayen thy tresoure for to countrepayse [III 1642-1645]

For certes, lady, thou alone haste all
That in heven Angels desyre:
The Iewell Riche, the tresour celestiall
Of heven kyng, of erthe lorde and sire,
And hym þat hath al þe hole empire
Of land and see, and the monarchie
Thou hast holy, o lady myne, to gye. [III 1646-1652]

"O blissed lady, flour of virgynyte,
We prayen ichone, o welle of our welfare,
Like a mothir net thy mylke to spare.

Yeffe hym plentee that is so plentevouse
Of fulsomnesse Angels to fede;
And yef hym souke the pyment graciouse
Of thy pappes: lat the condyte shede
The sote mylke all aboute in brede,
And motherly makyng it to avale
On his fayre tendur lymes smale."

Glad mayste thou be, þat sauf hym luste to **vouche,**
Withe his rounde softe lippeȝ lyte,
To have pleasaunce thy bresteȝ for to **touche**

Only to souke thy blissede pappes white;
And that hym luste so godely to delyte,
For his playe to haue so moche blisse,
Euere among thy holy mouthe to kysse.

And sodenly, with childely chere Iocounde,
Than a-none thy white nek embrace
With softe tendre Armes rounde,
And than at onys fallen on thy face,
And of his eyne, fulfillede of all grace,
A godely loke to thewarde enclyne;
And so furthe his chokes lay by thyne,

And withe his fyngres, mouthe and eyne touche;
His smal pawmes on thy chekes layne,
His yong face betwene thy pappes couche,
And holde hym stille, with all his besy payne,
And grype hym faste with his handez twayne;
For ther-in was his hevenly repaste,—
Þi ȝunge sone whan he list breke his faste,

Ther was his foode and his norchyng pure,
Sothefaste seler of his systynaunce;
The tone of lyfe that euere dyd endure,
Ilyche fresshe vnto his pleasaunce,
Withe sacrede lycoure of holy habundaunce,
That noon but he may touche nor aproche,
For it for hym was only set abroche. [III 1657-1694]

Some-tyme fro hevyn fel adoune the manne [III 1723]

O mayde, o mother, daughter of thy sonne [III 1750]

So bright a sonne spryngyng of so fayre a mone [III 1755]

Saff this day, the sonne of lyf moste shene [III 1756]

The soyl to adewe with his sote stremez [III 1778]

When Ianus Byfrons in colde Ianuarie,
With frosty berde entreth in the yere,
And phebus chare neyeth to aquarye
His watry beamez to-fore feverer,
Whan that his light was pale and no-thyng clere,
And from hym late was partyd lucyne,
The same nyght as I sawe her shyne

Ournede newe, with beamez glad and merye,
On the heven, and caste his stremes adovne,
I gan Remembre of the high ferye
That called is the Circumcisyon; [IV 1-11]

So yonge, so fayre, wepyng so for woo [IV 42]

When he was nayled high vpon the rode [IV 112]

The name of names, sacred from eterne [IV 164]

Of which the stremeȝ bene so fresshe and fyne [IV 209]

The holsome welle ay dothe flowe and flete
With mercy medled and remyssion [IV 212-213]

Cristall schelde of pallas for dispayre [IV 234]

It yevethe hym strength, it yeuyth hym sikernesse [IV 238]

Had in his hert of golde full depe grave [IV 256]

And letters newe depicte in euery veyne [IV 259]

This is the name that moste yeveth melodye
Vnto the eere, and the Swettest son [IV 274-275]

And or thy swerde of vengeaunce vs manace,
Lat reuthe afore thy rightfull dome enbrace [IV 335-336]

To make hem stonde stille as any stone [IV 390]

So yong, so fayre, in a golden spere [V 96]

Thorow mani a londe and many a diuerse yle [V 121]

And her venym vnder floures fayre
Full ofte is hydde tyll thay may appayre [V 181-182]

What can sugur vndur galle faine? [V 191]

But who the Ioy can tell or endyte,
Or with his mouthe, who can the myrthe expresse,
Or who can playnly with his penne wryte,
The grete blisse or elles the gladnesse
Which thay made in verrey sothefastnesse [V 211-215]

Though thy boste above the skyes blowe
Thy bildyng high shall be brought full lowe! [V 342-343]

And of the axtre by-twene the poleȝ tweyne
And all the enbrasyng of the golden cheyne [V 347-348]

And be well ware, or the spere byte
Of cruell dethe and the fell smerte [V 397-398]

Ligge þei not graue vndre clowris grene? [V 411]

And like a dove with fayre feders white [V 493]

For golde of trouthe is falsely nowe alayede
By feyned loue and Symylacioun,
And fayth with fraude is corrupte and affrayed
With double tunges and detraccioun [V 561-564]

For day of trouthe is turnede vnto nyght
Thorough wrong reporte and false suspecion.
And þus good feith is rollid up soo doun,
And trwe menyng darkyd with a skye
That we in Englisshe calle flaterye. [V 570-574]

For soden dom meynt with ignoraunce
Hathe a long tayle sewyng of repentaunce [V 594-595]

. . . o what thyng may this be,
To se that lorde in a Rakke lye
That hath the hevyn vndir his powste,
And all this worlde power hath to gye!
O how it is that the Regalye
Of heven and erthe is brought dovne so lowe
That noman luste vnethes his power knowe! [V 652-658]

So fayre, so gode and of so hygh estate [V 663]

A-yentse the snares of this dredfull werre,
To lyfe eterne be thou our lode sterre [V 699-700]

For of her wombe, the cloyster virgynall,
Was euere liche, bothe firste and laste,
Closed and shette as castell principall [VI 64-66]

For nowe to me dethe is wondir swete [VI 145]

That lastythe aye and may haue no endyng [VI 228]

And as the birde sheweth the commyng
Of grene ver with fresshe buddeӡ newe
Ryght so of vertu with floures fayre of hewe [VI 229-231]

That he his lyfe lede not in veyne,
But like a dove, bysely espye
Where he of vertu gedre may the greyne [VI 239-241]

For olde custome is harde to putte away
And vsage grevythe folkeӡ full sore
To do a-way that thei haue kepte of yore [VI 341-343]

And as the wax is made and wrought of newe,—
Thorough small bees of floures fresshe of hewe,

Thorughe clennesse only and diligent labour
Of blossomes gedrede and to the hyve brought—
So cristes manhode grewe oute of a floure,
Whose fresshe beaute of coloure fadyth nought;
For of a mayde clene in will and thought—
Like as wax of floures soote and glade
Is tried out and doith hem not to fade—

So criste Ihesu, conservyng her clennesse,
His manhode toke of a mayden free,
She standyng hole flouryng in fayrenesse
Withe all the fresshenesse of virgynyte [VI 391-403]

Fare well his gwerdon, his meryte and his mede, [VI 425]

Appendix B

Descriptions of Our Lady

Of thelke sterre that with hir bemys bryght
. . . .
Is wont to gladde, all our Emysperye [I 5-7]

This sterre in beautee passethe pliades [I 22]

For this of Iacob, Is the fayrest sterre [I 31]

Now fayre sterre O, sterre of sterres all [I 50]

A Flour of vertue [I 64]

O Nazareth, with Beddelem the by syde
This Flour, yov makyth, of name more Ryall
Than either Rome, elate and full of pride
Or myghty Troye, with the sturdy wall
Whose Renon halteth, to be paragall
In honour pryse, Fame and Reuerence
Vnto youre passyng, worthi excellence

If for the frute commendyde be the tre
Thow hast more laude, and commendacion
For thilke fruite, that sprong out of the
Than hath Aufryke of worthy Scypyon
Or Rome of Sesar, or of Fabion
Though hir nameȝ were some tyme grave in golde
Her Idyll fame, to thyne may not be tolde

Wherefor Reioyse, and be right gladde and light
O Nazareth of name, most flouryng
For oute of the, a floure mooste fayre of syght
Moste full of grace, som tyme dydde spryng
Of the whiche fully Remembryng
So longe a gon spake hooly Isaye
When þat he sayde in his prophecye

That on this flour playnely shulde rest
The holy gooste, for his chosyn place
As for the fairest, and also for þe beste
That euere was and, most full of grace
Whose passyng beaute, no storme may deface
But euere yliche contynueth fresshe of hewe
With oute fadyng, the colour is so trwe

For this is þe flour, that god hym self behelde
The white lylye of the chosyn vale
The swete Roose, of the fayre felde
Which of colour wexyth neuer pale
The violet, our langour to a vale
Purpyll hewede, thorough mercy and pety
To socoure alle, that in myschief be [I 78-112]

. . . A floure mooste fayre of syght [I 94]

. . . the holy frute of lyfe [I 126]

A clene mayde, in will and werking [I 157]

For she is Aurora, sothely this is noo nay [I 166]

. . . this floure of womanhede [I 182]

. . . this braunche of holynesse [I 192]

Full of vertu, devoyde of all outerage [I 225]

Of wordes fewe, and wondre softe of speche [I 266]

Hir godely face, was so full of light
That no man myght, susteyn to by holde [I 282-283]

Ne noon so fayre, was neuere founde in Reame [I 295]

Late be thow Grece, and speke not of Eleyn
Ne thow Troy, of yong Polexene
Ne Rome of Lucresse, with hir eyn tweyne
Ne thow Cartage, of thy fresshe quene
Dido that was so fayre some tyme to seen
Late be your boste, and take of hem noon hede
Whose beaute, fayleth as floure in frosty mede

Ester was meke, but not lyke hir mekenesse
And Iudith wyse, but she yet dyd excell
And Barsabe of grete semelynesse
And Rachell fayre, Iacob can yov tell
But she aloone, of womanhode the well
Of bountee, beaute, þat neuere fade may
Nat liche a floure, that flouressheth but in may

Passyde Ichone bothe ney and ferre
Bothe in fairenesse, and in perfeccion
Right as þe sonne, doth a litil sterre
And as þe rubie, hath wone þe renoun
Of stonys all, and dominacion
Right so this mayde, to speke of holynesse
Of women all Is lady and maystres

Off whome spake some tyme, wyse Salamon
In sapience, we so lust it to seke
That she was chosyn, for hym self alone
This white dove with hir eyn make
Whose chekys were, hir beaute forto eke
With lylieʒ meynt and fresshe Rosys Rede
This is to sayen, who so can take hede

First with the Rose, of womanly suffraunce
And with the lylye, next of chastytee
She was ennuede, to yef hyr suffisaunce
As well in goodnesse, as in beaute
And as he sayeth, she fayrer was to see
Than outhir phebus, platly or lucyne
With hornes full on heven, whan thay schyne

And of this mayde, as saint Ancelme seyth
In his wrytyng, hir beaute to termyne
Of face fayre, but fayrer yet of fayeth
He sayth she was, this holy pure virgyne
Whose chast hert, to no thyng dyd enclyne
For all hir beaute, but to holynesse
Of whome also this Autor saythe expresse

That she was daughtir of david by dyscent
Sterre of the see, and goddes awne ancyll
Quene of the worlde, al way of one entent
And goddes spous, his hestes to fulfille
And euere redy, forto wyrke his will
Crystes temple, and also Receptacle
Of the holy goost, and chosen tabernacle

The yate of heven, and also the fayrnesse
Of women alle, who so looke aright
Of maidenhede, lady and princesse
One of the fyve, that bare hyr laumpe light
Redy to mete, with hir spous at nyght
Full prudently, awaytyng at the gate
That for noo sloothe, she came not to late

In fygure eke the chaundelabre of golde
That some tyme bare, Seven laumpes schene
This is to saye, the Receyte and the holde
Of god preseruede, for she was so clene
Thorough hir merite, endowet forto ben
By grace of hym, that is of power most
With the seven yiftes, of the holy goste [I 302-364]

But she aloone of womanhode the well [I 313]

Of women all Is Lady and maystres [I 322]

This white dove with hir eyn meke [I 326]

Whose chekys were, hir beaute forto eke
With lylieȝ meynt and fresshe Rosys Rede [I 327-328]

. . . she fayrere was to see
Than outhir phebus, platly or lycyne
With hornes full on heven, whan thay schyne [I 334-336]

Of face fayre, but fayrer yet of fayeth [I 339]

Sterre of the see, and goddes awne ancyll
Quene of the worlde. . . . [I 345-346]

The yate of heven, and also the fayrnesse
Of women alle . . . [I 351-352]

And trwe merrowre of virgynytee [I 409]

. . . hir tendre handys white [I 432]

. . . flouryng in fayrenesse [I 727]

For she is fayre, and fresshe as Rose in may [I 729]

For hir meryte, of hevyn and erthe and qwene [I 805]

. . . this blissetfull mayde dere [I 820]

. . . as a fulsome well [I 824]

But nowe I leve, this blissetfull mayde dere
In Naȝareth a mong her frendys to dwelle
Ledyng a life, more perfyte and entere
Than any tunge, suffise may to tell
For euere elyche, as a fulsome well
Shedith his stream in to þe ryvere
Right so Marye, in ensample clere

Gaffe to all, by plentyvous largesse
Onely in vertu, vpon euery syde
O wele were thay, to whom thou were maistresse
And blisset eke, that might on the abyde
To have by ensample, so vertuouse a gyde
And blisset, was that holy companye
That day by day, the seen with her eye

And blisset was, the paleys and the house
In whiche thou haddist, thy holy mansion
Fortuned well and wondre graciouse
So humble was thy conuersacion
And blisset was also all the towne
Where thou abode, and blissed the village
O holy mayde, where thou helde hostage

And blisset was, the worthy table riche
Where day by day, thou wentist vnto bourde
For in sothenesse the Ioye was nat lyche
Of Cresus kyng, for all his riche hurde
And blisset ben thay that herden worde by worde
Of thy speche, blisset the houre and tyme
Of all thy lyfe, frome even to the prime

O welfull eke and gracious the sight
Of thaym that myght vpon the byholde
For well they awght to be glad and light
That werne with the all way when thay wolde
And blissed werne both yonge and olde
That werne reioysede, with thyne excellence
Whan that hem liste of theyne high presence

O the Ioye, who couthe tell aright
Of thyne hevenly meditacions
Assendyng vp above the sterres bright
In thyne Inwarde contemplacions
Or thy holy visitacions
Who can Reherse hem, bright as sonne or leven
So ofte sent downe to the, frome heven

O who can telle, thy holy slepes softe
With god alwaye, full in thy memorye
For love of whome, thou sigest full ofte
Whan thou were soole, in thyne orytorye
Or who can tell, the melody and glorye
That Angelleʒ have made, in the holy place
For the Ioye thay had, to loke vpon thy face
                         [I 820-868]

. . . a mayde, deboner, and full mylde [II 318]

. . . well, of womanhede [II 437]

. . . of vertu tresorere [II 446]

For she is the tour . . . and hous of yvour [II 544-545]

She was the castell, of the cristall wall [II 547]

She was eke the gate, with the lokeʒ breght
Sette in the Northe, of high deuoccion [II 568-569]

She was of golde, also the Riche ourne
Kepyng the manna, of our saluacion [II 589-590]

The yerde of Aron, with frute and leves lade [II 594]

She was the Auter, of Cedre gold and stone [II 596]

She shone as golde, by perfyte charite [II 602]

She was the trone, where that Salamon
For worthynesse, sette his Riall see
With gold and yvory, that so bright shone [II 610-612]

She was also the woman, that saint Iohn
Sawe in the hevyn, so Richely apere
Clad in a sonne, þe wheche brighter shon
Than phebȝ dothe, in his large spere
And xii sterres, that passyngly were clere
So as to hym, playnely dyd seme
Were sette above, in hir diademe [I 624-630]

. . . the first faythefull wall [II 642]

Ne fadith never in beaute ne in colour
Of maydenhede, to bere bothe lefe and flowre [II 748-749]

. . . fresh of fayrnesse for to see [II 900]

. . . of mercy grovnde and well [II 919]

. . . the clennesse of this Queen [II 938]

Blisset art thou, amonge wymen alle [II 960]

That Marye, debonaire and so mild [II 1362]

. . . lyke a myrrour, of all holynesse [II 1377]

She was ensample, to euery manere wight [II 1381]

. . . euere floured in hir fame [II 1442]

. . . the verry chosyn chest
Of all clennesse. . . . [II 1477]

. . . constant, as a wall [II 1509]

. . . this goodly fresshe of hewe [II 1527]

. . . this perfyte holy mayde [II 1528]

And lyche as phebus, in Ioly grene maye [II 1559]

. . . so plentyvouse benyng [II 1619]

O clene castell, and the chaaste toure
Of the holy goste. . . . [II 1663-1664]

. . . this floure of maydynhede [III 207]

. . . marye, example of maydynhede [III 452]

. . . that blissede perfyte holy hill
That groweth full of holsome floures fayre [III 687-688]

Lyche as the dwe of heven . . . [III 691]

Passing the Rose and the floure delys [III 730]

. . . O welle of our welfare [III 1658]

. . . of myrour of mekenesse [III 1734]

Benygne floure, of womanhode the welle [III 1735]

O fayre rose, o Rose of Iericho [III 1761]

. . . fayre Cedre, Cypresse of Syon [III 1765]

Chose chaumbre of wyse Salamon [II 1767]

Flour of the felde, swettest on holte and hethe [III 1768]

Of Syloe the water eke depurede [III 1770]

Laude and glorye of Iherusalem [III 1772]

Holsome Cysterne, this day of Bedlem [III 1774]

On whom kyngeȝ haue yoye to by-holde [V 353]

. . . She was fayrest for to see [V 387]

Þou blissful quene of kingis emperesse [V 618]

. . . o sterre of holynesse [V 621]

The weye of lyffe the ledder of holynesse [V 627]

So fayre, so gode, and of so hygh estate [V 663]

. . . of god the cheve chaste toure [VI 3]

. . . most holy of visage [VI 131]

For she hath power more in sothefastnesse
Then februa of Rome the goddesse [VI 363-364]

Like as wax of floures soote and glade [VI 398]

Appendix C

Alliteration

Lines

Of hevy hertes that soroen and syghen ofte [I 9]

Whose bright bemys shynyng frome so ferre [I 29]

Home to her houses a noon thay haue hem hyed [I 124]

Of face fayre, but fayrer yet of fayeth [I 339]

For lakke of helpe, when we hym lefte aloon [II 84]

He hathe fulfillede and fostrede in her nede [II 1037]

Full wyde and wast, to walke vpon the playne [II 1042]

Whyle þat he slepte, and sayde as ye shall here [II 1249]

And caught comfort, and consolacion [II 1282]

And trouthe of thynges that clearly can concerne [II 1394]

Tyll the trouth, be Ryped in the Rote [II 1427]

Or eny preef, or probecion [II 1489]

And fonde the floures, firste of Retoryke [II 1635]

Stoden styll astonyed of that light [III 211]

Devoyded of drede or devocion [III 388]

Spake ysaye, and sayde in wordes playne [III 631]

This sonne of life shall spryng and Ryse [III 658]

Was corven oute so clene in euery coste [III 686]

Sumtyme þe spouse spak in canticis [III 732]

To softe our sores, and the Swellyng slake [III 769]

Of the sterres and the signs twelfe [III 826]

With golde of feith fayre and bright borned [III 1022]

Ayeyne a-sault of any aventure [III 1085]

Shall strecche his stremes withouten wene [III 1567]

And while thay were at travers of these thre [III 1590]

Condescendyng into o conclusion [III 1607]

How trouthe and mercy in a mayden mette [III 1612]

Sothefaste seler of his sustynaunce [III 1689]

So bright a sonne spryngyng of so fayre a mone [III 1755]

Saff this day, the sonne of lyf moste shene [III 1756]

And for sharpnes of the soden smerte [IV 36]

Solempnyly make a stacion [IV 144]

With mercy medled and remyssion [IV 213]

That worldly wyndes, boystous in blowyng [IV 272]

Make her malice mekely to obey [IV 392]

By calkyng cast and computacion [V 55]

And thorugh thy sawle shall a sharpe swerde pace [VI 168]

Phrases and Clauses

slombre of slouthe I 2; loke upon the lyght I 4; bemys bryght I 5; the derkenesse and the doole I 8; aswagen and asofte I 12; worldely wawes I 13; passethe pliades I 22; at mydenyght and at morowe I 27; dothe declyne I 32; floures flete I 38; bournede bright I 41; spryng and sprede I 74; grave in golde I 90; floure mooste fayre I 94; fayre felde I 108; gate of golde I 120; gan growe all our grace I 127; fully forto fyne I 128; gladde and graciouse I 147; dovne by dessente I 156; Rawes rede I 159; went to west I 258; softe of speche I 266; Refute and Remedye I 279; sterres sevene I 286; fayleth as floure in frosty mede I 308; of womanhode the well I 313; doughtir of david by dyscent I 344; forto wyrke his will I 348; conveyede with clennesse I 401; full fervent I 417; hir holy halowed chier I 481; and knele vppon my kne I 500; lyggyng in hir lappe I 504; while my lyve may laste I 507; sterreȝ sevene I 581; the Somme of his sentence I 613; flouryng in fayrenesse I 727; fayre, and fresshe I 729; as made is mencion I 778; descended downe I 802; in tweyn torne I 815; shedith is stream I 825; thy holy slepes softe I 862; payne and passion II 3; hertly hevyness II 6; levith in langour II 8; wepe and wayle II 20; fayre frute II 93; to fynde full refuge II 104; sterres seven II 122; the dome of dethe II 210; his blisset bemys bright II 367; flame of fyre II 396; with synne soyled II 414; wel of womanhede II 437; to Renne oute of the Rote II 555; the sonne shene II 563; brynnyng also bryght II 604; to gouerne us and gye II 636; Reason to Receyve II 649; liste to light adowne II 678; beryth byrdeȝ smalle II 681; his brondeȝ bryght II 725; bothe leef and lynde II 754; this waste worlde wilde II 755; might make a mayde II 756; with fynnes syluer fayre II 766; to gouerne hem and gye II 767; his greyne to growe and sede II 789; with ferfull sparkelleȝ shene II 800; concerved clene II 803; the

Bible beryth witnesse II 810; by power previd ofte II 824; they faught in the felde II 845; the same skylle II 853; and grapes gouernour II 879; ne ded noo duresse II 897; fresh of fayrenesse for to see II 900; doun depe in hell II 921; to falle full vn softe II 1036; fulfillede and fostrede II 1037; let hem leve in veyne II 1044; to voyde vengeaunce II 1048; wake or wynke II 1079; set so sore II 1091; floure furthe II 1145; dovble drede II 1149; dothe denye II 1154; withoutyn wordes II 1185; tyde and tyme II 1187; fraudelent falsness II 1226; speke hir shame II 1267; his hole hert II 1285; chased clene II 1307; derke dulnesse II 1308; beames bryght II 1315; sothely in sentence II 1349; the Romour is Ronne II 1350; signes shewede II 1388; shelde me from shame II 1402; sowre or swote II 1425; devoyde of drede II 1448; ne hyde hym in his neste II 1475; derke demyng II 1501; fage may ne fayne II 1537; drawyng dovne II 1568; bonche ther brestez II 1577; make mencion II 1615; dewe dropes II 1633; neuere noon II 1637; swere for swete or sowre III 47; boundes of bedleme III 155; sequestrede and set asyde III 162; the story saythe expresse III 163; the sothefaste sonne of myght III 175; makyth mynde III 179; conceyved in clennesse III 187; to descende dovne III 277; So shene shone III 337; wondre womanly III 351; these signes sawe in-fere III 357; passeth playnely III 374; to seye and synge III 484; moste myghty III 497; wondre wele III 522; perfyt pees III 543; 550; clepe and crye III 574; gret goodnesse III 586; moche of might III 605; spryng sprede III 641; full of holsome floures fayre III 688; felde flouryng III 707; as he his handes layde III 714; fayre, fresshe felde III 731; souereygne suffisaunce III 737; closet of chosin chastite III 775; chaste, clene, chosin boure III 789; sothely for to sayne III 801; fulsom fode III 816; lay lowe III 828; shewe and shyne III 883; lowe and lowede III 886; sterne stede III 896; by myght of his manhede III 900; holtez hore III 917; preued pleynly III 957; descenden doun III 996; sette ne sowe III 999; shewe and shyne III 1028; sothely shewed III 1066; stonde sure III 1090; wallys white III 1101; sayde in sothe III 1120; sodeyne sonne III 1130; to stynte all our stryfe III 1134; cristall clere III 1139; schoure and shade III 1168; high heven III 1210; lusty large III 1247; floresshe and floure III 1249; fresche floures fyne III 1265; smothe and softe III 1270; worthy and wyse III 1299; lemynyne of face III 1330; cry and call III 1357; the myght of his natyuyte III 1425; spake or sayde III 1441; so fayre a face III 1459; stoke and stone III 1543; with wawes wynde III 1562; what was worthiest III 1584; the grayne of grace III 1614; holy habundaunce III 1692; clepe and calle III 1712; comforte and consolacion III 1738; Refute and refection III 1740; his sote stremez III 1778; gouerne vs and gye III 1799; full sharpe of stone IV 30; wonder womanly IV 56; to chaunge his chere IV 60; bothe frende and fame IV 83; most mortall IV 89; bokez maken mynde IV 138; fygured firste IV 166; rest and remedye IV 174; with hele habounde IV 179; swerde and spere IV 181; sothefaste saluacion IV 190; refressheth al Remys IV 199; the streme of sapyence IV 201; fresshe and fyne IV 209; flowe and flete IV 212; the spryt of slouthe IV 231; thay the trouthe tolde IV 249; sharpe shoures IV 262; sothefast sacrament IV 288; faught with the fende IV 314; mawgre his myght IV 315; worthy werryour IV 324; clepe and cry IV 330; to mercy meue IV 334; sore and scabbede eke with synne IV 356; stonde stille as any stone IV 390; besy been IV 396; full faythe IV 406; fro so ferre V 1; a sterre shewede V 10; bright bemes V 13; fro a ferre V 23; wake and wayte V 44; shrowde and shade V 61; doun descendyde V 69; sterre shene V 126; chaunge chere V 143; deuer doo V 173; floures fayre V 181; maugre thy myght V 198; holy of hert V 252; to make mencion V 437; as bokeȝ maken mynde V 442; with fayre feders V 493; maketh mencion V 537; stronge and sure V 550; clepe and call V 617; soulkyng in a stalle V 619; sore a-stonyed V 660; sighe and sorowe make V 669; cheve chaste toure VI 3; with humble herte VI 97; his bemeȝ bryght VI 151; of foreyne folke VI 153; for synne soroweth VI 226; floures fayre VI 231; myghty mars VI 328; floures fresshe VI 392; conservyng her clennesse VI 400; flouryng in fayrenesse VI 402; brene briȝte VI 421; his meryte and his mede VI 425; derke and ded VI 432.

6. COLLATION OF TEXTS

LEGEND

The following abbreviations have been used in designating the MSS:

B[1] — Bodleian 27643 (now Bodl. 120)

B[2] — Bodleian 2376 (now Bodl. 596)

B[3] — Bodleian 4119 (now Hatton 73)

B[4] — Bodleian 14634 (now Rawl. poet 140)

B[5] — Bodleian 2253 (now Bodl. 75)

H[1] — Harley 3862

H[2] — Harley 2382

H[3] — Harley 629

H[4] — Harley 1304

H[5] — Harley 3952

H[6] — Harley 4011

H[7] — Harley 4260

H[8] — Harley 5272

Ash[1] — Bodleian 6919 (Ashmole 39)

Ash[2] — Bodleian 6943 (Ashmole 59)

CC — Corpus Christi, Oxford 237

J — St. John's, Oxford

C[1] — Cambridge Univ. Kk. 1. 3. X

C[2] — Cambridge Univ. Mm. 6. 5

C[3] — Trinity College, Cambridge 601 (R. 3. 21)

C[4] — Caius Cambridge 230 (*Magnificat* only)

C[5] — Trinity College, Cambridge 602 (R. 3. 22)

Ar — Arundel 168

S — Sloane 1785

Ad[1] — B. M. Additional 29729 (*Magnificat* only)

Ad[2] — B. M. Additional 19452

Ad[3] — B. M. Additional 19252

Adv[1] — Advocates 1. 1. 6 (*Magnificat* only)

Adv[2] — Advocates 19. 3. 1

Ct — Chetham 6709

D — Durham Univ. Cosin V. ii. 16

Hu — Hunterian 232

L — Lambeth 344

An — Antiquaries 134

Lg — Longleat MS

Ch — Chicago University, 566

Hn[1] — Huntington HM 115

Hn[2] — Huntington HM 144

Co — Cotton Appendix VIII

V — Venerable English College MS. 1306

The text that follows is that of MS. Cosin V. ii. 16, Durham University (MS. D). In places where the preponderance of readings was against MS. D, lines have been substituted from MSS. B[1], H[7], and Ad[3], in that order of preference. All such instances are noted in the textual variants (see the chapter entitled "The Texts", page 18).

Frequently in the Durham text parts of words and also prefixes are separated. Where this has occurred, the elements have been joined with hyphens.

This booke was compilede by Iohn Lidgate Monke of Bury . at the
excitac*i*on and styyryng of our worshipfull prince . kyng Harry the
fifthe. In the honour, glory and worship of the byrthe of the moste
glorious maide wife and modir of our lord Ih*e*s*us* criste Chapterede
and markyde aftir this table[1]

FIRSTE A PROLOOG

1	The Nativite of our lady	Ca° i°
	Howe our lady was offrede into the Temple	Ca° ii°
	Of the conu*er*sac*i*on of our lady in the temple	Ca° iii°
	Howe our lady Receyvede the . vii . gifte3 of the hooly goste	Ca° iiii°
	Howe our lady prayede to god for . vii . peticiouns	Ca° v^{to}
	Howe Abiathar that was Bisshoppe of the lawe the	
	yere that our lady was weddide to Iosephe wolde haue	
	hadde our lady weddide to his sonne	Ca° vi^{to}
	Howe our lady sayde to the Bisshoppe that come fro Abiathar	Ca° vii°
10	Howe Iosephe was weddide to our lady	Ca° viii°
	Howe Iosephe aftir he had weddyd our lady went to Bedlem	
	and vside the craft of Carpentry	Capit*u*lo ix°
	How our lady is sette for an ensaumpler of all virginite	Ca° x°

Rubric. Iohn] Dan Iohn Ash[1].— the excitacion] excitacion L.—glory] om. Ash[1].—table] Table
that followeth Ash[1]; in honor of our lady dyvyded and chaptered after this table L.—honour
glory and worship] worship honour and glory B[4].

1. The] Of the L. 2. into] in Lg. 3. in the temple] om. Hn[1]. 4. the] om. Hn[1]. 5. prayede
to] made her petycyons to L; axede of Hn[1]. 6-8.] Howe the Bischope whos name was Abiathar
would haue had oure lady wedded to hys son Hn[1].—that was Bisshoppe of the lawe the yere
that our lady was weddide to Ioseph L. 9. sayde] answered Lg, H[6], H[3], Ad[2].—sayde to]
answered before L, Ash[1], H[4].—that come fro Abiathar] om. L. 10. was weddide to] weddide
Hn[1]. 11-12.] om. Hn[1]. II. he had weddyd] his weddyng L.—went to Bedlem and] om. L. 13,
is sette] may and worthy ys that she be set Hn[1].—sette for an] om. L.

[1]This introductory rubric and list of chapter headings is found only in MSS. D, B[4], C[5], H[3], H[4],
H[6], Ad[2], L, Ash[1], Ash[2] and Lg. The other MSS. either omit this rubric and table, or have lost
this portion of the poem.

Howe mercy and pees Rightwisnesse and trouthe disputyn

for the Redempcion of mankynde   Ca°   xi°

Howe mercy and pees broughten this ple before the

high Iuge   Ca°   xii°

Howe god the fadir answerde to mercy and pees   Ca°   xiii°

Howe the fadir of heven ooned these iiii sustres Ca°   xiiii°

20 Howe the fadir of heven tolde these iiii sustres howe

his sonne shulde take mankynde   Ca°   xv^{to}

Howe Gabryell the Angell was sent to our lady   Capit*u*lo xvi°

A lamentac*i*on of Saint Barnarde   Ca°   xvii°

A Recapitulac*i*on of the wordes of Gabriell to our lady Ca° xviii°

Howe hooly men by dyvine liknesse wrote of our lady Ca°   xix°

in commendac*i*on of hir / Antike conclusions agaynes

vnbileuet men that seyn that criste might not be born

of a maide   Ca°   xx°

Howe our lady went to saint Iohn Baptist modir   Ca°   xxi°   f. 3b

How our lady made Magnificat   Ca°   xxii°

30 How our lady aftir the birthe of saint Iohn Baptist

Retornede to Naȝareth   Ca°   xxiii°

Howe Iosephe returned to Naȝareth and was in

maner doutefull when he sawe Mary grete w*ith* chylde Ca° xxiiii°

14.] A dysputycyon of the four sustres mercy pes ryght trouthe L.—Howe] Howe the Coun-
sell of the Trinite that ys to save Hn¹. 15. Redempcion] p *inserted above.* 16-17.] om. Hn¹.
16. this] the L. 17. high] om. L. 18.] om. Hn¹. 19.] How the fader omnipotent of the plente
of his bountevous goodnesse accorded these foure sustren Hn¹.—ooned] om. L.—these] the L.
20-21.] Howe Criste toke mankynde by vertu of the worde of the fader. 20. of heven] om. L.
—these L.—iiii] om. L. 22. Gabryell the Angell] the angell Gabriell H⁶.—the Angell] om.
Hn¹, L. 24.] om. Hn¹.—to our lady] om. L. 25. by dyvine liknesse] om. L.—of our lady in commendac*i*on of hir] in commendac*i*on of our lady L. 27. be] om. Ash¹.—vnbileuet men that seyn
that Christe might not be born of a maide] incredyble peple L. 28. saint] om. H⁴, H³, Ash¹,
B⁴, Lg, H⁶, Ad²; Elizabeth L. 30. saint] om. Hn¹.—aftir the birthe of saint Iohn Baptist]
om. L. 31. to] ayen to Ash¹. 32.] Howe Ioseph returned from Galylee to Nazareth where oure
lady was and whanne he saye hyr gret he merveyled how and in what kynde Hn¹; Howe Ioseph
was in dowth of our lady conseyvyng L. 33. grete] om. Ash¹, B⁴.—Mary] oure lady H⁶.

How the maydens that were attendaunt to our lady

comfortiden Ioseph   Ca°   xxv°

Howe the Angell warned Iosephe to byde *with* our lady   Ca°   xxvi°

How the Bisshoppes did to sompnen Iosephe for our lady

was withe childe   Ca°   xxvii°

Howe Ioseph ansewerde the Bisshop excusyng hym

40   and our lady   Ca°   xxviii°

How the Bisshop made Iosephe and our lady to taast

a watir to preve hem by   Ca°   xxix°

How our lady was brought affore the Bisshoppe to

taast the watir of Ielousy   Ca°   xxx°

How our lady frendes weileden and morneden whan the

Bisshopis made so strong a preve of hir virginite   Ca°   xxxi°

How our lady prayed to god to shew hir virginite   Ca°   xxxii°

How the bisshopes and the people dredden hem full sore

of the grete preefe *and* assay that was done to our lady   Ca°   xxxiii°

50   A commendacion of Chaucer   Ca°   xxxiv°

How crist was borne aftir the makyng of the worlde

v.ml.C. and lxxxxix yere   Ca°   xxxv°

34-35.] Howe our lady maydes comforted Ioseph of hys doute L. 35. Ioseph] Ioseph of his doutfulnesse Hn¹. 36.] Howe Ioseph wold have forsaken oure lady but god sente an angel to hym and badde hym abyde Hn¹.—byde *with*] take L. 37. to] om. Hn¹.—sompnen] sonimen oure lady and Ioseph for she was wyth childe Hn¹.— Ioseph] om. Lg. 37-38.] Howe Ioseph was somenyd fore oure lady L. 39-40.] om. Hn¹. 39. the Bisshop] om. L.—and] of L. 40 and our lady] om. Ash¹. 41.] Howe the Bischoppis tastyden oure lady to preve hir clenesse and puryd virginite Hn¹.—to] om. H⁶. 41-42.] Howe our lady and Ioseph drank Ielesye. 42. a] the Ash¹. 43-50.] om. Hn¹. 43-44.] om. Lg. 43. affore the Bisshope] om. L. 45-46.] Howe oure lady frendes weyleden for hyre L. 46. of] om. Lg.—virginite] virginite and clenesse Lg. 47. to show hir virginite] for hyr preef L. 48.] Howe Byshopes and peple dreden aftyr the preef of hyre L.—full] om. Ash¹. 49. assay] om. Ash¹. 51-52.] How many yer aftyr begynnyng of the werle cryst was boore, L; Howe where and whenne Criste was borne Hn¹. 52. C. and lxxxxix yere] om. Ad².

How Iosephe and our lady wenten to Bedlem

to paye here tribute   Ca°   xxxvi°

How Ioseph went to seche mydwyves to our lady   Capit*u*lo xxxvii°

A devoute prayer that our lady made when criste

was borne   Ca°   xxxviii°

How the mydwyves dorste not entre w*ith* Iosephe into the

house for grete soden light that appered within   Ca°   xxxix°

60   How Balaam p*ro*pheciede of the sterre that shewede

crist*es* birthe   Ca°   xl°

How our lady Receyvede the Midwyves   Ca°   xli°

How the hande and the Arme of Salonne wexe drye for

she w*ith*oute drede and Reverence tastid criste   Ca°   xlii°   f. 4a

How the angell apperide to the Cheppherdes and tolde

thaym the brith of criste   Ca°   xliii°

Howe the Shepeherdes fonden criste w*ith* our lady   Capit*u*lo xliiii°

How godde wolde not be borne but of a mayde modir

and wife   Ca°   xlv°

70   Howe Isaak p*ro*phiciede the birth of cr*is*te by touchyng of

the clothis of his sonne   Ca°   xlvi°

53.] om. Hn[1].—to Bedlem] om. L. 54.] om. Hn[1].—here] om. Ash[1]. 55-57.] om. Hn[1]. 55. went to seche] sent L. 56. A devoute prayer that our lady made] How our lady prayed L.—that] om. H[4].—that our lady made] made to our lady Ash[1]. 58.] how the mydwyfes were aferd of the lyght L; How Ioseph brought the mydwyves to the dore where that criste was borne and they durst not entre for a gret lyght that schone wyth ynne Hn[1].—w*ith* Ioseph] om. H[4]. 59. that] om. H[3], Ash[1], B[4], Lg, Ch, H[5].—grete] a grete Ash[1], H[6], H[5]. 60-86.] om. Hn[1]. 60.] Of the prophecye of Balaam L.—shewede] prophecyed of Ch. 63.] Howe the arme of Salome wax drye and starked L. 65-66. and tolde thaym the brith of criste] om. L. 66. thaym] om. H[4], H[3], Ash[1], B[4], Lg, H[6], Ch, H[5].—the] of the H[6]. 68. wolde not be borne but of a] liste to be borne of L.—of] of of H[5]. 70. by touchyng of the clothis of his sonne] om. L.—of] om. H[4].

72.] pome garnet *inserted above line*.—Garnet appill] pomegarnet L, Ch. 74. to] vnto H⁵. 75.] Of fallyng of temple yn rome and other toknes L.—feldoune] felle H³, Ash¹, B⁴, Lg, H⁶, Ch, H⁵.—in Rome] om. B⁴. 76. othir] of the H⁵. 77.] How a well in Rome ran oyle yn Cristes birth L. 78.] How Octavian shold have defyed of the Senates L. 79. for theyre] for H⁵. 80. in stede of wyne the nyght] om. L.—vynes] wyves H⁴. 82.] Of the ymage called the goddes of Rome L. 83. to] om. H⁵. 84. to] om. Ash¹.—her goddesse] her image H⁵. 85.] How Sibyll prophecyed the byrthe of Crist L.—to] om. Ash¹, Lg. 87.] Howe the holy prophytis prophecye-den afor the incarnacion the holy and blessed birth of crist Hn¹.—the] om. L, Lg, H⁵. 88.] A solucion of a question of eldre prophetys L; A question assoyled whyche ys beste wyne or wymen or kynge Ch.—is] is the H⁵.—wyne] wife H⁶. 88-92.] om. Hn¹. 90. ought worthily be commendede and] shuld be L. 92.] A commendacion of oure lady L.

How criste was circumsided   Ca°   lx°

Howe in foure man*e*re of wise criste was circumsised   Ca°   lxi°

Howe criste suffrede circu*m*sicion in his chosen people   Ca°   lxii°

Howe crist shadde his bloode fyve tymes   Ca°   lxiii°

Howe the people of godde that duke Iosue had in gou*e*rnaunce

were savede by the stedefast by leve of the name Ihesus   Ca°   lxiiii°

Howe the name of Ihesus is moste souveraine medicyne

100 agaynste all man*e*re of malady   Ca°   lxv°   f. 4b

Howe the name of Ih*e*sus is likenede to the iiii stremes

that Refresshen all Rewuers   Ca°   lxvi°

Howe p*r*ophetes and martirs suffrede deth for the name

of Ihesus   Ca°   lxvii°

How p*r*ophetes prestes and myghty men were a noynted   Ca°   lxviii°

How crist Ih*e*su was bothe p*r*ophite preste kyng and

myghty Champion   Ca°   lxix°

Howe by the name of Ih*e*sus synners be made Rightfull   Capitulo   lxx°

Howe by the p*r*ophecie of Balaam whiche was made vpon

110 an hyll to asspie the sterre that signyfied the birth of c*r*iste   Ca°   lxxi°

Howe the iii kyng*e*s p*e*rceyvede the sterre that shewed c*r*istes

                                            birth   Ca°   lxxii°

Howe the iii kyng*e*s come to Iher*u*sal*e*m and askyde where   Ca°   lxxiii°

criste was borne

93.] The circumcision of Crist Hn[1].—circumsided] circumcised H[4], H[3], Ash[1], B[4], Lg, H[6], H[5], Ch, L. 94] How Cryst was circumcised in 4 maners L; How Crist was circumcised in four maner wyse H[5].—in foure man*e*re of wise criste] crist in foure maners of wises H[4].—of] om. H[6], Ch. 94-100. om. Hn[1]. 95.] om. H[5]. 96.] How Cryst bled fyve times in hys manhodde L. 97-98.] Howe stedefast byleve in thys name Ihesus L. 98. Ihesus] of Christ Ash[1]; of Ihesus H[6]. 99. the name of Ihesus] thys Iesus L.—moste souveraine] om. L. 100. man*e*re of] om. L.—malady] sekenesse Ash[1].—all] om. H[6]. 101.] Of stremes that renne oute of the name Ih*e*sus L; A comendacion of the worthy name of Ih*e*sus Hn[1]. 102-118.] om. Hn[1]. 104. of Ihesus] om. L. 105. prestes] prestes kynges H[5]. 106. Ih*e*su was] om. L.—Ih*e*su] om. Ash[1].—bothe] om. H[6]. 107. myghty] om. L. 109. by] *inserted above.* 109-110.] How wacche was made to aspye the sterre L.—whiche] wacche H[4], H[3], Ash[1], B[4], Lg, H[6], H[5], Ch.—prophecie of Balaam] om. Ch. 110. signyfied] tolde H[4], H[3], B[4], Lg, H[6], Ch, H[5]; showed Ash[1].—birth of c*r*iste] Cristes birth Ash[1]. 111.] om. H[5]. 112. and askyde where criste was borne] om. L.

Howe Kyng herode sent fro the iii Kyng*es* to inquere of

crist*es* birthe . as a *s*erpente coue*r*eth hym vndir flours

to styng and shede his veni*m* whome he may hurt   Ca°   lxxiiii°

So fals heroude shewede fals feynede wordes to haue

distroyede these three kyng*es*   Ca°   lxxv°

Of the Ioye that these kyng*es* hadde when they founde *c*riste   Ca°   lxxvi°

120   Howe the offryng of the iii kyng*es* shall be vndirstondon   Ca°   lxxvii°

goostely / Off vertues povert and mekenesse of our lady   Ca°   lxxviii°

Howe the angell warnede the iii . kyng*es* nought to passe

by heroude but by a nodir waye   Ca°   lxxix°

Anotable declaraci*o*n of the iii gifte notable of these iii kyng*es*   Ca°   lxxx°

Howe we shulde pray to god to do this offryng gostely   Ca°   lxxxi°

How our lady was purified   Ca°   lxxxii°

Howe Symeon Receyved criste of our lady in the Temple   Ca°   lxxxiii°

Howe where and whanne Symeon made Nunc dimitt*is*   Ca°   lxxxiiii°

Of the Ioye that Anna made the doughter of phanuell

130   whan criste was offrede into the Temple   Ca°   lxxxv°

A p*ro*phitable declaraci*o*n of the p*ro*purtes of the Turtill

and the doufe   Ca°   lxxxvi°

Howe Candilmasse day firste toke his name   Ca°   lxxxvii°

THE PROLOG

O thoughtfull herte, plunged in distresse f. 5a

With slombre of slouthe, this long wynters nyght

Oute of the slepe, of mortall hevynesse

Awake a noon, and loke upon the lyght

Of thelke sterre that with hir bemys bryght

And withe the shynyng, of hir stremys merye

Is wonte to gladde, all our Emysperye

And to oppresse the derkenesse and the doole

Of hevy her*tes* that soroen a[n]d syghen ofte

10 I mene the sterre, of the bright poole

That with hir bemys whan she is a lofte

May al the trowble aswagen and asofte

Of worldely wawes, which in this mortall see

Have vs byset, withe grete aduersitee

---

1. O thoughtfull herte, plunged in distresse B[1].—in] in high D, C[3]; in gret H[1].—thoughtfull] thou hevyfull L. 2. of] and CC. 3. the] om. Co; this B[1], B[2]; alle L.—slepe of mortall] mortall slepe of H[4]. 5. thelke] that B[1], B[2], B[3], H[4], C[2], C[3], CC.—that with] with CC.—hir] om. Hn[1]. 6. And] That C[2].—withe] om. Co. 8. to] om. H[1]. 9. hevy] ony B[2], CC.—soroen a[n]d syghen] sighen and sorwen B[1], C[3] 10. I mene the sterre, of the bright poole B[1].—the] thylke D. 12. the] *inserted above*; oure Hn[1]. 13. which] with Ash[1], H[6]. 14. grete] om. H[1].

The Rage of whiche is so tempestyuous

That whan the calme is moste blandyshyng

Then is the streme of dethe moste perylous

If that we wante, the light of hir shynyng

And but the syght, allas of hir lokyng

20   From dethes brinke, make us to escape

The haven of lif, of us may not be take

This sterre in beautee passethe pliades

Bothe of shynyng and of stremes clere

Botetes Arthour and also Iades

And Esperus when it dothe appere

For this is Spica *with* hir bright spere

That tawarde even at mydenyght and at morowe

Downe frome the hevyn adaweth all our sorowe

---

15. Rage] grace C³, Hu.—so] om. CC. 17. the] om. L.—streme] storme CC. 18. that] om. C².—we] ye Hu; he Ash¹, H³, H⁴, H⁶, C⁵.—light] syght J.—hir] om. H⁵.—hir shynyng] hyre bryght shynyng L. 19. the syght] syght the L.—syght] lyght Hn¹, J, Hu.—allas] als Ash¹. 20. From dethes brinke, make us to escape B¹.—make] so make D, C³; om. C⁵.—us to] us all to H⁴.—to] om. C², Hu. 21. The haven of lif, of us may not be take B¹.—of] by D. 22. sterre] streme C², H³, H⁴, H⁵, Lg, C⁵, CC, Ash¹.—in] om. Ash¹.—beautee] vertu C³. 23. Bothe of] Bothe in B¹, B², H⁷, C².—and of] and in B¹, B², H⁷, C². 24. Boetes Arthour] Boetes and Arthur B⁴, Ash¹, H³, H⁴, H⁶, C⁵. 25. And Esperus] And also Esperous H¹.—it] he Ash¹. 26. is] om. H¹.—hir] the J. 27. tawarde] om. Co, Hn¹.—even at] at evyn Ash¹; even both at C²; even CC.—and at] and B¹, B². 28. the] om. B¹, B², B³, B⁴, H¹, H³, H⁶, H⁷, Ash¹, CC, C², C⁵, L, Lg.

Whose bright bemys shynyng frome so ferre

30   That cloudes blake may the light nat fyne

For this of Iacob, Is the fayrest sterre

That vndir wawes nev*e*re dothe declyne

Whose course is not vndir the clyptyke lyne

But ev*e*ryliche of beaute may be sene

Amyddeʒ the arke of our merydyne

And driethe up, the bitter teres wete   **f. 5b**

Of Aurora, aftir the mourwen gray

That she in wepyng dothe on floures flete

In listy Aprill and in fresshe may

40   And causith phebus the bright somers day

With his golde wayne, bournede bright and fayre

Tenchase the miste of our cloudy ayre

---

30. may the light nat] may not the light Ash¹.—fyne] steyne B², B⁴, H¹, H³, H⁴, H⁵, H⁶, Lg, C⁵, CC, Ash¹. 35. arke] marke B². 37. aftir the mourwen] the morowe aftyr L. 38. in wepyng dothe on floures] on floures in wepyng dooth B¹, Ad².—in] om. C².—on] oure B², CC. 39. and] or B¹, B², B⁴, H¹, H⁷, C², C³, Hu, Hn¹, Co, Ad².—fresshe may] lusty may B³, L. 40. bright] freshe CC. 41. golde wayne bournede] wayne gold boorned Co, J, H⁷, B¹, Hu, C², B², B⁴, H¹, H³, H⁴, H⁵, H⁶, Ad², Ash¹, C⁵, Lg; wayne of gold Hn¹, B³, L.

For this is the sterre, that bare the bright sonne

Which holdyth the septre of Iuda in his hande

Whose stremes been, oute of Iesse ronne

To shede hir lyght bothe, on see and lande

Whose gladde beamys wit*h*out eclypsyng stonde

Estwarde to vs in the orient full shene

Wit*h* light of grace, to voiden all our tene

50   Now fayre sterre O, sterre of sterres all

Whose light to see, angelleȝ delyte

So late the golde dewe of thy grace fall

Into my breste, like skales, fayre and white

Me to enspyre of that I wolde endyte

Wit*h* thylke bame, sent downe by myracle

Whan the hooly goost, the made his habitacle

---

43. is] om. B¹, B², H⁵, H⁷, Ad². 44. holdyth] haste H⁵. 45. Whose stremes been, oute of Iesse ronne B¹.—stremes] beamys D, H¹.—Whose] Wiche H⁵.—been oute of Iesse] of Iesse bene out H¹. 47. gladde beamys] stremes glade H¹, Lg. 49. With light of grace, to voiden all our tene B¹.—all our] wit*h* our D; wit*h* out C³.—light] om. H¹, Lg.—to] om. H¹, Lg. 50. second *sterre*] om. B², CC. 51. angelleȝ delyte] aungels evere delyte Hn¹; angellys moche delyte C³. 53. white] brighte B¹, B², H⁷, Hn¹. 54. endyte] write Ash¹. 55. bame sent] baume that was sent Hn¹.—by myracle] by thy miracle L. 56. the made] made the L.—habitacle] tabernacle B², B⁴, Ash¹, H³, H⁴, H⁶, Ad², C⁵, CC.

And the licour of thy grace shede

Into my penne, tenlumyne this dite

Thorough thy supporte þat I may procede

60 Sumwaht to saye in laude ande p[r]eys of the

And first I thynke at the natiuitee

So that thyne helpe, fro me nat ne twynne

Benyng lady, a noon forto begynne

The Natyvyte of
oure lady Ca° *primo*

A Flour of vertue full longe kepyt in cloose

Full many ver *with* holsome leves swote

Only by *grace* vppon the stalke aroos

Out of Iesse, spryngyng fro the Rote

Off god ordeynyde to be a Resort and bote

Vnto mankynde our trouble to det*er*myne

70 Full longe afforne by p*re*scyens dyvyne

---

57. And the licour of thy grace shede H[7].—shede] do shede D, C[3]; thou B[1].—And] And eke
Hn[1].—grace] swete grace C[3]; fayre L. 59. supporte] disporte B[2], CC. 61. at] of B[1], B[2], CC.
—I] om. CC.—thy] my L. 62. ne] om. H[1], C[3], Ash[1]; thou B[1], B[2], B[3], C[2], L. 63. lady] sterre
C[3], Hn[1], J.—forto] here to C[3].—forto] to B[3], B[4], H[1], Ash[1], H[3], H[4], H[5] H[6], Ad[2], Lg,
C[5], L. 65. ver] a yere Ash[2], B[1], Hu, H[7], H[1], Ash[1], B[2], B[3], B[4], H[3], H[4], H[5], CC,
C[2], C[3], Ad[2], L, Lg, Hn[1], Co.; vertuis H[6].—swote] and softe H[1]. 68. god] om. C[2].
69. det*er*myne] termyne Lg, J, H[1].—trouble] trouthe C[3].—our] hys H[1].

The wiche Floure, *pr*eservithe man from dethe   f. 6a

Vnto the vertue, who so luste take hede

That in a garden, a myddys of Nazareth

So fayre som tyme gan to spryng and sprede

That thorough the worlde bothe in lenthe and brede

The fresshe odour, and also the swetnesse

Hert*es* comforteth, of all her hevynesse

O Nazareth, w*ith* Beddelem the by syde

This Flour, yov makyth, of name more Ryall

80   Than either Rome, elate and full of pride

Or myghty Troye, w*ith* the sturdy wall

Whose Renon halteth, to be paragall

In Hono*ur* pryse, Fame and Reuerence

Vnto youre passyng, worthi excellence

72. the] om. B², Ash¹, H³, CC.—so] om. H¹. 73. of] om. C³, Hn¹, Hu. 74. som tyme] whilom J.—gan] began Ash². 75. That] And H⁵.—bothe] om. B¹, B², B³, CC, C², Hu, L. 76. the] om. H¹. 77. her] om. CC. 79. of name] om. B¹, B⁵, Co.—yov makyth of name] of name you maketh H¹. 80. Than either Rome, elate and full of pride B¹.—and] om. D, Co, C¹, C³, B⁵.—Than] Than of L. 81. the] his Lg. 84. Vnto youre passyng, worthi excellence B¹.—passyng worthi] worthy passyng D, C¹, C³; worthy high Ash¹.

If for the frute comendyde be the tre

Thow hast more laude, and commendacion

For thilke fruite, that sprong out of the

Than hath Aufryke of worthy Scypyon

Or Rome of Sesar, or of Fabion

90 Though hir namez were some tyme *grave* in golde

Her Idyll fame, to thyne may not be tolde

Wherfor Reioyse, and be right gladde and light

O Nazareth of name, most flouryng

For oute of the, a floure mooste fayre of syght

Moste full of *grace*, som tyme dydde spryng

Of the whiche fully Remembryng

So longe a gon spake hooly Isaye

When þat he sayde in his prophecye

---

85. If for] Furste Ash[1].—comendyde] preised B[2], CC. 86. and] in J. 87. For thilke fruite, that sprong out of the B[1].—out] om. D.—fruite] floure B[4], Ash[1], H[3], H[4], Ad[2].—of] fro Hn[1]. 88. of] or B[1], B[2], B[3], B[4], B[5], H[1], H[3], H[4], H[5], H[6], H[7], Ash[1], Ash[2], CC, C[1], C[2], C[5], Ad[2], L, Lg. 89. Or Rome of Sesar] Of Rome Sesar B[3], B[4], H[1], Ash[1], H[3], H[4], H[5], H[6], Ad[2], Lg, C[5], L, CC.—or of Fabion] or blanchie Fabion Ash[2]. 90. were som tyme] somtyme were C[2].—som tyme] whylom J.—grave] om. Hn[1]. 91. fame] name Hu, B[1], J.—to thyne may not be tolde] may never to thine be tolde B[1], J.—tolde] reynynge B[2]. 92. light] mery C[2]. 93. name] fame C[1], Hn[1], J. 94. fayre of syght] goodly C[2].—a] om. Lg, C[5].—of syght] and bright Ash[1]. 95. Moste] And C[2].—som tyme] whilom J. 97. a gon] aforn B[1], B[2], B[3], B[4], B[5], H[1], H[5], H[7], C[1], C[2], Lg, Hn[1], Co.—spake] was C[3], J.—holy] fully CC; om. Ash[1]. 98. þat] om. H[3].—his] om. CC.

That on this flour playnely shulde rest

100   The holy gooste, for his chosyn place

As for the fairest, *and* also for þe beste

That eu*e*re was and, most full of grace

Whose passyng beaute, no storme may deface

But eu*e*re yliche contynueth fresshe of hewe

W*ith* oute fadyng, the colour is so trwe

For this is þe flo*ur*, that god hym self behelde   f. 6b

The white lylye of the chosyn vale

The swete Roose, of the fayre felde

Which of colour wexyth neu*er* pale

110   The violet, our langour to a vale

Purpyll hewede, thorough mercy and pety

To socoure alle, that in myschief be

---

101. As for the fairest, *and* also for þe beste B¹.—also for] also D, H⁶.—As] and C²; om. Hu.—also] om. C². 103. storme] stremes L. 104. But] That L.—eu*e*re] om. B¹.—yliche contyn- ueth] contynueth like C². 105. W*ith* oute] Wyth H¹. 106. For this is þe flour, that god hym self behelde B¹.—is] om. D.—is þe] om. C¹, C³.—þe] om. Ash².—hym self] om. C². 107. white] om. C².—chosyn] holsom C¹, C³, Hn¹, J. 108. swete] whete H⁷. 109. Which of colour wexyth neu*er* pale B¹.—Which] The which D, C¹, C³, Hn¹.—wexyth neu*er*] never wexed B², CC. 110. our] the Hn¹. 111. Purpyll] The purpul L. 112. To socoure all, that in myschief be B¹.— alle] hem all D, C³; hem C¹.

And from the stooke, of Ioachym and Anne

This holy floure hadde hir orygynall

To hem afforne, by synge Ishewede whanne

The Angell tolde hem playnely þat ther shall

Of hem be borne, a mayde in speciall

Chosyn of godde most chefe of hir alye

For hir mekenesse and hatte shall Marye

120   And whanne the Angell, at the gate of golde

Had of this mayde hir birthe prophecied

And all the man*ere* to bothe hem tolde

In bok*es* olde, as it is specifiede

Home to her houses a noon thay haue hem hyed

And she conceyved, this faythfull trwe wyf

By Ioachym, the holy frute of lyfe

---

114. hadde] and C². 115. synge] All other MSS have *signe*. 118. chefe] meke C¹, C³.—Chosyn]
The son Ash¹. 119. For her mekenesse and hatte] and for her mekenesse hate B⁴, H¹, Ash¹, H³,
H⁴, Ash², H⁵, B² Ch, H⁶, Ad², Lg, C⁵, CC; And of her symples her name C¹, C³; And for her
mekeness her name C². 121. Had] om. Hn¹; And CC.—prophecied] specified Ash¹. 122. to] of
B¹, B², H⁵, Ash¹, Ash², CC. 123. specifiede] tolde L. 124. her] the L.—a noon] om. C².—haue]
om. Ash¹, H³, H⁶. 126. holy frute] holy man frute B⁴.—frute] prophet C³, Hn¹.

Oute of the which gan growe all our grace

Our olde sorowes, fully forto fyne

The bitter gall, playnely to enchace

130 Of the venym, callet serpentyne

For when that Anne, hade monethes nyne

Borne this frute so holy and entere

Thorough *grace* of god, a noon it dyd appere

The oryent to gladde w*ith* all man kynde

W*ith* dedely erro*ur* oppressede of the nyght

With cloudes blake, and w*ith* skyeȝ blynde

Tyll thay were clered, *with* fayrenesse of the light

Of whiche the Angell, some tyme hade a syght

W*ith* Iacob wrestelyng, from hym as he breyde

140 So longe aforn to hym whanne he seide

127. the] om. B¹, B², C¹.—our] maner of H¹. 128. Our] Of oure Hu.—fully] oonly H³. 129. gall playnely] galle onely and pleinly B¹, C².—playnely to] playnely out to C³. 130. the venym] that foule venym C³.—callet serpentyne] called the serpentyne Ad³. 131. that Anne] Anne that L.—hade monethes] monthes hadde B⁵, Co. 132. Borne this] Born of this Co.—and] and so H¹, Hu; and eke C³. 133. Thorough grace] Thorugh the grace Hn¹, Ch, B³, B⁴, H¹, Ash¹, H³, H⁴, Ash², H⁶, Ad², Lg, C⁵, CC, L.—of god a noon] anon of god L.—it] om. Hn¹, C². 134. The oryent to gladde w*ith*] In the orient to glad B¹, CC, B², B³, B⁴, H¹, H³, H⁴, H⁵, H⁶, H⁷, Ash¹, Ash², C⁵, Ad², L, Lg, Ch, Co.—gladde w*ith* al] glade of C², B⁵, Ad³, J, Hu; glade al Hn¹.—man kynde] oure kynde B². 135. of] with H⁶. 136. w*ith*] om. B³, Ash², L.—and w*ith*] and eke with C¹, C³. 137. w*ith* fayrenesse] with the feyrnes C¹.—the] om. H³.—the light] night light Ash¹. 138. some tyme] whilom J. 139. as] whan B², CC. 140. So longe aforn to hym whanne he seide B¹.—whanne] whan that D, C³.—he] he to hym CC.

Late me departe, w*ith* outyn more affray   f. 7a

Agayne me, and make noo recistence

The nyght is passet, lo the morowen gray

The fresshe Aurora, so fayre in apparence

Hir light daweth, to voyde all offence

Of wyntir nyght*es* full long and tediouse

W*ith* newe apperyng, so gladde and graciouse

This is to say, the holy dawnyng

Of this mayde, at hir Natiuitee

150   The nyght gan voide, of oure olde mornyng

As þe Aungell, in figure did se

W*ith* such a touche, made Iacob be

Seer in his senwes, like as it is founde

In that membre, wher lust dothe moost habounde

---

141. Late] And H¹. 142. and] thowe C¹ om. C³.—noo] thou C³. 143. nyght is] nyght so is Co.—lo the morowen] lo ȝend the morow C¹, C³, Hn¹, J; lo now the morow Ash². 145. light] om. C¹. 146. Of] All H⁵.—full] so B⁵.—full long and] foule and B², CC.—and] om. Co. 147. newe] long C². 148. This is to say, the holy dawnyng B¹.—the holy] so holy a D, C¹, C³. 149. this mayde] thys fayre mayde C³.—at] and CC. 150. The nyght gan voide, of oure olde mornyng H⁷.—of] of all D, Co, B⁵, Ash², Ad³, Hu; om. B¹, Ch. 151. As þe Aungell, in figure did se B¹.—did] than dide C¹, C³, D; dyde thanne Hn¹.—Aungell in figure did se], aungel let him in figure see Ash². 152. W*ith* such a touche, made Iacob be B¹—be] for to be D; to be C¹, C³.—W*ith*] Which J. 153. his] om. B¹, Ch, B².—like] om. B⁵, Co.—is] om. CC. 154. that membre] that same membre C¹, C³.—lust dothe moost] moste luste doth C².

In fygure only, that þere shulde sprynge

Dovne by dessente, oute of his kynrede

A clene mayde, in will and werkeng

Pure of entent, bothe in thought and dede

Whiche as Aurora, with hir Rawes rede

160   The nyght avoideth w*ith* his copeʒ donne

Affore the vpryste of the bright sonne

Right so this mayde, at hir natyuytee

The nyght of dethe devoidede hath awaye

And bright kalendes, most lusty for to se

Of phebus vprist, wit*h*outyn more deley

For she is Aurora, sothely this is noo nay

Oute of which, as p*ro*pheteʒ can devise

The sonne of lyfe, to vs gan first aryse

---

155. þere] om. C². 156. oute] om. Ad³. 157. and] and in C³, Ash¹, H³, H⁴, Ash², H⁶, Ad³, Ad², C⁵, J, Hu. 158. in] of L.—thought] worde C³.—and] and in Ash¹, H⁶. 159. as] om. B⁴, Ash¹, H³, H⁴, H⁶, Ad², C⁵.—with hir] with with CC. 160. The nyght avoideth] The avoideth the nyght Hu. 161. the] om. Co. 162. at] in B³. 163. dethe devoidede] deth all voideth C¹, C³.—devoidede hath] hath devoided B¹, C². 164. And bright kalendes, most lusty for to se B¹.—for to] vnto C¹, C³, D; to C², CC.—most] om. C².—kalendes] kalendere kalendis CC. 165. more] om. L; any more Ash¹.—deley] day Ch. 166. this] ther L. 167. of which] of the which C¹, H⁵, H⁷. 168. gan] om. Lg—gan first] first dide C².

Of whose birthe, full many a day be forne

170 Albumaȝar, wrote in speciall

And sayde, a mayde sothely shall be borne

Vndir the signe above Celestiall

That callet is the sygne virgynall

The whiche mayde, as he eke tell can

Shall bere a shylde, withoutyn spote of man

And as Mynerua, the mothir of prudence   f. 7b

Is holde a mayde, Right so this hevynly quene

Bare in hir wombe, the fadirs sapience

And mothir was and a mayden clene

180 Of god provydede playnely for to been

Socour to man, and helpe in all our nede

Whanne she was borne, this floure of womanhede

---

169. Of] At B¹, B², C², Ad².—whose] wich C¹; the whiche C³.—birthe] brighte Lg.—full] om. Ash², C¹.—a day] day Ash¹, H³, H⁶, C³. 170. Albumaȝar, wrote in speciall B¹.—wrote] wrote it D, C³; thanne Hn¹. 171. a mayde sothely] in sothe a maide Ash². 172. above Celestiall] above high celestiall Hn.¹. 173. That] Whiche C¹, C³.—callet is] is called H⁵; clepyd is C³; is clepid C¹.—sygne virgynall] signe now virginall Hn¹. 174. The whiche] That is the C¹, C³.—eke] om. Co, B⁵, Ash².—tell] leve CC. 175. Shall] That shall C¹, C³. 176. as] om. C³.—the mothir] callyd modyr C³; modir called C¹. 177. hevynly] quenly B², CC. 179. and a] eke and a C².—mayden] virgin C¹, C³. 180. for] om. B¹, B², C².—playnely] eternally C². 181. to] of B¹. 182. this] om. B¹, B², Ch.—Whanne she was borne] This gracious maide C².

Howe our Lady was
offrede into the
Temple Caº iiº

Ande aftir iii yere, as was the vsage

Hir modir pappis, she left as in soukyng

And thanne anon, in her tendre age

Vnto the Temple, deuoutely they hir bryng

And unto god, they made offryng

Of this mayde, for to abyde there

With othir maydens, that in the temple were

190   And not with stondyng, hir passyng tendirnesse

Hir grene youthe, but of yeres thre

Thorough goddes helpe, this braunche of holynesse

With outyn helpe went vp, gre by gre

Fyftene on lofte, that wondir was to see

Tofore the auter, of so grete an hight

Thenne whanne hir modir, ther of had a syght

---

183. iii yere] thys ther H¹.—as was] as tho was C¹, C³. 184. she left] lefte she Ash².—left]
om. C¹.—as] om. Ad³, Ash². 185. And thanne anon, in her tendre age B¹.—tendre]
yonge tendre D, C¹; tendyr yong C³.—And] Left and Ch.—her] om. Ch. 186. they hir]
they dide her C²; they gan her B⁵. 187. And unto god, they made offryng H⁷.—unto]
to D, Hn¹, C¹, B¹.—offryng] devout Hn¹.—made] did made H⁵. 188. mayde] clene
mayde C³.—for] om. Ash². 190. And] om. Ash².—passyng] om. C². 191. grene] grete
CC.—and but] but but H¹. 192. helpe] grace B³, L.—braunche] well Hn¹; chaumbre L.
193. vp] om. Ad³, CC. 194. that wondir was to] that alle might, B², Ch, B⁴, H¹, C²,
Ash¹, H³, H⁴, H⁵, H⁶, Ad², Lg, C⁵, CC. 195. the] that H³, H⁴, Ad².—so] om. CC.
196. Thenne] And B², H¹, CC, B⁴, Hn¹, Ash¹, H³, H⁴, H⁵, H⁶, Ad², Lg, C⁵; om.
C².—ther of had] hadde therof Co, C³, B², H¹, CC.—ther of had a] ther of wonderide in her C².

For verrey Ioye, a noon she fell a dovne

And seide thus, that all myghten here

God frome above, hath herde myne orysoune

200 Of his godenesse, and graunted my prayer

And Recomfortede, myn oppressede chier

In sight of hem, that lowghen at my payne

And of malice, gan at me disdeigne

Now hathe he been, my synguler refute

To my tristesse, consolacion

For he hath made the bareyn to bere frute

Thorough his myghty vesitacion

And made eke clere, my confucion

And all my woo, for to overgone

210 Only by grace, a myddys all my foon

---

197. For verrey] Whiche for gret C². —a noon] thereof B⁵. 198. And seide thus, that all myghten here B¹. —thus] Right thus D, C¹, C³. —all] all men C¹, C³. 199. orysoune] bone C². 200. his] om. C². —graunted] herde B², CC; granted hath Ash². —my] om. CC; graunted my] graunted me my B¹, B³, H³, H⁷. 201. Recomfortede] comforted C⁵. 202. lowghen at my] lieth in C²; syen all my Ash². 203. And of malice, gan at me disdeigne B¹. —gan at me] of me gan D; at me gan C¹; gan of me H⁵. 204. he] om. H⁵. 205. To my tristesse, consolacion B¹. —consolacion] hole consolacion D, C¹, C³; grete consolacion B², CC. —To] And eke to Hn². 206. to] om. C³. 207. myghty] gracious Ash²; gracious and myghty Hn¹; myghty goodly Hu; gracious myghti B¹, B², H⁷, Ad³. 208. eke] om. Ch, B³, B⁴, Co, H¹, C², B⁵, Ash¹, H³, H⁴, H⁵, H⁶, Ad², Lg, C⁵, L, CC, J; all C¹, C³. —made eke] eke made Hu; eke hath made Hn¹. —confucion] foule confusioun C¹, C³. 209. for] now fully Hn¹. 210. a myddys] and H¹, Lg. —all] of all C¹, H⁴, J; om. B², CC.

And thurgh his myght, þe hertes hath ybowed   f. 8a

Of hem that gan, to chace at me by pryde

Wherfore she hath, vnto god avowed

That hir dought*er*, shall in the Temple abyde

The holy gost, for to be her guyde

For euermore, by godd*es* purviaunce

Thurgh her mekenesse, hym to do plesaunce

For all her life, there to slepe and wake

Hym forto s*er*ue, w*ith* p*er*fite humblesse

220   That all maydenes, may ensample take

Of hir alone, to leve in clennesse

And specially, of hir deuote mekenesse

Benyng, port, contenaunce, and chier

If that hem list of hir thay might ler

211. And thurgh his myght, þe hertes hath ybowed B¹.—hath] he hath D, J, Hn¹, C¹, C³.—þe] om. B², CC. 212. to] om. B¹, B², B⁵, H⁷, Ash², J, Ad³, Hu, L, Hn¹, Co.—gan to] om. Ch. 213. vnto] to Ash², H⁶. 214. the] om. Ash¹, H⁶. 215. The holy gost, for to be her guyde B¹.—for] om. D.—The] And the Hn¹. 217. Thurgh her makenesse, hym to do plesaunce B¹.—to] for to D, C¹, Hn¹, J.—hym to do] to do him Ash². 218. For all her life, there to slepe and wake B¹.—there] ther for D, C¹, Hn¹.—For] Forth for H⁷.—to] the B⁴. 219. forto] to B¹, C¹.—perfite humbless] humble perfitnesse C², Ch, B³, B⁴, Co, H¹, Hn¹, Ash¹, H³, H⁴, H⁵, H⁶, Ad², Lg, C⁵, L, CC, J, Hu. 221. clennesse] hygh clennesse C³. 222. deuote] om. B¹, B², B⁴, H¹, H³, H⁴, H⁵, H⁶, H⁷, Ash¹, CC, C¹, C², C⁵, Ad², Lg, Ch. 223. Benyng port] Benynge of port Ch, B³, H⁵, L; Benyne in porte Ash². 224. thay] om. CC.

Full of vertu, devoyde of all outerage

Hir hert was, that god to dwelle in chees

And day by day, Right as she wex in age

Right so in vertu, gan she to encrese

And nyght ne day wolde she neu*er* sees

230 To exclude slouthe, and vices to werrey

W*ith* hande₃ to werke, or *with* mought to pray

For but in god, hir hert nought delitede

So vpon hym, entierly was hir thought

And frome above, by grace he hir visited

That eu*er*y thyng, but hym, she sett at nought

Of worldly luste, she hath so litille rought

That oute of mynde, she lete it ou*er*e slyde

That nought but god, may *with* hir abyde

225. of] om. Ch. 226. that] with B¹, Ash¹, B², CC. 227. Right] om. Co.—in] of B². 228. she] om. C². 229. ne] and H⁵.—wold she] she wold C³, Ash².—wold] ne wold C¹, Lg, J. 230. and vices] and with vices B¹, B², CC, C².—werrey] be wreye Hu; fray B³, L, CC.— to] om. C¹. 232. hir] om. B¹, B². 233. So] For B¹, B², B³, B⁴, B⁵, Ch, Hn¹, Co.—vpon hym entierly] entyerly upon hym C², C³.—entierly] certenly C¹; eternally H¹. 234. by] with Co.—by grace he hir] he hyr by grace C³.—he] om. B³, L, Ad³. 235. That] And B¹, B², H⁵, Ad², Hu, Ch.—euery thyng] only C².—sett at] desirith C². 236. Of worldly luste, she hath so litille rought B¹.—hath] om. D.—rought] thoght B², C², H⁴, Ash², C⁵, CC. 237. ouere] never Ch. 238. may] om. Ash²; ne may Hn¹, J.—with] in Ch, B⁴, H¹, C², Ash¹, H³, H⁵, H⁶, Lg, C⁵, H⁴, CC.—hir] herte H⁴; her herte CC.

<table>
<tr><td></td><td></td></tr>
</table>

A nd whan þat she·V·yere dyd atteyne

240   She was as sadde in conuersacion

And also demure, sothely forto seyne

Form all childehode and dissolucion

In gouernaunce and in descrecion

And in talkyng alse wise and alse sage

As any mayde of xxx^{ti} yere of Age

And of hir Rull, this was hir vsaunce   f. 8b

Fro day to day, this holy mayde enter

Fro prime at morowe, by continuance

To thre at bell to be in hir prayer

250   And till the sonne was at mydday spere

On golde and silke and on wolleȝ softe

With hir handys, she wolde wyrke ofte

Of the conuersacion
of our lady in the
temple   Ca° iii°

---

239. þat she] the C¹, B¹, B⁵.—·V·] XV H¹, C², C³, Hn¹, Ash¹, H³, H⁴, H⁵, H⁶, Ad²,
Lg, C⁵, C¹. 240. as] so H³.—in] in her Ash². 241. forto] to C², Ash², CC. 242. all]
om. CC. 243. In] And in Hn¹.—and in] and H¹, CC, J. 244. in] of C¹, C³.—alse wise]
wyse CC; welavised C¹, C³, Hn¹.—alse sage] sage C¹, C³, Hn¹, Ash²; of sage L. 245. any]
any other C².—xxx^{ti}] xx C¹.—yere] wyntir C¹, Hn¹.—of] om. Hn¹, Hu. 246. hir vsaunce]
the vsaunce Ash¹, H⁵. 248. prime at morowe] the morow Ash². 249. thre at] tierce Hn¹,
J, C¹.—at] of Ash¹, H³, H⁴, H⁵, H⁶, Ad², C⁵, CC, Hu, L, C³; on B¹, B², B³, B⁴, H¹, H⁷,
Ash², Lg, Ch.—thre] xi C³.—to be] ay knelyng C¹, C³.—hir] om. B⁵, Co. 251. silke] silver
H³, Ch, B⁴, H⁴, Ad², C⁵.—and on wolleȝ softe] that was full faire and softe B¹.—on] om.
C², Ash², CC, H³. 252. hir handys] hir holy hands B³, L.—wolde wyrke] wroughte ful B³, L.

And even at none to brynge hir her fode

Fro god above, ther was an Angell sent

Whiche that she tooke, as for hir lyfelode

Thankyng hym aye, *with* hir hole entente

And aftir mete, a noon this mayde is went

Agayne to praye, tyll phebus went to west

And Evyn at eve, *with* hym she tooke hir Rest

260 This lyve she ladde and this course she goyth

In whome was never yet, founde offence

And neu*er* man sawe, this mayde wrothe

But ever meke, and full of paciens

Of hert clenne, and pure in conscience

This lif she ledde, *and* as bokes teche

Of wordes fewe, *and* wondre softe of speche

253. And even at none to brynge hir her fode Ad³.—hir her] hir D, H⁷, Ash², H⁴, Hn¹, CC; to hir C³.—And even] And at evene B¹, L.—And] At CC. 255. as] om. B¹, H⁵, H⁷, Ash², C¹, Ad³, Hn¹. 256. Thankyng] And thanked Ash².—hym aye] ay him C³, J.—with] with all J, B⁴, Ash¹, H³, H⁴, H⁶, Ad², C⁵.—hir] *inserted above.* 257. a noon] om. C², B¹, C¹.—maide] holy maide, B¹, C¹; om. L. 258. went] gan J; com B³, L.—west] reste B⁴, H¹, Ash¹, H³, H⁴, Ash², H⁵, H⁶, Ad², Lg, C⁵, CC. 259. And] And right Ash².—And Evyn at eve] And at even C².—with hym] om. Hu. 260. this] this hir C¹, C³; thus hir Hn¹, J. 261. was never yet] yet never was B¹. —yet] om. Hn¹.—founde] om. CC; founde noon Hn¹. 262. man] *inserted above.*—sawe] yet saw C¹, C³.—wrothe] out wroth C¹, B⁴, H¹, Ash¹, H³, H⁴, H⁵, H⁶, Ad³, Ad², C⁵, CC, Hu; yet wroth Hn¹. 264. hert] her CC.—clenne and pure] pure and clene B¹.—in] of Ch, B³, B⁴, C³, H³, H⁴, H⁶, Ad², C⁵, L, B², H¹; om. Ash¹, CC.—clenne] glade H¹. 265. This lif she ledde, *and* as bokes teche B¹.—This lif she ledde] This was hir won*e* D; This was hir vow C¹, C³. 266. Of wordes fewe, *and* wondre softe of speche B¹.—softe] fayre D, Hn¹, C³; few C¹.— wondre softe] softe C²; passyng softe Hu.

The mete also that was to hir brought

Out of þe temple, for her sustenaunce

With hert gladde, and with a perfyte thought

270 To pore and nedy, that leven in penaunce

To giffe it frely, was all hir pleasaunce

And who that euere, of hir hadde a sight

Of all diseases, was made glad and light

And euery wyght, grevyde with sekenesse

A touche of hir, made hem hoole a noon

And thay that were in tought and in diseasse

Whan they hir sawe, hir maladye was gone

And thus she was, to eueryche oone

Of all mischeve, Refute and Remedye

280 With a be haldyng, of hir godely eye

---

267. to] unto C³, J. Oute of þe temple, for her sustenaunce B¹.—for] as for D, C¹ C³.—þe] om. H¹. 269. with] om. H³. 270. that] and Hu.—penaunce] pouerte penaunce C¹. 272. who] om. Ash².—of hir hadde] had of her B⁵. 273. Of all diseses, was made glad and light B¹.—glad] both glad D, C¹, C³.—made] om. H¹. 275. made hem hoole a noon] anon mad hem hoole C¹; hem helide anon C². 276. and in] or B³, L; or in B¹, B², B⁵, J, C¹, C³, Hu, Hn¹, Co.—in] om. C¹, B⁴, H¹ C², Ash¹, Ash², H⁵, H⁶, Ad³, Ad². 277. maladye] malice B⁴, H¹, C¹, C³, Ash¹, H³, H⁴, H⁵, H⁶, Ad², C⁵, CC.—was gone] was al gon B¹, B², Ash², Ch.—maladye was gone] gref was done C². 278. to] vnto B², C¹, B³, B⁴, Co, H¹, C¹, C², C³, B⁵, Hn¹, Ash¹, H³, H⁴, H⁵, H⁶, H⁷, Ad³, Ad², C⁵, L, CC, J, Hu. 279. mischeve] myschief and sorowe Ch.—and] and eke Ash². 280. a be haldyng] vpholding CC.—godely] gostly B¹.—eye] syght C³.

And of this mayde eke, as it is tolde   f. 9a

Hir godely face, was so full of light

That no man myght, susteyn to by holde

For it was clever then the sonne bryght

That the crowne, in the wynters nyght

Of Adrian, ne of þe sterres sevene

To her fairnesse, be not for to nevene

Yet neuer man, temptyde was to synne

While he be helde, on hir hooly face

290 The holy goste, so hoole was hir *within*

That all envyron, sprede gan his grace

Where þat she was *present* in any place

For all way god gaffe to hir *presence*

So fulsum light, of hevynly influence

---

281. of] for Ash[1].—is] om. H[1]. 282. godely] gostly B[1], B[3], H[7], C[1], L.—was] it was CC; om. C[2]; was eke B[5]. 283. myght susteyn] sustene myght B[1], C[1].—to] ne H[7], Ad[3], Hu; and Co, B[5]. 285. That] That to CC. 286. Of Adrian, ne of þe sterres sevene B[1].—ne of] ne D, Hn[1], J; ne any of H[1].—þe] om. B[4]. 287. To her fairnesse, be not for to nevene B[1].—be not] ne wer not D; ne be not Ch, Ash[1], H[3], H[5], H[6], H[7], C[5], J, Hu; they be not B[2], CC. 288. Yet] And yet Ash[2], B[1], H[7], Ad[3], Hu, Hn[1],—to] with L, B[3], H[1]; for to H[4]. 289. on] vpon B[1], B[5], H[7], Ash[2], J, Ad[3], Hu, Hn[1], Co.—holy] om. C[2]; godely Ch, B[4], Ash[1], H[3], H[4], H[6], Ad[2], C[5]. 290. so hoole was] was so hool Hu; was hir so hole H[4]. 291. gan] om. C[2]. 292. Where þat she was *present* in any place H[7].—þat] so D; *evere* C[3]; so that J; om. C[1], Co. was present] present was B[1]. 293. way] myghty C[2].—gaffe to hir] gaf hyr to Ash[1], Ch, B[4], H[3], H[4], H[6], Ad[2], C[5]. 294. fulsum] holy CC.—fulsum light] gracious a gifte C[2].

Ne noon so fayre, was neu*ere* founde in Reame

As was this mayde, of Iuda and Syon

The doughtir chosyn of Ierusalem

Of David seed, for to be sett alone

Of all maydens, to Reken hem eu*ery*chone

300 She bare the price, as well in fayrnesse

As she excellede, in vertu and in goodenesse

Late be thow Grece, and speke not of Eleyn

Ne thow Troy, of yong Polexene

Ne Rome of Lucresse, *with* hir eyn tweyne

Ne thow Cartage, of thy fresshe quene

Dido that was so fayre some tyme to seen

Late be y*our* boste, and take of hem noon hede

Whose beaute, fayleth as floure in frosty mede

---

295. noon] no man L.—was neu*ere* founde] neuer was founde H³; was founde neuer Ch; was euer founde L. 296. and] and of H³. 297. doughtir chosyn] chosyn doughter C².—chosyn] chosen eke Hn¹. 299. all] all the B², CC.—hem] om. Ash¹, H⁶. 301. and] om. B⁵.—in] om. C¹, B⁴, Co, H¹, C¹, Ash¹, H⁵, H⁶, Ad², C⁵, CC, J, Ash².—goodenesse] godlinesse Ash². 302. speke] om. Ad². 303. Troy] Troy towne C³; Troie tollen C¹.—Polexene] o *inserted above.* 304. Ne] Ne thou B², CC. 305. some tyme] whilom J.—to seen] and sheen Ash², L. 308. in] in the CC.—frosty] fressh C¹.

Ester was meke, but not lyke hir mekenesse

310　And Iudith wyse, but she yet dyd excell

And Barsabe of grete semelynesse

And Rachell fayre, Iacob can yov tell

But she aloone, of womanhode the well

Of bountee, beaute, þat neuere fade may

Nat liche a floure, that flouressheth but in may

Passyde Ichone bothe ney and ferre   f. 9b

Bothe in fairenesse, and in perfeccion

Right as þe sonne, doth a litil sterre

And as þe rubie, hath wone þe renoun

320　Of stonys all, and dominacion

Right so this mayde, to speke of holynesse

Of women all Is lady and maystres

---

309. lyke] to B¹, B², B³, B⁴, B⁵, H¹, H³, H⁴, H⁵, H⁶, H⁷, Ash¹, Ash², CC, C¹, C², C⁵, Ad²,
Hu, L, Ch, Co; of Ad³. 310. wyse] om. B¹.—she yet] yet she B², C¹, C², L, CC, Hu.—yet]
om. B⁵, Co.—yet did] did yet H³, Ash², H⁵, B¹. 312. Rachell fayre] fair Rachell H¹.—can]
om. CC. 313. the] om. J. 314. Of bountee, beaute, þat neuere fade may B¹.—beaute] and of beaute
D.—bountee] bountevous L. 315. Nat] But Ash², CC.—but] om. Ash², CC. 316. Passyde] She
passeth B¹, B², Ash², C¹, C², Hu. 317. Bothe in fairenesse, and in perfeccion B¹.—Bothe in]
In all D, C³; In B³, L.—and in] and eke in B², CC; and Co, B⁵, J. 318. Right as þe sonne,
doth a litil sterre B¹.— a litil] the leste D, C³; a lytyl fayr Hn¹; fro a lytle L. 319. And as þe
rubie, hath wone þe renoun B¹.—wone þe] the Right D, C³; in B², CC; the Ch, B³, B⁴, H¹,
C², Ash¹, H³, H⁴, H⁵, H⁶, Ad², C⁵. 320. all] om. L.—and] in Ash¹; and hath Hu; the CC;
and the B¹, B², C¹, Ch. 322. all Is] is all L.—all] alle she Hu.—Is lady] om. Ch.

Salamon   Off whome spake some tyme, wyse Salamon

            In sapience, wo so lust it to seke

            That she was chosyn, for hym self alone

            This white dove *with* hir eyn meke

            Whose chekys were, hir beaute forto eke

            With lylieȝ meynt and fresshe Rosys Rede

            This is to sayen, who so can take hede

330   First *with* the Rose, of womanly suffraunce

            And *with* the lyle, next of chastytee

            She was ennuede, to yef hyr suffisaunce

            As well in goodnesse, as in beaute

            And as he sayeth, she fayrer was to see

            Than outhir phebus, platly or lucyne

            With hornes full on heven, whan thay schyne

---

323. spake some tyme] somtyme spake B[1], B[2], H[4], Ash[1].—some tyme] whilom J.—wyse] the wyse Ch. 324. so] om. H[3], Ad[3].—it to seke] to loke and seke C[2]. 325. was chosyn] chosen was B[5], Co.—hym] om. H[1]. 326. hir] om. H[1]. 329. so] that Hu.—can] om. Hn[1].—so] *inserted above*. 330. the] om. B[1], B[2], B[3], CC, C[2], Hu, Ch, Co. 331. lylye] faire lilie B[2], Ch, B[4], H[1], C[2], Ash[1], H[3], H[4], H[5], H[6], C[5], CC.—lylye] om. B[3], L. 332. hyr] om. B[1], B[2], B[3], H[7], Ash[2], Ad[3]; with CC. 333. As well in goodnesse, as in beaute B[1].—as] sothely as D, C[1], C[3], J.—goodnesse] godlinesse Ash[2]. 334. as] om. L; eke Hn[1].—he] she H[3], H[6], C[5].—to] vnto Ash[1].—to see] in B[3], L. 335. platly or] or bright C[2]. 336. on] om. Ad[3]; of Ash[1], B[3], B[4], Co, H[1], C[2], B[5], H[3], H[4], H[5], H[6], C[5], L, CC, Hu.—schyne] do shyne Ash[1].

Ancelme

And of this mayde, as saint Ancelme seyth

In his wrytyng, hir beaute to te*r*myne

Of face fayre, but fayrer yet of fayeth

340 He sayth she was, this holy pure virgyne

Whose chast hert, to no thyng dyd enclyne

For all hir beaute, but to holynesse

Of whome also this Autor saythe expresse

That she was doughtir of david by dyscent

Sterre of the see, and godd*es* awne ancyll

Quene of the worlde, al way of one entent

And godd*es* spous, his hest*es* to fulfille

And eu*ere* redy, forto wyrke his will

Cryst*es* temple, and also Receptacle

350 Of the holy goost, *and* chosen tabernacle

---

338. te*r*myne] determyne C¹, C², CC; terment H¹. 339. fayrer] wel feyrer C¹, C³.—yet] om. B⁵, Hu.—fayeth] sight C⁵. 341. no] om. Co. 342. but to holynesse] was all in her but holynesse B¹. 343. also] *inserted above.*—saythe] dothe CC. 344. of] to CC. 346. the] this H³, H⁶. 348. su*ere*] euermore B¹.—wyrke] do B⁴, B², C¹, B³, Co, H¹, C², B⁵, Ash¹, H³, H⁴, Ash², H⁵, H⁶, H⁷, Ad³, Lg, C⁵, L, CC, Hu. 349. also] also his Ash². 350. Of the holy goost, *and* chosen tabernacle B¹.—*and*] the D; and also H¹; his Ash².—chosen] worthy C³.—tabernacle] habitacle H¹.—Of] And of Ash².

The yate of heven, and also the fayrnesse   f. 10a

Of women alle, who so looke aright

Of maidenhede, lady *and* princesse

One of the fyve, that bare hyr laumpe light

Redy to mete, w*ith* hir spous at nyght

Full prudently, awaytyng at the gate

That for noo sloothe, she came not to late

In fygure eke the chaundelabre of golde

That some tyme bare, Seven lampes schene

360   This is to saye, the Receyte and the holde

Of god p*r*eseruede, for she was so clene

Thorough hir merite, endowet forto ben

By grace of hym, that is of power most   Ca iiii

W*ith* the seven yiftes, of the holy goste

---

351. yate] grace C³.—the] om. B³; of the Lg; of H⁶, L, CC. 352. Of women alle, who so looke aright B¹.—so] so that D, C¹.—women] whome H¹. 353. Of maidenhede, lady *and* princesse H⁷.—princesse] maystresse D, Ash², C³.—lady] eke lady B¹. 354. hyr] the Lg. 355. to] for to B5, Co. 356. at] on on B¹. 357 she] om. H⁴.—not] om. B³, L; not in Hu.—to] om. CC. 358. eke] om. C³.—chaundelabre] chandeler B¹, B², B5, H¹, Ash², C², Lg, C³, Hn¹.—of] were of C³. 359. some tyme] whylom J. 360. and] of CC. 361. god] gold C¹.—she] om. B⁴. 362. endowet] endles C¹.—forto] to C¹; to have H¹. 364. With the sevene yiftes, of the holy goste B¹.—the] om. D.—With] Whyche C³.

The firste yefte was the yefte of drede   Donum timoris domini

   To eschewe thyng*es* that god shulde displease

The next petee of werrey woman hede   Donum Caritatis

To Rewe on all, that she sawe in disease

The thryde, Connyng, god and man to please   Donum sciencie

370 The forthe, Strengh thorough hir stedfastnesse   Donum fortitudinis

Only by vertu, all vices to oppresse

Of counseile eke, she hadde excellence

To kepe hir pure in virginite

For ay *with* coun*n*sell, alliede ys prudence

For god hym self, chese *with* hir to be

Of vndirstondyng, eke, the yefte had she   Donum intellectus

Ande of wysdom, so god liste hir avaunce   Donum sapiencie

To knawe Iche thyng, that was to his pleasaunce

---

365. yefte was] was Lg.—the] om. B², B³, H¹, H⁷, Ch. 366. eschewe] om. Ch.—thyng*es*] eche thyng B², B³, B⁴, Co, Ash¹, H³, H⁴, H⁵, H⁶, Lg, C⁵, L, CC, J, Hu, C³, H¹; om. C², B¹, H⁷, Ash², Ad³; al things B⁵.—god shulde] shold god B², B³, B⁴, Co, Ash¹, H³, H⁴, H⁵, H⁶, Lg, C⁵, L, CC, J, Hu, B⁵, Ash².—that god shulde displease] in her virginite H¹. 367. next] seconde C². 368. she sawe] were C². 369. Connyng] lovynge Ash¹. 370. Strengh] force Co, B⁵.—hir] om. B¹. 371. Only by vertu all vices] All maner of vicis bi vertu C².—by] in Hn¹, J.—all] om. Ash². 372. eke she hadde] sche had eke CC.—hadde] om. Lg. 373. To kepe hir pure in virginite B¹.—in] in hir D, Hn¹, Lg, C³.—pure] pure alwey C³. 377. Ande of wysdom, so god liste hir avaunce B¹.—wysdom] hir wisdom D.—liste] om. L.—avaunce] to avaunce Ch, B⁴, H⁶. 378. Iche] om. L.—to] in H⁴.

She was also, the trone voyde of synne

380   That stondythe, so Royall in god*es* awne syght

To fore wheche, sevene laumpes brenne

W*ith* hevenly fyre, so sp*irit*uell of light

That never wast but eu*ere* yliche bryght

Continue in oone, high above in hevyn

By whiche trone, and the laumpes . vii .

Is vndirstonde, this mayden moste entier   f. 10b

W*ith* . vii . vertues, that in hir were founde

That some tyme were, with gostly fyre so clere

Thorough light of vertu, Inwardely Iocounde

390   Only thorough grace, that dyd in hir habounde

And all thay were growendyd in mekenesse

Her lyght to god, more plesauntly to dresse

---

379. She] om. C². —also the trone] the trone also Co. 380. so] om. Ad³. —godes] his B³, L.— awne] om. C². 381. To fore wheche, sevene laumpes brenne B¹.—wheche] the whiche D, J, Hn¹, C¹, C³.—To fore] Therefore C⁵; To Lg. 382. so] and B¹. 383. wast] fadith C¹.—euere] om. B², Ch, B³, B⁴, B⁵, Co, H¹, C², Ash¹, H³, H⁴, H⁵, H⁶, H⁷, Ad³, Lg, C⁵, CC, Hu. 384. Continue] Continually Ash¹.—oone high] here Ch, C²; ever high C¹.—high] om. Ash¹; here H³, H⁴, C⁵. 385. the] om. B¹, B², H⁵, Ash², C². 386. vndirstonde] vndirstonding H⁷. 387. With] Which C⁵.—in hir were] were in hir H³, Ash². 388. fyre] lyght B¹, B², B³, B⁴, B⁵, H¹, H³, H⁴, H⁵, H⁶, H⁷, Ash¹, Ash², CC, C², C⁵, Ad³, Hu, L, Lg, Ch, Co.—some tyme] whilom J. 389. Thorough light of vertu] As in felinge C². 390. Only] om. C².—thorough] by Co.— grace] special grace C².—dyd in hir] in hir did Ash¹, CC. 391. growendyd] dyd *inserted above*. 392. Her lyght to god, more pleasantly to dresse B¹.—god] god warde D, C¹, C³, Hn¹, J; of god H⁵.—to] didde H⁴.—dresse] redresse Hn¹.

For faythe in hir, had a grounde so stable

That it was voyde, of all doublenesse

Hir hope of truste, was also mayntenable

Roted in god, by p*er*fith sik*er*nesse

Whose charite, so large can hym dresse

That vp to god, hottest Ran the fyre

W*ith* hete of of clennes, to all by desyre

400   Strong in vertu, prudent in gou*er*naunce

She had also, co*n*veyede w*ith* clennesse

And sou*er*enly, she had temp*er*aunce

In all hir werk*es*, w*ith* greate avysenesse

And cu*er*e anexede v*n*to Rig*h*t wysnesse

With in hir hert of womanly bou*n*te

She had of custome mercy and pety

---

394. voyde] om. L. 395. truste] cryste B², CC. 397. Whose] Her C².—so large can him] largely she did C². 398. That vp to god hottest] But vpwarde hotter C².—vp to] uppon Hn¹, Ash¹, H⁶. 399. hete] hert B¹, B², B³, B⁴, B⁵, H¹, H³, H⁴, H⁵, H⁶, H⁷, Ash¹, Ash², CC, J, C¹, C², C³, C⁵, Ad³, L, Lg, Ch, Hn¹.—of] to Lg.—clennes, to all by desyre] clene and fervent desire C². 400. Strong] Force B⁵, Co, J.—in] om. B³, L; with H⁴. 401. had] om. B⁵.—had also] also was Ash². 403. greate] grace of H¹; first e *inserted above*. 404. And eu*er*e anexede v*n*to] And vnto hir annexid was Hn¹.—vnto] vnto hyr C³; with grete B⁵; vnto the H³. 405. hert] om. B¹, H⁷, C¹. 406. had of custome] customed had C¹, C³.—mercy and pety] pite and merce Ash¹.

Sothefaste ensample, also of chastite

As saythe Ambrose, she was in thought and dede

And trwe merrowre, of virgynytee

410   Of port benyng, full of lawlyhede

Aye humble of chere, *and* feminyn of drede

Prudent of speche, of what hir lust to shewe

Large of sentens, and but of word*es* fewe

To pray and Rede, that was eu*er*e hir lyve

Off hert wakir, by deuocion

To god all way wi*th* thought contemplatyf

Full fervent eu*er*e in hir intenc*i*on

And Idyll, neuer from occupac*i*on

And specially vnto almes dede

420   Hir honde was eu*er*e redy at þe nede

409. virgyntee] clene virginite B1, H7. 410. Of port] And of porte L; And in porte Hu.— port benyng] benigne porte H5. 411. Aye humble of chere, *and* feminyn of drede B1.—of drede] drede D, CC.—Aye] And Ash1; As H3, H4, C5, Ch. 412. Prudent] Gloriouse C1, C3. 414. Rede] to rede C1, C3. 415. deuocion] grete deuocioun C1, C3, Hn1. 416. wi*th* thought] om. CC.— contemplatyf] and contemplatyff Hu. 418. from] in B2, CC; from hir B1, H5, H7. 419. vnto] to J, Co, H1, B5, H8, Hu; in CC; ever vnto Hn1; alwey to C2. 420. Hir honde was eu*er*e redy at þe nede B1.—þe] om. D, Ch, B3, C2, Ash2, Ar, H8, L, CC; her Hn1.

And ful she was, of compassion   f. 11a

To rewe on all, that feltyn woo or smert

Wel willede eu*ere*, w*ith* hole affection

To eu*ery* wyght, so louyng was hir hert

Sad withe all this, that hir neu*ere* astert

Aloke amysse, of hir eyne fayre

So close of sight, was this debonayre

And in psalme3, and holy p*ro*phecye

To loke and rede, she founde most delyte

430   And whan she sawe, and herde in Isaye

Of crist*es* birthe, howe he dyd wryte

To god she lifte, hir tendre handys white

By sechyng hym, she myght abyde and see

This blisfull day, of his Natyvyte

---

421. And ful she was, of compassion B¹.—was] was was aye D, C³. 422. all] all thos B¹, H³, H⁸, J, Ar. 425. Sad withe all this, that hir neu*ere* astert B¹.—hir neu*ere*] neu*ere* hir D, C¹, C³, Hn¹, Ash², Ar.—this] om. B³, L.—that] dyd CC. 426. Aloke] To loke CC.—of] with H⁸, CC.—hir] youre Hn¹. 427. sight] myght C¹.—was] om. B¹. 428. and] of Co, H¹, Lg; and in H⁴, Ash², Ar, H⁸, H⁶. 429. rede] to rede B¹, B².—founde] had C¹, C³, Hn¹, H⁸; coude J. 430. sawe] rad C³; was L.—herde] founde B¹, B³, B⁴, B⁵, H¹, H², H³, H⁴, H⁵, H⁶, Ash¹, Ash², C², C⁵, Ar, Ad³, Hu, L, Lg, Ch, Co.—and herde] om. CC.—in] om. C¹, H². 432. lifte] lyft up C³, CC. 433. she] that she B¹, B², H³, Ash², C¹.—myght abyde] abide myght C². 434. day of his] lady at hir B², CC.

And in the boke, of Eliȝabethe

That titled is, of hir avisions

I fynde how this mayde of Naȝareth

Sayde eu*e*ry day, seven orys*i*ons

Whiche clepyde ben, hir petycions

440   Withe humblehert, this yong blisfull mayde

Ful lowely knelynge, evene thus she sayde

O Blisful lorde, that knawest the entent
    Of ev*e*ry hert, In thyne ete*r*nall sight

Yeffe me grace, the firste com*m*aundement

To fulfille as it is skyll *and* right

And grant also, wi*th* herte will and myght

And all my savle, and all my full knawyng

The for to love, aboven all othir thyng

Howe oure lady prayed to god for vii petycions prima peticio° Ca° v^to

---

435. And] And eke Hn1.—Eliȝabethe] Seynt Elyzabeth C3. 436. That titled is, of hir avisions B1.—of] in D, CC; for B3, L. 437. I fynde how this mayde of Naȝareth B1.—how this mayde of] this mayde born of D, C3.—how] how that C2. 438. orys*i*ons] swete orysons C3. 439. hir] Maryes C3. 440. Withe humble hert] Full humble H8.—yong] om. B1, B2, C2, C5.—yong blisfull] blesful yonge H2.—blisful] om. B4. 441. Ful lowely knelynge, evene thus she sayde B1.—Ful lowely] Devoytely D; Devout C1, C3; With lowely H; Ful longe C2.—evene] and even H8, J. 442. knawest] best C1. 443. hert] wyght B. 444. Yeffe] So yeve C. 445. To fulfille as it is skyll *and* right Ad3.—To] For to D, H8, C3.—is] om. B1, H7. 446. grant] graunt me C1, C3.—herte] om. H1. 447. And all my savle] And my savle H1, Lg; All my savle Ad3.—full] om. H1, Lg, B3, B4, C2, Ash1, H3, H4, H5, H6, C5, L, CC, Hu.

And gyffe me myght, playnely to fulfille   S*ecunda* **peticio**

450   The next byddyng, lyke to thy pleasaunce

And for to loue, withe hert and all my will

My neghbore in dede, and contenaunce

Right as my self, *with every* circu*m*stance

And her withall, for Ioye woo or smerte

That thou lovest, to love with all myn hert

'ercia peticio   The thride precepte graunte eke that I may   f. 11b

Fulfille also, boþe erly *and* late

In suche maner, as most is to thy pay

Benigne lorde, and make me for to hate

460   Manknydes foo, for he made furst debate

In kynde of man, and made hym to trespace

Agayns the and to lese his grace

---

449. myght] grace Ash1.—playnely] also C2. 451. withe] in B2, CC.—all] with all Lg.—hert and all my will] herte and alle my myght and wille B2; herte myght and wylle CC. 452. and] and in B3, C1, C3, S, Ar, Lg, L, Hu. 453. self] lyyfe Hn1.—with] in Ar, CC. 454. withall] with S. 455. That] What that B2, CC. 456. thride] om. H1, Ash1, H3, H5, H6, Lg, C5.—graunte] om. C2; graunt me L.—eke] om. Ash2, Ar. 457. Fulfille also, boþe erly *and* late B1.—and] and eke D, C3. 458. In suche maner, as most is to thy pay H7.—as most is] as is most D, B1, B5, Co, H2, H3, CC, C1.—to] unto C3. 460. Mankyndes foo, for he made furst debate B1.—made] gan D, H8, Hn1, J, C3, C1. 461. In kynde of man, and made hym to trespace Ad3.—In] The D, H8, J.—hym] om. S.—to] first B1, H7. 462. Agayns the and to lese his grace H7.—the] lorde D, C1, C3.—to lose] so he lost D.—his] thy B1.

And lorde graunte me, for thy mercy dygne

Quarta Peticio   Above al thyng, for to haue mekenesse

And make me sufferaunte, humble and benigne

With paciens and inwarde myldenesse

Of all vertues, gyf me eke largesse

To be accepte, the to queme and serue

To fynde only thy grace I may diserue

Quinta Peticio   470   And lorde also, with quakyng herte and drede

Mekely I pray vnto thy deite

Me forto graunte of thy godelyhede

The gracious hour, forto abyde and see

In whiche, the holy chosyn mayden free

Into this worlde here aftir shall be borne

Lyche as propheteʒ, have wrytyn here to forne

---

463. graunte me] me graunte H⁸, J. 464. for] om. B¹, C¹, C². 465. me] om. B¹, B², B³, H²,
CC, C¹, Ad³, L.—sufferaunte] om. C². 466. and] and with C², H².—inwarde] wordly C².
467. gyf me eke] eke yeve me B¹, C¹; yeve eke me Ch.—eke] om. Co, B⁵, S. 469. To] For
to S.—fynde only] That thorow C³.—thy] thorough H⁸, J.—diserue] pleynly deserue C³.
470. lorde also] also lorde B², H¹, Ch, C,² Ash¹, H³, H⁴, H⁵, H⁶, Lg, C⁵, CC.—and] in B⁵,
B³, S, Ar, H⁸, H⁷, Ad³, L, J, Hu. 471. Mekely] Yet mekely H².—vnto] now vnto Hn¹.—
deite] high deite Hn¹. 472. forto] to Hn¹. 473. forto] to B¹, B², B³, B⁴, H¹, H⁷, H⁸, Ash²,
CC, J, C², Ar, S, Ad³, Hu, L, Lg, Ch. 474. chosyn] om. C¹. 476. here] om. L.

Howe þat she shall by thyne election

Be maide and modur, to þi sone dere

Now goode lorde, here myn orisoun

480 To kepe my eyne, and my sight entier

That I may see, hir holy halowed chier

Hir sacrede beawtee, and hevynly conten*au*nce

If thou of grace liste me, so moche avaunce

And kepe myne eren þat I may also

Here hir speche, and hir daliaunce

And *with* my tonge, speke that mayden to

Paciently thorough hir sufferaunce

Of wordly Ioye, this were my suffisaunce

And hir to love, lyke as I desyre

490 Benynge lorde, thou set myne herte afyre

477. þat] om. H¹, Ash². 478. Be maide and modur, to þi sone dere B¹.—dere] so dere D, Ch, C¹, C³.—and] a Hn¹.—to] unto Co, CC. 479. Now goode lorde, here myn orisoun H⁷.—here] here thou D, C¹, C³, Hn¹.—goode lorde] lord gode B¹; good lady Ch, B⁴, H¹, Ash¹, H⁴, H⁵, H⁶, Lg, C⁵. 481. see] om. CC.—holy halowed] benigne C²; holy hond halowed, Ash¹. 482. hevynly] holy B², CC, Ch, B⁴, Co, H¹, C², B⁵, Ash¹, H³, H⁴, H⁵, H⁶, Lg, C⁵. 483. If thou] If that thou B², C¹, B³, B⁴, Co, C², Ash¹, H⁴, H⁶, C⁵, L.—avaunce] to avance C¹, H³; om. Ash², 484. I] they Ch, B³, B⁴, Co, C², H³, H⁴, H⁶, C⁵, L, B², Ash¹, H², CC, H⁵. 485. Here] And here Ash¹. 486. And *with* my tonge, speke that mayden to H⁷.—mayden] virgin D.—my] om. B¹, H⁵, H⁸.—speke] to speke Ash.² 487. Paciently] t *inserted above.* 489. And hir] And make me hir Hn¹.—lyke as] do B¹.—I desyre] I ay shall desyr C¹, C³. 490. Benynge] Gracious C²; Right benigne C¹, C³, Ash². —thou] and Hn¹; so B², Ch, B³, B⁴, H¹, Ash¹, H³, H⁴, H², H⁵, H⁶, Lg, C⁵, L, CC; om B¹, C², B⁵, H⁷, H⁸, J, Ar, S, Ad³, Hu, Co.

And also lord, on me safe þou vouche

Though I therto, have nowe noo worthynesse

That holy mayde, forto handyll and touche

Myn owne ladi, and myn maystresse

And that I maye, w*ith* humble buxumnesse

Uppon my feet, in all my best wyse

Go vnto hir, for to do s*e*rvise

And to that floure, of virginitee

Graunte also lorde, þ*at* I may haue space

500   Makely to bowe, and knele vppon my kne

Vndir supporte only, of hir grace

And to honour the godely yong face

Of hir sonne, as she dothe hym wrappe

In clothis softe lyggyng in hir lappe

---

491. And also lord, on me safe þou vouche B¹.—on me safe] safe on me D, H⁸, Ad³, C¹, C³.—also] om. Ch, H⁴, H².—also lord] lord also D, C¹, C³, B², B³, B⁴, Co, H¹, C², Hn¹, Ash¹, H³, H⁶, Lg, C⁵, L, J, Hu. 493. holy] wurthy B¹, B⁵.—for] om. B¹, B⁵.—handyll] haue Hn¹; hayle Ash¹. 494. Myn owne ladi, and myn maystresse B¹.—owne] sovereyn D, C¹, C³.—and] and also D, C¹, C³, B³, Co, H⁸, L, J, Hu.—myn maystresse] mistresse Ash², S. 497. Go vnto hir, for to do s*e*rvise B¹.—s*e*rvise] some s*e*rvyse D, C³.—vnto] now to C³. 498. to] vnto C².—virginitee] clene virginite Hn¹. 499. lorde] om. B¹, B⁵, H⁷, Ash², C¹, Co.—haue] om. H². 500. bowe and knele] knele and to bowe B¹, B⁵, C¹. 501. hir] om. B¹, B², B³, B⁴, B⁵, H¹, C¹, C², C³, L, Ch, Hn¹, Co. 502. the] hir H.—godely yong] yong godely CC. 503. as she] she as L.

And luffe hym best playnly to my laste

With all myne herte, and myne hole servise

Withoutyn chaunge, while my lyve may laste

Right as thy self lorde canst best devyse

So that I may, in faythfull humble wyse

510   In all this worlde, no more grace atteyne

Then love hym beste, with all my might and peyne

And to thy grace, also lorde I pray   *Sexta peticio*

Thou graunte it me to fulfyll in dede

Hooly thy statutes and mekely to obeye

Within the Temple, as I here hem Redde

For but thou helpe, I may no thyng spede

As of my self, therfore vnto the

All I committe, as thou luste it be

---

505. hym] om. B², CC.—playnly] ever C². 506. myne] om. Ash². 507. while] while that B², Ch.—may] om. H¹, C², Lg; shall CC, B², Ch. 509. that] om. Hu.—humble] om. L. 510.] To receyve the gift of grace special C². 511. love] to love B¹, B², B⁵.—beste] fervently C².—all] om. C².—might] hert Hu.—peyne] maine Ash², H⁶. 512. grace] om. Co.—also lorde] lord also Co.—also] om. H⁸.—I] I the L. 513.] to *inserted above.* 514. they] that the C⁵.—and] om. Hu.—mekely] om. B¹, B⁵. 516. but] but if Co, Ad³, CC. 517. of] for H⁸.—therfore] and therfore B¹, B⁴, B², B⁵, H², H³, H⁴, H⁶, H⁷, Ash¹. Ash², J, C¹, C⁵, Ar, S, Ad³, Ch. 518. All I committe, as thou luste it be B¹.—as] Right as D; so as Hn¹.—committe] submyt C¹.

The obs*er*vaunce₃ and the *pr*ecepte₃ all

520   That to thy Temple, oo lorde be p*er*tynent

So latte thy grace, by mercy on me fall

That I may done hem, w*ith* all my hole intente

And eu*er*y byddyng, and commaundement

That thy mynystre₃, assignede vnto me

Make me fulfill, with all humillite

Septima peticio   And thy Temple, and thyne holy house   f. 12

Benygne lorde, kepe frome all damage

And make thy peple, to be vertuouse

To thy pleasaunce of eu*er*y man*er*e age

530   The forto s*er*ve, w*ith* herte and hoole corage

And where they erre, o lorde on any syde

Or thou do Right, latte mercy be hir gyde

519. and the] and J. 520. oo] om. H8.—be] that be Co, Ash2 ; om. C3. 521. by] of H8.—by
mercy] om. Co.—on] vpon Ash2. 522. I] om. B4.—done hem] hym do S.—all] om. C3,
CC.—my hole] holy myn CC. 524. vnto] to un L.—me] the Ash1, H6. 525. fulfill] to fulfylle
B1, B2, B4, B5, H2, Hu, Ch; fully Hn1. 526. And] And to H2. 527. kepe] kepe me C1, H3, B4,
Ash1, H4, H6, Lg, C5. 528. to be] om. CC. 529 eu*er*y] all H2. 530. forto] to B4. 531. where]
whenne Ar, S, H3, Ash2.—they] that they B1, B5, C1.—o] om. B4, Ash1, H4, Ash2, Ar, H6,
C5, H3, Ch.—any] euery S, Ch, Hu. 532. latte] lorde B3.

Howe Abiathar that yere
Bisshoppe of the lawe
wolde haue weddede
our lady to his sonn*e*
Ca° vi°

Aend thus this mayde alway day by day

In the Temple, makyth hir prayers

To plese god, wat she can or may

The chief Resorte, of all hir desyres

Tyll she atteiynede into xiiii yeres

W*ith* hert avowyd, bothe in thought and dede

For to continue, in hir maydyn hede

540 Of whose entent, god wote full vnwar

Were some of hem, that in the Temple abyde

Of whiche a Bisshoppe callet Abiathar

Cast hym fully, forto sette asyde

Hir purpoys playnly, and so furth to p*r*ovyde

That hir avowe, made of chastite

Shall not holde but outrely that she

533. And] Ryght C³.—alway] om. H². 535. To plese god, wat she can or may B¹.—wat] in al that D; in what Ash¹, H²; that H⁸; in that C¹, C³, Hn¹. 536. all] om. H². 537. atteiynede into] atte the tyme of Ash¹. 538. and] and in Lg. 540. wote full vnwar] knowyng was hire gide Lg. 541.] Were in the temple of hem there to byde Ash¹.—that] om. Ar, CC.—the] om. H¹, Lg. 543. forto] to B¹, B², B⁵, Ad³, Ch. 544. playnly] fully Ad³, Ash², S, Ar; om. B¹, B⁵, H⁷; sikerly C².—furth] om. B¹, B⁵, H⁷, Ad³, B², Co, C¹, C³, H⁴, CC, Ash²; for C¹, B³, B⁴, Hn¹, Ash¹, H², H⁸, H⁶, Lg, C⁵, L, J, Hu, H¹, H³, S, Ar. 545. hir] om. H¹. 546.] Sholde not utterly holde but that she C².—Shall] Ne shall H, J. —holde] be helde Ash², Ar.

Sholde be weddyde, sothely if he myght

Vnto his sonne, of his affection

For that she was, in euery whyght*es* syght

550   So passyng gode of condicion

And to fulfill his entencion

Abyathar behotyth, golde and Rente

To the Bisshoppys, to make hir to assente

To his purpose, and to hir thay gone

And what thay may, thay gan hir excite

And afferme, to hir euerychone

W*ith* sugrede tonge, of many worde$_3$ whyte

That god above, dothe hym more delyte

In birthe of chyldren then in virginite

560   Or any suche, avowede chastite

547. if] om. H¹.—he] she H². 549. that] om. H⁸, H⁵.—whyght*es*] manys CC. 550. gode] faire and good B³, L. 551. to] thus to Hn¹. 552. behotyth] beholdeth Ar.—golde] bothe gold B², H³, CC. 553. the] om. H², Hu.—to assente] assente Co, H¹, C³, H³, Ash², Ar, J.—assente] concente B³, L. 554. and] alle Lg.—to] vnto J.—gone] grone S. 555. hir] to hir Lg.—excite] to excite B¹, B², B³, B⁵, H⁷, CC, J, S, Ad³, Hu, L, Co. 556. afferme] ganne afferme Ash². 557. of] with CC; and B¹, B², B³, B⁵, H¹, H², H⁴, H⁷, Ash², C³, Ar, L. 558. That] That to Lg.—more] om. H¹. 559. then in] than J. 560. any] om. CC; in any B¹, B², B⁵, C¹, Ar, Lg.

And more in children, is he honourde certeyn   f. 13a

And more in hem, hathe he his pleasaunce

Than in suche, as be not but baren

Without frute, thorough misgouernaunce

And holy writte, makyth Remembraunce

That no man, was sothely forto tell

Withoutyn seede, blesset in Israell

To whome anone, with loke don caste and chere   Howe our lady
answerde the
    Benyngly, and in full humble wyse   Bisshoppes that
she wolde nat
570 This holy mayde, sayde as ye shall here   be weddede
Ca° vii°

Certes quod she, yf ye yov wele aduise

Whiche in your self, so prudent ben and wyse

And woll aduerte in youre discrecion

That Abel sumtyme had a dowble crone

---

561. certeyn] om. Ash². 562. hathe he] hath bene H¹; he hathe B¹, B³, B⁵, H⁷, Ash², C¹, Ar, S, Ad³, L.—he] om. C², Hn¹, CC.—his] om. H⁸, J.—he his] om. Co. 563. in] om. B², CC.—as] that B², CC, H², Ash²; thynge that H⁸.—not] om. H⁷ Ar, H⁵, C³, C².—but] om. Ad³, Lg.—baren] as bareyn B¹, C¹. 564. Without] Wiche bene withoute Lg.—thorough] by Hu; with H²; with suche B¹, C¹. 568. To] of H², L.—and] hir Ar. 569. Benyngly, and in full humble wyse Ad³.—Benyngly] Right benyngly D, B¹, H⁷, H², C¹, C³.—and] om. Co, C², CC, Hu. 571. yov wele] woll yov B¹, H⁶, Ash¹.—you] om. CC. 572. Whiche] That B³, L; With H².—self] lyf B², Ch, H⁶, CC.—so] that so S.—so prudent ben] be so prudent B¹, C². 573. woll] to considere well Lg. 574. That Abel sumtyme had a double crone B¹.—sumtyme had] hadde some tyme D, C¹, Co.—sumtyme] whylom H⁸, J.

Oon for his faythful trewe sacrifice

Offerde to god, of humble hert *and* free

And an othir, as I shall yov devyse

For he his body, kept in chastite

And hely eke, as ye may rede and see

580   For he in hert, was a mayde clene

He was Ravysshede above the sterreȝ seven*e*

Bodi and all, in a chare of fire

For he hym kept from all corrupcion

Therefore in vayne is playnly yo*ur* desyre

To speke to me, of this opynnyon

For god wele knawithe, myne entenc*i*on

Howe I have vowede, as it to hym is couthe

To ben a mayde, fro my tendir youthe

---

575. Oon for his faythful trewe sacrifice B1.—faythful trewe] faithful and **trewe** D, C1, C3; true and faithful B2, CC. 576. Offerde to god, of humble hert *and* free B1.—and] om. D, Hn1, H6, H7, Ad3, J, S, Ar.—hert] om. C2.—Offerde] Offryng Ash1, H3, H4, H5, H6, Lg, C5.—of] for Ch; with B2, CC, S, Ar. 577. And] om. B5.—an othir] more CC.—shall] shall eke Hn1. 578. he] om. CC. 579. ye] I H8.—rede and see] se and rede L. 580. he] om. Ash2; she Lg.—he in hert] in hert he C2. 581. She was ravisshed in paradyse to bene above the sterrys sevene Lg.—He] om. L, Hu.—above] high above S, Ar, Ad3.—sevene] shene L, Hu, H5, S, Ar, Ad3. 582. Bodi and all, in a chare of fire B1.—in] Right in D, C1, C3.—a] om. B3, L.—of] om. H1. 583. hym] om. Co, B5.—all] om. S. 584. is playnly] playnly is B2, Ash2, Ar; is your playnely H4.—playnly] all C2. 586. wele knawithe] knoweth wel B1, C3. 587. it] om. B1, CC, C2, Co.—to hym is] is to him H1, C1, H2, Ash2, Ar, Lg. 588. a] om. B2, CC; his B5.

All my life, so forthe to p*er*ceue*r*

590   For lyve or deth, only for his sake

Fro which purpose, shall I not disceue*r*e

Thorough his grace, whedir I slepe or wak**e**

To kepe and holde I haue vndir take

My maydynhode, Sythyn goo full yore

Agaynst which, ne spekyth to me no more

And whan they sawe hir hert not mutable   **f. 13b**

But ay stedfaste, of oon affection

And eue*r*e Ilyche, as any centr*e* stable

Thay haue made, a conuocacion

600   Of all the kynrede as in conclusion

The viii day forto come in fere

By one assent, to trete of this matier

This is to say, þat of olde usage

Of Custome kept, for a memoriall

That euery mayde, xiiii yere of age

Riche and pore, and of the stok Royall

In the Temple, no longer dwell shall

But by statute, shall be take and maried

By the lawe, and no longer tariede

610   And whan thay were, assembled all in oon

Iȝachar, in open audience

Gan to pronounce to forne hem euerycheone

Full prudently, the Somme of his sentence

And sayde syrrys with your pacienceȝ

So þat youre eres, offende not ne greve

Declare I shall, my menyng with youre leve

---

603. This is to say, þat of olde usage B¹.—of] the D, C¹. C³.—is] om. L.—usage] usage kept C¹. 605. xiiii] of xiiii H⁸, H⁷, L, B¹, B³.—of] and more of H². 606. and of] of Ch, B⁴, C², C³, Ash¹, H³, H⁴, H⁶, C⁵.—the] om. B², B³, CC. 608. But] om. B⁵, S, Ash². B¹, H⁷, Ar, Ad³.— shall] olde shal B¹, Ash², H⁷, Ar, Ad³; om. C³.—and maried] in mariage maried Ash¹. 609. tariede] be tariede B¹. Hu.—no] om. B⁴. 610. whan] om. H².—were assembled] assembled were Ash².—all] om. C², B⁵. 611. Iȝachar, in open audience B¹.—Iȝachar] Then Isaȝhar D, C¹, Hn¹, Hu. 612. to forne] amonge H². 613. his] the B², Ch, CC; this his H⁶; this L. 614. syrrys] this H⁶. 615. offende not] not offende H¹.—ne] to CC. 616. menyng] mateer Hu.— with] by B², Co, H¹, B⁵, S, CC.

If ye Remmembre, sith Salamon the kyng

In Isaraell, Septer bare and crovne

In this Temple, so Royall in bildyng

620 Haue yong maydems, by deuocion

Of custome hadde here conuersacion

Bothe kynges doughtirs, and propheteȝ eke

As ye may funde, yf ye liste to seke

Vnto the age of xiiii yere

Abydyng here, and no lenger space

As ye wele knawe, withoutyn any wer

And þanne be removed from here place

And in hir stede, othir did pace

As custome was, and eke in hir lynage

630 Delyuerde was, vnto theyre mariage

618. Isaraell] Ierusalem H8. 619. in] of B1, B3, CC, C1, C2, C3, Ad3, L; om. Lg. 620. yong] your Ash2. 623. may] om. B2, CC.—liste to] will Lg. 625. no] om. B1, B3, L, H7.—and] and of B5, Ash2, S, Ar, Ad3.—space] of space B2, Ch, B4, Co, Ash1, H3, H4, H2, H5, H6, C5, CC, Hu. 626. wele knawe] knowen well Ash2.—any] om. B3, L; move Ash2, Ar. 627. And Þanne be remeved from here place B1.—be] they were D, C1, C3, Hn1, H8, J; to be H2.— from] out of C2. 630. vnto] thanne vnto B1, B5, H7, Ar, Ash2, S, Ad3; to CC, Ash2, Ar.

And as a lawe, it hathe be kept full trwe   f. 14a

Vnto this tyme, to high and lawe estate

But now Marie, hath founde an ordre newe

To kepe hir clene and inviolate

Agaynst which, ther helpith ne debate

But of free choys, and hertly volunte

She hath to god, avowede chastite

Wherfore me semyth it were Right wele fyttyng

To this purpoos, by good discrecion

640   First how we myght fully haue knawyng

Of godys will, in this opynyon

For than it were, of more perfeccion

Hir clene entent as semyth vnto me

And eke the strenger of Auctorite

---

631. as a] om. H¹.—a] om. Ash¹, H². 632. Vnto this tyme] Here toward H⁸, J.—to] in H²,
L, CC, Hu. 633. now Marie hath] Mary hath nowe Ash.²—an] that in an Lg. 636. and] and of
H⁸. 638. Right] om. C², B⁵, Hn¹, Ash¹, H², H⁸, Ad³.—wele] om. B¹, C².—fyttyng] vtturly C¹.
639. this] hir Ash¹, 640. fully] *inserted above;* om. C¹.—fully haue] have fully C², H⁸, H⁶, L.
642. of] om. H³. 643. as] as it B⁵, H⁸.—vnto] om. H³.—Hir clene entent] And more evydent
Lg. 644. eke] om. Hn¹, Ash², H⁸, J; much C¹, C³.—the] om. CC.

Firste þat we might knawe verily

  To whose kepyng she shall comitted be

And thay assentide, hereto vttirly

Withoute more of high and lawe degre

And of one accorde and of oon vnyte

650 The prestes alle, gonnen to procede

To caste lotte, down by Iche kynrede

The which lotte, on Iuda fell a none

As I suppose thorough goddes purviaunce

And Iȝacar, among hem euerychone

Purposed hath a newe ordynaunce

That euery wyght, of that aliaunce

That wyfeles were, withoutyn more delay

Sholde brynge a yerde, a gaynst the next day

How Ioseph was
wedded to our lady
Ca° viii°

---

645. knawe verily] haue ful knowynge B³.—verily] vtturly B², C³, CC. 646. kepyng] om. CC.—she] om. H².—she shall] shall she B², CC. 647. herto] all herto Hn¹.—vttirly] entierly C³, Ash², H⁸, Hn¹; verely B², Ch, B⁴, H¹, H³, CC, Ash¹, H⁴, H⁵, H⁶, Lg, C⁵. 649. of oon vnyte] one vnite Ch, C². 650. alle] om. C².—gonnen] gan hem H².—to] alle to H¹, Lg. 651. lotte down] doon lotte B¹, C¹.—Iche] every B¹, C¹, Co. 652. on] to Ash¹; vnto H⁶.—on Iuda fell] fell on Iuda H³, Ar. 653. thorough] of B⁵, Ash².—thorough goddes purviaunce] among hem everychone H¹, Lg. 656. of that] of L. 657. withoutyn] with L.

And to the Bisshop, highest of Ichoon

660 Eu*e*ryche of hem, did his yerde bryng

Among whiche Iosephe hath brought oon

Though he were olde passit his lykyng

And he anon made his offryng

To god above, and a sacryfice

In the olde lawe suche as was the gyse

And god to hym did anoon apere   f. 14b

And with the yerde, badde than þat he shulde goon

And putten hem, eu*e*rychone in fere

In *Sancta* Sancto*ru*m lyggyng oone by oon*e*

670 And on the morowe, to come a gayne Ichone

Eu*e*ryche his yerde, for to Receyve a gayne

Vppon which, ther opynly was sayne

659. to] om. H4. 661. whiche] the which B5. 662. passit] and past B2, Ch. C5, B3, B4, H1, C2, Ash1, H2. H3, H4, H5, H6, Lg, L, CC.—were olde] age C3. 663. he] om. Ash2.—his] an Hn1, H8, J. 664. To god above, and a sacryfice B1.—and] and eke D, C1, C3.—a] om. Co, C2, B5, Ash2, S. 665. In the] In B4.—suche as] as than B5.—as] om. Ash1,—suche] lyche C3, Hn1, Ash2, H8, J.—the gyse] Justice CC. 666. to hym did anoon] dide to hym anon H2; to him did to him C5; to him anon did B2, H1, B5, Hn1, Ash2, S, H7, CC; anon dede to him B1. 667. the] om. H1.—than þat] om. Ash2, H8, J.—he] om. CC. 668. hem] om. Ch, B4, Ash1, H3, H4, H6.

A dove apere and vp to hevyn flee

He that shall haue withoutyn more obstacle

Marie in kepyng so fayre vpon to see

As it is Right, for the high myracle

And than thay come vnto the tabernacle

As ye have herde, the Bisshopp deuotly

Eueryche his yerde, delyuerde by and by

680　But vttirly vppon noon of all

At this tyme, was there noo thyng seyne

For goddys heste, was not yet fall

Of hir desyre, to putt hem in certeyne

Wherefore the Bisshopp, with newe fyre agayne

Entride is in to þe seintwarye

And whiles þat he, a while there gan tarie

---

673. and] om. H8. 674. that] om. B3, H3, L, H2.—haue] haue Marye C1, C3.— withoutyn]
with H2. 674. Marie in] That mayde to C1, C3.—in] into Ar. 676. high] om. H2. 677. than]
om. B2, CC. 678. As] And Ash2. 679. his yerde delyuerde] delyuered his yerd B5. 680. of]
of them Ash1; at H5. 681. At this] That ilke H2; At thilke B3, L. 682. not] never not S. 685.
Entride is in to þe seintwarye B1.—Entride] Tho entrede D, C1.—is] om. B5, CC.—þe] that
D; the same C1. 686. þat] om. C2.—while] lytyl C3.—there gan tarie] ther sumwhat tarie
C2; did there tarie S; gan tarie C1, B5; did tary CC; there did tary B2; gan there to tary Hu.

Goddis Aungell aperyth to hy*m* newe

Downe from hevyn, by myracle sent

And tolde playnly the heste of god was trwe

690   But how hym self, was som*e* what negligent

For to delyuere, by commaundement

Eu*ery* man his yerde, as he aughte

And whan the Bisshopp, a Right hym bethought

He gan Remembre, playnly in his mynde

That of disdayne, and wilfull necgligence

The yerde of Iosephe was lefte by hynde

Wherby he knewe, he had doon offence

And gan anoon, to bryng it in presense

And toke it Iosephe devoutly in his hande

700   Among hem all, there he dyd stonde

687. Goddis Aungell aperyth to hy*m* newe B1.—Goddis Aungell] The Angell of god D, C3, C1.
—newe] there new C3; al new C1. 689. tolde] told hem C1.—playnly] trewely C2. 690. hym
self] that he B1, H7.—was some what] sumwhat was B2, C3, CC.— how] om. Hu. 691. by] by
his H2. 692. he] he be H5. 693. the Bisshopp a Right hym] aright the bishop hymself Ash2.—a
Right hym] sothly C1.—hym] hymself H8, J. 694. playnly] clerly C2. 697. That wherebi
aknewe his owne offense CC. 698. gan] began B3, Co, L, Hu, H2; than C2.—to] om. Hn1; did
C2.—in] into Ash2. 699. his] om. H2. 700. Among] And among B2.—he] as he B1, B5, H2,
H7, Ar, S, Hn1; they Ch, B4, Ash1, H3, H4, Lg, C5.

Alle by hynde, dyseuerede fro the prees

W*ith* humble chere, in the lawest place

And of his yerde, in maner Rekeles

Full styll of porte, w*ith a* dredefull face

And whan he dyd, w*ith* his hande enbrace

His yerde a gayne, full debonayre of loke

By Innocens of humble fere, he quoke

And sodenly, thorough grace, above devyne

All opynly in eu*ery*, weyghte3 sight

710 Vppon the yerde, of Ioseph full benyng

Was sene a dove, of fetheres lylly white

That towardes, hevyn, evenshe toke hir flyght

And w*ith* oo voys, the people thoo obreyde

And unto Ioseph, all atoones seyde

---

702. in] and in S. 703. of his yerde] in his herte H². 704. with] and with Ch.—dredefull] full dredful B², C², CC. 705. with] om. B⁵.—his] om. B¹, B², H⁷, Ad³, Hn¹.—enbrace] dyd embrace Hn¹. 707. fere] drede H³; herte H².—humble fere] drede humble Ar. 708. sodenly] om. Ash¹.—grace] om. Ar, L.—above] om. H¹. 709. weyghte3] manys C². 710. the] the the Ar. 711. of] with Lg.—fetheres lylly] lily fedris CC. 712. evenshe] she H¹, C², Lg; anon she Ash².—hir] the B³, B⁴, Ash¹, H³, H⁴, H⁵, C⁵, L, H, C², Lg. 713. thoo] om. Lg. 714. And unto Ioseph, all atoones seyde B¹.—seyde] thay sayde D.—unto] to B⁵, S, Ad³.

Blesside art thow, and blisside is thy chaunce

Thy fate is blesset, and thyne aventure

And blissed is thyne, humble attendaunce

And thow art blisset, so long to endure

For to possede, so fayre a creature

720 So goode so holy, nowe in thy passed age

So clene a mayde, to haue in mariage

And she a noon, by prestes of the lawe

Assigned was, vnto his gouernaunce

But sely Iosephe, gan hym to withdrawe

With humble chere, and shamefaste contenaunce

And sayde certis, there is noon accordaunce

By twyxe hir yought, flouryng in fayrenesse

And me whome age, with vn lust doth oppresse

---

715. art] be C². 716. is] om. H⁸, B², Ch, B³, B⁴, Co, H¹, C², Ash¹, H³, H⁴, Ash², H⁵, Lg, C⁵, CC, J, Hu.—and] and eke C¹. 718. to] om. Lg. 719. For] And for Hn¹. 720. goode] good and H².—nowe] om. B², CC.—thy] om. H⁸; this B³, L. 724. sely] sothly C¹.—hym] hym self Ash¹.—to withdrawe] wyth to drawe L. 725. shamefaste] stedfast B², CC. 726. there] this H³.—accordaunce] ordynaunce H². 728. with] and B⁵, Ar; om. H³.

For she is fayre, and fresshe as Rose in may

730   And well Iwote, also mayden clene

And I am olde, *with* white lockes graye

Passed full ferre, my tendre yeres grene

Wherfore I pray yov, to considre and sene

Tacorde discordant, and speke to me noo more

By twene hir beaute, and my lockes hore

And whan the bisshop sawe the humble entent   f. 15b

Of this Iosephe, and eke the Innocence

And how that he, to take hir nolde assent

To hym he sayde, in opyn audience

740   Ioseph quod he, take hede to my sentence

And be welware, þat thou the not excuse

Ageynst the will of god, forto Refuce

---

729. is] in age is Ash[1]; om. B[1], S.—fayre and fresshe] freshe and faire Co. 730. also] om. B[4].
731. And] om. H[1].—white lockes graye] lockes hor and gray B[3], L. 732. my] beth my B[5].
733. yov] om. H[5]. 735. my] om. Ar. 736. sawe] om. H[2].—the] his Ash[1]. 737. this] this ilke Hn[1].
—the] his C[1], C[3]. 738. he] om. H[2].—he to take hir] her to take C[2].—take] om. C[1], Ar.—hir]
om. H[1].—nolde] wold not C[2], C[3], B[5]. 739. in] there in Hn[1]. 740. quod he] he sayde B[4], Co,
Ash[1], H[3], H[4], C[5], Ch; sayd he CC.—to] of Ad[3]. 741. the] om. H[1]. 742. Ageynst] And ayen
Ash[2].—forto] to Co, C[2], B[5], H[2], Ash[2]; hire for Hn[1].—to] the H[1].

This holy mayde, assignet vnto the

By opyn signe, whiche all the people seye

Thorough godd*es* grace and myghty volunte

Agaynst whiche, be warr to disobeye

And þenke how he su*m*tyme made to deye

Dathan Abyron . only for offence

Doon vnto hym, of Inobedyence

750   Quod Iosephe thanne, I woll not for **no thyng**

Io godd*es* will or byddyng be contrar

But hir accept vnto my kepyng

For whom god hath shewed signe so fayre

Whiche is so goode, benyngne and debonayre

That I to hir seruaunt woll be and gyde

Tyll god for hir, lust better to provyde

---

743. assignet] assigned was H5. 744. whiche] the whiche H6.—all] all al Lg. 745. grace and myghty] almighti H1. 746. warr] wel ware Ash1, H6; ware now Hn1.—disobeye] dysdeyne Ash1. 747. And þenke how he su*m*tyme made to deye B1.—to] om. D, H8, J.—howe] om. L, Hn1.—su*m*tyme] whilom H8, J, Ash2.—su*m*tyme made] made sumtyme Ash1, H6. 748. Dathan Abyron] Abiron and Dathan B1, B5, Ar, Ad3, B3, Ch, B2, B4, Co, H1, C2, Ash1, H3, H4, H5, H6, Lg, C5, L, Hu, H, S; Dathan and Abiron Hn1, Ash2, CC, H2.—only] om. B5, Ar, Ad3, B1, H7 S.—offence] the offence B2, Ch, B3, B4, Co, H1, C2, Ash1, H3, H4, H5, H6, Lg, C5, L, Hu, H2, B5, Ar, Ad3; the grete offense B1, H7, S.—Dathan] There in H8, J. 749. vnto] to B4, Ash1, H4, H6, C5, Ch.—vnto hym] hym vnto B5, Ar, Ad3, S.—of] for Ch, CC; by H2, Ash2, S. 750. thanne] that Ch, B2, B3, B5, Co, C2, B5, Ash1, H3, H4, H2, S, Ar, H6, Ad3, C5, L, Hu, B1, CC, Lg, H1, H5, H7.—not] wote Lg. 751. be] om. C5. 754. so] om. Co.—debonayre] bonayre H8, H5. 755.] That I to hir liste better to provide Lg.—and] om. H5. 756.]Till god for her will seruant be and guyde Lg.—god] om. Ch, B4, H3, H4, H6, C5.—god for hir] that she Ash1.—to] om. B5.

And as the custume, of the lawe theym bonde

So made was tho, the confirmacion

By hest of wedlok, by twene theym hande by hande

760 And he hir toke, to his possession

W*ith* hert clene and meke affeccion

But while he wente to Bedlem the Cite

Mary abode styll in Galile

Howe Iosephe aftir he had weddyde our lady went to Bed- leem and vsed the crafte of Carpentre Cap*itu*lo ix°

At Naȝareth in hir faders house

Like hir a vowe, of hert all way oon

And fyve maydens the most vertuose

Of the Temple, were chosyn oute a noon

Of the Bisshop w*ith* hir for to goon

To wayte on hir, by humble attendaunce

770 In what þey can, to s*er*ve and do plesaunce

---

757. And] om. B². —as] om. CC.—theym bonde] of land H². 758. made was] was made B⁵. 759 theym] om. Ar, Lg.—by] in Lg, Ash¹, Ar, H³, H⁴, H⁶, H⁷; and B¹, B², B³, B⁴, B⁵, H¹, H², H⁴, Ash², CC, C¹, C², C³, C⁵, L, Ch, Hn¹, Co. 760. And he hir toke, to his possession H⁷.— to] in D; into B³, L.—he hir] there hir Hn¹.—he] om. B¹, B⁵, C², S. 761. clene and meke] meke and clene B², CC; clene herte and meke L. 762. while] om. Ash².—to] om. L. 763. styll] stylle thanne Hn¹. 765. oon] in oon B², Ch, B³, B⁴, H¹, C², Ash¹, H³, H⁴, H⁵, H⁶, Lg, C⁵, L, CC. 766. And] Hadde B³, L.—fyve] om. H⁵.—the] om. Ash¹, Ash². 767. oute] om. S. 769. on] or on H¹.—by] with S, H⁶, L. 770. In what þey can, to s*er*ve and do plesaunce H⁷.— what] that D, Co, C¹, C³, B⁵, Hn¹, Ad³, D.—do] to do B², C², H⁸, CC.—and do] or to B¹, B³, H¹, Ash¹, Ch.

Of whiche the first, was callet Rayca   f. 16a

And Sephera, the secund as I fynde

Susanna ʒabel, and Abygea

The othir thre, as bokes makyn mynde

Which neuer wolde, for slouthe be byhynde

But ay in oon, as it is specified

In werke and prayer, weren occupyed

And vnto hem, as made is mencion

That of levying, so faythfull weren and trwe

780   And diligent in occupacion

Delyuerede was silke, of sondry hewe

For to make, of dyuerse werkes newe

In the Temple of entencion

Onely to be, in mynstracion

---

771. whiche] the whiche H⁵, L.—was callet] called was Ch, B³, B⁴, Co, H¹, Ash¹, H³, H⁴, H²,
S, Ar, H⁶, H⁷, Ad³, Lg, C⁵, J, Hu, H⁵, L. 772. secund] next H². 774. mynde] mencion Ash².
777. were] werre ever H², Ash², B¹, B², CC, C¹; ever were Ash¹, Hu. 778. vnto] to Co.—made
is] is made H³. 779.] So feythfull were and trewe C¹; So feythfull were they and so trew C³.—
so faythfull weren] were so feithfull Ash¹, H⁴. 780. And] And also Hn¹, Ash¹, C²; And ful
H².—in] in vertuous B³, L; in all hire Hn¹; in honest B¹; in her C¹, C³, Ar; were in B², CC.
781. was] om. H⁸, CC; was thanne Hn¹. —of] and Hn¹, H².—sondry] diverse B¹, B², H⁵, S.
782. For] om. Ash².—dyuerse] sondry C¹. 783. of] ther of C¹, C³; of oon Hn¹; of good H².
784. in] there in H²; ther in into Hn¹.

And as it is put in Remembraunce

Eu*er*yche hir silke, toke by aventure

Lyke as hir hande, fell ther on by chaunce

But Marye, as god tho schope hir vre

The purpyll silke, she toke in cure

790   By graciouse happe, of sort wi*th*outen sight

The whiche colo*ur*, of custome and of Right

To noon estate, kyndely is fittyng

Of dewte to speke, in speciall

But to thestate, onely of a kyng

So þat noo wight, but of the stokke royall

By statute olde, this colo*ur* vse shall

For by olde tyme, ye shulde noo man seen

In purpyll cladde putt onely, kyng or qwene

---

785. as] om. CC. 786. Eu*er*yche] Everyche of hem Hn¹. 787. as] om. H², Hu.—ther] om. B², B⁵, CC. 790. By] Of H⁶.—sort] fortune CC. 791. colo*ur* of custome] of custome no coloure Ash¹.—and of] and S; without CC. 792. kyndely is fittyng] is properly accordynge C²; is kyndely theyrof fyttyng C³. 793. speke] speke of B¹, B², H⁴. 795. þat] at S.—of] om. H². 796. olde] of old time Ash¹, H¹, Lg.—colo*ur*] om. H⁸.—this colo*ur* vse shall] ye shuld no man seen Lg; ye shuld no man sene at all H¹. 797. by] in Ar. 798. In purpyll cladde] This colour were B², CC.

Wherfore the sorte, full rightfully is falle

800   Verrely by dewe disposicion

Vpon marye that to forne thayme alle

By lyne right, is descended downe

Of blode Royall, and by election

Of god above, was Ichosyn forto been

For hir meryte, of hevyn and erthe the qwene

And modir eke, as ye shall aftir here   f. 16b

Of thelke kyng þat all was cladde in Rede

Of purpill hewe, bothe face and chere

Downe to the foote, from his blissed hede

810   Whan he of purpill, dyd his baner sprede

On Calvery abrode, vpon the Rode

To save mankynde, whan he schede his bloode

---

799. full] om. B¹, B⁵, H².—Wherfore] Wher B², CC.—is] gan Hn¹. 800. dewe] true H⁴; dyvyne high C³; high divyne C¹; divine Hn¹, Ash², H⁸, J. 802. lyne right] right lyne C¹, C². 803. Of] of the Hn¹. 805. hevyn and erthe] erthe and hevene B², CC.—erthe] of erthe Ch. 806. modir] more CC.—as] and L.—aftir] om. B¹. 807. thelke] that B², C², B⁵, Ash¹, Ar, CC; that ilke B¹, H¹, C¹, Ch.—all was cladde] clad was all B², C², B⁵, Ash¹, Ar, CC, H³, H⁴, H², Ash², S, H⁵, H⁶, H⁷, Ad³, Ad², Lg; was al clad B³, H⁸, L, J; clad was B⁴, C⁵.—all was cladde in Rede] here shuld shewe in dede Hu. 809. to] fro CC.—the] om. Ad³. 811. abrode] om. B¹, Ar, C¹, Hu.—vpon] on Hn¹, Ar.

And of this purpill, that I of spake to forne

I fynde playnely, how that Marye wrought

Thylke vayle that was in tweyn torne

The same houre whan he so dere vs bought

Loo howe þat godd in his eternall thought

Provydede hathe, by Iust purvyaunce

The purpull silke, vnto his moders chaunce

Howe our lady is 820
sett for an ensample
of all virginyte
Ca x

But nowe I leve, this blissetfull mayde dere

In Naȝareth a mong her frendys to dwelle

Ledyng a lyfe, more perfyte and entere

Than any tunge, suffise may to tell

For euere elyche, as a fulsome well

Shedith his stream in to þe ryvere

Right so Marye, in ensample clere

---

813. I] om. H8.—of] om. Ar.—I of spake] I spake of B1, B2, B4, B5, H1, H3, H4, H5, H6, Ash1, CC, C2, C5, Ad2, Hu, Lg, Ch, Co. 814. playnely] trewly C2.—that] om. J, Hu. 815. Thylke] That C1, C3, Hn1, Ash2.—in] in pecys C1, C3, Hn1, Ash2.—was in tweyn] in tweyne was L.—torne] to torne C1, C3, Hn1, Ash2, Hu. 816. he so dere vs] he us so dere B5, L; so dere he vs Ch. 817. þat] om. H8, Ar. 819. vnto] to Ch, B4, H1, C2, Ash1, H3, H5, H6, Ad2, Lg, C5, CC. 821. In Naȝareth a mong her frendys to dwelle B1.—to] om. D, L.—to dwelle] all H8.—frendys] feere Ash2, J. 822. and entere] too endire H6. 823. suffise] suffice suffise C1. —suffise may to] may suffice to B1, B2, Ash2, CC.—may] for B5.—to] om. H7. 824. as] om. Ash1, H6, Ar.—fulsome] quyk spryngynge B3, L; full H6. 825. Shedith his stream in to þe ryvere B1.—in to] Right into D; forth into C3.—the] om. Ash1. 826. in] is an Ash1, L.

Gaffe to all, by plentyvous largesse

Onely in vertu, vpon eu*er*y syde

O wele were thay, to whom thou were maistresse

830 And blisset eke, that might on the abyde

To have by ensample, so vertuouse a gyde

And blisset, was that holy companye

That day by day, the seen w*ith* her eye

And blisset was, the paleys and the house

In whiche thou haddist, thy holy mansion

Fortuned well and wondre graciouse

So humble was thy con*ue*rsacion

And blisset was also all the towne

Where thou abode, and blissed the village

840 O holy mayde, where thou helde hostage

---

827. Gaffe] Than H¹, Ash¹.—Gaffe to all] Vnto alle gaf Hn¹. 828. in] om. B², Ad², Ch, B⁴, H¹, C², Ash¹, H³, H⁴, H⁵, H⁶, Lg, C⁵, CC; to H⁸; uppon B⁵.—eu*er*y] mercy Ar. 829. thou] they B², Co. 830. on] with C¹, H², S, CC, H⁶; by Ash¹. 832. that] all that Ar. 833. the seen] seyen hir B², CC. 835. haddist] madest H².—holy] om. Co. 837. thy] by Ash², H⁸. 838. was also] also was B⁵, Ash¹, Ash², Ad².—all] om. B¹, H³, Ad³, B², C¹, Hu, Ch. 839. Where] Of there S.—blissed] blessed was Lg, S; blessed be B¹, H¹, H⁶, C¹, C³, Co.

And blisset was, the worthy table riche   f. 17a

Where day by day, thou wentist vnto bourde

For in sothenesse the Ioye was nat lyche

Of Cresus kyng, for all his riche hurde

And blisset ben thay that herden worde by worde

Of thy speche, blisset the houre and tyme

Of all thy lyfe, frome even to the *prime*

O welfull eke and graciouse the sight

Of thaym that myght vpon the byholde

850   For well they awght to be glad and light

That werne *with* the all way whan thay wolde

And blissed werne bothe yonge and olde

That werne reioysede, with thyne excellence

Whan that hem liste of theyne high *presence*

---

841. worthy] holy CC; verry C¹. 842. vnto] to B¹, B³, H⁸, C², L, Lg. 844. riche] like Ash². 845. ben] om. H⁸, J, Ash².—worde by] eche Hn¹. 846. blisset] and blessed B¹, B², B³, B⁴, B⁵, H¹, H², H³, H⁴, H⁵, Co, H⁷, H⁸, Hn¹, Ash², CC, J, C¹, Ch, C³, C⁵, Ar, S, Hu, L, Lg.—the] be the B⁵, Hn¹, CC, B², C¹, L.—blisset] om. Ash¹, H⁶.—houre and tyme] tyme and houre Ash². 847. Of all] All of Ash².—all] om. B⁵.—frome even to the *prime*] till eve of thy prime Ash²; till even aforn the prime C¹, C³; to the end from prime B³, L; tyll even from the prime Hn¹, H⁸, J.—the] om. CC, Hu, B⁵. 848. eke] is hym C¹, C³, Hn¹.—welfull] helthefull Hu.—the] is the B⁵; was the Hu, H⁶. 849. Of thaym] om. C¹, C³, Hn¹.—vpon] on B¹, H², H⁸, Ash², S, Ad². 852. bothe] om. B², Ch, B⁴, H³, H⁴, Ad², C⁵, CC. 853. That] They H². 854. of] with CC.—high] om. C¹; good C².

O the Ioye, who couthe tell aright

Of thyne hevenly meditacions

Assendyng vp above the sterres bright

In thyne Inwarde contemplacions

Or thy holy visitacions

860   Who can Reherse hem, bright as sonne or leven

So ofte sent downe to the, frome heven

O who can telle, thy holy slepes softe

With god alwaye, full in thy memorye

For love of whome, thou sigest full ofte

Whan thou were soole, in thyne orytorye

Or who can tell, the melody and glorye

That Angellez have made, in thy holy place

For the Ioye thay had, to loke vpon thy face

---

855. O] Of H³, H⁸, Ad².—aright] now aright Hn¹. 856. hevenly] hevenly and swete Hn¹;
holy C¹, C³. 857. vp] om. C¹. 858. inwarde] inward swete Hn¹. 859. Or thy holy visitacions
B¹.—thy holy] of the swete and holy D, C³; yet the holy H², Hu; the holy celestial B³, L; the
delectable Hn¹. 860. bright] so bright C¹, C³, Hn¹.—or] om. Co, C¹, C³, Hn¹; of H¹, Lg.
861. to the] from the C¹; om. CC.—frome heven] to heven C¹; from the hevene Hu. 862. O]
om. H¹, Lg, C².—slepes] dremys B⁵. 863. With] Which Ar.—full] om. Co.—thy] om. Ash².
864. sigest] yedist H². 866. melody and glorye] joy and melody B¹, C¹; joy and glorie B³, L.
—glorye] the glorie Ch, Co. Ad². 867. have] om. C³, Hn¹.—made] had Lg.—holy] om. B², Ch.
B³, B⁴, Co, H¹, C², B⁵, Ash¹, H³, H⁴, H², Ash², Ar, H⁸, H⁵, H⁶, H⁷, Ad², C⁵, L, CC, J, Hu.
868. the] om. B², Ch, H⁵, CC, Ash², H⁸, J.—vpon] on B³, Ch, H⁵, CC, B⁴, H¹, C², Hn¹, Ash¹,
H³, H⁴, H², H⁶, Ad², Lg, C⁵, L, Hu.

I am to Rude for to Rehersen, thaym all

870 For vnconyng, and for lake of space

The mater is so Inly sp*iritu*all

That I dar nat, so high a style pace

But lady myne, I put all in thy grace

This first booke compylede for thy sake

Of my symples, and thus an ende I make

Besechyng all, to haue pyte and routhe   f. 17b

That ther of shall haue Inspection

Yf aught be left, of necgligence or slowthe

Or sayde to moche, of presomppcion

880 And put it mekely to her correcion

And aske mercy for my trespace

Where as I erre, and put me in her *grace*

---

869. to Rude] rude C1, B4, Ash1, H3, H4, H6, Ad2, C5.—for] *inserted above.* 872. That] om. B2, Ch, CC. 873. myne I put all] put myne all H1.—all] me al C5. 875. and thus] om. B2, CC. 876. all] om. B1.—to] for to H1. 877. Inspection] any inspection B1, B2, B3, B4, B5, H1, H2, H3, H4, H5, H6, H7, Ash1, CC, C2, C5, Ar, Ad2, L, Lg, Ch, Hn1; suspeccion Hu. 878. Yf aught be left, of necgligence or slowthe B1.—aught be lefte] I haue lefte D; ther be left C1.—of] thorugh Ar. 880. And put it mekely to her correcion B1.—And] I D.—to her] in your D. 881. for] as of B2, B3, C2, C3, B5, Hn1, H2, Ash2, H5, H7, L, J, Hu. 882. Where as I erre, and put me in her grace B1.—her] your D.—Where] Ther B3, Ash1, L, Ch, Co.—in] holy in Ch.

And thoroughe hir benyngne supportacion

So as I can, forthe I woll *p*rocede

W*ith* all my hert, and hole entencion

Prayeng that mayde, that is of godelyhede

Croope and Rote, to helpe in this nede

Whom I now leve in Naȝareth Soio*ur*ne

889   And to my mater, I will agayne returne

BOOK II

Howe mercy Pees
Rightwisnesse and
Trouthe disputede
for the Redempcion
of mankynde
Ca xi[1] *primo*
2 lib.

Who that is bonde, and feterde in *p*rison

Thenketh longe aftir delyveraunce

And he that felyth payne and passion

Desyrith sore, aftir alleggeaunce

And who þat is in sorowe *and* penaunce

Lytyll wondir of hertly hevynesse

Though he covete, relees of his distresse

---

883. supportacion] supplicacion C[1]. 884. as I] as now I Hn[1].—I woll] wil I B[5], Ash[2]. 885. hole] good H[1]. 886. that is of] of hir B[2], Hn[1], Ash[1]; of all H[5]; of so B[1], B[3], B[4], B[5], H[1], H[2], H[3], H[4], H[5], H6, H[7], CC, C[2], C[5], Ar, Ad[2], Hu, L, Lg, Ch, Co. 887. Croppe] And croppe Hn[1].—in] us in C[1]; at Ash[1]. 888. now] om. B[2], Ash[1], Ash[2].—I now leve] now I leve Ch, Co, C[2], B[1], B[5], H6, CC. 889. I will agayne] agen I will Co, C[2]; will I agayne H[8], J; ageyn will I Ash[2].—returne] torne B[5]. Book II. 1. that] om. Hn[2].—fetered] lith fetered B[2], CC. 3. and] om. Ash[2].—he] om. H[1], Lg, CC.—he] who H[4]. 4. sore aftir] after sore B[1], S. 5. And who þat is in sorowe *and* penaunce B[1].—*and*] and in D, B[3], B[4], Hu, H[1], C[3], H[2], Lg, L, J.—sorowe] woo H[8].—and in] om. H[5]. 6. of] and H[8], J.—of hertly] though theyr C[3].—hertly] hys Hn[1]; her hertly Hu.—wondir of] wonder ys of L. 7. covete] kannot H[2].—Though he] Sone C[3].—his] theyr C[3].

---

[1]xi *erased*

And who that levith in lang*our* and in woo

Fer in exile, and pr*o*scripcion

10 And is bysette with many a cruell foo

And can no gynne, to his saluac*i*on

To escape deth, *with* oute grete rawnsoun

Full longe he thynketh of full lytyll space

While he in bonde3, abydeth aftir grace

And yet to recorde, of olde felicite

In sothefastnesse, encresethe more his payne

Than all constrent, of his adu*er*site

And causeth hym more, to syghe and pleyne

For Ioye passet, can hertes more constrayne

20 Her welthe affore, to be wepe and wayle

Than all the turment, that hem dothe assayle

---

8. and] or B¹, B³, B⁴, B⁵, H¹, H², H³, H⁵, H⁶, H⁷, Ash¹, C¹, C⁵, Ad², L, Lg, Ch, Hn¹.— lango*ur*] anger C².—and in] and Hn², Ash², Ar, H⁸. 9. Fer] And ferr Hn¹.—in] om. H⁵. —and] and in H⁶. 10. a] om. B¹, B⁵, H¹, H², H⁷, H⁸, Ash², Ar, S, Lg, Hu.—bysette] with set Ch, B⁴, H³, H⁴, H⁶, Ad², C⁵. 11. can no] not Co.—no gynne] not goo ageyn Ch.—gynne] help C¹, C³, Hn¹.—gynne to] wey for Hn². 12. To escape dethe, *with* oute grete rawnsoun B¹.—grete] a grete D, Ash², Hn¹.—a grete] om. B², CC, S.—dethe] om. S.—escape] eschewe C¹. 13. full] so B³.—of] a B³, Ash¹, L.—full] om. C², CC.—longe] lityll Hn².—lytyll] longe Hn².—of] and S.—he] om. H⁸. 15. And yet to recorde, of olde felicite B¹.—to] om. D, H¹, C¹, Hn¹, Ash², H⁸, Lg, J.—olde] om. Hn².—recorde] the record B³, L. 16. more] om. H⁸; more and more H⁵. 17. the] om. L.—constrent] constreynyng B³, L. 18. And causeth hym more, to syghe and pleyne H⁷.—pleyne] to playne D, B¹.—hym] om. C², B², CC.—more to] more for to B², CC. 19. constrayne] distreyne CC.—hertes more] more hertes L. 20. be wepe] wepe Hn².—and wayle] and to be wayle H².—welthe] helthe CC. 21. that] of B². —hem dothe] doth hem C³, H³.—the] om. H³.—all] om. Ar.

Life of Our Lady

O who couthe eu*e*re, sithe the worlde by gan   f. 18a

Of more ioye, or of gladdnesse telle

Then some tyme couthe, the worthe kynde of man

That shapen was, in paradise to dwell

Tyll he alas, was banschede into hell

Fer in exile, from his possession

And þ*er*to abide, stoked in p*r*eson

And hathe loste his richesse and hono*ur*

30   His mirthe his ioye, *and* his olde welfare

His force his myght, and holy his socour

And was of vertu, nakede made and bare

And lay full seeke langwyssheng in care

So fer p*r*oscript, oute of his contre

That by the lawe, ther may noo recoverbe

22. who couthe euere] coude ever who H¹.—O] om. Co, Hn², Ad², CC. 23. Of more ioye, or of gladnesse telle B¹.—of] of more D, C¹, C², C³, Hn², Ash¹, CC.—or of more] or Ar, J. 24. some tyme couthe] coude somtyme H², Hn².—couthe] om. Hn¹.—kynde] king Ar, H⁶, Lg, CC; Kynee C⁵.—Then some tyme] That whilom Ash², H⁸, J. 26. he] om. H¹.—into] to Ar. 27. exile] helle B², CC. 28. And þerto abide, stoked in preson B¹.—And] om. D.—stoked] sore stoked D; dors stoked C¹, C³.—abyde] dwelle B², CC. 29. hathe] om. B², CC.—hir] om. Hn², Ash².—And hathe] And he hathe Ch, B⁴, Ash¹, H³, H⁴, H⁶, Ad², C⁵. 30. His mirthe his ioye and his olde welfare H⁷.—and] and all D; om. B¹, L, Lg.—mirthe] myght B², Ch, Ash¹, Ash², CC.—olde] om. Hn².—his ioye] and his joy L. 31. force] strengthe C¹, C³, Hn¹.—holy his] his holy Hn².—myght] power Ash².—and] om. H⁵.—holy] onli CC. 32. made] was H⁵, Lg. —nakede made] made naked Ash².—nakede] al naked Hn¹.—made] om. H¹.—and bare] and all bare H¹. 34. oute] fer oute B¹, B², B⁵. 35. recoverbe] socourbe C¹, Hn².—the] om. Ash². —by] he CC—the] be CC—ther] om. CC.

Whoos nekke oppressed, *with* so stronge a cheyne

Lay plonged downe *with*outen Remedy

That whan that mercy wolde haue bene ameen   Mi*sericord*ia

Rightwisnes gan it, anoon denye   Iusticia

40   And whan that pees, for recover gan to crye   Pax

Can trowth forthe, *with* a sterne face   Veritas

And sayde plattely, that he gette noo grace

For pece and mercy, to gedir assembled were

Full longe agoone, to trete of this matier

And Rightwisnesse *with* hem was eke there

And troughe also, *with* a deynous chere

And whan thay were, all foure in fere

As ye haue herde, and gan to entrete

Than first of all, cruely to threte

---

36. stronge] grete Hn². —a] om. L. 37. Remedy] any remede Hn². 38. that mercy] mercy B¹, B³, H², H³, H⁵, J, C¹, C², L, Lg; that vertu mercy B². —wolde] om. B², CC. 39. Rightwisnes gan it, anoon denye B¹.—gan it] it gan D, Hn¹, C³, J.—it gan a noon] anone it gan H², H⁸; gan anon hit Ch; anon gan hit H², H³, Ash². —denye] to deny S. 40. for] om. B², CC—that] om. C². —to] om. Ash², S. 41. trowth forthe] forthe trouthe B¹, C¹. 42. he gette] man schulde have Hn¹; he shall gete B², CC; he shuld have B¹. 43. to gedir assembled] assemblyed togeder B¹. 44. Full] om. B¹; For H⁶.—Full longe] Fur yore H⁸, J. 45. *with* hem was eke] was eke with hym Ch, Co, C³, Ar, H⁸; with was hem eke L.—*with* hem] om. CC. 46. a] om. B³, B⁴.—deynous chere] deynous face and chere Ash¹.—deynous] hevyous L. 47. whan] om. Hn². 48. to] in to H¹.—gan to] gunnen for to S, Ar, H⁷. 49. cruely] oonly C².—to] gan to Hn².

50 Trouthe be ganne, al most in a rage Veritas

Of cruell Ire, and of malencolye

And sayde schortely, that man for his outerage

Of verrey Right, moste nedeȝ dey

And thus be gan the controuersye

By twene the Sustren, and trouthe all way in oon Veritas

Sayde playnely, Rekever is ther noon

For I quod Trouthe at his creacion f. 18b

Tolde hym the perell affore his offence

But he me putte oute of his bandon

60 And gaffe to me no maner audience

Iusticia And I quod Right with all my diligence

Wolde hym haue reuled but he toke no hede

Wherfore of me he getyth noo helpe at nede

---

50. Trouthe be ganne] For quod trouthe Ash².—beganne] om. H⁸. 51. of] om. B¹, B⁵, H⁷, H⁸, Ash¹, Ash², J, Ar, S, Ad³, Hn¹, Co, Hu. 52. that] om. Ash¹, Ash², H⁸.—sayde] om. Ar, Hu. 53. Right] rigte and trouthe Lg. 54. thus be gan] thus he began Hn². 55. all way in oon] euer in one H²; anon Ash².—and trouthe all way in oon] al foure in fere Hn². 56. playnely Rekever] pleinly that recovere B¹, B², B³, H², H⁷, C¹, C², Hu, S, Ad², Ad³, L, Hn¹, Co.—there] the B¹, B², B³, H², H⁷, C¹, C², S, Ad², Ad³, L, Hn¹, Co.—is] was C³, Ash¹, H³, H⁶, Lg, C⁵, CC, Ch, B⁴, H¹, B⁵, Hn², H⁴, H⁵.—Sayde] And seyde Ch, B⁴, H¹, B⁵, Hn², H⁴, H⁵.—Rekever] that recover Ch, B⁴, H¹, B⁵, Hn², H⁴, H⁵, Ash¹, H³, H⁶, Lg, C⁵, CC, Ar.—is] om. Ar. 58. affore his] affore of his H⁸, J.—affore] of Ch, C².—his] the H², 59. bandon] pardon H⁸.—oute] om. Lg. 60. audience] of audience B¹, H², C², S.—maner] om. Lg.—gaffe] om. B².—maner] more Co, B⁵.—to] om. Hn². 61. with] om. C⁵. 62. but he toke no hede] with god to fede H².—toke no] ne toke no Ch, B⁴, Ash¹, H³, H⁴, Ad², C⁵. 63. he] om. Ash²—of] at H⁶.

For whan he gave credence to the snake

He made his quarell even agayne right

And a gaynes trouthe falsely he gan to take

When he hir putte clene oute of his sight

A gayne pees be gan a cruell fight

Whan he from hym mercy sette aferre

70 Brekyng the trouthe and wolde algate haue werre

Wherfore quod Right pletyth for hym no more

But latt hym haue as he hathe des*er*ued

Ye done grete wronge if ye woll hym restore

That hath his heste to yoo nought cons*er*uet

A • yes quod mercy nature hath res*er*uet

To pees my Sustre playnly and to me

On wreche3 eu*er*e for to haue pyte

---

64. For] And Ch, B⁴, Ash¹, H³, H⁴, Ad², C⁵.—to] vnto Ad³, Hu.—the] that H⁸.—whan]
om. B².—whan he] om. CC. 65. right] the right B⁴, Co, B⁵. 66. falsely he] he falsely B², Ch,
B³, B⁴, H¹, C², Hn², Hn¹, Ash¹, H³, H⁴. H², H⁸, H⁵, H⁶, Ad², Lg, C⁵, CC, J.—and] om.
Co.—to] om. C³, S.—falsely he gan] he gan falsely L.—he] by Hu. 67. he] om. B².—oute] om.
H².—putte clene] clen put C². 68. A gayne] And ayens B¹, B³, Co, B⁵, H², Ash², H⁸, L, J, Hn²,
Ash¹, H³, C¹, Hn¹.—fight] to fight B¹, Ash¹, CC, Ar, Hn¹.—cruell] quarell CC, H³.—cruell
fight] quarel to make Hn².—be gan a cruell] a quarell he gan to Ar; he began a quarell to Ash¹.
—began a cruell] he a quarrell Co; he gan cruelly Hn¹.—a] om. Hu. 69. mercy sette aferre]
gan sette aside the ferre H². 70. trouthe] trewes Ash¹, H³, H⁴, Ash², Ar, Ad², C⁵, L, CC, C²,
B⁵; trewe Hu, H⁸, Lg; tretee C³.—algate] om. C².—wolde algate] algate wold B⁵, H²; alwey
wold H⁸. 71. pletyth] playnli CC.—Wherfore] Therfore C⁵, B¹, H⁷, C¹, Ar, S, Ad³.—for]
with B¹, H⁷, C¹, Ar, S, Ad³. 73. done] do hym H⁸, CC.—woll] om. H⁸, CC, B²; do Ash¹.—
woll hym] him will Ar, J. 74. That] He B¹, B², H⁴.—hath] om. Hn¹. 75. nature hath] hath
nature H¹.—A . yes] And this Ar. 76. playnly and] and playnly Ash².—to] vnto Ash².—playnly]
sikerly C². 77, for] *inserted above;* om. B¹, B², B⁴, H¹, H², H³, H⁶, H⁸, Ash¹, CC, Lg,
Hn², Co.

And he offended hath, of ignoraunce

More then of malice, I wisse quod mercy thoo

80 Ye for all that, he most haue his penaunce

Quod Right a noon lyke as he hathe doo

A þenke quod pees, þat toward Iericho

He was dispoilet, amonge his cruell foon

For lakke of helpe, when we hym lefte aloon

That was quod Trouthe, for he was Rekles

To go the way, I taught hym of Reason

Quod mercy than, the mortall foo of pees

The olde serpent, Rote of all treson

Of fals envye, and Indignacion

90 Lay in a waite, to bryng hym to a trayne

Whan vnto hym, falsely he gan sayne

---

78. offended] that offended CC.—he] om. C5. 79. I wisse] om. Hn2. 80. his] om. B1, J.—his] yet Ash2, C5, CC, Ad2.—that] om. H8.—Ye for] Wherefore B3, L.—all that] om. B3, L.—he most haue] he may be receyveth to B3; he may be reserved to L. 81. lyke] right B4. 82. A þenke quod pees, þat toward Iericho B1.—A] And D, C5.—þat] om. Co, B5. 83. cruell] om. Hn2.—dispoilet] disposed H3, H4, Ad2, Lg, C5, Hu.—his] all his H6. 84. hym lefte] lefte hym B3, B4, Co, H1, C2, B5, Hn2, S, Ar, H5, Ad3, Ash1, Hu, H3, H4, Ash2, H6, Ad2, Lg, C5, CC, L.—lefte] he left Ash1, H3, H4, Ash2, H6, Ad2, Lg, C5, CC.—we hym lefte] he was Ch.—we hym] he was C3, H2.—we] om. L. 85. quod] om. Co. 86. I taught] that I thoughte Hn2.—I] om. B3, L.—of] bi B3, L. 87. foo] om. B2.—mortall foo] olde mortal CC. 88. Rote] the rote Ash2, Ar. 89. fals] alle B1.—Indignacion] of indignacion H2. 90. Lay in a waite, to bryng hym to a trayne H7.—a waite] wayte D.—to a] in a B1, B3, C1, Hn2, Ash1, Ar, H5, H6, L; a Ch, C2. 91. falsely he gan] he falsly gan C1, C3, Hn1.—sayne] to sayn C1, C3, Hn1.—falsely he gan] he falsely dide B3, Co, H1, H5, Hu, Hn2, H8, H5, H7, Ad3, Lg, L, J.—gan] did him B2, CC.—vnto] he vnto H2.—he gan sayne] and playne H2.—gan] did Ash2, Ar.—vnto] be to H6, B1.—falsely] falsly falsly H6.—gan] dude H6.—he gan sayne] dede seyne B1.

That if he eete, of the forboden tre

The fayre frute, in paradise *present*

He shuld lyke, un to goddes be

Of gode and yvell, to haue entendement

And for my Sustre Trouthe was absent

And ye your selfe, also Rightwisnesse

He was be trayede, sliȝly be falsnesse

Wherfore quod *mercy*, I purpose out*erly*

100 Hym to Releve, yf I can or maye

And I q*uod* pees, well helpe faythfully

The grete Ire, and Ranco*ur* to alay

Of Iugement, to put it in delay

And here vpon to fynde full refuge

I well procede affore the high Iuge

---

92. That] om. H5.—if he] he shuld H2. 94. He shuld lyke, un to goddes be B1.—goddes] the goddes D.—un to] to H5.—like un to the goddes be] vnto goddes like be B2, Co. 95. entendement] the entendement H3. 96. for] om. H1, L.—and] om. S. 97. youre selfe also] also youre selfe Ash1, H6. 98. be falsnesse] with gylefull falsenesse Hn1. 99. out*erly*] me utturly B3, L. 100. or] om. H5.—I can or maye] that I maye and can or may Lg. 101 faythfully] soothfully B5.— woll helpe] to helpe hym Ash2. 102. and] or B1, B2, H7, Ash1, C1, S, Ad3.—The] To Co.— to] om. Co. 103. it] hem H2. 104. here vpon] happen Ar.

A nd right forthe w*it*h before the kyng of glory

Mercy and pees, this cause brought a noon

And in the high hevenly consistatory

Pees sayde thus, amonge hem eu*e*rycheone

110   A blessud lorde, þat art both thre *and* oon

So please it the benignely to here

What I woll saye, ans my sustre dere

Remembre lorde, a mong thy werk*es* all

How thow maidst, mercy sou*e*reygne

That whan that eu*e*re vnto the she call

Thow maist of Right, hir prayer not disdeyne

And specially whan that we bothe tweyne

To thy highnesse for any thyng Requyre

Thow must of grace, fulfill our prayer

---

106. for the] om. Hn².—king of] om. L.—right] om. CC. 107. this] the C⁵, L. 108. the]
om. B⁴.—and] om. H¹, Lg.—high] om. Ash¹, H⁶, H¹, Lg, Hu.—hevenly] devyne H⁸. 110.
A blessud lorde, þat art both thre *and* oon B¹.—A] O D.—þat] thou Co, Ash².—both] om.
C². 111. the benignly] benyngley the L.—please it] plesit B¹, B², B³, B⁴, B⁵, H¹, H², CC,
C¹, C², C³, Lg, Ch, Hn¹, Co. 112. woll] shall H⁸. 114. sou*e*reygne] moost soverayn B¹, H⁴,
Ar.—thow] that B³, L.—mercy] mercy above them H². 115. vnto the she call] sho vnto the
calle Ch, Ash², Ar.—whan] what B², CC.—she] shall B².—vnto] to Co, H⁸.—That] om. Hn².
—vnto the she call] she to the calle CC.—that] om. H².—That] And H⁵.—that] so B¹, B⁵,
C², S. 116. of Right hir prayer not disdeyne] not of right hir prayer disdeyne B², Ch, B³, B⁴,
H¹, C², Ash¹, H³, H², H⁵, H⁶, Ad², Lg, C⁵, L, CC. 117. whan that] that whan Ar.—that]
om. Co, C, B⁵, Hn², Hu, Ash², H⁸, H⁵, J.—bothe] om. H¹. 118. thyng] om. B², CC. 119. of]
om. Ch.—of grace] algate H².—grace] mercy Ash².

---

[1]x is erased

120 Is not thy mercy, grete above the heven

Thyne awne doughtir, chefe of thyne alye

And hath hir place, above the sterres seven

With the orders, of eu*e*ryche Herarchye

Whom day by day, thow canste so magnifie

Among thy werkes, to make hir empresse

To helpe wreches, whan thay be in distresse

Thy mercy abydith eke aye w*ith* the   f. 19b

Lyke thy gretnesse, and thy magnificence

And who that dothe mercy and pyte

130 Dothe sacrifice high in thy p*rese*nce

And is not mercy of more excellence

Lyke as the Sawter, well reherse can

Upon the herthe, bet*er* than lyfe of man

---

121. of] above B¹, B⁵, Ch. 122. hath] om. C². 123. the] om. B⁴, Ash¹, Ash², H⁶, L.—With the] Ther with Hn¹. 124. Whom] Thorow H⁵. 125. to make] om. Lg.—empresse] oppres CC. 126. whan thay] that Ash¹, H⁶. 127. abydith eke] eke abideth B², Ch, B³, B⁴, H¹, C¹, C², C³, Hu, Co, B⁵, Hn², Hn¹, H³, H², Ash², H⁸, H⁵, Ad², Lg, C⁵, L, CC, J.—aye] there Ash¹, H⁶. —abydith eke aye] evere abidith eke S, Ar, H⁷, Ad³; abideth ever eke B¹. 128. Lyke] Like as B², CC.—and] of Ar.—and thy] and Ash², Ad³. 129. dothe] om. B¹. 130. Dothe] Doth dew Hn¹.—high in thy] to thyne hye B¹, H⁷, Ar, S, Ad³.—high] om. CC. 131. not] om. B¹, B³, C¹, L.—of more] more of B², CC; of high Hn¹. 132. the] om. H⁶.

Thy self also, as it is playnly couthe

Avisely who so, taketh hede therto

Sayest opynly *with* thyne awne mouthe

That to a thousand, thow canst thy m*er*cy doo

And holy David, Recordith eke also

With his harpe above all othir thyng

140   That he thy mercyes, et*er*nally shall syng

And how might eke, any creature

Vpon erthe, of any man*er*e kynde

*With*outyn mercy, eny whyle endure

For all wer goon, and m*er*cy wer byhynde

Wherfore lorde, on mercy haue thy mynde

The woofull caytyffe, to take vnto thy grace

That hath so longe, be seu*er*ede fro thy face

---

134. self] lyffe Ash¹, H⁶.—also] also also Ch.—is] om. Co, Hn¹.—couthe] is couthe H².
135. Avisely] To man avysily Hn¹; And wisely L, Ar, Hu.—so] om. B², B³, C², C³, Hn²,
Ash², H⁸, H⁵, Ad³, Lg, J. 136. *with*] within B².—opynly] pleynli H¹.—awne] om. B². 137.
to] om. B³, L.—thou] om. S.—thy] om. Ash². 138. eke] hyt C³; welle Hn²; welle the B²,
CC; and to eke B¹, B⁵.—also] thereto B², CC, Ar. 139. *With*] That with H². 140. That]
om. H².—he] om. B⁴. 142. erthe] the erthe Hn¹.—of] by CC; in H³, H⁵, Ad², Lg, C⁵.—of
any man*er*e]in any maner of Ash¹, H⁶. 145. lorde] om. C².— haue] om. C¹.—thy] om. B¹,
Ch. 146. woofull] om. CC.—to] om. CC.—vnto thy] hym to Ash².—thy] om. C¹, C², Hn¹, H⁸,
J. 147. hath so longe] so long hath H³.

Pax And though that I be humble meke and free

For sothe lorde, of dewete and of Right

150 Yet eu*er*e in oon, my dwellyng is w*ith* the

For selde or neu*er*e, I part oute of thy syght

Pees is my name, that power hath and myght

Thorowe my con*n*yng, hem that bene mortall foon

Thorough helpe of the, to corden thayme in oon

And also lorde as holy wryte can tell

That of thy pees, ther may noo ende be

And eke thy pees, eu*er*y whight dothe excell

And art thy self, of verray dewte

Called the prynce, of pees and vnyte

160 And yet behotest, wreches to Releve

Thy bonde of pees, that it shall neu*er* meove

---

148. that I] I quod pees B³, L. 149. For sothe] My sovereyn Hn¹; Soveren C¹, C³; Parde H⁸, J, Ash², Hn²—dewete] te *inserted above.* 151. part] spare CC; part of H². 152. my] om. Lg. —power hath] hath bothe power B², CC; hath power Ash².—hath] om. H¹, L. 153. be] om. B¹, H⁸. 155. as] hath H¹. 156.] That of the pees doth every whyte exile CC.—pees ther] om. H⁸. 158. verray] vertu L. 159. Called] Yclepid Ash².—the] om. Hn¹. 160. yet] eke Hn¹, B³, L; om. C¹, C³, Hn², Ash², H⁸, J. 161. Thy bonde of pees] That is mankynde B², Ch, B⁴, H¹, Ash¹, H³, H⁵, H⁶, Ad², Lg, C⁵, CC, C²; Into thy pees Hn¹; In bond and pees L.—that it shall neu*er* meove] and shall neuer from hym meve B², Ch, B⁴, H¹, Ash¹, H³, H⁵, H⁶, Ad², Lg, C⁵, CC, C².

And Iob Recordith the holsomest frute   f. 20a

Of all this worlde, spryngyth oute of pees

Now lorde sithe, I am made to be Refute

And to the wofull, comfort and encrese

Graunt of thy grace, now a full Relees

That I and mercy, may thy foon confonde

Of thylke caytyffe, that lyeth in preson bounde

So that he may haue liberte

170   To goo at large, and haue Remyssion

Of his þraldom, and captiuite

And be deliuered, ouȝt of his preson

So that ther be made Redempcion

For his seruage, and a fynall pay

Lorde of thy mercy, with outyn more delay

162. Iob] Iacob C³, Hn¹, Ash¹, H³, H⁶, Ad³. 163. all] om. Co, Ar. 164. be] om. S.—to be] om. H⁸. 165. the] om. Hu, B¹, B⁵, H², H⁷, H⁸, Ash², J, C¹, C⁵, Ad², Ad³, Ar, B³, L.—to the] om. S; all to thyn Ash¹, Hn⁶.—and encrese] and of releyf encrees B³, L.—And to the] To Co. 166. thy] om. H¹.—Graunte] Streyte Hn².—full] om. Hn².—grace] grace lorde Hn¹. —now] om. Ash¹, Ar, CC. 167. and] om. Co. B⁵.—thy] the Co, B⁵, Ad³.—that I] that pees Ad³. 169. that] om. B¹—liberte] now thy liberte Hn¹; of liberte Hn²; fre liberte Hu. 170. haue] to have H⁸.—at] all H⁶. 171. Of his þraldom, and captiuite B¹.—his] this D, C⁵, CC.—of his] off H⁵. 172. And be deliuered, ouȝt of his preson B¹.— his] this D; om. B², B³, C², Ash², L, CC. 173. Redempcion] no redempcion B⁴; a redempcion B³, H², L.—be] may be B⁴, Ash¹, H⁶ Ch, H³, Ad², C⁵.—made] om. Ash¹.—be] om. Lg. 174. fynall] full fynall Hn¹.—a] om. H⁸, L.—and] om. CC. 175. Lorde] om. Hn¹.—thy] om. H².—more] any CC.

And whan thay had thayre mater full *pur*posed

Merncy and pece, w*ith* full high sentence

Touchyng man, with synne so ennoysed

The Iuge gave, benygne audience

180 And whan he had longe kepet sylence

For all the skylleȝ, to hym that they layde

Yet at the laste, to hem thus he sayde

Myne awne doughtirs next of alye

    Though youre Request, come of tendre hert

Ye must consydre, w*ith* a prudent eye

Of Rightwysnesse, it may nat me astert

Lyke yo*ur* askyng, by favo*ur* to adu*er*te

Vnto the cause, that is Repr*e*sent

But Right and trouth, fully will assent

Howe god the fadre of heven answerde to mercy and pees Ca° xiii[1]

---

176. mater] om. C³.—full] om. Ash². 177. w*ith*] seyth B¹, H², J. 178. ennoysed] enbrously noised Ash¹. 179. audience] in audience Ash¹. 180. whan] whan that Hu.—longe] so long B¹, H¹, H⁷.—longe kepet] kept longe H², H⁸. 181. for] to CC.—they] om. C⁵; he Lg.—layde] made B⁴. 182. to hem thus] thus to hem H².—the] om. B³, H², C², S, L.—thus he] he thus L. 183. of] myn B¹, C⁵, Ar, Lg; to myn Ch, B⁴, Ash¹, H³, H⁶, Ad², C⁵.—awne doughtirs] daughter dere Ash².—of] of myn B², H¹, C², C³, Hn¹, H², S, Ar, H⁵, H⁷, Ad³, CC. 184. come] whiche come B², CC. 185. with a] thus Hn².—prudent] prudently Hn².—eye] om. Hn². 186. me] be B¹, B³, H⁸, C², Ar, S, L.—nat me] me not H⁸, J, Hn², Ash².—it] I Hn², Ash². —me] om. H¹, C¹, Lg. 189. fully will] wol fully H².

---

[1]x *is erased.*

With outyn whome, I may not procede

To execute any Iugement

Wherfore lette call hem in this gret nede

For I must worche by hir avysement

And whan thay, were comen and present

Then trouth a noon touchyng this matier

Saide openly, þat alle myȝten here

If it be so this man, that hath trespaced   f. 20b

Ne be nat dede, for his Inyquyte

Than outrelyche, the fraunchece is defaced

200 Bothe of my sustyr, Rightwisnesse and me

And fynally, our bothe liberte

Gothe vnto nought, and our iurediction

But he be punysshed, for his transgressyon

---

191. execute] excuse execute C¹. 192. gret] om. Ash². 193. I] om. B⁴.—hir] om. Ash². 194. and]
to Hn¹; in H⁸. 196. Saide openly, þat alle myȝten here B¹.—þat alle myȝten here] as ye shall
after here D, Hn¹, C³.—Sayde] And C³, Hn¹. 197. so] thus B².—that] om. B⁴, Ash².—hath]
om. Hn². 198. Ne] om. B¹, B³, H⁷, L, Hu. 199. the] om. Ch. 200. Bothe] om. Ash².—sustyr]
self Ar.—and] and of Ash², Ch, B³, Ad³, L, CC. 201. our bothe] bothe oure Ash¹. 202. Gothe]
Bethe B⁴.—and] of B⁴, Ch, Ash¹, H³, H⁶, Ad², C⁵.—our] om. Hn², Ash², H⁸, J. 203. he] if
he Ar.

The worde of god that playnely may not erre

Tolde hym afforne, withoutyn any drede

The grete parell of this mortall werre

Etyng the apull, that he muste be dede

But he of slouthe, toke therto no hede

Wherfore he muste, as right lust provyde

210   Withoutyn mercy, the dome of dethe abyde

And though that pees, be of pite meovede

Man to delyuere, with a ȝeole of Routhe

Rightwisnesse, wolde than be agrevyd

With me to consent, that am callet trouthe

As me semyth, it were to grete a slouthe

Dome, cause, or plee, or any othir sute

Withoutyn vs twayne, to ben execute

---

204. that playnely] playnly that H². 205. hym] om. CC. 207.] For etynge the appul that God hym forbade B³, L. 208. he] om. H³.—no] of no Ash¹, H². 209. luste] liste to B³, Hn², Ash², S, Ar, H⁸, Ad³, L, J, B⁵, H².—luste] om. H⁵; luste better B¹, H⁷; lyste best Hu. 210. dome of dethe] deth of dom B¹.—Withoutyn] With H¹. 211. though] om. H¹.—of] om. J. 212. ȝeole] rule Ash².—Routhe] trowthe H⁸. 213. wolde than] than would B², B⁵, CC; wylle been Hn², Ash², H⁸, J.—than be] be then C³. 214. With] om. C³, Hn², Ash², H⁸, J.—am] all B², C³.—am callet] called am Ar.—that am] to that S. 215. me] it Ash².—grete a] a grete S. 217. to] now to Hn¹.

Me semyth eke my sustir Pees dothe wronge

To socour man, and holde agayne vs twayne

220   That haue ben con*ue*rsaunte so longe

Amonge vs discorde, to Restreyne

Therfore quod Pees, now will I not feyne

To doo myne office, Right to modyfye

That she of Rigur, cause hym nat to dye

Than q*uo*d Right of necessite

It most folowe, though he were my brothir

He moot dye, by dome of equyte

Or in his name, mot be dede some othir

So of my shyppe, gyed is the Rother

230   That I ne may erre, for wawe ne for wynde

More than the Anker, of trouthe woll me bynde

---

220. so] now so Hn1. 221. to] shulde ever Hn1.—Restreyne] distreyne Ad3. 222. now] om. B1, H5. 223. to] om. L.—modyfye] edifie CC. 224. to] om. Co, J. 225. of] of verrey Hn1. 227. He] That he Hu. 228. mot] om. Co.—mot be dede] mote dye Ash2, H8; die muste CC. 229. gyed] now gyed Hn1. 230. I] he Ash1, H2, L.—ne may] may Co, Hn1, Ash2 H8, J, Hn2, Hu. 231. the] om. H2, H8. 232. so] so that Hn1.

Certys q*uo*d mercy, so it nat displease

f. 21a

Vnto youre noble, and wise providence

His dethe to yov, may be full lytyll ease

For holy wryt, Rehersyth in sentence

Iff ye considre, in youre advertens

That dethe of synners, the high god to queme

Is werste of dethes, if ye of Right luste deme

For synfull blode, is no sacrifice

240   To god above, that eu*er*y thyng may seen

Than muste ye, the dethe of one dyvyse

That is of synne, Innocent and clene

And as I trowe, vndir the sonne schene

Thorough oute the worlde, to serche all mankynde

It were full harde, suche one forto fynde

---

233. wise] hye Hu. 234. dethe] om. Ch.—to yov may be] may you do C². —be] om. Hn¹, Ch; not be S.—full] om. B¹, B², B³, H¹, H³, H⁵, H⁶, H⁷, H⁸, Ash¹, Ash², CC, J, C¹, C², C⁵, Ar, An, Ad³, S, L, Hn¹, Co; but Ch, B⁵, H²; to Lg. 235. in] in his H². 238. of dethes] dethe B², CC.—ye of] he hys Ch.—of Right] om. Ash¹, H².—Right luste] the right H¹.—of] om. H⁶.— of Right luste] list of right C².—deme] to deme Hn¹, S, Ar, Ash¹, H², C². 239. is] to god is B², CC. 241. muste ye] ye moste H⁸.—ye] he Ar.—ye the] om. Co.—the dethe] dethe the L. 242. is of synne] of synne is Ash².—of] withouten Hn². 244. oute] all B¹, H⁷, H⁸, C², S, Ad³; oute all Ar.—to serche] rehersen B¹, B⁴, H⁴, H⁷, H⁸, Ar, Ad², Ad³, S; to reherce B², Ch, B³, Co, H¹, C¹, B⁵, Ash¹, H³, Hu, H², H⁵, H6, Lg, An, C⁵, L, CC, C².—all] om. S, H⁷; of CC. 245. forto] to B¹, B², B³, B⁵, H¹, H², H³, H⁷, CC, C², C⁵, Ar, S, L, Co.

For Ruste with Rust, may nat scowrede be

No foule, with fylthe, may nat be puryfied

And who is foulede, with dishoneste

To wasshe a nothir, it is nat apliede

250   Blake, in to wyte, may not be vndied

Ne bloode infecte, with corrupcion

To god for synne is noon oblacion

Fygure here of, ye may beholde and se

As the Byble, makyth mencion

Howe that a lambe, of spotte and fylthe fre

Some tyme was take, by eleccion

And offrede vpe, in satisfaccion

To god for synne, forto sygnyfye

That who that shulde, for manys Raunsome dye

---

246. may nat scowrede] scoured may not Co. 247. nat] om. Ch, B³, Co, H¹, C², C³, Ash¹, H³, S, H⁵, H⁶, H⁷, Ad³, Lg, An, C⁵, J, Hu.—foule] filth Ar.—may nat] no may Ar. 248. And] But Ash¹, H³, H⁶, An, C⁵.—who] who so Hn¹, Ar. 249. it] as it H³; om. B⁵.—nat] om. C². 250. Blake in to wyte, may not be vndied B¹.—may] ne may D.—vndied] died C¹. 251. with] into H¹. 252. is noon] may be B³, L. 254. As the Byble, makyth mencion H⁷.—mencion] of mencion D, C¹.—As] And as B¹, C⁵, An, Lg; And eke as Hn¹. 255. of] withouten H². 256. Some tyme] Whilom H², H⁸, J. 258. for synne] synne L. 259. who] he H².—Raunsome] redempcion CC.

260 Must be clene, pure, and innocent

Right as a lambe, fro eu*er*y spotte of blame

And trewly vndir the firmament

Ther was no soche, sythe Adam dyd atayne

The frute, to ete, for ether halte or lame

In soverayne vertu, is all the kynde of man

Wherfore q*uo*d m*er*cy, the best rede þ*at* I can

That Pees my sustir, sesse this discorde   f. 21b

And all the stryve, that is vs be twene

And that we praye our Iuge, and mighty lorde

270 To þis matere benyngly to sene

That of his grace, he shape suche a meen

For Trouthe and Right, so prudently ordeyne

That Pees ne I haue no cause to playne

---

260. Must be clene, pure, and innocent H7.—clene pure] pure clene D, B1, B4, C1, Ad2.—clene] om. L.—and] and full Hn1. 261. of] and B2, Ch, H1, Hn1, H3, H2, Lg, An, C5, CC. 262. And trewly vndir the firmament B5.—vndir] yet vndir D, B1, B4, H2, Ar, S Ad3.—And] And now Hn1. 263. dyd] dyd yt L. 264. to ete] forbade B3, L.—for] om. H2.—ethir] om. B1, B2, B3, L, An. 265. all] om. Ar, H7, Ad3, B1, B2. 266. Wherfore q*uo*d m*er*cy, the best rede þat I can B1.—þat] om. D, Co, H1, C3, B5, Ash2, Ar, H8, Lg, J. 267. sesse] om. B3, L. 268. all] om. H2.—vs] om. H8. 269. that] om. B2, CC. 270. To þis matere benyngly to sene B1.—To] Vnto D.—to] for to Ash1, H6.—benyngly] now benignely Hn1. 271. he shape suche a meen] mekeli for to bene H1; benignely to seen Lg. 272. For] And for B3, H1, Lg, L; That B2, CC. 273. That pees ne I haue no cause to playne B1.—ne] and D, H8, J; nor Hn2.—no] om. Hn2.—haue noo cause] no cause haue H8, J; ne haue cause B3, L.—playne] complayne Ash1.

And this Request, is nat againe Right

Ne vnto Trouthe, playnely, noon offence

If that our Iuge, of his grete myght

Ordeyne so, in his prudence

To shape a way, thorough his sapience

That trowþe *and* right be nothing displesid

280   Thorugh Pees, and me, though man be holpe and eased

Howe the fader of
hevyn conyde thees
iiii sustren Caº xiiiiº[1]

And whan þat she, had hir reason fyned

That groundede, was platly vpon skylle

The high Iuge, by mercy is enclynede

To condecende, of grace, to hir will

And in suche wyse, hir axyng to fulfyll

That Right be *ser*uet, and Trouth nat dysmayed

That Pees and she shulden eke be well a payede

---

275. noon] any B³, L. 276.] If that oure sentence or jugement of the myghty Juge Hn¹.—grete]
grace H¹; om. S. 277. Ordeyne so, in his prudence B1.—prudence] providence D, Ash²; wise
prudence Hn¹.—so] now so Hn¹.—in] of Ash². 278. a way] so Ash². 279. That trowþe *and*
right, be nothing displesid B1.—*and*] ne D, C¹.—nothing] in this D, C¹; not Ad², H³, H⁶, An,
C⁵.—trowþe *and* right] right and trouth Ad².—be] ne be C¹. 280. Pees] om. H¹.—me] mercy
Ar; right me H⁵.—holpe and] om. C². 281. had] om. Ash².—þat] om. Co, Hn², L.—hir]
by Ash¹, H³, Ad², An, C⁵. —had hir reason] her reson had H⁸. 282. was] om Ash².—
platly] om. Hn²; verely C².—vpon] vnto Ash². 284. to] by H². 285. in] om. B1, Lg.
286. dysmayed] deseyvid CC. 287. eke be] be eke C¹.—eke] om. Ch; ever eke L.—and she]
om. H⁸.—well a] om. Ash².

---

[1] x is erased.

And by sentence, a noon diffynytyfe

He sayde, for hole conclucion

290 An Innocent, clene, and pure of lyfe

Shall makely dye, and pay the Raunsome

For mans gylt and transgression

And he so frely, shall the dethe obeye

In all his payne, þat he no worde shall saye

And thus shall Right, in all man*e*re thyng

Have hir desyre, and Trouth shall not fayle

To execut fully hir axyng

Fynally to stynte, this batell

And for that Pees, so moche may avayle

300 And mercy eke shall not be agrevyde

Her bothe axing, shall also been achevyde

---

288. a noon] om. Ash². 289. He] The juge Ad², B², Ch, B⁴, H¹, C², Ash¹, H³, H⁵, H⁶, Lg, An, C⁵, CC.—for] for sothfaste B³, L; furthe wyth Hn¹. 290. and] om. H²; and also B², CC. 291. and pay] for to be C³. 293. he] om. C², Hn², Ash², H⁸, H².—frely] mekely H².—the dethe] to the deth B¹, H⁷, Ad³, S. 294. all] om. H¹.—his] in Ch, B⁴, H³; om. S.—no worde shall saye] schal not gensaye C¹. 295. shall Right] Ryght shall C³.—thyng] of thinge H⁵. 297 To execut] In al thyng to execute H².—fully] now thus fully Hn¹. 298. Fynally] And fynally B¹, H², H⁷, Ash².—stynte] stynte forever Hn¹. 299. so moche may] may so much B¹, B², H⁸, Ash², CC, C². 300. eke] also Co.—not be agrevyde] shal vndirtake Hn². 301. Her bothe] Bothe hir B³, L.—bothe] brother H⁶, H⁷, C⁵, Ar, Lg; aither H¹.—shall also] also shall Ar, CC; shall not Lg.—achevyde] agrevid Lg.

To fynde a man that shall vndirtake

This myghty quarell, of mercy and pite

To suffre dethe oonly for mans sake

Vncompellyd, frely of volunte

That as a lambe, withoute spotte shall be

And with his blode, shall wasshe vndefouled

The gilt of man, with rust of synne ymouled

f. 22a

310

But forto witte, of what stok he shall spryng

Or of what kynryd, or of what estate

My sothefast worde, eternally levyng

Myne awne sonne, withe me Increate

Shall downe be sent, to be Incarnate

And wrappe hym self, in the mortall kynde

Of man for love, so that he may fynde

Howe the fadre of hevyn tolde thees iiii sustren howe his sonn shuld take mankynd Ca° xv^{to}

302. vndirtake] now vndir take Hn1. 303. and] and of S, H8.—pite] pees and piti Ash1. 304. oonly] namely L. 305. frely] fully Ash2.—of] of his owne B1, Ash2. 306. as] is H8, C5, CC, L.—withoute spotte] with spotte oute L. 307. shall] om. L, H1.—his] om. C2, S.—with] om. H1.—vndefouled] the defouled H1. 308. The] With Ch, C1.—rust] most Ch, C1; spotte CC. 309. what] om. B2.—forto] now for to Ash2.—writte] wright Ar.— what] the Ar. 310. Or] om. C1, B4, Ash1, H3, H6, Ad2, An, C5, Hu, L, B2, B3, B4, Co, H1, C2, B5, Hn2, H2, Ash2, S, Ar, H8, H5, Lg, CC, J.—or of what estate] or what estate L.— or of] and of Ch, B4, Ash1, H5, H6, Ad2, C5.—what] om. H7. 312. Increate] create CC.—sonne] om. Co. 313. downe be] be don L.—to be] for to be Ash2. 315. he] ye S, H8.

A clene grovnde, his paleys onto bylde

In alle the erthe, noþ*er* of lyme ne stone

But in a mayde, deboner, and ful mylde

The humble doughter, of Iuda and Syon

320   And vnto hir, shall trouthe and mercy goon

By one accorde, sent afore my face

Lyche my devyse, to chese me a place

And say to hir, in al man*ere* thyng

Hir tabernacle, þ*at* she make fayre

Agayne the com*m*yng, of hir myghty kyng

Whiche is my sonne, and myne owne heyre

That in hir breste, shall haue his Repayre

Where trouthe and mercy shal togedur mete

By one assent, and her Rauncour lete

---

316. his] so his CC. 317. In alle the erthe, noþ*er* of lyme ne stone Ash[2].—noþ*er*] but nother D, C[1], C[3], Hn[1].—the] om. B[1], S, Ar, H[7], Ad[3], H[8].—ne] ne of B[1], Ash[1].—of] om. B[4]. 318. ful] om. B[2], C[1], B[3], B[4], Co, H[1], C[2], C[3], B[5], Hn[2], Ash[1], H[3], H[2], Ash[2], H[5], H[6], Ad[2], Lg, An, C[5], L, CC, J.—and ful] eke and S, Ar, H[8], Ad[3]. 319. The humble doughter, of Iuda and Syon B[1].—and] and of D.—The] om. Ash[2].—and of] om. H[8]. 320. vnto] to H[1], H[8], Lg.—trouthe and mercy] and mercy and trouþe C[2].—hir] this H[2]. 322. a] in a S. 323. thyng] of thing CC. 324. she] om. B[4]. 326. owne] mygti B[2], CC. 327. his] om. Hn[2], H[8]. 328. Where trouthe and mercy shal togedur mete B[1].—shal togedur] togydir shall D.—shal] om. H[1]. 329. lete] now lete Hn[1].

330 And there shall, Pees, kysse Rightwisnesse

And al the sustren, accorden in that place

And Right shall leve, al hir sturdinesse

And Trouthes sworde, shall no more manace

And fynally, mercy shall purchace

A Chartour of pardon, lyche this mayden clene

Whiche shall for man, be so goode ameyn

That he shal nowe escape dawngerles   f. 22b

Amyddes the foreste, fre frome eu*er*y trappe

Whileʒ the mayde, that causith al this pees

340 Hathe the vnycorne, slepyng in hir lappe

That thorough mekenesse shall his horne so wrappe

There it was wonte, to slee, by violence

Thoroughe deth, it shall agayne dethe be defence

---

331. that] oon H³. 332. And] That Ash².—Right] om. B⁴, Co.—al] om. B², Ch, B³, CC; right than Hu.—hir] om. B¹, C¹, B⁵. 333. shall] he shall Co, B⁵.—sworde] his sword H², S, H⁸.—sworde shall] shall his sword Hn². 334. fynally mercy] mercy finally H¹.—And fynally] And thenne finally Hn¹.—And fynally mercy shall] And finally shall mercy H². 335. lyche] of Hn¹.—lyche] liche as H³.—this] a S, H⁸. 336. Whiche] And which H⁵, Lg, C¹, B⁴, Ash¹, H³, H⁶, Ad²; The which B²; om. CC.—for man be] be for man B¹, B², B⁴, H³, H⁵, H⁶, CC, Ash¹, Ad², L, An, Lg, C⁵, Ch. 337. That he shal nowe escape dawngerles B¹.—shal nowe] mowe D, J; om. C².—shal nowe escape] shal escape away H².—nowe] om. C².—mow escape] shall escape away H². 338. fre] ferre Ash¹, H².—eu*er*y] any Ar. 339. that] om. L. 340. Hathe] Holdeth Hn¹.—slepyng] om. Hn¹. 341. mekenesse] his mekenesse Co, B⁵.—so] om. S, Ar.—horne] hand Ash¹. 342. it] he Ar. 343. Thoroughe deth, is shall agayne dethe be defence B¹.—it] om. D.—defence] fence Ar, CC; offence Ad³.

Agaynes venym, more holsome then tryacle

Eu*ery* poyson a softe, and a swage

Whan þe lyon, maketh his habitacle

W*ith* Inne, a mayde but of tendre age

And Gabryell shall goo on message

To hir a noon, myne awne secretarye

350   With new tythyng*es*, and noo lenger tarye

How Gabriell was sent
to our lady Ca° xvi to[1]

A nd Right forth with the Angel taryed notʒ

     But holdyth his waye from the see of glorye

Vnto this mayde clene of will and thought

Where as she sat in hir oratorye

W*ith* hert intentiffe and w*ith* hole memorye

Erecte to god and all hir ful mynde

To whom the Angell whan he dyd hir fynde

---

344. then] om. Ash², Ad³.—more] om. CC. 345. Eu*ery* poyson a softe and a swage B¹.—a softe and a swage] to soften and to swage D, C¹, C³; to asofte and aswage B³, Co, B⁵, Ash², An¹.—poyson] venym CC. 346. Whan þe lyon maketh his habitacle B¹.—maketh] hath D; that hath C³. 348. message] the message L. 349. awne] swete B², CC. 351. with] om. H².—forth] sotwyth L. 352. see] kynge C¹.—holdyth] take Hn²; halfe H⁸. 353. of] in B², Ch, B⁴, H¹, Ash¹, H³, H⁴, H⁵, H⁶, Ad², Lg, An, C⁵.—clene] om. B¹, B², B⁴, H¹, H³, H⁴, H⁵, H⁶, H⁷, Ash¹, C¹, C⁵, Ad², Hn¹, Lg, Ch. 354. Where] Whiche B³.—sat] was B², CC; om. H⁴. 355. w*ith*] om. Hn¹, H², H⁸. 356. Erecte to god and all hir ful mynde B¹.—ful] hole D.—Erecte] Create H³, H⁴, Ad², C⁵, CC.—and] with C². 357. the Angell] om. Ash².—he] om. L.

---

[1]x *is erased*

Benyngly w*ith* all humylite

Sayde vnto hir a noon as ye shall here

Ave maria gratia 360 Haylefull of grace the lorde is w*ith* the

plena d*omin*us tecum Ne drede the not be right glade of chere

That arte to god so acceptable and dere

That hooly hys grace ys vpon the falle

To be moste blisset amonge3 wymen alle

And w*ith* that worde thorugh gra*ce* of godd*es* myght

Al hole the sonne of the deyte

That from hevene his blisset bemys bryght

Shad on the erthe of our humanite

Whan in þe brest of a maide fre

370 The holy gooste by fre eleccion

For hir mekenesse hathe made his mansion

---

359. vnto] to B5.—vnto hir a noon] a noon to hir B1, B5, H3, S, Co. 360. is w*ith*] is hole with Ar, H8, Ad3, B2, B3, H1, C2, Hn2, Ash2, H5, Lg, CC, J, Hu.—the lorde] oure lord B4, Co, B5, Ash1, H3, H4, H6, Ad2, An, C5, L, Hu. 361. be right glade of chere] so acceptable and dere Hn1.—right] om. B4, C1.—right glade] of right glad Ash1.—of] om. H8.—not] but B1, B4, H8, Ash1, Ad2, C1, Hn1. 362. to god] so good C1, C3, L.—That] That thou B2, H4, CC, H8.—so] om. H5. 363. hooly] alle B1, B2, H7, Lg. Ch. 364. moste] om. C1. 365. godd*es*] om. H1, Lg.—And] That Ash2. 366. the deyt] his deyte Ash2.—of the] of Ar. 367. That from hevene his blisset bemys bry3ht B1.—That] Hathe D, Ash2, J. 368. Shad on the erthe of our humanite B1.—on the] vpon D; under the B5; unto CC, H2.—of] for D, L, CC. 369. Whan in þe brest of a maide fre B1.—Whan] Whan that D.—of a maide fre] be free eleccion Hn2; for her humilite C2.—in þe brest] in a maide C2.—fre] so fre Hn1. 371. For] Of Ash2.—For hir mekenesse] Through soveryn grace C2.

For whan that Bernarde, som tyme gan be holde   f. 23a

With thought vp lifte, by contemplacion

This bright sonne, in herte he gan to colde

Inly astonyde, in his asspeccion

And full devoute, in a meditacion

Therof Remembryng, as he gan take hede

Sayde evyn thus, quakyng in a drede

A lorde *quod* he, how I am agrysyde   A lamentacion of saint
380   And sore adredde, to loke on this clerenesse   Barnarde Ca° xvii°[1]

And yet wel more, *with* fere I am supp*ri*sed

For to be holde, for myne vnworthynesse

Any worde to wryte, or expresse

Of this misterye, and grete pryvite

Benyng lorde, lest thou saye to me

---

372. For] That Hn², Ash², J.—som tyme] whilom Hn², Ash², J.—that Bernarde som tyme] that somtyme Bernard B², CC. 373. With] His Ash². 374. sonne] om. B², C¹, CC. 375. astonyde in] astonyed thanne in Hn¹.—in his asspeccion] in his affecion Ar, H⁸. 376. full] om. C¹; ryght C³.—a] his Ash². 377. Therof] Therof the H⁷. 378. a] om. Ash². 379. how] so Ash¹, H³, H⁴, H⁶, Ad², An, C⁵.—I am] am I H⁸. 380. And sore adredde, to loke on this clerenesse B¹.—sore] so D.—on this] on thy D, H⁸; upon thy Hu.—so] sore B¹, B², B⁴, B⁵, H⁷, H⁸, Hu, Ash¹, C¹, Ad³, L, Ch, Hn², Co. 381. yet wel more *with* fere] yet with fere wel more Ash¹; yet right Ar.—yet wel more *with* fere I am] welmore yet I am with fer B¹, Ash¹, L, An. 382. for] om. B³, L, CC. 383. or] or to B², Ch, H¹, C², Ash¹, H³, H⁴, H⁸, H⁵, Ad², Lg, An, C⁵.—Any] Or any Hn¹.—or] or for to H⁶. 385. to] unto B², H⁸, CC.—thou] that thou Hn², Ash², J.

---

[1]x *is erased*

Why arte thou bolde, or durst in any wyse

My Rightwissnesse to tell, or to wryte

Or to presume, so hardely to avise

My testament, with thy mouthe tendite

390 That certis lorde, but if thu respite

My wrecchednesse, by supporte of thy grace

I gretly drede, of dethe, for my trespace

But wolde god thorugh his grete myght

And his goodnesse, lyche to my desyre

That from the Auter, that brynnyth in his sight

No lytyll sparke, but a flame of fyre

Wolde downe discende, myne herte to enspire

For to consume with his fervent hete

The rusty fylthe, that in my mouthe dothe flete

386. Why] What Ash1, H3, H5, H6, Ad2, Lg, An, C5, CC, H4, V.—durst in] durst thou in H4. 387. or to] or B2, Hn2, H4, Ash2, CC, C1. 388. to avise] vise Co, B5, Ash2, J.—so hardely] hardly so C3.—to avise] high empryse C3. 389. thy] om. H. 390. That certis lorde, but if thu respite B1.—if] þat D, Hn1.—but] om. Ash2.—but if thu] but thou yf L. 392. of] the B2, CC; om. B3, L.—trespace] foule trespas B1, B2, B3, H7, H8, CC, Ar, L, An. 393. But] But nowe Hn2, Ash2.—myght] grace Ar. 394. And] Of Ash1; As H6. 395. his] om. H1.—in his sight] to fore his face Ar.—that brynnyth] brynnyth H8.—the] om. C1, B4, Ash1, H3, H4, H6, An, C5. 399. in my] many a H2.

400 And alle vnclennes, cankerd þer of olde

To make clene, and to scowre awaye

That thorugh his grace, I durst be so bolde

Ethir to wryte, or some worde to saye

That was Rehersyde, vpon that blisset day

Whanne Gabriel and marie mette

In Naȝareth, and humbly hir grette

But sithen this man so perfyght of levyng   f. 23b

This holy Bernarde, so goode and gracious

So dredefull was, this matier in wrytyng

410 That was of lyfe, so Inly vertuouse

How dar I thanne, be so presumpcwouse

I wofull wrecche, in any manere wyse

To take on me, this perfyte high empryse

400. And alle vnclennes, cankerd þer of olde B1.—cankerd þer of] thereof cancred D. 401. make] make hyt Hn1.—and to] and for to L.—to scowre] scowre B1, B2, L, Hn1. 402. be so] so be Hn2.—That] And Ash1.—so bolde] bolde B1, B2, Ash1, Ar, Hn2. 403. worde to] word for to J.—or] other B2, Ch, B3, B4, H1, H3, H4, H5, Ad2, Lg, An, C5, CC. 404. vpon] on B5.—that] the B5, H4, H6, H7, Ad2, Lg, An, C5, L, J, CC. 405. Whanne Gabriel and marie mette B1.—Whanne] Whan that D, H2.—and] with B3, L; om. H8.—marie] our lady B3, L. 406. humbly hir] humbly he hyr L; humbly hyr soo Hu. 407. so] of C1.—of] and Hn2.——this man] Bernard Ash2. 408. and] and so Hn2, Ash2.—and] so B3, L, J.—so bothe H.—so goode and gracious] so gracious and so good B1. 409. was] was in Hn1, Hn2, Ash2.—in] om. Hn1, Hn2, Ash2; into Ar.—matier] in mater L.—So] And B1, H2, Ash2, Ar, L, Hn1, Hn2. 410. was of] whos H.—so] on H5.—of] in B1, H8, Ash2, Ar. S.—so Inly vertuouse] so vertuous in modd B1, H5, H8, Ash2, Ar, S.—so] om. H5. 411. so] om. Ch, B4, H1, C2, C3, Ash1, H3, H4, Ash2, Hu, H5, H6, H7, Ad3, Ad2, Lg, An, C5, B1.—thanne] om. B1.—presumpcwouse] presumptious and can no good B1. 413. perfyte] practysse Ad2.—on] vpon Ash1.—hygh] om. Ash1, Ash2,—perfyte] om. B1, H2, Ash1, Ash2, Ad2; *inserted above*.

My lippys poluted, my mouthe with synne soyled

Myne hert vnclene, and full of cursydnesse

My thought also, with all viceȝ boyled

My breste Receyte, and cheste of wrecchednesse

That me to wryte, of any p*er*fytenesse

Not only dreed, of p*re*sompcion

420 But for to encurre, the endyngnacion

Of god above, for my grete offence

That I am bolde, or hardy in his sight

To dar p*re*sume, the grete excellence

For to discreue of hir, that is so bryght

But vndir hope, that m*er*cy passith Right

And that disdeyne, my style nat werrey

W*ith* humble hert, thus to hym I pray

415. vnclene] viole Ash¹.—and] om. Ash². 416. all] om. J.—viceȝ] thoughts B¹, J, An, Lg, C¹. 417. of] om. Lg. 419. Not] That Lg. 420. encurre] eschewe C⁵.—for] om. B¹, B², H¹, C¹, C⁵. 421. my] om. Lg. 422. bolde or hardy] hardy so bold Co, B⁵. 423. the] this B¹, B², B³, B⁴, B⁵, H¹, H³, H⁴, H⁷, H⁸, Ash¹, J, C¹, C², C³, Ch, Hn¹, Co, Hn².—grete] om. C¹.—the grete excellence] of her that is so bright Hn¹. 424. is] was B¹, B², B⁴, B⁵, H¹, H³, H⁴, H⁵, H⁶, H⁷, H⁸, Ash¹, C², C³, C⁵, Ar, Ad², Ad³, An, Lg, Ch, Hn¹, Co, Hu.—of] om. Ch.—so] om. H¹.—is] om. B⁴. 425. hope] holpe H¹.—But] And CC. 426. nat] not ne B¹, B², B⁵, H¹, H⁵, H⁷, H⁸, CC, C², Ar, Lg, Co.—disdeyne] discerne Co, B⁵.—style] soule B⁵, Co.—that] not CC. 427. thus to hym] to him thus Hn².

A recapitulacion of the
wordes of Gabriel to
our lady Caᵒ xviiiᵒ   430

O lorde whose m*e*rcy, gothe not to declyne

But eu*e*re lyche, stondyth holy in oon

That som tyme, sendist downe from Seraphyne

To Isaye an Angell, w*ith* a stone

Where with he gan to touche his mouth anoon

To purge his lyppeȝ, fro all pollucion

So late thy grace to me discende a downe

My rude tonge, to exployte and spede

Som what to saye, in commendacion

Of hir that is well, of womanhede

And thorugh hir helpe, and mediacion

Be to my style full direction

440   And lete thy grace, all ways be pr*e*sent

This boke to ferther, aftir myne entent

---

428. O] om. CC.—m*e*rcy gothe] mercy passith gothe Hn². 429. holy] om. H¹. 430. som
tyme] whilom Ash², J, Hn².—Seraphyne] hevyn Hn². 431. an] the L. 432. with] om. H⁸.—
gan] began B⁴, Ash¹, H³, H⁴, H⁶, Ad², An, C⁵. 433. all] om. C¹. 434. grace to me] grace
lorde to me Hn¹. 435. and] now and Hn¹. 436. Som what] And som what Hn¹. 437. well]
now welle Hn¹. 438. hir] om. H¹.—mediacion] meditacion C⁵. 439. Be to my style] To be
of the stile C².—full direction] good lord now full direction Hn¹.—Be to] To be Ash¹. 440.
be pr*e*sent] be plentewully present Hn¹.—all ways be] be alway C¹, C², Ash¹.

For of my selfe, for to vndirtake   f. 24a

To speke or wryte, in so devoute matier

Lytyll wondir, though I tremble and quake

And chaunge bothe counten*an*s and chere

Sythen this mayde, of vertu tresorere

Perturbed was, in loke and in visage

Of Gabryell to hir the mesage

And full demurely, styll gan abyde

450   And in hert, castyng vp and downe

Full prudently, vpon eu*er*y syde

The man*er*e of this salutacion

And how it myght, in conclusion

In any wyse, full *per*formed be

She standyng hole, in hir virgynyte

---

442. selfe] lyf Ash¹, Ar.—for] om. H³, Ash², Ash³. 443. wryte] to write Ar, An. 444 and] or H⁴, S, H⁵, H⁶, H⁷, Ad³, Ad², Lg, An, C⁵, L, CC, V. 445. and] and eye Ar. 447.] To seke or write Lg.—in] om. B¹, Ash¹, Ash², C², S. 448. Of] Whan Hn².—to hir the mesage] to here dyd the mesage Hn².—the mesage] that swete mesage Hn¹; when he said the mesage H⁶. 450. hert] her herte B², C¹. B³, B⁴, Co, H¹, C², B⁵, H³, H⁴, H⁵, Lg, An, C⁵, J. 451. vpon eu*er*y syde] vpon her every side S; vpon hir by every side H⁸. 452 The manere] The swete maner Hn¹.—this] his Hn¹. 454. full] om. Ash¹. 455. hir] om. Hn², Ar, H⁶.

And whan the Angell sawe hir lawlyhede

And the hooli rednes also in her face

He sayed marie, for no thyng that thou drede

For to fore god, thou has fovnden grace

460 And shall conceyve, w*ith* in a lytyll space

W*ith*in thy wombe, a sonne of all vertu

And shall hym calle, whan he is borne Ih*es*u

That shall be grete, and namet sothefastly

Sonne of the hyghest, that euere was of myght

And god to hym, shall gyffe full Iustely

The see of David, his awne fadirs right

And he shall Regne, in eu*er*y wightys sight

In the house of Iacob, eternally by lyne

Whoos kyngdome, ay shall ast, and neu*er*e fyne

---

456. And] That Ash[1], J.—lawlyhede] goodlihede H[1], Lg; holyede Ar. 457. And the hooli rednes also in her face H[7].—And the] The D, C[1], C[3], Co, B[5], Hn[2], Ash[2], J.—rednes] dedis C[1], C[3].—also] om. B[1], C[1], V, C[3]. 458. He] om. Hn[2], Hn[1], Ash[2], J.—marie for no thyng] *for no thyng Marie* B[3], L.—for no thyng] that for not thynge S, H[8].—that] om. L, Hu, V. 460. with] *inserted above.* 461. all] om. Ash[2].—of all vertu] full of vertu Ash[1].—all] grete B[3], L. —Within] And in Ch, B[4], H[3], H[4], An, C[5]. 463. sothefastly] sothly Ar. 464. the] om. B[3], L. 465. to] of H[2], Ash.[2]—full] seete ful H[3].—to hym shall gyffe] shall yeve to Ch, H[1], H[8], L.— full] om. B[1], Ash[2], H[3], Hn[2].—god] om. B[1], H[3]. 466. awne] om. C[1], C[2]. 469. ay] om. Hn[1], CC.—ay shall] **shall ay** C[1], B[5].

470   And though his heste, wer passyng of Renoone

Surmontyng eke, as in excellence

That outewarde gaffe, so mervelouse a soune

And wundurfulle to here audience

Yet she full mekely *with* grete Reu*e*rence

And looke downe cast, of hir een clere

Benygnely the Angel gan enquere

In what man*e*re, shall this thyng betyde   f. 24b

Sithe I noo man knowe in noo degre

Quod Gabriell, wit*h*in thy blissed syde

480   The holy goste, shall yshrouded be

And all the vertu, of the trynyte

Enclose shall, in thy brest so clene

The sonne of lyfe, wit*h* all his beames shene

---

470. his heste] his voys H8.—wer] om. H8. 471. as in] of Ash1; in his B5.—in] in grete B1, B5, H7, Ash1, Lg. 472. outewarde] outwardly Ch, B4, H3, H4, Ad2, An, C5. 473. And wundurfulle to here audience B1.—here] hir in D, C1, H3.—And wundurfulle] And eke ryȝt wonderfulle Hn1. 474 with] of B4, H3, H4, Ad2, An, C5.—grete] full grete C3.—Yet] And yet Hn1.—full] om. Hn1.—grete] all CC. 475 hir] *inserted above*. 476 gan] did C2.—Benygnely the Angel] Benygnely she the angel Hn2.—Benygnely the Angel gan] Benygnely gan the angel B1, C2, S, Hn2. 477. thyng] om. CC.—In] om. Hu. 478. noo] any B3, L. 479. within] with H.—syde] om. S. 480. shall] om. C2.—yshrouded] yshadowed B2, CC.—be] the C2. 481. all] om. C2.—of] eke of Hn1.—of the trynyte] of the hooli trinite B1, C2, Hn1. 483. all] om. B3, L.

Wherfore this chylde, that shall of the be born

Shall called be, goddys sonne entier

By holde and see, a lytyll here be forn

Eliȝabeth, thyne awne cousyn dere

Conseived hathe sithen gon half a ȝere

Thow she for age, wene to haue ben baren

490 And is with chylde, to put all in certeyne

That vnto god, ys no thyng impossible

But as hym list, may euery thyng fulfyll

Vnto whose word, be fully now credible

By holde quod she, of god the meke ancille

With all my hert, obeyng to his wille

In euery þing, riȝt, as hym liste it be

And liche thy worde, so fall it vnto me

---

484. shall] om. C². —that] om. Ash¹. —be] om. S. 485. entier] eterne C⁵; clere Ash². 486. see a] om. Hu. 488. Conseived hathe sithen gon half a ȝere B¹. —gon] gone is D. —half a ȝere] a full yeer Ash², S. 489. Thow she for age, wene to haue ben baren B¹. —to] om. D, C³, J, Ash², Hn²; to for H¹. —she] om. Hn². —wene] thought B², CC. 490. in] om. Ash¹. 491. vnto] to Ch, B⁴, H³, H⁴, H⁶, Ad², An, C⁵. —ys no thyng impossible] there is no thynge possible Ash¹. 493. be fully now] be now fully B², CC. —fully] om. C³. 494. quod] and B². —meke] om. C³. 495. With all my hert] Within my herte Ash¹, H⁶. —obeyng] obbey Ash¹, H⁶. —to] unto Ad². 496. In euery þing riȝt, as hym liste it be B¹. —In] To D. —it] to D, B³, Ar, L; om. Hn². —riȝt] like B², Ad³, CC; om. B⁵, V. 497. so] om. Ch, B⁴, Ash¹, H³, H⁴, H⁵, H⁶, Ad², Lg, An, C⁵, V, CC, H¹, C². —it] om. H¹. —liche] after liche C².

Loo she that was chosyn forto been

Of all this worlde, lady and Empresse

500   Of heven and erthe, aloon to be queen

And goddys mothir, for his holynesse

Loo, for all this, how lawly *with* mekenesse

She all commytted, vnto goddys will

As he ordenyd redy to fulfylle

Nold calle hir self, noon othir name

But goddys hande mayde, in full lawe man*e*re

O where is al thy transitorye fame

Of pompe and pryde, and Surquydre in feer

Where is your booste, or how dar ye apeer

510   W*ith* you*r* forblowe, blowyng vanyte

Sithe that a mayde, thorugh hir humylite

---

498. Loo she] Loo how she B⁴.—Loo] For B³, L.—forto] to Ad³.—was] om. Hu. 500. aloon] all onely H⁸; of bothe CC; above Hu.—and erthe] om. C². 502. Loo] And loo Hn¹.—how] then B³, Ash², L.—with] in Ash². 503. vnto] to Co, B⁵, Hu.—all] om. Ash². 504. redy] all redy CC; evyr Hu.—he] om. H6.—As] And as Hn², H³. 505. Nold] And now B¹; And nold Hu, V; And wold not C³; And nolde not C⁵. 506. hande] owne hande B¹, B², H¹, H⁴, C¹, C³, Hn¹; om. C¹, Ash¹, H⁶, C³, Hn¹, H⁴. 507. al] om. B², CC; *inserted above.* 508. and] of B¹, B², B³, B⁵, C², C¹, An, Ch.—and Surquydre] om. C². 509. how] wa B¹, B⁴, B⁵, H³, H⁴, H⁶, Ash¹, J, C⁵, Ad², An, Ch; om. Ch, B⁴, Ash¹, H³, H⁴, H⁶, Ad², An, C⁵.—dar] om. Ch. 510. blowynge] om. Ash¹, H⁶; flateryng Hu.—forblowe] forwode CC. 511. that] om. B², Ad³, L, CC.—hir] om. Ar, H⁸.

Of pryde nowe, hathe wone the victory f. 26a

And opynly, yyeven hym a fall

Thorugh whose lawnesse the high kyng of glorye

With Inne hir wome, hathe made in speciall

His dwellyng place, and his hospitall

And *with* a worde, of þe mayden spoke

The holy goste, is in hir brest Iloke

520 And whanne þe angelle from her departed was
     And she aloon in hir tabernacle

Right as the sonne persheth thorugh the glas

Thorugh the Cristall, Byrell or spectacle

*Wit*houtyn harme Right so by miracle

In to hir closet, the faders sapience

Entrede is, with outyn violence

Howe holy men
by dyvyne like-
nesse wrote of
our lady in
*com*mendacion
of hir Ca° xix°[1]

---

512. wone] goten B[1], B[3], B[4], B[5], H[1], H[3], H[4], H[5], H[7], H[8], Ash[1], J, C[5], Ar, Ad[2], Ad[3], An, Lg, Ch, Hn[1], Co.—nowe hath wone] hathe nowe founde H[3]; hath nowe wone Ch, B[3], B[4], Co, H[1], B[5], Hn[1], Ash[1], H[4], Ar, H[8], H[5], H[7], Ad[3], Ad[2], Lg, An, C[5], J; hathe she nowe won Hu. 513. yyeven] hath yeuen V. 514. lawnesse] lowlinesse B[1], B[2], B[3], B[4], B[5], Hu, H[1], Ash[2], CC, C[1], C[2], C[3], C[5], Ar, Ad[2], L, An, Lg, Ch, Hn[1], Co.—high] om. Ch, Co, CC.—Thorugh] That An. 515. in] his H[6]. 516.] Theryn to rest that lord eternale C[2]. 517. And *with* a worde, of þe mayden spoke B[1].—þe] that D.—with] that Co.—And] om. Ash[1], H[6].—of þe] that the Ar. 518. is in hir brest] in her brest is Ar.—in hir brest Iloke] within her loke Ash[2]. 519. And whanne þe angelle from her departed was B[1].—dep*ar*ted] partyd D.—fro hir] om. CC.—fro hir partyd] partyd from her Hu. 520. aloon in] aloone than in Hn[1].—in hir] in all hir Ch. 521. the] om. L, H[1], C[2].—thorugh] in H[8]. 522. Cristall Byrell] berell crystall Co.—the] om. B[3], B[5], L.—or] of Lg; and Hu. 523. harme] fracture C[2]. 524. the] om. B[1], B[5], H[6], CC, S, Co.—hir] the Co, B[5].—sapience] of sapience CC.

---

[1]first x *is erased*

Or any wemme, vnto hir maydenhede

On any syde, in party or in all

For godes sonne, takyng our manheed

In hir hathe bilte, his paleys prynci[p]all

530 And vndir pight, this mansion Rial

With vii pilers, as made is memorye

And ther in sette, his Reclynatorye

Wheche is performed, al of pure golde

Only to vs, forto signyfye

That he all holy, maked hath his holde

With Inne this mayde, that callet is marye

And vii pillours, that shulde this mayden gye

Been vii spirites, so as I can decerne

Of god above, this mayde to gouerne

526.] Without wite grete or small CC. 527. On] Or H8.—or in all] an in all H8. 528. our] youre H; every B3.—sonne] love H1. 528.] Weche for our sake was quyk and dede CC. 530. this] his hys Ch, CC. 531. as made is] as is made Co. 533. Wheche is performed al of pure golde B1.—pure] clene D, Ad3; clene purid Ash2. 534. to vs] for us CC. 535. all] om. B1.— maked hath] hath made Ash1, Ar, Hu.—hath] om. H7. 537. this mayden gye] his paleis guye Ash2, J.—And] Ben Ch. 538. so] om. B1, Ash2.—Been] And C1. 539. to] forto B2, Ar. —Of] To H3; O An.

540 For all the tresoure, of his sapience

And all the wisdome, of hevyn and erthe therto

And all the Richesse, of spirituall science

In hir were sette, and closyde eke also

For she is the tour, wi*th*outyn wordes moo

And hous of yvour, in wheche Salamon

Shette all the tresoure, in his possession

She was the castell, of the cristall wall   f. 26b

That neu*er* man myght yet vnclose

Whiche the kyng that made and causyth all

550 His dwellyng chefe, by grace gan dispose

And like as dewe, descendeth on the Rose

With siluer dropes, and of the leves fayre

The fresche bewete, ne may not apayre

---

541. thereto] also H5; too V. 542. science] intelligence H1. 543. closyde] om. Ash2.—eke] om. C2. 544. wi*th*outyn] with H8.—the] om. H1, C2. 545. And hous of yvour, in wheche Salamon B1.—wheche] whiche that D, C3.—And] And the B2, CC.—yvory] om. CC.—in] of Hn1; om. C1. 546. his] om. B2, CC; and Ash1, H5.—the] om. Ash2.—in his] and Ar, V. 547. of] and C2, H4; with Ash2, J.—castell of the cristall wall] ferre cristall walle B2, CC. 548. myght] ne myght J, Ash2, Hn1.—yet] hit H8; om. B2, CC.—myght yet] yet myghte Co; might not yet Hu.—man myght] might man H7. 549. that made] made that B2, CC.— and] om. B2, CC, Ch, B1; but and H8, Ad3.—Whiche] The which H5; In the wyche Ch; in whiche V.—made] om. Ch, B1. 550. gan] om. C2.—by grace] by wold C2.—dwelling chefe] chefe dwelling B5, V. 552. With siluer dropes, and of the leves fayre B1.—and of] vpon D; and on Ash2, Ar, CC.—the] om. Hn1. 553. ne] om. B1, B3, B5, H1, H2, C2, S, L, An, C1, Co.—bewete] braunche H6.—may not] may it not Ash2.

Ne as the rayne, in Apryll or in May

Causyng the vertu to Renne oute of the Rote

The grete fayrenesse nought apayre may

On violeteȝ, and on erbes soote

Right so this grace, of al our grevous bote

The grace of god, a mydde the lyly white

560   The beaute causith, to be of more delyte

And as the Cocle, with hevyn dew so clene

Of kynde engendreth, white perles Ronde

And hathe no cheryshyng, but the sonne shene

To his fostryng, as it is playnely founde

Right so this mayde, of grace most habounde

A perle hath closed, within hir brest white

That from the dethe, myght al our Raunsom quyte

---

554. Ne as the rayne, in Apryll or in May H⁷.—Ne] And right D, Co; But B³, L.—May]
fresshe may B¹, J, Hu.—or] ne C². 555. of] om. Ash².—to] om. H⁶.—of] unto CC. 556.]
Diverse colours to flourishe and to make gay B³, L.—nought] freschly C². 557. On] Of B³,
L, H⁵, upon Ar.—erbes] other herbes Ar, B³, L.—on] *inserted above.* 558. our] grevys B².
559. lyly] hye L. 560. The] Hir Hu, L.—of more] more of H⁸.—of] om. H¹, J. 561. the]
om. Ash². 562. white] with Ash², L, CC. 564. is] om. H¹.—playnely] so plainly C². 565. of
grace moste] most of grace L; of moste vertu V. 566. A perle hath closed, within her brest
white B¹.—closed] chosyn D. 567. the] om. B¹, B², H⁷, Ash¹, CC, J, S, L; our V.—al]
om. Ash².

She was eke the gate, with the lokeȝ breght

Sette in the Northe, of high deuocion

570 Of wheche sumtyme, the prophete had a sight

Ezechiel in his a vision

Wheche stoode eu*ere* clos, in conclusion

That neu*er* man, entre shall ne pace

But god hym selfe, to make his dwellyng place

And Right in sothe, as I Reherse can

So as the flees, of Gedeon was wette

To forn he fawte with hem of madian

W*ith* hevynly dewe, environ all by sette

In signe onely, hc shall spede the bette

580 **Right so hathe godde, in hir his *grace* shewed**

Withe the holy goste, when she was al bydewed

---

568. the gate] om. B¹, B⁴, B⁵, H³, H⁴, H⁶, Ash², Ch, J, C⁵, Ad², An, Hn²,—with]
of Ash¹, Ch, B⁴, H³, H⁴, H⁶, Ad², An, C⁵.—with the lokeȝ] with lockes Ash².—gate] grace
Ash¹.—the gate] gate J, Ash². 570. Of wheche sumtyme, the prophete had a sight B¹.—
wheche] whiche that D.—some tyme the prophyte] the prophete somtyme Ar.—some tyme]
whilom Ash², J. 571. Eȝechiel] Elizabeth H¹; Good Ezechiel Hn¹. 572. Wheche stoode eu*ere*
clos, in conclusion B¹.—eu*ere*] ay D.—in] in his H³.—stoode] om. H¹. 573. entre shall] shall
entre Ar. 574. god] om. B⁴. 575. I] om. C.—Right] yet B², B³, B⁴, H¹, Ch, C², Ash¹, H³,
H⁴, H⁵, H⁶, Lg, Ad², An, C⁵, L, CC. 577. To forn he fawte with hem of madian B¹.—he
fawte with] the fawte of D.—he] that he H⁶; for he Ch, B⁴, H⁴, Ad², An, C⁵. 578. by sette]
byfell Ash².—environ] and enviryon H⁸. 579. he shall spede] spede he shall Ar, V. 580. hathe
god] god hath B¹, H¹, H², Ch, Ash², C².—hathe] as H¹.—in] on H¹, C².—godde] om. C².
—his] om. Ash², Ch. 581. al] om. Lg.—when she] sche whan B⁵.

In token playnly, she sholde socour be   f. 27a

Vnto mankynde, manly forto feyght

Agayne the devill, that hath in his powste

Al Madyan, w*ith* his fel myght

But thorughe the helpe, of the mayden bryght

And thorughe the dwe of hir hevynly grace

We shall this serpent, from our bondes chase

She was of golde, also the Riche ourne

590   Kepyng the manna, of our saluacion

That all our woo, may to Ioy to*ur*ne

W*ith* holsome foode, of full p*er*fection

And eke she was in sygnyficac*i*on

The yerde of Aron, with frute and leves lade

Of vertu moste, to comfort vs and glade

582. playnly] only H². — she] that she C², B¹, B², H⁷, H⁸, Ar, Ad³. 583. manly] namely Ar, H⁸. 584. Agayne] And B¹, H², H³, H⁴, Ad², Ch. 585. w*ith*] with all J. 586. But] And C⁵, An. 587. hir] om. Lg. 588. bondes] body H⁸. 589. of golde also] also of golde B¹, B², B³, B⁴, B⁵, H², H³, V, H⁴, H⁵, H⁶, H⁷, Ash¹, Ash², CC, J, C², C⁵, Ad², Ad³, L, An, Lg, Hn¹, Co; also golde H¹. — ourne] wone H⁸. — of golde] om. Hu. 590. manna] name B¹, B², B⁵, H², H⁵, H⁷, H⁸, Ar, Ad³, Co, Hu. 592. full] om. Ad³; hole Ar. 593. eke] om. CC. — And eke she was] And sche was eke C³. 594. The] om. Ash², J. 595. vs] moste CC. — to] of L. — moste] us C². — to comfort vs] vs to comfort C³.

She was the Auter, of Cedre gold and stone

Stedefast and trwe, thorugh *p*erfection

And as the Cedre cons*er*vyng ay in oon

Hir body clene, from all corruppcion

600   And for to make, a full oblac*i*on

Of eu*er*y vertu, to god in chastite

She shone as golde, by perfyte charite

And on this Auter, she made hir sacrifice

With fyre of love, brynnyng also bryght

To god and man in eu*er*y man*er*e wyse

As done the sterres, in the frosty nyght

Hir franke ensence, gaffe so clere a leight

Thorugh good ensample þ*at* the p*er*fite levyn

Of hir levyng, Raught vnto hevyn

---

596. of Cedre gold] of the Cedre H². 597. and trwe] as ston Hu, B¹, H², H⁷, H⁸, Ash², J, Ar, Ad³; and stable B³, L.—thorugh] of CC; in B², Ch, V, B⁴, H¹, C², Ash¹, H³, H⁴, H⁵, H⁶, Ad², Lg, An, C⁵; ever in full H². 598. cons*er*vyng ay] ay cons*er*vyng B¹, S; is cons*er*vyng CC. 601. vertu] om. B², CC. 602. by] in Ash², H⁸, CC. 603. hir] this B², H⁷, CC. 604. also] full H⁸.—*With* fyre of love] Which of love Ash². 605. in eu*er*y man*er*e] in a fervent C². 607. clere] swete CC. 608. good ensample] ensaumple good Ch. 609. vnto] vnto the B², Ash², Ad³,V; to the S.

610   She was the trone, where that Salamon

      For worthynesse, sette his Riall see

      With golde and yvory, that so bright shone

      That al aboute, the beaute men may se

      The golde was loue, the yvory chastyte

      And xii leouns so grete huge and large

      That of this werke, baren vp the charge

      Of the olde Lawe, werne the propheteȝ twelffe   f. 27b

      That longe aforne gan beholde and see

      That Salamon, goddys sonne hymself

620   Shulde in þis maide be holde his rial see

      So that in sothe hir clene virginyte

      To be a mayde and a mothir, sholde no thyng lette

      Amydde hir breste, þat he his Trone sette

---

612. that] om. Ash². 613. men] that men H¹. 614. yvory] Ivor was H⁶, Ad², L. 615. And xii leouns, so grete huge and large B¹.—grete huge] huge grete D, J.—leouns] om. L.—huge] so huge H⁷; longe Ash². 616. this] the B², CC.—the] all the B², CC. 620. Shulde in þis maide be holde his rial see B¹.—be holde] bild D, J, C¹, C³, Hn¹, Ash², Ash¹; holden H⁸, CC.—in] have in H¹; of B³, L.—be holde his rial see] take humanitye B³, L. 621. hir clene] to hir B¹, H⁷, H⁸; for her Hn¹; in Ar, Ad³. 622. and a mothir] om. B¹, Hu, V. 623. þat] they H⁸.—þat he] hym B³, L.—sette] to sette B³, L.—he] om. Co, H¹, CC.

She was also the woman, that saint Iohn

Sawe in the hevyn, so Richely apere

Clad in a sonne, þe wheche bright*er* shon

Than phebȝ dothe, in his large spere

And xii sterres, that passyngly were clere

So as to hym, playnely dyd seme

630   Were sette above, in hir diademe

And as hym thought, at hir feet there stode

A large mone, bryght and nothyng pale

In fygure onely, þat she that is so goode

To swage the bitt*er* of our olde bale

The sonne of lyve, made to avale

Downe to the herthe, to gou*er*ne vs and gye

And eke the moone, to us doth signifie

---

624. that] of Ad³. 625. in] hyȝe Hn¹. 626. Clad in a sonne, þe wheche bright*er* shon B¹.—þe wheche] whiche that D, H⁸. 628. that] om. H⁸. 629. to hym playnely] playnely to hym B¹. 631. hym] om. B⁴. 632. mone] and a H¹.—bryght] om. B², CC. 663. þat she] that B¹, B⁵, H³, H⁴; of hir Co, B⁵; she H⁴. 634. To swage the bitt*er* of our olde bale B¹.—olde] om. D, Ch, C¹, C³.—bitt*er*] bitternesse B², B³, L, CC.—To] Should H². 635. made to avale] her mekeness made Hn¹.—lyve] rightwisnesse B³, L. 636. gye] to guye CC.—the] om. L.—to gou*er*ne us] us to governe C³. 637. And eke the moone, to us doth signifie B¹.—to us doth] dothe vs D; to us to CC; dothe to us Co, C¹, C³.—moone] sone H¹.

All holy chirche, large to be holde

Whiche in this mayde, had his orygynall

640 Whanne finally, w*ith* hise rightis olde

The Synagoog, of Iues had a fall

For in this mayde, the first faythefull wall

Of holy chirche, god gan first to bilde

Whan w*ith* his sonne, he made hir goo w*ith* chylde

And to Reforme the Rudeness vtterly

Of blynde folk*es*, that koweth not p*er*ceyve

How that marye, myght kyndely

A mayde be, and a chylde conceyve

And if hym lust, Reason to Receyve

650 They may ensamples, Right I nowe fynde

Of this matier accordyng vnto kynde

638. to] forto Ash². 639. Whiche] Whan B².—in] om. B¹.—his] om. B³, C², H⁸, L. 640. Whanne finally, w*ith* hise rightis olde B¹.—Whanne] Whan that D. 641. of] the H⁸. 643. holy] h *inserted above.*—first to] first behold to Ash¹. 644. goo] first go Co. 645. Rudenesse vtterly] froward rudeness B³, L. 647. kyndely] in sothfastnesse B³, L; so kyndely Hn¹. 648. conceyve] to conceive Ash². 649. And if hym] If that him B¹, H⁷, V.—Reason] frowardness B³, L.—Receyve] conceye Ch, B⁴, Co, H¹, C¹, C³, B⁵, H⁴, H⁶, Ad², Lg, An, V, Ash¹, C⁵; perceyve H². 650. They] That H³; Meny Ash².—Right] om. B², CC.

O blynde man, thorough thyne Inyquyte

f. 28a

Why hast thou lost, thy Reason and thy sight

Autentike
conclusiou*n*s a
gayn vnbylefull men
that seyne þat
Criste may not be
born of a Mayde
Ca° xx°

That thou of malise, list not for to see

How criste Ih*esu*, thorough his gret might

To his disciples, helde the waye Right

Thoroughe the gates, shette by gret defence   i

Withoutyn brekyng or any violence

Why myght he not, of his magnificence

660 Within a mayde, make his mansion

And she yet stonde, in the excellence   ii

Of maydynhede, frome all corrupcion

Ye be to blynde, in y*our* discrecion

That lust nat se, also howe he Rose

Frome dethe, to lyfe, and his sepulcre close

---

652. thyne] om. B², CC.—O] om. C¹. 654. for] om. B³, H⁸, H⁶, Ash¹, L. 655. cris*te* Ih*esu*]
Ih*esu* Crist B³, L.—gret] grace H¹; full gret Hn¹. 656. waye] wey ful Hn¹.—To his] Then to
H². 657. gret] om. H¹. 658. brekyng] strength B².—any] om. CC. violence] dissence C¹.—any]
eny kynde Hn¹. 659. not of his] not than of B³.—he not] not he C².—myght he not] he myght
not L.—magnificence] majesty Hu. 661. yet stonde] stonde it B⁴.—stonde] fonde H³.—the]
high B², Ch, B³, H¹, C², Ad¹, V, H⁴, H⁵, H⁶, Ad², L, An, C⁵, B⁴, CC, H³.—yet] ryȝt H⁸.
she yet] yett she L. 663. Ye be] Thou art B³, L.—to] om. C¹. 664. se] to se B¹, H⁴, C², C⁵,
L, Hn¹, CC.—also] om. H⁴, An, CC.—also howe] how he also H⁸. 665. and] in C⁵, CC.

And here withall, thou maiste also adu*e*rte

How he in sothe, of his myghty grace   iii

Made Petre oute of prison sterte

And where hym lust, frely to pace

670   And yet the dores, were shette of the place

What wondre than, though god by myracle

Within a mayde made, his habitacle

She beyng close and p*e*rfytely shette

With all the bonde3, of virginyte

For sothefastely, hir clennesse was not lette

Upon no side nor hir chastite

But encresith and fayrere for to see

That godd*es* son liste to light adowne

Wi*th* this mayde, to make his mansion   iiii

---

666. and here withall] and yet also B¹.—withall thou maiste] thou mayste wyth all L.—withall with you C¹; all also Co.—And here] And yet Ar, H⁸, H⁷, Ad³.—also] also 3yt Hn¹; om. B², Ash², CC. 667. he in sothe] also he of B¹, B⁵; in sothe] also Co, H², Ash², Ar, H⁸, H⁷, Ad³, J, Hn¹, Hu; full graciously B², Ch, B⁴, C², Ash¹, H³, H⁴, H⁵, H⁶, Ad², L, An, C⁵, CC, V, H¹, B³, Lg.—myghty] ful Hn¹. 668. oute of] also out Hn¹; of C².—sterte] to sterte B³, L. 669. to] for to H², L, Hu, V.—hym] hyt hym L. 671. than though] thanne you that Ch, B⁴, H³, H⁴, H⁶, Ad², An, C⁵; was than Ash¹.—god] om. C¹, B⁵.—though] that H⁵. 672. habitacle] tabernacle CC.—mayde made] mayde than made Hn¹.—Within] in H². 673. She] And B³, B⁴, H¹, C², V, Ash¹, H³, H⁴, H⁵, H⁶, H⁷, Ad², L, An, C⁵, CC, H².—close] also Hn¹.— perfytely shette] perfytly eke Hn¹.—close] aye clos H². 674. virginyte] her virginitee B¹, H¹, H², H⁸, Ash², Ad³, An; clene virginite B², Ch, B⁴, V, H¹, C², Hn¹, Ash¹, H³, H⁴, H⁵, H⁶, Ad², L, C⁵, Lg, CC. 675. clennesse] bondis C¹.—lette] shutte CC. 676. Upon no side nor hir chastite B¹.—Upon no side] In nokynnes kynde D, Hn¹, C³.—hir] her pure H². 677. and] om. H⁸.— and fayrer for to see] in more honeste C².—for] was Hu.—encresith] ever Hn¹. 678. to] om. H⁷, Ad³, J; so to Hn¹. 679. this] his CC; a H².—to] and H⁶.—this mayde] her wombe B³, L.

680 Eke Hildefons, tellyth of a tree

In stede of frute, that beryth byrdeȝ smalle

Fro yere to yere by kynde, as men may see

Withoutyn meddelyng of femall or of male.

This is verrey sothe, playnely and not tale

Than wondir nat, though Crist were bore betwene

The chaste sydeȝ, of a maydyn clene

Eke certyn briddes called vultures   f. 28b

Withoutyn medelyng conceyved by nature

As bokes sayen, withoute any lees

690 And of her lyfe, an hundreth yere endure

Than the lorde, of euery creature

That causith all, no wondre þat I sayde

Though þat he were conceyved of a mayde

680. a] *inserted above.* 681. byrdeȝ] leves B¹, Co, H², H⁷.—that] he H². 683. of male] male B⁵, Co, C², H², Ar Lg; with male B³, L. 684. playnely] om. B¹.—is verrey] verrily is B², Ch, B³, B⁴, H¹, C³, Ash¹, H³, H⁴, H², H⁵, CC, H⁶, Ad², Lg, C⁵, L.—is] om. J. 685. Than] om. H². 687. Eke certyn briddes called vultures B¹.—Eke certyn] Also the D, C¹, C³.—called] þat ben callet D, C¹, C³; called is CC. 690. And] That H². 691. Than the] Thanne sithen the B¹, H⁷, H⁸, Ar, Ad³; Loo thanne Hn¹. 693. þat] om. B², Ash¹, Ash², Ar, CC.—Though] om. B³, L, C².—mayde] clene madye B³, L.—were] was C².—conceyved] conseyved and born C².

vi   Eke Plunius, in bokes naturell

      Wryteʒ of a Roche, grete and large also

      That will Remeove *with* a fyngre small

      But if a man do, all his might therto

      It will not stirre, nethir to ne froo

      Right so this mayde, that this of vertu moste

700   With *a* fyngre, of the holy goste

      And with a touche, of his myghty grace

      Conceyvede hath, sothefast god and man

      That neu*er* myght Remeove, from hir place

      Of thilke avowe, that she first be gan

      To be a mayde, as ferforthe as she can

      In hert and will, as any Roche stable

      That frome his grownde, is not Remeovable

694. Eke Plunius] And Plunius eke C³.—Eke] And Ash¹, H³, H⁴, Ash², Ad², Lg, C⁵, CC.—
Plunius] prominus H⁸. 695. grete and large] large and grete J. 696. will] will not CC. 697. do]
put Ash².—if] and a Ash¹.—a man] he C². —all] om. C², B², CC. 699. mayde] om. B¹, B², H⁸,
C⁵, L, Ch. 701 myghty] holy gosts CC.—myghty] holy Ar. 702. sothefast] stedfast H³, Ad²,
C⁵. 703. place] face B², B⁴, H¹, Ch, V, C², C³, B⁵, Hn¹, H³, H⁴, H², H⁵, H⁶, Ad², Lg, CC.
—from] from in C⁵. 706. wille] in wille B².

vii This Clerke also, this wyse plunius

Saythe in Tawrygge, ther is an erthe fovnde

710 That of Nature, is so vertuouse

That will cure, eu*ery* maner wovnde

Right so marye, was the erthe Ifounde

That god oute, chees by eleccion

To bere the frute, of our Redempcion

That shulde be helpe, and eke medycyne

To all our wounde3, when thay ake or smerte

And our greves, and our hurtys fyne

Fro the dethe, to make vs to asterte

With holsome bavme, perschyng to the hert

720 That shall to [helþe], sodenly Restore

Our festrede sores, that thay shall ake no more

---

708. This Clerke also] Also this clerke H⁸.—plunius] prominus H⁸.—this] this this B³.—wyse] om. L. 709. in Tawrygge ther is] ther is in Tauriche H⁶, Ash¹.—Tawrygge] trouth Ash².—erthe] roche Ash².—there] om. S, H⁸, CC. 710. That of nature] Of the nature H⁵. 711. will] it wole B¹, B², B³, B⁵, H², H⁷, Ash², CC, J, C³, Ar, Ad², Ad³, L, Hn¹. 712. was the erthe Ifounde] in vertue dide habounde B³, L; also was ther C³. 713. That god oute chees] That oute chese god H¹.—oute] hir B³, L. 714. Redempcion] saluacion C². 716. wounde3] om. C¹. 717. greves and our hurtys] hertes and our greves Ad³.—fyne] om. C¹.—And] Alle B³, L. 718. the] om. H⁸, Lg; our V.—to asterte] asterte H⁸, Lg, Hn¹, Ash². 719. perschyng to the hert] om. H⁶; sodenly converte Ash¹. 720. shall] om. H¹.—[helþe] MS D reads *helpe;* helthe now Hn¹.—to helþe] to the helthe H⁷; be helthe L. 721. shall ake] ake shalle B¹, H¹, H⁷, Ar, S, Ad², Ad³, Hu, Hn¹.—shall] om. C¹, C³, Ash¹, H², H⁶.—that] om. Co, B⁵, Ash², J.—thay shall ake] they akene shall Co, B⁵, Ash², J.

And ferthermore, this auctor can eke telle   viii   f. 29a

Withe Inne his boke, who so loke a right

To Iubit*er*, sacrede is a welle

That whan he hath, quenched his brondeȝ bryght

That eft ayen, it yeveth hem newe light

Who so luste a saye, sothe as he shall fynde

What wondre than, though the god of kynde

A myddes this well, fro fylthe of synne colde

730   Full of vertu, *with* fayre stremyꝼ clere

His loogyng toke, and his myghty holde

And thorough his grace, set it newe a fyre

W*ith* the holy goste, that with outyn werre

Thow she were colde, from alle flesshlihede

She brent in love, hatter than the glede

---

722. And] om. B¹, H⁷.—this] else this B¹.—auctor can eke] auctor gan B¹.—ferthermore] further C¹.—can eke] eke can Co.—eke] you Hn¹. 723. his] om. Lg.—loke] can loke B², CC. 724. sacrede is] is sacred B².—is] ther is C².—sacrede] a sacred well CC. 726. That eft ayen, it yeveth hem newe light B¹.—yeveth] sendith D.—newe] a newe D, Ash¹, H³, H⁴, H⁶, Ad.².—That] om. B³, L, V.—hem] om. Ar. 727. a saye] to assay B¹, C², L.—so] om. B², C¹, B⁴, H³, H⁴, S, H⁶, Lg, C⁵, J, B³, Co, V, C³, B⁵, Ash², Hu, L, H⁸, Ad², CC.—as] om. B¹, B³, C², Co, C³, B⁵, Ash¹, L, Ash², H⁵, Ad², CC, Ar.—shall] shall hit Ash¹, C¹.—sothe] the soith H⁵; the *inserted above.*—so luste] so woll C¹.—as] all H⁸. 729. A myddes] A this Ad³.—Amyddes] And Ar.—fylthe of synne] synne or filthe B², CC.—colde] colde S, H⁸. 730. *with*] were H⁸. 731. his] om. B⁴.—loogyng] longyng S. 732. And] That Hn¹. 734. Thow she were colde, from alle flesshlihede B¹.—alle] eu*ery* D.—alle flesshlihede] alkyns manheede C³; alle filthelyhode Ar. 735. brent] bent B².—the] only B², CC.

And in Falisco, as hym liste to wryte   ix

Is a well, that causithe eke of newe

Whan thay drynke oxen to be white

And sodenly forto chaunge her hewe

740   What merveile than, though the well trwe

The well of helthe, and of lyfe et*er*ne

The lorde of all so, as I can discerne

His stremes shede, into this mayde fre

To make hir whitest, as in holynesse

That bothe shulde, mayde and modir be

And eu*er*e in one, kepyng hir clennesse

With outyn chaunge, so that hir whitnesse

Ne fadith never in beaute ne in colo*ur*

Of maydenhede, to bere bothe lefe and flowre

---

736. in] om. B⁴. 738. to] om. Ad²; that Ash¹, CC. 739. forto chaunge her] changeth their Ash².—forto] to C⁵.—her hewe] newe S. 740. than] ye than H⁶; om Ar. 741. helthe and of lyfe] lyif and of helthe B¹, C⁵, Ar.—of lyfe] lyif Hu, Ash². 742. so] om. B², B³, CC. 745. mayde and modir] moder and mayde B³, Ash², L. 747. chaunge] her chaunge H⁶.—hir] om. Hn¹, H⁸.—chaunge] weem B³, L.—whitnesse] h *inserted above*. 748. ne] om. Ash², B³, L.—ne in colour] nor colour Ash². 749. Of] in H².—to bere] but to be H²; to be Co, B⁵, Ash², H⁸, J, Hu.

750 And who that will, dispute in this matier

I holde hym madde, or ellys oute of mynde

For if he haue, his eene hole and clere

He shall mow see, preef I nowe by kynde

For he that made bothe leef and lynde

And with oo worde, this waste worlde wilde

Might make a mayde, for to goo with chylde

x   And he that made, the high cristall hevyn   f.29b

xi   The firmament and also euery spere

xii   The golden axeltre, and the sterres seven

xiii   760   Cithera so lustly, for to apere

xiiii   And Reed mars, w*ith* his sterne chere

Myght he nat eke onely, for our sake

Withe Inne a mayde, of man, the kynde take

---

750. in] om. Co, Ash¹. 751. mynde] hys mynde C¹, B³, L.—or] and B³, L. 752. if] om. C².— if he haue] be that his C².—eene hole] yen it faire C².—eene] witte Hu. 753. mow see preef] inowe see thereof B², CC; and preef H¹; se preves B³, Ash¹, H², H⁶, L.—shall mow see preef] may se ensaumples C².—mow] nowe H⁵.—see preef I nowe] see ynough ther of Ar. 754. lynde] cynde B¹, B², B³, B⁴, B⁵, H¹, Ash¹, Ash², C¹, C², C³, S, Ch, Hn¹, Co.—he] om. C³. 755. wilde] wyde H¹, C³. 756. for to goo] go B¹, B², B⁵, CC, C², L, Lg, Hn¹.—goo with] to bere C¹.—for to goo with chylde] of man the kynd take H⁵.—for] om. S; so Hu.—for to] *inserted above.* 757. that] hath H². 758. euery] the even H⁸; the B¹, H¹, Ash¹. 760. Cithera] and Cithera B¹, B³, H¹, H⁷, Ash², L.—for] om. B², Ch, B⁴, Co, H¹, C², B⁵, Ash¹, H³, H⁴, H², S, Ar, H⁵, H⁶, Ad², Lg, Hu, C⁵, CC, J, H⁸, Ad³.—so] that so Hn¹.—for to] doth Hn¹. 761. And] The L. 762. he nat eke onely] not be oonly eke B¹.—eke onely] onely eke H⁸; not eke H¹.—eke] ekely Ch.—he] om. Ash¹, H⁶.—eke] om. B², H², Ar, CC; *inserted above.* 763. take] to take Ash², C¹, C².—of man the kynde] the mankinde H¹; the kynde of man C¹, C².

xv   And he that causith, fouleȝ in the eyre

                      In hir kynde, to waxe and multiplie

xvi   And fisshes eke, w*ith* fynnes syluer fayre

                      In depe wawes, to gou*er*ne hem and gye

xvii   And dothe oon lyve, *and* another dye

                      And giffith bestes, her foode vpon the grovnde

770   And in her kynde, dothe hem to abou*n*de

                      Sythen he is lorde, and causith all thyng

                      To haue beyng, if I shall not feyne

                      And is the prince, and the worthy kyng

                      That all enbraseth, in his myghty cheyne

xviii   Why myght he nat, by power souereygne

                      At his free chose, that all may save and lese

xix   To his mothir, a clene mayden chese

---

764. fouleȝ] the foules B[1], B[2], Ash[2], C[3], Ch, Co.—he that] that H[1], H[8]. 765. In hir kynde to waxe] To waxe in her kynde B[1], Ad[2].—multiplie] to multiplye H[4]; so to multiplie Hn[1].—to] for to C[1]. 766. And] The CC.—fisshes eke] eke fyshes H[7].—fynnes syluer] siluery fyness C[2]. 767. hem] om. H[2]. 768. And dothe oon lyve, *and* dye H[7].—lyve] to lyve D, Hn[1], C[2], C[3], C[1].—and] om. H[1], C[2], C[3], C[1], B[2], Ch, Ar, CC.—dye] now to dye Hn[1].—dothe] causeth C[2], C[3]; suffre Hu. 769. her] om. H[2]. 770. to abounde] habounde B[1], Ad[2], Hu.—dothe] to H[2]. 771. Sythen] Now sythen Hn[1]. 773. worthy] myghty C[3]; and] of Hu. 774. myghty] om. C[3]. 776. his] the B[1], B[2]; om. Lg, H[1]. 777. a clene] thanne a clene Hn[1].

Who causith frute, oute of the harde tree

By vertu onely, that spryngeth from the Rote

780 To growe and wexe, lyche as men may see

With levys grene, and newe blosomes sote

Is it not that lord that for our alþer bote

Wolde of a mayde, as I Reherse can

Mekely be borne, withoute touche of man

xx   For he that dothe, the tendre branches spryng

And fresshe floures, in the grene mede

That werne in wyntir dede, and eke droupyng

Of Bawme voyde, and of all lustyhede

Myght he nat make, his greyne to growe and sede

790 Withe Inne hir brest, that was bothe mayde and wyfe

Wher of is made the sothefaste brede of lyfe

---

778. frute] the frute B², Ch, B⁴, H¹, C², Ash¹, H⁴, H⁵, H⁶, Ad², Lg, C⁵, V, CC, H³.—oute] om. H³. 779. from] om. Lg.—the Rote] oute H³.—onely] om. C². 780. men] om. B¹, H⁷. 782. Is it not that lord, that for our alþer bote B¹.—Is it not that lord] Is nat he D; Also is hit not that lord H⁶, Ash¹; Hit is oure lorde C².—alþer] also alder H6, C³.—alþer bote] alther goode Lg; for all our bote Ch.—that] for all C¹. 783. Wolde] Then wold Ash².—as] mekely as Ash².—can] now kan Hn¹. 784 Mekely] om. Ash².—man] any man Ash².—touche] sede C². 785. the] om. B¹, B², H², H⁶, H⁷, H⁸, L, Lg, Ch.—branches] herbis Ash².—dothe] maketh C³; om. C². 786. the] om. B⁴. 787. droupyng] wepinge Lg. 788. all] om. Ch, B⁴, Co, H¹, B⁵, Ash¹, H³, H⁴, H², Ash², H⁶, Ad², Lg, C⁵.—of] om. H⁸. 789. Myght he nat make, his greyne to growe and sede B¹.—sede] sprede D.—to growe] om. Hu.—to] om. B², B⁴, H², CC. 790. Inne] om. H⁸. 791. brede] sone H⁸.

And he that graved of his grete myght   xxi   f. **30a**

Withe outyn poyntell, in the hard stone

And in the tables, with lett*r*es clere *and* bryght

His ten p*r*ecepteʒ and byddynges eu*er*yche one

The same lorde, of his power aloon

Hath made this mayde, here oon erthe lowe

A chylde conceyve, and no man to knawe

And he that made, þe busche to a pere   xxii

800 All on flame, w*it*h ferfull sparkelleʒ shene

When Moyses be ganne, to a proche nere

And yet no harme, came to the bowes grene

The same lorde, hath concerved clene

His habitacle, and his erbor swete

In this mayde, from all flesshely hete

792. he] om. CC, B², H².—graved] growith CC; also greveth B², H².—grete] hard CC.—of]
with H⁴.—he that] that he Ash¹. 794. And in the tables, with lett*r*es clere *and* bryght B¹.—
clere] fayre D, C¹; om. H⁶.—in] om. C⁵. 796. his] om. B¹, Ash¹. 798. conceyve] to conceyve
H², CC, B⁴.—to] om. C, B, V. 799. And he that made, þe busche to a pere B¹.—þe] that D.—
busche] bowes CC; bisshop H³.—he that] he hath H².—he] om. Ash¹, H⁶. 800. ferfull]
verry H². 801. When] And whan B², Ch, B³, B⁴, V, H¹, C², H³, H⁴, H², H⁵, H⁶, Ad²,
Lg, C⁵, L, CC, Ash¹.—be ganne] ganne B², V, Ch, B³, B⁴, H¹, C², H³, H⁴, H², H⁵, H⁶,
Ad², Lg, Ash¹. Hu, C⁵, L, CC.—to] om. Ash¹, Co. 802. came] om. H⁸.—yet] soo B³, L.—
bowes] busshes Ash¹. 803. concerved] reserved her Ash². 804. erbor] herber fulle Hn¹.

And he that made, the yerde of Moyseȝ   xxiii

Of a serpent to take the lykenesse

In the hall a monge, all the prees

Where Pharao, his people did oppresse

810   And in deserte the Byble beryth witnesse   xxiiii

The Ryver made to Rynne oute of a stoon

The thurste to staunche, of his people a noon

And ouere this, for to verefye

His grete myght, Sampson the stronge man   xxv

As Iudicum dothe, playnely specyfye

Dranke the water, that from the kanell Ranne   xxvi

And he that made, the flodeȝ of Iordan

To turne a gayne, for love of Iosue

That al his peple clerly myght see

---

806. he] om. H², H⁸. 807. to] and to H². 808. In the hall] In alle Ch.—the prees] peyres
Ch. 809. his people did] dede his peple B¹.—his] the B⁴, Ash¹, H³, H⁴, H⁶, Ad², C⁵. 810.
deserte] the desert Co. 811. a] the Ash¹, H⁵, H⁶, Lg, C⁵, CC, H³.—to] om. H³. 812. his]
the Ash¹, H³, H⁴, H⁶, Ad², C⁵.—of] oute of CC. 813. ouere this] furthermore C¹, C³; euer
more Ash², J.—And ouere this for to verefye] And ferthermore yet this Hn¹. 815. dothe
playnely] pleynly B¹, B², H¹, C⁵.—dothe] can CC.—Iudicum] Iudith Ash².—playnely specyfye]
specifie pleynly H². 816. the] of the B¹, B³, B⁵, H², H⁴, H⁷, H⁸, Ash², C³, C⁵, Ar, Ad³, L,
Hu, Hn¹, Co. 817. he] om. C³, H². 818. love] the lufe H¹, Ar. 819. That al his peple clerly
myght see B¹.—clerly myght] myght clerly D, L.—That al his peple] That his pepill all H⁸.—
his] the Ash¹, H².—al] om. B², Ash².

820 And howe the wawes, gan a sondre breke   xxvii

And like an hyll stande, high a lofte

And he that made, the Asse for to speke

To Balaham, for he Rode vn soffte

Why mygbt he not, by power previd ofte

Sithe he the yrne, made on the water hove

Be of a mayde, borne for mans love   xxviii

xxix   And he that made, an Angell for to take   f. 30b

Abacuk, by his lytyll here

And sodenly brought hym to the lake

830 In Babylone, whiche was so fer

And to visite, lygyng in his feer

Danyell a monge the bestes Rage

Till he to hym brought the potage

---

820. And] om. B¹, B⁴, Ash¹, Co, C¹, C³, B⁵, Hn¹, H², Ash², Ar, H⁸, H⁷, Ad³, J.—And howe] Now Hu.—gan a sondre] a sondur gan B¹, B⁴, Ash¹, H³; gan to sondre Lg.—the] om. H¹, B², Ch, B⁴, H¹, C², Ash¹, H⁴, H⁵, Ad³, C⁵, CC, H³, H⁶. 821. an hyll stande] a wal to stonde B³, L.—stande high] to stonde hiȝe B⁴, C², Ash¹, H⁴, H², H⁶, Ad², C⁵. 822. for] om. B¹, C², C⁵; the Ash².—he] om. H¹. 823. vn] om. Co, B⁵, Ar, Ad³; so H⁸, H⁵, H⁶, H⁷, V, Ad², Lg, C⁵, L, CC, Hu. 824. Why mygbt he not, by power previd ofte B¹.—he not] nat he D. 825. the yrne made] made the yren B¹, C², Lg.—on] in B¹, C², S, An, Lg, B³, CC, Hu. 826. of] om. B².—mans] maidys C². 827. he] om. CC.—for to] om. CC.—an] the L; om. Hu. —take] breke L.—And he] That lord H². 828. here] the prophete H².—Abacuk] The prophete Abacuk B³, L. 829. to] into H²; unto H¹.—And sodenly] Andenli H¹. 830. was] om. H⁸.— so] om. Ar. 831. And] om. H².—feer] ther B³.—lygyng] the holy prophete B³; the prophete L. 832. Rage] wode B³, L. 833. Till] Whan H².—Till he to hym brought] And brought to hym B³, L.—the] om. B³, L.—potage] potage and fode B³, L.

The dores shet, of the stronge presovne

For to asswage, of hungre al his payne

And in a moment to his mansion

Full sodenly Restored hym a gayne

Why myght he not, as wel in certeyne

The same lorde, of a mayde than

840   Take flesshe and blod, and be come man

xxx   And he that made the sonne, at Gabaon

To stonde and chyne, vpon the bryght shelde

Of Iosue, and taward Achalon

The mone also, as all the hoste be helde

xxxi   The long day, while thay faught in the felde

Agayne the kynges, of myghty Ammorie

That his people, clerly myght see

---

834. of] and H4.—shet] beynge shette B3, L.—stronge] om. B3, L. 836. in] om. H5.—a] om. B4. 837. sodenly] devoutly V. 838. Why myght he not, as wel in certeyne B1.—he not] not he D, Co.—Why myght] Whi he not myght H6.—as well as well Hu.—he not as well] as wele nat Ash1. 839. of] and of Hn. 840. Take flesshe and blod, and be come man B1.—and] to D. —Take] To take L. 841. he that] om. H7.—at] of H3, H4, Ad2, C5, CC, J; and H1, H5.—he] om. Ash1. H2. H6. 842 vpon] on B1. H7, L.—stonde] stonde still Ar. 844. as] om. H2; that Hu.—the] om. B4, Hu.—all] om. H3. 845. the] om. V, B1, B2, Ash2, C5, Hn1. Hu.—while] om. Ch, B4, Ash1, H3, H4, H6, C5. 846. myghty] om. C1. 847. That] That all Hn1.

xxxii   And he that made, the shade to Reto*ur*ne

In the orlage, of kyng Eȝechye

850   By ten degrees, only to *per*forme

The heest made, to hym of Isaye

Why myght he not, þis lord that all doth gye

Of A mayde by the same skylle

Frely be borne, at his owne wille

xxxiii   And he that fedde, *with* fyve loveȝ small

Fyve thousand, in solitarie place

Fer in desert, sittyng in a valle

Thorough the foyson, and plente of his grace

The same lorde, why myght he not purchase

860   Withe Inne a mayde, duryng hir maydenhede

Whan that hym luste, to take his manhede

---

848. shade] sonne Ash². —shade to] shadow of L.—he] om. Ar. 850. only] for C¹. 851. The] By Ch, B⁴, H¹, C², Ash¹, H³, H⁴, H⁵, H⁶, Ad², V.—made] I mayde H⁸.—to] of H⁸.—made to hym] to hym made C¹, C³.—made] that y made L. 852. Why myght he not, þis lord that all doth gye B¹.—he not] not He D, C¹.—dothe] shal B⁴, Ash¹, H³. H⁴, H⁶, Ad², C⁵; may C¹. —he] om. H².—all dothe] doth al Ash². 854. be] to be Hn¹. 855. fyve] his Ar.—he] om. H². 856. thousand] thousand folk B³.—solitarie place] litell space B², CC. 857. in] in the Co. 859. The same lorde, why myght he not purchase B¹.—he not] not he D, C¹, Hn¹. 860.] Whan that hym liste within Mary a bowre Hu. 861.] And she a mayde beyng and he owre savyowre Hu. —to] om. B³, Ash², L, J.—that] om. C².

For as the Be, dothe wax and hony shede   xxxiiii   f. 31a

At the evyn, who taketh hede therto

Right so Marye, flouryng in maydenhede

Bare in hir wombe, god and man also

And yet in sothe, she was bothe too

I dar afferme, in oo *per*son Ifer

A Mayde clene, and Cristis mothir dere

For as the beem shynyng from aferre   xxxv

870   Shedyng his light, as men may well aspye

With outyn harme, or hyndryng to the sterre   xxxvi

And so as Manna, feldou*n* fro the skye

Right so this floure, that callet is marye

W*ith* wombe halowed, in to schastyte

Conceyved hath, in hir virgynyte

---

862. the] a Ad², —dothe] both Ad², H³.—wax and] om. H⁵.—wax and hony] honey and wax
H². 863. the] om. Co.—evyn] hyve Ch, B⁴, H¹, C¹, C², C³, Hn¹, Ash¹, V, H³, H⁴, H⁵, H⁶,
Ad², Lg, C⁵.—who] who so H².—At the evyn] Out at their Ash².—taketh] that taketh CC.—
At the] And the B³. 864. in] in her B¹, H². 867. *per*son] *per*forme C².—afferme] wel say B³.
868. clene] clere B¹, B², C¹, CC. 869. aferre] sofer B¹, B⁵, H², H⁷, H⁸, Ash², J, C¹, C³, Ar,
S, Ad³, V, Hu, L, An, Ch, Hn¹, Co.—For] And B³, B⁴, H¹, C², Ash¹, H³, H⁴, H⁵, H⁶, Ad²,
Lg, C⁵.—as] om. H². 871. to] of B¹, B², B⁵, H², H⁷, H⁸, J, C³, Ar, Ad³, L, Ch, Hn¹, Co.
—or] of C⁵. 872. so] om. B², CC.—feldou*n*] fell Lg. 873. callet is] is called C².—floure] om.
Ash². 874. halowed] avowed Ash².—in to] in clene B³, L. 875. hath in] ever hathe C².

And as the Barnacle, in the harde tre   xxxvii

Of kynde bredith, and the vyne floure

Causyth the wyne, floures for to be   xxxviii

Thorough Bachus myght, and grapes gou*ernour*

880 Right so in sothe mankynde₃ savyour

As the Bernacle, or floure oute of the vyne

Spronge of marye, she beyng a virgyne

And as a worme, vndre the harde stone   xxxix

Of erthe comyth, wit*h*outyne *e*ngendrure

And as the Fenyx, of which ther is but one   xl

To asshes brent, Renuyth by nature

Right so this lorde, that all hathe in cure

Our kynde, agayne, fro synne to Renewe

Toke flesshe and blode, in this maydyn trewe

---

877. the] om. H8.—bredith] groweth B3, L.—and] as B2, CC. 878. floures] om. Ash2; for flore Co, B5.—the] om. H2, CC.—floures for to be] for to be flores J. 879. and] of B1, B5, H1, H2, H5, H7, H8, Ash2, J, C1, C3, Ad3, Lg, Hu, Hn1, Co.—and grapes] of vines B2, Ar, CC. 880. in sothe] forsothe CC; *inserted above.* 881. or] and the B4, C2.—oute] om. B4, J, C2, H1, H2.—the] om. H1.—or] and Ash1, H5, Lg, C5, CC, H3, Ad2, L, H1, H2. 882. a] om. H3, H4, H2, H8, Ad2, C5.—of marye] oute of Marye L. 883. vndre] thorough Ash1; of H2. 884. Of erthe] Of the erthe B4, C2, Ash1, H3, H4, H6, Ad2, Lg. 885. the] om. H6, L; of Ash1.—of] om. C1.—ther] om. B4. 887. all hathe in cure] hath all in his cure B1, B2, B5, J, Ar, Ad3, Lg, Ch.—this] by this C2.—lorde] om. C2, Ash2.—in cure] in his cure C1, B3, B4, Co, H1, C1, C3, V, B5, Hn1, Ash2, Ash1, H3, H4, H2, Ar, H8, H6, H7, Ad2, C5, L, CC, C2. 889. in] trewe H2.

890   And as the snawe, fro Iubiter dothe falle   **xli**

Thorough the force, of Sagitarrius bowe

And ȝepherus dothe the flores shale   **xlii**

On white blosomes, whan she dothe blowe

Right so in sothe, the grace a light lowe

Of the hooly goste, like a wynde cherschyng

A mydde this mayde, to make his dwellyng

And to the floure, ne ded noo duresse   **f. 31b**

But perfitely concervyde, hir beaute

From euery storme, of flesshely lustynesse

900   Aliche fresh of fayrenesse for to see

As by ensamples, moo than two or three

Hir to serve, as thay haue herde devyse

Whiche as me semyth, ought Inow suffice

---

890. falle] flake J; shake Ash²; avale B³, H¹, C³, L, V. 891. Thorough the force, of Sagitarrius bowe H⁷.—Sagitarrius] Saturnes D.—the] om. B¹, H¹. 892. And ȝepherus dothe the flores shale B¹.—shale] calle D; smale B³, L; shake Ash², J.—the flores] flowres the L. 893. whan] while C¹.—dothe] down C¹.—white blosomes] blossoms white H.—she] that she J. 898. concervyde] consydere L. 900. Aliche fresh of fayrenesse for to see B¹.—Aliche fresh of fayrenesse for] And euere ylike of fayrnesse freshe D, C¹, C³, Hn¹.—fresh] om. Hn¹. 901. or] and Ad³.—than two] than oone two B², CC. 902. Hir to serve as] As her to forn B¹, V, B², H¹, H⁷, H⁸, Hu, CC, C², Ar, Ad³, Lg, C¹, Hn¹.—Hir to serve as thay] As ȝe to forne C¹, B⁴, Ash¹, H³, H⁴, H², H⁶, Ad², C⁵.—serve as] forn B³, Co, C³, B⁵, Ash², L, J. 903. Whiche as me semyth, ought Inow suffice B¹.—ought] myght D, C³, H⁶.—Inow suffice] not to devise Ash¹, H⁶.—suffice] to devise B⁴, C³, H³; to suffice Hu.—me] om. B².

To all that ben grovndyd in faythe

Ageyns the fals, to stande at defence

And Right in sothe, as saint Gregory saythe

Faythe hathe noo meryte, where þat evydence

Or mans Reason, yeveth experience

But he that leveth and fyndeth no Reason

910 No kynde accorde, is worthy more gwerdon

And if that any be nowe in this place

That hath doute, or ambiguyte

Thourgh fals errour, that dothe his hert enbrace

Or ellis of malice, or Inyquyte

For to accuse the virgynyte

Of Marye playnely this is my bone

But if so be, þat he amende hym sone

---

905. the fals] falsenesse Co; falshede B², B⁴, H¹, C², Hn¹, Ash¹, H³, H⁴, V, H⁸, H⁵, H⁶, Ad², Lg, C⁵, CC, Ch.—Ageyns the fals] Against false men Ash². 909. he that] that Ash¹. 910. accorde] of a cordyng B³, L.—more] om. H⁴. 911. And if that any be nowe in this place B¹.—be nowe] nowe be D, C¹, B⁵, Ar,—And if that any be nowe] But if so that any C²; But and ther be any now Ash¹; But yf that any Ash²; But hif ther be any nowe CC; But yif any be nowe Ad³. 912. hath] hathe here inne Hn¹.—or] or any CC. 913. his] in his B⁴. 914. Or ellis] Eyther H², B², Co, C², B⁵, Ash², Ad³, L, J.—Inyquyte] of iniquyte H², V.—of] wyth foule Hn¹; om. C¹, C³.—or] other of B². 915. the] hir Ash¹.—virgynyte] pure virginity Hu; holy and clene virginity Hn¹. 916. is] is ay C³.—is] now Hn¹; om. Ash². 917. a mende hym sone] him amende sone C²; if] om. C².—þat] om. C².—hym] om. V, B⁴, Ash², Lg, J.—if so be] so it be Ash².—if] it Lg, J.

And axe mercy, for his grete offence

Of her that is, of mercy grovnde and well

920   That he of vengyaunce, haue experyence

With Ixion doun depe in hell

And þat the claper, of his distouned bell

May cancre sone, I mene his fals tunge

Be dume for euere, and neuere to be Ronge

With hym I am no better in charyte

As ye haue herde, at evyn ne at morowe

For here my trouthe, he getyth no more of me

Save Cerberus, I take hym to borowe

What euere he be, and let hym go with sorowe

930   To tantalus, his hungre to a pees

At fewe wordes, passe ouer it is an ees

---

918. grete] om. C². 920. he] om. B⁵, H⁶. 921. With Ixion doun depe in hell B¹.—depe] and depe D, C³.—and depe] om. Lg. 922. his] om. H⁸.—þat] om. L.—his] youre CC. 923. cancre] cese C³.—I] in C¹. 924. for] om. B¹, B², B⁴, H¹, H³, H⁴, H⁵, H⁶, Ash¹, Ash², CC, C², C⁵, Ad², Ch.—to] efte B², H¹, C², Ad², Lg, CC, V; aftir Ash¹.—Be dume] To be doumbe Ash²; and] om. Ash². 925. I am] om. CC.—no] om. Hn¹.—I] om. Hu. 926. As] Than B¹, B³, C³, L, J, Ash; ne] and B¹; om. Ash². 928. Save Cerberus, I take hym to borowe B¹.—to] vnto D, J, Ad³, H⁷, H⁸, Ar, Ash², Hn¹.—Save] For H¹. 929. go] om. B², B⁴, Co, H¹, C², Ash¹, H³, H⁴, H², H⁶, Ad², Hu, Lg, C⁵, CC.—go with] om. Ash².—hym go] om. B³, L. 930. To] With B³, L. 931. At fewe wordes, passe ouer it is an ees H⁷.—it] nowe it D; om. B¹, Hu.

F̲or what in sothe, vppon eny syde

    Is phebus chare, empeyryd of his light

Thowe eyen rawe, may not abyde

For to behalde, agayne his bemeȝ bryght

Right so playnely though the govndy sight

Of heretykeȝ, ne may not systeyne

For to behalde, the clennesse of this Queen

May in no syde, sothely dysencrees

940   His clere light, ne hir p*er*fyte bryghtnesse

Whose fayre stremes, shullen neu*er* cesse

Wi*th*outyn eclipse, to shyne in clennesse

For of this mayde, as bokes sayen expresse

Whan Gabryell to hevyn drewe the cooste

She Replensshed, of the hooly goste

f. 32a
Howe our lady
wente to Saint
Baptist modir
Ca° xxi°[1]

---

932. syde] wyse B⁴.—vppon] though in C³. 933. Is] His B¹.—his] om. CC. 934. Thowe eyen rawe, may not abyde B¹.—may] ne may D, J, H², Hn¹.—eyne rawe may] nerawe H⁴. 936. govndy] cloudy B², C³, CC; ungodely H⁶. 937. ne] om. Ch, B³, B⁴, H³, H⁴, Ar, Ad², Lg, C⁵. 938. clennesse] clerenesse Ash¹. 939. in] om. Ch, H².—syde] wyse Ch, H⁴, B⁴, C², Ash¹, H³, H⁶, Ad², C⁵.—sothely] om. Ar. 940. hir] om. B², H⁵.—bryghtnesse] clerenesse H¹. 941. Whose fayre stremes, shullen neu*er* cesse B¹.—shullen] ne shulde D, J, Ash², C³. 943. of] om. C³, Hn¹; sayen expresse] beryn wytnesse Hn¹, C³.—sayen] doon H⁸. 944. the] ys coste H¹.—drewe] take B⁵. 945. of] was of H², Ash², C⁵, H⁸; with B³, C³, L, CC.

---

¹first x *is erased.*

Roos vppe a noon, and oute of Naʒareth

Tawarde the Mounteyns, fast gan her high

And ther saluede, mekely Eliʒabeth

With Inne the house, of trewe ʒakarye

950   And Right furthe w*ith*, whan she dyd espye

Of Marye, the meke salutacion

And thorough hir eres whan passed was the sou*n*

W*ith*in hir wombe playnely this is no tale

For verrey Ioye, and sp*irit*uell gladnesse

The yong enfaunt, w*ith* his lymmes small

Reioysyde hym, the gospell sayet expresse

And she fulfillyd, in verrey sothefastnesse

W*ith* the holy goste, lovde gan to crye

And evyn thus, sayde vnto Marye

---

946. Roos] And rose H². 947. fast] she fast Ash². 948. ther] ther she B², Ch, B⁴, H¹, C²,
Ash¹, H⁴, H³, H², H⁵, H⁶, Ad², Lg, C⁵, CC.—mekely] ful mekely Hn¹. 949. Inne] om. Hn¹.
950. And] Thanne B¹, B², B⁵, H⁴, H⁶, H⁷, H⁸, Ash², CC, C¹, C³, Ad², Ad³, L, Lg, Ch, Hn¹.
—with] om. Ad².—she] om. L.—dyd] gan H⁸.—whan] as Ash². 951. salutacion] lovely
salutacion Hn¹; Marye] blessed Marie Hn¹.—meke] trewe C¹, C³; lowly B³, L; om. Ash², J.
952. whan] as Hn¹; om. C³, Ash¹, Ash², J; was H².—sou*n*] se sown C³, Ash¹, Ash². J.—
passed was] was passed H².—hir] the H⁸. 953. is] om. Hn¹, H³, Ash², Ad², C⁵.—no] trew C³.
954. For] Of Ash¹. 955. enfaunt] saunte B¹, H⁷, H⁸, Ar, Ad³, Lg. 956. sayet expresse] berith
witnesse B¹, H², H⁸, C³.—sayet] doth C³, H³, H⁸. 957. verrey] vertu Ash²; euery Ash¹,
H⁶. 958. lovde] and lowde H². 959. sayde vnto] said she to B²; to H¹.—sayde] saide she
Ash¹; om. Ar; she said CC.

960　Blisset art thou, amonge wymen alle

And of thi wombe, blessud the frute also

And howe to me of happe, nowe it is be fall

My lordes mothir for to comme me to

For verrye Ioye, I not what I may doo

For sothefastely, thy gretyng as I here

With Inne my wombe, my lityll child nowe here

Reioysith hym, for gladnesse as he can　　　　　　　　f. 32b

That of all woo myne hert yt dothe Releve

And blisset art thou, that firste this Ioye began

970　The worde of god, so faythefully to leve

Nowe be Right gladde, and thyne hert not meove

For al thynges, shall performet be

That ben of god, byhestede vnto the

---

961. And of thi wombe, blessud the frute also B¹.—the] be the D, C¹, C³, H⁴, H⁸, H⁶, Ad³, L, CC; is the Co, Ash¹; om. H². 962. nowe it is] is now B¹, Co; is hit now B⁵.—howe] om. Co.—it] om. Ash², Hu. 963. me to] to me B¹, B⁴, H², H⁸, L, Hn¹, Co, H², L.—comme me] come now me Hn¹.—to] untoo B⁴.—me] om. Co, H⁸. 964. I not] I wote not B², C³, CC.—I] om. Lg. 965. I here] I may hire B², CC. 966. child] om. B¹, B³, B⁵, H¹, H², H⁷, Ash¹, J, C², L, Lg.—With] Whiche Ash¹.—nowe here] doth chere B³, L.—here] stere H¹, Lg.—nowe] om. H². 967. he can] he doth never Ad².—Reioysith] And reioiceth B³, L.—for] om. L. 968. woo myne heart yt dothe] woo it doth myn hert Ash².—yt] om. H⁴.—Releve] release Ash¹.—woo myne] my woo myn Lg. 969. thou] om. H⁸.—firsthe this Ioy] this ioy first B², CC. 970. leve] beleve B³, L.—faythefully] sothfastly Ar. 971. not] om. B¹, Hu, H⁸. —thyne hert not] not thyn hert Ash², J.—and] in H⁸. 972. be] now be Hn¹.—thynges] om. CC. 973. god] om. H⁵.

Marye thenne, w*ith* full devoute entent

With loke benigne, and ful humble chere

The same houre, beyng ay pr*es*ent

Eliȝabethe, hir awne cousyn dere

With al hir hert, a noon as ye shall here

And all the accorde, and holy melodye

980   Of the holy goste, sayde in hir Armonye

Howe our lady made
Magnyficat Ca° xxxii°[1]

W ithe laude and prese my sowle magnyfieth
        Eternall lorde, both oon twoo and thre

That all hath made, and eu*er*y thyng nowe gyeth

Whiche of his myght, and bountevous pyte

Of his goodnesse, and his benygnyte

Oonly of mercy, liste to haue pleasaunce

For to considre and graciously for to se

To my mekenesse, and humble attendaunce

---

974. full] om. B[1], B[2], B[4], H[2], H[3], H[4], CC, C[5], Ad[2], L, Ch, Hn[1], Co.—entent] praiere B[2], CC.—full] a H[3], H[4], Ad[2], C[5]. 975. With loke benigne, and ful humble chere B[1].—and] and with D, C[1], C[3]. 976. ay] thanne Hn[1]. 977. cousyn dere] coseyn ful dere Hn[1]. 978. hert] om. Co. 979. holy] hool the B[1], B[2], B[5], H[2], H[7], H[8], Ash[2], CC, Hu, J, C[1], C[2], C[3], Co, Ad[3], L, Ch.—And all] And of all L.—all] om. B[2], CC.—accorde] recorde H[2]. 980. hir] om. Hn[1], H[2]. 981. magnyfieth] hes magnified Adv[1].—and] of Co.—Withe] Miche Ad[1]. 982. lorde] om. Co.—Eternall lorde] the eternal God Adv[1]. 983. nowe] om. Ad[1], B[3], L; dois Ash[1].—all hath] hath al B[5].—That] om. Hu. 984. of] om. H[2].—bountevous] grete H[6]. 985. and his] and B[1], B[3], B[5], H[2], H[7], H[8], Co, B[5], Ash[1], Ash[2], J, Ad[1], Hu, Adv[1], Ar, Ad[3], Co.—Of] And of Ash[1].—and his] and eik Adv[1].—Of] om. Co, B[5].—his] om. Co, B[5]. 986.] And riȝte anoon whan she did espye C[1], C[3], Hn[1]. 987. For to considre] And consider C[4].—graciously] gloriously Co.—and] om. Hn[1]. 988. mekenesse] meke Ad[1].—humble] mekenesse H[6].

---

[1]first x *is erased.*

Et exultauit *spiritus* meus   My spryte also, w*ith* hert and thought in fere

990   Reioysed hathe, by fulsome habundance

In god that is, my souereyne helthe entere

And all my Ioye, and all my suffisaunce

Myne hole desire, and my full sustynaunce

Within my thought, so depe he is grave

That but in hym, with oute variaunce

In Al this worlde, I can no gladnesse haue

Ouia Respexit   For he from hevyn, godely hathe be holde

Of his hande mayde, the humylite

Where of in sothe, al onely for he wolde

1000   Al kynredes, shall blisset calle me

Of whiche the thanke, o lorde be vnto the   f. 33a

W*ith* prys and hono*ur*, of e*uery* voys and tunge

Thorough Armony, and sothefast vnyte

For this Alone, be to thy name songe

---

989. in fere] entiere B[2], CC.—hert and thought] thought and hert B[5]. 990. by] with Ch, H[3], Ad[2], C[5], CC.—fulsome] ful B[3], L.—hathe by fulsome] hes with fully of Adv[1].—fulsome] grete H[6]. 991. helthe] hert Ch, B[4], Ash[1], H[3], H[4], H[6], Ad[2], An; hool Adv[1]. 992. my suffisaunce] my ful suffisaunce H[2]. 993. and my] and al my B[4], Ash[1], H[3], H[4], H[6], H[7], An, C[5].—full] hool Ash[2].—sustynaunce] sufficiaunce Hn[1], C[4].—full] om. Ch, H[2]. 994. he] om. B[2], CC.—so depe he is grave] he is so deep ingrave Adv[1]. 995. in] om. B[5]. 996. I can no gladnesse haue] no gladnes can I haue Ad[1], Ash[2].—can] may Ad[2]. 999. al onely] om. Co.— Where of in sothe al onely] Quhairfor in sot only Adv[1]. 1000. shall] save Adv[1].—calle me] call thay me Adv[1].—shall blisset] blessed shall Ash[1], CC.—me] Be Ad[1]. 1001. o lorde be vnto the] be vnto the o lord C[4].—be vnto] be it vnto B[2].—lorde] lord god Co, B[5].—o] om. B[4].—be] om. H[3].—vnto] to B[3], C[1], C[3], Hu.—be] all only be Hu. 1002. voys] hairt Adv[1]. 1003. and sothefast] of forthfast H[2]. 1004. name] om. C[2].—For] For all C[3], Hn[1], C[4].—songe] ay soung Adv[1].—to] vnto Ash[1], An; *inserted above.*—be to] to be Ar; name] onne Ar.—thy] myn Hu.

For he to me hath done, thyng*es* grete   Quia fecit in magna

Of high Renon, and passyng excellence

His grace made, so fully to me flete

For he is myghty of his magnificence

His name holy, and of most Reu*e*rence

1010   That while I leve, it shall me neu*e*re astert

With al me feithful trewe diligence

To thanke hym, w*ith a*ll my hole hert

And his mercy, most passyngly famous   Et m*isericord*ia

Fro kynne to kynne, and so dovne to kynryde   eius a p*rogen*ie

Shall thoroughe his grace, be so plentevouce

P*er*petually, that it shall p*ro*cede

And specially to hem, that loven in drede

Myne owne lorde, w*ith* hert wille and mynd*e*

To suche his pyte, shall eu*e*re spryng and sprede

1020   Of dewe Right, and neu*e*re be behynde

1005. done] om. H¹, Lg. 1006. high] grete C¹, C³, Hn¹, C⁴, Ad¹, Ash², J. 1007. so] om.
H¹, H², Lg.—made] om. Adv¹; hath maad C⁴.—me] be Ar. 1008. his] most C¹, C³, Hn¹,
C⁴, Ad¹, Ash², Adv¹, J.—of] and off Lg, H¹.—is] om. H¹. 1009. of most] most of B¹, B²,
B⁴, H¹, H², H³, H⁴, H⁵, H⁶, H⁷, Ash¹, Adv¹, C³, C⁵, Ad², Ad³, L, An, Ch, Co.—of] om.
H².—holy] is holy Adv¹. 1010. That while I leve it shal me neu*e*re astert B¹.—it shal me]
I shal it D, C⁴, C¹, Hn¹; it shall never me Hu.—That while] The whiche B², CC.—That
while I leve] Than for to leif Adv¹. 1011. With al me feithful trewe diligence B¹; W*ith* al my
trewe and feithfulle diligence D, H⁸; Hit study stylle with all my diligence Ad¹.—trewe]
om. H¹. 1012.] To trust in him with my hoill mynd and hairt Adv¹.—to] and Ad¹; hole]
om. Ad¹, L.—all] om. B², CC. 1013. And] Of Co, Hn¹, C⁴.—his] he his B², B³, H¹, C¹,
C², Ash¹, H³, H⁴, H², H⁵, H⁶, Ad², An, C⁵, Lg.—most] so H⁸; om. Lg. 1015. thoroughe] be
B¹ Ash², C⁴, Ad¹.—his] om. Ad¹, Ash². 1016. it] he Ash¹. 1017. in] and B¹, Hu—loven in
drede] dred love and drede H¹.—hem] thame thame Adv.¹. 1018. wille] worde Ad³; mouthe
Ash².—owne] gratius Adv¹. 1019. eu*e*re] om. Adv¹; ay C⁴.—pyte] mercy Ar; om. C².—To
suche] The whiche B², CC. 1020. behynde] hynde Co.—d*e*we] al C¹, C³; new Lg.—be] to be
Ash¹, Ad¹; om. Lg.

He hathe his Arme enforsede and made stronge Fecit

His dredefull myght, that men may see and knawe potenci*am* in

And provide men, they Regne not full long brachio suo

He seuerede hath and made full lowe

W*ith* all his hert, dovne fro the wheell hem throwe

For to abate hyr, Sirquydry and pryde

Or thay where war her pompe was all ou*er* þrowe

Full sodenly, and layde her boste on syde

   And myghty Tyrauntes fro her Riall see Deposuit potentes

1030 He hathe avalede, and yputte dovne

   And humble and meke, for her humylite

   He hathe enhaunsede, to full high Renovne

   For he can make a transmutacion

   Fro lowe to high, as it is sene full ofte

   And whan hym luste, the d*om*inacion

   Of worldely pompe, to falle full vn softe

1021. enforsede] he forcit Adv¹; He hathe] And als Adv¹. 1022. that] om. B¹, H⁶, H⁸, Ash², Lg, Ch.—and] or Ash².—men] om. L. 1023. they] om. B³, L.—full] to Adv¹.—they Regne] that thay raingin Adv¹.—And] How C⁴; That H².—full] om. C², Ad¹, Ar, H⁸, Ad³, Hu; so Ash², J. 1024. made] made hem B², Ch, B⁴, H¹, C¹, C², Ash¹, H³, H⁴, H², H⁵, H⁶, Ad², Lg, An, C⁵, CC.—hath] hath hem B³, L.—seuerede hath] dothe them sever Ad¹. 1025.] For all thayr by harte down he dothe them throwe Ad¹.—fro] om. Ash²; of B¹. 1026. to] om. H⁸. 1027. Or thay wher war her pompe was al ou*er* þrowe B¹.—al ou*er* þrowe] ou*er*e blowe D, H², Ad¹, Ash², J.—ou*er*] down B³, L. 1028. and] is Ad¹.—layde her boste] her bost leyd B³, L. 1029. And] The Adv¹.—Tyrauntes] potent Adv¹.—Riall] Myȝty Ch.—fro her] in ther Ad¹. 1030.] Even as he wold, he hes thame brocht lou doun Adv¹.—yputte] put them Ad¹, Ash². 1032. enhaunsede] avancit Adv¹.—to] with Ch.—full] om. Ad¹. 1033. a] and Adv¹. 1034. lowe] lowli C⁴. 1036. full vn softe] fro the lofte B³, L; ofte on softe B².—Of] And B⁵.—full] om. C⁴.—falle full] make it falle Ad¹.

Esurientes impleuit He hathe fulfillede and fostrede in her nede   f. 33b

Withe the goodes of plentyuous largesse

Hem that werne hungry, and Indigent in drede

1040 Hathe hem Relevede, of all her wrechydnesse

And he the Ryche hathe, raught from her Rychesse

Full wyde and wast, to walke vpon the **playne**

And sodenly hem plounget, in destresse

All solitarye, and let hem leve in veyne

Suscepit isrel For he his chylde chosyn of Israel

Benygnely hathe, taken vnto his grace

And of his mercy, is Remembrede well

To voyde vengeaunce, only fro his face

And humble pees, shall occupye his place

1050 And pyte, shall be feffed in his stall

And Ruthe shall, his Right so enbrace

To set mercy, above his werkes all

1037. fulfillede] fillid Co.—fostrede] suffered Ar. 1038. the] om. Ad¹, Adv¹.—of] and Adv¹.
1039. in drede] om. H².—drede] dede Ash².—in] and H⁵.—Indigent] om. H⁴, An.—werne]
om. Adv¹.—and Indigent] indigent and Adv¹. 1040. Hathe] And B¹. 1041. from her] fro hem
her Ash¹, CC.—he] om. C¹, Ash². 1042. Full] And Ash¹.—wast] om. Ash². 1043. in] into C⁴.—
hem] om. C⁵.—hem plounget] plung hem C¹, Ad¹, CC. 1044. let hem leve] lefte hem ligge
B³, B⁴, C², Ash¹, H³, H⁴, Ad¹, H⁶, Ad², Lg, An, C⁵, CC.—and] to Adv¹; veyne] pane
Adv¹.—hem] om. L. 1045. For] And Adv¹.—chylde chosyn] chosen chyld Adv¹.—his]
is a B⁴; as Hn¹; that is Ad¹; is called H⁶.—he] om. CC.—chosyn] om. CC.—of] in H³.
1046. vnto] to Co, B⁵.—his] om. Ash², J.—vnto his] to Ad¹. 1047. his] om. Ar.—is] and H⁶;
hes B¹, B², Adv¹. 1048. only] om. Ash², Ar, Ch, Co.—vengeaunce only] oonly vengeaunce
B², B⁴, Co, H¹, B⁵, Ash¹, H³, H⁴, Hu, H², Ad¹, Ar, H⁸, H⁵, H⁶, H⁷, Ad³, Ad²,
Lg, An, C⁵, CC, J; al veneaunce B³, B¹, B², L, Adv¹. 1049. pees] pepill Adv¹.—humble]
om. Adv¹.—occupye his place] seisit in his stall Adv¹. 1051. his Right so] so his right B¹,
Co, B⁵, H².—Ruthe] trouthe B², B⁴, C¹, Hn¹, C⁴, H³, H⁴, H⁸, Ad², An, C⁵, CC, Ad¹.—so]
om. Ar; so sore J, Ad¹. 1052. his werk*es*] them Ad¹.—set] sett his C², Adv¹; exalte B³, L.

Sicut locutus est

As he hathe spoken, and faythfully be hight

To our fadres, that haue bene here by fore

To Abraham, and his seede of Right

That his mercy, shall last eu*er*more

For ner his mercy, all the worlde were lore

Vnto the whiche, to make man atteyne

He hathe made mercy, our kynde to Restore

1060   And of all his werk*es,* to be souereigne

Howe our lady aftir
the birthe of saint
Iohn Baptiste reto*ur*-
nede to Naȝarethe
Ca° xxiii°[1]

A nd whan this blisset graciouce dite
     Was sayde to god, deuoutly of Marye

I fynde aftre playnely, that she

Styll in the house, abode of ȝakarye

Thre monetheȝ the gospell may not ley

And aftir that, I rede eke in certeyne

To Naȝareth, þat she went a gayne

1053. As] For Lg. 1054. here] om. B[1], B[2], B[5], H[2], H[7], H[8], Ash[2], C[4], Ad[1], Adv[1], Ar, Ad[3], Hn[1], Co, Hu.—haue been here] we haif had Adv[1].—here] ner Ad[1].—haue] om. H[8]. 1055. his] to his H[6], Adv[1], B[1], Hu; so to hys Ch. 1056. last] last for Ad[1], Adv[1].—eu*er*more] evyn and morn Ash[1]. 1057.] For without it this world had been forloir Adv[1].—ner] were not Ad[1]. 1058. make man] man make L.—Vnto] to Co, C[2], Adv[1].—make] om. H[1], Lg. 1059. our] every B[1], B[2], H[1], H[5], H[7], CC, Adv[1].—kynde] kyng H[5].—our kynde] mankynd Adv[1].—mercy] om. H[1]. 1060. And of all his werk*es,* to be souereigne B[1].—And] om. D, C[3], Ad[1], Ash[2], Adv[1].—his] oure Lg. 1061. And] om. Ash[2], C[3]. 1062. sayde to] to seyde L.—to god] om. CC. 1063. that] how that B[1], CC, Ash[1], L, C[2].—I fynde aftre] Is undyrstand CC.—aftre] om. Ash[1], L.—playnely] verrely C[2]. 1064. In the house abode] abood in the house B[1], H[1], H[6], J.—of] with H[6]. 1066. eke] om. B[1], B[2], B[4], B[5], H[3], H[4], H[6], H[7], H[8], Ash[1], CC, C[2], C[5], Ad[2], An, Ch, Co; also H[6].—aftir] all H[4].—in] om. Co, B[5]. 1067. þat] om. B[1], H[1], Ash[1], Hn[1].—went] returned Hn[1].—she] om. H[1].

---

[1]first x *is erased*

And ther abode, in contemplacion

And on hir prayere, all waye day by day

1070   With many an holy meditacion

To queme hir lorde, in what she can or may

Fro whome hir thought, went neuere a way

Hir fulmynde ner hir Remembraunce

For but in hym, she hadde no pleasaunce

In al this worlde, for no manere thyng   f. 34a

For all hir Ioye was on hym to thynke

What euere she dyd, prayeng or worchyng

No thyng but he, myght in hir hert synke

For fynally whedir she wake or wynke

1080   Amyddes hir hert, he was all way present

So fixe on hym, was sette her hole entent

1070. holy] om. H¹; holy devout Hn¹.—an] om. Ash², Hu. 1071. queme] plese B¹, B³, H⁶, L, Ch.—she] om. Ch. 1072. went] om. Lg. 1074. no] hir H⁶; *inserted above.*—For but] Euir H⁶. 1075. manere] maner of L, CC. 1076. on] of B¹, B², B³, B⁴, B⁵, H¹, C¹, C², C³, Ar, Ch, Hn¹, Co. 1078. hir] om. H⁷, Ad³.—in hir] he myght Ash¹.—myght] om. H⁸.— hert] myȝt H²; om. Ash¹.—synke] spring Ash². 1079. For] om. B¹, B³, H², H⁴, H⁶, Ash²; And Ash².—wake or wynke] ete or drynke B³, L.—whedir] wher that H², H⁶.— wake] did wake H⁶. 1081. fixe] fast B¹, B², H⁸, Ash², CC.—her hole] al her Ash².

And day by day, this hooly life she ledde

This p*er*fite mayde, thorough high devocion

So feruent loue, vnto god she had

Ther may be made no deuysion

For she sequestrede, hir opynnyon

Fro all the worlde, and let it playnely gon

So hole to god, she gaffe hir hert alone

And euere in love, she brent more and more

1090   Towardes god, in his high s*er*uyce

Was all hir lust, w*ith* hert set so sore

All erthely thyng, she fully dothe dispise

And day by day, hir wombe gan to Ryse

Thoroughe the fulfillyng of the holy goste

Ther in by look, whom she loved moste

1083. p*er*fite] holy Ash². —high] her Ash². 1084. vnto] to B², H⁸, CC.—feruent] grete H⁶.
1085. no deuysion] thereof no mencion Ash².—Ther] To her C¹, C³, Hn¹.—deuysion]
comparison Hn¹.—made no] no up C³.—be] om. B³, L. 1086. hir] al her Ash².—sequestrede]
maid suyr H⁶.—she] om. H¹. 1087. let it] late H¹, Lg. 1088. to god] her herte H².—hir
hert] to god H². 1089. And] For H³, H⁶, B⁴, Ad², An, C⁵.—love] oone Hn¹. 1090. in his]
and in Ash².—god in] her god Hn¹. 1091. hert set] here herte Co.—set so sore] om. C².
1092. fully] om. B¹, H², L, An.—she fully] that she B³.—All erthely] That all H².
1093. gan] he gan B¹, B², H⁶, H⁸, Ash², CC, C², Ad³, L, Ch.—wombe] devocyon H⁶.
1094. the] om. B¹, B², H², Ash², CC, L, Hu.—fulfillyng] workyng H⁶. 1095. Ther in by look]
In Ihesu H⁶.—whom] whan H⁴, An.—Ther in] whit hym C¹, C³.

This meane while, Iosephe ay soyo*ur*nede

    In Galile god wote ful Innocent

Of al this thyng, and why he nat Reto*ur*nede

Was for that, þat he was so diligent

1100 In Caphernam with his full entent

Sondry werk*es,* of mervylous enp*ri*se

By Carpentrye, to forgen and devyse

For in that Crafte, passyng excellence

He had in sothe, and high discrecion

And was hadde, in moste Reuerence

Of all the werke men, of the Region

And for he had in conyng, suche renon

Lyke a maistir, ther is no more to saye

The werke men all, his byddyng dyd obeye

Howe Ioseph
retornyd to Naȝareth
and was in man*er*
doutefull when he sawe
Marye with childe
Ca° xxiiii°

1096. soyo*ur*nede] savyowr L.—ay soyo*ur*nede] did tary ful dilgent H⁶. 1098. Reto*ur*nede] the present H⁶.—al] om. B², CC.—and] om. B², CC. 1099. for that] om. Hu, B¹, B², B⁴, H¹, Ch, CC, Lg.—þat he] he B⁴, H¹, Lg, V.—he was] he H¹, Lg.—for that] that for B², C¹, CC. 1100. Caphernam] carpentrye B¹, B², B³, B⁴, B⁵, H¹, H⁶, H³, H⁴, H⁵, H⁷, H⁸, Ash¹, V, CC, C², C⁵, Ad², Ad³, L, Lg, Ch, Hn¹.—his full] all his Ash², Co, C¹, C³, H².— full] hole B³, L.—In] om. Co, C¹, C³, H², Hu. 1102. to forgen] craft to forgen C³; to ardeyne H².—devyse] to devyse B², H⁶, CC. 1103. that] om. H¹; this Ad², An, C⁵. 1104. and] om. B¹, H⁷, H⁸, C², Ar, Ad³. 1105. hadde in] y hadde B¹.—in moste] most in Hu. 1106. the] that B¹, Hu.—the Region] all that region H⁸.—all] om. Co, B⁵.—of the] in the Ar. 1107. renon] perfyt H⁶. 1108. ther is] the trouthe H⁶.—no more] om. H⁶. 1109. his byddyng dyd' obey] dede his biddynge obey B¹, B², H⁶, C¹, Ar.—the werke men] they weryn C¹.—dyd] to C¹.—his] om. Ar.—The werke] for the H⁶.

1110 And whan he had, all his werke achevede   f. 34b

He is Repayred, to Naȝareth agayne

But lorde howe he was, in his hert a meovede

Whan that Marye, he hath *with* childe sayne

That for astonyde, he noot what he myght sayne

And at his hert, it satte so Inwardely

Tyll at the laste, he abrayde sodenly

And sayde alas, howe, is it falle of newe

In myne absence, or what thyng may this be

Sythen this mayde, so faythfull and trwe

1120 Is with chylde, and god wot not with me

That some tyme had, avouede chastyte

And to my kepyng, eke delyuered was

What shall I say nowe of this soden case

1110. all] om. H8.—achevede] ydon H6. 1111. Repayred to] to Nazareth repayred Ar.—agayne] anon ayen H2.—is] hym Hn1.—is Repayred] went in H6. 1112. his] om. H1, H2, H8, Ash2.—was] om. Ash2.—howe] om. B2, CC.—lorde] God H6.—howe he] wot how H6.—a meovede] ysett H6. 1114. That] om. B4, H6, H2; And B5.—he noot] om. C2.—what he myght] nyst what to C2; nat whatto C1; what to H2; to whom complayn B3, L.—noot what] that he note H2; wyst not H6. 1115. its satte so] was stonyd Hn1.—And] Growid H6; For H2; So B4, H1, H3, H4, H5, Lg, An, C5, CC, V; Atte B3, Co, C1, C3, B5, Ash2, L.—at] om. B3, Co, C1, C3, B5, Ash2, L.—it satte] om. H6. 1116. at the] he at B5.—he] om. B5.—Tyll at the laste] And tharin Hn1.—sodenly] and seyde sodeynly Hn1. 1117. falle of] be falle B1, B4, H1, H3, H4, H5, H6, H8, Ash1, C1, C5, Ad2, L, An, Lg, Ch, Hn1, Co.—is it] hit is Ch, B4, Co, C1, Hn1, Ash1, H3, H4, Lg, L, H8, H5, Ad2, An, C5.—newe] me H6. 1118. may this] it may H1. 1120.] "And god wote not by me" is with child H2.—with me] by me V, B1, B3, B4, B5, H2, H5, H7, H8, C2, C3, Ar, Ad3, Hu, L, Lg, Hn1, Co.—Is] I H8.—and] om. H8.—not] om. B4. 1121. some tyme] whilom Ash2. 1122. eke] also H6; om. H4, An. 1123. nowe] om. B1, V.

What shall I answer, my self to excuse

Vnto the Bisshopp, if he me apose

For eythyir moste I, playnely hir acuse

Or ellys my self, w*ith* this gilte enoyse

This thyng is opyn, I may it nat enclose

O blissefull god, so do me nowe this grace

1130   Oute of my breste, my woofull gooste to Race

For certis lorde, and it were thy wille

I had leu*ere* vtt*er*ly to dey

Than thorough my worde, this mayden forto spille

As I muste nedes, if I hir be wrye

And on my self, if I the charge ley

For to afferme, she conceyved hath by me

I must accuse, hir vowe, of chastyte

1124. answer] say Ash².—self] lyf H², Hu. 1125. apose] now oppose Hn¹. 1126. acuse] to accuse H⁸.—playnely] om. B², CC.—playnely hir] her playnly H².—eythyir] om. Co.—moste I] I muste Hn¹, C². 1127. ellys] om. B¹, Hu, V.—self] gilte B⁴, H¹, H⁶, Ash¹, H⁴, Ad², Lg, An, C⁵; lyf H².—enoyse] suppose H⁶.—Or ellys] Outher Ash²; Of this C²; Of my gilte H³. 1128. it nat] not it B¹, Ash¹, J, CC, C¹, C³, Ar, L, An, Ch, Hn¹.—enclose] close B², C¹, C³, CC, Ash¹.—it] om. Ar.—I may it nat] it may not be kept Ash¹. 1129. blissefull] blessed B², CC.—nowe] om. B², CC.—so] om. Ch, Co, B⁵. 1130. to] om. B¹, B², B⁴, B⁵, H², H³, H⁴, H⁷, H⁸, Ash¹, CC, C⁵, Ad², Ad³, An, Ch, Hn¹, Co.—my] thys Ch, B⁴, Ash¹, H³, H⁴, Ad², An, C⁵.—gooste] herte B², CC.—gooste to Race] arose Co. 1131. and it] yf hit C¹, H². 1132. to dey] for to dey B³, Ash¹, L.—vtt*er*ly] now here utterly Hn¹. 1133. forto] to B¹, B², H², Ash², CC, C², C³, Ar.—this mayden forto] utterly to Ash². 1134. hir be wrye] the charge leye B¹.— As I] And I B³, B⁴, L.—hir be wrye] to her be trewe H⁶.—hir be] now hir Hn¹.—nedes] om. Ash².—if I] om. CC. 1136. she conceyved] that she H⁶.—conceyved hath] hath conceyved Hn¹, Ash².—afferme] sey C². 1137. hir vowe] nede her Hn¹.

And so my self apeche of vntrouthe

Sith I in sothe, did hir neu*e*re knawe

1140   O blissefull lorde, haue on this matier Routhe

For vtterly my wit is brought so lowe

To se corne growe, where noo sede is sowe

And Reason also, plattly can I noon

Howe a mayde, *with* childe shulde thus goon

And floure furthe in her virgynyte   f. 35a

I neu*e*re saw, ne neu*e*re yet dede Rede

And thus in doute, my Reason can not se

How *þat* marye, hath kepyd hir maydynhede

In myne absence, and thus in dovble drede

1150   My witte is brought, and wote not wherto turne

For double cause, that I haue to morne

1138. apeche] speche An. 1139. did hir] ne did her Ash²; I did H³, Ad².—I] om. Ad², H³.—
in] of H². 1140. blissefull] blessud Ar.—O] om. H².—this] om. H¹. 1141. my wit is brought]
is brought my witt B¹, H².—For] That H². 1142. is] was B¹, B², B³, B⁴, B⁵, H¹, H², H³,
H⁴, Ash¹, CC, C¹, C², C³, L, Ch, Hn¹, Co.—sede] om. C¹.—no sede is] is no sede B⁴, L. 1143.
can I] I can Hu, B¹, B², B³, B⁵, H², H⁵, H⁷, H⁸, CC, C², C³, Ar, Ad³, L, Co. 1144. thus]
so B¹, H⁷, B⁵, H², H⁵, H⁸, Hu; om. B², V, B⁴, Co, H¹, Hn¹, H³, H⁴, H⁶, Ad², An, C⁵,
CC, J, B³, L, Ash¹, Ash², Lg, Ch.—childe] a childe Ash¹.—*with* child shulde] shulde with
childe B³, L; shall thus with child C¹, C³.—a] that a Ch, Ash², Lg. 1145. And floure furthe
in her virgynyte B¹.—in her] thus in D, C¹, C³. 1146. I neu*e*re saw, ne neu*e*re yet dede rede
B¹.—yet] om. D, B⁴, C¹, C³, Ash², J. 1147. my] om. B¹, B², H², H³, H⁷, Ash², L, Lg, Hn¹.
—not] to Lg. 1148. *þat*] om. C², Ash¹, H⁶. 1150. not] neuer H⁴, C⁵, H⁶, Ad², Lg, An.
1151. that] and perforce Hn¹.—haue to] haue here H⁵.—haue] have now Ch, B³, B⁴, H¹, C²,
Ash², H³, H⁴, H⁶, Ad², Lg, An, C⁵, L, V.

That oon is this, þat my fantesye

May neu*e*re accorde, that she dyd offence

And Reason playnely, agaynewarde dothe denye

And vpon kynde, growndyde is sentence

To preve sothely, wi*th*outyn Resistence

That neu*e*re woman, in natures sight

Wi*th*oute man, a chylde conceyve myght

And withe that worde, he brast oute forto wepe

1160 Lyche as he shulde, al in teres drowne

And for the constreynt, of his sighes depe

Stode on the poynte, to haue fallen downe

His soden woo, made hym all moste swone

So for distresee, this Iosephe fer in age

Of Inwarde thought, caught was in a rage

1152. this] that B⁵, Ash².—þat] that of Hn¹. 1153. she] om. H¹.—that] om. Ash². 1154. playnely ayaynewarde] ayeward playnely H⁴, H².—ayaynewarde] om. Ar. 1155. growndyde] prevyse B⁵; growth H³. 1156. wi*th*outyn] with H⁸.—sothely] sothe H.—To preve] That is to say B⁵.—Resistence] existence Ash¹, H⁶. 1158. Wi*th*oute] With Co, Hn¹.—a] om. Ash¹, H³, H⁴, Ad². 1159. forto] to B¹, Ash¹, CC, C³, Ad³, Hu.—withe] at B⁵. 1160. shulde] wolde H¹, H³, An, Hu.—in] to Co.—al] om. B⁵. 1162. to haue] for to haue B⁴, H¹, Ch, Ash¹, H³, H⁴, H⁶, Ad², Lg, Hu, An, C⁵.—the] om. B³, L. 1163. made hym] almost made him B¹, B³, CC, L.—swone] to swone B³, CC, L. 1165. So] And so Lg. 1165. caught] cast B², CC.—was] om. B², CC.

A
nd whan the maydens, that weren aye p*r*esent

  And eure in one, abydyng on Marye

Vndirstondyng what that Iosephe ment

All at onys, they be gan to crye

1170 And sayde Iosephe, leve this fantasye

And thyne erroure, for it is folye

W*i*thoutyn avyse, to deme sodenlye

For certenly, w*i*th all our hert entyer

Of knowlegyng, in verrey sykernesse

We will Recorden, eu*er*ycheone in fere

All opynly, touchyng hir clennesse

And ther vpon, beren opynly witnesse

Lyke as we knowe, vnto this same daye

Though all the worlde, at ones wolde saye naye

Howe the maydens
that wer attendaunt
to our lady com-
forted Iosephe Ca°
xxv^{to 1}

1166. aye] om. Hn¹.—that] om. B⁴, H³, H⁴, C⁵. 1167. on] with Ash¹. 1168. Vndirstondyng]
And undirstoden B², Ch, B⁴, H¹, Ash¹, H³, H⁴, H⁵, H⁶, Ad², Lg, An, C², C⁵, V, CC; When
they understode C²; Haue understode B³, L.—that] om. Hu. 1169. Al] Thanne alle Hn¹.
1170. sayde] om. B¹, H², Ash¹, Ash², Hn¹.—leve] let be H², Ash².—Iosephe] to Ioseph Hn¹.
1171. is folye] is all H².—is] it is H¹.—erroure] foule errour Hn.¹. 1172. to] for to C¹, Ash².—
sodenlye] so H², L; now thus Hn¹. 1173. certenly] hertely H⁸. 1174. in] of B¹, B², B³, B⁴,
B⁵, H¹, CC, C¹, C², C³, Ar, Ch, Hn¹, Co.—Of] And Ar. 1176. hir] to her B¹, B². 1177. ther]
here Ash¹, H⁴, An.—beren] here Ash¹, H⁴, An. 1178. vnto] vn Hn¹.

¹first x *is erased.*

1180   For we in sothe thourgh bysy diligence

Haue been with hir, bothe day and nyght

And neue*re* partyde, oute of hir p*re*sence

But euer in oon, of hir had a sight

And late and erly, wi*th* all our full myght

On hir awayted, wi*th*outyn wordes moo

That fro our sight, she dydde neu*ere* goo

And eue*re* houre, bothe tyde and tyme

Of vs ther was, no dyvysion

And all the day, fro the self prime

1190   She neu*ere* stynte, of high deuocion

To be in prayer, and in oryson

And iche a day, be continuaunce

A certeyne houre, she hadde daliaunce

1182. neu*ere* parted] parted neuer Ash². —p*re*sence] right Ash². 1183. of hir had] hadde of her B², Ch, B³, B⁴, H¹, C³, Hn¹, Ash¹, H³, H², Ash², Ar, H⁵, Ad³, Lg, An, L, CC, J. —in oon] more hadden C². —a] om. H⁸. —in] om. B⁵. —hir] us B⁵. 1184. all] om. B¹, B², H⁷, Ash². 1185. On] Of H². 1186. That fro our sight, she dydde neu*ere* goo B¹. —dydde neu*ere*] neu*ere* dydde D, Lg, Hu. 1188. dyvysion] kynnes devysion B¹, B³, H⁷. 1189. day fro the self prime] morwe tide til the hiӡe prime B⁴, H¹, C², Ash¹, H³, H⁴, H⁵, H⁶, Ad², Lg, An, C⁵, CC; morow tylle the hyӡ prime Ch; morow tyde till tyll the hye pryme B². 1190. of high] from her B¹, B², B³, B⁴, B⁵, H¹, Ash¹, CC, C¹, C², C³, Ch, Hn¹, Co. 1191. be in] ben ben B⁴. —and in] eke in Hn¹. 1192. And iche a day, be continuaunce B¹. —iche a] eu*ery* D, Co. 1193. daliaunce] of daliaunce Ash¹, H², H⁶; a dalyaunce Ad², C⁵.

With holy Angels, that *with* hir knelyd or stode

And at oo tyme, thorough godd*es* purvyaunce

Of his hande, she tooke hir holy foode

As nedefull was, vnto hir sustinaunce

And this in sothe, hath ben hir gou*er*naunce

As we ycheone, of hir can Recorde

1200   Wherefore Iosephe, this lyfe dothe not accorde

In sothefastnesse, to thyne opynyon

That so mysdemys, of this mayde fre

Of fantasye, or false suspecion

For to acuse, hir virgynyte

Of whiche thyng, we dar assure the

That no wyght made, sothely to devyse

But the holy goste, hir wombe to aryse

1194. or] and Ar, H[6].—holy] certen B[5].—hir] om. H[8]. 1195. And] om. Ash[1].—thorough] hir B[5]. 1196. his] theyr B[3], L.—she tooke] marde she B[2]. 1197. As nedefull was, vnto hir sus-tinaunce B[1].—vnto] to D, B[2], Co, C[2], C[3], B[5], CC; to hir ful Hn[1]. 1198. this] these B[2].—hath] om. CC. 1199. As] And B[1], B[2], Ash[2], CC, Hn[1].—can] take B[1], B[2], Ash[2], CC, Hn[1].—hir] us Hu. 1200. dothe] can B[2], CC. 1201. to] of B[4], Ad[2], An, C[5].—to thyne] now to Hn[1]. 1203. false] of false C[1], H[2], H[8], C[5].—Of fantasye or] O falst of Ash[1].—or false] or els false H[1].—fantasye] lewde Hn[1].—suspecion] inspection Hu. 1204. hir virgynte] nowe her clene virginite Hn[1]. 1205. we dar] now we Hn[1]. 1206. made sotheley] sothly made B[2], CC.—no wyght] to no C[1].—sothely to] sothfastly Ash[2]. 1207. the] om. H[1].—to] made to C[1].—the] that Ash[2].—hir wombe] maketh her Ash.[2]—to] for to B[2], Ch, Hu, B[4], Co, Ash[1], H[3], H[4], H[8], H[5], H[6], H[7], Ad[3], Ad[2], Lg, An, C[5], CC, J, H[1].

And here vpon, we recorde can

Of all the tyme, thou were in Galile

1210   She neuere alone, was with no man

And what she spake, we myght here and see

Wherefore Iosephe, late thees taleȝ be

And deme nought amys, in worde ne in thought

For all this thyng, by god*es* hande is wrought

And by his Angels, com*m*yng on message

Is this thyng, fully brought a boute

Therfore Ioseph, latt thyne Ire asswage

And of Marye, be nothing in doute

Certys quod he, I may not voyde oute

1220   My fantasye, to assent in any wyse

It shulde be, liche as ye devyse

1208. can] al kan Ash². —we] as we Hn¹.—recorde] alle recorde H². 1209. thou were] she was Ash¹; we wer Ar. 1210. no] eny B³, L.—with no] yt wyth Hn¹.—alone was] was alone Lg.—with no] not with J. 1211. what] om. Hn¹.—she] we H⁴.—spake] dede B³, L. 1212. late thees] nowe lete al these Hn¹. 1213. And deme nought amys, in worde ne in thought B¹.—ne in] ne D, Co, B⁵, Ash², J. 1214. this] om. Ash². 1216. Is] om. H¹.—fully] now thus Hn¹.—Is this thing fully] This thyng is now fully H². 1217. thyne] all thyn Hn¹.—Ire] sorwe B³, L. 1218. And of Marye, be nothing in doute B¹.—be nothing] ne be no more D, H⁷, Ash², J, Ad³, L, Co. 1219. oute] hȝt oute Hn¹. 1220. to] om. Ash¹.—My] Of my Hn¹.—in any] now in no Hn¹.—to assent] cease H². 1221. It shuld be, liche as ye devyse B¹.—It] That it D, C¹, C³, H², Hn¹; How it Ash².—shulde] myght ever Hn¹.—ye] ye now Ch, B⁴, H¹, C², Ash¹, H³, H⁴, H⁵, H⁶, Ad², Lg, An, C⁵, Co, V.

For by an Angell, it were inpossible

Hir to conceyve, lyke as ye expresse

But if it so were, if it be credible

Som wyght by sleyght, takyng the lyknesse

Of an angell, thorow fraudelent falsnesse

Thorough Innocence, shortly to conclude

By engyne of fraude, hir yougth to delude

And efte agayne, for his Inwarde payne

1230   He gan to chaunge, bothe face and huwe

And from his eyne, the salt tereʒ Reyne

Lyke as he wolde, drowne hym self of newe

So sore he gan, in hert for to rewe

For this matier, that for his mortall woo

He can noo Rede, ne wote what he may doo

1223. expresse] witnesse B³, B⁴, H¹, C², H³, H⁴, H², H⁶, Ad², B², Ch, CC, V, Ash¹, Lg, An, C⁵, L; om. C³.—Hir] Sche Hu.—lyke] om. B², Ch, CC.—conceyve] touche Ash¹. 1224. But if it so were, if it be credible B¹.—But if it] But it D, L, J, B³, Co, H², Ash², Ar, H⁸, H⁵, H⁷, Ad³, C¹, C³, Hn¹.—if it be] it were C¹, C³, CC.—if it so] if so Ash¹.—if it so were if it be] hyt were that hyt be now Hn¹.—if it be] that it be Ash¹, H¹. 1225. the] om. C¹.—Som wyght] So with Ash¹.—takyng] to take Ash¹. 1226. Of an angell, thorow fraudelent falsnesse B¹.—thorow] by D, Co, B⁵, C¹, C³.—an] om. H². 1227. Thorough Innocence] Of apparens C²; thorough myne H⁴.—Thorough] Hir Ash². 1228. engyne] gyle Hn¹, C¹, C³.—yougth] om. C¹; though Ar. 1230. He gan to chaunge, bothe face and huwe B¹.—bothe] bothe his D, C¹, C³. 1231. salt tereʒ Reyne] fast teres dyde reyne C¹. 1232. of] as Ash¹. 1233. So sore he gan, in hert for to rewe H⁷.—hert for] his hert D.—for] om. B¹; hym for Hn.¹. 1234. that] and Ash¹, H⁶.—his] om. H¹.—for] on L. 1235. wote] not B¹, B², B³, H⁴, H⁷, H⁸, CC, C¹, C³, Ar, Ad², L, Ch, Hn¹.—what he may doo] not what he shall do B², CC; why fer he schal go Hn¹.—he may] whatto C¹, C³; for to B³.

And in his hert, he caste many a waye

To have founden Refute, w*it*h all his full mynde

And thought all waye, he wolde hir not be traye

For he was Rightfull, playnely as I fynde

1240   And thus he gan, in sondry thoughteȝ wynde

As in balaunce, pu*r*posede uppe and downe

Tyll at the last, in conclusion

He fully pu*r*poseth, and caste hym vtterly

To gone his waye, shortly if he myght

And thought he wolde, forsake hir p*r*ively

And neu*er*e more to come in hir sight

Till an Angell, on the same nyght

Sent downe from god, to Ioseph dyd apere

Whyle þat he slepte, and sayde as ye shall here

1236. And] For B¹, B², B³, B⁴, B⁵, H¹, H⁷, H⁸, C¹, C², C³, C⁵, Ar, Ch, Hn¹, Co.—in] om.
H⁸. 1237. full] om. H².—his] om. H⁸—have] om. J. 1238. hir, not] not her B¹, B², H⁵, H⁶,
Ash¹, Ar, C¹, C², L, Hn¹.—all waye] om. Ash¹.—wolde] nold Ar.—not] om. Ar.—he wolde]
that he H⁶. 1239. playnely] in scripture C². 1240. gan] om. C². 1241. in] in a L.—As] om.
Co, B⁵, Ash², J.—pu*r*posede] fer passed Co, B⁵, Ash², J.—uppe and downe] upon Hu. 1242.
Tyll at the last, in conclusion H⁷.—in] in full D, C¹, C³, Ar. Hn¹; in short B¹, Ash². 1243.
He fully pu*r*poseth, and caste hym vtterly B¹.—fully] om. D, C¹, C³.—vtterly] fulle H¹.
1244. shortly] fastely C¹; sothly B⁴, H³, H⁴, Ad², An, C⁵.—if] as Lg. 1245. he wolde] all-
ways he wolde J. 1246. And neu*er*e more, to come in hir sight B¹.—more to come] to come
more D, Hn¹, C¹, C³.—And] om. Ash², J. 1247. Till] And thanne Hn¹. 1248. downe] om.
C². 1249. Whyle] As C².—þat] *inserted above.*

Howe the Angell 1250
warnede Ioseph
to byde *with* our lady
Ca° xxvi°[1]

O thou Ioseph, ne drede the not blyve   f. 36b

Thou son of Dauid, of lyne by discent

For to take marye, vnot thy wyve

Whiche is a Mayde, w*ith* all hir full entent

With whome is ay, the holy goste *pr*esent

Of whome is all, I tel it the be forne

In verrey sothe, that shall of hir be borne

And like sothe, as wryteth Crysostomus

Of this matier, that for cause3 thre

Vnto Ioseph, as he tellyth vs

1260   The Angel cam, and first he sayde þat he

Sythen he was Rightfull, þat in no degre

Of purpose Rightfull, he shulde vnrightfully

This holy mayde, forsake pryvely

1250. not] om. H6.—ne] om. B3, B5, L.—blyve] now blyve Ash2, J. 1251. Thou son of Dauid, of lyne by discent B1.—of line by] by lyne D; by lyneall C3; by line of B3, L, Co, B5, Ch.—son of] the son of C2, C5. 1252. vnto] to Hn1, H5, Ch, B4, H1, C2, H3, H4, H6, Lg, An, C5.—thy] om. J.—marye] now Marie Hn1. 1253. full] hole B3, L.—Mayde] clene mayde Hn1. 1254. is ay] om. H4, An.—present] is ay H4, An. 1255. it the] ye hit H8; om. Hn1.—it] om. Ad3.—all] ay H3, H4, H6, Ad2, Lg, An, C5. 1256. that] om. B1, B2, H4, H7, H8, Ash2, Ar, Co.—borne] beforne H4.—that shall] of her Ash2. 1257. in sothe] om. Ash2.—sothe] sothenesse Hu. 1258. that] as Ad2; om. H3, Ash2.—Of this] wel of Hn1. 1259. he tellyth vs] telleth the gospel us Hn1. 1261. he] that he H3, Ad2, An, C5, Ash1. 1263. pryvely] now Hn1.

---

[1]first x *is erased.*

A nothir cause, he wrytyth eke expresse

That his forsakyng, myght vnto hir name

Be dishonour, and cause in sothefastnesse

Of vntrwe tungeȝ, for to speke hir shame

All though in hir, there was no spotte of blame

Suspecion to voyde, on eu*er*y ayther syde

1270   The Aungel bad þat Ioseph sholde abyde

The thryd cause, and also most trewe

Was for that he, *with* most diligence

Shulde hir kepe, when he the sothe knewe

That she was clene, w*ith* oute all offence

And wist playnely, þat by magnyfycence

Of the holy goste, his errour to enchase

Conceyved hath, this mayde full of grace

1264. eke] here B[1], H[7], H[8], Ad[3], Ch, Hn[1]; om. C[1], Ad[3].—A nothir] And anoþer Hn[1].—he wrytyth eke] eke he dothe H[8]. 1265. Vnto] to B[1], B[2], B[4], B[5], H[1], H[2], H[3], H[4], H[5], H[6], H[7], H[8], Ash[1], Ash[2], C[2], C[5], Ar, Ad[2], Ad[3], An, Lg, Ch, Hn[1], Co, Hu. 1267. tungeȝ] thynge H[8].—vntrwe tungeȝ] oune trewe tokenes Ash[1].—Of] om. Ash[2], J; To H[2].—hir] of her H[2]. 1268. All] And Hn[1], Ad[3], Lg, L.—there was] be C[2]. 1269. on eu*er*y ayther] of never neyther B[1], H[2], H[7], H[8], Ash[2], J, Hu, C[1], C[3], C[4], Ar, Ad[3], Hn[1].—eu*er*y] om. H[2].—Suspecion] But all Hn[1].—ayther] om. Hn[1], Ch, C[3], Ash[2], J. 1270. The Aungel bad þat Ioseph sholde abyde B[1].—The] Thus The D; And the C[1], C[3]; They Lg.—þat] om. Co, B[5]. 1271. The thryd cause, and also most trewe B[1]. —and also] also and C, J; is also H[7]; also that Hn[1].—cause] due cause Ash[2].—most] riȝt C[2]. 1272. most] more B[1], Hu.—that] more Hn[1]; with more B[2], CC.—for] om. Ch, CC, B[2], B[4], H[1] Ash[1], H[3], H[4], Ar, H[6], Ad[2], Lg, An, C[5]. 1273. the sothe] hir Ash[1]; sothe B[4], H[8].—the] that Hn[1].—he] om. C[1]. 1274. all] more C[1]; any H[2]. 1275. þat by] by that B[1], H[8], Ash[1], C[1], C[2].—þat] om. C[1], Ash[1], H[8].—playnely] surly C[2]. 1277. hath this] this mayde Co.—this] om. C[2].

And whan þat Iosephe, abrayde oute of his slepe

And in hir hert, by Reuelucion

1280 Gan for to cast, and to take kepe

Ayenst the morowe, of his avysyon

And caught comfort, and consolacion

Of all that eu*ere*, he was to forne dispayrede

And to Marye, he agayne repayrede

And thanketh god, w*ith* all his hole hert   f. 37a

That he is to hym, so graciously

In Recomfort of his Inwarde smerte

His grete myght hathe, declared opynly

And of marye, full benyngly

1290 He axed mercy, of humble affection

That eu*ere* he had, to hir suspecion

1278. whan] om. B¹, B², Ash², C², An.—abrayde] at last C².—and] om. Ash².—oute] om. Ash², Hu. 1279. by Reuelucion] thanne caste Hn¹. 1280.] And bygan bysyly for to take good kepe Hn¹.—for] om. B¹, Hu.—to] om. H⁸. 1281. Ayenst] Erly on C¹, C³, Hn¹.—the] om. Ash², J. 1282. And] He C¹, Hn¹, Hu.—consolacion] conclusioune C¹.—comfort and] thanne comfort Hn¹. 1283. eu*ere*] om. C¹.—that eu*ere*] afore that B⁵.—to forne] om. B⁵. 1284. And to Marye, he agayne repayrede B¹.—he] he is D, B³, C¹, C³, Ash², L, J.—to] unto Hn¹, Ar, H⁷, H⁸, Ad³.—agayne] om. Ar, H⁷, H⁸, Ad³.—he] om. B², CC. 1285. w*ith*] of B¹, B⁴, B⁵, H¹, H², V, H³, H⁵, H⁷, H⁸, Ash², J, C², Ar, Hu, Ad², An, Lg, Ch, Hn¹, Co.—And] om. Ash². 1286. so] hath so B¹, Hu.—he] om. Ad³. 1287. In] Of B¹, B², B³, B⁴, B⁵, H¹, H⁸, Ash¹, C¹, C², C³, Ar, Lg, Ch, Hn¹, Co.—Recomfort] comfort Ar; the comfort C¹. 1288. hathe] om. B¹, Hu; for to C¹. 1289. of marye] of poure Marye Hn¹. 1290. of] with B³, L; and Hu. 1291. to] of Ash².—suspecion] evil suspicion B³, L.

And of his errour, and of the trespace

This hore gray, *with* all hymylite

With wepynge eyen, gan to axe grace

And she a noon, of womanly pyte

His hevynesse, while she dyd see

Comforteth hym, in all that euere she myght

And he a none, in thayre althre sight

And all hir maydens, stondyng envyron

1300   Gan evyn thus, for to crye lowde

Certes quod he, my derke suspecion

Cam of blyndnesse, for I no nothir cowde

But now in sothe, the mysty blake clowde

Of ignoraunce, is so claryfied

That all the trouthe, to me is verrefyed

1292. the] his B¹, Hu.—of the] his H¹, H⁵, V.—the] great Hn¹.—of his] for of H¹. 1293. *with* all] Ioseph with B³, Ar, L. 1294. W*ith* wepynge eyen, gan to axe grace B¹.—wepygne eyen] eyne wepynge D, C³.—gan to] craved and H².—eyen] om. B², CC.—gan] than B², CC. 1295. of] with Co, B⁵, H⁸. 1296. while] whanne Hu, Hn¹, Co, B⁵.—see] there see Hn¹.—she dyd] that scheo Co, B⁵. 1297. euere] om. C², C³, H². 1298. thayre] all here Ash¹.—in thayre] ther in C¹.—he] sche B⁵. 1299. envyron] everychone B¹, B², B³, B⁵, Ash², Ar, C¹; Hn¹.—And] om. Ash², J.—envyron in B⁵. 1300. Gan evyn thus, for to crye lowde H⁷.—Gan] Be gan D, B¹, C¹, Hu.—evyn thus] thus evene B¹.—for] om. H⁴. 1301. he] sche C⁵, Hu. 1302. I] he Ad³. 1303. But now in sothe, the mysty blake clowde B¹.—mysty blake] dark mysty D, C¹, C³.—now] om. B², CC. 1304. Of ignoraunce, is so claryfied B¹.—so] clene D, C¹, C³, Hn¹. 1305. That all the trouthe, to me is verrefyed B¹.—That] And D, J, Ash², Hn¹.—is] om. H³, H⁴, An, J.

Thoroughe grace of god, þat myne olde rudenesse

Is now fro me, chased clene a waye

Haueth me excusede, of my derke dulnesse

With all myne hert, benyngly I praye

1310 My nyght of errour, is turned in to daye

That I may nowe, with myne eyne olde

The bryght beames, of Tyten welbeholde

That was eclypsede, fer oute of my syght

That for derkenesse, I nost whatte to done

Onely for lak, that his beames bryght

Were me be rafte, thorough the cloude mone

That this eclipse was caused al to sone

By hir soden interposicion

That was chefe grownde, of my enspecion

1306. þat] and Ar.—myne olde] thoruh myn B². 1307. chased clene] clene chased Hu. 1308. me] om. H².—derke] grete Ash². 1309. With all myne hert, benyngly I praye B¹.—I] nowe I D, C¹, Hn¹; I you Ash². 1310. of] and J.—My nyght of errour is turned in to] Of mercy God thanking this Ash². 1312. beames] om. Ash².—welbeholde] nowthe bemys, beholde Ash²; beholde C², C³. 1313. of] om. Ash¹. 1314. nost] muste C¹.—to done] I myst what C¹.—derkenesse] dures C¹. 1315. that] of B¹, B³, Ash², Ad³, Hn¹.—bryght] ful Hn¹; light B³. 1316. thorough] by Co, B⁵. —me] om. Hn¹. 1317. was] *inserted above.* 1319. chefe] my chef B¹.—my] om. C¹.—grownde] cause H¹.—enspecion] suspecioun C¹, H¹, Hu, V.

1320   This is to sayne, þat myne erthely thought

So was opressede, derked and borne dovne

With worldely skyes, þat I myght nought

Ne was not worthe, to inspection

Of this light, by Revelacion

Tyll the sonne of grace, dyd shyne

My witte enclipsed fully to enlumyne

For he to come, hathe his Angel sent

Myne ignoraunce fully for to clere

Wherfore of yov, in all my best entent

1330   O ye Maydens, that ben present here

I axe mercy, with all my hert entier

Of all that euere, hath be spoken of or sayde

And lawly pray yov, beth not evyll apayde

1320. þat] om. L. 1321. borne] world C1. 1322. With] That Ch, B4, H3, H4, Ad2, An, C5, Ash1.—þat] om. Ash1. 1324. light] nyght Hu, B1, B2, B4, B5, H1, H2, H3, H4, H5, H6, H7, H8, Ash1, CC, C1, C2, C5, Ar, Ad2, Ad3, L, An, Lg, Ch, Hn1, Co. 1325. dyd] to me Hn1.—grace dyd] hye grace B2, Ch, B4, H1, CC; his grace Ash1, H3, H4, H6, Ad2, Lg, H5, C2, An, C5.—sonne] newme C2. 1326. fully] om. C2.—to] for to Ar. 1327. he to come hathe his Angel] to me his angelle hathe Hu, B1, V. 1328. for] om. Ash2. 1329. best] hole Ad2.—in all] of my H2. 1330. ben present here] be here present Ash2. 1331. all] om. H2. 1332. hath] that Lg.—euere hath] y haue H2, Hu.—hath be] that hath Ch, B4, H1, H3, H4, Ad2, An, C5. 1333. pray yov] I pray H2, H8.

And thay Icheone, thanked god of all

With hert and will, bothe in worde and dede

That he in Ioseph, hath in speciall

His grace of newe, made for to sprede

To voyde away all his hole drede

Of euery conceyte and ymagenyng

1340   To make hym knowe, the trouthe of al this thyng

Wherfore in sothe, the Ioye gan Renewe

Amonge hem all, eche of one accorde

The ermonye, entuned, was so trwe

By twene hem, that ther was no discorde

Not so moche, as of alytyll worde

And thus in Ioye, a while I late hem dwell

And of this Bisshop, furthe I will yov telle

1334. god] om. C¹.—thay] than H². 1335. worde] thought C³, B⁵.—in worde and] trewely in Ash². 1336. in Ioseph] unjoyfull B², CC.—he] om. B⁴, Ash², CC. 1337. sprede] shede Ash¹. 1338. hole] olde B³, C², Ash², L, J. 1339. euery] any Lg.—ymagenyng] of ymaginynge H⁸. 1340. al this thyng] that is don CC.—al] om. C².—this] om. Ch, Co, B⁵, Ash², H⁸.—hym] om. B⁴. 1341. Wherfore] Ther with Ash²; where thoruh the Ch; wher thurgh B³, B⁴, C³, Co, B⁵, Hn¹, Ash¹, H⁴, H⁵, Ad², An, L, J.—the] our C¹. 1342. eche] beyng C²; eche one Hu. 1345. of] om. B⁵, Ash¹.—Not] But Hu. 1346. a while I late hem dwell] I let him a while dwelle B¹, B⁵, H⁴, C¹, C², Ad³, An, Co.—a while] om. C¹, H⁴, An.—a while I] a litil while C².—thus] om. B⁵.—hem] om. Co. 1347. of] at H⁸.—yov] now H⁸; this] the Hu, C⁵; om. H¹.

Howe the Bisshoppe made
sompne Ioseph for our
lady was w*ith* Childe Ca°
xxvii°

Touchyng this thyng, playnely if I conne

Howe worde by worde, sothely in sentence

1350   Of all this thyng, the Romour is Ronne

And Reportede that thorough necligence

Of this Ioseph, or by violence

How this Marye, gothe w*ith* chylde grete

Wherfore thay haue in a soden hete

Cyted hym, aforn hem to apere   f. 38a

And he cam furthe, w*ith* sobre contenaunce

Of whom a noon, the Bisshop gan enquyre

Abiathir, of his gou*er*naunce

Fro poynt to poynte, w*ith* eu*er*y circu*m*staunce

1360   Touchyng this thyng, what it myght amounte

Or howe that Ioseph, wolde giffe a compte

1349. sothely] pleinly CC. 1350. thyng] matyr C³.—this] om. Ash².—all this] om. Ch.—is Ronne] is so runne Hu.—all] om. B⁴, H¹, Ash¹, H³, H⁴, H⁶, Ad², Lg, An, C⁵.—thyng] thyng is so Hu. 1351. that] om. CC.—thorough] of Ash².—necligence] the neglygence C³, H⁶. 1354. Wherfore] where thorugh H⁵. 1356 w*ith*] om. Hn¹. 1357. a noon the Bisshop] the bisshop anoon B¹, B², B⁴, C², Ar, Ch.—gan] dide B⁴, C².—enquyre] e Ar.—a noon] om. Ch. 1358. his] al his Ar. 1359 eu*er*y] al Ar.—w*ith*] of CC. 1360. thyng what it myght amounte] cas of this new mater C².—this] om. Ch. 1361. a compte] his acounte B¹, B², Ash², CC, C², Ch.—Or] om. Ch, C².—wolde] thereto wolde C².—that] om. Ash², CC.—giffe] so give B².—acompte answer C².

That Marye, debonaire and so mylde

Whiche som tyme, was of suche opynyon

In the temple, is nowe grete w*ith* childe

Agayne the lawe, of hir professyon

By some engyne, or by collusion

In preiudice, of hir virgynyte

Nought w*ith*standyng vtterly that she

A vowede hadde, of holy affection

1370   Al hir lyfe, to have kepet hir maydynhede

And was that tyme, of suche p*er*fection

That sothefastly w*ith*oute any drede

Of suche a nothir, couthe I neu*er*e Rede

Hir vertue3 all, to Reken hem by and by

Fro day to day, all that tyme vtt*er*ly

1362. That Marye, debonaire and so mylde B1.—Marye] faire Marye D, C1, C3.—so] om. D, C1, C3, Co, B5, Ash2, J, H8.—and] om. Ash1, H6.—fayre] om. Hu. 1363. Whiche] That B1.—some tyme] whilom Ash2, J. 1364. nowe grete] grete now Ad2, C5.—grete] om. Ash1. —is] om. H4, An.—with] is with H4, An. 1365. lawe] avow B1.—hir] soche H2. 1366. by] om. Hu, B1; ells Ash2; faule Hn1; fals C3; old C1.—By some] That by H2.—or by] of H3, H4, Ad2, An, C5, B4. 1368. vtterly that] but utterly Hn1; that utterly Co. 1369. holy] all B1, H7, H8, S.—hadde] om. H8. 1370. have kepet] kepe B2, B3, B4, H1, C2, Hn1, Ash1, H3, H4, H2, Ash2 V, H5, H6, Ad2, Lg, An, C5, L, CC, J. 1371. p*er*fection] intencion C2. 1373. Rede] of rede C3.—I] we H8. 1374. hem] om. B3, Co, C2, B5, H2, Ash2, Ar, H8, L, CC, J. 1375. vtt*er*ly] truly B1.—all] om. Hu.

She neu*e*re stynte, for to wirke or praye

But lyke a myrrour, of all holynesse

The wille of god, holyche dyd obeye

W*it*h all hir hert, and all hir bysynesse

1380   And w*it*h all this, fulfilled of mekenesse

She was ensample, to eu*e*ry man*e*re wight

That there abode, or hir had a sight

And euery day w*it*houte wordes moo

Stou*n*d mele, fro the hevyn dovne

Goddys Angell, cam to and froo

Where as she laye, in contemplacion

And at laste, of grete affection

By signes shewede, of godd*es* volunte

She was of vs, assignede vnto the

1376. for] om. Ad³, CC, Ash².—praye] to pray Ash². 1377. of all] al of Hu, B¹, B², B³, B⁴, B⁵, H³, H⁴, H⁶, H⁷, Ash¹, C⁵, Ar, Ad³, L, An, Lg, Ch, Hn¹, Co. 1371. holyche] fully B¹.—dyd] to H². 1380. w*it*h] om. Ar.—of] with Ar, H⁶. 1381. to] of B¹, B², B³, B⁴, B⁵, H¹, H⁸, Ash¹, Ash², C¹, C², C³, Ar, Ad², Ch, Hn¹, Co. 1384. Stou*n*d mele] Diverse tymes B¹, B², H⁵, Ch, Hn¹, Co; sodenly Hn¹.—the] om. B², Ch, H². 1386. laye] was Ch. 1387. laste of] the last B¹.—of] by H⁸. 1388. of] om. H²; be Ar. 1389. of vs assignede] assigned of us B⁵, H³.

1390 Aftir the custume, playnely of the lawe   f. 38b

   That thou sholdest, conserue hir and gouerne

   Nowe be wel war, that thou hast nought mysdrawe

   Hir tendre youthe, fro god that is eterne

   The trouthe of thynges, that clerly can concerne

   Wherfore be war, that thou be not to wyte

   In this matier, lest he woll the white

Howe Ioseph answerd
the Bisshopes excusyng
hym and our lady
Ca° xxviii°

   For in my self perfytely I knowe

    She is a mayde, but if it be for the

   Quod Ioseph than, with heed enclyned lowe

1400 The sothefaste lorde, that euery thyng may see

   My trust is fully, he will excuse me

   Of Rightwysnes and shelde me from shame

   Of all that euere, ye put me in blame

1390. playnely] and use C². 1391. hir] om. H¹, L.—conserue her] her conserve Co, H²,
Ar. 1392. mysdrawe] with drawe Ash².—hast nought] not have Ash¹.—wel] om. Hn¹.—
hast] om. H⁴. 1393. youthe] thought Co. 1394. that] om. Hu, B¹.—can] om. Hn¹,
Ash¹.—that clerly] om. CC; playnly can H².—concerne] discerne Ar, H⁸.—The] That
B³, L. 1395. to] om. Ash². 1396. In] Of CC. 1397.] om. B², Ch, B⁴, H¹, C², Ash¹, H³, H⁴,
H⁵, H⁶, Ad², Lg, An, L, B³, CC, V, C⁵. 1398.] om. B², Ch, B⁴, H¹, C², Ash¹, H³, H⁴,
H⁵, H⁶, Ad², Lg, An, L, B³, V, CC, C⁵. Between 1400 and 1401] *added lines* Sires speeke
I will if it your will be *and* Of this thynge I am not a knowe B², Ch, B⁴, H¹, C², Ash¹,
H³, H⁴, H⁵, V, H⁶, Ad², Lg, An, L, B³, CC, C⁵. 1401. he will] that he Ash². 1402. me] om.
H⁸. 1403. in] now in Hn¹.

For I haue kepet hir, in the same poynt

Of maydenhed, that she was me by take

Of whiche as yet, she stant in noo disioynt

I dar afferme, and swere it for hir sake

And for my part, what *p*reve ye lust I make

I will be Redy, and let it not be spared

1410   Tyll verrely, the sothe be declared

Howe the Bisshop made
Ioseph and our lady
to taste a water to
preve hem by Ca° xxix°[1]

Than quod the Bisshop all suspecion

    For to voyde, all ambiguyte

That god may make demonstracion

Of yov tweyne, how the trouthe be

Ye shall atastc, bothe thou and she

Of thylke wat*er* to speke in word*es* fewe

By God ordenyde, trouthe forto shewe

1404. hir] om. C², H⁸.—I] om. B. 1405. Of maydenhed, that she was me by take B¹.—by] om. D, J, L, Ash², H², B⁵, C³, B³.—that] as C¹, Co.—Of] Her of C². 1406. as yet] om. H¹.—disioynt] dishonest Ar.—Of] In H⁸.—noo] om. Hn¹.—as] om. C². 1407. afferme] I that C¹.—and] I B²; it and Ch, B⁴, H¹, Ash¹, H³, H⁴, H², H⁶, Ad², Lg, An. 1408. I] to B⁴, C³, Ash², H⁸, CC. 1410. Tyll verrely, the sothe be declared B¹.—verrely] verrely of hir D, Hn¹, C¹, C³; verrely here the H²; utterly H⁸. 1411. quod] om. C¹. 1412. all] and all B⁵, Hn¹, Ash¹, H³, H⁴, H², Ar, H⁸, H⁵, H⁶, Ad³, Ad², Lg, An, CC, B³, B⁴, Co.—voyde] devoide and C¹, C³, Ash², J; devoid H¹.—For] om. Hu. 1413. may] list H². 1414. the] that the Hn¹. 1416. thylke] that Ar; thikke H⁷. 1417. god] om. B¹, CC, J, C⁵, S, Hn¹.—forto] to CC.

---

[1]first x *is erased*

To exclude playnely, eu*e*ry conceyte newe

Of tunge₃ large, and eu*e*ry fantasye

1420   As it was some tyme, shewed by the hewe

Of hem that dranke, the drynke of Ialousye

As Numery dothe, clerely specifie

Wherfore a noon, ther is no more to sayne

Make yov Redy, for ye bothe tweyne

Shall make a taste, wer it be sowre or swote   **f. 39a**

Ther is no gayne saye, nor excusacion

Tyll the trouth, be Ryped in the Rote

We shul *pro*cede in this conclusion

That god liste, to make demonstracion

1430   Of all this thyng, for favo*ur* or for routhe

There is no mene, but the playne trouthe

1418. playnely] om. Hu. 1419. tunge₃] thynges H². 1420. some tyme] whilom Ash², J.—some tyme shewed] shewed somtyme B², CC. 1421. drynke] cuppe B¹, B², B⁵, H⁷, H⁸, Ash¹, C⁵, CC, C², Ar, Ad³, Ch, Hn¹; water B², B⁵, Ash¹, CC.—the] of the Ar, H⁸. 1422. clerely] doth Ch. 1424. ye bothe] bothe ye B³, H², L.—Redy for] both ready both H⁶. 1425. make] om. B¹, H⁷, Ash², C⁵, S. 1426. saye] om. Ash², J, Hn¹.—nor] he noon Hn¹. 1427. in] to Ash², J; into Ash¹.—be Ryped] to rype Hn¹. 1429. **That god liste make demonstracion** B¹.—make demonstracion] to make declaracion D. 1430. or for] or of Lg.—all this thyng] this mater C². 1431. playne] playnely B¹, Ash², C⁵, Ch.—is] nys B², B³, B⁴, Co, H¹, C¹, C², CC.

For if god lust, that your Innocens

Lyke yo*ur* desert, be opynly excused

Than is yo*ur* meryte, of more excellence

That ye to forne, falsely were accused

And sithen this preve, may not be refused

But that ye must obey to the lawe

Com of a noon, and yov nat wi*th*drawe

1440   D o sette hir furthe, and bryng hir to *presence*   Howe our lady

            That hath in vertu, so excellent a name   was brought

        furthe affore the

In whom was neu*ere* yet fovnde offence   Bisshoppes to

But to this tyme, euere floured in hir fame   tast the wat*er*

And stant at large, from eu*ere* man*ere* blame   of Ielosye

Nowe let hir come, and like as god yov vre   Ca° xxx°[1]

For youv disposith taketh yo*ur* aventure

1432. lust] wole Co, B5. 1433. opynly] playnly Ar. 1435. to forne] before me Ash2. 1436. And sithen this preef, may not be refused H7.——this] the D; om. B1, C5; that C3. 1437. to] unto H2, Ar. 1438. yov] om. Hn1.——of] om. H5.——of anoon] anoon of H3. 1439. sette hir] hir B1, B5, H7, H8, C5, Ar, Ad3, An, Lg, Co.——bryng hir] bryng C2. ——sette hir] sette Hu.——presence] the lawe CC. 1441, In whom was neu*ere* yet fovnde offence B1; In whom was yet neu*ere* fovnde offence D, C3; In whom was never founde yet, offence B5, Ash2, J. Hie you faste for nothing ye shawe CC. 1442. to] into Ch, B3, B4, Co, H1, C2, Ash1, H3, H4, H2, H5, H6, Ad2, Lg, An, L, B2.——hir] good B5.——But to] For now CC.——eu*ere*] she CC; om. B2.——hir] om. CC, Hu.——to this tyme eu*ere*] hither toward C1, C3, Hn1, Ash2, J. 1444. like as god yov vre] yef that she be puyr H6.—— let hir] om. C2.——yov] hir Hu. 1445.] Lat god disposes take hir in hir aventure H6.——disposith] to dispose Ash1.——taketh] to taketh Hn1.——For yov] And for now Co.

---

[1]first x *is erased*

And she a noon, was of hir frendeȝ brought

Knowyng Right nought, what all this wolde mene

Devoyde of drede, bothe in hert and thought

For drede in sothe, may do hir no tene

1450   To concyence, that is of synne clenne

Ne vegeaunce, ther no place occupyeth

There Innocence, a soule vngilty gyeth

For the fyre, may no while brenne

Aftur the brondes, ben taken awaye

Ne the Ryver, holde his cours and Renne

The hede spryng drye, sothely this is no nay

Ne vengeaunce playnely, may make noon assay

To execute agaynst Innocence

Devoyde of synne, his myghty violence

1446. of] to Ash[1], H[6]. 1447. wolde] mygt Ch, B[4], H[1], H[3], H[4], H[6], Ad[2], Lg, An, C[5].—Right nought] no thing C[2], H[2].—all this wolde] hit myght Ash[1].—Right] the ryght L.—all] om. L. 1448. in] om. Hu. 1449. may do hir] may not do B[2], Ch, B[4], H[4], H[2], Ad[2], An, CC; ne may not do Co, H[1], B[5], Ash[1], H[8], H[5], Ad[3], H[6]; ne may do Ash[2], H[7], J; ne may not be Lg.—hir] om. B[1], B[3], H[3], C[2], C[5], Ar, L, Ch, Hn[1]. 1450. clenne] so cleen C[1].—is] om. H[8]. 1451. Ne] And B[3], L. 1453. may] ne may Ash[2]. 1454. Aftur the brondes, ben taken awaye B[1].—the] that the D. 1455. and] can B[1]; or Ch, B[3], B[4], Co, H[1], C[1], C[2]; to B[2], CC. 1456. sothely] om. Ash[1], H[2], B[1], S, Ch.—no] om. H[7].—is] om. Ch, B[4], H[1], B[1], H[3], Ash[2], An, J, Ad[2], C[5]. 1457. playnely] om. B[1], C[2].—may] om. B[2], Ch, CC.—may make] make may C[5]. —Ne] om. H[2]. 1458. To execute] Of execucion B[3].—Innocence] trew innocence C[3].—agaynst] ouyte ayense Hn[1]. 1459. his myghty] for al his B[3], L.—his] by his H[8].

1460   For nought but synne, may engendre shame   f. 39b

       For selde or neu*ere*, be the chekeȝ Rede

       Of hym in sothe, that is devoyde of blame

       For who is clene, takyth lytyll hede

       To wynke or blenke, for any man*er* drede

       And for thassaut, of eny mysty cloude

       Lyght of vertu, may no while shroude

       It may a whyle, be derked *with* askye

       As is a monge, the fayre bryght sonne

       And *with* the wyndes, of malice and envye

1470   The shynyng sterres, often wexen donne

       But whan that trouthe, settyth a broche his **tonne**

       To make the sothe, opynly be knowe

       The wynde of falsnesse, may no lenger blowe

1460. engendre] void CC.—may] om. Ash¹.—but] of Ar. 1461. neu*ere*] nought Ash¹,
H³, H⁴, H⁶, Ad², C⁵. 1462. Of hym in sothe, that is devoyde of blame B¹.—of] in D.—is]
ben B³.—is devoyde] devoide is H³.—in sothe] om. CC. 1463. who] whose Ch, B⁴, H¹, Hn¹,
Ash¹, H³, H⁴, H⁵, H⁶, Ad², Lg, An, C⁵, V.—For] For therto B², CC.—clene] so clene
Ash². 1464. drede] blame or drede B², CC. 1465 thassaut] the offence Hn¹. 1468. a monge]
unwhile B³, L. 1469. the] om. B¹.—and] of Ch.—wyndes] wordes Ash¹. 1470. shynyng] clere
B¹, B², B³, B⁴, H¹, H³, H⁴, H⁵, H⁶, Ash¹, CC, C², C⁵, Ad², L, An, Lg, Ch.—shynyng]
shere C, B⁵, H², Ash², Ar, H⁸, H⁷, Ad³, J. 1471. his tonne] her time B¹, B², B³, B⁴, B⁵, H¹,
H², H³, H⁴, H⁵, H⁶, H⁷, H⁸, Ash¹, Ash², CC, C², C⁵, Ar, Ad², Ad³, L, An, Lg, Ch,
Hn¹, Co.—that] the C¹, C³; om. J, Hu. 1472. To make the sothe, opynly be knowe H⁷.—
be] to be D, L, B², CC, B³.—the sothe opynly] openly the soth B¹. 1473. wynde] wyntier C¹.

Howe our ladys frend*es* weyled and morned whan the Bisshopes maden so strong a preve on hir virginite Ca° xxxi°¹

Then sithyn the trouthe, may no while dare

Hornes shrynke, ne hyde hym in his neste

But lyke a sonne, his light a brode declare

Than she that was, the verrey chosyn chest

Of al clennesse, and ther *with* all the best

Of all good, howe myght it be tyde

1480   Hir light of vertu, to be sette a syde

That it nil shyne, mavgre who saythe nay

Whan hir beameȝ, ben opynly discured

As gold in fire is fynyde be assay

And at the teste, Silu*e*re is depuryde

And she that was, in vertu most assured

Where the holy gost, his dwellyng dyd sette

How myght then, any mystys lette

1474. Then sithyn the trouthe, may no while dare B¹.——while] lenger D, C¹.—— may no while dare] is not good to spare Hu. 1475. Hornes shrynke, ne hyde hym in his neste B¹.—shrynke] shrynke in D, C¹.—ne hyde] the lyde C¹.—hym] om. C¹—Hornes] Hir hornys Ash². 1476. a] the B², CC.—declare] doth declare B², CC.—his light a brode] abrode his light H². 1477. the] om. L. 1478. Of al] Of Ash².—ther] om. Ar. 1479. be tyde] thou betyde Ash¹. 1480. be] om. B², CC, H⁴.—to be] for to C¹.—of] om. H⁴.—light of] om. Ash². 1481. it nil] wol C².—it] he B³, L.—that it nil] buy hyt woll C³.—who] who so Ch, B⁴.—nil] om. Co.—it nil] but wol B⁵, Hn¹, Ash¹, H³, H⁸, H⁶. 1482. beameȝ] veynes B³, L.—ben] om. C². 1483. As gold in fire is fynyde be assay H⁷.—in fire] and siluer D, C¹; om. Hu, B¹, Ch; in the fire H⁴.—is] om. C⁵. 1484. the] om. H⁷.—teste] chaast Ar.—depuryde] clene pured Hn¹. 1485. was] om. Hu. 1486. gost] om. Ch.—dyd sette] his dwellyngy *repeated* Lg. 1487. How myght then, any mystys lette B¹.—then] ther then D, C³; it then C¹.—lette] that lette H².—it ther C¹.—lette] that lett H².

The clere light, of hir p*er*fytenesse

Or eny preef, or probacion

1490　In any party, for to make it lesse

For light wol oute, it may not be borne dovne

And so wil trouthe, have d*omi*nacion

For any falsnesse, that men can conspyre

Than she that was, so full sette afyre

W*ith* the holy goste, ne thar but lytyll drede　　　　　　f. 40a

To drynke water, whethir it be thyke or clere

To make a pref, of hir maydynhede

For hir to harme, it shall haue no powere

For to deface, hir colo*ur* or hir chere

1500　But Rathir more amende, and claryfye

The derke demyng, of eu*er*e clody skye

1488. clere] om. B¹.—light] night Ash¹, H⁶. 1489. Or eny preef, or probacion B¹.—Or] Of D.—eny] om. H²; every Ash².—or] outher B², B⁴, H¹, C², Ash¹, H³, H⁴, H⁵, Ad², Lg, An, C⁵, CC. or els C¹; also or H². 1491. be borne] bene Hn¹. 1493. that] om. B¹, H⁷, Ar, Co. 1494. sette] om. C¹. 1495. ne thar] that C³.—With] Of Ash¹, H³, H⁴, H⁶, Ad², Lg, An, C⁵. 1496. water] that Ar. 1498. to harme] to do harme H⁸; to hurt B⁵; harme C⁵.—to harme it] hit to harme Hn¹, H². 1499. For] Nor Ash², J.—or] nor Ash², J.—chere] clere Lg. 1500. more amende] amende more C⁵, L. 1501. eu*er*e] her B²; our Ad³.

And so mayre stondyng, in the place

And all hir frendes, aboute environ

Wher men may see, vpon many a face

Of frendely Routhe, and compassion

The salt teres, fall, and Renne dovne

For drede and love, thay had for to sene

So hard assay made, on hir age grene

But she all way constant, as a wall

1510 In thought ne chere, abaschede neu*er* a dele

Ne in hir hert, dredyth not at all

But vpon god, trustyth all waye wele

That he of trouthe, shall trye oute the stele

Al be that she, speke but wordes fewe

Withoutyn speche, shall the dede shewe

1502. so] also H¹; om. H². 1503. aboute] abowte hir H⁵.—all hir frendes] hyr frends all L. 1504. many a] any Ar. 1506. salt] white B¹, H⁷; laste Lg; fast B², Ch.—fall and Renne] renne and falle B¹, Ash¹, H², Ad³, Ad². 1507. and] of B², CC, C³; in H⁸.—drede] feer Ash². —had] om. B², CC.—for] om. L. 1509. she] om. Ash². 1510. chere] clere Lg; chere ne Ash¹, H⁶. 1511. Ne] She B¹, Co; And B³, L.—hir] om. Ash¹, H², H⁵, H⁶, J.—not at all] **nevyr** adell J; not so nelle Ash². 1512. vpon] on B¹, Ash¹. 1514. speke] ne spake B¹, B², B³, B⁴, H⁵, H⁶, H⁷, H⁸, C², Ad³, L, Ch, Co, V.—that] though C³.—she] he B⁵, Hn¹, Ash².— but] wit but C¹.—be that] that be that H¹, Ash¹. 1515. shall] he shal B¹.—dede] **trouthe** Ash¹, H².

And whan the wat*er*, fully was confecte

Lyke the statute, of the Rites olde

The Bisshopp hathe the cuppe, furst directe

Vnto Ioseph, and the parell tolde

1520   And manfully, he gan it holde

And dranke it vp, and chaunged not his chere

And vii tymes, aboute the Autere

He went thanne, by custome as he aught

Of face and colo*ur*, alway elyche newe

And to Marye, also the Bisshopp brought

A cuppe of water, and she w*ith* hert trewe

Acceptyth it, this goodly fresshe of hewe

And or she dranke, this perfyte holy mayde

All opynly to god, thus she sayde

1516. fully was] was fully B[1], H[8], CC, Ch, Co. 1517. of] and Hu, B[1].—the statute] statute L.—of the] and H[1].—olde] wold H[2]. 1518. the cuppe furst] furst the cup C[3], H[3]. 1519. and] and hym Ch, B[4], H[1], C[2], Ash[1], H[3], H[4], H[5], H[6], Ad[2], Lg, An, C[5]; and to hym B[2], CC. 1520. holde] for to holde B[1], B[2], B[3], B[4], B[5], H[1], H[2], H[3], H[4], H[5], H[6], H[7], H[8], Ash[1], Ash[2], CC, J, C[1], C[2], C[3], C[5], Ar, Ad[2], Ad[3], An, Lg, Ch, Hn[1], Co.—gan it] yt gan for to be L. 1521. not his] no B[1], Ash[2].—and] he B[2], Ch, CC. 1522. the] the hye Ash[1]. 1523. thanne] as L. 1525. brought] it brought B[1].—to] unto Hn[1]. 1526. trewe] newe C[1].—of] with B[2], CC. 1527. it this] om. B[1]; it and is Ash[2]; eke this B[2], Ch, B[3], B[4], H[1], C[2], Ash[1], H[3], H[4], H[5], H[6], Ad[2], Lg, An, C[5], L; eke with CC; this Hn[1], H[2], Ar, H[8], Ad[3].— fresshe of hewe] herte trewe CC. 1528. this] om. B[1], L.—or] for H[8].—perfyte holy] holy perfyght Ash[2], Ad[2], C[5]; goodly holy CC. 1529. thus she] she thus B[1].

Howe our lady   1530
prayed to god to shewe
hir virgynyte Ca° xxxii°

Sothefast lorde, that haste the knowlegyng

Of eu*ery* thyng, thorowe thy grete myght

And art so trewe, and so Iuste a kyng

To lowe and high, that thou wilt do right

And no thyng may, be shadwede fro thy sight

Thorough noon engyne, ne fro thy face astert

But sothefastly, thou knowest eu*ery* hert

So that no wyght, fage may ne fayne

To for the eye, of thy sapyence

Nowe late thy grace, downe fro hevyn **Rayne**

1540 Clerly in dede, and nought be aparence

To shewe in me, if ther be offence

Or eny gilt, myn avowe to a peche

To the I pray, so thy light to **Reche**

1530. Sothefast] O sothfast B¹, V.—lorde] god Ash². 1531. grete] grace and Ch. 1532. art] om. C², B⁴.—And] That C².—so Iuste] iuste C¹. 1533. lowe and high] hye and lowe, Hu, B¹.—To] So B³.—right] but right B³, L. 1534. shadwede] hydde B¹, B⁴; coverid C². 1536. thou] om. B¹, B², B³, B⁴, B⁵, H¹, H², H³, H⁴, H⁵, H⁶, H⁷, H⁸, Ash¹, Ash², CC, J, C⁵, C², Ch, Ar, Ad², Ad³, L, An, Lg, Hu, Co. 1537. fage] sage Lg, C²; forge H⁸; sade L, B³.—fayne] seyne L, B³, C², H⁸.—wyght fage] thinge sage C². 1538. To] So B¹, B⁵, C¹, Co; By B³, L.—the] thyn B¹, B⁵, C¹, Co.—eye] om. B², CC; the Ch. 1539. downe] om. B¹. 1540. in] by B¹, B², B³, B⁴, B⁵, H¹, C¹, C², C³, Ch, Hn¹, Co.—nought] om. H⁸. 1541. offence] any offence B¹, B⁴, H⁷, H⁸; apparence Hn¹.—ther] that ther Hn¹. 1542. Or] Of Ash¹. 1543. so] so lete B¹, J, An.—so thy] sothe H⁸.—light] ryght Ch, Co, H¹, C¹, B⁵, Hn¹; lyke H⁸.—Reche] streche B², C², Ar, CC.—to Reche] to me reche B⁴; so to reche B³, L.

That it be couthe, here all playnely

To wit in sothe, whether I in chastyte

Haue led my lyfe, of hert faythefully

Lyche as thou knoweste, for the love of the

And if I haue, myne virgynyte

Conservede hoole, this is my oryson

1550   Make opynly a demonstracion

And with that worde, the drynke she dyd a taste

And went hir cours, aboute the Autere

And all the people, be gan to gasen faste

If any signe, did in hir apere

Outhir in colour, in countenaunce or chere

But all for nought, playnely as I tolde

The more on hir, they loken and byholde

1544. playnely] openly B¹, B².—all] om. B¹, J, An, Hn¹; and Ch.—it] I B². 1545. whether]
whether that C¹. 1546. of hert] om. C⁵. 1548. it I] yit H⁸; y H², H⁶. 1549. Conservede hoole,
this is my oryson B¹.— is] om. D, B⁴, Co, C². 1550. Make opynly a demonstracion B¹.—
opynly] opynly nowe D, C¹, Hn¹; here opynly Ash¹.—make] make here Ash¹. 1551. a
taste] astate H¹. 1553. be gan] gan B³, Co, H¹, C², B⁵, Ash¹, V, Ash², H³, H⁴, H², H⁵,
H⁶, Ad², Lg, An, C⁵, L, CC.—to] om. Ash². 1554. did in hir] in hir dide B¹, H⁷, H⁸, Ar,
Ad³. 1555. Outhir in colour, in countenaunce or chere B¹.—or] or in D, C¹.—in countenaunce]
countenaunce C¹.—Outhir] Or Ash¹, H². 1556. playnely] sothly C². 1557. and] or B¹.

The more she was, to her sight fayre

And lyche as phebus, in Ioly grene maye

1560 Whan he hathe chasede, the derke mysty eyre

Shyneth more bright, the clere somers daye

Whan þikke vapours, ben dreven clene awaye

Right so Ioseph, and also Marye

So fresshe werne, in euery wighteʒ eye

That to beholde, they thought it dyd hem goode   f. **41a**

The longe day, in hir opynnyon

For in her face, al waye was the blode

Withoutyn palyng, or any drawyng dovne

Al way more fayre, of inspeccion

1570 Of whiche thyng, the people gan mervayle

And for astonede, thought hir witt*es* fayle

1558. The more she was, to her sight fayre H7.—fayre] right fayre D, C3.—to] in B1, C5, Ch; into H6, CC; of B3, L. 1560. mysty] om. H2. 1561. bright and clere] clere the bright Hu, B3, B4, Co, Ch, H1, C2, B5, Hn1, H3, II4, H2, Ar, H5, H7, Ad3, Ad2, An, C5, L, J; clerely the derke Ash1, H6; clere than the bright H8, Lg.—Shyneth] Sheweth B2, CC. 1562. Whan þikke vapours, ben dreven clene awaye B1.—dreven clene] clene dryven D, H1; clene C2; dryven B4. 1563. Right so Ioseph, and also Marye H7.—Marye] good Marye D, C1, C3; eke Marie H2, J. —also] om. B1. 1565. beholde] beholde her B1, L.—to] om. L. 1568. Withoutyn] With H1. 1569. inspeccion] suspeccioun B1, B2, B3, B4, B5, H2, C1, C3, Co.—Al way] And alwey B2, H6, Ch, H1, C2, Hn1, Ash1, H3, H4, V, H5, H6, Ad3, Ad2, Lg, An, C5, CC.—fayre] fewe B2.—of] of the Ar; of her Ash2. 1571. fayle] wolde fayle B1, B5, H7, H3, C3, Ar, Ad3, Hn1; would sternow C1.—hir witt*es*] they C1.

And in party gretely werne dismayed

    Leste that of theym, take were vengeaunce

For thay so ferre, haue godd*es* myght assayede

Of errour blynde and verrey ignoraunce

And Right furthe with, of hertly Repentaunce

They bonche ther breste*ʒ*, with fiste*ʒ* wondir sore

And al at onys, fell dovne afore

This holy mayde, with humble Reu*e*rence

1580   And wold hir fete, haue kyssed thėr anone

Axyng m*e*rcy, of thayre grete offence

And she forgaf it, to hem eu*e*rycheone

And all the Bisshoppe*ʒ*, and the people goon

Benyngly, to brynge hir awaye

And to hir paleys, fully hir conveye

Howe the Bisshopes and the people drede hem full sore of the **grete** preve and assay that **was** done to our lady Capit*u*lo xxxiii°[1]

1572. party] apparence Hn[1].—gretely werne] weren gretely Ar. 1573. Leste that of theym, take were vengeaunce B[1].—of] on D, C[5], Ash[2].—take were] wer taken D, Ash[2], B[4], Co, C[1], H[8].—that] om. Ash[2], B[3], L, Ad[3]; that god C[5], H[6]; there C[3].—vengeaunce] some vengeaunce Ad[3]. 1574. haue] om. B[1], H[1], H[3], H[4], L; hadde B[3].—assayede] hath assaied H[1], H[8]. 1575. Of] Of her B[1], B[2]. 1576. furthe with of] soth with B[1]; for right of H[4]. —hertly] verry C[1]. 1577. bonche] betith H[8]; knokken Ch, B[4].—*with* fiste*ʒ*] om. H[8], B[4]; and fistes H[4]. 1578. And] om. H[2]. 1579. holy] humble Co, B[5]. 1580. And wold hir fete, haue kyssed ther anone B[1].—his fete haue kyssed] haue kyste hir fytte D, C[1], C[3], Hn[1]; hir feete a kissed Ash[1]; her fete ther have kissed anon H[2]. 1581. Axyng] And axinge Hn[1].—thayre] om. Lg. 1582. to] om. B[1], B[2], H[4], Ash[2], CC, C[2], C[5], An, Hu. 1583. and] made C[2].—goon] gan goon Ash[1]. 1584. awaye] on her waye B[1], B[2], CC, C[1], C[2], L, Hn[1]; on the way B[3]. 1585. fully] they fully Hn[1].

---

[1]first x *is erased.*

Of whome the noyse, to the hevyn rong

W*ith* hert and speche, as thay magnyfye

The lorde above, and eu*er*y wightys tunge

For Ioye and myrthe, gan hym gloryfie

1590 And all the day, thus in meloyde

Thay led furthe, tyl it drewe to eve

And gudely thanne, of hir thay toke her leve

And furthe thay wente, eu*er*y man his waye

In the story as made is memorye

But marye in all the haste she maye

Entrede is in to hir oratorye

As she that hathe, wonen the victorye

Of all thoo, that to fore gan muse

Hir maydynhede, of malice to acuse

1586. to] is to Ash². —the hevyn] high hevene Hn¹; om. H⁸, Lg, CC.—rong] ys runge J. 1588. and] is B², Ch, B⁴, H¹, C², C¹, Ash¹, H³, H⁴, H⁵, Ad², Lg, An, C⁵, CC. 1589. gan hym] thei dide C². 1590. in] om. Lg. 1591. eve] the eve B¹.—led] hadden L. 1592. thanne of hir] of hir than H²; than of her than C².—her leve] leve B⁴, C³, J. 1594. In the story as made is memorye B¹.—the] om. D.—made is] is made D.—memorye] mencion Ash². 1595. But] And H⁸; But swete C¹.—all the] the L; al Ar. 1596. is] om. H¹, CC.—Entrede is in to] Hyʒeth hir unto Hn¹.—to] om. Ash²; *inserted above.*—hir] the H⁵.—oratorye] oratorye soon Ash². 1597. hathe wonen the victorye] the victorie woon Ash². 1598. that] om. H⁶.—to fore gan] gan aforn Ash¹, H⁶. 1599. Hir maydenhede, of malice to acuse B¹.—to] for to D, L, B³, C¹, C³.

1600 And thorugh hir merite, she hathe the mouthes shette   f. 41b

And lippys closed, of men that wer in were

And day by day, kepyng hir closette

Contynually lay, in hir prayer

Expectant aye liche as ye shall here

With humble hert, and deuoute obeysaunce

Vpon the tyme, of hir deliueraunce

The holy goste, beyng ay hir gyde

Hir Chaumbre she kept, hir day awaytyng

And as ye shall here, if ye liste tabyde

1610 And god to forne, yet or the bryddys syng

And or than Flora, dothe the floures spryng

To for the kalendes, of apryll or of may

My purpose is, playnely if I may

1600. the] her B1, B2, B3, B4, B5, H1, H4, H7, CC, J, C1, C2, C3, L, Ch, Hn1, Co. 1601. lippys] om. C1.—men] hem B1. 1603. lay] she lay Hn1.—prayer] devout prayere Hn1. 1604. liche] om. B1, H7, C1.—aye] dayly C1. 1605. With] The H2.—and] and with Co. 1606. Vpon] Vnto Ash1.—deliueraunce] obeysaunce Hu. 1607. beyng ay] ay beyng B2, H3, CC; kepyng ay H1.—hir] om. B4. 1608. Chaumbre] day Co, B5.—day awaytyng] dawytynge B1. 1609. And] om. B1, B4, H1, H4, H6, H7, H8, Ash1, C1, C3, V, C5, An, Ad2, Lg, Ch.— tabide] abide B2, B3, Co, C2, B5, Hn1, H3, H2, V, Ash2, Ar, H5, Ad3, L, CC, J; to abyde B1, B4, B5, H1, H5, H4, H6, H7, H8, Ash1, C1, C3, C5, Lg, An, Ad2, Ch, Hu. 1610. or] of Ad2, An.—the] om. H1, Hn1, Lg. 1611. than] om. Hu, B1, B5, C1, Ar; that H8, J, B2, C1, B3, B4, Co, H1, C2, Hn1, Ash1, H3, H4, H2, Ash2, H5, H6, H7, Ad3, Ad2, Lg, An, C5, L, CC.—the] om. C3, H8, J. 1612. the] om. C1, Hn1, Ash2, J.—of may] May B2, C2. 1613. playnely] sikerly C2.—if I may] to assaye C2; as I to you say B3, L.—if] if that Hn1, C5.

For to procede furthe, in this dyte

So as I can, and make mencion

Of the feste and solempnyte

That callede is, the Incarnacion

Only thorugh helpe, and supportacion

Of hir that is, so plentyvouse benyng

1620 Or that phebus enters in the signe

Wythe his carte, of the ariete

Of this feste sumwhat, shall I wryte

But oo alas, the Retorykes swete

Of petrak Fraunces that couthe so endite

And Tullyus, with all his wordys white

Full longe agone, and full olde of date

Is dede alas and passed into faate

1614. dyte] degre Ch. 1615. and] om. H8. 1616. and] and the great B1; and hye Hu. 1617. That callede is, the Incarnacion B1.—That] Whiche D.—callede] clepyde D, C1, C3.—the] om. H2. 1618. Only through] Through the C2. 1619. so] om. L.—plentyvouse] gracios C2.—benyng] and benynge L, C2, Ch, B3, Co, H6. 1620. Or that phebus enters in the signe B1.—in] into D, B2, C1, C2, C3, Ar, CC; om. Ash2. 1622. feste] om. B4. 1624. couthe so] so coude H3, CC. 1625. all] om. CC.—white] swete H8. 1626. Full longe agone, and full olde of date B1.—longe] yore D, J, Ash2; long tyme Lg.—olde] long H2. 1627. Is] Ben B3, L.—into] into the Ad3; into hir B3, L.

A commendacion of
Chauucers Ca° xxxiiii°[1]

Ａnd eke my maist*er* Chauser is ygrave

The noble Rethor, poete of Brytayne

1630   That worthy was the laurer to haue

Of poetrye, and the palme atteyne

That made firste, to distille and rayne

The golde dewe, dropes, of speche and eloquence

Into our tunge, thurgh his excellence

And fonde the floures, firste of Retoryke   f. 42a

Our Rude speche, only to enlumyne

That in our tunge, was neu*er*e noon hym like

For as the sonne, dothe in hevyn shyne

In mydday spere, dovne to vs by lyne

1640   In whose presence, no ster may a pere

Right so his dyteʒ w*ith*outyn eny pere

1628. is] is now B[2], H[2]; now ys Ch, B[3], B[4], Co, H[1], C[2], B[5], Ash[1], H[3], H[4], H[5], V, H[6], Ad[2], Lg, An, C[5], L, CC, Hu. 1629. The] For the H[8].—poete] and poete H[8], C[1], C[3], B[5].—of Brytayne] for very certayn Hu. 1630. That worthy was the laurer to haue B[1].—to] for to D, C[1], C[3], Ash[2].—worthy was] was worthy H[5].—was] is CC.—laurer] lauer garland Ar. 1631. atteyne] to atteyne Ash[1]. 1632. That made firste, to distille and rayne B[1].—That] Whiche D.—to] for to D, C[3]. 1633. golde] colde H[2].—dewe] om. C[2].—of speche] om. H[2]. 1636. only] om. C[2].—to] for to C[1], C[2]. 1638. dothe] om. Hn[1].—in] on Hn[1], B[3], H[1], B[5], Ash[1], H[2], Ar, H[5], H[6], H[7], Lg, J. 1639. by lyne] shine B[1]. 1640. no ster may] may no sterre B[4]. 1641. his] om. CC; this H[8].—pere] nocer werre Ash[2].

---

[1]first x *is erased*

Eu*er*y makyng withe his light disteyne

In sothefastnesse, who so takethe hede

Wherefore no wondre, thof my hert pleyne

Vpon his dethe, and for sorowe blede

For want of hym, nowe in my grete nede

That shulde alas, conveye and directe

And w*ith* his supporte, amende eke and corecte

The wronge trace3, of my rude penne

1650 There as I erre, and goo not lyne Right

But for that he, ne may not me kenne

I can no more, but w*ith* all my myght

With all myne hert, and myne Inwarde sight

Pray for hym, that liethe nowe in his cheste

To god above, to yeve his saule goode reste

1642. disteyne] diserne B¹, An. 1643. so] so list Ar. 1644. thof my hert] thorogh I H⁸.
1645. for sorowe] right sore B¹.—blede] myn herte blede Ch, 1646. nowe] om. H¹, B⁴, Hn¹.—
my] this H¹. 1647. alas] all H⁸.—conveyve] conceyve L; amende H⁸.—directe] corecte H⁸.
1648. eke] om. Hu. B¹.—amende] convey H⁸.—corecte] directe H⁸. 1649. rude] om. B¹.
1650. goo] om. H¹. 1651. But for that he, ne may not me kenne B¹.—kenne] nowe kenne
D, H⁸, Ar, Hn¹, H⁷.—But] That H.—ne] om. B¹, B², B³, H⁴, CC, C¹, L. 1653. and]
and all H⁶. 1654. Pray for hym, that liethe nowe in his cheste H⁷.—liethe nowe] nowe
liethe naylede D, C¹; now lieth Co, B⁵, H², L.—Pray] To pray Ash¹.—liethe] that he Hu.
1655. goode] om. J.

And as I can, forth I woll procede

Sythen of his helpe, ther may no socour be

And though my penne, be quakyng ay for drede

Neythir to Cleo, ne to Caliope

1660   Me luste not calle, forto helpe me

Ne to no muse, my poyntell forto gye

But leve all this, and saye vnto Marye

O clene castell, and the chaaste toure

Of the holy goste, mothir and virgyne

Be thou my helpe, counsel and socour

And late thy stremes, of thy mercy shyne

Into my breste, this thryde boke to fyne

That thorugh thy supporte, and benyng grace

1669   It to performe, I maye haue tyme and space.

1656. And as I can, forth I woll procede H7.—forth I woll] I furthe woll D; I wile forth
B1, Hu, B2, Ash2.—forth] om. L, CC. 1657. ther] om. B1, H6, Ash2, Lg. 1658. And] om.
Ash1, H6; all L.—be] om. CC, H3; be quaking ay] ay quaking H3; by quaking C3, H8; ay be
quaking Ch. 1659. Neythir to Cleo, ne to Caliope B1.—ne to] ne D; neither to Ash1, H6.—
Cleo] Cro H8. 1660. calle] to calle B4, H7.—forto helpe me] for no help CC.—me] om. Hu.
1661. no] om. B2, C1, B5, H2, Ash2, CC. 1662. and] to B5; and I B1, B2, Ad3, Ch.
1663. and] of Ash2; O B3, L.—chaaste] castell CC; clene Co, B5. 1665. counsel] and
counseil B1, C1. 1667. this] my Ch. 1668. thorugh] om. Ash1, H6.—thy] om. Ash2.—
supporte] supportacion CC.—thryde] rude V. 1669. tyme] lyfe Hu, B1, V.—I] if I Ash1.
—I maye haue] haue I may B5.—space] space Amen B2, H7.

BOOK III

Howe Criste was born
aftir the makyng of the
worlde v m C iiii xix
yere Cap xxxv^{to1} 1^m
   1 x x

Whanne al was hust *and* al was in silence,   f. 42b

  And in his course the longe sterry nyght

  Was passed half and fresche of aperaunce,

Lucyne shone on hevyn fayre and bryght;

Thy worde, oo lorde, that is moste of myght,

Whiche ay abydythe and partyth not from the,

Sent and discendid from thy Royall see,

Hathe sodenly upon all the erthe

Shed his light for our saluacion,

10 As I shal synge or maies dai the ferthe;

If ye lust here of humble affection,—

How in the yere by computacion

Fourty and two of Octouian;

Ferthermore, aftir the worlde beganne,

---

1. Whanne **al** was hust, *and* al was in silence, B^1.—*and* al] and D, Hu.—hust] wiste B^2, J; don CC.—in] om. Ash^2, H^2; in in CC.—was in] in Ar. 2. in] om. L.—his] this B^1.—sterry] winters C^2. 3. passed half] half past Ch, B^2, H^1, C^2, Hn^1, H^3, H^4, Ash^1, L, J, An, H^5, H^6, Ad^2, C^5, B^3, B^4, Lg, V; half half past CC.—of] in Ar. 4. on] in Ch, C^3. 5. Thy worde oo lorde] O lorde thy worde C^3, Hn^1.—lorde] god B^2, J, CC.—is moste] most is B^2, J, CC.—moste of] of most Ash^2. 6. ay] ever B^5.—not] never B^1. 7. Sent] Sende B^1, H^6; Sene Ash^1.—discendid] discendity Co, B^5, H^1, Ash^2; discende Ash^1, H^6.—thy] the H^1, Ash^2, H^5, H^8, V. 8. the] om. Ch, Co, B^5, H^3, H^4, Ash^1, L, An, CC, H^6, Ad^2, C^5, B^4, V; *inserted above.* 9. Shed] Made Lg.—light] might H^4, An. 10. As I shal synge or maies dai the ferthe, B^1.—or] on D.—As] And as Hn^1.—synge] seyn Ash^2.—ferthe] freche Lg.— maies] may Co, B^5, CC. maies dai] manyr dayes Ash^2. 11. here] hers L; to here B^1, C^1, C^2, CC, B^3, B^4. 12. by] of H^1. 13. Fourty and] Fourty yere and B^1, Co, C^3, B^5, Hn^1, H^7, H^8, Ar, Hu, V. 14. Ferthermore] Ferther CC.

---

^{1}crossed through

Beda   Fyve thousande, as Beda liste to deffyne,

And an hundreth sothely this is no lese—

And there-*with*-all nynty yere and nene,

Whanne al the worlde in reste was ande pes,

Withoutyn werre; and of Olympyades,

20   In the hundred nynty yere and thre,—

And by cronycle, eke as ye may see,

Whan Augustus by com*m*aundement,

Seuerally, *without*en exepcion,

Bade by his *lett*re*ʒ* that the p*re*sident

Of eche province, cite, borugh, *and* toun,

Thorugh-oute the worlde, make a discripcion

Of eu*er*y hedde; so that iche man,

At a certeyne day, in all the hast he can

---

15. to deffyne] deffyne Ch, B², Co, H¹, C¹, C², Hn¹, H³, H⁴, H², Ash¹, L, An, CC, H⁵, H⁶, Ad², C⁵, B³. B⁴, Lg. 16. hundreth] thousand CC.—this] it B¹. 17. there-with-all] with that Ash².—yere] om. C². 18 Whanne al the worlde in reste was ande pes B¹.— ande] and in D, An.—the] this L.—in reste was] was in reste H¹, L, H⁸. 19. and] or B¹. 20. In the] Three L; The B³.—hundred] hundred yere Ch, Co, C², B⁵.—nynty yere] nynty C², B⁵. 22. Whan] Thanne Ch, H³, Ash¹, L, J, H⁶, H⁷, Ad², C⁵, B⁴; The H⁴, An; When that C³. 23. excepcion] any excepcion B¹, Co, B⁵, H⁸. 24. Bade] Was J, CC. 25. Of eche province, cite, borugh, *and* toun H⁷.—and] or D, Co.—Of] And Ar.—eche] his Ash².—province, cite, borugh *and* toun] cite province and borough toun B¹. 27. Of eu*er*y hedde; so that iche man B¹.—iche] eu*er*y D, B³, Co, C³, B⁵; a Ad². 28. a] om. V.—he] that thei B¹, Co, H⁸, Ar.—can] came H¹.

Vpon a payne be founde in that Cyte

30 Where he was borne; *without*yn more delay,

Bothe high and lowe of what estate he be,

Aftir his statute, his tribute for to paye.

And that no man be hardy to saye naye,

To quyte hym self, *with euer*y circu*m*staunce.

To make in opyn a reconesaunce,

With honde assuryd *and* hool profession, f. 43a

Of the provynce tofore the president,

That he is suget vnto Rome towne

With all his hert, and his hole entente.

40 And here-vpon that he paye his Rente,

As the statute and the custome bonde;

That is to saye, that he brynge in his honde

29.a] om. B¹, B².—be] to be B¹.—founde] bunde B¹; founden Co; found it C¹.—that] the B², H¹, C¹, C², C³, Ash², Hn¹, H³, H⁴, H², Ash¹, J, An, CC, H⁵, H⁶, Ad², C⁵, B³, B⁴, Lg, Hu, V; om. L. 30 borne] om. C². 31. Bothe] Bothe and H⁷.—and] *inserted above*.—of what] what B¹; of what of H¹. 32. his statute] the statute Ash², B³.—statute] astate H⁴; stature Ash¹.—his tribute] tribute V. 33. And that] That also Ash².—be hardy] so hardy Hn¹, H³; be so hardy B³.—to] om. B⁵. 34. quyte] wyten B³, CC.—*wit*h] of B², H¹, C², H³, H⁴, Ash¹, L, J, CC, H⁵, H⁶, Ad², C⁵, B³, B⁴, Lg, V. 35. To] And B¹, Co, C², Ar; And to C³, B⁵, Hn¹, H⁷, H⁸, Ad³, Hu.—in] an C¹.—a] om. C¹, C³. Ar.—reconesaunce] recompence B²; remembraunce Ash¹. 36. With honde assuryd *and* hool profession H⁷.—hool] holy D; holde B¹.—honde] hounde H¹, H⁸. 37. tofore] before H², CC. 38. he] om. H².— he is] his CC.—suget] of sogett J. 39. all] all all J.—and] and all B¹.—his hole] hole C², H³, Ar. 40. here] ther B¹, C³, B⁵, Hn¹, V.—he] om. B¹.—paye] may pay B²; paide C⁵, B⁴. 41. As] And C¹; And as C².—statute] statue H².—and] in B², J, CC.—statute and the custome] custome and the statute H³, H⁴, Ash¹, An, H⁶, Ad², B⁴.—and the] and Ash². 42. he] om. CC.—brynge] brynge it B¹.—honde] lond C³.

A large peny, enpryntede wi*th* the name

And the ymage, of the emp*er*our.

And þer-upon, he shulde anoon atame

An othe of newe, and for the more honoure,

Withe honde touchede, swere for swete or sowre,

While he levyth, and neu*ere* for to Rue,

With hert and body pleynely to be trwe.

50   To tempre hym his byddyng to obeye,

Wi*th*outyn grochyng, or Rebellion,

With all his myght for to leve and deye;

Ande thanne a-noon the discripcioun,

Of eu*ery* hede, in his owne towne

Was made in haste, where that he was bore.

And aftir that, I fynde ferthermore,

---

43. A] In a J.—enpryntede] prentid H¹. 44. And the] And B¹.—of the] of H¹. 45. And
þer—upon, he shulde anoon atame B¹.—he shulde anoon] a noon he shulde D.—shulde]
shall CC.—anoon] om. H⁶. 46. An othe of] In ooth of B¹; And of the B², J, CC; And
othe of Co, C³, H⁸; And other H³, Ad², C⁵; Another H⁴, B⁴.—and] om. H².—for] of
H¹.—the] om. B¹, CC. 47. Withc honde] Without C².—touchede] touche C²; touchynge L,
B³; touchis H⁵.—sowre] sorow Ar. 48. levyth] lyved B⁵.—for] to for Ash², H². 49.
pleynely] surely C²; om. L.—to be] om. B². 50.] To his biddynge evir to boey Ash²;
And to make hym here byddynge to obeye Hn¹.—To tempre] In temperalite B², J,
CC; To the empre Ad²; The emperoures B⁴; to the Emp*er*oure V.—hym] om. B², H¹,
C¹, H³, H⁴, Ash¹, L, J, An, CC, H⁵, H⁶, Ad², C⁵, B3, B⁴, Lg.—his] her C¹, C³, B⁵, H².
51. grochyng] grucchinge to obeie Lg. 52. With all] Enforce Ash².—for to] to B¹.—
and] or H⁸, Hu. 53. Ande thanne a noon the discripcioun B¹.—thanne] that D, Ash²; om.
H⁵.—the] om. Ash¹, H⁶. 55. Was made in haste where that he was bore B¹.—that]
om. D, B², H¹, C¹, C², Ash², L, J, CC, H⁵, B³. 56. I fynde] and side more B¹; I fynde
that Co, B⁵.

His name was regestrede and Inamede there,

Perpetually forto be in mynde.

And this discryvyng, if ye luste to here,

60 Was made firste in Cyrye, as I fynde,

By one Cirynus, the peple for to bynde,

To be to Rome ay in subiecion.

For this Cyrinus, in that Region,

Was prefecte than, vndir the Emp*e*rour,

In bokys olde, as made is mencion.

And while that he was ther gou*e*rnour,

Was begon firste this discripcion;

The yere, in sothe, Aftir the fundacion

Of myghty Rome, VII*e* and fiftene.

70 At whiche tyme w*ith* his beemus shene.

---

57. His] This Hn1.—was] is C3.—and Inamede] with them Ch, B2, C3, H3, H4, Ash1, L, J, An, CC, H5, H6, Ad2, C5, B3, B4, Lg, V; and writen H1, Ash2. 58. forto] to Ch, H3, H4, Ash1, An, H6, Ad2, C5, B4. 59. this] thus H8.—discryvyng] desceonyng Ash1; discripcioun H8.—ye] he An, C5, B4.—to] om. 55.—here] weten H1, Ash2. 60. made firste] first made B1.—Cyrye] Cry H2. 61. By one] With oon B2, J; withoutyn CC.—Cirynus] grennys CC. 62. To be] Be Ch, Ash1 J, An, H5, H6, Ad2, B4, Lg.—to Rome] in Rome H1, B5.—ay] ever B1, Co, C3, B5, Hn1, H2, H7, H8, Ar, Ad3, C5, Hu; om. Ch, B2, H1, C1, C2, Ash2, H3, H4, Ash1, L, J, An, CC, H5, H6, Ad2, B3, B4, Lg, V. 63. this] that B1; om. H1. 64. prefecte] preferred Ch, C2, H3, H4, L, An, H5, H6, Ad2, C5, B3, B4, Lg; president Co, B5, V.—Was prefecte than] Thanne was perfite B1.—than] there Ch, H3, H4, L, An, H5, H6, Ad2, C5, B3, B4, Lg.—the] that Ar. 66. while] whis H8.—that] om. Ch, B1, H3, H4, Ash1, An, H5, H6, Ad2, C5, B4, Lg.—ther] than C2. 67. Was] He C2.—begon firste] first begon Ch, C3, H3, H4, Ash1, An, H6, Ad2, B4, Lg; first thanne begun C5.—this] the B1, Co, C2, C3, B3, Hu, H3, H4, An, H6, Ad2, V; the first Ash1. 68. in sothe] for soth B1.—the] om. H1, Ash2. 69. c] hundred yere B1, C3. 70. At whiche tyme w*ith* his beemus shene B1.—w*ith*] was D.

Was fresche Phebus in his firste face,   f. 43b

Of Ca*pr*icorne his lawest stacion;

The same yere callet the yere of grace,

The yere of comfort, and of Remyssion;

Beynge the thriddeteneth the indiccioun,

The golden nombre of the same yere

xviii accomptede in oure calendere.

Howe Ioseph and our   The Regne of Heroude xxx^{ti} yere and one,
lady went to Bedlem   Whan made was the discripcion,
to pay thayre tribute
Cap° xxxvi^{to1} 2^m   80 As ye haue herde, that Ioseph must gone

To Bedeleem for conclusion,

To pay his tribute in his owne towne,

As the statute afore dothe specyfye;

Because that he and also eke Marye

---

71. fresche] first B², CC.—his] hyr C³.—in his firste] first in his L.—firste] frest B². 72. his] the Ch, H³, H⁴, An, H⁶, Ad², C⁵, B⁴, Lg; in his H². 73. The] This H¹.—same yere] same B¹. 74. and of] and H¹, C², B⁵, Ash¹, H², C⁵, Lg. 75. Beynge the thriddeteneth the indiccioun, B¹.—Beynge the] Beynge D, C¹, C³.—the indiccioun] of the indiccioun H⁸, Lg; of indiccioun; indiccioun B², H², L, J, CC, B³, B⁴, Hu. 76. of] in B¹; eke of H⁸. 78. Regne] yere Ch, C¹, H³, Ash¹, An, H⁶, Ad², C⁵, B⁴; regnynge B¹. 79. Whan] And whan B², J, CC; Whan that C³; om. H².—made] maked H¹, Ash², H²; om. H⁵.—was] om. H¹.—the] this B¹, H¹, C³, B⁵, Ash², Hn¹, H², H⁷, H⁸, Ar, Ad³, Hu. 80. haue] om. Ch.—that] how C¹. 81. To] Unto H¹, Ash²; Forth than to Hn¹.—for] for a C¹, Ash¹; forth in C³. 82. pay his] pay a C².—in] and in B¹. 83. afore dothe] before do B¹; tofore doith C¹, Ar; as fore doth B⁵; doth aforn H¹. 84. also eke] eke also B², Co, CC; also B¹, H¹, C¹, Ash², H⁸, Ar, B⁴, Hu; eke H⁵; his spouse C²; eke hys wyfe C³.—also] *inserted above.*

---

¹crossed through

Werne of the householde and of the trybe borne

Called Iuda, and of the kynrede

Of worthy Dauid, as I haue sayde to-forne.

And on her Iournay, as thay gan thayme spede,

And holy Ioseph dyd hir brydill lede,

90 Sodenly marye full sone she abrayede,

And vnto Ioseph evyn thus she sayde:

"I wys," quod she, "me thynkyth þat I see

Two folkys gretly discordyng,

Vpon the waye aperen vnto me.

The tone Reioysysng, that othir compleynyng."

To whome Ioseph benyngly lokyng,

Ansewerde agayne and bad hir Ryde in pees;

And prayed hir also nat to be reccles,

---

85. the householde] householde H². —of the trybe] the tribe Ch, B¹, B², Co, H¹, C³, B⁵, Ash², Hn¹, H³, H⁴, J, An, H⁵, H⁶, H⁷, H⁸, Ar, Ad³, Ad², C⁵, B³, Hu; of the tribute Ash¹, CC, V; the tribute J, Ar; the thrid Lg. 86. and] om. Ash². 87. haue] om. H⁸. —to forne] be forne Ch, B¹, B², Co, H⁸. 88. on] in B², J, CC. —gan thayme] can B¹; hem gan B⁵; have hem H². 89. And] This C². —Ioseph] om. B¹. —dyd] and C²; as he H². —dyd hir brydill] hyr brydyll dyd C³. 90. Sodenly] And sodenly Ch, B², C², H³, H⁴, Ash¹, L, J, An, CC, H⁵, H⁶, Ad², C⁵, B³, B⁴, Lg, V. —full sone] thanne Ch, B², H³, H⁴, Ash¹, J, An, CC, H⁵, H⁶, Ad², C⁵, B³, B⁴, Lg; fyrst H¹, Ash²; om. Ar. —marye full sone she] than abreide Mari C²; Mary dyde L; Marye than V. —she] om. Ch, H¹, C², C³, Ash², H³, H⁴, Ash¹, L, J, An, CC, H⁵, H⁶, Ad², C⁵, B³, B⁴, Lg, V. 91. vnto] to B¹, H¹, Ash². —evyn] anon CC, H⁵. —thus] this C², H⁶. 92. I wys] For sothe B¹, H⁷; sothly Hn¹. 93. Two] Tweyn Co, H¹, C¹, B⁵, Ash², H², H⁸, Ar, Ad³, Hu. —gretly] afore C³. 94. aperen] apperynge Ch, B¹, B², Co, C¹, C², C³, B⁵, Hn¹, H³, H⁴, H², Ash¹, L, J, An, CC, H⁵, H⁶, H⁷, H⁸, Ar, Ad³, Ad², C⁵, B³, B⁴, Lg, Hu, V. 95. The tone] That on Ch, C³, B⁵, H⁴, H², Ar. —Reioysyng] reioyseth C³. —that othir] the tother Ch, H¹, C¹, C², B⁵, Hn¹, H³, Ash¹, L, J, An, H⁵, H⁶, H⁷, H⁸, Ad³, Ad², C⁵, B³, B⁴, Lg, Hu. 97. Ansewerede] Answering H⁶. —and] a C². —bad] om. H¹, Hn¹. 98. hir also] also hir B²; also C¹, B⁵; hir H¹. —nat to be] nought be Co, V; to be to be not C¹, H¹; be not Ash¹, B⁴.

Any wordys for to speke in vayne,

100   But holde hir way and hir Iournay Right.

And vnwarly, aforne hem in the playne,

Apered an Angell w*ith* face sterne and bryght

Of whome the beaute ȝaf a plesant lyght,

The place envyron and a sote odoure.

And his clothyng like the lely floure

Was whit in sothe, as snowe that fallith newe;   f. 44a

Whiche gan a-noon chere and loke to meve,

And ther-w*ith*-all, with a chaunged hewe,

By-gan also Ioseph to repreve.

110   And shortly bad his wordes that he leve,

And sayde, in sothe, that he was to blame

For to be bolde any wordes to atame

---

99. Any] And Ash². —wordys] worde Hu.—for to] to Ch, B¹, H¹, Ash². —speke] speky H¹. 100. But holde] Beholde H¹; Let holde C¹. 101. vnwarly] inwardely Ch, H¹, C¹; unwarnely B¹.—aforne] to forn C¹; be forne B⁴.—in] upon B¹, B², Co, C², J, H⁷; on Ch, H¹, B⁵, Ash², Hn¹, H⁴, H³, H², Ash¹, L, An, CC, H⁵, H⁶, Ad², Ad³, B³, B⁴, Lg, Hu. 103. Of whome the beaute ȝaf a plesant lyght, B¹.—plesant] plentevouse D; so plesant a V. 104. a] of a B¹; so C¹; om. C³, CC, Ar; *inserted above.*—odoure] of odoure C³. 105. And his] This C².—like] fair like C²; like as Hn¹. 106. Was whit in sothe, as snowe that fallith newe, B¹.—fallith] fallyt D; fallyn H¹, Ash². 107. gan] chere Ch; began C².—a noon] his C².—chere] gan Ch; to chere B².—and] to Ch.—loke] om. B², J, CC.—to] om. B¹, H⁷, H⁸, Ar, Ad³. 108. with a] a H³, B⁴.—chaunged] chaungynge B¹, H⁸. 109. also] anoon C². 110. And] That J, CC.—shortly bad] bad shortly H¹, L.—his] hir B², J, CC.—wordes] om. B², J, CC.—that] for to C².—he] she B², J, CC; om. C; he shulde H³. 111. sayde] seith H¹, Ash². 112. For] And B², J, CC.—be bolde] be holde Ash², H², H⁵; bolde J.—to atame] for to atame B¹, B², J, CC.

Ayens Marye; thorough his necligence

To saye that she spak any worde in vayne.

For that she sawe was non apperance,

But verrey sothe as she hath it seyne.

"For truste me well and be right certeyne,

Of this folke of whiche she spake to the,

In sothefastenesse, lyche as thou shalt see,

120 Ben the peoples and the folkeȝ tweyne,

That ben disceuerde in full large space:

The ton of Iues, that wepe shull and pleyne,

With many atere distyllyng on his face;

That wilfully shall refuse his grace,

Of frowarde hert for to be benyng,

To devoyde and playnely to Resygne

113. his] thy C^5. 114. To save that she spak any worde in vayne, B^1.—worde] thyng D, Co, H^1, C^1, C^2, B^5, Ash^2, H^2, Hu, V.—in] om. Ch, C^2, Ash^1, L, An, H^5, H^6, Ad^2, C^5, B^3, B^4, Lg; on C^1.—she] om. Ash^2. 115. For that she sawe was non apperance B^1.—non] not D, H^1, Ash^2, C^1.—sawe] saith Ad^2.—was] hit was C^3.—apperance] fantasye Hu. 116. verrey] certyn H^1, Ash^2; werre Lg; was C^2.—she] ye H^1.—it] om. B^4.—seyne] said Ar. 117. me] om. H^1.—right] right in Co, B^5. 118. Of] That H^1, C^1, Ash^2; And H^2.—this] these B^1, Hn^1, H^7, Ar, Ad^3, Hu.—folke] om. B^1, H^7, Ar, Ad^3.—of] *inserted above.*—of which] that B^1, Co, C^3, B^5, Hn^1, H^7, Ar, Ad^3; which C^2.—she] I Ch, B^2.—spake] speketh of C^3. 119. shalt] shal B^1, H^1, C^1, Ar. 120. peoples] peple Ar, B^4.—and the] of the Ch; and CC. 121. That] Whyche C^3.—ben] ar H^1.—in] by Ash^2. 122. The ton] That on Ch, Co, H^1, C^3, B^5, Ash^2, H^2, Ar.—Jewes-wes Lg.—that] om. H^1, Ash^1. 123. stere] teeris B^2, H^1, C^1, Ash^2, H^2, J, CC, Hu.—on] in C^2, C^3, Ash^1.—his] her Ch, C^1, H^3, H^4, H^2, Ash^1, L, An, H^6, Ar, Ad^2, C^5, B^3, B^4, Lg. 124. wilfully] wilfull H^6.—shall] shulde Lg.—refuse] refuge Ash^2.—his] om. B^2, J, CC; all his Co, B^5; theyr C^3, L, B^3; of this Ash^2. 125. for to] to B^1, CC; full H^1; and Ash^2.—be] om. B^2, H^1, Ash^2.—benyng] unbenigne H^1, Ash^2. 126. To] And Ash^2.—devoyde] voyde B^4.—and] om. H^1, B^5, Ash^2.—playnely] playnli and B^5.—to Resygne] resigne B^1.

The Sinagoge, w*ith* hir Rite3 olde,

Whiche in shorte tyme shall drawe to declyne,

And hir phares quenche and waxen colde

130   With sacrede light, that were wonte to shyne.

For tyme is come þ*at* they must fyne,

Ande the weylinge of her derked chere

Vncloos shall and shewe al bryght and clere,

As phebus dothe at mydday in the sowthe,

Whan eu*er*y Rakke and eu*er*y cloudy skye

Is voyde clene, so hir face vncouthe

Shall shewe in opyn and fully ben vnwry.

And the peple whiche that marye

Reioysyng say for yoye and gladnesse,

140   Ben paynymes þ*at* mekely shall hem dresse,

---

127. w*ith*] whyche B¹; with with Ch.—hir] his H¹, Ash¹, H⁴, Ar; om. C².—olde] hoolde B¹; ful olde Hn¹. 128. Whiche] With B², C¹, J.—to] and B¹, C². 129. phares] faces Ch, B², C², Hn¹, H³, H⁴, H², Ash¹, J, An, CC, H⁵, H⁶, H⁷, Ad², C⁵, B³, B⁴, Lg; face L; fyres B⁵, Ash², Ar; feres H¹, C¹; fairenesse H⁸.—colde] pale CC; olde Ar, Ad³. 130. light] li3thes B⁵.—were wont] wont were C³, Hn¹; never went C². 131. they] the Ar. 132. Ande the weylinge of her derked chere, B¹.—derked] derke D, C¹, C², H⁶, H⁷, Hu; dewed Ar.—the] hir C¹.—weylinge] werkynge H¹, Ash²; weykynge J, CC. 133. shewe] shede H⁸; shynne B¹.—al] as Ch, H⁴, Ash¹, An, H⁵, H⁶, Ad², C⁵, B⁴, Lg; om. C³, CC, Ar. 134. at] on H².—mydday] mydon B¹; the mydday C².—in] on H².—the] om. Co, CC. 135. Rakke] rake Co; rokke C³.—cloudy] cloudes B¹, J, H⁷, Ad³; cloude on H¹; cloude CC; cloudyd Hn¹. 136. voyde clene] clene voyde C³; voyded clene H⁸.—so] for Ad³; saf CC.—hir] his Ch, B².—face] faces H². 137. shewe] schewyn H¹.—in] al C¹; and B², J, CC.—fully] full Ch, H¹, Ash².—vnwry] humblye B², J, CC. 138. the] eke the Hn¹. 139. say] sawe B¹, B², H¹, C¹, C³, B⁵, Ash², Hn¹, Ash¹, J, CC, H⁷, H⁸, Ar, Ad³, B³, V; sall L. 140. þat] om. Lg.—mekely shall] shul mekely B¹; meke shall L, B³; thekely shall Lg.—hem] hym Hu; om. Lg.—dresse] drede Ch, B², C¹, Hn¹, Ar, Ad³, Ad², C⁵, B⁴, Hu; redresse H⁸; om. Lg.

This tyme of grace fully to obey,

With hert and will, and full humble chere.

For goddes worde that no man maye wi*th*saye

Hath hastyd it gon ful many a ȝere,

To Abrah*a*m and Isaak in-fere,

And to Iacob, that in hir holy seede,

Full hastely, who so luste take hede,

Shall al peples pleynly blissede be,

Thorugh-oute the worlde in eu*er*y londe and realme."

150   And with that worde, as Ioseph myght see,

The Angell sty above the sonne beame.

And he gothe furthe tawarde Bedlem,

Wi*th* marie, til that thei bothe tweyne,

In full lytyll space go*n*nen to atteyne

---

141. This] The Ash².—**of]** full of L.—**fully]** full H¹.—**to]** for to C³, Ash². **142. full]** om. Ch; with full B¹, B², Hn¹, L, J, CC, H⁵, H⁷, H⁸, Ar, Ad³, B³, Hu, V; with Co, C², C³, B⁵, H³, H⁴, H², An, Ad², C⁵, B⁴, Lg. **144.** Hath hastyd it gon ful many a ȝere, B¹.—**gon]** go D; gon is H⁸; full goon Ar.—**ful]** om. Ar.—**a]** om. H. **145. and]** and to Ch, C¹, C², C³, Hn¹, H³, H⁴, L, J, An, CC, H⁵, H⁸, Ad², C⁵, B³, B⁴, Lg.—**in]** also in B¹, B⁴; on V. **146. And to]** Unto B⁴. **147. hastely]** hertly C¹.—**who so]** who Ch, L, B³.—**luste]** woll Ch, H³, H⁴, An, Ad², C⁵, B⁴.—**take]** to take B¹, L, J, CC, B³. **148. al]** al the Ch, H¹, Ash², H³, H⁴, L, An, Ad², C⁵, B³, B⁴, Lg; of all CC.—**peples]** pepyll C³, Hn¹, CC.—**pleynly]** trewly C²; full pleynly CC; om. L.—**blissede]** blesse H⁸.—**be]** om. H⁸. **149. Thorough oute]** Thoruȝ C².—**in eu*er*y]** both B², CC; on every C¹; every H¹; thorowe oute J.—**londe and Realme]** rewme B¹; and londe reame CC. **150. as]** that Ch, H⁸, An, B⁴, Lg; and C¹, H⁴, L, B³. **152. gothe]** go H³, Ar. **153.** Wi*th* marie, til that thei bothe tweyne H⁷.—**that]** om. D, C³, H¹, C¹, Ash², H², H⁵.—**marie]** feyre Mary C³.—**thei]** om. Ch, B⁴.—**bothe]** om. B¹.

To the boundes of bedleme the cite,

Wery *and* mate sumdel of her viage;

Where thay founde of peple seche plente

In the Cyte, of eu*ery* man*ere* age,

That thay myght haue noman*er* herbygage

160   In all the towne, nethir boure ne hall,

Save a stable and a lytyll stall,

That were sequestrede and set asyde

Oute of all prees, the story saythe expresse,

Made for beste3, sothely into abyde,

Ful straite and narewe, schadewid w*ith* derknesse.

Into whiche Ioseph gan hym dresse

W*ith* Marye, to reste ther all nyght.

And as she entrede, a newe soden light

---

155. To the boundes of bedleme, the cite, B¹.—the] that D. 156. Wery and mate sumdel of her viage, B¹.—mate sumdel] som dele mate D; late sumdele H⁸.—viage] visage Lg. 157. Where] There for Ch, H³, H⁴, An, Ad². C⁵, B⁴, Lg; Whanne B², J, CC.—of] of the Ash², H²; the L.—seche] grete C¹. 158. age] of age B⁵. 159. myght] ne might Hn¹; om. Ash².—myght haue] have myght Ar.—haue] fynde B², J, CC.—noman*er*] non B¹, Co, H¹, C³, B⁵, Ash², Hn¹, H², H⁷, H⁸, Ar, Ad³. 160. nethir] ne B²; nethir in C¹, L, B³; in CC; om. H⁸.—ne] non B¹; ne in C¹, CC. 161. stall] halle H². 162. were] was H⁴.—were sequestrede] sequestred was Ar.—set] y-sette Ch, H¹, C², Ash², H³, H⁴, H², L, J, An, H⁵, H⁷, H⁸, Ad³, Ad², C⁵, B³, B⁴, Lg, V.—asyde] all asyde C³. 163. all] the C²; all the L, B³.—saythe] doth H⁸. 164. sothely] om. Ch, B², C², Hn¹, H³, H⁴, H², L, J, An, CC, H⁵, B⁴, Lg, Hu; there in H².—into] to H¹, Ash²; in forto C³.—sothely into] in sothly to B¹, H⁷. 165. Ful straite and narewe, schadewid w*ith* derknesse, H⁷.—schadewid] and shadewede D, H¹, Ash².—w*ith*] in CC.—derknesse] derenesse Ar.—narewe] ful narewe B¹.

Gan the place enlumen envyro*n*,

170 That shone as bright as eny som*e*res day,

So that this lityll humble mancio*n*

Was fresche of light as phebus is in may;

Whiche gan to waxen and encrece aye

While she was there, all-be þat it was nyght.

And right anoon, the sothefaste sonne of myght,

Of all our Ioye, caste hyme to aryse   f. 45a

And shed his light to glad all man kynde.

For tawarde mydnyght, shortly to devyse,

Whan all was huste, holy wryt makyth mynde,

180 As softely as he dyd hym wynde

In the sydes, of this holy mayde,

So easely this newe sonne abrayde,

---

169. Gan] And Ch, B5, H3, H4, Ash1, An, CC, H5, H6, H7, Ad2, C5, B4; hathe C2.— enlumen] to enlumyne H1, C3, Ash2; enluminide C2. 170. eny] om. Ch. 171. that] om. H1, Ash2.—this] the Hn1.—lityll] om. Ch. 172. of light] om. B1; and light C2.—phebus] mede C2.—is] om. B2, J, CC; shynneith B1.—in] om. Co. H1. 173. Whiche] The whych Ash2.—and] and to C1, C2, Ar.—encrece] encresyng H1. 174. While] While that B1.—all be] though B1, B2, CC; all be it Co; all that C1.—þat] om. B1, B2, H1, C1; though C3.— it] om. C1.—was] were B1, B2, CC, Ash; same C1. 175. And right anoon] om. Ash2.— sothefaste sonne] sonne Ch; sonne sothe faste C2.—of myght] of lyȝt Ch, H3, H4, Ash1, An, H6, Ad2, C5, B4, Lg; bryȝht B1, B2, Co, H1, C1, C3, B5, Hn1, H2, CC, H5, H7, H8, Ar, Ad3, B3, Hu, V; and bright C2; bright anoon right Ash2. 176. all] om. H1, Ash2.—to] forto Hn1.—aryse] rise B1, H1, Ash2. 177. shed] shewe B1, L, B3; shewed H8; shaden Ash2.—glad] om. H8; gladden B2, Ash2, J, CC. 179. was] holy Ash2.—huste] wist B2, J; in pees C2.—mynde] mencioun C1, H3. 180. softely] sothely Ch, B2, H5, H4, H2, An, H6, H8, Ad2, C5, B4; sothfastly C1. 181. In] With yn C3.— this] the H1, C2, B5, Ash2, L. 182. this] this this H2.—abrayde] dide abrayde B1.

Whan he was borne in to this mortall lyfe,

Vpon the erthe to shede his bryghtnesse,

Wi*th*outyn helpe of any mydwyfe,

Or of his mothir, travell or sekenesse.

For she that firste conceyved in clennesse,

It sat right wele that she shulde also

Wi*th* outyn trayvell or eny man*e*re woo,

190   For to go quyte at hir delyueraunce,

And specially haue ap*r*erogatife,

In hir childyng to fele no penaunce,

Sithe she was bothe mayde, modir, and wife,

Chosyn of god for to stynte our stryve,

Of all wymen, by hir self aloon.

Wherfore it sat not hir for to crye and grone

---

183. Whan] And C². —he] she Ch; om. C². —borne] com C¹. —in to] in Ch; unto C², H⁸. —this] his B². 184. the erthe] erthe H¹, C², J, Ash², V. —to] he Ar. —shede] shewe B², L, J, CC. B³. 185. helpe] the helpe B⁵; any helpe Ad². —any] om. CC. 186. Or] Of Ch; om. C², CC. —mothir] moders CC. 187. that] om. C². 188. It] Hir C³. —she] om. C². 189. Wi*th* outyn] Sche without C². —man*e*re] other C². —woo] of woo B¹, Ash¹, CC. 190. go] om. Co, B⁵, Ash², CC, Lg. —at] go at Ash²; all CC; of B². 191. haue] to have B¹, Co, Hn¹, B⁴; for to have Ad². 193. Sithe] om. Ash¹. —was] is B¹, Co, C³ B⁵, Hn¹, H⁷, H⁸, Ar, Ad³, Hu. —was bothe] bothe was CC. —bothe] om. C³. —bothe mayde] maide bothe H³. 194.] And ever was blessyd in al hir lyif B¹. —for] to C³, CC; for J. 195. self] lyfe Hn¹. 196. Wherfore] om. L, B³. —not hir] hir not B², Ash², L, B³. —hir] to hir Ch, H¹. —to] om. Ch; forto C². —and] ne B¹, C¹, L, B³, V; nor B²; or C³; ne to CC.

Lyke oþer wemen þat ben inli sike,

In the tyme of hir trvelyng.

Wherfore sithe she was to noon othir lyke,

200 No payne felte the houre of hir chldyng.

And, as I fynde, at hir delyueryng

Ther was no wight but hir self aloon;

For þylke tyme Ioseph was out goone,

Howe Iosephe went to seke Mydwyfeʒ to our lady Ca°xxxvii[1]ʒ[m]

In full gret hast to enquere and seke

Some Mydwyfe to helpe in this nede.

And in this while, with hir eyne meke,

She childed hath, this floure of maydynhede.

And home agayne, as Ioseph gan hym spede,

And to the place the mydwyfeʒ brought,

210 Evyn at the dore abasshede in theyr thought,

197. Lyke oþer wemen, þat ben inli sike, B[1].—inli] in like D.—Lyke] Syk Co.—oþer] to other Ch, H[3], H[4], Ash[1], An, H[5], H[6], Ad[2], C[5], B[3], B[4], Lg; owe CC. 198. In] On H[1], Ash[2].—of] that of Hu. 199. sithe] om. Ash[1], H[6].—she] om. C[2].—was] is CC.—to] om. B[1], C[1], Hn[1], CC, H[7], H[8], Ar, Ad[3].—noon othir] nother H[7].—lyke] sche like C[2]. 200. No] Ne Co, B[5], H[4].—felt] felt she CC; felt in B[1], Co, C[1], B[5]; she felde C[2].—the houre of] om. C[1]. 201. at] of H[8]. 202. no] om. H[1]. 203. For þylke tyme Ioseph was out goone, H[7].—þylke] that D, B[1], B[2], C[1], C[2], Hn[1], Ar; as that C[3].—out] foorth B[1], Ar. 204. full] om. Ch.—to] for to H[1], H[8].—hast] nede L. 205. to helpe] om. Ash[2].—in] at CC. 206. in] yet C[3]; om Ash[2], H[8].—while] tyme C[2]; whyle whyle Ch.—with] om. Ash[2].—hir] a C[2].—eyne] than B[2], H[2], J; spirit C[2].—meke] ful meke C[2].—with hir eyne meke] she that was meke CC. 207. this] the B[1], H[1], C[3], B[5], Hn[1], CC, H[7], H[8], Ar, Ad[3], Hu.—maydynhede] manhede J, CC. 208. as] whan C[2]; om. H[3].—gan] om. B[1]; dide C[2].—hym] om. C[2]. 209. And to] Unto C[3]; to Hn[1].—place] places L.—the mydwyfeʒ] midwives B[1]; the mydwyfe CC.—brought] he brought Co, C[3], Hn[1], Hu. 210. the] hir C[1].—theyr] his CC.

[1]crossed through

Stoden styll astonyed of that light,   f. 45b

And þe briȝtnesse þat schone in þe place,

Aȝen kynde, þat tyme of the nyȝght,

That thay ne myght susteyne in her face

And no wondre, for the sonne of grace,

Within whiche cast his light so ferre,

Of whome the mone and eche othir sterre

Receyven her light, euerech in her spere,

Al be þat he lay here in erthe lowe,

220   In a stable with his sacrede chere,

Sool with his mothir that no man dyd knowe;

On whome hir loke she mekely gan to throwe,

Gudly biholdynge his fayre ȝonge face,

And knelyng downe began to enbrace

---

211. Stoden] stonding H¹; stonden Ash², Ash¹, H⁶.—styll] om. B², J, CC; all styll
C³.—that] the V. 212. And þe briȝtnesse þat schone in þe place H⁷.—Ande] Of
D.—and of C³ Hn¹.—bryȝghtnesse] liȝtnes C².—in þat] in the Ch, B², Co, C¹, C³,
Ash², Hn¹, H³, H², Ash¹, L, J, CC, H⁵, H⁶, H⁷, H⁸, Ar, Ad³, Ad², C⁵, B³, B⁴, Lg, Hu.
213. Aȝen kynde, þat tyme of the nyȝght B¹.—of] on D.—þat] in that C².—the] om. C².
214. susteyne] it susteyne C³, Hn¹, L, H⁵; susteine it V. 215. for] so B¹; þouȝ H³.
216. Within] Within was V.—cast] was caste H³.—light] eyen Ch. 217. eche] eke
H⁴, H⁸; euery V.—othir] the other H⁸. 218. Receyven] Resceyvynge Hu. 219. Al
be þat he lay here in erthe lowe H⁷.—lay here] here laye D.—Albe] Thow B¹.—that]
om. B¹, B⁵.—he] she CC.—her laye] lay here B¹, Co, H¹, B⁵, Ash², Hn¹, H³, H⁴, H²,
Ash¹, An, H⁶, H⁷, H⁸, Ad³, Ad², C⁵, B⁴, Lg, Hu; lay Ch, CC.—in erthe] herthe Ch;
in the erthe B¹, B⁵. 220. stable] stalle B¹, H¹.—his] a B¹, B², Co, C³, B⁵. 221. dyd]
dide hym H¹, Ash², L, B³. 222. her] she her C².—she mekely gan] she gan mekely
B², CC; she gan C¹, Hn¹; mekely gan C²; she mekely can B¹.—to] om. B¹, C², B⁵, CC,
B⁴. 223. Gudly biholdynge his fayre ȝonge face, B¹.—fayre ȝonge] yonge fare D; fare Ch.
224. to] forto C³.

His tendre lymmes in hir Armes tweyne,

And wrappede hym in clothes tendrely,

Ande toke hi*m* up and sooftly gan hi*m* leyne

In hir lappe; and full humbly

She be-helde his feturs by and by,

230 So fayre shapen in party and in all.

And wi*th* hir mylke, verrey celestiall,

And hevenly licour of hir pappes small,

His tendre lymmes she sprede in eu*er*y coste,—

The white bavme to make it avale,

Fette fro the condyth of the holy goste,

Vpon the thyng that se loved moste;

And gaffe hym souke of the pyment sote,

That sprange and grwe oute of the holy Rote

225. in hir] in Ch; with H⁸; in his Ad³. 227. Ande toke hi*m* up and sooftly gan hi*m*
leyne, B¹.—sooftly] sothely D; softe Co, C², B⁵.—gan] dide C²; om. H⁶.—hym leyne]
hym hym leyne L. 228. full] om. Ch, H¹; than full C³, Hn¹. 229. and] the and C².
230. shapen] shapp H².—party and in] every party over B¹. 231. hir] om. H⁵.—mylke]
meke H¹. 232. of] in H³.—hir] his B⁴.—pappes] pappe C². 233. His] Hyr Ash², H⁴,
CC.—lymmes] loines B¹.—sprede] sprenged B²; spreyd H⁸; stremes CC.—in] be CC.
234. bavme] beame CC.—it] om. H¹, Ash²; hete H⁸.—avale] to avale B¹, C¹, Hn¹,
H², H⁷, H⁸, Ad³; awake Lg. 235. fro the] fro C².—condyth] condite Ch, B¹, B²,
Co, H¹, C¹, C², C³, Ash², Hn¹, H³, H⁴, H², Ash¹, L, J, An, CC, H⁵, H⁶, H⁷, H⁸,
Ar, Ad³, Ad², C⁵, B³, B⁴, Lg, Hu; conduct B⁵.—of the holy goste that she lovyth
moste H⁸. 236. the] that B², H²; om. H⁵.—that] om. Ch, B¹, H¹, Ash², CC.—she]
om. Hu.—loved] lovyth B⁴, V.—that she loved moste] om. H⁸. 237. souke] drynke
Ch, H¹, Ash². 238. That sprange and] That and B¹; And that Ash².—oute] om. H⁵,
Ad².—the] that C¹; this Ar.—holy] hole C².

Of maydenhede, and fro the chaste **vyne**

240   Of all clennesse, was itryede oute.

Wher-wi*th* she made hir yong chylde to dyne,

Whom hevyn and erthe muste obeye and loute,

Albe that he, wi*th* beste*ʒ* hym aboute,

Lay humbly, as ye haue herde devyse,

And aftir this his mothir dyd **aryse**

And lyft hi*m* up, sooftly in-to the stalle   f. 46a

Where-as the asse and the oxe stode.

And on hir knees she gan a-noon to falle,

And worshipped hym, this beste of all gode,

250   That gyvethe to Angel and to man his foode.

And than this mayde, wi*th* debonayre chere,

Withe face erecte and handys eke in-fere,

239. and] om. Hu.—from] of Co.—chaste] holy B¹. 240. was] om. B¹, H¹, B⁵, H³; was thanne Hn¹. 241. made] makyth Hu.—childe] sone B¹.—to] om. B⁴. 242. Whom] To whom Ash¹.—and erthe] om. H¹.—obeye] obeyeth C³. 243. Albe that] All thowe B¹, J, CC; Alle be it that Hu.—he] she C².—with] lay with B¹, J. 244. Lay] om. B¹.—as] ay as CC. 245. aftir] atyr An.—aryse] rise B¹. 246. And lyft him up sooftly in-to the stalle, B¹.—sooftly] sothely D, C¹, C³, H³.—vp] om. H⁴.—into] in H¹, Ash².—stalle] stable Ash². 247, as] om. Ch, B², H¹, C¹, C², B⁵, Ash², H³, H⁴, Ash¹, L, J, An, CC, H⁵, H⁶, Ad², C⁵, B³, B⁴, Lg, Hu, V; that Co, C³.—asse] the oxe C¹, H².—and the oxe] and also the asse C¹; and the asse H². 248. she] anon sche Co; they H⁸.—gan] began C².—a noon] om. Ch, B¹, Co, C². —to] doun B¹. 249. this] the CC.—beste] bestes H⁸. 250. That] And B², CC.—Angel] angels Ch, B², H³, H⁴, Ash¹, L, J, CC, H⁵, Ad², C⁵, B³, B⁴, Lg; man H⁶.—to man] man B², CC; to angelis H⁶.—his] their B², L, CC, H⁶, B³; om. H². 251. than] that H¹, Ash²; om. C³.—with] with a B¹, CC; of H⁸. 252. face] om. L. —erecte] swete B²; dyrecte J, CC, Ar; trewe Ash¹.

A deuote prayer that our lady made whan criste was borne Ca° xxxviii[1]4.

To god above by-gan thus for to pray:

    "O lorde," quod she, "*with* all my full myght

To whom iche thynge iustely must obeye,

To the be thanke, as it is skyll and right,

That thou so goodly luste to haue a sight

To my mekenesse, though I vnworthe be.

And not dysdeygne of thy benyngnyte,

260   To graunte only of thyn high goodnesse,

Me to encrece vnto suche excellence,

To be a mayde and mohtir in clennesse,

To bere thy sonne and eke thy sapyence,

That neu*ere* twynnyth oute of thy *presence*,

But in heven abydythe aye *with* the,

And in erthe mekely nowe withe me,

253. thus] this C², C³.—for to] to H¹, C³, CC.—pray] crye L; say V. 255. To whom iche thynge iustely must obeye, B¹.—iche] all D.—all] eche Ch, B¹, B², H¹, C¹, C², C³, B⁵, Ash², Hn¹, H³, H⁴, H², Ash¹, L, J, An, CC, H⁵, H⁶, H⁷, H⁸, Ar, Ad³, Ad², C⁵, B³, B⁴ Lg, Hu; every Co.—iustely muste] muste iustely C², B⁴. 256. To] So H¹, Ash²; om. L, B³.—the be] the I Ch, B², Co, C¹, C³, Hn¹, H³, H⁴, H², Ash¹, L, J, An, CC, H⁵, H⁶, H⁷, H⁸, Ar, Ad³, Ad², C⁵, B³, Lg, Hu; I the H¹, Ash²; the ʒeve C².—thanke] thanne Ch, B¹, B², H¹, C³, Ash², H³, H⁴, Ash¹, J, An, H⁶, H⁷, H⁸, Ar, Ad³, C⁵, B⁴ Lg, Hu; thonkys C²; tent CC; name H⁵; thanne the Ash².—skyll] slyle Ch, B⁴; om. C²; right Ash².—and right] right C²; and skyll Ash². 257. a] om. CC. 260. only] me only C². 261. vnto] of C³, Hn¹, CC; in H³; into H⁴, An, C⁵; unt J.—suche] thi high CC. 262. a] om. B⁴.—mayde and mothir] modir and mayden Ash¹, L, B³.—mothir] a modir H¹, Ash². 263. and] om. Ash², CC.—eke] om. Ch, B², H¹, C¹, C², C³, Hn¹, H³, H⁴, H², Ash¹, L, J, An, H⁵, H⁶, Ad², C⁵, B³, B⁴, Lg, Hu, V; with Ash²; of CC. 264. neu*ere*] may never H⁴; om. B⁴.—twynnyth] weute Co; twynne H⁴; twynneth never B⁴. 265. abydyth aye] ay abydeth H³; evere abideth H⁸, Ar.—aye] ever B¹, Co, C³, B⁵, H⁷, Ad³, Hu; eternally Hn¹; highe CC.—*with*] there with Ar. 266. in] in the C¹; now in C³, Hn¹, L.—nowe] om. Ch, C³; the Hn¹; ys L, B³.

[1]crossed through

Lyeth in a stall, of chere moste debonayre,

To-fore my face, my Ioye and my comforte;

Whiche w*ith* þe lokynge of his iȝen faire

270 Is hool my gladnesse, *and* fully my disporth,

Sothefaste pleasaunce and my chefe resorte;

My dere sonne, and my childe also,

To who w*ith* hert and all that I can do,

I thanke the, lorde, that liggiste me beforne,

That thou luste chese to haue affection

Of me so mekely in erthe to be borne,

And fro thy fadre to descende dovne,

Only for helpe and our savacion

Of all mankynde frely of thy wille.

280 My blisset chylde, that so goodly stylle

267. Lyeth] Lyst Ch, B², Hn¹, H³, H⁴, Ash¹, J, An, CC, H⁵, H⁶, Ad², C⁵, B⁴, Lg, V; Liste be C²; om. L, B³; And lyeth C¹; Lyght Hu.—stall] B², CC, H⁸. 269. Whiche w*ith* þe, lokynge of his iȝen faire, H⁷.—þe] his D, Co.—w*ith* his]. with the Ch, B¹, B², H¹, C¹, C², C³, B⁵, Ash², H³, H⁴, H², Ash¹, L, J, CC, An, H⁵, H⁶, H⁷, H⁸, Ar, Ad³, Ad², C⁵, B³, B⁴, Lg, Hu.—his] this B¹; hir H¹; thyn Hn¹. 270. Is hool my gladnesse, *and* fully my disporth, B¹.—hool] holy D, Co, C¹, B⁵, H⁸, Lg.—fully] full D. 271. and] of Lg. 272. and my] and H⁵.—childe] lorde Ch, B², C², H³, H⁴, Ash¹, L, J, An, CC, H⁵, H⁶, Ad², C⁵, B³, B⁴, Lg. 273. hert] will Ash¹. 274. thanke] am Ash¹.—the] o H¹, C¹, Ash²; om. CC.—that] as H¹, C¹; at Ash².—liggiste] hightest H¹, Ash².—me] me me Lg.—be forne] to forn H¹, C¹, Ash². 275. thou] om. Ch, B¹, H¹, Co. Ash², Hn¹, H³, H⁴, Ash¹, J, CC, H⁵, H⁶, B⁴.—chese] to chese B¹, B⁴.—to] me to L; and to C². 276. Of me so mekely in erthe to be borne, B¹.—in] on D; om. Ch, Ad³, Ad², C⁵.—erthe] om. Ch, Ad³, Ad², C⁵. 277. thy] the H¹; my Lg. 278. helpe] helthe H⁸.—and] of C¹.—our] om. Ch, B², C², Hn¹, H³, H⁴, H², Ash¹, J, L, An, CC, H⁵, H⁶, Ad², C⁵, B³, B⁴, Lg, V. 279. of] at B¹. 280. that] om. B¹, Ar.—stylle] and stylle B¹, C², H², L, CC, Ar, B³.

Liggest nowe here mekely be sufferaunce,　　　　　　　　**f. 46b**

A-myddeste these besteȝ, so fayre vpon to see,

And hast no wight to thyne attendaunce,

Lyke thyne estate a-waytyng vpon the,

Saue that thou haste so goo[d]ly chosyn me,

Of thy grace, vpon the to abyde;

I to serue and thou to be my guyde,

As it is Right; and Iosephe *with* vs tweyne,

To take his parte, what fortune so betyde,

290　Like as thou luste of grace to ordeyne."

And than a-noon, Right in the selfe-tyde,

Ioseph cam In and stode hir be-syde.

And sodenly, whan he the childe dothe se,

Full humbly knelyng on his knee,

---

282. A-myddeste] Amyd Ch, Co, H¹, C¹, C², B⁵, Ash², H³, H⁴, H², Ash¹, L, J, An, CC, H⁵, H⁶, H⁷, H⁸, Ad³, Ad², C⁵, B³, B⁴, Lg; Betwene C³, Hn¹, Hu; And Ar.—these] the Ch, H³, H⁴, Ash¹, An, Ad², C⁵, B⁴, Lg; two B², J, CC; this H⁷, H⁸, Ar.—vpon to] unto H¹, Ash². 283. wight] body C².—attendaunce] tendaunce Lg. 284. vpon] om. B¹. 285. that] om. C¹.—thou] of grace thou C²; the Ar.—haste] list Ar.—so] om. C²; thyn Hu.—chosyn me] uppon to see Co. 286. Of thy grace] Thi creature C²; Uppon thi grace H³. 287. I] om. B², J, CC.—to] the to H¹, C¹, C³, Ash², An.—thou] the Ash¹.—be my] my be L. 288. As it is] And it V.—*with* us tweyne] us betwene B². J, CC, Ad³. 289. what] whan H⁴. 290. thou] om. Lg.—of] or C²; of thy B¹. 291. Right] om. H¹, Ash².—selfe] same B¹, C², CC, Lg. 292. hir be syde] right even bi hir syde B¹; by hir syde B⁵, H²; right by hir syde Co, H¹, C³, Ash ², Hn¹, H⁷, H⁸, Ar, Ad³, Hu. 294. humbly] humble C².—knelyng] he knelynge B¹, Co, C³, B⁵, Hn¹, H⁷, Ar, Ad³, Hu; he knelid H⁸.—on] uppon B², C¹, CC; down on C², L, B³.

Howe the mydwyfeȝ
durst not entre in with
Ioseph into the house
for the grete soden
light that apperyde within
Ca° xxxix°[1] 5[m]

W orshipped hym with all his hert and myght,

With all his will, and all his full thought,

Ande tolde marie, for fer of the lyȝght,

The mydwyfes that he had brought,

Astonyd werne, þat thay durste nought

300 Entre In, but kept hem a-ferre;

For cause only that a new sterre

Ascendyd was vpon that mansion,

That spred his light and his beames shene

Fro est to weste thrugh that Regyon,

That all thay that euere it had seen,

Gan faste musen what it myght mene;

And in her hertes gretly for to charge

That a sterre so bright, so fayre, and so large,

---

295. his] om. H[4].—hert] power H[2].—and] *inserted above;* and his B[1]. 296. will] myȝte Lg.—and] and with Co; of B[5]. 297. Ande tolde marie for fer of the lyȝght, B[1].—the] om. D, Lg; of that B[4].—marye] Marie Marie H[1]. 298. that] whiche that C[3].—he] sho Ch; om. Hu, CC.—had] had theder H[2]. 300. in] B[1].—kept] kepe CC; stoden Hn[1].—hem] al Hn[1]. 301. For cause] Because C[3]; For by cause H[5].—only] eke C[2].—that] of L. 302. that] that C[1], C[2], L, B[3].—mansion] mownteyn C[1]. 303. That] And L.—spred] spredith H[8]. 304. to] into the Co, B[5]; unto the H[1]; to the Ash[2]; toward C[1].—west] om. C[1].—thrugh] thorough out Ch, H[4], Ash[1], An, H[6], Ad[2], C[5], B[4]; om. C[1]; of H[2]; in CC. 305. thay] om. H[4].—euere it had] it did Ch, B[2], H[1], C[1], C[2], Ash[2], H[2], Ash[1], J, An, CC, H[5], H[6], C[5], B[3], Lg, V; ever hath it B[1], Co, H[7]; ever it hath B[5], Hn[1], Hu; did it H[3], H[4], L, Ad[2], B[4]; it hath ever H[8]; it ever hath Ar, Ad[3]. 306. faste] first C[1], Ash[2]; fast to B[1], B[2], C[2], J, CC.—faste musen] muse first H[1]; fast to muse V.—what] what that B[1], Hn[1], H[2], Ad[3], Hu.—myght] did H[1], H[4], An.—mene] bene H[2]. 307. her] om. C[1], CC.—for to] gan B[1]; gan it Co, C[2], B[4], Hn[1], H[7], H[8], Ar, Ad[3], Hu. 308. a] om. C[1].—bright] fayr B[1], CC; gret C[3].—so fayre] and so bryȝght B[1]; so bright C[3], CC; so grete H[2]; and fayre Ch; fayre L, B[3].—and] om. C[3].—so large] large Ch, H[1], Ash[2], Ash[1], Ar, B[4], Lg, V.

---

[1]crossed through

Of new dyd apere in that Realme,

310   That neuere was secheon sene beforne,

Of the whiche, prophyteʒ in Iherusalem

That tyme were astonyed wondre sore,

And sayde playnly, withoute eny more,

That thilke sterre dyd signyfye

Thilke sterre whiche in his prophecye

Howe Balam the sonne of
Beor prophicied of the
sterre That shews Cristes
birthe Ca°xl[1] 6ᵐ

Balam, the sonne of Beor, as I fynde,   f.47a

    Comendythe so in all his beste wyse,

Whan he sayde, sothely, of the kynde

Of worthy Iacob a sterre shulde aryse;

320   And eke also, as he dothe devyse,

Full opynly the Byble can yov telle,

How a yarde oute of Israell

309. Of] Whiche of C[1]; O Ad[2].—dyd apere] apperide C[1].—in] so fayre in CC. 310. was secheon] non suche was Ch, B[2], C[2], H[3], H[4], Ash[1], L, J, An, CC, H[5], H[6], Ad[2], C[5], B[3], B[4], Lg, V; was seyn such on Co, Ash[2].—sene] om. Co, Ash[2].—beforne] to forne Lg. 311. the] om. Ch, B[2], H[1], C[2], Ash[2] H[3], H[4], H[2], Ash[1], L, J, An, CC, H[5], H[6], Ad[2], C[5], B[3], B[4], Lg, V.—whiche] whiche sterre Ch, B[2], C[2], H[3], H[4], Ash[1], L, An, J, CC, H[5], H[6], Ad[2], C[5], B[3], B[4], Lg, V; prophetes whiche H[2].—prophyteʒ] the prophetes C[3]; om. H[2]. 312. tyme] om. H[1], Ash[2].—were] were that tyme H[1], Ash[2].—wondre] om. Ar. 313. And] om. Ch, B[2], Co, H[1], C[1], B[5], Ash[2], H[3], H[4], H[2], Ash[1], J, An, CC, H[5], H[6], Ad[2], C[2], B[4], Lg, V.—sayde] sendyn B[5], V. 314. thilke] this Ch, B[2], H[1], C[1], C[2], Ash[2], H[3], H[4], H[2], Ash[1], L, J, An, CC, H[5], H[6], Ad[2], C[5], B[5], B[4], Lg; that C[3]; thik Ar.—sterre] bright sterre Co, B[5], Hu.—dyd] dide thanne B[1], Hn[1], H[2], H[7], H[8]. 315. Thilke] That B[2], C[1], C[2], CC; the C[3]; this Ash[1].—sterre] same in soth C[3].—in hys] is in H[3], Ar; in B[4]. 316. of] om. C[3].—Beor] Seor Ash[2]; Booz Hn[1], L; Deor Ash[1]; om. C[3]. 317. Comendyth] commendid B[1], Co, H[7], H[8], Ar, Ad[3].—all] om. C[3].—his] this H[1]. 318. sothely] in sothe C[2]; sothely as I fynde Ash[1]. 319. a] the H[3]. —sterre] sterre a sterre H[1].—shulde] shal B[1]. 320. he] ʒe Lg. 322. How] Howe that B[1], H[1], Ash[2].—oute] thanne out Hn[1].

[1]crossed through

Shall sprynge also, to smyte and oppresse

The fel dukes of moab *with* her myght;

And he shall waste in verrey sothefastnesse,

The children of Sethe, and of kynde right,

Withe the shynyng of his beames bright;

Conquere also, to his subieccioun,

Withoutyn obstacle, and haue possession

330　Of ydvme, for his heritage,

With many a-nothir Riche regioun,

And of Syr the Riche baronage,

Shal to hi*m* lought for his renoun,

So þat þis sterre, in concluscioun,

Whiche in Bedlem brightest of sterres alle,

The whiche above the lytyll oxe stalle,

---

323. Shall] Shuld C¹; Shall opynly C³.—also] om. C³.—to smyte] to semite Lg; the smite Hu; to C³.—and] om. C³. 324. dukes of] duke CC.—with] of Hu.—her] hert Ch; his CC. 325. he] she H³.—waste] wassh C¹. 326. Sethe] sithir H¹. 327. Withe] That L.—the] om. B⁴.—shynyng] signe H¹.—beames] beme H⁵. 328. Conquere also to his subieccioun, B¹.—Conquere] And conquere D.—to] in C²; of Ash¹. 330. for] and for H¹, Ash²; for all C³. 331. Riche] om. C¹; large B³. 332. of] om. C², H⁸.—Syr] Seir Ch, B¹, B², Co, B⁵, Hn¹, H³, H⁴, H², Ash¹, L, J, An, CC, H⁵, H⁶, H⁷, Ar, Ad³, Ad², C⁵, B³, B⁴, Lg, Hu; Cirie H¹, C¹, Ash²; sever C²; sete C³; seyne H⁸. 333. Shal to him lought for his renoun, B¹.—his] his high D, Ash², C¹, C³.—loute] om. Ash². 334. So þat þis sterre in concluscioun, B¹.—in] as in D.—this] om. L.—sterre Ash¹, H⁶. 335. Whiche] with B², J, CC, V; whiche that C¹. 336. The whiche] Apperyng C²; A lytyll L, B³.—the lytyll oxe] the oxe and the asse L, B³.

So shene shone at the Natyvyte

Of the childe, as ye haue herde me tell,

Be-tokeneth playnly, as ye shall aftir se,

340   That the lorde of hevyn, erthe, and hell,

Whiche may of Moab the tyranne felle,

Was ther by loke and helde his hostage

In a stable narwe as eny cage,

Amonge bestys, though he were lorde of all,

Ande alle this worlde my3ght at his wille gou*er*ne,

Which in his hande hangeth as a ball,

In verrey sothe, his myght is so et*er*ne.

And all this thyng Marye gan concerne

With in hir self seker and full close.

350   And aftir that, she mekely vp Rose,

---

337. So] No Ch; Os so B¹.—shene] om. H⁸.—the] om. Lg. 338. the] this C².—haue] om.
C¹. 339. Be tokeneth] Betokened B⁵.—playnly] verrely C²; after B⁵.—aftir] pleynle B⁵.
340. erthe] of erthe B⁵, B⁴. 341. may] many B², Ash¹, J, CC.—of] a Ash¹, CC.—the] om.
Lg. 342. helde] helde there Co, H¹, B⁵, Ash², Hu; there helde C³; hade Hn¹.—hys] in
CC, V. 343. stable] stalle Ash².—any] om. C². 344. bestys] om. H¹; beest B¹.—were] be
H⁸. 345. Ande alle this worlde myght at his wille gouerne, B¹.—this] the D.—all] of all
H¹.—worlde] om. Ash².—myght] may Ch, B², C¹, C², H³, H⁴, H², Ash¹, L, J, An, CC,
H⁵, H⁶, Ad², C⁵, B³, B⁴, Lg, V; *inserted above*. 346. Which in] Withynne H⁸.—his] om.
L, B³.—hangeth] hanged B⁵. 347. verrey] vertewe Co, B⁵.—sothe] fethe B⁵.—is] om.
C².—so] om. B⁵. 348. And] This C¹.—this] om. C¹.—Marye gan] dide Mary C².—con-
cerne] conserve H⁸, Ar. 349. seker and full close] ful sikirly and close C², Ar; full siker
and full close Ash². 350. she mekely] mekely scheo Co.—Rose] arose Ch, B², Co, C², C³,
B⁵, Ash², Hn¹, H³, H⁴, H², Ash¹, L, J, An, CC, H⁶, H⁷, H⁸, Ad³, Ad², B⁴, B³, Lg, Hu, V.

How our lady Receyvede
the Mydwyfeȝ
Caº xliº¹ 7ᵐ

A̲nd to the dore, wondre womanly

     She went apas, and when she dyd se

The mydwyfes, full benygnely

She brought hem in wi*th* all humylite,—

Scephora and also Solomee,—

And hem welcomyth in full lawe man*ere*.

And when that thay these signes sawe in-fere,

Of the sterre and the besteȝ knele

Tawarde the childe to do hym Reu*e*rence,

360   And gan also by othir tokens fele

Of maydynhede ther was none offence,

But that she stode hole in the excellence

Of p*er*fyte clennesse and hool virgynyte,

Mothir to be and floure in chastite,

---

351. to] unto H². —wondre] ful B¹; riȝt C²; wonderly J.—womanly] demurely C². 352. whan] whanne that Hn¹, H⁷, H⁸, Hu; om. L. 353. full] there full Hn¹. 354. in] om. H¹, Ash².—all] gret C². 355. Scephora] The first Shophora Hn¹.—and also] the secunde Hn¹. 356. welcomyth] welcomed B¹, Co, C³, B⁵.—lawe] lowe Ch, B², Co, H¹, C¹, C², C³, B⁵, Ash², Hn¹, H³, H⁴, H², Ash¹, L. J. An, CC, H⁵, H⁶, H⁷, H⁸, Ar, Ad³, Ad², C⁵, B³, B⁴, Lg, Hu; lowely B¹. 357. that] om. B¹, H², CC.—thay] sho Ch.—these signes] om. H¹, Ash²; those signes C¹; thys thyng C³; this signes CC, H⁵, H⁶; these thynges Hu. 358. the] om. CC.—sterre] sterres Ch, B¹, B², C¹, C², H³, H⁴, Ash¹, An, H⁵, H⁶, Ad², C⁵, B⁴, Lg; therre CC.—the] of the CC, H⁸, Ar. 360. gan] om. B¹, H⁷; dide C²; can CC.—by] om. C³.—othir] aftir H⁶. 361. ther] that there Ch, B², Co, C², C³, B⁵, Hn¹, H³, H⁴, H², Ash¹, L, J, An, CC, H⁵, H⁶, H⁷, H⁸, Ar, Ad³, Ad², C⁵, B³, B⁴, Lg, Hu.—none offence] no resistence B⁵. 362. But that] And Ch; And that H³, Ash¹, An, H⁶, Ad², C⁵, B⁴, Lg.—in the] the C¹, C³; in Hu. 363. Of] To B³.—hool] om. Ch, B², Co, H¹, C¹, C², B⁵, Ash², H³, H⁴, H², Ash¹, L, J, An, CC, H⁵, H⁶, Ad², C⁵, B³, B⁴, Lg; of B¹, C³, Hn¹, H⁷, H⁸, Ar, Ad³, Hu. 364. Mothir] And modir Ch, H³, H⁴, H², Ash¹, An, Ad², C⁵, B³, B⁴, Lg; A moder B¹, B², Co, Hn¹, L, J, CC, H⁵, H⁶, H⁷, H⁸, Ar, Ad³, Hu, V.—and] a B¹, L.—in] of B¹, B², C¹, L, J, CC, H⁵, Hu; of in H⁶.—chastite] virginite L.

---

¹crossed through

Withoutyn wem on eny party founde,

For all the preves that thay make coude;

And whan thay sawe hir pappes so abounde

With henvenly mylke sent from above the cloude,

Scephora began to cry lowde

370 That a mayde hath a chylde borne,—

The whiche thyng was not seen afforne

In all this worlde, who so luste take hede.

For it, in sothe, the right of all nature

Passeth playnely, and also dothe excede

The witte of man, I do yov well assure.

But I se well, thoroughe the myghty cure

Of goddys honde this thyng is brought aboute;

Wher-of plattely I am no-thyng in doute,

---

365. Withoutyn] Out C². —on] in B², Co, H¹, C³, Ash², Hn¹, L, H⁸; or B⁵, Ar, Ad²; of CC, Hu. —party] partise C². 366. the] thyse L; om. B⁴. 367. whan] om. H⁸. —thay sawe] om. B⁵. —hir] the B¹. —so abounde] om. H¹; habounde L. 368. hevenly] hevenly Ch, B¹, B², Co, H¹, C¹, C², C³, B⁵, Ash², Hn¹, H³, H⁴, H², Ash¹, L, J, An, CC, H⁵, H⁶, H⁷, H⁸, Ar, Ad³, Ad², C⁵, B³, B⁴, Lg, Hu. —sent] fet B¹, H⁷, Ar. Ad³. —from] om. Ar. 369. Scephora] Than Sephora B¹, Hn¹, H², H⁷. —began] gan Ch, B², Co, H¹, C¹, Ash², H³, H⁴, H², Ash¹, L, J, CC, An, H⁵, H⁶, Ad², C⁵, B⁴, Lg. —to] forto B¹, C¹, B⁵, H⁷. —cry] crye crye B². —lowde] alowde L, B². 370. That] And sayde that Hn¹. —borne] y-bore L, B³. 371. thyng] om. Ash². —was] hath H². —not] never B¹, L B³. —seen] sey C², C³, Hu; be sene H²; se Ash¹. —afforne] to forne Ch, Co, C¹, H³, H⁴, H², Ash¹, B⁵, Hn¹, L, J, An, H⁵, H⁶, Ad², C⁵, B³, B⁴, Lg; beforne B¹, B², C², Ash², CC, H⁷, H⁸, Ar, Ad³, Hu; there by forn C³. 372. so] om. Ch, CC. —take] to take B¹, B², J. —who] *inserted above.* 373. it] om. Co, B⁵; it is H¹, B⁴. —the] by H¹, Ash¹. —right] right wey Lg. —all] om. CC. 374. playnely] sicourly C². —also] eke C². —doth] dethe H³. —excede] excese H⁸. 375. witte] wiȝt B⁴. —yov well] you C²; well you H⁸. —assure] to assure Ch, B¹; exure vl assure Ash¹. 376. But] For C³. —I se well] she will H¹, Ash²; see that C². —the] thy Ash¹; that H⁸. 377. honde] sonde Ch. 378. Wher of] Where all C¹. —plattely] oonly C¹; by my feithe C²; pleynli CC, H⁶. —am] om. Hu.

But assented w*ith* hert and hole credence,

380   Ther-of havyng noon ambiguyte.

And than a-noon, for the grete offence

And for wantruste, hir felowe Solomee

Opynly, that all myght it see,

Waxc in that Arme dede and colde as stone,

Withe the whiche she was hardy for to gone

**Howe the hande
and the Arme of
Solome wexe drye
for she w*ith*oute
drede and
Reuerence touchede
Criste Ca° xlii[1] 8**

T he childe to touche of presumpcion;   f. 48a
        And his mothir, w*ith*-outen Reuerence,

Devoyded of drede or devocion,

Or eny faythefull, humble adu*er*tence,

390   Done as hir aughte to his magnyfycence.

Where-fore a-noon, for hir high trespace,

All opynly in the same place,

---

379. assented] assent H[1], C[2], Ash[2], H[2]; assuryt C[1]; assenteth Hu.—credence] entent
and credence Ash[1]. 380. Ther-of having] Havynge there on Ch, B[1], Hn[1], H[3], H[4], H[2],
Ash[1], An, H[6], H[7], Ad[2], C[5], B[4], Lg, V; Having therof B[2], C[1], C[2], C[3], B[5], Ash[2], L, J,
CC, H[5], H[8], Ar, Ad[3], B[3], Hu; Having non there of H[1].—noon] om. H[1]. 381. than
a-noon] forth with C[2].—the] om. C[1]. 382. wantruste] untriste H[8]. 383. Opynly] Al
openly B[1], B[2], C[3], Ash[2], H[2], J, CC, H[7], H[8], Ar, Ad[3]; Amonge hem opunly Hn[1].—all]
all men B[1], Co, C[3], B[5], H[8], B[4], Hu; om. C[2], Hn[1].—it] om. B[1], B[2], H[1], C[3], Ash[2], Hn[1],
J, CC, H[7], Ar, Ad[3]; al y C[2]. 384. Waxe] Wexyd C[3].—that] the C[1], V.—in that Arme
dede] dede in hyr arme C[3].—and] as Co, Ash[1].—colde as] any Ash[1]. 385. Withe the
whiche] Where with H[2].—the] om. Ch, B[2], Co, H[1], C[1], C[2], C[3], B[5], Ash[2], Hn[1], H[3],
H[4], Ash[1], L, J, An, CC, H[5], H[6], H[7], H[8], Ar, Ad[3], Ad[2], C[5], B[3], B[4], Lg, Hu. 386. of]
with B[2]. 388. or] or of Ch, C[1], C[2], H[3], H[2], H[4], Ash[1], J, An, CC, H[6], Ad[2], C[5], B[4], Lg, V;
and also of B[1]; and Co, H[7], Hu; and of C[3], Hn[1], L, H[5], Ad[3], B[3]. 389. Or] Or of Ash[1].
—aduertence] attendance B[2], CC; reverence C[1]. 390. Done] Which was don Ch; Non
B[1]; Doud Lg.—as] om. Ch.—hir] sche C[2]; hyt C[3]; om. Ch.—aughte] out Ch.—to] of
Ch, H[3], H[4], An, Ad[2], B[4]; unto Ar. 391. hir] the B[2], J, CC. 392. All] Evyn C[2].—in]
there in Hn[1].—the] that H[8].

---

[1]crossed through

She pun[i]shede was, that all myghten se;

And gan to sorowe, wepe, and complayne,

And sayd: "O lorde, haue pyte vpon me,

And of mercy Rewe vpon my payne,

And of myne offence þat thou not disdeyne,

Ne to thy highnesse be no displeasaunce,

That I a wreche, blynde of ignoraunce,

400 Offendyde haue gretly in thy sight,

Of moche vnconnyng and of discrecion."

Ande sodenly in her alther syght,

Evyn a myddes of that mansion,

An Angel bright, sent from hevyn dovne,

Dydde appere; byddyng hir a-noon,

With deuoute herte þat she sholde goon

---

393. myghten] myght hit Ch, B², Co, C¹, C², C³, B⁵, Hn¹, H⁴, H³, Ash¹, L, J, An, H⁵, H⁶, H⁷, H⁸, Ar, Ad³, Ad², C⁵, B³, B⁴, Lg, Hu; men might H¹, Ash². 394. gan] om. C²; than B⁵; by gan Hn¹.—to] for Ch, B¹, B², Co, H¹, C², B⁵, Ash², Hn¹, H³, H⁴, Ash¹, L, J, CC, An, H⁵, H⁶, H⁸, Ad², C⁵, B³, B⁴, Lg, Hu, V; forto C³, H², Ar, Ad³. —wepe] began to wepe C². 395. vpon] now on B¹, Hn¹, H⁷; on H¹, H⁴, An, H⁸; of C³. 396. of] on thy B¹; on H⁵. 397. þat] om. C³.—thou] om. B¹, L. 398. Ne] Nor H¹, Ash²; And L, B³.—to] of H³.—be] hit be Ch, B¹, B², Co, Hn¹, H³, L, J, An, CC, H⁵, H⁷, Ad², C⁵, Lg, B⁴, Hu; be hyt C³, H⁸, B³, V.—no] om. C²; not B¹. 399. a] om. B¹, B², Co, H¹. 400. Offendyde] Offendith B⁴.—haue] hath C², H⁵; I have Ash²; have so Hn¹, H²; gretly have H⁸.—gretly] om. Ash¹, H⁶, H⁸. 401. vnconnyng] unkendness CC.—and] om. Hu.—of] grete C¹; om. Ch. B¹, B², Co, H¹, C¹, C², C³, B⁵, Ash², Hn¹, H³, H⁴, H², Ash¹, L, J, An, CC, H⁵, H⁶, H⁷, H⁸, Ar, Ad³, Ad², C⁵, B³, B⁴, Lg, Hu.—discrecion] indiscrecioun B², C², Ash², H³, H⁴, H², Ash¹, L, J, An, CC, H⁵, H⁶, Ad², C⁵, B³, B⁴, Lg, Hu, V; undiscrecioun B¹, Co, C³, B⁵, Hn¹, H⁷, H⁸, Ar, Ad³. 402. Ande sodenly in her alther syght, B¹.—in] there in D, C³, H².—her alther] all her D, C³. 403. of] om. B¹; in H². 404. An] An an B¹. 405. Dydde] And dyde Hn¹. 406. With] With a H⁴.—she] om. B¹, Lg; he Ash².

Full humbly in hir beste entente,

Vnto the chylde for to haue socure,

And touche the hem of his vestement

410   Reuerently *and with* gret honoure.

For he, in sothe, is the Savyoure

Of all the worlde and of all mankynde,

And power hathe playnly to vnbynde

All thoo that pleyne hem and ben in distresse,

When thay to hym mekely wolle call.

And Salomee deuoutly gan hir dresse

Towarde the childe, and on hir knees felle,

And sayd: "O lorde, that power haste of all,

So latte thy mercy goo[d]ly on me sprede,

420   Me for to socoure nowe in this grete nede;

---

407. humbly] humble B¹; humely C²; *inserted above.*—in] in all H¹, Ash²; with C³. 408. for to] to B², CC. 409. touche] twocheth H⁸.—hem] hem of hem B¹.—his] the Ash². 410. Reuerently *and with* gret honoure, B¹.—*with*] with full D, B², Co, B⁵, L, CC, H⁵, H⁷, Ar, B³, Hu.—*with*] om. C³; in H⁸. 411. he] om. C².—in] for B⁴.—is] is nowe Hn¹. —the] the blessed Co, B⁵. 412. the] this CC.—and of all] and B¹; and all Co, H¹, B⁵; and of Lg. 413. power hathe] pow ave H⁸; power he hath B¹.—playnly] of riȝt C².— to] forto C³. 414. All] And all C³; And Ar, Ad³.—thoo] om. B¹, H², Ash¹; they CC.—pleyne hem] pleynen Ch, B², Co, H¹, C¹, C², C³, B⁵, Ash², Hn¹, H³, H⁴, H², Ash¹, L, J, An, CC, H⁵, H⁶, H⁸, Ad³, Ad², C⁵, B³, B⁴, Lg, Hu; mekely pleyne B¹, H⁷; playnly Ar.—and ben] om. B¹, H¹, C¹, C³, B⁵, Ash², Hn¹, H⁷, H⁸, Ad³, Hu; that beth H²; ben Ar; *inserted above.*—in] in here Hn¹. 415. mekely] hertily B¹.—wolle] don Co. 416. And Salomee deuoutly gan hir dresse, H⁷.—And] Thane D; And than C¹, C³; om. B², J. CC.—Solome] om. Ad³.—deuoutly gan hir] gan hir devoutly B¹.— deuoutly] om. H⁸.—gan] sone gan Co, B⁵, H⁸.—hir] to Ar. 417. felle] gan falle B¹, Co, C², C³, B⁵, H⁷, H⁸, Ad³, Hu; falle V. 418. O lorde] lord C¹.—haste] hast hast H⁶; hath Ar. —of] over B¹, Ash². 419. So] And Ch, H³, H⁴, Ash¹, L, J, An, H⁵, H⁶, Ad², C⁵, B⁴, Lg.—mercy] grace B¹, H⁷.—goo[d]ly] goodly Ch, B¹, B², Co, H¹, C¹, C³, B⁵, Ash², Hn¹, H³, H⁴, H², Ash¹, L, J, An, CC, H⁵, H⁶, H⁷, H⁸, Ar, Ad³, Ad², C⁵, B³, B⁴, Lg, Hu; om. C²; so goodly CC.—me] her J. 420. Me] om. Ch, H¹, C¹, C², Ash², H³, H⁴, H², Ash¹, L, J, An, CC, H⁵, H⁶, Ad², C⁵, B³, B⁴, Lg; Nowe B¹, Co, C³, B⁵, Hn¹, H⁷, H⁸, Ar, Ad³, V.—for to] to H⁸.—in] me in Ch, B², Co, C², C³, B⁵, H³, H⁴, H², Ash¹, L, J, An, CC, H⁵, H⁶, H⁸, Ad², C⁵, B³, B⁴, Lg, V.—this] his An, Ar; my H⁴.— grete] om. B¹, Co, C³.

Me wrecchede wight, pun[i]schede Rightfully,   f. 48b

And loste for eu*ere,* saue only thy grace.

For in sothe, lorde, excepte thy mercy,

I haue loste myne Arme, alas, for my trespasse."

And w*ith* that worde, as she dyd enbrace

To touche the clothe that he lay in bounde,

With-oute more this Solome hath fou*n*de

Remedye and was made hole agayne

Sodenly or she coude it asspye.

430   And vp she Roos and may no longer fayne,

But in the strete opynly gan crye,

Howe the lorde that all the worlde may gye,

Discendyd is and become man.

And while₃ that she thus in the strete ran,

---

421. Me] The Ch, C². My J; And Hu; om. L, B³.—wight] creature C². 422. only] of only Ash¹.—thy] of thy Ch, B², Hn¹, H³, H⁴, H², J, An, H⁵, H⁶, H⁷, Ad², C⁵, B³, Lg, V; by thy Co, H¹, C¹, C³, B⁵, Ash², Ar, Ad³, Hu. 423. lorde] om. Ch, B², H¹, C¹, C², Ash², H³, H⁴, H², Ash¹, J, An, CC, H⁵, H⁶, Ad², C⁵, B⁴, V.—excepte] save excepte C³.—thy] thy gret Hn¹; thy high L, B³. 424. I haue loste myne Arme] Myne arme ys lost C³.—I] om. C¹, Ash¹.—alas] om. C², H².—my] om. H¹. 425. as] and Hn¹. 426. that] om. Ch; the H⁵.—in] on H². 427. this] om. B¹.— Solome] Salaman H¹.—hath] was Ash². 428. made] om. B². 429. Sodenly] Right sodenly Hn¹.—or] as Ar. 430. may] made B¹, Ash¹, L, B³; might B², J, CC; om. Ash².—fayne] finde Lg. 431. But] And C¹.—in] into B¹.—the] om. Co, CC.—gan] gan to B¹, C², Hn¹; she gan to C³; gan she Lg. 432.] The blessed lorde and Kynge of glorye B¹.—the lorde] he C³.—the worlde] om. Ch. 433. man] a man H². 434. that] om. C². —she] om. Ch.—thus] om. Hu; this C², H⁸, Ar.—the] om. Hn¹.—strete] way H².

Tellyng the byrthe, and of the sterre also,

And of hir Arme, and of hir soden cure,

The peple gan to drawen faste hir to,

To herken more of this aventure;

And in her speche som gan hem assure,

440   And thought hir wordes myght be credible,

And specially, for alway so visible,

The sterre shone eu*e*re above the house,

I-lyche fixe wi*t*houten mocion,—

So bryght, so large, so glad, and so Ioyus,

Þat alle þat hadden þer of inspeccioun,

In hert p*er*fyte, and trwe of entencion,

Thoughten thay were Reioysyd and made light,

And al this thyng, fel vpon the nyght

---

435. the byrthe] om. H1, Ash2; this birthe C3.—and] om. Co.—of] om. Ch, Co, B5, H3, H4, Ash1, An, CC, H6, Ad2, C5.—the] om. C, CC.—sterre] there of CC. 436. And] om. B2, H1. —Arme] harme Ar.—of hir soden] the soden Ch; hir soden B2, H1, C2, C3, Ash2, H3, Ash1, An, CC, H5, H6, Ad2, C5, B4, Lg, V. 437. gan] began Co, H1, Hn1, C2, C3, H8, Ad3, Hu.— gan to] to *inserted above.*—to drawen faste] faste to drawe B1, H7, Ar, Ad3; faste drawe Co, B5, H8, Hu; draw faste Ash1, H6.—hir to] to Ch, H1, C1, C2, C3, Ash2, H3, H4, H2, Ash1, L, J, CC, An, H5, H6, Ad2, C5, B3, B4, Lg; unto B2; hir unto Co, B5, H8, Hu; hem to Hn1. 438. To] And to Hn1; And Ar.—herken] here C2, CC. 439. And] For Ch, H4, H3, Ash1, An, H6, Ad2, C5, B4, Lg.—in] om. H8.—som gan hem] som of hem gan H1, Ash2; som dide hem C2; som gan hir B1; som gan V.—assure] ensure CC. 440. thought] though H1.—myght] must C1.—be] be so B2, J, CC.—credible] possible Ash1. 441.] And in theyr thought they were nought terrible C3.—specially] also more specially Hn1; also specially H2; special Co, B5.—for] therefor C1; om. H8.—alway] the C1; om. H2, H8.—so] not H1, Ash2; more C1; om. H2, H8.—visible] credible Ch, C1, H3, H4, Ash1, An, H5, H6, Ad2, C5, B4, Lg, Hu, V; om. H8; peesible B1, H7, Ar, Ad3; receptible H1, Ash2; possible Hn1, H2. 442. eu*e*re] evene Hn1, H2, V; over Ar.—above] aboute H1, Ash2. 443. I lyche] Evere ylyche Hn1.—fixe] feyre C2; afixe H5.—mocion] any manere mocioun B1; any mocioun Ash2. 444. so glad] om. Co, Ar.—and so] and Ch, Ash1; so B1, H8. 445. Þat alle þat hadden þer of inspeccioun, H7.— hadden þer of] ther of had D.—inspection] any inspection B1, Co, H8, Hu. 447. Thoughten] Though CC. 448. thyng] om. H1, Ash2.

On a sonday, my auctor will not varye,

450   As ye may fynde, yf ye luste to Rede

The viij kalendes, for sothe, of Ianuarie;

Whan marye, example of maydynhede,

Was of age, who so wil take hede,

Sixtene yere, this floure of Naȝareth,

As the vision of Eliȝabeth

Playnely recordyth, loke and ye may see.   f. 49a

And in this nyght of moste worthynesse,

Of cristis birthe and Natyvite,

As the gospell saythe and beryth witnesse,—

460   Whan the shepeherdes, *with* grete besynesse,

Kepten her wacche the longe wynters nyght,

Vpon her shepe, an Angel *with* great light

---

449. my auctor] wrytyng L, B³. 450. As] And as Ash². 451. for sothe] sothly B², CC; the sothe Co, H⁸, Hu; in sothe H¹, B⁵, Ash². 452. Whan] Whan the Ch.—marye] om. Ch, H², Hu. 453. Was of age, who so wil take hede, B¹.—wil take] taketh D; liste take C¹, C³, Ar. 454. this] the C².—of] of of B¹. 455. As] At Ch, H³, H⁴, An; Ryght as C³; And Ash²; As ys yn Hn¹.—of] of sent B¹, Ar; of holy L, B³. 456. recordyth] cordeth C¹.—loke] loketh B², J, CC.—and] om. C¹. 457. And] As C³, Hn¹.—in] om. C².—this] the Hn¹. 458. In MS V lines 458 and 459 are *inverted.*—birthe and] hoole L; holy B³.—and] and the H¹. 459. As] And CC.—And as L.—saythe and] om. L. B³; eke C². 460. the] that H⁵.—grete] om. H¹.—besynesse] hevynesse B². 461. her] for H².— wacche] shepe Hn¹. 462. *with* grete light] fayre and bright Ch.

Howe the Angell
apperyd to the
Shepeherde₃ and tolde
hem the birthe of
criste Cap. xliii°[1] 9ᵐ

Amydde the felde, to hem dyd apere;

And gafe hem comforte in her grete drede,

And bad hem be light and gladde of chere.

"For I," quod he, "shew to yov in dede,

A Ioye that dothe eu*ery* Ioye excede,

That fynally shall of all disease

To all folke comforte be and ease;

470   And be to hem refute and socoure

In all myscheues and aduersite.

For nowe this day, mankyndes savyoure,

In Bedlam of Dauid the Cyte,

Is borne in sothe, liche as ye may se;

Gothe and beholdyth howe that it is falle.

And ye shall fynde in an oxe stalle,

---

463. Amydde] Myddis B¹; In myddis Co, B⁵, Ar, Ad³, H⁸, Hu.—the] a Ash²; of the H⁸.
—felde] folde H⁸.—to hem] om. Hu.—dyd] dude angel B¹; an awngel dyde Hu. 465.
hem] om. Ash².—be] om. H¹. 467. dothe eu*ery* Ioye] every joye dothe C². 468. That]
It J, CC.—all] every Hu; om. C². 469. be] to be 471. myscheues] myschief
B².—and] and all Ash¹, H⁶. 472. For nowe] O how V.—mankyndes] mankynde Hn¹.
473. of] om. B¹; in B², J, CC.—the] hys Ch, Co, C³, B⁵, Hn¹, H³, H⁴, H², Ash¹, An,
H⁵, H⁶, H⁷, H⁸, Ar, Ad³, Ad², C⁵, B⁴, Lg, Hu; in hys B¹; om. B², J, CC, C².—Cyte]
citee of all H¹. 474. liche] om. B².—may] mowe CC. 475. Gothe] Sooth Hu.—howe]
that how Ash²; now howe C².—that] om. B¹, Co, C², CC; this C¹.—is] was C¹. 476.
And] As B⁵, H⁷, H⁸, Ad³, Hu.—oxe] oxes C¹, C², B⁵, Ash², Hn¹, H³, H⁴, H², Ash¹,
L, J, An, H⁵, H⁷, H⁸, Ad³, Ad², C⁵, B⁴, Lg, Hu.

---

[1]crossed through

Howe that he lieth in clothes narowe yvounde,

þis ȝunge faunte, w*ith* cheere ful benygne.

The whiche thing, whan that ye haue founde

480 That all is sothe, latte be to yov asigne."

And sodenly, w*ith* laude and prees condigne,

With the angelle the hol cheualrie

Of alle heuene by on armonye,

For Ioye her of gan to seye and synge:

"Glory and hono*ur* in the hevynly see

Be vnto god et*er*nally duryng,

And in erthe pees and reste be

To all the men, that of one vnyte

This high feste honour and magnyfye.

490 And we ichone, w*ith* oo melodye,

447. Howe that he] He that C1.—lieth] lyght Hu.—in] om. Ch, B5. 478. þis ȝunge faunte w*ith*
cheere ful benygne, H7.—faunte] enfante D, B2, C1, Ash2, CC, J. 479. The] om.
Hn.1.—thing] om. C2.—whan] what H8.—that] om. B1, B2, C1, H3, J, CC, H7.
—ye] they Co, C3, B5, H2, Ar, Ad3, Hu; om. C2; he L; thei H7.—haue] hau B1, B3.
480. That] And C3.—all] om. H8; it B1, Co, B5, H7, Ar, Ad3.—latte be] that I C3; let hit be
Co, B5. 481. w*ith*] om. B1.—laude and prees] pris and laude B1, Co, B5.—prees] preysyng L.
482. With the angelle the hol cheualrie, B1.—hol] holy D.—With] But Hu. —Angel] aungelys
J, CC. 483. Of alle heuene by on armonye, B1.—on] hole D, C1.—by] with H8. 484. to] om.
C2.—seye] joye Hu.—and] to B2. 485. in] and alle B1; and Co, H7, H8, Ar, Ad3. 487. in]
in the B1. 488. the] tho Ch, B1; om. Hn1.—men] om. B1, Ar.—of] om. H8. 490. ichone]
everichon B2, CC.—with] of Ch, B2, H1, C2, H3, H4, Ash1, L, J, An, CC, H5, H6, Ad2, C5,
B3, B4, Lg, Hu, V.—melodye] armonye B2, CC.

O myghty lorde, we preyse and blisse the,   f. 49b

And worship eke *with* humble Reu*e*rence,

And gloryfye thy high mageste,

And thankyng yef to thyn magnyficence

For thy glory and thyn excellence.

O thou lorde god, O kyng celestiall,

O god the fadir, moste myghty founde at all,

And god the sonne, his childe alone et*e*rne,

Criste Ih*e*su borne of thys hevynly qwene,

500 Of god also the chose lambe so derne,

Sonne of the fadir, w*ith*-oute spotte all clene,

That doste away this worldes synne and tene,

Hau*e* mercy on vs of thy high godenesse,

Sythe thou thy-self, in p*e*rfyte holynesse,

491. O] So Lg.—we] om. B¹, Co, C³, B⁵, Hn¹, H², H⁷, H⁸, Ar, Ad³, Hu. 492. eke] the B¹, H⁷, Ar.—humble] grete Ash². 493. And gloryfye] And thankynge yeve to Co, B⁵; And eke we glorifie Hn¹; And glorie Hu.—thy high] to thy Co, B⁵; thy L. 494. And thankyng yef] And glorie eke Co, B⁵; And thankyng is yeven Ash²; And yif CC; And thankes yeve H².—thy] thyn hye B², J, CC. 495. glory] grace Co, B⁵.—thyn] thy grete Co, B⁵, Ash²; eke thyn Hn¹; om. H⁸. 496. thou] om. C¹, H³, H⁴.—god] om. Ch.— Kyng] thou Kyng CC, Ar. 497. founde] fonden B¹.—at] of C¹. 498. And] O Co; A Lg. —god] om. B¹; goddes B⁴.—his] hy Ch; the Ash¹.—alone] above Ch. B¹, H¹, C², C³, Hn¹, H³, H⁴, Ash¹, An, H⁶, C⁵, B⁴, Lg, Hu.—et*e*rne] eternall B², C¹, CC; entiere C², L, Ad³, B³. 500. Of] O Ch, Co, H¹, C², B⁵, H³, H⁴, Ash¹, An, CC, H⁵, H⁶, Ad², C⁵, B⁴, Lg.—lambe] lampe H².—so] om. C¹. 501. with-oute] with Ar. 502. That] *smudged in V.*— doste] doth B¹, C¹, Ar; takest L.—this] the Ch, B¹, H¹, C², C³, H³, Ash¹, L, An, CC, H⁵, H⁶, Ad³, Ad², C⁵, B³, B⁴, Lg.—worldes] wordes H¹; worlde is H⁶. 504. Sythe] Sothen Ch, B¹, B², Co, H¹, B⁵, Hn¹, H³, H⁴, H², An, H⁷, H⁸, Ar, Ad³, Ad², C⁵, B⁴, Lg, Hu.— thy] om. H².—self] life H⁴.—in] in thy B¹.

Alone art holy, sothely and no moo;

Ande lorde aloone, ou*er* al other thynge,

And worthyest and higheste eke also;

O Ih*es*u criste, of hevyn and erthe kyng,

With the hooly goost in glorie reynynge,

510 Ay w*ith* the fadre by eternyte,

Thre knytte in oon thorughe p*er*fyte vnyte."

How the Shepeherde*ȝ*
founden criste with
our lady Ca° xliv°[1]

And whan the Angels w*ith* this hevynly songe

The birthe of criste had magnyfied,

With p*er*fyte gladnesse that was hem amonge,

To hevyn anoon agayne thay haue hem hyed,

And the herdes, by one accorde alyed,

Ben hastely vnto Bedlem gon,

Wher thay founden, whan they come a-noon,

505. art] thou art Ch; art thou B[5].—sothely] om. Co, B[5].—holy] om. Ash[1]; onely Ar.
506. Ande lorde aloone, ou*er* al other thynge, B[1].—aloone] aboue D; most sovereyne
Hu.—other] om. D.—And] An L.—lorde] om. C[1].—ou*er*] of Ch; ever over B[2], J, CC;
eke over H[2]. 507. And] om. B[2], J. 508. Ih*es*u criste] Crist Ihesu Ch, B[1], Co, H[1], C[2],
B[5], Ash[2], H[3], H[4], H[2], Ash[1], An, H[5], H[6], H[7], H[8], Ar, Ad[3], Ad[2], C[5], B[3], B[4], Lg.—of
hevyn and erthe] of erthe and heven H[2]. 509. With the hooly goost in glorie reynynge,
B[1].—in] *above in* D.—With] wiche CC. 510. Ay] Ever B[1], Co, C[3], B[5], Hn[1], H[7], H[8],
Ar, Ad[3], Hu; And H[1], C[1].—by] by perfit Ch; by ful Hn[1]. 511. Thre] Ther B[2].—knytte]
kyȝght B[1]; knightes CC.—thorughe] by Ch, H[5], Hu; om. CC.—vnyte] charyte Ash[2].
512. whan] om. B[1].—this] his B[1], C[3]; the Ash[1], H[6], V. 513. had] had opynly C[3]; had
thus H[2]. 514.] Forth they wente and turnede nought longe Co; Forthe thei went and
taryed not long B[5].—gladnesse] godnes C[2].—hem] om. B[2]; with hem Ad[2]. 515. anoon
agayne] agayn anon C[3], B[5], Hn[1].—agayne] forsoith B[1].—thay] he B[1], C[3].—haue] om.
B[1], C[3], Ash[2], L. 516. the] om. Hu.—herdes] herdemen C[3]; herdthis Hn[1]. 517. Ben]
Ben full Co, B[5], H[8], Ar, Ad[3]; Hem Hn[1].—vnto] to B[1], B[2]; then C[3]; hyȝed and unto
Hn[1]. 518. thay] the Ch.—a noon] in oon Ash[2].

[1]liv is erased

Marye and Ioseph and the childe also,

520 Layed in a stalle, accordyng eu*er*y dele

As the Angell had sayde hem to.

And of the sight thay lyke wondre wele,

And in hem-self gun knowe and fele

That all was sothe that thay herde afore

Of the Angel, howe a childe was bore

Into this worlde, mankynde for to saue,   f. 50a

After the recorde of olde prophecye,

Where of they gan so grete Ioye haue,

That all at onys they gune magnyfie

530 God above, and hym to gloryfye,

Retornyng hem devoyde of eu*er*y smerte.

And Marye cloos wi*th*in hir herte

---

519. and] and eke Ar. 520. stalle] stable C¹, C², H³, H⁴, H², L, An, CC, H⁵, Ar, Ad², C⁵, B³, B⁴, Lg. 521. Angel] aungels B², J, CC.—had sayde hem] hem hadde seide Co, B⁵, H⁸, AD³.—to] unto H¹, C², H³, H⁴, H², L, An, H⁵, H⁶, H⁸, Ad², C⁵, B³, Lg, Hu, V. 522. of] om. C³.—the] that Ar.—sight] light Ash².—like] liked Ch, B¹, B², Co, H¹, C¹, Ash², L, J, CC, H⁵, B³. 523. hem] hym CC.—knowe] to knowe C³, Hn¹, Ad³.—fele] fell C³. 524. all] it B², CC.—sothe] om. Ash².—herde] had herde B¹, Co, Ad³; have herde H³.—afore] tofore B⁵. 525. Angel] angelis J.—a] the B², CC; that a H¹. 526. Into] In B¹, L.—this] this kynde this B¹; the L.—for to] to B¹, C³, Hn¹, H⁸, Hu. 527. After the recorde of olde prophecye, B¹.— the] om. D; B², H², CC, J.—of] of the B², J, CC.—olde] hold H⁶.—prophecye] antiquite Ash². 528. Wher of they gan so grete Ioye haue, B¹.—Ioye] a Ioye to D, C¹, H¹, Ash², CC, H⁵.— Wher of] That C¹; Wher Ar; And therof V.—so] sone so B¹.—grete] gretly Ar.—Ioye] ioie a ioie H⁵. 529. That—] To Hn¹.—magnyfie] to magnifie C². 530. above] hyȝe above Hn¹.—hym to] to Ch, B², H¹, C¹, C², C³, Ash², H³, H⁴, Ash¹, L, J, An, CC, H⁵, H⁶, Ad², C⁵, B³, B⁴, Lg, Hu; hym gan Hn¹, H². 531. hem] home B⁵.—devoyde] devoyded H⁸; voyde B⁵.—of] fro C². 532. And] And prudently C³.—Marye] Marie prudently Hn¹, Hu; Marie mekely H².—cloos] gan close B¹, Co, H⁷, H⁸, Ar, Ad³; om. C³.

Conserved all that she dyd see,—

Worde and dede, and eu*ery* man*ere* thyng

That be-felle in that Natyvyte,—

Full secretly ther-on ymagenyng,

And prudently hir-self gou*er*nyng,

Kept hir sonne *with* all byse cure;

Bonaventure Whiche on this day, as saythe Bonaventure,

540 Lyche a spouse fro his chaumbre is gone,

His chosyn chyldren thrugh his benygnyte,

In his chirche to Ioye hem of Syon

By p*er*fyte pees and sothefaste vnyte.

And he this day hathe shewede the beaute

Of his face of excellent fayrenesse;

In whose honoure this day of high gladnesse

---

533. Conserved] Conserve B⁵; Conserved wel Ash²; And well conserved H⁸; And conserved Ar.—that] the H⁸.—she] she there C³, Hn¹, Hu.—dyd] dide here and B¹, H², H⁷; gan Ash². 534. dede and] dede H⁸.—thyng] of thyng H¹. 535. be felle] thanne be felle Hn¹.—in] to her in H².—that] this Ch, B², H¹, C², Ash², H³, H⁴, Ash¹, J, An, H⁵, H⁶, H⁸, Ad², C⁵, B³, B⁴, Lg, Hu; his B¹, Co, B⁵, Hn¹, H⁷, Ar, Ad³; the C¹, CC; this hygh C³; Cristes H², V. 536. secretly] sikirly B², H¹, Ash¹, J, CC, H⁵, H⁶, B³.—ther on] therof Ash²; of ther on H². 537. And] And ful B¹, C³, Hn¹, H⁷, Ar, Ad³, Hu.—prudently] discretly C³.—self] lyf H²; om. Ar. 538. Kept] She kept B¹.—sonne] save C¹.—all] a B¹; all hir Ch, B², C², B⁵, Hn¹, H³, H⁴, Ash¹, An, CC, H⁵, H⁶, Ar, Ad², C⁵, B⁴, Lg, Hu.—byse cure] besynesse and cure Hu. 540. a] as Co.—fro his] his from his B¹. 542. In] To C³.—his] thys C³, Hu; hir Hn¹.—of] in B¹. 543. pees] ioye pees L.—sothefast] stedfast C³, Hu. 544.] The flowre of every precious poynt of humilite B¹.—hathe] had H⁶.—the] his B⁵. 545. face of] face and L, B³. 546. high] her C².

Was made the ympne, the gospell saythe also,

Our althir myrthe and yoye to encrece;   Et in terra pax

Gloria in excelsis deo.   hominib*us* bone

550   And in erthe this day a p*er*fyte pees   voluntatis

To man was shewed, withoutyn eny lees.

And as saythe poule, goddys benygnyte

This day aperyd in his humanyte.   Aparuit

                                             benignitas

                                             humanitas

                                             saluatoris nostri dei

Howe god luste to be bou*r*ne of a mayde and moder Ca° xlv°[1] 11ᵐ

A nd more ouer, as he eke telle can,

     God was this day in simylytude,

In erthe honourede in likenesse of man.

And he this day his godhede did Include

In oure manhode; and shortely to conclude,

This day also, yf I shall not feyne,

560   Byfel also othir thynges tweyne,—

---

547. the ympne] yingne os B[1]; this ympne Co, B[5], H[2]; the ympe C[1], C[2]; the song Ash[2].—also] so C[1], C[3], Hu.   548. althir] al other B[1]; aldre CC; althdre H[5].—myrthe and yoye] joye and mirthe B[1].—to] eke to B[5]; om. C[2]. 550. in] in the C[1].—this day] om. B[1].—a] om. B[1], Ar. 551. was] om. Ash 2.—eny] om. C[2]. 552. And] om. H[2]—as] om. Hn[1].—saythe] seid B[5].—poule] sent poule B[1].—goddys benygnyte] in divinite [?] B[1]. 553. This day] In this H[7].—aperyd] apperith C[2], H[2]; appere B[1].—in] and Co, C[3], B[5], Ash[2]; to H[5].—his] oure Ch, B[1], B[2], H[1], C[1], C[2], H[3], H[4], Ash[1], L, J, An, CC, H[5], H[6], H[7], Ar, Ad[3], Ad[2], C[5], B[3], B[4], Lg, V.—humanyte] nativite C[3], Hn[1], Hu. 554. more ouer] over thys Ch, B[1], B[2], H[1], C[2], H[3], H[4], Ash[1], L, J, An, CC, H[5], H[6], H[7], Ar, Ad[3], Ad[2], C[5], B[3], B[4], Lg, Hu, V; evere more Co, Ash[2], B[5]; ovir more C[1], H[2]; ferthermore C[3], Hn[1].—he eke] clerkes B[1]; clerkes eke H[7], Ar, Ad[3]; eke Co, B[5]; he Lg; eke he H[6]; I eke Ash[2].—can] he can B[5]. 556. erthe] erther Ch.—in] and Co, B[5].—of] of a Ch, B[1], B[2], Co, H[1], C[1], C[2], B[5], H[3], H[4], Ash[1], L, J, An, H[5], H[6], H[7], Ad[2], B[3], B[4], Lg, Hu, V. 557. he] om. B[1], B[4].—his] by H[3].—did] he dide B[4]. 558. and] om. B[1], C[3], B[5]; as L, B[3].—shortely] sothly C[1]. 559. day] om. H[5].—not] om. H[7].—feyne] vayne B[1]. 560. Byfel] Beside B[2].—also] eke C[3]; more over Ash[2].—othir] there An.—othir thynges tweyne] if y shal not fayne B[1].

---

[1]crossed through

The wondreste *and* moste merueilous

That eu*er*e yet were sene to-forne,

Wher-of no witte, by kynde is capciouse.

Firste howe that god, to save that was for-lore,

Lowly in erthe luste to be bore;

And howe a mayde in hir virgynyte,

Might also childe and mothir be.

f. 50b

The whiche thynges passen and transcende

Reason of man by kyndes likenesse.

570 But faythe alone muste all comprehende,

And it enbrace by p*er*fyte stablenesse,

And make his grovnde vpon the witnesse

Of p*r*ophetes, whiche in hir prophecye,

So long aforne gan to clepe and crye

---

561. The wondreste *and* moste merueilous, H⁷.—moste] the moste D; the Ar.—wondreste] wonderfullest Ch, H¹, C², H³, H⁴, H², Ash¹, L, An, H⁵, H⁶, Ad², C⁵, B³, B⁴, Lg, V; wondires B¹; wondirfull B², J, CC. 562. yet] that Hn¹.—sene] sey C³; seem Lg; sithen V.—to forne] before B², C², CC; here to fore H². 563. of] for H², CC.—witte] wight Ch, B¹, B², Co, H¹, C², C³, Ash², Hn¹, H³, H⁴, H², Ash¹, L, J, An, CC, H⁵, H⁶, H⁷, Ar, Ad³, Ad², C⁵, B³, B⁴, Lg, Hu, V; white C¹.—is] is so H².—capciouse] capyows Hu. 564. howe that] how to C².—that was] thas L; that were B¹, C².—for lore] lore Ash², H². 565. in erthe] in his herte H⁵.—luste] now list Hn¹.—to] for to H¹, C¹. 566. howe] have C¹.—in hir] in B¹, C³, Lg; pure in hir Hn¹. 567. also] have H².—childe] a childe H¹, H².—and] and a H¹, C¹, C², C³, H³, H⁴, H², Ash¹, J, An, H⁵, H⁶, H⁷, Ar, Ad³, Ad², C⁵, B⁴, Lg, Hu; thus and a Hn¹. 568. The] om. Ash². 569. of] of a H¹.—kyndes] kynde B², J, CC; kyndly Ash², H⁶.—likenesse] liklynesse B², Ash². 570. alone] above Ch, B², H¹, C², C³, H³, H⁴, H², Ash¹, L, J, An, CC, H⁵, H⁶, Ad², C⁵, B³, B⁴, Lg, Hu; anon Ash².—all] om. B¹, H¹. 572. make] makyng H¹.—the] om. Ash². 573. Of] Of the B¹; Of olde H².—whiche] alle whiche Hn¹. 574. longe] ferre B²; lo H¹.—aforne] to forne C¹.—clepe] speke Ch, B², H¹, C¹, C², C³, Hn¹, H³, H⁴, H², Ash¹, L, J, An, CC, H⁵, H⁶, Ad², C⁵, B³, B⁴, Lg, Hu, V.

Aftir the comyng of this myghty kyng,

Our olde woo and trouble to enchace;

Domine ostende faciem   To whome Dauid sayde in his wrytyng:

tua*m et* salui erimus   "O blisfull lorde, shewe to vs thy face,

And we in sothe, only thrugh thy grace,

580   Shall saved be from all myscheve and drede;

And lorde also, now in our grete nede,

Sende vnto vs thy comfortable light,

Vs to enlumyne liggyng in derkenesse."

Ysaie   Eke ysaye, wi*th* all his Inwarde sight,

Vp vnto hevyn gan his loke to dresse,

And seyde, "lorde, of þi gret goodnesse,

Oute of deserte, from the harde stone,

Vnto the dougthir dwellyng in Syon,

---

576. woo] om. C¹.—and] to B², Co, B⁵, J.—to] and to Co, C¹, B⁵. 577. To whome Dauid sayde in his wrytyng, Ad³.—To] Of D, B¹, H⁷, Co, C², B⁵, Lg.—sayde] saith B¹, B², J. 578. blisfull] blessed B¹, B², Co, H¹, C¹, C², C³, H², L, J, Ar. 580. Shall] Shullen Hn¹, H³, An, H⁵, H⁷, Ar, Ad³, Ad², C⁵, B³, B⁴, Lg, Hu.—from all myscheve and drede] through thi godhede C². 581, And lorde] And Ch, B¹, B², C², H¹, H³, H⁴, Ash¹, L, J, An, CC, H⁵, H⁶, Ad², C⁵, B³, B⁴, Lg. V. 582. vnto] to H¹, C¹, C², Ad³. 584. ysaye] Isaie the prophete H².—all] om. B¹, H³.—hys] her Ar. 585. Vp] om. H¹, C¹.—vnto] to Ch, B¹, B², C², C³, Ash², Hn¹, H³, H⁴, H², Ash¹, L, J, An, CC, H⁵, H⁶, H⁷, Ar, Ad³, Ad², C⁵, B³, B⁴, Lg, Hu, V; Oppon C¹.—hevyn] the heven Ash².—to dresse] vpdresse Ch, Ash²; dresse B¹, Co, C³, B⁵, L, H⁷, Ar, Ad³, Hu; to redres C¹. 586. And seide, "lorde, of þi gret goodnesse, H⁷.—gret] houge D, B⁵, Ash²; high Co, C¹; om. Ar.—seide] om. C². —of] for B. 587. of] of the Ch, B¹, B², H¹. 588. the] thy B¹, Co, H¹, C³, B⁵, Ash², Hn¹, H⁵, H⁷, Ar, Ad³, Hu.

Sende dovne thy lambe fulfilled *with* mekenesse,

590 That lordship hathe and domynacion

Of all the herthe, our dool to Redresse.

And wolde god for our saluacion,

This myghty lorde for to come adovne,

The high hevens wolde breke entweyne,

Vs to Releve of that we so compleyne."

And Dauid eke spake this lorde vnto,   f. 51a

In the sauter our sorowes for to fyne,

And sayde, "lorde in Relees of our woo,

The high hevens thy mercy make enclyne

600 And downe discende, and late thy grace shyne

Vppon vs wrecches in the vale of sorowe."

And, "lorde, do dawe thyne holy glad morowe,"

---

589. fulfilled] fulfulle Ch. 591. Of] To Hn1.—the] om. Ch, B1, B5, Co, Hn1, H7, Ar, Ad3, B4, Hu.—our] the C3.—to] forto C2, B5, H7, Ar, Ad3. 592. god] om. Ash2. 593. for] om. H2.—adovne] doun Ch, B1, B2, Co, C1, Ash2, Hn1, H3, H4, H2, Ash1, H6, H8. 594. hevens] hevynesse H1.—wolde] for to B5, H7, H8.—entweyne] on tweyne Ch, Co, C3, B5, Ash2, H3, H4, H2, Ash1, An, H6, Ar, Ad3, Ad2, C5, B4, Lg, V; in tweyne B2, CC; atwene B1, H1, C2, Hn1, L, H5, B3, Hu. 595. Vs] As H1.—we] woo L.—so] om. Ash2, Hn1, Ash1, Ar, Ad3; us C1; thys C3. 596. eke] out Co; also Ash2; om. C1.—spake] spak also C1.—this lorde] his wordes CC. 597. sorowes] socour B2, J, CC; sores Co, B5; sorowe Ar.—for to] for B1. 599. The] In Ch, B2, H1, C1, C2, Hn1, H3, H4, Ash1, J, An, CC, H6, Ad 2, C5, B4, Lg, V; Fro the H2; Fro L, B3; This C3; Thy Hu.—hevens] heven C1.—thy] by B1, Co, B5, Ash2, Ar, Ad3; om. B2, CC.—make] maketh C3. 600. And] And late Co, B5.—discende] sende Ash1; ascende CC.—late] om. Co, B5.—thy] th Lg. 602. lorde] om. Ar.—do] to B2, J, CC, H5, H8, Ash2, H1, C3, Hn1, Ad2; late Ar.—dawe] glade Co, B5.—thyne] the B1, Co, B5, H7, Ad3, Hu, Lg, H8.

Quod Salamon. "and shewe to vs thy light

Of thy mercy and Rewe on our distresse,

And w*ith* thy vertues, that ben so moche of myght,

That no man may counte hem ne expresse;

Fulfille Syon, and w*ith* high gladnesse

Thy people hertes make for to renewe,

That thy prophetes, may be founde trwe;"

610   Which all at onys w*ith* hert wille and thought,

Aftir this day so longe dyden crye:

"O come thou lorde, and ne tarye nought."

And of this day, in hir p*r*ophecye

Wrote some tyme holy ȝakarye,

Byddyng the dougthir of Syon to be light;

Where he also assured and be-hight

---

603. Quod] Ande B¹.—and] sayde B¹.—shewe] shede H².—to vs] us up C³.—thy] the H⁶. 604. distresse] derkness C². 605. thy] the H³.—vertues] vertuous C².—ben] beth Hu.—so moche of] of so mykell CC. 606. counte hem] hem counte B², J, CC; count Hn¹, Hn², Hu; accompt C³.—ne] nor Ar. 607. Syon] and a Ch.—high] om. B¹. 608. people] peples Ch, B², Co, H¹, C², C³, C¹, B⁵, Ash², Hn¹, H⁴, H², Ash¹, L, J, An, H⁵, H⁶, H⁸, Ad², C⁵, B³, B⁴, Lg, Hu; pepyll ys CC.—hertes] hert H².—make] make make Ch.—for] om. Ch, H¹, C¹, C², Ash², H², Ash¹, An, CC, H⁵, H⁶, Ad², Lg, Hu. 609. may] om. B², J, CC; might Ash².—be] be ever B², J, CC.—founde] om. B², J, CC.—trwe] true at preve CC. 610. hert wille] wille herte B¹, Co; herte soulle B². 612. ne tarye nought] tarye thu nought B¹, H²; and tarye nought Hu, C¹; ne tary thou nought Hn¹; tary no wight CC; ne narrye noght H¹. 613. of] after H². 614. Wrote] Wrote not B², C¹, C³, B⁵, L, J, CC, H⁵, B³, Hu, V.—some tyme] whilom C¹, H¹, Ash². 615. to be] om. H¹, Ash². 616. also assured] sured also B¹.

To Iher*usa*lem that is a myghty kyng

Shall come in haste his peple to visite;   ȝakarie

And he shall bryng pees in his comyng,

620   Of whome the power shall not be alyte,   Potestas eius A

For it shall laste, as hym luste to wryte,   mare vsque

From see to see, and all the erthe sprede,   ad mare

Thorugh the worlde bothe in lengthe and brede.

And Baruk bad to Iher*usa*lem   Baruk vi

To by-holde, in all his beste entente,

Tawarde the brightnesse of the sonne beme,   Circu*m*spicite

And wysely loke into the oryente,   Iher*usa*lem ad

To see the gladnesse that this day is sent   orientum

Dovne to the erthe, nowe that Criste is bore.

630   Of whose commyng, so many a day affore,

---

617. To] om. B¹, Co, C¹, C³, Ash², Hn¹, H², H⁷, H⁸, Ar, Ad³, Hu.—that] there Ch, B², C², C³, Hn¹, Ash¹, L, J, CC, H⁵, H⁶, Ad², C⁵, B³, B⁴, Lg, V.—is] as H¹; om. H⁸.—a] om. B¹, Co, C¹, Ar; so C³, Hn¹, Hu; my Ash².—myghty] mighty kynde C¹; myghty a C³, Hn¹, Hu. 618. his] this Hu.—to] forto Ad³. 619. shall bryng] bryngeth C³. 620. whome] wich C¹.—not] om. C¹, CC.—be] om. B¹.—a] om. B¹, C², H², Ar.—lyte] light J. 621. laste] byn B¹, Co, B⁵, H⁸; om. B², CC. 622. all] om. Ch.—the] om. L.—sprede] to sprede B¹, H¹; aboute B⁴. 623. Thorugh] Thorughout Ch, B², Co, H¹, C³, B⁵, Hn¹, Ar, Ad³, Ad², C⁵, B³, B⁴, Lg, Hu.—bothe] om. B¹; boght C¹. 624. And] And also Hn¹.—to] unto C¹, C³, Hn¹. 625. To] To to H¹.—in] om. H⁸; and see in Hn¹.—all] om. H⁴.—his] om. Ash¹; her H⁶; the CC. 626. brightnesse of the sonne] sunne bryȝgh of his B¹. 627. And] And also Hn¹.—loke] lokyd CC.—into] onto H⁸. 628. the] om. H¹.—this day] theder B¹. 629. the] om. C².—bore] born C³. 630. so] om. B¹, H¹, Ash², CC, H⁷.—a] om. B², B⁵, H², Ash¹, Hu, V.—affore] to fore Ch, C¹, H³, Ar, Ad²; before B¹, B², Co, B⁵, H², H⁵, H⁸.

Spake ysaye, and sayde in wordes playne: f. 51b

"The high hevynes dothe *your* grace adewe."

And sayde also, the Skyes sholde Reyne

Rorate celi desup*er* Vpon erthe, her moystur for to shewe;

nubes pluant Iustum And bad the grovnde, eke in wordes fewe,

Isaie xlv For to open and thorowe his heuenely showre,

For to buryovne our alther savyour.

Ieremye And Ieremye spake eke of this day,

And sayde that god shulde make seed

640 A greyn of Dauid, fayrer then floure in may,

Whiche in freshenesse shall eu*e*re spryng and sprede,

And conseruen Iuda oute of drede,

And eke Israel kepe in sekyrnesse.

And he shall make, all Rightwysnesse

---

632. hevynes] heyvenesse Ash¹, H⁶.—*your*] oure Co.—grace] wordes C³. 633. the] that C¹, C³; om. H¹.—sholde] shull B², Ash², H⁸.—Reyne] eke reyne Hn¹. 634. Vpon] Upon the C², C³, Hu.—moystur] moisteris H¹, Ash²; monster C².—for to] shuld H¹. 635. grovnde] erthe Co. 636. For to open and thorowe his heuenely showre, B¹.—and] and thus D, Ch, C², H³, Ash¹, An, H⁶, Ad², B⁴, Lg.—and] om. H².—thorowe] om. Ch, C², H³, H⁴, Ash¹, An, H⁶, Ad², C⁵, B⁴, Lg.—his] this Ch, H³, H⁴, Ash¹, An, H⁵, H⁶, Ad², C⁵, B³, B⁴, Lg; hire Co; the C², V; her B⁵. 637. For to] Sholde Co.—buryovne] be borne Co; bere H⁸. 628. Ieremye] Jerome C¹, CC.—spake eke] eke spak B¹; spake H¹, Ash². 639. sayde] om. H¹.—that] on hye Ch, B², C², H³, H⁴, Ash¹, L, J, An, CC, H⁵, H⁶, Ad², C⁵, B³, B⁴, Lg; om. H¹, C¹, C³, Ash², H², Hu.—seed] a seed C³, Hn¹, Hu. 640. A greyn] Ageyn Co, B⁵, L, B³.—then] than the B²; than the J, Hu; the CC.—floure] flour is H⁸. 641. in] is V.—freshenesse] fairenesse Ar.—eu*e*re] om. Ch, B¹, B² 642. conseruen] conceve B²; so conserve C³, Hu; so to conserve Hn¹. 643. And eke Israel kepe in sekyrnesse, H⁷.—And] om. D, C¹.—And Ash¹.—kepe] kept B¹, Ar; ay kepe C¹.—sikernesse] sekeness H¹; secrenes CC. 644. he] om. B⁴.—all] dom and Ch, B², C², Hn¹, H³, H⁴, Ash¹, L, J, An, CC, H⁵, H⁶, Ad², C⁵, B³, B⁴, Lg; com doun H¹, Ash²; edom and C¹, Hu; peese and C³; even dome and H².

Vpon the erthe, of high and lowe degre.

And Rightewisnesse men shall his name call,

When he is comyne to sytte in the see

Of kyng Dauid in his riall stalle.

And he also, to-fore the prestes all,

650 Bothe of Iuda and levy, shal devyse

With newe encence to do sacryfyce

To god aboue, for the grete offence

Of the peple, and for her ignoraunce;

With his offerying make Recompence,

Or that the swerde be whette of vengeaunce.

Even like as made is Remembraunce

In Malachie in the same wyse,—

This sonne of life shall spryng and Ryse

645. the] om. B², Co, B⁵, J, CC, Hu.—erthe] om. Hu.—of] om. H¹, Hu; to B¹, B⁵, H⁷, Ar.—
high and lowe] lowe and hyʒe C².—lowe] to lowe B¹. 646. his name] hym H¹, Ash². 647. is]
om. Ch, B², C², C³, Hn¹, H³, H⁴, H², Ash¹, L, J, An, CC, H⁶, H⁷, H⁸, Ad², C⁵, B³, B⁴, Lg,
Hu, V; shall H⁵.—comyne] cometh B², C³, J, CC, Hn¹, B⁴, Hu, V. 648. Of] As. L.—his]
this H⁸.—riall] hye B¹.—stalle] hall B¹, C³, Hn¹, H², H⁷, Ar, Ad³. 649. he] om. B¹.—to
fore] before H¹, C³, Ash². 650. Iuda] Juda Juda H⁶.—Iuda and levy] Levi and Juda B², V.
651. to] forto C¹. 652. the] thy Co, B⁵; his C¹. 653. for her] of the Hu.—her] om. Ch, Co,
C², B⁵, H³, H⁴, Ash¹, An, H⁶, Ad², C⁵, B⁴, Lg. 654. his] hir H¹, Ash¹.—make] to make
B¹, Co, C³; and make B⁵; make a Ar. 655. Or] Of Ad².—that] om. C¹.—be] he H⁴.—whette]
went Ar. 656. made is] is made B¹. 657. Malachie] Meloche H¹.—in the] on the H¹.—same]
thanne H⁷. 658. This] The H¹, C¹, H⁵, Lg.—spryng and] om. B¹, J.

To all tho that hym loue and drede,

660   And ben expectant w*ith* al humylite

On his comyng, to suche he shall oute shede

His light of grace at his natyvyte.

Wher-fore be gladde, lyke as byddyth Miche,

Thou Bedlem called Effreta,

Though thou be lityll namede in Iuda;

For oute of the shall p*ro*cede a-none   **f. 52a**

The myghty kyng and lorde of Israel.

And nowe this day is corven oute of a stone,

W*it*houten handes of that holy hylle,

670   Of whiche whilome, the prophete Danyell,

In his bok*es* wrote so long aforne,

To signyfye that there sholde be boren

---

659. tho] om. Hn¹.—and] or C². 660. And] That C³.—al] om. L. 661. his] thys
L.—suche] which H¹, Ash².—oute] not B¹.—shede] sprede C¹. 662. His] By L; This
H².—of] and H¹; of his B¹.—at] of B², J. 663. lyke] om. B¹, B², C¹, Ash¹, J.—byddyth]
bid Ch, Co, C¹, Ash², H³, Ash¹, L, An, H⁵, H⁶, Ad², C⁵, B³, B⁴, Lg; he byd C³; bad
B⁵; saith H².—Miche] the C³. 665. lityll namede] named litil Ar; litill called H¹.—in]
of L. 668. nowe] om. B¹.—corven] corven now B¹.—a] the B¹, C², H³; om. Co, H¹,
Ash¹, An, H⁶, H⁴, Ad², C⁵, B⁴, Lg, V. 670. whilome] som tyme Ch, B¹, B², Co, H¹, C²,
H³, H⁴, Ash¹, An, H⁶, Ad², C⁵, B⁴, Lg, V. 671. aforne] be forne B¹, B². 672. sholde]
shall B¹, Co.

A childe, in sothe, wi*th*oute touche of man,

Of a mayde, aftir his be-heste;

That like a stone was ycorven oute than,

Whan he was bore in this high feste,

Only to breke the crovne and eke the creste

In Babylyne of the grete ymage

That made men firste, to done outerage.

680 For nowe, in sothe, comyn is the day,

Of p*r*ophetes so longe aforn be-hight,

For Criste Ih*e*su, playnely this is no naye,

Is thilke stone, who so loke a-right,

Whiche by his wisdome and his faders myght,

And the vertu of the holy goste,

Was corven oute so clene in euery coste,

---

674. mayde] meke mayde Hn¹; mayden B¹, H¹, Ar. 676. this] the Co. 677. creste] cheste Ch, Co, H³, H⁴, Ad², C⁵, B⁴. 678. of the grete] of brasse the Ash². 679. made] om. Hn¹; make Ch, Hu.—men] man Ch, B¹, B², Co, H¹, C¹, C², C³, B⁵, Ash², Hn¹, H³, H⁴, H², Ash¹, L, J, An, H⁵, H⁶, H⁷, H⁸, Ar, Ad³, Ad², C⁵, B³, B⁴, Lg, Hu.—firste] most first B¹.—to] forto C¹, Hn¹, H³, H⁴, Ash¹, L, H⁵, H⁶, Ad², C⁵, B³, Lg, V. 860. is] om. Ch. 681. Of] Of the C³.—so longe aforn] tofore so longe C¹.—aforn] by forn Ch, H³, H⁴, L, An, Ad², C⁵, B⁴. 682. this] thus Ch. 683. Is] om. H¹.—thilke] this same B²; this eke H¹; that C¹, C², C³, Lg; this ilke J.—stone] son Ash¹. 684. by his] ys C³. 685. And] And of Hn¹; And by L, B³. 686. oute] om. C².

Of that blissede perfyte holy hill

That groweth full of holsome floures fayre.

For oute of hir that was in hert and wille

690   A perfyte mayde, humble and deboneyre,

Lyche as the dwe of heven dothe repayre

Vpon Ermon, al-waye newe and newe,

Amendyng aye the herbes of her hewe,

Right so thorugh vertu lastyng ay in one

Of the holy goste, this day of marye

Was corven oute, the sothefaste angle stone,

Whome that prophetes pryse and magnyfie.

For she this day was the gladde skye,

Whiche the childe of helye dyd see

700   So plesauntly ascende from the see

---

687. blissede perfyte] parfite and blessid Ash²; blessid and perfyt B¹, C³, H², H⁷, H⁸, Ar, Ad³, Hu; blysfull and parfit Ch. 688. holsome] homsom An.—of] om. Hu. 692. Ermon] herbis Ash²; heven Ar.—al waye newe and] ever more allwey B¹; allweie mewe and mewe Ash². 693. Amendyng] Amendid H².—aye] ever Co, B⁵, H⁷, H⁸, Ar, Ad³.—herbes] fressh-nesse Ch, B², H¹, C², C³, H³, H⁴, Ash¹, L, J, An, H⁵, H⁶, Ad², C⁵, B³, B⁴, Lg, V; herbis ever B¹; hertes Ar; colour Ash². 694. thorugh] like B².—lastyng] ever lastynge B¹.—ay] om. Ash², B¹; ever Co, B⁵, H⁷, H⁸, Ar, Ad³.—in one] anon Ch, C¹, C². 695. this] this this B¹.—of] in Ash¹, H⁶. 696. angle] aungell J, H⁶, Hu. 697. that] the Hu.—pryse] so preyse C³. 699. the] om. Ar.—helye] holi H¹; helth C¹, C³, Hn¹, Hu. 700. So plesauntly ascende from the see, B¹.—ascende] ascendyng D; descended Ash²; ascendid Ash¹, B⁴.—from the] for C¹, Hu.—plesauntly] plenteous B²; plenteously J.—see] high see D; tree C⁵; Marye Hu.

Vppon the erthe, nakede and bareyne   f. 52b

Of holsome frute and of herbes soote,

That hathe shede the comfortable Reyne,

The Reyne of grace, for our alther boote,

That p*er*cede hath, even to the Rote

Of our welfare, to do the levys spring.

For she alone is the felde flouryng,

That sumtime ȝaf so passynge a swetnesse

To Isaak, whan he was fall in age;

710   Of whiche he caught so inwardely gladnesse,

That hym thought holy his corage

Renewede was, and w*ith* a glad visage,

Unto Iacob of hertely Ioye sayde,—

On his clothis, as he his handes layde,—

---

702. frute] herbes B¹.—and of] and Ar, Ad².—herbes] frute B¹. 704. Reyne] greyne Ch, H¹, C², H³, H⁴, Ash¹, An, H⁵, H⁶, Ad², C⁵, B⁴, Lg; dew L, B³.—for] of B¹.—alther] aller Ar. 705. percede] persshed B¹, B², C³, H², L, B³; prechid H¹; preyede C².—hath] om. C².—even] heven Ash². 706. Of] To C¹.—to] and B⁵.—do] make C³.—levys] leve H⁸.—spring] to springe B¹. 707. is] is is Ash².—felde flouryng] floure flourynge B², J, H⁸. 708. That sumtime ȝaf so passynge a swetnesse, B¹. sumtime] whilome D, C¹, Ash², H².—so] the C¹; a Ad³.—passynge] plentevous B²; perfight H¹.—a] om. C³, C¹, H², Ad³. 709. To] That L, B³.—Isaak] Israel C².—he] the he Ch, B⁴. 710. so] his B².—inwardely] inwarde Ch, B², H¹, C¹, C², C³, H³, H⁴, H², Ash¹, L, J, An, H⁵, H⁶, Ad², C⁵, B³, B⁴, Lg.—gladnesse] a gladnesse L, B³; a corage H¹. 711. corage] gladnesse H¹. 712. and] in him and H².—with] om. B¹.—a] om. B¹, C¹, H², H⁸. 713. hertely] erthely B¹, B², J; herty C³, Hn¹, L.—Ioye] love C³.—sayde] he sayde B¹, C³, Hn¹, H⁷, Ar. 714. On] Onto Ar.—his] these these Ch.—as] and C¹; om. C³; when Hn¹, H².—he] om. C³.—his handes] hys Ch; he is hande Ar.—layde] when he layde C³.

Howe Ioseph prophicied
the birthe of criste be-
touchyng of the clotheʒ
of his sonne Iacob Ca°
xlvi°[1] 12ᵐ

M yne owne childe, and my son dere,

The grete Swetnesse and the fresshe odour

Of thy clothyng to me is so entere,

That it frome me devoydyth all langoure;"

Sayeng tofore that there shulde a floure

720 Oute of the felde springe of his kynrede,

The whiche shulde suche an odour shede,

That all the worlde shall comforte fynde and hele

In the swetnesse aʒens iche maledie,

And soueraine helthe in euery myscheve fele;

So that this felde was no wight but marye,

That by discent come of his alye.

Oute of whiche to gladen all our chere,

This day in erthe ther dyd a floure apere,—

---

715. childe] sone B[1].—son] childe so B[1]. 716. grete] fressh C[3]. 717. thy] the Ch, Co, H[1], H[3], H[6], H[7].—to me is] is to me B[2], C[2], B[5], Ash[2]; to me CC. 719. Sayeng] Soyng C[3].—tofore] therefore Ash[2].—that] that for that C[2]. 720. the] a Ar.—his] the B[2]. 721. The] To J. 722. shall] schal schal C[2].—fynde] sende B[1]. 723. In the swetnesse aʒens iche maledie, B[1].—the] this D; om. H[2].—In] Into H[2].—aʒens] and the Ar.—iche] all B[2], L, CC; every Co, C[3]; fressh Ar.—maledie] odour Ar; melodie Lg. 724. And] The Ch, C[2], Hn[1], H[3], H[4], H[2], Ash[1], An, H[5], H[6], Ad[2], C[5], Lg; om. B[2], J, CC.—soueraine] Benigne B[2]; savaryng H[1].—helthe] helpe B[1], Co, H[1], C[3], B[5], Ash[2], L, H[7], H[8], Ar, Ad[3], B[3], B[4], Hu.—in] and H[1]. 725. this] the B[1], B[5], H[2], H[7], Ar, Ad[3]; om. H[4].—felde] wight Ch, C[2], H[3], Ash[1], An, Ad[2], C[5], B[4], Lg; there H[4].—no] non B[4].—wight] thyng B[2], CC; om. B[4]. 726. of his] is of Co; of a CC; out of his Ar.—alye] lye CC; alyee H[7]. 727. Oute] om. H[1].—of] of the Ch, Co, C[1], C[2], H[3], H[4], An, H[5], H[6], Ad[2], C[5], B[4], Lg.—to] oute to H[1]. 728. in erthe] om. B[1]; on erthe CC.—ther] om. Ch, B[2], Co, Ash[1], CC; the Hu.

---

[1]crossed through

The Sweteste yet that ev*e*re man be-helde,

730 Passing the Rose and the floure delys.

And of this holy, fayre, fresshe felde,

Sumtyme þe spouse spak in canticis,

Whan he it sawe so fresshe at his devys,

And habundaunt of a temp*re* eyre,

And þ*at* it was so passing Inly fayre.

How the Garnet appull
is likened to our lady
Ca° xlvii°[1] 13ᵐ

O howe the bawme of hevenly lycoure   f. 53a
    Of thy Swetnesse, *with* souereygne suffisaunce,

Lyke Paradys shedith his vapoure

Erly on morew, avoydyng all grevaunce,

740 Lyche the frute that is of suche pleasaunce,—

The garnet apull, of colour golden hewed,

Thurgh whose odour the corage is renewed

---

729. Sweteste] swetnesse L.—be-helde] dide biholde Co. 730. delys] delicis H⁷, Ad³; fflorid lyce B⁴. 731. holy fayre fresshe] fayre fresshe B¹; faire holy freysshe Co, B⁵, H⁷, Ar, Hu; holy fressh fair H¹, H⁴, Ash²; faire fresshe holy H⁸. 732. Sumtyme þe spouse spak in canticis, B¹.—Sumtyme] Whilom D, H¹.—in] to H⁴. 733. at] in CC.—his] hit B⁵. 734. And] With V.—habundaunt] abounde CC.—a] om. B¹, B², Co.—temp*re*] tempred Ch; temperate C², L, Hu. 735. And] om. B⁵.—þat] this C³.—it] is H¹.—passing Inly] passyngly B², J, CC; inly H⁸. 736. O howe] Thowe Ch, B¹, B²; How C², L, B³; O thow Hu.—of] and Ch, B¹, B², H⁶, Ad², C⁵, B³, H³, H⁵, B⁴, Ash¹, L, J, An, V; and the Co, H¹, C², C³, B⁵, Ash², Hn¹, H⁴, H², CC, H⁷, H⁸, Ar, Ad³, Lg, Hu. 737. thy] thei H¹.—souereygne] very B¹, H⁷; saving H¹. 738. Lyke] Lyke a H¹, Ash².—shedith] sheded B¹; sheding C¹; sheddyth oute Hn¹. 739. on] a Ch, B¹, C², C³, Hn¹, H³, H⁴, Ash¹, L, An, Ad², C⁵, B³, B⁴, Lg.—avoydyng] voydyng B¹, Co, H¹, B⁵, Ash², H², H⁷, H⁸, Ar, Ad³, Hu; to avoide B⁴. 740. the] om. Hu.—that is] th ys Lg; that H¹; as is C².—of] om. H⁸. 741. of] om. H⁸.—golden] oolden B².—hewed] hewe Lg. 742. odour] colur B¹.—corage] colour CC, Hu.

---

[1]crossed through

Of eu*e*ry wight, that may the eyre Receyve.

For evyn like as the golden Rynde

Is playne and shynyng, as ye may conceyve,

His colo*ur* kepyng eu*e*re in one by kynde,

And dothe his pypens in the skalis [bynde],

To do comfort to seke in her accesse,—

Right so maye, our sekenesse to redresse,

750   This day hath borne the holsom holy frute,

The frute of lyffe, that w*ith* his soote brethe

Is remedye, and also cheve Refute

To mankynde, a-gayne the fever of dethe.

For as the grayne of the Garnet slethe

Þe stronge accesse *and* doith þe hete avale,

Right so this day, oute of the golden scale,

---

743. eu*e*ry] ony B², J, CC.—the] om. B², J, CC.—eyre] erthe C³. 744. evyn] men C².—
like] ryght B¹.—Rynde] rynge L. 745. and] om. Hu. 746. His] Hyr Hn¹—colo*ur*]
lycoure Hn¹. 747. doth] do H¹, Ash².—his] the Ch, B⁵, B³.—[bynde] MS. D has *blynde*.
748. To] Forto Ash²; And to C².—do] om. B¹, C².—to] om. B¹; the C². 750. the] this
H⁸.—holsom holy] blossum B¹; holy holsom C¹, C³, Hn¹. 751. that] om. B¹, H⁷.—his]
her CC. 753. fever] synne Ash¹. 754. Garnet] garden C¹; appell H². 755. þe stronge
access *and* doith þe hete avale, H⁷.—þe hete] hete D; om. L.—stronge] stong B¹.—
and doith] and doth and doth C¹. 756. this day] om. B¹.—the] om. B⁴.

The holsome pepyn and the grayne of lyve,

Criste Ih*e*su, gan firste to apere;

And of marye, mothir, mayden, and wyffe

760 The golden garnet w*ith* his scales clere,

Beyng al hole and iliche entere,

Was borne, in sothe, for to refresche blyfe

Our olde accesse. and right as the Olyfe

His oyle shedyth, and braunche leffe ne tre

Apeyreth nat of fayrenesse ne coloure,

Right so marye, flouryng in chastite,

This day hath borne our alther saviour,

The oyle of pees to stynte our langour,

To softe our sores, and the Swellyng slake

770 Of all owre wondes, whanne thay smerte or ake.

---

758. gan] by gan B¹, Co, B⁵, Hn¹, H⁷, H⁸, Ar, Ad³, Hu.—to] om. H². 759. mothir mayden] mayden modir C³, B⁵, Hn¹, H², Hu, V. 760. his] the B¹, C², H⁷, H⁸, Ar, Ad³; her B⁵, H⁸. 761. al] ay B¹, Co, B⁵, H⁷, H⁸, Ar, Ad³, Hu.—and] and ever Ch, B², H¹, C², Hn¹, H³, H⁴, Ash¹, L, J, An, CC, H⁶, Ad², C⁵, B³, B⁴, Lg; om. C¹.—entere] feere Hn¹; in cheer Hu. 763. right] like Ash²; om. H². 764. braunche] braunchith C¹, Ash¹, L.—ne] nor Co, B⁵, Ar, Ad³; om. H²; and B², CC. 765. ne] ne of Ch, B¹, B², Co, C³, B⁵, Hn¹, H⁷, H⁸, Ar, Ad³, B⁴, Hu; om. H³, H⁴, Ash¹, An, Ad², C⁵, Lg; nor Ash². 766. flouryng] floure H². 767. alther] om. B², J, CC. 768. our] with our CC. 769. softe] souple L, B³.—sores] sorowes L, B³. —and the] oure Ch, B¹, L, B³, H⁵, Hu; and oure Co, C³, B⁵, H³, H⁴, An, H⁶, H⁷, H⁸, Ar, Ad³, Ad², C⁵, B⁴.—and the Swellyng slake] when they smert or ake Ash². 770. Of all owre wondes whanne thay smerte or ake, B¹.—or] and D.—all] om. Ash².— thay] om. H¹.—whanne thay smerte or ake] and the swelling slake Ash².

And nowe this daye, shortely for to wryte,   f. 53b

This blisfull tyme of the Natyuyte,

Of yonge Ioseph, The coote polymete,

Wrought by power of all the trynyte,

Within the closet of chosin chastite,

Performede was, and by noo hande of man,

Alex *super* cantica   As Alysaundre wel reherse can,

With-in his boke, made in speciall

On cantica, as ye may Rede and see.

780   The which clothe of purpur moste Ryall,

Hewede *with* clennesse of virgynyte,

This day hathe shewede in our humanyte

The godhede hole, for by this clothe is mente

Of our kynde the frele garnemente.

---

771. nowe] om. H¹. 772. blisfull] blessid B¹.—the] om. CC. 773. yonge] om. Ash².—
the] om. CC.—coote] soote C³; gode H⁸. 774. by] by the Ch, B¹, B², Co, H¹, C²,
C³, Hn¹, H³, H⁴, Ash¹, L, J, An, CC, H⁵, H⁶, Ar, Ad³, Ad², C⁵, B³, B⁴, Lg.—all]
om. B¹, C³, H⁸. 775. chosin] close B², Co, C², H⁴, J, Ar, Lg; om. CC. 776. and] om.
H³.—by noo] not by the C²; by on B², J, CC. 777. As] om. B⁷.—Alysaundre] salamon
B², CC.—wel] ful wel H⁷. 779. may] mowe CC.—Rede] here Lg. 780. of purpur] om.
B⁵. 781. Hewede] Shewide C².—with] with the H². 782. shewede] shrowdid B¹, Co, B⁵,
Ash², J, CC, H⁵, H⁷, Ar, Ad³, Hu, V; shrowdith B²; Shrowed H⁸.—in] of H⁸. 783. for
by] whereby B², J, CC; for in B⁵; for H⁸.—this] the C², C³, Hn¹.—clothe] clothynge
B¹. 784. the frele] freyle the B³; the frely Ash¹, H⁶.

Howe Ioseph figurede
the birthe of Criste
Ca° xlviii°[1] 14[m]

Also this day of Ioseph the gauell,

    Amydde the felde that dothe the vertu floure,

Was gadrede vp by clennesse eu*er*y dele;

Whom all the other gan worship and honour.

For in the chaste, clene, chosin boure

790   Of maydenhede, this gavel grwe by kynde;

That whan the bretherne of Ioseph dyd bynde

Eu*er*yche his chefe, the byble can deuise,

How it stode vp a monge hem eu*er*ychone;

And all that othir gan at onys ryse,

And worshippede it mekely one by one.

For this Ioseph sawe this day a-lone,

Sonne and mone and sterres eke xi[e],

To hym obeye vppon the high hevyn.

---

785. Also this day of Ioseph the gauell, B[1].—of] om. D.—Also] And B[2], J.—gauel] cauell Ch; samell Ash[1]; sauel Ar. 786. dothe] both Ar.—the vertu] in vertu B[1], Co, B[5], Ash[2], H[7], Ar, Ad[3], Hu; vertu B[3]. 787. gadrede] gradid Hn[1]. 788. Whom] Whan C[2], H[2].—the other] that other Ch, B[2], C[2], H[2], CC; the tother B[1], Ash[2], Hn[1], H[3], H[4], Ash[1], L, J, An, H[5], H[6], H[8], Ar, Ad[3], Ad[2], C[5], B[3], B[4], Lg; the erthe C[3]; to there H[7].—gan] can Ar. 789. the] om. Ch, H[3], H[4], Ash[1], Hn[1], J. An, CC, H[5], Ad[2], C[5], B[4], Lg, Hu; a B[2].—chaste clene chosin] chaste chosen C[3]; clene chaste chosen L, B[3]; chaste clene close C[1], J, CC, Ar.—boure] tour CC, V. 790. gavel] cauell Ch, C[5], B[3]; sanel Ar.—grwe] growith C[2]. 791. That] Than Ash[2].—of Ioseph] om. Ch; Ioseph CC. 792. Eu*er*yche his chefe the byble can deuise, B[1].—can] gan D, Hn[1], Ash[1], H[6], Hu.—his] om. H[1], C[2], H[2].—chefe] self B[5]. 793. it] his Ash[1].—stode vp] up stode H[6]; stode C[2]. 795. mekely] om. B[2], Hu.—by] and Ch, B[1], B[2], H[1], C[1], C[2], C[3], B[5], H[3], H[4], Ash[1], L, J, An, CC, H[5], H[6], Ad[2]. C[5], B[3]. B[4], Lg, V. 797. sterres] the sterres H[1], C[2], CC, Lg. 798. vppon] up in C[3].—the] om. B[1].—high] om. CC.

---

[1]crossed through

And sothefaste garner of this holy grayne,

Guydo   800   As saythe Guydo, was a mayde swete,

In whome was shet, sothely for to sayne,

The sacrede store and eke the halowede whete

Of the vii^e yere that dyd in plente flete.

For on this parfyte Rote that is so vertuouse,

The vii^e yeres of grayne so plentevouse

This day ben growe to full perfection,   f. 54a

To saue Egypt in his grete nede;

And for to be to hym savacion

In scarcyte whan that he hathe nede.

810   For this is the grayne that shall fostre and fede,

With full repaste to woman, child *and* man,

And all his brethern dwellyng in Canaan.

---

799. And] And the H⁶.—this] his Ash²; the Hn¹, B³. 800. saythe] saide B², Co, CC.—
Guydo] Guydonis Lg.—a] this B¹, H⁷.—mayde] mayden B², C³, Ash², CC. 801. was]
is Ash².—sothely] sothefastely B⁵.—for to] to H². 802. store] ston C³.—and] om. H⁸.—
eke the] eke H².—halowede] holi B⁵, CC. 803. yere] yeris B², CC, Ar.—dyd] om.
Ash².—flete] schete H⁸. 804. For on] Fon B¹; For in C², C³; For of Hn¹; For one
H⁸.—Rote that is so] and rote Hn¹; rote and H²; rote that so Ar; rote Ch, B², H¹, C¹, C²,
C³, Ash², H³, H⁴, Ash¹, J, An, CC, H⁵, H⁶, Ad², C⁵, B³, B⁴, Lg, V. 805. vii^e] sevenes of Hu.
—yercs] eeres Ch, Co, H¹, C³, Ash², Hn¹, H³, J, H⁷, Ar. Ad³, Ad², C⁵, B³, B⁴, Lg, Hu; yere
C², H².—of] om. Hu. 806. ben growe] began growe Co, Ar; be growen B², C², B⁵, J, CC, H⁵,
H⁶, H⁷, H⁸, Ad³, H⁴, Ash¹, An, Ad², C⁵, B³, B⁴, Lg, Hu; beth growe Ch, H³.—full]
full of Ash². 807. saue] safe B⁵. 808. hym] hem full B³. 809. scarcyte] adversite C¹;
hys scarsyte C³; craste CC.—that] om. H¹, C², C³, Hn¹, CC, C⁵, B³.—hathe] had
Hn¹, Ar.—he hathe nede] ther grew no fede B³. 810. this] om. B¹.—is] om. B², Ash²,
CC.—shall] om. H¹.—fostre] suffer Ash². 811. With full repaste to woman, child, *and*
man, Ad³.—With full] Withoutyn D, C¹; Ande full B¹, H⁷.—woman] to woman B¹,
Ash², H⁷, Ar, Ad³. 812. his] om. Hu; his his H².—in] om. B³.

This yonge Ioseph, this Ioseph the secunde,

Shall by his witte helpe and Releve,

And Iacob make in plente to habounde

With fulsom fode, at morew and eke at eve,

That the hungre on no syde greve

Of the vii^e yere vnto his lynage.

And like as Iosephe, in his tendre age,

820   Thought he sawe high vp in the hevyn

Sonne and mone in his avysion,

And ther with all sterres eke elleven,

Honour hym by grete devocyon,

So this Ioseph, excellyng of Renoun,

This newe Iosephe, criste Ihesu hym-self,

Of the sterres and the signes twelfe,

---

813. this Ioseph] om. CC; Ioseph H4, Ar, B, V. 814. by his witte] bye with his H2.—helpe] om. B1; both help C3.—and] om. B1. 815. make] to make H8; made H1, Ash1, H3, H4, An, H6, Ad2, C5, B4, Lg.—in] hys C3.—make in plente] in plente make B1. 816. fulsom] fulsid Ash2.—fole] flood J.—eke] om. B1, C2, C3, Hn1, H2, H6, H7, Ar, Ad3, B3, B4, Hu.—eve] one H1. 817. on] in C2, H2, B3.—syde] wise C1, C2, H8, B3.—greve] ne greve Ch, B1, B2, Co, H1, B5, H3, H4, Ash1, J, Ar, Ad3, Hu, V; do greve C2, B3. 818. yere] yeres B1; om. H1, B1.—hys] this H8. 819. like] as B1. 820. vp in the] upon H1, C2; upon the B1, C1, Ash2, H2, Ar, B3; up in Ch, B2, Co, H3, H4, Ash1, J, An, CC, H5, H6, Ad2, C5, B4, Lg; up into Hn1. 822. all] om. C2; eke the B3.—sterres] the sterres Ch, C1, C3, B5, H3, H4, B4, Lg, Hu.—eke] om. C2, B3. 823. honour] honoured H8.—by] with B1, Co, C2, B5, H7, H8, Ar, Ad3, C5, Hu. 824. So] Of Ch, B2, Co, H1, C1, C2, C3, B5, Hn1, H3, H4, H2, Ash1, J, An, CC, H5, H6, Ad2, C5, B4, Lg; om. B3.—excellyng] excellent Ar.—of] in H1. 826. Of] Of all B3.—and the] and Ar; and of the B1, Co, CC, V.

Honourede was w*ith* low subiection,

Though he lay lowe in an oxe stall.

For bothe troni and d*o*minacion,

830   And holy the curte above celestiall,

This high feste for a memoriall,

The laudes songen in the hevynly quere;

Lyke as Dauid bad in the sauter:

"Preysyth the lorde, of the high empere,"

And with o voys his birthe gloryfieth,

That hathe w*ith* loue brent and set afyre.

Seraphin wherfore hym magnyfieth,

Atwene two bestes though he in erthe lyeth,

Full humble thurgh his humylite,

840   And nowe this feste of the Natyvite,

---

827. low] ful lowe B¹. 828. oxe] oxes C², Ash², Hn¹, H³, An, H⁵, H⁷, H⁸, Ad³, Ad², C⁵, B⁴, Lg, Hu. 829. bothe] both and H, both of B³.—troni] trone Co, B⁵, H⁸; om. H¹. 830. And] He B³; A CC.—holy the] hool the Ch, Co, C¹, C², C³, Ash², Hn¹, H³ H⁴, H², Ash¹, J, An, H⁵, H⁶, Ad², C⁵, B⁵, Lg, Hu, V; the hole B¹, B⁵, Ar, Ad³; the holy H⁸; hole above the B², CC; all the hool H¹; helde the B³.—above] om. B¹, B², CC, H⁷. 831. high] hieste C². 832. The] In H⁷.—laudes laude C².—songen] songe, Ch, B², C², B⁵, Hn¹, H³, H⁴, Ash¹, J, An, CC, H⁵, H⁶, H⁷, Ad², C⁵, B³, B⁴, Lg; synge B¹; syngyn C¹.—in the] in CC. 833. the] om. Hu. 834. of] and C¹. 835. And] Om. Ash².—o] a H¹, H⁸.—gloryfieth] glorifie CC. 836. hathe w*ith* loue] with love hath H²; with love C³.—afyre] on fyre B¹, Hu. 837. hym] he H¹.—magnyfieth] magnyfied Ash¹. 838. Atwene] Betwene B¹, C³, Ash¹, H⁶, H⁷, Ar, Ad³, B³, Lg, Hu, Hn¹, C¹, C², H².— though he in erthe] in erthe thow he B¹; in erthe thow C³.—lyeth] lyed Ash¹. 839. humble] humbly B¹, B², Co, C¹, C², C³, H⁷, H⁸, Ar, Ad³, Ad², C⁵, B³, B⁴, Lg, Hu.— humylite] humanyte C³; benignite B³. 840. nowe] om. H⁵.—the] om. B⁵, Ash², H⁸, Ad³.

The high Angels and virtutes all,   f. 54b

Presith hym as thay ben wonte to done.

And lete the swetnesse of your notes fall

Dovne to the erthe, wher godd*es* awne sonne

This day hathe ioye *with* vs to wonne,

And lithe now wrappede in his mothir barme;

Whome wel softely *with* hir holy Arme,

And *with* the fayrenesse of hir fyngers white,

Hir yonge childe mekely dothe embrace,

850   And so moche in hert dothe delite

His tendre lymmes to welden and compace,

Ande to biholde the goodlyeste face,

That eu*ere* was forged by natur*e*.

For it was he, I dar yov well assur*e*,

841. The] Ande the B¹, Co, B⁵, H⁷, H⁸, Ar, Ad³ Hu.—Angels] angell B¹, Co, C²,
Hn¹, H², H⁷.—and] and the B¹, Co, B⁵, C², C³, Hn¹, H², H⁷, H⁸, Ar, Ad³, Hu.—
virtutes] vertues Ch, B², H¹, C¹, Ash², H³, H⁴, Ash¹, J, An, CC, H⁵, H⁸, Ad³, Ad²,
C⁵, B³, B⁴, Lg; vertuous B¹, Co, C², B⁵, Hn¹, H², H⁶, H⁷, Ar, Hu; high virtutes C³.
842. Presith] Preysen B¹, B², Co, C³, B⁵, Hn¹, J, CC, Hu; Preise ye Ash².—thay
ben] ye are B², J, Ash², CC.—to] om. Ch. H³, H⁴, H², Ash¹, H⁵, H⁶, B³, B⁴, Lg;
do C². 843. lete] lettith Ash², B³.—the] om. B¹.—your] theyr C³.—notes] om. CC. 845.
hathe] om. B².—ioye] chose Ch, B², H¹, C¹, C², C³, Ash², Hn¹, H³, H⁴, H², Ash¹, J,
An, CC, H⁵, H⁶, Ad², C⁵, B³, B⁴, Lg, V.—to] forto B¹, Co, C¹, C², C³, B⁵,
Ash², Hn¹ H², Ash¹, J. An, CC. H⁵, H⁶, H⁷, H⁸, Ar, Ad³, Ad², C⁵, B³, Lg, Hu.
846. lithe] hath H¹.—in] hym in H¹. 847. wel] full B¹, Co, H¹, C¹, C², C³, B⁵, Ash², H²,
H⁸, Ar, Ad³, Hu; so ful H⁷.—with hir holy] he holdeth on hyr C³; with holy Ch. 848.
hir] his H³, H⁴, An, Ad², C⁵, Lg. 849. Hir] His Lg.—mekely dothe] doth mekely B¹;
mekely doth hym H¹. 850. so] in so Ch, B¹, Co, H¹, C¹, C², C³, B⁵, H³, H⁴, Ash¹, An,
H⁶, H⁷, H⁸, Ad³, Ad², C⁵, B⁴, Lg.—dothe] hir doth B¹, Co, B⁵, C³, H⁷, H⁸, Ad³.
851. and] and to H¹. 852. Ande to biholde the goodlyeste face, B¹.—the] that D, Ash²;
his B⁵.—goodlyeste] mooste goodly Hn¹; goodli CC. 853. eu*ere*] ever yit to fore Hn¹.—
forged] for gret H¹.—by] wyth Hn¹. 854. he] om. B¹; so C².—dar] thare Ash¹, H⁶.—
well] om. Ash².—assur*e*] insure Ar.

Life of Our Lady

Whome she behelde with her eyne meke,

That from eterne was in his faders [thought]

And oon with hym, who can take kepe,

His owene worde that al made of nouȝt,

Whome a mayde hathe to mankynde brought,

860   Thorugh hir mekenesse of hevyn and erthe quene,

The lyneall stok of Iuda to sustene.

Iacob in libro de
testimentis xii

Whome that Iacob on his fatall day,

Whan attropos gan his threde vntwyne,

Whiche cloto had put long in delaye,

And lachasis, or thay wolde it fyne,

Gan to blisse and thus of hym defyne,

Whan all his bretherne stoden envyron,

This olde gray, with a full softe soun:

855. Whome] When CC.—behelde] beholdeth V.—hir] om. H¹,—meke] depe Ash². 856. in] om. Ash¹; from B², J, CC.—his] the B¹, H⁶, H⁷, H⁸; her C²; om. H¹.—[thought] MS. D has *yougth*. 857. who] who so B¹, B², H¹, C², C³, Ash², H², J, CC, H⁵, H⁷, H⁸, Ar, Ad³; who that Hn¹, Hu.—can] gan Ash¹; liste CC; can eke V.—kepe] nede H². 858. His owene worde that al made of nouȝt, B¹.—al] all thyng D, C¹; al hath Hn¹. 859. hathe to mankynde] to mankynde hath B¹, C². 860. hir] his C², Ash¹.—of] om. J. 862. Whome] Whan C².—that] om. B¹.—on] upon B¹, Co, Ash², H⁷, H⁸, Ar, Ad³; in C³, Hn¹, H². 863. gan] shall Ch, B², H¹, C¹, C², C³, Hn¹, H³, H⁴, H², Ash¹, An, J, CC, H⁵, H⁶, Ad², C⁵, B³, B⁴, Lg; om. B¹.—his] my Ch, H¹, B², C¹, H³, H⁴, H², Ash¹, J, An, CC, H⁵, H⁶, Ad², C⁵, B³, B⁴, Lg, V; her B⁵, Ash², Hn¹.—threde] drede H².—vntwyne] gan to untwyne B¹. 864. put] om. H⁸. 865. or] for H⁸.—fyne] fynde Hu. 866. thus] this H².—hym] hem Ch, B¹, Co, H¹, C¹, C², C³, B⁵, Hn¹, H³, H⁴, H², Ash¹, J, An, CC, H⁵, H⁶, Ad², C⁵, B³, B⁴, Lg, Hu.—defyne] dyd fyne CC. 867. envyron] everychone H²; hym envyron Ash². 868. olde] colde H²; hollde Hu.—gray] crie H¹.—a] om. Ash¹.—full] om. B¹, Co, H⁸, Ar, Ad³.

"O Iuda, Iuda, thy bretherne eu*er*ychone

870 Shall prese and worship the high renou*n*

Of thyne estate, which shall of all thy fone

The pryde opresse, and make hem loute dovne;

That shal be cleped the whelpe of the lioun,

The Royall beste whiche, maugre who saythe nay,

Shall myghty be to cache and take his pray

And proudely bere it home vnto his cave,—   f. 55a

My sonne Iuda, in thy dredfull tene,

For thorugh thy myght thou shalt victory haue,

Maugre echone that the reuers mene.

880 For who shall mowe wi*th*stonden or susteyne

Thy kyngly power, to make resistence

A-gayne thy manhode and thy magnyficence,

---

869. O] Of Co.—Iuda Iuda] Iuda B¹, Co, H¹, H⁷, H⁸, Ar, A̧d³, Hu. 870. the] with C²; thy Ash, CC.—high] gret hye B¹, C¹, C³, B⁵, Hn¹, H², Hn⁷, Ar, Ad³, Hu; gret C², V; hie grete H⁸. 871. which] that B³.—fone] soun C². 872. The] Thy Ch, Co, H¹, Ash², H³, H⁴, An, H⁵, Ad², C⁵, Lg; there J, CC.—hem] om. H¹, C², Lg.—loute] to loute B¹, C³, Hn¹, H⁸; light Ash². 873. That shal be cleped the whelpe of the lioun, B¹.—of] and D, C¹.—cleped] called Co, B⁵.—the whelpe] whelpe H¹. 874. Royall] riallest H².—whiche] om. B¹, Co, C¹, H⁷, H⁸, Ar, Ad³, Hu. 875. cache] touche C¹; chase Ash², CC; take H².—take] to take B¹; cacche H². 876. proudely] prudently C².—home] om. B¹; oute Ash².—vnto] untyll Ch; to B¹, Co, C², B⁵, Ash¹, H⁷, H⁸, Ar, Ad³; un H³, An; into H². 877. in] for B¹.—thy] the C¹, J. 878. thou] that H⁴.—victory] the victory B¹, Ash¹, J, CC, Hu. 879. Maugre] Thurh C¹.—the] thi C².—mene] doith mene B¹. 880. who] om. B⁵; who so J.—mowe] now B⁵, B¹, Co, C¹, C², C³, H², H⁸.—or] and C¹. 881. Thy] The B¹, B², Co, H³, H², CC, H⁷ Ar, Ad³.—kyngly] knightly Ash¹. 882. A-gayne thy] Agayne the H⁶, B³, Lg, Hu.—and thy] and Ash², Lg; and the H⁶; of thy B³, Hu.

That shall in the so clerly shewe and shyne

W*ith*outyn clipsyng or any man*ere* clowde;

The septre of whome, in sothe, shall neu*ere* fyne,

To be famous by Reporte lowe and lowede,

Nor neu*ere* sese in couerte ne i*n* shrowde,

Till a duke aryse of thy kynrede,

Whom all the world shall obey and drede.

890   The whiche, in sothe, is for to be sente

Ou3t of thi sed by dwe successioun,

Liche a kyng to holde his parleamente,

W*ith* his legees a-mydde his region,

And he shall be to eu*ery* nacion

Sothefaste abydyng and socour in her nede.

And he shall bynde his myghty sterne stede,   Ipse erit expectacio

genci*um*

---

883. That] Thow C³, Hn¹; Shall H⁴.—shall in the so clerly] shall so clerly in the B¹; in the shall so clerly H¹; shall ful clerly C³, Hn¹, H⁸; shall in the clerly Ash¹, H⁶.—shewe] also shewe Hn¹.—and] and eke C³. 884. or] of Ch, B¹, B², Co, H¹, C¹, C², C³, B⁵, Ash², Hn¹, H³, H⁴, Ash¹, J, An, CC, H⁵, H⁶, H⁷, H⁸, Ar, Ad³, Ad², C⁵, B³, B⁴, Lg, Hu.— any] every C³. 885. in sothe] om. B¹, B⁴. 886. lowe and lowede] of lawe lewde Ch; both softe and lowde Ash²; of lawe lowde B², H¹, C², H³, H⁴, Ash¹, J, An, CC, H⁵, H⁶, Ad², C⁵, B³, B⁴, Lg. 887. in couerte ne in] ne in covert Ch, H¹, C¹, Hn¹, H³, H⁴, Ash¹, J, An, CC, H⁵, H⁶, Ad², C⁵, B⁴, Lg, V; nor in covert B²; ne in coveryd C³; never in coverte B³. 888. of] thanne of Hn.¹—thy] the H¹, CC, H³, V. 889. world] worde CC. 891. Ou3t of thi sed by dwe successioun, B¹.—thi] the D, C², Ash¹, H⁶.—Ou3t] om. Hn¹.—by] om. Lg.—dwe] om. Ch, B², H¹, C¹, C², C³, Ash², Hn¹, H³, H⁴, H², Ash¹, J, An, CC, H⁵, H⁶, Ad², C⁵, B³, B⁴, Lg. 892. a] as a Ad³.—to] om. C¹. 893. a-mydde] and H¹, Ash².— region] renoun B¹. 894. he] om. B¹, Co.—to] of B¹, C³, Ash², Hn¹, H⁷, H⁸, Ar, Ad³, Hu. 895. abydyng] kynge CC. 896. his] om. H¹.

Of verrey fors, at the holesome vyne;

And tye his asse vindir the grapes Rede.

Ande he his stole þat lyke to golde doth shine,

900 And his palle, by myght of his manhede,

He shall wasshe in grapes that shull blede

The Rede blode, depper than skarlet hewe.

And thus arayede in his vesture newe, **Gen xlix**

Of loke he shall be sterner to by-holde,

Than the stremes of the light sterre; **Pulcriores oculi**

And of eyne fayrer many folde, **eius vino**

Thanne wyn fined shynynge thorowe a verre

And like yuoury that comes fro so fer,

His tethe shall be evyn smothe and white."

910 And liche, in sothe, as Ioseph lust endyte,

---

898. vndir the] unto his H1. 899. Ande he his stole þat lyke to golde doth shine, B1.—to] the D, B5, Ar; om. H1, C3.—he] om. C2.—his] is H7, Lg, Hu.—golde] god C1, Hu, V.—doth] om. H1, Lg; do CC. 900. by] with CC. 901. He] And he Ch, H1, C2, H3, H4, Ash1, An, H5, H6, Ad2, C5, B4, Lg, V; om. C3, Hn1, B3; And B2, J, CC. 902. The] And the B1; om. H2, CC.—than] than the B1, B2, Co, C1, C2, CC, H8. 903. thus] thus are thai Ar; this H8. 904. Of] O Ash1.—sterner] sterne on B1; sterne C1, C2, Ash1, CC.—to by-holde] to abide bolde B2, J; and abyde bolde CC. 905. light] bright Ch, B2, H1, C2, H3, H4, Ash1, J, An, CC, H5, H6, C5, B3, B4, Lg. 906. of eyne] ofte thanne B2, CC; of then J.—fayrer many] many fairer Lg; fayre many Ch.—folde] a folde H1, C1. 907. Thanne wyn fined shynynge thorowe a verre, B1.—Thanne[That D.—fined] om. CC; finew H8.—shynynge] schewing B5.—a verre] ferre H3, H4, An, Ad2. 908. so] the B2, J, CC. 909. be] om. CC.—evyn] om. C2. 910. as] om. C1.—endyte] to endite H2, H6, H8.

The sonne of Iacob in his testament,   **f. 55b**

Wherto his children he maketh mencion,

To-fore his dethe, w*ith* full deuoute entent,

In his *pres*ence as they knelyn adovne,

To hem Rehersyng the grete avysion

Whiche he had in egipt gone full yore,

In a foreste, among the holtez hore,—

How that he sawe twelfe hertes white,

Full lustely goon in her pasture.

Lincolne   **920** And aftir that, as Lincolne liste to wryte,

He sawe of Iuda borne a creatur*e*,

Of thought and dede, a verrey mayden pure.

And in his dreme, hym thought he dyd sene

Of hir brought furthe, w*ith*outyn spote all clene,

---

911. The] This H⁸.—in] and C¹. 912. Wherto] Whetto H³, H⁴, An; Whette Ad².—children] childe CC. 913. w*ith*] om. H⁵. 914. In] om. Ch, H³, H⁴, An, Ad², C⁵, B⁴.—they] he B¹. 915. the] his B⁵. 916. gone full yore] long afore B¹, Co, B⁵, H⁷, H⁸, Ar, Ad³, Hu.—gone] om. H⁴, An. 917. a] the C⁵.—holtez] holt H¹.—hore] here H¹; sore H⁸. 918. he] I Ar.—twelfe] twenty B², J, CC. 919. lustely] lusty C³, Hn¹.—in] to V. 920. aftir] om. V.—to] forto V. 921. sawe of] of saw of H⁵. 922. Of thought and] And thow in CC.—mayden] man Ar. 923. in] om. H².—hym] he C³, H⁵, Ar.—he] that he Hn¹, C³. 924. w*ith*outyn] with H¹.

A lambe moste fayre to his inspection,

That eu*ere* he sawe vnto his pleasaunce;

On whose lefte hande stode a fyers lyon,

And best*es* many by one alyaunce,

That were in erthe thorugh cruell resemblau*n*ce,

930   Aforsyng hem by sheltroun in batayle,

By felle malice, the fayre lambe to assayle.

But or that thay avayle myght in fyght,

The lambes power made hem for to dye;

And hem venquyschede thorugh his humble myght,

That man and Angell, when thay this conqueste seye,

Thay fell downe streght and the lambe obeye,

That was sent of god, this meke werryour,

The whiche was borne to ben our savyour,

---

925. moste] must H¹.—to] in B¹, C², H², H⁷, Ar, Ad³.—inspection] speccioun B¹, H⁷, Ar, Ad³; suspeccion CC. 926. euere he] he ever Ch, B², H¹, Hn¹, H³, H⁴, Ash¹, J, An, CC, H⁵, H⁶, H⁷, Ad², C⁵, B⁴, Lg; never he B¹.—vnto] to B¹. 927. fyers] ferly H²; fayr CC; fere Lg. 928. many] all Ch, B², H¹, C², C³, Hn¹, H³, H⁴, H², Ash¹, J. An, H⁵, H⁶, Ad², C⁵, B³, B⁴, Lg; allore CC. 929. were] was B⁵.—thorugh] by CC. 930. Aforsyng hem by sheltroun in batayle, B¹.—in] and D, J; om. CC.—Aforsyng] Afore seyng Co, H⁸.—by] om. H⁵. 931. the] this Ch, H¹, C², H³, H⁴, Ash¹, An, H⁶, Ad², C⁵, B³, B⁴, Lg.—fayre] om. B¹, B², C³, Hn¹, J, CC, Hu; stouth H².—lambe] beest H².—to] forto C³. 932. that] om. Ch, B², Co, H¹, C¹, C², C³, B⁵, H², J, CC, H⁵, Ar, Ad³. 933. for] om. Ash¹. 934. hem] be H².—venquyschede] overcam Ch; vengyd B¹; requysshed H³.—his] om. Hu. 935. this] his CC; the H⁵, V. 936. Thay] om. B¹, H⁷, Ad³, B³.—streght] om. Ch, B², H¹, C¹, C², C³, Hn¹, H³, H⁴, H², Ash¹, J, An, CC, H⁵, H⁶, Ad², C⁵, B³, B⁴, Lg, V; flat B¹, H⁷.—and] and dide B¹, H¹, C², C³, Hn¹, H⁷, Ar, Ad³, Lg, Hu.—obeye] dide obeye Ch, B², H³, H⁴, Ash¹, J, An, CC, H⁵, H⁶, Ad², C⁵, B³, B⁴. 937. That was] om. Ch, B², H¹, C¹, C², C³, Hn¹, H³, H⁴, H², Ash¹, J, An, CC, H⁵, H⁶, Ad², C⁵, B³, B⁴, Lg, V.—meke] new C³. 938. The] om. Ch, B², Co, H¹, C², H³, H⁴, H², Ash¹, J, An, CC, H⁵, H⁶, Ad², C⁵, B³, B⁴, Lg.—borne] sent B¹, H⁷.—our] om. H⁵, V.

And to mankynde full protection,

940 To sle the lyon, that he may not endure.

And acordyng with this avysion,

This lambe of god, clad in our armoure,

This day was borne of a mayden pure,

And lorde of all, here in a lytyll cage,

By Right lyne discended oute of the lynage

Of the worthy and myghty bretherne two;   f. 56a

As a burgeon oute of a stoke growyng,

Right so this childe, fro levy and also

Frome myghty Iuda, growe oute succedyng,

950 Borne of the blode to be preste and kyng,

So entermellyde by succession

Of bothe was the generacioun,

939. And to] Unto Ch, B², H¹, C¹, C², C³, Hn¹, H³, H⁴, H², Ash¹, J, An, CC, H⁵, H⁶, Ad², C⁵, B³, B⁴, Lg; And unto H⁷, H⁸, Ar, Ad³.—full] and Ch, B², H¹, C¹, Hn¹, H³, H⁴, H², Ash¹, J, An, CC, H⁵, H⁶, Ad², C⁵, B³, B⁴, Lg; and the C³. 940. sle] fele C². 941. And] Ande with.—this] the C²; hys C³, J, H⁸. 942. our] youre J. 944. of] over B¹.—here] erthe C¹, Ad².—a] om. B¹.—lytyll] bateyll CC. 945. Right lyne] Kyn Ch; Kynde lyne Ad², B³; lyne B⁴, Lg, Co, C¹, C², C³, H², B⁵, H⁵, H⁶, Ar, Hn¹, V; lyne lyne An, H³, H⁴, Ash¹, H⁷, Ad³, B¹, Hu; lyn kyn B⁵; lyneall H¹.— discended] discent H¹. 948. this] the C².—fro] and fro B¹, C³, Hn¹, H⁷, Ar; of B², CC. —levy] lyne Ar.—and] om. B¹, C³, Hn¹, H⁷, Ar.—also] Juda B², CC. 949. Frome] For Ch, CC; The Ash¹, H⁶.—oute] out the B¹; out by H⁸. 950. the] om. B³. 952. Of bothe was the generacioun, B¹.—the] this D, Co, B⁵, Hn¹, H⁸, Hu; he so the C³.—generacioun] gubernacion CC.

Tyll the braunches be ronne and so ferre gone,

By lyneall cours descendyng as a stayre,

Til the kynredes were growe bothe in-to oone,

In-to o braunche to haue his repayre,—

Þat was preued pleynly to be ayre,

The right of levy in presthode to succede;

And by Iuste tytle, who so lust take hede,

960 For to be kyng and bere the diademe

Aftir his fadre, and to be successour*e*

To worthy Iuda, all Israel to queme,

To ben hir prince and myghty gou*er*noure.

And from Iacob this burion and this floure

Firste gan spring to Iesse, till it raught

And so furthe dovne, till the buddes caught

---

953. braunches] braunche C³, H².—ronne and so ferre gone] so ferre runne and gone B¹; ronne and gon so ferre Co; ron and ferre goon C³; ron so ferre and gone B⁵, H⁷, Ar, Ad³, Hu; ronne and also fer gon H². 954. By] om. B¹.—as] om. B², J, CC. 955. Til the kynredes were growe bothe in-to oone, B¹.—growe bothe] bothe growe D, B², H⁴, Ash¹, An, CC, H⁵, H⁶, Ad², C⁵, B³, B⁴, Lg, Hu.—in-to] in D, Co, C³, H².—kynredes] king kinredis C¹. 957. þat was preued pleynly to be ayre, H⁷.—preued] purvoyed D; om. B⁵; provyded H².— to be] by the Co; to be right B¹. 958. in presthode] playnly B¹, Co, B⁵, H⁷, H⁸, Ar, Ad³, Hu. 959. lust] om. B⁴.—take] to take B¹. 960. For] And CC.—bere] take H². 961. and] om. Ch.—to] om. B², H¹, Hn¹, C³, H³, H⁴, H², Ash¹, J, An, CC, H⁵, H⁶, Ad², C⁵, B³, B⁴, Lg, V; so C². 962. To] Of B¹.—all] and B¹; of C³, H⁸; as H⁵.—queme] be queme C³. 963. hir] ayre CC.—gou*er*noure] governaunce Ch. 964. this] thi B¹. 965. gan] can Ar.—till] to H¹; that C³, Hn¹. 966. furthe] om. C².—buddes] bude C².—the] he J.

Howe nature obeythe to
virgynyte Ca° xlix°[1] 15

The holy sydes of a pure virgyne,

To bere the frute that shall mankynde save.

And nowe this day, the prophecye to fyne,

970   In Bedlem within a lityll caue,

Kynde and a mayde suche werre haue,

For this matier: howe in a creature

Two names myght Iustely, by nature

That be contrarie, haue her restynge place,

For mayde and mother, shortly for to saye,

In o person to-gyder may nat trace,

For by kynde the tone moot voyde awaye.

But in this case, nature dyd obeye

To a mayde, and gafe vp hol her right,

980   Wysely aduertyng she was to feble of myght

967. The] To the J, CC.—pure] holy H[2]. 968. the] om. B[1]. 969. this] the C[1].—the] of
C[1]; be the Ar.—fyne] refine B[1]. 971. a] om. Ch, B[1], H[1], H[3], H[4], Ash[1], An, H[6],
H[7], Ad[3], Ad[2], C[5], B[3], B[4], Lg, Hu; of CC.—suche] such a C[3].—haue] to have B[1].
972. For] For in B[1].—in] that Ar. 973. Two] These two H[8].—myght] right
Ch, B[1], B[2], CC; my H[8].—Iustely] lustely H[8]; om. Co, B[5]. 974. That he contrarie haue
her restynge place, B[1].—restynge] dwellyng D, C[1].—haue] to have Ar. 975. for to] to
B[1], CC. 976. trace] race CC. 978. in this case] here in Hn[1]; in this matir Co. 979. a]
om. B[1].—hol] om. C[1], C[3]; al B[4]; thanne Hn[1].—her] his CC. 980. to] so Co.—feble] fle CC.

[1]crossed through

In this matier to holde champartye   f. 56b

With hir that was of face moste benygne.

Wherfore she voydyth all Rancour and envye,

And humbly hir quarell dothe Resigne.

For it were veyne, nature to malingne,

Though she of kynde be the Empresse,

Ayeyne hir lorde that made hir so maystresse,

That she mot nede of necessite

In euerythyng to his will obeye,

990   And be ministre vnto his volunte,

Sithen of hir myght he berythe hym-self the keye.

For vnto hir, by no manere waye,

It is no wrong ne no preiudice,

Though of a mayde withoutyn synne or vyce,

981. to holde] the oolde H³. 982. hir] his Lg. 983. voydyth] voyded C³, Ash¹, An, H⁶. 984. humbly] humble B¹.—quarell] wharell H¹. 985. were] is H¹.—veyne] warn Ar; but vayn B², J, CC.—nature] for nature Ch, B², C², H³, H⁴, Ash¹, J, An, CC, H⁵, H⁶, Ad², C⁵, B³, B⁴, Lg, V; for C¹. 986. of] be of H⁸.—Empresse] emprise H¹. 987. hir] the H¹.—hir so] his modir his H¹. 989. to] om. V.—obeye] to obeie V. 990. be] to be Co; that be H¹; by C¹, H⁴, An.—ministre] mirakill C¹.—vnto] to B¹, Co, C³, B⁵, Hn¹, H², CC. H⁷, Ar, Ad³, B³, Hu. 991. Sithen] Sith Ch, B¹, B², Co, H¹, C¹, C², Hn¹, H³, H⁴, H², Ash¹, J, An, CC, H⁵, H⁶, H⁷, H⁸, Ad², C⁵, B³, B⁴, Lg.—he] she C².—hym self] om. Ch, C², H², Ar. 992. by] be C¹; in C³.—no manere] namyd C¹.—waye] of weye CC; alwey C¹. 993. It] om. H⁸, Hu.—no] nat C³.—ne no] ne B¹; nor no B².—preiudice] providice B¹. 994. of] om. B¹, Co, H¹, C¹, C², C³, Ash¹, H⁷, Lg, Hu, V; in H².— mayde] man H¹, C², Lg.

That was so holy and p*ar*fite founde at all,

He wolde of grace descenden dou*n* full lowe

To take the clothyng frele and mortall

Of our kynde, to make a buriou*n* growe,

That neu*ere* was of man sette ne sowe.

1000   But *with* a worde, and the consentyng

Of a mayden, a graffe so burgenyng

Of Iuda stok this day gan a-pere,

Whan criste was borne of a mayden free.

And the fader sent his sonne so dere

Dovn to the erthe to make an vnyte,

By p*ar*fyte love and fervent charyte,

Et*er*nally by bonde that may not fayle,

Fully assuryng by weddyng and sponsayle,

995. so] om. Lg.—at] om. Ch; with C¹. 996. full] so Ch, B¹, B², Co, H¹, C¹, C², C³, B⁵, Hn¹, H³, H⁴, H², Ash¹, J, An, CC, H⁵, H⁶, H⁷, H⁸, Ar, Ad³, Ad², C⁵, B³, B⁴, Lg, Hu, V. 997. frele] fre H¹, C², C³, Lg. 998. a] om. B², J, CC. 999. sette ne] ne set ne B², CC; set nor B¹, Ar. 1000. a] oo B², CC.—the] a C³. 1001. a graffe] be grace CC.—so] om. Ch, B², H¹, C¹, C², C³, Hn¹, H³, H⁴, H², Ash¹, J, An, CC, H⁵, H⁶, Ad², C⁵, B³, B⁴, Lg, V. 1002. Of] O Hu.—stok] a stok C³.—day] om. Co, B⁵, H⁸; grace CC. 1004. so] om. Ch, B², H¹, C¹, C², H³, H⁴, Ash¹, J, An, CC, H⁵, H⁶, Ad², C⁵, B³, B⁴. Lg, V. 1005. the] om. C².—an] and H⁵, H⁸. 1006. p*ar*fyte] fervent Co, B⁵.—fervent] parfyt Co, B⁵. 1007. Et*er*nally] Eternall H¹.—not] noo H¹. 1008. assuryng] ensuryd CC; assuryd Ch, B¹, B², Co, C², C³, B⁵, Hn¹, H³, H⁴, H², Ash¹, J, An, H⁵, H⁶, H⁷, H⁸, Ar, Ad³, Ad², C⁵, B³, B⁴, Lg, Hu, V.—and] of B¹, H⁷, Ad³.

Be-twene his sonne and his chosyn ayre,

1010 And holy chirche p*er*petually to laste.

And in a chaunbre, by excellence fayre,

Of maydenhede that hym-self caste,

The holy knotte and the bounde so faste,

So bonden was that it may neu*er*e vntwyne;

And of that araye fully to det*er*myne,

Where the fest and the weddynge was,   f. 57a

In all the erthe, halowede and yholde,

In a closet more clere þan verre or glas,

Or any byrell bryght to be-holde.

1020 For by recorde of patriarkes olde,

The chaste chaumbre was wi*th*in adornede

With golde of feith fayre *and* bright borned,

1009. Be-twene] Atweyn C¹. 1010. p*er*petually] perpetually perpetually Ch. 1011. in]
om. H¹, H⁸.—by] of C³. 1012. maydenhede] a maiden Ar.—self] om. C². 1013. knotte
and the bounde] bonde and the knotte B¹; knotte and the bonde and the bonde Ch. 1014.
So bonden] Y-bounden Ch, B², H¹, C², H³, H⁴, H², Ash¹, J, An, CC, H⁵, H⁶, Ad²,
C⁵, B³, B⁴, Lg, V; Bounden C³.—was] fast Ch.—may] might B¹.—vntwyne] twynne
B¹, C³, Hn¹. 1015. of] om. H².—fully to det*er*myne] for to termyne B², H¹, Hn¹, H³, H⁴, J.
CC, H⁵, H⁶, Ad², C⁵, B³, B⁴, Lg; for to determyne Ch, C¹, C², C³, H², Ash¹, V.
1016. Where the feste and the weddynge was, B¹.—the] this D, C³. 1017. the] om.
B¹, C³, H⁷, Ar, Ad³, Ad². 1018. In a closet more clere þan verre or glas; H⁷.—clere]
clerer D, J; om. Ad³.—than] or B¹, Hn¹.—verre] cristal B³.—or] om. H¹. 1019. to]
unto B¹. 1020. of] of the B², J, CC. 1021. within] om. B¹.—adornede] deorned B⁵; ordeyned
Ar. 1022. With golde of feith fayre *and* bright borned, B¹.—of] and D, C¹.—With] Of C².
—*and* bright] bright CC.

With charite, that yeveth so clere a light

To Recomforte all that ben in *pr*esence,

And w*ith* silu*er*e depurede oute so bright,

Thorough the high wisdome of gostely sapience,

And all the Gemmes that hauen excellence

In morall vertu for to shewe and shyne,

Þe closet chose so clerli enlumine

1030   That of vnclennes ther may noo clipsyng be,

So fulsome light is ther of p*ar*fytenesse.

For ther the violet, men may be holde and se,

Of clene entent and of holynesse,

Withe Roses strawede, in god to haue swetnesse;

Ande w*ith* lylies of chastite y-meint,

And ther-of colour that neu*er*e wolbe fayent;

1023. yeveth] yaff B², J, CC; reyneth C2. 1024. in] in hyr C³. 1025. depurede] pured B², C², J, CC.—oute] om. C².—so] of Lg. 1026. Thorugh] And thorugh C³.—the high] hir Ch, CC; the B¹, B², H⁷, Ar, Ad³; high H¹, C², C³, Hn¹, H³, H⁴, H², Ash¹, An, H⁵, H⁶, Ad², C⁵, B³, B⁴, Lg; his C¹, J, V.—of] and Ch; of the CC. 1027. the] om. J. 1028. morall] mortall J, CC, H⁸, Ar, Ad³.—for to] to CC. 1029. þe closet chose so clerli enlumine, H⁷.—chose] close D, C¹, Hn¹, Ad³, Ar. 1030. ther] om. B⁵, H², H⁸, Ar, Ad³, Hu.—may] om. Co. 1031. is] as H²; is is Ash¹; was CC.—there] here H¹. 1032. the] om. C².—violet] violettes Ch, B¹, B², H¹, B⁵, Hn¹, H³, H², Ash¹, J. H⁵, H⁶, H⁷, Ar, Ad³, Ad², C⁵, B³, B⁴, Lg; viols C¹, C³, Hu. 1033. Of] Of the B¹.—and of] and of the B¹. 1034. in] with C³.—have] om. C².—swetnesse] clennes C¹. 1035. Ande w*ith* lylies of chastite y-meint, B¹.—y-meint] Imenent D; y-bente CC. 1036. And ther] That were C³; And they Co, Ar; And there to H², Hu.—be fayent] desente CC.

Wher violettes bytokenyng maydenhede,

Like to purpill in signe of victorie.

And in this chaumbre full of honeste drede,

1040   The chosen closet, the chase oratorye,

This day, in sothe, the high kyng of glorye,

To shewe his myght, how he for man gan [wyrche],

And howe he hathe spousede our mothir holy chirche,

And like a spouse he *procedyde* is

Oute of his chaumbre, for to rectifie

All that was wronge or in our kynde amys;

Wherfore his feste we aught to gloryfye.

Full long a-gone, to syng his psalmodye,

The kyng Dauid entune dyd his harpe,

1050   And withe the tenoures and the trebles sharpe,

1037. Wher] These Ch, B², H¹, H³, H⁴, Ash¹, An, H⁵, H⁶, Ad², C⁵, B³, B⁴, Lg, V; The C²; This J, CC; Which H².—bytokenyng] betoken Ch, B¹, B², Co, H¹, C¹, C², B⁵, Hn¹, H³, H⁴, H², Ash¹, J, An, CC, H⁵, H⁶, H⁷, H⁸, Ar, Ad³, Ad², C⁵, B³, B⁴, Lg, Hu.— maydenhede] manhede C². 1038. to] the CC.—signe] token H².—victorie] virgenite CC. 1039. in] om. H¹.—drede] and drede B¹, Co, B⁵, H⁷, H⁸, Ar, Ad³; of drede H⁶. 1040. chosen] close H⁶, Ar. 1041. the] this C². 1042. gan] dide C²; can Ar.—[wyrche] MS. D has *wryche*.—wirche Ch, B¹, B², Co, H¹, C¹, C², C³, B⁵, Hn¹, H³, H⁴, H², Ash¹, J, An, CC, H⁵, H⁶, H⁷, H⁸, Ar, Ad³, Ad², C⁵, B³, B⁴, Lg, Hu. 1043. And howe he hathe spousede] Y-spoused hath Ch, B², H¹, C¹, Hn¹, H³, H⁴, H², Ash¹, J, An, H⁵, H⁶, Ad², C⁵, B³, B⁴, Lg, V; Y-spousede with C²; In spusehede hathe CC.—holy] om. H⁵. 1044. like] om. H⁵.—is] his CC. 1045. his] thys H⁴. 1046. or] and B¹, H⁷; as Ar. 1047. his] this Ch, B¹, B², Co, H¹, C¹, C², C³, B⁵, Hn¹, H³, H⁴, H², Ash¹, J, An, CC, H⁵, H⁶, H⁷, H⁸, Ar, Ad³, Ad², C⁵, B³, B⁴, Lg, Hu, V.—we aught] for Ch, B², H¹, C¹, C², C³, Hn¹, H³, H⁴, H², Ash¹, J, An, CC, H⁵, H⁶, Ad², C⁵, B³, B⁴, Lg, V. 1048. Full] As full H⁸, Ad³, B⁵.—long] om. H¹.—to] forto H², CC.—his] this Lg; in B¹. 1049. The] om. Co, C³; To Ar.—entune dyd] entuned B¹, C¹, H⁸, B³. 1050. withe the] with H¹.— and the] and with the B², CC.

He to heuene gan en-haunce *and* ryse   f. 57b

This day of dayes, moste worthy and famous.

And all *p*rophetes in hir sawes preyse

This noble feste, this feste so graciouse;

And fro*m* hevyn, wi*th* voys melodiouse,

Angelles full lowe Swiftely dovne a-light,

For to hono*ur* this holy sacrede nyght,—

The nyght of nyght*es*, highest of ycheone,

Excelling all as in worthynesse.

1060 For in this worlde was creature noon,—

In hevyn ne herth, nor in sothefastnesse,

In lande nor see, that with grete bysynes

Her deyu*ere* dyd this nyght, to honour

Hym that was borne mankynde to socour.

1051. He to heuene gan en-haunce and ryse, B¹.—He to] The tone D. 1052. This] Hys
CC.—of] is of Co. 1053. hir] his Ash¹.—preyse] so preyse H². 1054. so] om. Ch, B².
Co, H¹, C¹, C², C³, H⁴, H², Ash¹, J, An, CC, H⁵, H⁶, Ad², C⁵, B³, B⁴, Lg. 1055.
melodiouse] so melodious B¹. 1056. Swiftely] sone Ch, B², H¹, C¹, C², H³, H⁴, H²,
Ash¹, J, An, CC, H⁵, H⁶, Ad², C⁵, B³, B⁴, Lg, V; om. C³; from heven Hn¹.—dovne]
did Ash¹. 1057. this] this this CC.—sacrede] om. Ch, H¹, C², C³, B⁵, H³, H⁴, Ash¹,
An, H⁶, Ad², C⁵, B⁴, Lg.—nyght] myght Ch. 1058.] The nyght heyest of nyghtes
everychone B³. 1059. as] om. H³. 1060. was] was a Ch, B²; was ther C¹. 1061. ne]
ne in Ch, B², H², J, CC, B⁴; in B¹, Co, C¹, B⁵, H⁸, Hu.—nor in] ne in Ch, B², H¹,
C¹, C², C³, Hn¹, H³, H⁴, H², Ash¹, J, An, CC, H⁵, H⁶, Ar, Ad², C⁵, B³, B⁴, Lg;
in very B¹, Co, H⁷, Hu; ne H⁸; in Ad³. 1062. nor] ne on B¹, B², J, CC; nor in Co, B⁵,
H⁷, Hu; in C¹; nother in H⁸.—that] om. Ch, B², J, CC; but B³. 1063. to] for to B¹,
Co, B⁵, H⁷, H⁸, Ad³, Hu; so to Hn¹.

Howe the chefe temple of
Rome fel dou*n* the nyght
of crist*es* birthe and of
othir wondrefull tokens
Ca° 1°¹ 16

For on this nyght, by eu*er*y creatur*e*

Was sothely shewed his Natyvyte

In Bedleme: how that of a mayden pure

A childe was borne, moste souerayne of degre.

And firste of all, in Rome the Cyte,

1070 His birthe was shewede by myracle.

For wall and Roof, tours and pynacle

Of the Temple moste famous in the towne,

To god of pees that was consecrate,

The same nyght to grovnde fel adovne,

Pleyne with the erthe, wast and desolate;

In whiche temple, moste Riall of estate,

The statute stode of myghty Romulous,

And at the byldyng, the story tellyth thus,

1065. on] in CC. 1066. sothely] fully C¹.—Natyvyte] om. Ad³. 1067. that of] om. B¹, B²,
Co, C², B⁵, H⁴, CC, B⁴; of Ch, H¹, C³, Hn¹, H², Ash¹, J, An, H⁵, H⁶, H⁷, H⁸, Ad³,
Ad², C⁵, B³, Lg, Hu; that Ar; of V. 1068. was] hathe B⁵.— moste] in B¹.—of] of all
Ch, Co; in H⁸, Ad³, Hu; om. H¹. 1069. Rome] the Rome Ash¹.—the] in that B¹; that
C¹. 1070. by] highly by Ch, B², H¹, C², H³, H⁴, Ash¹, J, An, H⁵, H⁶, Ar, Ad², C⁵,
B³, B⁴, Lg, V; there by C³, H², H⁷; holy by CC. 1071. and Roof] and towre B¹, C²; roof
Ar.—tours] and roof B¹, C²; dores H⁸.—and pynacle] or pynacle Hu. 1072 in the] in
B⁴. 1073. To] The C¹. 1074 to] to the Ar; fel to B¹.—fel] it fell CC; om. B¹.—
adovne] om. Ar. 1075. wast and] and was H²; and CC; playne and Ash¹, H⁶. 1076.
In] In the Hn¹.—temple] om. C².—of] of the J; and C².—estate] estage H⁸. 1077.
The] And H².—statue] statute C², Hn¹, H³, H⁴, H², An, CC, H⁷, H⁸, Ar, Ad³, Ad²,
Lg.—stode] good H².—The statue stode] Stode the stone Ash¹. 1078. And] om. CC.—
at] om. B¹, Ar.—byldyng] bygynnyng B¹; biddynge Co; billing H⁶; pledynge Hu.—
tellyth] seith C².—thus] us C³, J, CC.

---

¹crossed through

Of this temple, thay of Rome wente

1080　To appollo w*ith* humble sacryfice,

To haue answer in hir beste entent,

How longe this fane Riall of asyse,

So strong bilt, and in so thrifty wyse,

That it shulde lasten, and so to endure

Ayeyne a-sault of any aventure,

Or p*erturbyng on any maner syde.　　　　　　　　　　f. 58a

And he yaf answer vnto one and all,

Howe this temple w*ith* his walleȝ wyde,

W*ith* his creseȝ and batelyng Riall,

1090　Shall eu*ere* stonde sure w*ith*outyn fall,

Vnto the tyme that a mayde childe.

And thay a-none that firste made it bilde,

1079. this] the B¹, H⁷, Ad³.—temple] peple H².—thay] om. B¹. 1080. humble] humbly H⁸. 1082. fane] pane B¹, C³, Hn¹, H², H⁷; fame B², J, CC; tempill C¹.—of] of this B², J, CC. 1083. strong] long B¹, Ad².—bilt] om. Ar.—in] om. B¹, B², C¹, J, Ar.—so] om. C²; so in Ar.—thrifty] trusty B², H¹, J, Ar, Ad², Lg; myghty B⁵. 1084. lasten] so laste H².—and so to] ever and Ch, B², H¹, C², H³, H⁴, Ash¹, J, An, CC, H⁵, H⁶, Ad², C⁵, B³, B⁴, Lg, V; ever and in Ar; and so B¹, H⁷; and C¹, H²; long and C³; and ever to Hn¹. 1085. a-sault] the asault Ch, H¹, H³, H⁴, H², An, H⁵, H⁷, Ad², C⁵, B³, Lg, Hu, V; the saute B¹, C², Ash¹, H⁶, B⁴; the ascent B², Hn¹, CC; the myȝte C¹; the assautys C³.—any] om. B¹; every B², C³, J.—aventure] creature B², H¹, Ch, C², Hn¹, H³, H⁴, Ash¹, J, An, CC, H⁵, H⁶, Ad², C⁵, B³, B⁴, Lg, Hu, V. 1086. on] in Co, C², C³, H⁴, H², Ash¹, H⁶; of C¹, H⁸, V.—syde] of side Ash¹, H⁶. 1087. And] om. C², B³.—he] om. Co.—vnto] to C², B³.—all] to all B¹. 1088. this] the CC, Hu.—with] wys J.—his] this Co.—wyde] whiȝt C². 1089. batelyng] batlement B³. 1091. the tyme that] om. Hn¹.—mayde] man CC.—childe] have a childe Ch, C², H⁸; hath borne a childe Hn¹, H⁴, B⁴; doth childe H²; had a child Ad³; be with child B³. 1092. thay] om. Hn¹.—made] did B⁴.—it] the B¹; and Hu.—bilde] and by helde H⁸.

Of this answer glade and full credible

That this temple eu*e*re shulde stande.

For hem thought it was inpossible,

A mayde eu*e*re, othir on see or lande,

To haue a childe, and so thay vndirstonde.

And thay a-noon yaf the temple a name,

By one assente, for the grete fame,

1100   And called it, as I can discerne,

The Temple of pees w*ith* his wallys white;

And ther-w*ith*-all namede it et*e*rne,

And at the entre so thay dyd wryte.

But on the nyght, the trouthe to endite,

Whan criste was borne of a mayden clene,

This temple fel dou*n* endelong the grene,

1093. Of] And of B⁵.—glade] were glad B¹, H⁷; full glad B², CC; glad were B³.—full om. B¹, B², CC. 1094. temple] answ of the temple Ch.—eu*e*re shulde] shuld ever Ch.—stande] holde H⁴, An. 1095. thought] om. H⁴.—it] that it Hu.—was] were H¹; was an C³. 1096. eu*e*re] om. B², H¹, C¹, C², H², CC, Lg, Hu; eny B⁵.—othir] eythir Ch, H¹, C¹, Hn¹, H³, H⁴, Ash¹, J, An, CC, H⁵, H⁶, H⁷, H⁸, Ar, Ad³, Ad², C⁵, B³, B⁴, Lg, Hu; where B⁵; or H²; om. B¹.—on] in B², C², H⁸.—or] or of B¹; or on B², H¹ J, Ar, Hu; or in H⁸. 1097. and] om. CC. 1098. a noon] om. Co.—name] name anon Co.—one] om. H¹.—for] and for Hn¹. 1102. all] om. C².—it] is Ch, H³, H⁴, An, H⁵, H⁶, Ad², C⁵, B⁴. 1103. at] that Lg.—thay dyd] dide thei C². 1104. on the] on the the Ash¹; at the B⁵.—nyght the trouthe] trouthe the nyght Ch. 1105. mayden] may J. 1106. endelong] even long C¹, H².—the] in the C², C³.

To fulfill the trwe prophecye

Of appollo that tolde hem all this thyng.

Ande in that place in wurship of marie

1110   And of hir sone of heuene *and* erth kynge,

Stant a cherche ful of byldynge.

And even like the self same tyme,

The grete statute, long or it were prime,

Of Romulus that was deifyede,

Fell to erthe and braste on peces small;

And thogh Romaynes made hym stellifiede,

His greate hede for all that dyd avale;

Of whome also, the werkeman made a tale

That forget it many day affore,

1120   And sayde, in sothe, till a childe be bore

1108. hem] om. C², An, H⁴.—all] om. B²; of H5. 1109. Ande in that place in wurship
of marie, B¹.—Ande] And that D; om. H8. 1110. And of hir sone of heune *and* erth
knyge, B¹.—And of] And D, Co, H¹, Hu, B⁵, C¹, C³, C²; And in C³, Hn¹; And so
H⁶.—erthe] of erthe Ch. 1111. Stant a cherche ful ryal of byldynge, B¹.—in] of D.—a]
now a B³.—full] om. C². 1112. like] om. Co.—self same] same self B², J, CC; self sanor
H¹. 1113. grete] om. H⁶.—statue] statute B¹, B², Co, C², Hn¹, H⁴, H², An, CC, H⁷,
H⁸, Ar, Ad³, Lg, Hu. 1114. that] wich that C¹.—was] thanne was B¹, Co, B⁵, H⁷, H⁸,
Ad³, Hu; she was B², J, CC.—deifyede] edified B⁴; i *inserted above,* 1115. to] to the
Ch, C³, B⁵, Hn¹, H³, H⁴, Ash¹, An, J, CC, H⁵, H⁶, H⁷, H⁸, Ar, Ad³, Ad², C⁵, B³, B⁴,
Lg, Hu; onto the C².—braste] om. H⁵; brak V.—on] in Hn¹; into J, CC; to H⁶, H⁸. 1116.
thogh] thoughte CC; yit H¹.—Romaynes] the Romayns B², C¹, J, CC; that Remaynes H².—
made] om. H⁵.—hym] it H²; them Ash¹, CC. 1117. all] om. B¹.—that] it H¹. 1118. werkeman]
werkemen Lg. 1119. forget] for gate H¹.—affore] tofore Ch, C¹, Lg; before B¹, H⁷, H⁸, Ar.
1120. sayde] om. Ch, B², C², C³, Hn¹, H³, H⁴, Ash¹, J, An, CC, H⁵, H⁶, Ar, Ad³, C⁵, B⁴,
Lg.—be] were Ch, B2, H¹, C², C³, B⁵, Hn¹, H³, H⁴, Ash¹, J, An, CC, H⁵, H⁶, Ar, Ad³, C⁵,
B⁴, Lg.

Of a mayde, it shulde stonde vp-Right,

Þis grete ymage, *and* neuere his hede encline;

But he aloute vpon the same nyght,

Whan crist was borne of a pure virgyne,

Like as the werkemen dyd afore devyne,

Ayene the conseyte and the entencion

Of that he ment in his opynyon.

I fynde also, that the skyes donne,

Whiche of custome corteyne so the nyght,

1130 The same tyme w*ith* a sodeyne sonne

Enchasede were, that it wex as light

As at mydday, whan phebus is moste bright,

To shewe sothely that the sonne of lyfe

Was borne that nyght, to stynte all our stryfe.

1121. it] that H²; and Hu.—vp Right] up aright Ar. 1122. þis grete ymage *and* neuere his hede encline, H⁷.—þis] The D, C¹.—neuere his hede] his hed never B¹, B², CC; never his hede did Ad³.—enclyne] decline B², CC. 1123. he] om. C¹.—aloute] all out Ch, H³; dide loute B³; alone H⁸.—vpon] om. B¹, C³; on Hn¹. 1124. Whan] Where Ash¹.— was] is C¹.—of] upon CC. 1125. the] om. H⁶. 1126. and the] of the H²; and H¹, C³, H⁶, V.—entencion] devocioun Hn¹. 1127. Of] yff C²; om. Hn¹.—ment] myȝte C¹.—in] of CC.—opynyon] ocupacioun B¹. 1128. that] at Ch; om. Ad³. 1129. corteyne] coursen H¹.—so] om. B¹, C³. 1130. same] som C¹. 1131. Enchasede] Enclosed Hn¹.—as] al Co, B⁵. 1132. is mostel] so C¹. 1133. shewe] sey Ar.—lyfe] lyght Hu. 1134. all] om. B¹, H¹, CC, B⁴, Hu.

Howe the nyght of crist*es*
birthe a well in Rome
ran Oyle Ca° li°1 17

A nd even than, also as bokes telle,

    In verrey sothe, withoutyn any werre,

The selfe tyme in Rome was a well,

Of his stremes passyngely entiere

To loke vpon as any cristal clere,

1140   From his vaynes as it dyd boyle;

Of whiche the water chaunged into oyle

The same nyght, and to Tybre Ran

So large plentee that all myght it see.

Of whiche well longe before or than,

Al opynly, in Rome the Cytee,

Sybelle the wyse, that had souereygnete

Of prophecye, playnely wrote and tolde,

That the water of this well shulde

1135. even than] thanne even Ch.—also as] as Ch, B¹, B², H¹, C¹, C², C³, Hn¹, H³, H⁴, H², Ash¹, J, An, CC, H⁵, H⁶, Ar, Ad³, Ad², C⁵, B³, B⁴, Lg; as also Co, B⁵, H⁷, H⁸; also Hu.—bokes] boketh H¹.—telle] also telle Ch, B¹, B², H¹, C¹, C², C³, Hn¹, H³, H⁴, H², Ash¹, J, An, CC, H⁵, H⁶, Ar, Ad³, Ad², C⁵, B³, B⁴, Lg. 1136. In] The H⁷.—any] om. H⁵.—werre] drede C¹; where H⁶, H⁸. 1137. selfe] same B¹, B², C¹, C³, CC, H⁷, Ar, Ad³, Hu.—tyme] tide Co, H⁸. 1138. Of his stremes passyngely entiere, B¹.—passyngely] passyng D, C², H⁸, B³. 1140. his] her H⁴, An.—it] he B¹, H⁷, Ad³; om. Co.—dyd] dothe CC. 1141. chaunged] turned H¹.—into] om. Lg. 1142. and] om. Ad³, Hu.—to] into B¹, Co, C³, B⁵, Hn¹, H², H⁷, Ad³, Hu; in H⁸.—Tybre] tribe H⁸. 1143. all] all men Hn¹, H⁸.—it] om. H², CC. 1144. well] full H⁸. 1145. Al] And C².—the] in the C¹; the faire C²; om. Hu. 1146. had] had the C¹, C². 1148 this] that H⁸.

---

¹crossed through

The same nyght chaunge his lycour

1150 Into oyle, and so a day endure,

Whan of this worlde was borne the savyour,

In Bedlem of a mayde pure.

And as I fynde also in scripture,

The same day, high in the firmament

Towarde the partye of the oryent,

Wer seyn thre sonnes lustyly apeer,—   f. 59a

Eu*er*yche of hem large Rounde and bright;

That caste abrode her fayre beameʒ clere,

Thourgh all the world in eu*er*y manes sight.

1160 The whiche sonnes drowe lyne Right,

Her cours holdyng in hast and that a-noon,

Till all thre were Ioynede into oon;

1149. The same nyght chaunge] Chaunge the same night C1.—chaunge] chaunged C3, Hu.
1151. this] the CC.—was borne] borne was B1, H7.—the] oure H8. 1153. And as I] As B1.
1154. day] say Ch.—high in the] in the high C1; hye on the B2. 1155. partye] parties C1.
1156. Wer] There were C1; Where CC.—lustyly] listy CC. 1157. large Rounde] rownd
large Co; large and rounde B1. 1158. her] his H1, C2, H3, H4, An, H6, Ad2, C5, B4, Lg.
1159. all] om. C3.—in] and B1; into H2.—manes] man ys CC. 1160. drowe] drow hem
V.—lyne] by line C3.—Right] aright Ch. 1161. in hast] om. Ch, CC. 1162. all thre] that
they C1.—Ioynede] closed Ar.—into] in Ash1, H6; al into C2.

To mankynde playnely to declare

That he was bore, in whom were founded thre,

To encrece our Ioye and also our welfare,

Flesshe and soule, and eke the deyte,

Knytte all in one by sothefaste vnyte;

Which as a sonne, voydyng schoure and shade,

Was borne this day all the worlde to glade.

1170   Also in rome, as wryghtet innocent,

     In his cronycle makyng mencion,

How the Senates, all by one assent

In concistorye, of affection

Whiche thay hadde in her opynyon,

Vnto her noble and miȝti Emperour

Octouyan, of worthynesse the flour,

Howe the Senates
of Rome wolden
haue halden
Octouyan her
Emp*e*rour as for
her god
Ca° iii°[1] 18

1163. to] for to H[8]. 1164. in] and B[1].—whom] om. Ch. Ad[2], C[5], B[3], Lg.—were] was
B[1], Co, C[3], B[5], H[2], H[7], H[8], Ar, Ad[3], Hu. 1165. also our] our Ch, B[2], H[1], C[1], C[2], C[3],
Hn[1], H[3], H[4], Ash[1], J, An, CC, H[5], H[6], Ar, Ad[2], C[5], B[3], Lg; om. B[4]. 1166. Flesshe
and soule] soule and flesshe C[1].—eke] also H[2]. 1167. in] om. C[2]. 1168. Which]
Lyke Ch; The wich C[1].—as a] om. B[2], C[1], J, CC; is a V. 1169 the] this Ch, C[1], C[2],
C[3], Hu. 1170. Also in rome as wryghtet innocent, B[1].—wryghtet] worthy D. 1171.
makyng] makith C[1], Ad[2]. 1172. Senates] senatours Ch, B[1], B[2], Co, C[1], J, CC, B[3].—all]
and all B[5], H[7], Ad[3], Hu; om. C[1].—by] om. H[8]. 1173. In] In the B[2], J, CC.—concistorye]
constorye B[1], H[7].—of] of oon B[1], B[2], C[1], J; be oon CC; of grete H[2]; of hole Ash[1]; of
the grete B[3]. 1174. in] om. H[5]. 1175. Vnto her noble *and* miȝti Emperour, H[7].—*and*]
om. D, B[1], Hn[1], H[3], H[2]. 1176. of] the H[1].—worthynesse] myȝtines C[1].—the] om.
H[1], C[2].

---

[1]crossed through

Wolden Ichone hym haue deyfyede,

And callede hym by name Immortall.

The whiche thyng when he had espyede,

1180   As he that was ful prudent founde at all,

To his *pr*esence made a-noon to calle

Sybelle, that was myrrour of sapyence,

Here vpon to here, her sentence;

And ther-w*ith*-all that she moot dyffyne,—

W*ith*outyn doute of ambyguyte,

As fer in sothe as phebus dothe now shyne,—

If ther wer any of power more than he,

Or *pe*regall vnto his degre,

Fro Est to west, here in erthe lowe,

1190   In all this worlde that she couthe of knowe.

1177. hym haue] have had C¹.—deyfyede] desired Ash¹. 1178. callede] calle Ch, Ar, Ad³.—by] by the C¹. 1179. The] In B³. 1180. As he that was ful prudent founde at all, B¹.—at] in D.—ful] om. H¹, H⁴. 1181. made a-noon to] anon made H². 1182. Sybelle] She Ash¹; Sith he H⁶.—myrrour of] of mirrour H⁷. 1183. here] geve Hu.—her] the H⁸; his Ad³. 1184. ther-w*ith*-all] that Ch; ther uppon Hn¹.—that] om. Co, B⁵, CC.—moot] mote with all Ch; sholde Hn¹. 1185. of] or Ch, B², Co, H¹, C¹, C², C³, H³. H⁴, H², Ash¹, J, An, CC, H⁵, H⁶, Ar, Ad², C⁵, B⁴, Lg, V. 1186. fer] ferforth B², J, CC.—now] om. C¹, B³, B⁴. 1187. wer] om. Co.—of] in Ch.—any of power more] of power eny more Co, B⁵; any more of power H¹. 1189. here in] into H⁸. 1190. this] that C¹.—worlde] om. C¹; erthe B⁵.—she] om. C².—couthe] om. Hu.—of] auȝte B⁵; om. B¹, Co, B⁵, Hn¹, H⁷, H⁸, Hu.

And this was done vpon the selfe day   f. 59b

Whan criste was borne in Bedlem by myracle.

And she full wysely putte hym in delaye,

To yef answer makyng a small obstacle;

Til at the laste, the fin of hir oracle,

Amydde the chaumbre of the Emp*er*our,

Stondyng envyron many a Senatour,

Was playnely this, w*ith* chere and face bolde,

"O Emp*er*our, lifte vp a-noon thyne eyne,

1200   And loke vp yonder, and se the cercle of golde

A-boute the sonne, whiche easi is to asspyen,

And ther by-holde, thou maiste it not denyen,

A mayde sitte, of beaute moost souereyne,

Holdyng a childe in her Armes tweyne."

1191. was] om. Hu.—selfe] same Ch, Ar. 1192. in Bedlem] om. C². 1193. And] As Hn¹.—putte] nolde putte Ch, B², H¹, C¹, C², H³, H⁴, Ash¹, J, An, CC, H⁵, H⁶, Ar, Ad², C⁵, B³, B⁴, Lg, V. 1194. yef] yef an B⁵.—small] fynall B⁵, H², Ar, B³. 1195. Til at the laste the fin of hir oracle, B¹.—Til] But D.—the fin of hir oracle] she fond a myrakill C¹. 1196. Amydde] And in C³.—of the] of hir C². 1197. many] om. H⁸. 1198. Was playnely this] She opunly sayde B¹, H⁷; she pleinly seid Ad³; sayd playnly H².—this] thus Ch, B², Co, H⁴, Ash¹. 1200. vp] om. C¹; upon J.—and se] see C³. 1201. A boute] Above Ash¹, CC.—whiche] the whych B¹.—easi is] is esy Ch, Hu; ethe is H¹, C², C³, Hn¹, H³, J, An, H⁵, H⁶, Ad², C⁵, Lg, V; is ethe Ash¹, Ar, B³, B⁴.—to] forto Hu. 1202. ther] om. C².—not] not to H⁸. 1203. A mayde sitte of beaute moost souereyne, B¹.—moost] om. D, Co, B⁵, H⁸, Ad³, Hu. 1204. in] om. B², J.—Armes] handes B¹, H⁷, Ad.³.

And right a-noon, as this Octovyan

Sawe the childe by clere inspection,

Wi*th*oute abode, a voys he herde than

From a-lofte into the chaumbre doune:

"By-holde and se *with* humble affection,

1210 This is the auctor of the high heven,

Sette in the sonne, clere as any leven."

Where Sybell all a-brode gan saye

To hym a-none, and list not to abyde:

"Thy crovne avale, and the childe obeye,

Whos face bright the sonne may not hyde.

And lat nowe be thy pompe and all thy pryde."

And at oo worde she plattely gan hym telle,

The childes myght his power dyd excelle.

1205. this] om. Ch, B², H¹, C¹, C², C³, Hn¹, H³, H⁴, H², Ash¹, J, An, CC, H⁵, H⁶, Ar, Ad², C⁵, B³, B⁴, Lg, V. 1206. clere] clene Hu. 1207. he] om. Ch, C³; she C², Lg. 1208. a lofte] lofte B¹, Ad³, Hu; the lofte C²; above V.—into] to Ar. 1210. auctor] awtere Hu, B⁵.— of the] of B¹, Co, H¹, C², C³, H⁸, Hu. 1211. any] om. C¹. 1212. Where] Wherefor Ch, B¹, B², Co, H¹, C¹, C², C³, B⁵, Hn¹, H³, H⁴, H², Ash¹, J, An, CC, H⁵, H⁶, H⁷, H⁸, Ad³, Ad², C⁵, B³, B⁴, Lg, Hu.—a brode] on brode J; alowde B¹, H⁷.—saye] assaye Ash¹; to say C¹. 1213. and] om. B¹, H⁷.—to] for to Ch, B², Co, H¹, C¹, C³, Hn¹, H³, H⁴, Ash¹, J, An, H⁵, H⁶, H⁸, Ad³, Ad², C⁵, B³, B⁴, Lg, V.—abyde] byde Ch, B¹, H¹, C¹, C³, Hn¹, H³, H⁴, Ash¹, J, An, H⁵, H⁶, H⁷, Ad², C⁵, B³, B⁴, Lg, V. 1214. the] this Hn¹. 1215. Whos] Who is CC.—bright the] the bright Ch. 1216. lat nowe] now let C¹.—be] be all B¹.—all] om. Ch, C¹, C³, Hn¹, H⁶. 1217. she plattely] platly she C²; she playnly Ash¹, H⁶; platly C¹. 1218. The] This B², CC.—myght] power C².—his] the C³.—power] myght C².

Whiche thyng whan he gan playnely vndirstande,

1220 Of faythefull will and hole herte entere,

He knelyde dovne and list no longer stande;

And with encens cast in the sencere,

He dyd worship vnto the Autere,

And to the childe moste excellent of fame,

And liste no more vsurpe on hym the name,

To be callede, ayenste alle skylle and Right,   f. 60a

Wrongfully a god, sithen ther is but one.

And Right a-noon, this noble worthy knyght,

Thorowe ouȝt the worlde his *pre*cept made to gone,

1230 To provynces and contreyes eu*er*ychone,

Vpon payne of dethe, that noon of hem all

Be hardy more a god hym for to calle.

1219. Whiche] The whyche B¹, H⁷, Hu.—whan] om. C¹.—he] they Co, B⁵; she CC; gan playnely] gan B¹, Hu; pleynly gan H⁶; gan platly H⁷. 1220. faythefull] ferefull C³. —hole] om. B¹, C²; of hool Co, H⁷, H⁸, Ad³. 1221. knelyde] kneleth Co, B⁵, H⁷.—list] wold C¹.—stande] to stonde B¹. 1222. And] om. C³.—with] om. C².—the] a B¹. 1223. He] And B¹; om. C¹.—Autere] aucter H², J. 1224. to] om. C¹. 1225. vsurpe on hym] on him usurpe B¹; of him usurpe Co, B⁵; usurpe in hym H⁶; usurpe of him H⁸. 1226. alle] as H⁵. 1227. Wrongfully] Wrongly B², J, CC.—is] is no moo Ash¹. 1228. this] the C².—worthy] wirth Lg. 1229. Thorwe ouȝt the worlde his precept made to gone, B¹.—to] om. D, C³, B⁵, H², H⁷, H⁸, Hu.—made] om. V. 1230. and] and to C¹. 1231. Vpon peyne] Up peyne Ch, B¹, Co, H¹, Hn¹, H³, H⁴, H², Ash¹, An, H⁵, H⁶, H⁷, Ad³, Ad², C⁵, B³, B⁴, Lg, Hu, V; Of peyne C¹; On peyne B², J, CC. 1232. more] om. B¹; hym Hu.—hym for] for Hu; hym C¹, C², C³, Hn¹, H⁴, Ash¹.

For he well wiste, by signes opynly

And evydenceȝ, eke in speciall

Ther was oon borne, of power more worthy

Then was hym-self, and thereto Immortall

To whome no kyng on erthe is p*er*agall

In all this worlde, of high ne lowe estate

And for this skylle, aftir dedicate

1240   Was that chaumbre, by high devocion

To marye playnely, this is noo naye

And called eke, for this avysion

Ara celi, yet into this daye

The name abyt, and slydeth not awaye

Ne lesith not, the light of his brightnesse

Thourgh noon eclippsyng, of foryetylnesse

1233. he well] well he B². 1234. eke] many eke B¹, H⁷. 1235. Ther] That C¹,—was oon] was H¹; one was C¹.—borne] om. B², J, CC.—more] most Ch, H¹, C¹, C², H³, H⁴, An, H⁶, Ad², C⁵, B⁴, Lg. 1236. was] om. C³, Hn¹.—hym] his H¹. 1237. Kyng] thynge Ch, C¹, An, H⁸, Ad², C⁵, B⁴.—no kyng on erthe] in erthe no thynge C².—peragall] principall B². 1238. In] Of Ch, B¹, B², Co, H¹, C², C³, B⁵, H³, H⁴, H², Ash¹, J, An, CC, H⁵, H⁶, H⁷, Ad², C⁵, B³, B⁴, Lg, Hu.—this] the CC.—ne] ne of B¹; or C¹; and Ash¹, H⁶, H⁸. 1239. for] after Ch.—aftir] for that Ch; and after Co; a sterre H⁸. 1240. that] this H¹, H²; the H⁴, An.—by] with V.—high] om. B¹, H², Ad³, Hu. 1241. this] that C¹. 1242. And] A Ad².—eke] eke hit B⁵.—this] the C². 1243. celi] om. Ad³, Hu.—yet] om. B¹, H⁸.—into] unto CC. 1244. The] Ther C¹.—name] om. C¹.—abyt] abideth Ch, B¹, B², Co, H¹, C¹, C², C³, B⁵, Hn¹, H³, H⁴, H², Ash¹, An, CC, H⁶, H⁸, Ad², C⁵, B³, B⁴, Lg, V.—and] yit and B¹.—slydeth] shedith Ash¹; slyt J. 1245. his] his hie B³. 1246. Thourgh] Ne thorowe Ash¹, H⁶.—foryetylnesse] forgetfulness Ch, B¹ B², C¹, C³, H¹, H⁴, H², CC, Ash¹, H⁶, H⁸, B³.

Howe vynes shedde
bavme
in-stede of wyne
Ca° liii°1 19

And in Engady, the lusty large vynes,

That tyme in the yere of her kynde bare,

Gan floresshe and floure and in-stede of wynes,

1250 Withe Riche Bavme her braunches to repayre.

And the vertu that wyntre made bare,

Thourgh constreynyng of colde in the Rote,

Nature made with fresshe blossomes soote,

To assende vpon this same nyght

Vnto the croppe, with frute and levys newe;

Makyng the bowes as lusty to the sight,—

As fresshe as fayre of colour and of hewe,

And as plentevous her colour to Renewe,—

As in Septembre whan Bachus hathe power

1260 To shewe his myght that tyme of the yere.

1248. That] What H6.—in the] of Ch, B1, C1, H1, C3, Hn1, H3, H4, Ash1, An, H6, Ad2, C5, B4, Lg, Hu; of the B2, C2, H2, J, CC, H5, H8, Ad3, B3; in Co, B5.—of] in Ad3.—of her kynde bare] large vynes bere C1; ayen kynd bare H2. 1249. Gan] Was Ch; Thanne B1; That C1.—and in] in C1, C3, Ash1; and in the H7. 1250. her] he B4. 1251. bare] dare B5, Hu. 1252. constreynyng] constreynte C2, B5.—of] in C3.—colde] coloure C1.—in the] of the C3. 1253. blossomes] floures H2. 1254. vpon] up in B1; up C3, B5, H7; om. Hn1.—this] the Ch, B1, B2, C1, H3, H4, Ash1, J, An, CC, H5, H6, H7, Ad3, Ad2, C5, B3, B4, Lg, Hu. 1255. the] om. Ad2.—with] of H8.—newe] grene and newe Ash1; shewe C3. 1256. as] als H7, Ad3, Hu; al B5.—to the] to H2. 1257. as fayre] and as fayre B2, H1, C1, H3, H4, H2, Ash1, J, An, CC, H5, H6, Ad2, C5, B3, B4, Lg, V; and fayre Ch. 1258. her] his C2.—to] dide B1, Co, B5, H7, H8, Ad3, Hu. 1259. As] Bright as C3.—whan] when that CC.—Bachus] busshes Ash1. 1260. shewe] shede Co.

1crossed through

Loo howe the lorde and the myghty kyng, f. 60b

That hathe lordship ou*ere* grape and vine,

Vnto whose myght *euery* man*ere* thyng.—

Hevyn and erthe,—lowly muste enclyne,

Gan braunches bere w*ith* fresche floures fyne

Araye newe, though thay be seer and olde,

In frosty wynter and in wedir colde,

As in somer whan phebus is a-lofte,

Whan flora Reignyth in may and in aprill,

1270 And make blossomes to ben as smothe and softe

Amyde Decembre, whan men for colde so chille.

Wherefore this feste, frely at his wille,—

The nyght I mene, of his Natiuyte,—

To shewe his myght in herbe, floure, and tre,

1261. Loo] om. H¹; And H⁷; To Hu.—the lorde] the kynge lorde H¹; this lord C¹.—and the] and H¹, CC; and this C¹.—myghty] almighti H⁶. 1262. hathe lordship] lordship hath H².—ou*ere*] of H⁸. 1263. *euery*] all H⁸.—thyng] of thyng CC. 1264. Hevyn] In heven B³.—lowly muste] must Ch, H³, H⁴, Ash¹, An, H⁵, H⁶, Ad², C⁵, B³, B⁴, Lg; must ever C¹.—enclyne] decline CC. 1265. Gan] Gan B¹, B², B⁵, Co, H⁷, Ad³; When C².—w*ith*] and C¹, B³.—fresche] floures H².—floures] of flour H¹; fresh H².—fyne] fayre Ch, B², Co; and fyne H²; fynde H⁸. 1266. Araye] Araide C².—seer] fayre CC. 1267. and in] and B², J.—wedir] wedres B³. 1268. As] And CC.—whan phebus] phebus when he C¹.—is] was H⁸.—alofte] on lofte B¹, V. 1269. flora Reignyth in may] in may regneth B²; yt rayneth in may J, CC.—and in] and CC, H⁸, Hu; or in H⁷, Ad³. 1270. make] made H⁸.—to] om. B².—as] all Ch; om. H⁸; also Co, B⁵.—smothe] fressh C¹.—softe] soote C². 1271. Amyde] In myddis Hn¹.—men] om. H¹; folk V.—so] do Ch, B², V; om. B¹, Hn¹, C¹; or H²; and J; to CC; for H⁵. 1273. nyght] myght C³.

He made the vynes, as ye haue herde me sayne,

In Engady her bavme for to shede,

Whan thay were moste nakede and barayne

And oute of season, who so can take hede.

Of whiche nyght long afore, I rede

1280   That in Egipt the prophete Ieremyee,

Full opynly in his prophecye,

To the prestes of that kyngdome tolde

That the Idoles of her temples alle,

With-outyn arest, by myracle sholde

Breke her neckeȝ and to grounde falle,

Whan a mayde in an oxe stalle

Hathe borne a childe, this thyng shall be-tyde.

Wherefore the prestes in her fanes wyde,

1275. as] om. B¹. 1277. moste nakede and] naked and moste B¹, H⁸; moste and naked and B⁵.—barayne] bare C¹. 1282. the] om. B¹; thes Hu. 1283. her] the B¹, Co, B⁵, Ash¹, H⁷, H⁸, Ad³, Hu.—temples] temple B², Hn¹, CC, H⁵, H⁸. 1284. arest] eny rest Ch, B², H¹, C¹, C², H³, H⁴, Ash¹, An, CC, J, H⁵, H⁶, Ad², C⁵, B³, B⁴, Lg, V; duresse H⁸. 1285. to] to the Co, B⁵. 1286. oxe] oxes Co, C¹, C², B⁵, Hn¹, H³, H⁴, Ash¹, An, H⁵, H⁶, H⁷, H⁸, Ad³, Ad², C⁵, B⁴, Lg, Hu. 1287. this thyng] this B¹, Co; thynge Ch; that thynge C². 1288. fanes] pane B¹; sawes C³, CC; panes Co, B⁵, H⁷, H⁸, Ad³, Hu; fynes H².

Of verrey faythe and of high credence,

1290   Secrely vpon a lytyll stage,

Vpon his worde *with* humble reuerence,

Of a mayde let make an Image,

And in her Arme, a childe of tendre age;

Doyng ther-to in her paynyme wyse,

Aftir her Riteȝ, a man*er*e sacryfise.

And on this feste, ay fro yere to yere,   f. 61a

Thay were a-waytyng whan it wolde be;

Til on a day of happe the kyng cam nere,—

The noble, worthy, and wyse Tholome,—

1300   Þe whiche þing whanne þat he dide see,

A-noon of hem the cause he gan enquere,

Why or wherfore the Image was sette there.

1289. Of] O hu.—and of] and B², Co, B⁵, H³, J, CC. 1290. a lytyll] an hy H². 1291. his] this H⁵. 1293. Arme] armys C¹, Ad².—a childe] an ymage J, CC. 1294. her] his H⁸.—paynyme] paynyms C³. 1295. Aftir] om. C¹.—her] hys Ch, H³.—Riteȝ a man*er*e sacryfise] wirshypingis and hir servise C¹. 1296. this] hys Ch, B⁴.—feste] heste Ch, B¹, B², H¹, C², C³, H³, H⁴, H², Ash¹, J, An, H⁵, H⁶, Ad², C⁵, B³, B⁴, Lg. 1297. were] where CC.—whan] when that Ch, H¹, C³, Hn¹, H⁴, Ash¹, J, An, H⁵, H⁶, H⁷, H⁸, Ad³, Ad², C⁵, B³, B⁴, Lg, Hu.—it] om. H¹.—wolde] sholde Ch, Hn¹, H⁴, H², Ash¹, H⁵, Ad², V. 1298. Til on a day of happe the kyng cam nere, H⁷.—of happe] as D; om. C², Co, B⁵.—kyng] kynge of happe Co; kynge of hope B⁵. 1299. noble] noble and the B¹; noble and Co, C¹, C², B⁵, H⁷, H⁸, Ad³, B⁴, Hu.—and wyse] the wyse Co, C¹, C², B⁵, H⁸, Hu; wyse H⁷, H⁸, B⁴.—worthy and wyse] and the wyse and worthi B¹. 1300. þe whiche þing whanne þat he dide see, H⁷.—þat] om. D, B¹, Hu.—þing] kynge Ash¹. 1301. A-noon] Ande anon B¹.—of hem the cause] the cause of hem B¹; of hem of the CC.—gan] dyd C³, An. 1302. Why] om. H².—the] that B¹.

And thay Ichone, of one entencion

Yaffe answer and lust not for to lye.

For it was ordenyde of olde tradicion,

Shewede to-forne by holy prophecye,

In whiche thay dyd faythefully aspye,

Vndispeirid the hest shal not varie

Of the prophete, awhile though it tarye.

1310   And sothefastly, in conclusion,

Vpon the tyme of the Natyuyte,

The false Idoleȝ in Egipt fel adovne,

And al to-braste in peceȝ moo then thre;

To shewe truly that Iborne was hee,

Of heven and erthe that hath the Regalye,

And shall distroye al false mawmetre.

1303. of] on B¹.—entencion] enchesoun B², J, CC. 1304. Yaffe] To him yaf Hn¹.—lust] lite Lg.—for] om. CC, C¹. 1305. For it] It Ch, B², H¹, C¹, C², Hn¹, H³, H⁴, H², Ash¹, J, An, CC, H⁵, H⁶, Ad², C⁵, B³, B⁴, Lg; That it B¹, Co, B⁵, H⁷, H⁸, Ad³, Hu; Hys C³.—of] with B², J; by C³.—olde] holde CC; ful olde V. 1306. to-forne] beforne B¹, B², H¹, CC; afore B⁵.—holy] hoole H¹, CC.—by] of V. 1307. thay dyd] day C¹, Ad².—aspye] to espy C¹. 1308. Vndispeirid the hest shal not varie, B¹.—the] in D.—shal] shuld H¹. 1309. the] om. Ch, B¹, C¹.—prophete] prophecye Ch, B², H¹, C¹, C², H³, H⁴, Ash¹, J, An, CC, H⁵, H⁶, H⁷, Ad², C⁵, B³, B⁴, Lg; prophetis B¹, Co, B⁵, H², H⁸, Ad³, Hu.—it] they H². 1311. the tyme] H⁵. 1312. in Egipt fel] fell in Egipt Ch.—adovne] all doun J. 1313. al to-braste] brast H¹; tobraste H⁵.—in] on H¹, C³, B⁵, Hn¹, H³, H⁴, An, H⁷, H⁸, Ad³, Ad², C⁵, B³, B⁴, Lg.—in peceȝ moo then] mo then pecis C¹. 1314. truly] trewe H².—that] that than B¹, H⁷, H⁸, Ad³. 1315. that] he B¹.—the] om. Co, B⁵, H⁸. 1316. mawmetre] tiranny C¹.

Howe Romayns whan
thay had *dom*inacion
ou*ere* all the worlde
made hem an
Image and callet
it the Goddes
Ca° liiii[1] 20

I fynde also, as wryteth Carnotence,

In his boke, Policraticon,

That whanne Romanes had excellence

1320 Of high lordship, so many day a-gone,

And that peples and Regnes eu*ery*cheone

Stoden vnto hym vndir lowe s*er*uage,

Fro yere to yere makyng a payage

Of a tribute that was customable,

To the Empyre of verrey dewte;

For whiche the Romanes and Senate hono*ur*able,

Whan thay flourede in moste felicite,

Devysed haue for a grete Ryalte,

A-myd her towne in moste worthy place,

1330 A large statue, femynyne of face,

1317. as] om. B[1].—wryteth] writ V. 1318. boke] boke of C[1]; boke called H[4], B[3].—
Policraticon] pollicronicon C[1], CC. 1319. whanne] when the B[1], C[1].—Romanes] Romaynes
Ch, B[1], Co, H[1], C[1], C[2], C[3], B[5], Hn[1], H[3], H[4], H[2], Ash[1], An, H[5], H[6], H[7], H[8], Ad[3],
Ad[2], C[5], B[3], B[4], Lg, Hu; they B[2], J, CC. 1320. a-gone] be forne C[2]. 1321. that] the
Ch, H[1], C[1], H[3], H[4], Ash[1], An, H[5], H[6], H[7], Ad[2], C[5], B[4], Lg; om. Hu; that the Co,
B[5], V.—peples] peple B[2], C[2], CC.—and] and the H[1]. 1322. Stoden] Stonde B[1], C[3];
Did C[1].—hym] hem B[2], Co, H[1], C[3], B[5], Hn[1], H[2], J, H[7], H[8], Ad[3], B[3].—vndir] in Ch,
B[1]; om. Hu; wondir C[1].—seruage] servise servage C[1]. 1323. makyng a payage] payynge a
trewage Ch, H[1], C[1], C[2], H[3], H[4], Ash[1], An, CC, H[5], H[6], Ad[2], C[5], B[3], B[4], Lg, V; makyng
a parage C[3], B[5]. 1324. a tribute] attribute B[2], H[1]; tribute H[2]. 1325. To] Of Hn[1].—
Empyre] emperour C[1]. 1326. the] om. Hn[1]. 1328. haue] hath Ch, B[2], C[1], Ash[1], Hu; to
have B[1]; hem V.—a grete] a Ch, B[2], H[1], C[1], C[2], C[3], H[4], Ash[1], J, An, CC, H[5], H[6], Ad[2],
C[5], B[3], B[4], Lg, V; gret B[1], Co, B[5], H[7], H[8], Ad[3], Hu; om. H[3]. 1329. her] the H[1], CC.—
in] in the H[2]. 1330. statute] stature B[1], B[2], C[2], Hn[1], CC, H[7], Hu; statute H[2], Ash[1], H[6],
H[8], Ad[3].

---

[1]crossed through

That maked was of coper and of bras,

Large and long, and wonderfull to se,

And of entayle devydede the compace.

This grete ymage called sholde be

Goddes of Rome, and like a maieste,

In hir Right hande sholde also holde

A large worlde, full sterne to by-holde;

Whiche sholde of Rou*n*denesse haue the fygure,

To signifie that sche moost glorious,

1340   The cyte hathe holy in hir cur*e*,

And howe by hir thay were victoriouse.

And here vp-on, moste excellent famous,

Thay dyd a werke-man seken vp and dovne,

It to *per*forme, thorugh oute all the tovne,

1331. coper] cipres C³.—and of] and B¹, B², J, CC, Hu. 1332. long and] long C³, H³. 1333. And] om. B¹, Co, C³, B⁵, Hn¹, H⁷, H⁸, Ad³, Hu, CC.—the] by B¹, Hn¹, H⁷, Ad³, B³; with the B², J, CC; was the C². 1335. and] om. C³. 1336. sholde also] also shulde B¹, C¹, Hn¹, Ash¹, H⁷.—holde] folde B³. 1337. full sterne] with stremes B¹; sterne B², CC; full sternely H².—to by holde] bolde B¹. 1338. the] om. C², Hu. 1339. To signifie that sche moost glorious, B¹.—moost] was D; is most B⁴. 1340. hathe holy] holly hadde B¹; hadde holy Co, H⁷, H⁸, Ad³; had al hole B⁵; had hole C¹, CC. 1341. hir] om. Hu.—were victoriouse] victoriouse were C¹. 1343. seken] to seke H⁷.—vp] both up C³.

Till at laste, of happe sucheon thay fynde,

That passede all to werke in entyle,

And was sotyll bothe of witte and mynde,

To werke in metall, and sayde he wolde nat fayle

Of this emprise, that may so moche avayle

1350   To the cyte, and shortly in this caas,

Thorugh his engyne, it *per*formede was

So Ryally, *þat* in the worlde noo man

Couthe a-mende it in that ilke tyde.

And to by-holde it, many a thousande ran,—

So gladde of it the were on eu*er*y syde;

Till at the laste, one of verrey pryde,

Presumptuously gan to cry and call,

Ande sayde shortly, the legges were to small

1345. Till] And Ch, B², H¹, C¹, C², H³, H⁴, Ash¹, J, An, CC, H⁵, H⁶, Ad², C⁵, B³, B⁴, Lg, Hu.—at] at the Ch, B¹, Co, H¹, C³, B⁵, Hn¹, H³, H⁴, Ash¹, J, An, CC, H⁵, H⁶, H⁷, H⁸, Ad³, C⁵, B⁴, Lg, Hu, V.—of] up B¹, C²; om. C¹, Hn¹, H².—happe] om. C¹, Hn¹, H².—sucheon] such C²; suche a man Hn¹. 1346. passede] passeth C³.—to] the C¹, C², Hu.—werke] workmen C¹.—in] and H⁸.—entayle] Itaill C¹. 1347. was] was right C³.—of] in H⁸.—and] and of B², J, CC; and in H⁸. 1348. To] The C¹.—in metall] to make C¹; in entaille V.—he] thei C².—wolde nat] nolde Ch, H¹, B⁴, Lg; nolde not H⁴, Ash¹, H⁵ Ad², C⁵. 1350. the] this H³. 1351. Thorugh his] That this C¹.—it] om. B¹, C¹; a CC. 1352. Ryally] riall C¹, H².—the] om. Ash¹; this B¹, Co, B⁵, H⁷, H⁸, Ad³, Hu. 1353. that] the CC.—ilke tyde] evetyde H⁸; same tide B², CC. 1354. many] went C³, Hn¹.—a] om. B¹, H⁸, B⁴.—ran] thedir ran B¹; cam Co, B⁵, H⁸, Ad³. 1355. of] on B¹, Co, H⁷, Ad³.—of it the were] thei wer of hit C². 1357. call] gale Ch, C¹, H³, H⁴, Ash¹, An, H⁶, Ad², C⁵, B⁴, Lg. 1358. Ande sayde shortly the legges were to small, B¹.—were] be D.—Ande] om. C¹, H⁸.—sayde] om. Co, Hn¹, CC, H⁵; that H⁸.—shortly] shortly seyd B⁵.

So grete a werke longe to susteyne,

1360   For lak only of gode proporcion.

Wher-of a-noon, with soden Ire and tene,

The werke man brent in his opynyon,

Rebukyng hym of his presompcion.

And sodenly perturbede in his mynde,

Answerde ayene, shortly as I fynde,

As it had ben halfendele in scorne,   f. 62a

And sayde: "frende, if thou canst vndirstande,

Til þat a childe be of a mayde borne,

I vndirtake þat this werke shall stonde.

1370   Thyne hede is dulle on watir and on londe

To lak thyng thou canste not a mende."

And the werkeman, sother then he wende,

1359. a] om. CC.—longe] oonly Hn¹. 1360. only] om. C¹. 1361. of] for Ch, B², H¹, C¹, C², C³, Hn¹, H³, H⁴, Ash¹, An, CC, H⁵, H⁶, H⁷, H⁸, Ad², C⁵, B³, B⁴, Lg, Hu. 1362. brent] om. C³.—his] om. C². 1363. of] in Ash¹, H⁶. 1364. And] So C³. 1365. Answerde] Answere Lg. 1366. As] Has H¹.—it] y H³.—halfendele] alwendely Hu; halve nedle H¹. 1367. thou] you Ch, Ad², B⁴, Lg. 1368. þat] om. B¹, C³, B⁵, Hn¹, H², H⁸, Ad³, Hu.—be] om. B¹.—borne] be borne B¹. 1370. on watir] in water H².—and on] and C³, J, H². 1371. lak] blame C², H².—thou] that thu C², B⁵, V. 1372. then] and H¹.

Had of this werke sayde and prophecyede.

For on the nyght whan that criste was bore,

In verrey sothe, it may not be denyede,

Of bras the goddes is broken and to-tore,

And all the coste of the werke for-lore.

In signe only that the lorde and syre,

And myghty kyng of the high Empyre,

1380 Was borne that tyme in the lityll towne

Of bedlem, of a pure virgyne;

To whose power and dominacion,

Grete Rome mekely shall enclyne.

For erthely lordship nedys muste fyne,

With all his pompe and lowte to hym lowe,

Whan the power of this kyng is knowe.

1373. Had] Han Ch, B1, Co, H5; Hath B2, H1, C1, C2, C3, Hn1, H4, H2, L, J, CC, H6, H8, B3; Have B5, H3, Ash1, An, H7, Ad3, Ad2, C5, B4, Hu, Lg.—sayde] and said L. 1374. For] Founde H6.—on] in H2.—the] this B1, H7, Ad3, Hu.—that] om. B1, C2, C3, H6, B4.—was] om. B5. 1375. denyede] devoidit C1. 1376. Of bras the goddes] The goddesse of bras B1.—is] was B1, CC, L, B3; ben B2, Ash1, L, J.—and] and all H1, Lg. and that C1.—to tore] anoon C1. 1377. all] om. B1, B2, J, CC.—the coste] to cast C1.— werke] workman B1, Co, B5, H7, H8, Ad3, Hu.—for lore] lore B1, Co, B5, H7, H8, Ad3, Hu; y lore V. 1378. only] opunly B1. 1379. And] And the H1, C2.—the high] that high Hn1; om. B1; the Co, B5, H2, L, H8, Ad3, Hu. 1380. that] the B1. 1381. Of bedlem, of a pure virgyne, B1.—of] and of D.—a] om. H1; the Lg. 1382. power] lordship B2, CC, J. 1383. Rome] om. CC.—shall] om. B2. 1384. nedys] nedely H8.—muste] most he Ch. 1385. With] To C2.—pompe] power H2.—lowte] lowe CC. 1386. this] the Ch, CC, H5.

Howe wyse Sybill tolde
to the Senates of Rome
the birthe of criste
Ca° lv^{to1} 21

And of this tyme, gone full many a yere,

Wyse Sibylle, called Tiburtyne,

Spake to the Senate full opynly and clere,

1390 His dreme expoundyng of the sones nyne;

Which thay say all at ones shyne

Vpon a nyght, eueryliche full dyuerse,—

To hem declaryng playnely in her vers

That yche sonne in hir avysions,

Whiche on heven were so bright and fayre,

Betokenyth sothely the generacions

That shall succede, dyuers and contrarye.

Of whiche sonne shull vanysshe and appeyre,

And of beames waxen wonder donne,

1400 Vnto the tyme that the viii sonne

1387. of this tyme] thus this wyis woman B¹; of this towne knowyn CC; in this **tyme**
H⁸.—gone] om. C², CC.—full] om. H². 1388. Wyse] And wyse B¹; This wise C³.—
called] spak and callid C¹; called that time C³.—Tiburtyne] Tibernatyne C². 1389.
Senate] senatour Ch; senatores J, CC.—full opynly] wisely H².—and] an Lg; and full
CC. 1390. His] Here Ch, B², C³, Hn¹, H³, H⁴, H², Ash¹, J, An, CC, H⁵, H⁶, Ad²,
C⁵, B³, B⁴; By L.—of] and of Hn¹.—the] om. C¹.—sones nyne] someris seven C¹.
1391. all] om. B¹, C².—shyne] shynynge H⁴. 1393. playnely] openly V. 1394. yche]
every C¹. 1395. on] in C³, Hn¹.—were] shynyng C³; where L. 1396. Betokenyth] Be
tokenesse H¹; Betokenede L, B³.—sothely] om. B¹; shortly H¹, C². 1397. shall] sholde
Co, B⁵. 1398. sonne] som C³, B⁵, Ad², C⁵; sunnes Hn¹, H⁸, Hu.—appeyre] enpayre
C³, H⁸; payre L, CC. 1399. And of] Hyr bright C³, Hn¹; And of the Co, B⁵.— waxen]
wer B⁵; om. CC; and wex C³. Hn¹.—donne] dymme Co. CC. 1400. the tyme] eche tyme
L.—that] om. CC, B³, L; than H⁷.—viii] tenth B¹, H⁷, Hn¹, Ad³; highest Co, B⁵;
right Ash¹, H⁶; hei3te H⁵; highe H¹, C², H⁸.

---

¹crossed through

His stremes shede Rede as any blode,

f. 62b

That specifieth the gen*er*acion,

That shall by kynde be furiouse and woode,

And to vertu full of rebellion;

Tyll ther be bore a myghty champion,

Oute of the stoke of Iuda, that shall hau*n*te

His myghty hande, her tyranye to dau*n*te;

Whose mother shall come of the kynrede

Of the Ebrwes, and issewe of the lyne,

1410 And oute of hem even Ilyke *p*rocede

As dothe a floure oute of the rough spyne.

And she shall be mothir and virgyne.

And tolde hem eke in hir *p*rophycye,

Whan she is borne, haten shall Marye.

1401. shede] schewe C², shed as B¹, B².—any] my H¹. 1402. That] The wheche B¹. 1403. by] of H².—kynde] kynge C¹.—be] om. C¹.—and] an CC. 1404. to] into Ch; unto B², C¹, C², H³, H⁴, Ash¹, J, An, H⁵, H⁶, H⁷, Ad², C⁵, B⁴, Lg; of Co, B⁵, V.—full of] the vertifull C¹. 1405. ther] that H⁸.—be] been C¹.—bore] bothe Hn¹. 1406. that] om. C². 1407. her] his B², J, CC.—to daunte] om. Lg; daunte Co. 1408. Whose] Who is CC. 1409. Of the] Of H⁷, H⁸, Ad³, Hu.—issewe of the] jury by L, B³; issu of her Ch, C¹, C³, Hn¹, H³, H⁴, H², Ash¹, J, An, CC, H⁵, H⁶, Ad², C⁵, B⁴, Lg, V. 1410. Ilyke] ilk C¹; like Ash¹, H⁸. 1411. As] And Lg.—a floure] the roose L.—oute] om. V.—the] om. Hn¹; a H².—rough spyne] roote sprynge L. 1412. she] om. B², J, CC, Lg.—virgyne] pure virgyne C³, Hn¹. 1413. tolde hem eke] eke as it seyd C¹. 1414. Whan she is borne] That she also C³, Hn¹.—haten shall] sche shall hiȝt B⁵; she highte shall Co, H⁸, Hu; hight shal V.

And she shall be by holy election

Mothir to hym that is of power moste;

Of whome the birthe and the concepcion,

Shall fully be of the holy goste.

And he shall streche vnto eu*ery* coste

1420   His grete kyngdome that shall neu*ere* fyne.

And of his birthe she gan also devyne,

And tolde hem furthe, affermyng sothefastly,

Whan he wer borne that he sholde be

Bothe god and man to-gyder verrely.

And of the nyght of his natyuyte,

[To hem of Rome many thynges tolde she];

And specially, what he shulde hight,

As opynly ye may haue a sight

1415. she] om. B¹, B², Co, L, J, CC, B³; he H³, H⁴, An.—be] eke be B², L, J, CC, H⁵, B³; be eke Ch, H¹, C¹, H³, H⁴, Ash¹, An, H⁶, Ad², C⁵, B⁴, Lg; eke C².—holy] om. Ch, B², H¹, C¹, H³, H⁴, H², Ash¹, J, L, An, CC, H⁵, H⁶, Ad², C⁵, B³, B⁴, Lg, V; high Hn¹, C³. 1416. Mothir] Be modir Hn¹; Modir be C².—to] of H⁸.—is] us Ch, L. 1417. Of] And of Hu.—birthe] bright H¹.—and the] and B², Co, B⁵, Hn¹, H², CC, H⁶, H⁷, H⁸, Ad³, Hu. 1419. he] om. B⁴.—shall] om. B¹.—streche] strenkthe B¹.—vnto] into Hn¹, H²; to H³; over H⁸. 1420. that] om. L, B³.—shall neuere] never shal B¹, B⁵, H², H⁷, H⁸, Ad³, Hu; hit shal never C³, Hn¹. 1421. she gan also] also she gan B¹; she can also Co, C¹, C², H³, H⁴, H⁸.—devyne] to devyne CC. 1422. tolde] tell C¹, L, H⁸. 1423. wer] is C¹.—sholde] shall C¹. 1424. verrely utterly J, CC. 1425. his] the L; his hooly B¹. 1426. This line omitted in D. All other MSS are identical except CC, which reads: Of hem of Rome many a thynge told he. 1427. what] what that B¹, H⁷, Ad.—shulde] shal B¹, CC. 1428. ye] as ye C¹, C³, Hu.—may] om. B⁵; mowe CC.

In thilke vers that allegede be

1430 In grete Austyne, where ye may the name

In the begynnyng of Ihesus criste see;

And of his Renoune and of his grete fame,

And by and by, howe she dyd atame

To the Iewes his comyng euery dele.

Of whiche thyng lykynge no-thyng wele,

Certeyne prestez of the Iewes lawe   f. 63a

Gan to grocche as thay gafe audience,

And bad to hir her tunge to withdrawe,

And wolde haue putte hir for angre in sylence;

1440 And liste of malise yeve noo credence

Vnto noo worde that she spake or sayde,

Tille þat she of sodeyne Ire abrayde,

1429. thilke] that B1, C3; the B2; to the C1; thes V.—vers] verses V.—that] om. C1; that al C2.—allegede] called CC; alleggeth Hu. 1431. Ihesus criste] Crist Ihesu Ch, H1, C2, H3, H4, Ash1, An, H6, Ad2, C5, B4, Lg. 1433. by and by] by C1. 1434. To] om. C2.—comyng] comyng and his abydinge J, CC. 1435. Of whiche thyng lykynge no-thyng wele, B1.—lykynge] lyked D, C1; thei lykyd H6; like they C5.—Of] Of the Ash1; To J; The C3. 1437. gafe] have H8. 1430. to hir] hir B1, C1.—to withdrawe] withdrawe B1, B4. 1439. haue putte hir for angre] for angur have put hir Ch, B2, H1, C1, C2, H3, H4, Ash1, L, J, An, CC, H5, H6, Ad2, C5, B3, B4, Lg, V.—in] to B2, C2, L, J, B3. 1440. liste] wold C1.—yeve] to yeve B1, Co, C3, B5, Hn1, H2, H7, H8, Ad3.—noo] more Lg.—credence] creature C5. 1441. Vnto noo] To ony H1; Unto the L; Unto Lg.—or] and C3.

And sayde: "O Iewes, blynde w*ith* the skye

Of ignoraunce and malice indurate,

Ye shulle to hym of verrey fals envye

Be wykked rebel and obstynate,

And aye w*ith* hym ye holden shul debate.

And maugre yov and al yo*ur* enemyte,

Yet shall he Regne and kyng crovnede be,

1450   When he is borne in the herytage

Of his fadre, who-so that saythe nay,

And pr*o*ceden oute of yo*ur* lynage."

And of his comyng shall be no delaye

And tolde hem eke playnely of the daye

Of his birthe, bet then I can ryme.

And like her worde, comen is the tyme,

1443. And sayde] om. C¹.—blynde] blynded B², H¹, C², B⁵, Hn¹, H³, H⁴, H², H⁵, H⁶, H⁷, Ad³, Ad², C⁵, B³, B⁴, Lg, Hu. 1444. ignoraunce and malice] malice with ignoraunce B¹, Co, B⁵; ignoraunce with malice L, H⁷, H⁸, Ad³, Hu. 1445. Ye] And ye B¹. 1446. rebel] rebelles B¹, C¹, C³, Hn¹, Ash¹, H⁷, Ad³.—and] and full B¹, C³, Hn¹, H⁷, Ad³. 1447. aye] ever B¹, Co, B⁵, H⁷, H⁸, Hu. 1448. maugre] magry of C¹.—al] om. B¹, C³, H⁷, Ad³. 1449. Yet shall he] He shal yit Hn¹; Yett he schal B⁵.—kyng] om. B¹, C³, Hn¹, H². 1450. in] to C². 1451. so] om. C¹, CC.— that] ever Ash¹. 1452. oute] ȝewe C¹; shall out C³.—your] our Hn¹, H². 1454.] Very trouthe to knowe upon a day B¹.—tolde] to C².—eke] om. L.—the] this C². 1455. birthe] brigh H¹. 1456. And like her worde, comen is the tyme, B¹.—comen] comynge D; com C¹, C³, H², H⁶, Ash¹.

The tyme of tymeȝ, the tyme of lyfe and grace,

The tyme of Ioye and no-thyng to morne,

Sythe he is borne *with* so fayre a face,

1460 The golden worlde makyng to reto*u*rne,

The worlde of pece, the kyngdome of Sato*u*rne,

Of whiche some-tyme Proba that was wyfe

Of Adelphus, wrote in her lyfe.

Howe *p*rophete ȝ
prophecied the birthe
of Criste Ca° lvi°[1] 22[m]

T he tyme also that is Auctorysede

Of *p*rophete ȝ in her *p*rophecye,

Wher his comyng is opynly devysede.

Abdias *p*ropheta — Recorde I take firste of hym Abdye,

In monte ante Sion, Et — That sayde thus, the bible may not lye,

ascendit ex monte Syon — How in the hille playnely of Syon

vt montem, Esau — 1470 Shall Ioye and helthe bothe come in one

---

1457. tymeȝ the tyme] tymes H[1].—of lyfe] om. B[1].—and] and of L. 1458. and] om.
L.—no thyng] thyng H[1].—to] for to B[2], CC, B[3].—morne] mournyng C[1]. 1460. worlde]
worde H[1].—to] hit C[2]. 1461. worlde] worldom H[2]. 1462. Of] The Hu.—Proba] om.
H[4].—wyfe] wise H[8]; the wyf B[1], B[2], J, CC. 1463. her] his H[1]. 1464. The] Of Hn[1].—
also] awaytinge Ash[1].—that] which C[3].—is] is also B[5], Ash[1]. 1465. Of] Of the C[3].—
in] eke in Hn[1].—her] the CC; here here Ash[1]. 1466. his] ys L, Lg; as Hu.—is opynly]
openly ys H[3]. 1467. firste] om. C[1], C[3].—of hym] of oon callyd C[3]; on hym H[2]; of H[8].—
Abdye] abyde Hu. 1468. thus] this B[2]. 1469. hille] bibill C[1]. 1470. helthe] helpe C[3], H[2], J,
H[7], CC; helpe helthe H[5].—bothe come] come both Ch, B[1], B[2], Co, H[1], C[1], C[2], C[3], Hn[1],
H[3], H[4], H[2], L, J, An, CC, H[5], H[6], H[7], H[8], Ad[3], Ad[2], C[5], B[3], B[4], Lg, Hu; come all
Ash[1].—in one] into B[1]; anoon V.

---

[1]crossed through

Vnto mankynde, and saluacion   f. 63b

Where he set his kyngdome and his see;

Wherby is take the myghty Region

Of worthy Iuda. and he shall also be

Socour and helpe vnto Idumee

Naum *propheta*   Of Esav, that callede is the hille,

To yoyne bothe to obeye his wille.

Celebra, Iuda dies   And Navm hight Iuda to be light,

festes tuos ascendit   And bad hym halowe his festeჳ principall.

qui insufflat in fa-   1480   For he that shall newe enspire his sight,

ciem tua*m* eripiens   Ascendyd is vpon his hill Riall,

te ex eius   That shall be to the bothe toure and walle,

tribulac*i*one   Chefe defence and *p*rotection

In eu*er*y woo and tribulacion.

1471. Vnto] And unto B¹.—and] in C³. 1473. is] to C³.—the] his C², CC. 1474. shall] om. Ch.—also] om. Ash¹, H⁶. 1475. helpe] helthe Hn¹.—vnto] unto al C²; in soth to C³; and to H⁸. 1476. callede] clepyd C³.—is] his Hu.—the] om. B¹. 1477. yoyne] inne Ash¹.—bothe] bote V.—to] forto C³. 1478. hight] and hight Co; it C¹; high H⁸; hit Lg. 1479. halowe] alowe C², CC.—his] thes L.—festeჳ] feste B¹, L, CC. 1480. he] om. Ch, B¹, H¹, C¹, C², Hn¹, H³, H⁴, Ash¹, An, CC, H⁵, H⁶, Ad², C⁵.—that] om. Hu.—shall] om. C³; sawe H⁸.—newe] newly Ch, B², H¹, C¹, C², Hn¹, H³, H⁴, Ash¹, L, J, An, CC, H⁵, H⁶, Ad², C⁵, B³, B⁴, Lg.—his] in B¹; om. CC.—sight] light C², J, CC. 1481. is] his Hu.—hille] his Hu; see Ch, B², H¹, C¹, C², Hn¹, H³, H⁴, H², Ash¹, L, J, An, CC, H⁵, H⁶, Ad², C⁵, B³, B⁴, Lg, V. 1482. be to the] to the be V.—be] om. C², H².—bothe] om. B¹; bothe be H². 1483. Chefe] Chevest H⁸.—and] and full B¹.

Do*min*us ad Abacuk   And Abacuk makyng mencion

Scribe visus ap*er*te   Of his comyng, whan he wrote in the tre

in buxo Splendor   Of grene boxe his avysion,

eius vt lux erit,   Where he spake playnely of his Natyuyte,

et cornua in mani*bus*   And sayde his shynyng clere and light shall be.

1490   And of the hornes he playnely gan to sayne

     That he shall holde in his hande3 twayne;

Ibi abscondita est   Wher-in is hydde his power and his myght,

fortitudo eius *etc.*   That on his foon kyngely he shall shewe.

Incuruati sunt colles   And of the hilles he telleth ther a-right,

mundi   How he shall bowe hem and the croppe3 hewe.

     And tellethe eke, in wordes not a fewe,

Tabernacula Ethiopum   Of Ethiopc and also madian

expanescent *et*   The tabernacles, how thay shall quake thanne.

tabernacula madian

1486. the] om. Ch, H1, C1, C2, H3, H4, Ash1, L, An, H6, Ad2, C5, B3, B4, Lg. 1488. playnely]
om. Hn1.—his] om. H4. 1489. sayde] om. Ch, B1, B2, H1, C1, C2, Hn1, H3, H4, Ash1,
L, J, An, CC, H5, H6, Ad2, C5, B3, B4, Lg.—clere and light] light and clere C2, H2;
clere light C1, Ad2; clere as light B1, Co, C3, B5, H7, H8, Ad3, Hu. 1490. the] his C1.—
he] om. C1, H8, V.—playnely] platly he H8.—to] om. C2, L. 1491. he] om. C2.—in] om. C2.
—twayne] twyn Co. 1492. is hydde] hid is B1; om. C2; to hid B5; his hed Hn1; and
his] and Hu. 1493. on] in H2.—he shall] shall he C2; shall B5. 1495. hem] om. B1, B2, H2,
J, CC.—the] in the CC.—croppe3] croppith H1; copyes H7, Hu, Ad3; copious H8.—hewe]
om. H1; schewe CC; doun hewe B1. 1496. a] om. C1. 1497. also] also of B1, B2, Co, B5,
H3, H2, L, J, CC, H7, Ad3, B4, Hu; and] Lg; of C2. 1498. shall] om. H1.—quake thanne]
quakyn C1.

Baruk		And Baruk eke, scrybe of Ieremye,
Ecce dies venient	1500	Full opynly wrote of his comyng,
dicit *dominus*		And bad loke vpe clerly *with* thyn eye.
		And sayde of Dauid a buriou*n* and the spryng
		Shall be susteynede and Regne like a kyng.
Et faciet Iudiciu*m et*		And he shall do, thourgh his worthynesse,
Iusticiam in *terra*		Dome in erthe and also Rightwysnesse.

Sophone		And Sophone bad abyde awhile	f. 64a
Expecta me dicit		Vpon this day *with* devocyo*n,*	
dominus quia Iudiciu*m*		For he shall gadre oute of eu*ery* Ile,	
meu*m* vt congregem		Of eche kyngdome and eu*ery* regyon,	
gentes	1510	His peple in one of high affection.	
		And also ther, as he maketh mynde,	
		Fro the flodes of Ethiope and Inde,	

1499. eke] om. H¹. 1500. wrote] eke wrote Ch.—of] all H³. 1502. sayde] om. Ch, B¹, C¹, C²,
C³, B⁵, H³, H⁴, Ash¹, L, J, H⁵, H⁶, Ad², C⁵, B³, B⁴, Lg.—a] the H⁸; and CC.—and
the] of the CC; and a B², L, B³; shulde B¹; shal out H². 1503. Shall] That shall H².—
susteynede] constreyned Ch; sustenyng C¹.—and] to Ch, B², H¹, C¹, C², C³, Hn¹, H³,
H⁴, H², Ash¹, L, J, An, CC, H⁵, H⁶, Ad², C⁵, B³, B⁴, Lg, V. 1504. do] om. H²;
inserted above. 1505. Dome] Doone H⁵; Downe H⁸.—in] on Co, H⁸, Hu. 1506. bad] also
bad B¹. 1507. with] with good H². 1508. Ile] hyll CC. 1509. eche] every Co; the CC.—
and] and of C³, Hu; and in CC.—eu*ery*] eche H². 1510. His] This B¹.—in one] in his
one B¹; into one L; anoone Ad³.—of high] om. C¹; of gret and high C²; and of high
H²; of his CC. 1511. he] om. C²; ye H⁶. 1512. Fro] Flome Ash¹, H⁶.—of] and Ch, B².—
and] and of Ch, B², H²; of of CC.

Thay shall deuoutly offeryng to hym bryng,

And done to hym fulle hole sacryfice.

And fals goddes, eke thorugh his worchyng,

With Riall myght he shall also dispice,

And fro her see make hem to aryse,

And fro the boun*des* of her dwellyng place,

Of verrey force, dryfe hem and enchace.

1520 And of his birthe, long or that it be-felle,

In avysion wondirfull of sight,

Spake the *p*rophete called Danyell,　　　　　　　**Danyel**

And sayde hym thought he sawe vpon a nyght,—　**Cum nubibus celi**

Like to be-holde as he demed a-right,—

A sonne of man comyng wi*th* a skye;　　　**Et ipse datus est**

To whome power, hono*ur*, and Regalye　　　**principatus** *et* **honor**
　　　　　　　　　　　　　　　　　　　　　　　　regnu*m* *et* potestas
　　　　　　　　　　　　　　　　　　　　　　　　***emy*[1] perpetua qui**
　　　　　　　　　　　　　　　　　　　　　　　　non transibit *et*
　　　　　　　　　　　　　　　　　　　　　　　　Regnum eius
　　　　　　　　　　　　　　　　　　　　　　　　non corrumpetur

1513. shall] om. C[2].—deuoutly offeryng to hym] to hym devoutly offeryng Ch, B[1], B[5], H[3], H[4], Ash[1], An, H[6], H[8], Ad[2], C[5], B[4]; devoutly to hym offrynge B[2], Co, C[3], H[7], Ad[3], Hu; to hym devoutly hir offeryng C[1]; devoutly shal offeringe to hym C[2]; devoutly offringe Hn[1]. 1514. done] do Ch, B[1], B[2], H[1], C[1], C[2], H[3], H[4], H[2], Ash[1], L, J, An, CC, H[5], H[6], H[7], Ad[3], Ad[2], C[5], B[3], B[4], Lg; om. Co, C[3], B[5], Hn[1], H[8], Hu. —fulle] still Co; do eke Hn[1]; om. V.—hole] dewe Ch, B[2], C[1], H[1], C[2], Hn[1], H[3], H[4], H[2], Ash[1], L, J, An, CC, H[5], H[6], Ad[2], C[5], B[3], B[4], Lg; lowly B[1], H[7]; hoole do Co, C[3], B[5], H[8]. 1515. eke] also CC. 1518. fro] om. H[2].—boun*des*] founde L, B[3]. 1519. Of] And of Hu.—dryfe] denye Co.—and enchase] tenchase; and chase L, B[3]. 1520. his] this Co, CC.—that] om. B[1], C[2], L, B[3], Hu. 1521. wondirfull] full wondirfull Hn[1]; wonderfully B[1]. 1522. the] to the L.—called] om. Hu. 1523. hym] he L.—vpon] on B[1], Hu. 1524. demed] dempte C[2], B[5], Ash[1], H[5], H[6], H[7], Ad[3], Lg; deme H[2]; domed CC; drempte H[8].—a right] right Ch, C[2], H[3], H[4], H[2], Ash[1], An, H[5], H[6], Ad[2], C[5], B[4], Lg.

---

[1]Abbreviation for "emendam", to indicate that a passage has been omitted: probably the equivalent of et omnes populi, tribus, et linguae ipsi servient (Daniel 7: 14). the gloss is not from the Vulgate.

Ther yeve was, *per*petually to abyde.

And his kyngdome by et*er*nyte

Shall stonde hoole in oon and not devyde,

1530 Wiche shall not passe, neyther corupte be.

Whose comyng eke whan he dyd see,

The holy *p*rophete, olde Eʒechiell,   Eʒechiell

Sayde thus, the bible can yove tell: Suscitabo inquit sup*er pecora*

meam   pastorem   vn*um*   qui

pascet ea

"I shall ordeyne and prudently *p*rovyde

An herdman, my shepe to kepe sure,

That vpon hem shall nyght and day be gyde,

To lede hem wysely into her pastur*e*."

And ferthermore, he dothe vs eke assure,—

The holy *p*rophete furthe in his wrytyng,—

1540 Sothely affermyng that there shall be a kyng

1527. Ther] The B², J, CC.—yeve was] was gyven C¹. 1528. And] And eke B¹, H⁷.
1529. hoole] holi H¹.—in oon] om. Ch, H¹, C¹, C², H³, H⁴, Ash¹, An, H⁶, Ad², C⁵, B⁴,
Lg.—devyde] be devyde B¹, H⁷, Ad³. 1530. not] neider B¹.—neyther] non B¹; nor H¹;
ne C¹, Ash¹. 1531. he] om. B⁴. 1532. holy] good H¹; olde C², B⁴; olde holy Ash¹.—
olde] the olde Co; holde B⁵; om. B⁴.—Eʒechiell] Qechiel Ad³. 1533. can] gan H¹, Ash¹,
Lg. 1534. I] om. Lg. 1535. An] And Ch, B², C³, B⁵, CC, H⁵, H⁸; A C², H².—herdman]
d inserted above. 1536. vpon hem shall] shall uppon hem C².—and] ne H⁶.—be] om. V.—
gyde] tyde C², H¹, Lg. 1537. lede] leve C³.—into] unto B¹, L; to Ash¹. 1538. he dothe vs
eke] eke he doth B¹.—eke] om. H⁸, B⁴, Lg. 1539. furthe] om. Hn¹, Ash¹; eke CC. 1540.
Sothely] Soth H¹.— affermyng] offerrynge affermynge B¹.—there] om. C³; this H⁸.—
be] om. C².—kyng] kynde H¹.

Et **rex** inquit vnus	Of al folkes, whose Empyre shalle be oon, f. **64b**
erit omni*bus*	And no lenger devydede in-to tweyne;
Et non erit vl*tra* duo	Whiche ydels made of stoke and stone,
gentes, nec diuiditur	Ne shall no more be pollute to ordeyne
amplius in duo **Regna**	Fals offerynges to goddes that thay feyne.
nec polluentur **vltra**	And the *pro*phete that called is Agge,
in Idelis suis	Full opynly, who so luste to see,
Ad huc modicu*m*	
	Wryteth of his birthe in a lityll stou*n*de,—
Et ego comouebo	Even lyke, as he was enspirede,—
celum et mare et **1550**	That he shall meve heven, see, and grounde;
aridam et veniet	And he that is of all moste desirede,
desideratus cunctis	Shall cum in haste, like a kyng atyrede.
gentibus ȝakaria	For Ioye of whiche, holy Zakarye
	To cristes spouse thus dothe *pro*phecye:

1542. devydede] be devyded B¹, Hn¹, H⁷, Ad³.—in to] in H¹. 1543. Whiche] Whyche of Ch; Whiche in B¹, B², Co, H¹, C¹, C², B⁵, Hn¹, H³, H⁴, H², Ash¹, J, An, CC, H⁵, H⁶, H⁷, Ad³, Ad², C⁵, B³, B⁴, Lg, Hu, V; With C³; Whyche into L; Which H⁸.—of] of a H⁶; a C¹.—and] of C¹.—stone] om. Ch. 1544. Ne] I Ash¹; om. L, B³.— pollute] polluted L.—to] ne B², J, CC. 1545. offerynges] offerynge Ch, B², H¹, C², H², H⁵.—goddes] god Ch, H¹, C¹, C², H³, H², Ash¹, H⁵, H⁶, Ad², C⁵, B⁴, Lg.—that] om. H².—feyne] fynde C¹. 1546. called is] ys called Ch, H¹, C², C³, B⁴; called was C¹, Ad². 1548. of] in H⁸.—of his birthe] who so luste to see CC.—in] om. B², J. 1549. was] was thanne B¹, H⁷.—enspirede] enspreded Hn¹. 1550. heven] even C¹, Ash¹. 1551. that] there H⁸.—of all] in hevon CC.—desirede] desidered H². 1552. a kyng] a mayde kynge C¹. 1553. whiche] whom L, B³. 1554. thus dothe] doeth thus B⁵; this doth H⁸.—prophecye] specifye Ch, B², C¹, H³, H⁴, Ash¹, An, CC, H⁵, Ad², C⁵, B³, B⁴.

Exultant inquit filia	"Be glad and light, thou doughter of Syon,
Sion Iubia filia Iher*usalem*	And syng, thou doughter of Iher*usalem*.
ecce rex tuus venit	By-holde, thy kyng shall come Right a-noon,
	That shall be borne sothely in Bedlem;
Potestas eius a mari	And his power shall frome Reme to Reme
us*que* ad mare *et* a 1560	The bou*n*des strecche of his Rialte,
fluminib*us*	As fer, in sothe, as floode or eny see
	Holden her cours, or thay *with* wawes wynde
	Oute of her mother, the grete occian."
Malachie	Of whose comyng Malachye makethe mynde
Ab ortu enim solis	*With*in his boke, the bible telle can,
vsq*ue* ad occisum	Howe the name of hym, bothe god and man,
magnu*m* eius	Shall strecche his stremes w*ith*outen wene,
	Fro thilke place wher the sonne [shene]

1555. and] now and C².—thou] though C³; the H⁶. 1557. thy] this C³; the B⁴. 1558. be borne sothely] soitly be borne B¹. 1559. shall] shall be Hn¹.—to Reme] om. Hn¹. 1560. The bou*n*des strecche] And the bondes shall streche B¹, H⁷, Ad³; The bondes strengthe Ash¹.—Rialte] ryall to L. 1561. As] Als Hu.—sothe] south C¹, H³, H¹.—or] is or CC.—see] tree Co, B⁵. 1562. Holden] Holdyng C¹.—cours] towres H⁶; courses Ch, B¹, B², C², C³, Hn¹.—or] as V.—with] with the B¹.—wawes] baumes C². 1563. Oute] om. H⁶. 1564. makethe] makid Lg. 1565. *With*in his] With this C¹.—boke the] om. C²; bible the Lg.—telle can] yow telle can B¹, H⁷; can tel H⁴, H⁶. 1567. Shall] Shall fresshely B²; Shall fressh J, CC.—*with*outen wene] kene CC, J; withoute any wene B¹, Hn¹, H², H⁷, Ad³. 1568. Fro] For H³; Where CC.—thilke] thik B¹, H⁷; that B², C¹, C², C³, CC, H⁶.—[shene] MS. D has *shyne*.

Raysethe his light, whan it be-gynnyth to dawe

1570 At his vpriste in the mornyng,

Vnto the west where he gothe vndir wawe,

Till Efte ayeyne his charet he bryng

Into the Est, that dothe the larke syng

For Ioye only that his bemes ryse.

Amos *propheta*
And of his comyng dothe Amos eke **devyse,**

In illa die inquit
And saythe he shall newly by myracle   f. 65a

resuscitabo tabernaculu*m*
Restore aȝeine *and* eke redifiee

dauid *et* reedificabo
Vpon that day the myghty tabernacle

Of kynge dauid, with al the regalie.

Isaia *propheta*   1580
And of this childe, wryt also Ysaye,

Continebunt Reges
Whan he is borne, that in his *p*resence

ɔs suum
Kyngeȝ for drede shull kepe hem in silence.

1569. Raysethe] Resceyvith CC.—light] height B¹, H¹, H⁷.—Whan] Where Hn¹.—to] om. Ch, B², Co, C², C³, H³, H⁴, Ash¹, An, CC, H⁵, H⁷, H⁸, Ad³, Ad², C⁵, B⁴, Lg. 1570. his] the Ch, H¹, C¹, C², H³, H⁴, Ash¹, An, H⁶, Ad², C⁵, B³, B⁴, Lg.—in] ful erly in B¹, H⁷. 1571. the] om. Ash¹, Ad³.—where] when C¹, H⁸.—he] om. CC.—wawe] the wawe B¹; dawe H⁵. 1572. Till Efte] To cast B², CC.—charet] claryet Hu.—he] hym L. 1573. the Est] the chest C³; este Hn¹.—that] whanne L.—syng] to syng H⁷, H⁸, Ad³, Hu.—the] *inserted above.* 1574. Ioye] they H⁸.—ryse] aryse L, B³. 1575. dothe Amos eke] Amos doth B¹; eke doth Amos C², H²; doth Amos C¹.—devyse] synge L. 1576. saythe] lieth B¹; sith B².—he] hit Ash¹. 1577. Restore aȝeine and eke redifiee, B¹.—eke] om. D. 1578. that] a C¹.—the] that H⁸. 1579. Of kynge dauid with al the regalie, B¹.—the] his D, C¹, C³, H⁸.—with] and H⁸.—regalie] ryally C¹; regalite Ad³. 1580. this childe] childe this C²; his childe L, H⁶, CC.—wryt also] also wrot Co; writith also C¹, C², H⁴, Ash¹, An, CC, H⁶; wrot also C³, B⁵, H², H⁷, H⁸. 1581. is] was C¹; om. CC. 1582. kepe] ken Lg.—hem in] hem B¹; in C²; om. Ch, B², H¹, C³, H³, H⁴, Ash¹, L, J, An, CC, H⁵, H⁶, Ad², C⁵, B³, B⁴, Lg.

A question assoyled
which is worthyest, of
kyng wyne or woman
Esdre orta questio
Ca° lvii°[1] 23

And as in Esdre is made a question,
   Of thynges thre what was worthiest:
Kyng, wyne, or woman, in comparison,
Eche Ipreysede and yhelde for best.
And all this stryfe, as daryng gan lest,
Zorababell, withoutyn any slouthe,
Aboven ychone had preferrede trouthe.

1590 And while thay were at travers of thees thre,
Eueryche holdyng his opynyon,
Zorobabell of Right and equyte,
To woman yafe his commendacion;
Makyng furthe-with of trouthe mencion,
Only in sygne, as he can devyse,
Fro woman firste trouthe moste aryse;

1583. as] om. B², J, CC, C¹.—Esdre] erthe H⁶, C⁵; Isodore H⁸.—is made] made is
C³.—a question] mension C³, Hn¹; the questioun B¹; question Co, B⁵, H⁷, H⁸, Ad³, Hu.
1584. thynges] kynges L.—what] whas H¹; wich C¹, C³; thet C²; that what II⁶.—
was] were B², J, CC; was the C¹. 1585. wyne] wife H⁸, Hu. 1586. for] as for the
C¹, H³, H⁵, H⁷, J, Ad³, B³, as for Ch, Co, H¹, C², B⁵, H⁴, Ash¹, L, Ad², C⁵, Lg,
Hu; for the B², B¹, C³, Hn¹, H², CC, H⁶, H⁸, B⁴. 1587. all] om. H².—this] the
B², J, CC.—daryng] daryus Ch, B², H¹, C¹, C², C³, Hn¹, H³, H⁴, H², Ash¹, L, J,
An, CC, H⁵, H⁶, Ad², C³, B³, B⁴, Lg.—gan] gan do Ash¹. 1588. Zorababell] And
Zorobabell B¹.—any] om. B², CC. 1589. Aboven] Ande aboven B¹.—had] hath C³.—
preferrede] reserved H².—trouthe] the trowthe H⁸. 1590. while] whane An.—at]
at the B², J.—of] for C³.—thees] this Co, C², Ash¹, CC, Ad³.—thre] tweine B¹. 1591.
Eueryche] Til eche B¹; Everyche thus Hn¹.—holdyng] helde C².—his] her CC; his
owne C³. 1592. Zorababell] Zorobabell thanne Hn¹; Thanne Zorobabell B¹. 1593. his]
the CC. 1594. furthe with] for the whiche L, B³.—of trouthe] a trewe C¹; all trouthe
Co.; trouthe Ch, B⁴.—mencion] mocioun C¹. 1595. Only] O oonly B¹.—can] gan B²,
Hn¹, Ash¹, J, CC, H⁷. 1596. Fro] For Ash¹.—firste trouthe moste] trouthe must first
B¹, Ad³; trouthe fast moste Co, H⁷, Hu; trouthe furst most B⁵.

---

[1]crossed through

Whiche is þe bonde *and* knott principal

Of all vertu, it may not be denyede,

And ther-*with* also, excellent Riall,

1600   W*ith* god hym-selfe that it is next alyede.

And for it is so moche magnyfyede,

Thorugh the worlde, of p*ri*se and worthy fame,

God chees hym-self of that to bere the name,[1]

And w*ith* his mouthe, hym-selfe so luste to calle,

As the gospell maketh mencion.

And by Recorde of olde p*ro*phetes alle,

Condescendyng into o conclusion,

This day in erthe, for our saluacion,

Of a woman in maydynhode flouryng,

1610   To mankynde trouthe dyd spryng.

1597. is] is the Ch, B1, B2, Co, H1, C1, C3, B5, Hn1, H3, H4, H2, Ash1, L, J, CC, An, H5, H6, H7, H8, Ad3, Ad2, C5, B3, B4, Lg, Hu. 1598. denyede] devyded L. 1599. also] all so Ch, B1, B2, Co, H1, C1, C2, C3, Hn1, H3, H2, Ash1, L, J, An, CC, H5, H6, H7, H8, Ad3, Ad2, C5, B3, Lg, Hu. 1600. W*ith*] That H1; That to Hn1.—that] om. B1, B2, Co, Hn1, H2, Ash1.—it] om. C1, C3, H4, L, An, H6, H8, B4.—is] om. Ch, H3, Ad2, C5, Lg.—alyede] callid Lg. 1602. worlde] word H1, C2, H8.—prise] pryde C1.—worthy] eke B2, CC. 1603. of that] om. CC; of it B2. 1604. And] And thus Ch, Hn1, H3, H7, C5.—so] om. B1, B4.—lus̈te] let C3, Hn1.—to] he Ch, Co, B5, C3, Hn1, H3, H4, H2, J, An, H5, Ad2, C5, Lg; om. L, H8, B3. 1605. As] And H1. 1606. And] om. B2, C1, J, CC.—Recorde] reporte L.—olde] om. Ch, B2, H1, C1, C2, Hn1, H3, H4, Ash1, L, J, An, CC, H5, H6, Ad2, C5, B3, B4, Lg; the H2, CC. 1607. Condescendyng] Godes sendynge Ch, C5; Don descendynge B1; Concenting C1; Condescended CC; God descending H6.—into] to Ch, B2, H1, C1, C2, Hn1, H3, H4, H2, Ash1, L, J, An, CC, H5, H6, Ad2, C5, B3, B4, Lg.—o] oure H8. 1609. a] om B1, Co, H1, B5, H7, H8, Ad3; alle CC. 1610. mankynde] kynde H6.—trouthe] thorowʒ H8.—dyd] dyd first B1, Hn1, H7, Ad3; first gan H2.

---

[1]MS. D repeats *hym* in the line.

And fro heven Rightwysnesse be-helde　　　　　　　　f. 65b

How trouthe and mercy in a mayden mette.

And thus is trouthe sprong oute of the felde,

Wher the holy goste the grayne of grace sette,

To make the graffe that he fro Iudas fette,

Fructyfie in a pure virgine;

That shall be title of the same lyne,

The crovne of Iuda to hym accepte a-noon,

And vndirfonge it as a champion,

1620　Which was by-rafte, so many a day agone,

Fro Sedechye away in Babylone,

Whan ther was made a transmygracion,

By the tyrant Nabugodonosore,

Whose cruelte last shall no more.

1611. fro] to Ch.—heven] om. L.—be helde] did he holde CC. 1612. and mercy in a mayden mette] in a maid met and mercy C¹. 1613. thus] this H⁸.—is] om. H⁵, Hu.—oute] om. C¹.—the] a Ch, B¹, H¹, C¹, C², H³, H⁴, Ash¹, An, Ad², C⁵, B⁴, Lg, Hu. 1614. grayne of grace] grace of greyne Ch; grene gras C¹. 1615. fro] om. H¹.—Iudas] Iuda B¹, B², Co, H², J, CC, H⁸, Hu. 1616. Fructyfie in a pure virgine, H⁷.—Fructyfie] To fructyfye D.—fructyfie] fructuose Hn¹.—pure] clene pure C³. 1617. That] Whyche C³.—title] titelid C¹.—same lyne] salyne C¹. 1618. hym] om. L, B³.—accepte a-noon] by accepcioun B², CC; be acceptacioun J. 1619. a] a stronge L, B³; a myghti H⁶. 1620. was] om. L.—by rafte] braste C¹. Ad², Lg. 1621. in] to B², J; into C², B³, B⁴. 1622. ther] that Ch, H¹, C¹, H⁸, H⁴, H², Ash¹, L, An, H⁶, Ad², C⁵, B⁴; om. Lg; he was ther B², J, CC.—was] om. B⁵. 1624. last shall] shal laste B¹, B², C¹, CC.

Howe our lady aught
worthyly to be
commendyd and
worshipped for the birthe
of criste Ca° lviii°[1] 24[m]

Nowe he is borne that is rightfull heyre,

    That shall make bet then Neemye

His peple of Iuda forto haue repayre;

Iher*usalem* a-gayne to edyfye,

Though herodes that falsely occupye,

1630 As a foreyn thorugh his cruell myght,

By tyranye and no tytle of Right;

Of whome the kyngdome shall not long endure,

The Regne vsurpyng by extorcion.

For the lorde of eu*ery* creature,

This day hath take his Iuste possession

In Bedlem, wit*h*in a small donion,—

He and his mother, as who say the but alone,

To wayte on hym othir fewe or noone.

1625. he is] ys he L, B³, Hu.—is] is so B¹, Co, C³, H⁷, H⁸, Ad³, Hu. 1626. make]
make make H¹, C².—then] that B²; tha CC; nowe than Hn¹.—Neemye] Ninive B¹,
Co, H⁷, H⁸, Ad³.—bet then Neemye] om. C¹. 1627. His] That his C¹.—peple] power
Co; pepyr Hu.—forto] tho forto B¹; to C¹. 1628. to] forto C¹, B³. 1629. that] om.
B², CC; it H².—falsely] fals H⁸.—occupye] doth occupye H⁶; occupiere H⁸.—that
falsely occupye] thorow his cruel myght Hu. 1630. foreyn] forn Co, C³, B⁵, H².—
thorugh] thouȝt H⁸. 1631. tyranye] tyrauntre J, CC.—no] by no B¹, L, B³; om. H¹.
1632. long] om. Ash¹.—endure] dure B⁴. 1633. Regne] ream H⁶.—vsurpyng] to usurpe
Hn¹. 1635. his] om. Ch.—Iuste] om. B⁴; moste C².—possession] posse possessioun
Ch. 1636. wit*h*in] in C³, H⁶; with B⁴.—small] pore L, B³; welle small H⁶.—donion]
town C¹; dominacioun C²; dominioun Hn¹; mansyoun L, B³. 1637. as] om. C¹.—who]
who so B²; he Co; om. C¹.—saythe] sittyng C¹. 1638. wayte] await B², J, H⁵, V.—
othir] or H².

---

¹crossed through

A lady myne, howe god hathe made the ryche,

1640   Thy-selffe alone all ryches to possede!

For in this worlde noon is to the liche,

Of plente Riall; for the londe of mede,

Wher the hylles of golde ben, as I rede,

May no tresoure in his maynes Reyse,

Ayen thy tresoure for to countrepayse.

For certes, lady, thou alone haste all   f. 66a

That in heven Angels desyre:

The Iewell Riche, the tresour celestiall,

Rex regum *et* do*minus*   Of heven kyng, of earthe lorde and sire,

dominancium   1650   And hym þat hath al þe hole empire.

Of land and see, and the monarchie,

Thou hast holy, o lady myne, to gye.

1639. A] O B³. 1641. to] om. B¹.—the] see J, CC. 1642. for] fro Ch, H¹, C¹, C², H³, H⁴, Ash¹, An, H⁶, Ad², C⁵, B⁴, Lg.—of] and B¹.—mede] medee B², H². 1643. Wher] Whe H¹. 1645. thy] the C¹, H².—for to] for no C³.—countrepayse] counterprise H². 1646. certes] certayn H⁶.—thou] you H¹.—alone heste] hast aloon B¹. 1647. That] The wiche C¹.—in] within Ch, H¹, C², H³, H⁴, Ash¹, An, H⁶, Ad², C⁵, B⁴, Lg.—desyre] edifie B¹, Co, H², H⁷, H⁸, Ad³. 1648. the tresour] of tresour C². 1649. of erthe] and of erthe H⁴, B³.—sire] sye C¹. 1650. And hym þat hath al þe hole empire, H⁷.—al] om. D, C¹, H⁶.—And] Of L, B³. 1652. holy] om. B¹.—o] om. C², B¹.—to] forto B¹.

And as Austyne, the holy doctour, write

In a *ser*mon of the Natyuyte,

We may to the sayne, right as he bitte,

W*ith* deuoute hert, knelyng on our knee:

"O blessed lady, flour of virgnyte,

We prayen ichone, o welle of our welfare,

Like a mothir nat thy mylke to spare.

1660   Yeffe hym plentee that is so plentevouse

Of fulsomnesse Angels to fede;

And yef hym souke the pyment graciouse

Of thy pappes: lat the condyte shede

The sote mylke all aboute in brede,

And motherly makyng it to avale

On his fayre tendur lymes smale."

1653. holy] om CC.—write] writith H⁶. 1655. We] Whee CC.—to the sayne] saye to the B¹, B², H⁸; to save Hu.—bitte] biddeth CC. 1656. W*ith*] With a B¹.—hert] her B⁵.—our] her H³. 1657. blissed] blisfull Co, C³, B⁵, Hn¹, Hu.—flour] o flour B¹, Hn¹, H⁷. 1658. ichone] everychone B¹.—o] the B², CC; of J; as C¹. 1659. a] as a B²; as J. —nat thy mylke to] thy mylke that thou ne B¹, Co, C³, B⁵, H⁷, H⁸, Ad³, Hu; thi mylke not to C². 1660. Yeffe] But yeve B¹; To yeve Hn¹. 1662. the] tha H¹; that C¹, Ash¹; thy H⁵. 1663. the] thy Ch, B¹, B², Co, C¹, C², L, H⁵, H⁶, H⁷, H⁸, Ad³, Hu. 1664. The] Thy H⁸.—mylke] brede B², CC.—in brede] yn lengthe and brede L, B³. 1665. And] om. Ch, B², C¹, H¹, C², Hn¹, H³, H⁴, H², Ash¹, J, L, An, CC, H⁵, H⁶, Ad², C⁵, B³, B⁴, Lg.—makyng it] hit makyng Ch, B¹, B², C¹, H¹, C³, H⁷, H⁸, Ad³, C², Hn¹, H³, H⁴, H², Ash¹, J, L, An, CC, H⁵, H⁶, Ad², C⁵, B³, B⁴, Lg; hit make Co, B⁵; makith hit not Hu; in makeynge B¹. 1666. On his fayre tendur lymes smale, B¹.—fayre] foure D.—On] Nowe on Hn¹; Of H⁸.—his] om. C¹.—smale] so smale C¹; and small H².

Glad mayste thou be, þat sauf hym luste to vouche,

Withe his rounde softe lippeȝ lyte,

To have pleasaunce thy bresteȝ for to touche,

1670 Only to souke thy blissede pappes white;

And that hym luste so godely to delyte,

For his playe to haue so moche blisse,

Euere among thy holy mouthe to kysse.

And sodenly, with childely chere Iocounde,

Than a-none thy white nek enbrace

With his softe tendre Armes rounde.

And than at onys fallen on thy face,

And of his eyne, fulfillede of all grace,

A godely loke to thewarde enclyne;

1680 And so furthe his chekes ley by thyne,

1667. mayste] must B2, Co, B5, H2, J, CC, H7, H8, Ad3, Hu.—þat sauf hym luste] that sauf
lyst Ch, B2, H1, H3, H4, Ash1, J, An, CC, H5, Lg, H6, Ad2, C5, B4; saf that him
liste B1; that so list C1; that saf hymself liste C3; that he list L, B3. 1668. rounde]
om. CC.—softe] swete B1, Co, C3, B5, H7, H8, Ad3, Hu.—lippeȝ] lippe L. 1669.
bresteȝ] breste B1, B2, H1, H8; prestis Lg.—for] om. CC. 1670. Only] And B3.—
to] forto H2, B3. 1671. so] so so C2.—to] om. B1. 1672. haue] save H5.—to haue so
moche] that ys kynge of L, B3. 1673. thy] this C1; his CC, H6; the Ad3.—mouthe]
mamy Lg. 1674. with] anon with CC.—childely] om. Ash1.—with childely chere] thy
child clere C1.—Iocounde] founde B2, J, CC. 1675. thy] the J.—nek] newe H8.—white
nek] neck white H1.—enbrace] to enbrace Hn1, H6, C5. 1676. With] That J, CC. 1677.
on] to B1; uppon Hn1. 1678. of] with C1, L, B3.—his] om. Ch, B1.—fulfillede] all
fulfilled C3, Ad3, B4, Hu; full L, B3.—of all] of B1, H1, C1, L, B3; all of
C3, Ad3, B4, Hu. 1679. A] A ful B1; And C1.—to thewarde] he did to the C1. 1680.]
And so his cheke ley forthe to thyne C2.—so furthe] folewynge anoon Hn1; so with H8;
so forthwith Co, H1, B5, Ad3, Hu; so for sothe CC.—his] thy Hu.—ley] lay hem B1,
Co, B5, H7, Ad3, Hu; leve hem H8.—by thyne] to thyne Ch, B1, B2, Co, H1, C1, C2,
C3, B5, Hn1, H3, H4, H2, Ash1, L, J, An, CC, H5, H6, H7, Ad2, C5, B3, B4, Lg,
Hu; unto thine Ad3; to schine H8.

And withe his fyngres, mouthe and eyne touche; f. 66b

His smal pawmes on thy chekes layne

His yong face betwene thy pappes couche,

And holde hym stille, *with* all his besy payne,

And grype hem faste with his handeȝ twayne;

For ther-in was his hevenly repaste,—

Þi ȝunge sone whan he list breke his faste,

Ther was his foode and his norchyng pure,

Sothefaste seler of his sustyn*au*nce;

1690 The tune of lyfe that eu*er*e dyd endure,

Ilyche fresshe vnto his pleasaunce,

Withe sacrede lycoure of holy habundaunce,

That noon but he may touche nor aproche,

For it for hym was only set abroche.

1681. his] om. L, B³, B⁴. 1682. His] His said Ash¹.—on] to H⁸. 1683. yong] swete
B⁵.—betwene] attweyn H¹.—thy] the Hu.—couche] touche C¹, Lg. 1684. hym] hem
Ash¹, L, J, B³, Hu.—all] om. B¹. 1685. hem] hym C¹, H⁵, H⁶, C⁵, Lg.—his] om.
J; al his C². 1687. þi ȝunge sone whan he list breke his faste, H⁷.—list] lust to D;
wold L, B³. 1688. his foode and his norchyng] his norssheynge and his fode B¹. 1689.
Sothefaste] And soitfaste B¹. 1690. tune] tyme Co, C¹, C³, B⁵, H⁸, Ad², H³.—that]
om. H⁷.—dyd] doth C³. 1691. Ilyche] And ever ylyche Hn¹.—vnto] to Hn¹, CC.
1692. lycoure] lyfe CC.—of] and Hn¹. 1693. nor] and Ch, H², Ad³. 1694. it for hym]
hym hit wit Ch; hym hit B⁴.—was only] only was B¹, Co, C², C³, B⁵, L, H⁷, H⁸,
Ad³, B³, Hu.—abroche] on broche B¹, H¹, C¹.

For in that licour was full remedye,

Holy refute, and pleynly medycyne

Ayayne the venyme brought in by envye,

Thorugh fals engyne and malyce serpentyne,

Whan the snake made Adam to dyne

1700   Of the Appull that was intoxicate,

Falsely with god to make hym at debate.

But nowe the mylke of thy pappes tweyne,

Benygne lady, is to vs tryacle,—

Whiche in thy brest sprenketh fro a vayne,—

Ayenst dethe to be to vs obstacle.

O how it is a passyng high myracle,

Thorugh goddys myght and by nought elles,

Oute of a breste to see two small wellys

1695. full] full and Ch; full of Co, B⁵. 1696. pleynly] pleyne Ch. B¹, B², Co, C¹, C², H³, H⁴, Ash¹, L, J, An, CC, H⁵, H⁶, H⁷, Ad², C⁵, B³, B⁴, Lg. 1697. in] and Hu.—by] his H⁵. 1698. and] of L, B³. 1699. to] om. H¹. 1700. the Appull] an appull C¹; thappull C³.—intoxicate] in paradice toxicate H⁸; in Toxicate Ad³, Hu. 1701. hym] hem CC.—at debate] at bate B¹, H¹. 1702. the] thy C¹.—thy] the H¹, C²; om. Lg. 1703. lady] lay C¹.—is] it is B², Hn¹, J, CC.—is to vs] on to his C¹. 1704. Whiche in] Withynne B², H², C¹, J, Lg.—thy] the Lg.—brest] birest Hu.—sprenketh] spryngyng C¹.—fro] for C³, CC, H².—vayne] vyne Hn¹. 1705. dethe] the dethe Ch, B², C², H³, H⁴, Ash¹, L, J, An, CC, H⁵, H⁶, Ad², C⁵, B³, B⁴, Lg; thy dethe C¹. 1706. O how] Thouȝ C².—it] om. B¹. 1707. by] om. B¹, B², Co, C³, B⁵, J, CC, H⁷, H⁸, Ad³, Hu.—nought] nothyng C²; noth Hn¹. 1708. a] hir C¹.—to see] om. Ash¹; to have B², J, CC.—two] so C¹; om. Lg.

Of mayden mylke spryng as a Ryuer,

1710 To yefe hym drynke that is kyng of alle.

O goode lady, o hevenly boteler,

When we in myscheve to the clepe and calle,

Some drope of grace lat vpon vs falle;

And to that seler make a Redy waye,

Wher thou alone of mercy beryste the keye.

And of grace lat be no scarste,   f. 67a

Gode lady that arte of grace well,

For nowe this day in erthe is bore of the

The sothefaste god of hevyn, erthe, and helle;

1720 Whiche is comyn dovne *with* vs for to dwelle,

And hathe of the our mortall kynde Itake,

Of all our woo an ende for to make.

1709. Of] O H². —mayden] a mayde Ch, B¹, B², Co, H¹, C¹, C², H³, H⁴, Ash¹, J, An, H⁶, Ad², C⁵, B³, B⁴, Lg; a maydyns C³; maydes B⁵; maydens Hn¹, L.—mylke] om. Ch, C¹, H³, H⁴, An, H⁶, Ad², C⁵, B³, B⁴.—spryng] spryngynge Ch, B¹, B², Co, C³, B⁵, H³, H⁴, Ash¹, L, J, An, CC, H⁵, H⁶, H⁷, H⁸, Ad³, Ad², C⁵, B³, B⁴, Lg, Hu.—a Ryuer] a well Ash¹; ryver Hu. 1710. of] over B¹. 1711. goode] godely, Ch, B¹, H³, H⁴, Ash¹, L, J, An, CC, H⁵, H⁶, H⁷, H⁸, Ad³, Ad², C⁵, B³, B⁴, Lg.—O hevenly] and hevenly Ch. 1712. the] the I Hu.—and] or Ch, B¹, Co, H¹, C¹, C², C³. 1713. lat vpon vs] let on us B¹, Co, B⁵, Hu; upon us let H¹. 1714. that] the B¹, C¹, CC.—make] made C¹; make us C³. 1715. Wher] Where of B², J, CC.—alone of mercy] of mercy alone Ch, B², Co, H¹, C², C³, B⁵, L, J, CC, H⁶, H⁷, Ad³, Ad², C⁵, B³, B⁴, Lg, Hu; mercy allone H⁸. 1716. of] of thy C¹.—be] om. H⁶.—scarste] scarside H⁶. 1717. Gode] Be good H⁶; Nowe good Hn¹.—well] the well B¹, C², Hn¹, H³. 1718. this day in erthe is bore] this day is borne in erthe B¹; in erthe this day is borne B².—in] on CC. H⁸; om. H³.— erthe] om. H³. 1719. erthe] and erthe Ch. 1721. the] om. Co, C¹.—Itake] tke B¹, Co, C¹, C³, B⁵, CC, H⁶, H⁷, H⁸, Ad³, Hu. 1722. an] and H³, H⁷, H⁸.—for] om. B¹.

Some-tyme fro hevyn fel adoune the manne,

To refresshe the hungre in her nede,

And þat be-fell in desert Right thanne,

When moyseȝ, the peple of our lorde dyd lede.

But nowe this day, in erthe man to fede,

An humble mayde, to all that ben trwe,

In this desert hath brought furthe manna newe;

1730   Whiche to Angel is the fode of lyffe,

To man, repast of Ioye and of gladnesse,

Chefe recomforte, and eke restoratyfe

To all feble oppressed *with* sekenesse.

O gode ladi, o myrour of mekenesse,

Benygne floure, of womanhode the welle,

In this desert wher as we nowe dwelle,

1723. Some tyme] Whilome H¹.—fro hevyn fel adoune the manne] adoun fro heven
fel the man C²; from hevene manna fel adoun Hn¹. 1724. the] om. H¹.—nede] grete nede
Co, C³, B⁵, H⁸, Hu. 1725. þat] thanne CC.—Right thanne] ful boun Hn¹. 1726. the]
thi H¹; out of Egypte the L, B³.—of our lorde] om. Ch, B², H¹, C¹, C², Hn¹, H³,
H⁴, Ash¹, L, J, An, CC, H⁵, H⁶, Ad², C⁵, B³, B⁴, Lg. 1727. this day in erthe] in
erthe this day Hu.—in] on CC.—man] men Lg; om. B², J, CC.—to] for to C².—fede]
fynde H⁶. 1728. An] Manne an B², J, CC; And H⁷, H⁸.—all] om. B². 1729. desert]
defecte H⁸.—furthe manna] man forth H¹; manne B²; forth man Co, C³, B⁵, Hu.
1730. Whiche to] lyfe of C¹.—Angel] angellis H¹, C¹, J, CC, H⁸.—the] om. B², J,
H⁷, H⁸.—fode] foote H⁷. 1731. man] mannes H¹, L.—and of] and B¹, C¹, Hn¹, CC,
H⁷, H⁸, Ad³. 1732. recomforte] comfort C¹.—eke] om. Ch, B², C¹, C², Hn¹, H³,
H⁴, H², Ash¹, L, J, An, CC, H⁵, H⁶, Ad², C⁵, B³, B⁴, Lg; a H¹. 1734. O gode ladi,
o myrour of mekenesse, B¹.—of] of all D.—gode] goodly C¹, H³, CC. 1735. Benygne]
Beryng C¹; Beynge Ash¹.—floure] figure H¹.—of] and H².—the] om. H¹, H²; that
C².—welle] floure B². 1736. as] inne B¹; om. B⁵.—we nowe] now we Ch, B¹, C¹,
C², C³, B⁵, H³, H⁴, Ash¹, L, An, Ad², C⁵, B⁴, Lg.

Sende vs this manne of souereigne hertes hele,

To owre comforte and consolacion;

And lat vs grace in thy mercy fele,

1740 For our Refute and refection.

And in this vale of confucion,

Late thy grace fro the skyes rayne

The manne of lyfe, that we may attayne.

For thou alone art comforte synguler

To al tho that noo refute konne;

This day also, of mercy the Ryuer,

Fro whiche all grace is to mankynde ronne,

The sterre also, that hathe brought furthe the sonne,

The sonne of lyfe, in erthe forto wonne,

1750 O mayde, o mother, doughter of thy sonne,

1737. this] om. Ch; thy C¹, C³, H³, H⁴, Ash¹, An, H⁶, Ad³, Ad², C⁵, B⁴. 1738. To owre comforte and consolacion, B¹.—and] and our D.—comforte] hertis comfort H⁷. 1739. grace] thy grace C¹, H⁶.—in thy] and C¹; and thy H⁶. 1740. and] and eke H¹; and chief C³; and our H². 1741. of] of veri H¹; an CC. 1742. thy] the CC. —the] thy C¹, Ash¹. 1743. may] mowe J, CC, H⁵. 1744. comforte] refute H¹. 1746. of] of the B¹. 1747. Fro] For B², Hn¹.—is to mankynde] to mankynde is B¹, Co, C³, B⁵, H⁷, H⁸, Ad³, Hu; to mankynde C². 1748. furthe] om. Co, C³, B⁵, H⁸, Hu.— the sonne] sonne H⁸. 1749. in] in the B⁴. 1750. doughter] thouder Ash¹.—thy] the Co, H¹, C², C³, B⁵, CC, H⁶, H⁸, Hu; om. B⁴.—sonne] syon H⁷, B⁴.

Whiche non, in sothe, sithe the worlde by-gan   f. 67b

Was bothe two, but thy-selfe alone.

For who is he that remembre can,—

First or laste, late or elles sone,—

So bright a sonne spryngyng of so fayre a mone,

Saff this day, the sonne of lyf moste shene

Fro the arose, and thou a mayden clene,

Wi*th*oute eclipsyng or leesyng of thy light;

For thou a mother and mayden bothe two,

1760   In vertu aye yliche shene and bryght,

O fayre rose, o Rose of Iericho,

That hast this day god and man also

In Bedlem borne a3en the gray morowe,

The nyght to voyde of al our olde sorowe,

1751. non] now H[7]; thow Hu. 1752. bothe two] non CC.—but] save B[5]. 1754. Firste] Fyeste Ash[1].—late] om. B[1]. 1755. spryngyng] sprynger H[8]; sprynge Ch, B[1], B[2], Co, H[1], C[1], C[2], B[5], Hn[1], H[3], H[4], H[2], L, J, An, CC, H[5], H[7], Ad[3], Ad[2], C[5], B[3], B[4], Lg, Hu.—so fayre] om. C[1]; fayre Hu.—a mone] mone B[5]. 1756. moste] so B[1]; must CC.—shene] schine CC. 1758. thy] the H[1], C[1]; om. Ch, Co, B[5], H[8], Hu.— light] sight C[3]. 1759. thou] to C[1].—and] and to a C[1]; a C[2]; and a Hn[1], H[6], H[8], Hu; and and Ash[1]. 1760. aye yliche] ever aliche B[1], Co, C[3], B[5], H[7], H[8], Ad[3], Ad[2], Hu; i-lich C[1]; ay in liche H[1].—shene] shone Ch; shyne H[1]. 1761. of] o H[7]. 1762. borne] om. Ch. 1763. The nyght to voyde] Te night avoide Ash[1].—to] om. H[8].— olde] om. B[1].

Of likenesse of our lady
in commendaciou of hir
Ca° lix°[1] 25

Nowe fayre Cedre, Cypresse of Syon,

    Spryngyng light oute of Naʒareth,

Chose chaumbre of wyse Salamon,

Flour of the felde, swettest on holte and hethe,

Of whome the vertu saveth man fro dethe;

1770   Of Syloe the water eke depurede,

Wherby, the lepre of Naaman was purede;

Laude and glorye of Iheru*sa*lem

Thou namede art, of Israel gladnesse;

Holsome Cysterne, this day of Bedlem,

The thruste of Dauid to staunche in destresse;

Of paradyse the well in sothefastenesse,

Physon that [floweth] into sondry Remes,

The soyl to adewe *with* his sote stremeʒ;

1765. Cypresse] O sypresse B[1], B[2], H[7]. 1766. light oute] out light B[2], J, CC; light H[6], C[5]. 1767. Chose] Close Hn[1].—Salamon] Salon C[3]. 1768. of the] on the H[2], Hu.—felde] olde B[2], J, CC.—and] or C[3], Ash[1].—hethe] helth B[2]; brethe C[3]. 1770. the water eke] eke the water Ch, C[3]. 1771. the] om. C[1].—of] om. Ch, Co, C[1], C[2], Hn[1], H[3], H[4], Ash[1], An, H[6], Ad[2], C[5], B[4], Lg, Hu.—was] ys L, B[3].—purede] recured Ch, B[1], B[2], Co, H[1], C[1], C[3], B[5], Hn[1], H[3], H[4], Ash[1], J, An, CC, H[5], H[6], H[7], H[8], Ad[3], Ad[2], C[5], B[4], Lg, Hu; delyverede C[2]; cured H[2], Ash[1], L, B[3]. 1772. and] of B[2].—glorye] glorifie H[3]. 1773. of] and of Ch, B[2], C[1], C[2], C[3], B[5], H[3], H[4], Ash[1], L, J, An, CC, H[5], H[6], Ad[2], C[5], B[3], B[4], Lg. 1774. this] thi H[7]. 1775. staunche] chaunge Co, C[3], B[5], H[8], Hu.—in] and Ch, B[2], J, CC. 1776. in] of C[2]. 1777. [floweth] MS. D. has *foloweth*.—into] in Lg, Hu. 1778. soyl] sool B[2], J, CC, H[5]; foyle H[7].—to adewe] shadewe B[2], J, CC; to tawe H[8].

---

[1]crossed through

The londe also of promyssyon,

1780   That mylke and hony bothe in-fere shedyth,

The soyle and grovnde of our saluacion,

With his herbes that fosterthe vs and fedeth;

Nowe blisset mayde, whose mercy euere medyth,

All tho that levyn in thy seruyce,

This high fste so for vs devyse.

That in honour of thy sonne so dere,   f. 68a

We may of hert Rede, syng, and pray.

And late the stremez of thyne eyne clere,

Thy seruauntez, o lady myne, conveye,

1790   To contynue fully tyll we deye,

The to serue with hertly loue and drede,

As moste is plesyng to thy womanhede

1779. of] of the C1. 1781. and] of C1. 1782. fosterthe vs] us fostrith Ash1; forstressuth
L. 1783. mayde] may H2.—euere] never H6; every H5. 1784 tho] om. H8, J, C3, Hn1.
—in] here in B1, H7, Ad3.—thy] the C1, Ash1; thy hy H2. 1785. This] Thy Ch, H2.—
so] om. C1.—vs] to CC. 1786. in] in the B1, C3, H3, V.—thy] the H7.—so] om. Ch,
B2, H1, C1, C2, C3, H3, H4, H2, Ash1, J, L, An, CC, H5, H6, Ad2, C5, B3, B4,
Lg, V. 1787. of] in C1.—and] or C1. 1788. late] om Ad3.—the] thy C1.—clere] om.
Co. 1789. myne] swete L. 1790. To] And so to Hn1.—contynue] conteine H8.—tyll]
unto H6, C5. 1791. hertly] herte B1, Co, C1, C3, B5, H6, H7, H8, Ad3, Hu. 1792.
moste] om. H1.—to] unto H1, Hn1.

And this feste, of festeʒ principall,—

Called the fest of the natiuite,—

Make loue and pees to Regne ou*er*e all,

And herteʒ Ioyne w*ith* p*er*fyte vnyte;

Voyde all discorde, and late no Ranco*ur* be

In bresteʒ closede by malice or envye,

But of thy grace, so gouerne vs and gye,

1800   This high feste in whiche thy sonne was **borne.**

Now this mydwynter, w*ith* full affection,

While phebus shynyth in the Cap*ri*corne,

We may the s*er*ue with all deuocion.

And lady myne, in full conclusion,

Nowe this monyth that called is decembre,

Vpon thy men faythefully Remembre.

1793. feste] om. B¹; fest is the fest C¹. 1794. Called the fest of the natiuite, B¹.— the] thy D, B³, L, H⁸. 1795. Make] Makethe J, CC.—to] in B¹. 1796. Ioyne] joy C¹, Ash¹, H⁸.—with] in B¹, Co, C², C³, B⁵, H⁷, H⁸, Ad³, Hu. 1797. Voyde all discorde] And discore C¹; Voyde of discorde C²; Voyde of all discorde L. 1798. bresteʒ] hertes Ch, C², Hn¹, H³, H⁴, Ash¹, An, B⁴, Lg.—or] ne B¹, Co, C³, B⁵, H⁷, H⁸, Ad³, Ad², Hu; of H²; nor C², Hn¹, H³, H⁴, H¹, Ash¹, J, An, H⁵, H⁶, C⁵, B⁴, Lg. 1799. and] to H⁶. 1800. whiche] whiche feste CC.—was] as Lg. 1801. Now] om. B³; In C¹, L.—mydwynter] mydwynter nyght Ch, B², C¹, H³, H⁴, L, J, An, CC, H⁵, H⁶, Ad², C⁵, B³, B⁴, Lg.—full] high CC. 1802. the] om. B¹. 1803. may the] the to C¹. 1804. lady myne] lady blisfull H²; hevenly lady L, B³.—full] om. Ch, B², C¹, C², C³, B⁵, H³, H⁴, H², Ash¹, L, J, An, CC, H⁵, H⁶, Ad², C⁵, B³, B⁴. 1805. this] in this H¹. 1806. men] servauntis C²; servaunte L, B³.

BOOK IV

How Crist was
circumsised
Ca° 1x°¹ 1ᵐ

W han Ianus Byfrons in colde Ianuarie,

With frosty berde entreth in the yere,

And phebus chare neyeth to aquarye,

His watry beameȝ to-fore feverer,

Whan that his light was pale and no-thyng clere,

And from hym late was partyd lucyne,

The same nyght as I sawe her shyne

Ournede newe, with beameȝ glad and merye,

On the heven, and caste his stremes adovne,

10 I gan Remembre of the high ferye

That callede is the Circumcisyon;

Howe it be fell than by Reuolucion,

By Iuste acomptyng in the Calendere,

The firste day of the newe yere,

---

1. Ianus] Jamys C³, CC.—Byfrons] bifins B¹, H², H⁷, B²; be forne CC, H⁸.—colde Ianuarie] olde imageri C². 2. With] With his CC.—entreth] entryd CC. 3. neyeth] neighist H¹; nyghe J; entrith in H⁶.—to] om. H⁸. 5. his] this Ch, H⁸; om. Adv²; is H⁶.—pale and] om. H². 6. hym] om. C¹; *inserted above.*—late] om. Hn¹.—was partyd] parted was B¹, Co, H¹, C³, B⁵, Hn¹, H², H⁷, H⁸, Adv², Hu; was passed B², CC, Ad², C⁵; passed was H⁶. 8. Ournede] Honowrd B¹, H², Ash¹, H⁷; Arned Hu; Borned B², C³, Hn¹, J, CC; Urned H⁶; Horned H⁸, Adv².—glad] clere H⁶. 9. On the] In C¹; On the hy H²; On to CC.—and] om. C²; he C¹.—his] hire Co, B⁵, H¹, C³, H⁸, Hu; the H⁶. 10. I gan] Thanne can I Hn¹; I con Adv².—of] me on Adv²; on H⁸. —the] this B¹, Co, H¹, C², C³, B⁵, H⁷, H⁸, Hu; an H².—high ferye] feste high H¹. 11. the] om. C²; nowe the Hn¹. 12. be fell] fell H¹, C².—than] tho H¹; om. B¹, Co, B⁵, H², H⁷.—Reuolucion] revelacion B¹, Co, H¹, C¹, C², B⁵, H², H⁷. 13. acomptyng] a cowte B¹.—in] on H⁸. 14. of] on B¹.

---

¹crossed through

And thought I wolde in my booke *procede*,   f. 68b

Of this feste somwhate forto wryte.

And to the gospell firste I gan take hede,

Of this day howe luke luste to endyte;

Though he therof spake but a lyte,

20 And was full breff and compendious;

ȝet of this day, so high and gloryouse,

He wryte pleynly, and sayth how that a-noon,

Aftir the day of the Natyuyte,

When viii dayes passed were and gone,

The childe was brought *with* all humylyte

To the Temple, louly for to be,

As the lawe of Iewes had deuised,

The viii day to be circumcisede.

---

15. thought I wolde in my booke] in my book I thouȝt I wolde B¹.—in] on B², C³, Hn¹, H², Ash¹, L, J, H⁵, B³, Lg.—my] om. Hu.—*procede*] procede and write B¹. 16. this] this holi H².—somwhate] om. H².—forto] to C², CC. 17. to] of H⁴.—I gan] gam B¹; con Adv.²—take] om. H¹. 18. to] om. C², Lg. 19. Though he] Thought C¹. —spake] to speke C¹.—a] om. B¹. 20. And] That H².—full] om. H¹.—and] and full B¹. 21. ȝet] And yet B¹.—so] om. Ch, B², C¹, C², C³, Hn¹; full H¹.—and] so B¹. 22. He] We Hu.—wryte] wrytith H¹, C¹, B⁵, H⁴, H⁶.—how that] right C¹; owe that CC; that H².—a-noon] one Hn¹. 23. of the] of C². 24. passed were] weren passed B¹, C¹, C², H⁸, B⁴; passed was CC.—gone] agon Co. 25. all] om. H¹. 26. louly] holy CC. 27. As the lawe of Iewes had deuised, B¹.—of] of the D, C¹, C³, Hn¹. 28. day] om. Ch, H⁵, B³, B⁴.—to be] om. L, B³; for to be B², H¹, J, CC.

And he ther-to mekely dyd obeye.

30 And withe a knyfe made full sharpe of stone,

His mothir lokyng w*ith* a pytous eye,

The childe was corve ther-w*ith* all, a-non,

That all a-boute the rede blode gan gon

Bonaventur*e*   W*ith*oute a boode, as saythe Bonaventure,

That for the payne that he dyd endure,

And for sharpnes of the soden smerte,

The childe gan wepe þat pyte was to here.

Wherfore his mothir, of verrey tendre herte,

Oute brast on teres and myght her-self not stere,

40 That all bydewede were her eyne clere,

Whan she sawe hym that she louede soo,

So yonge, so fayre, wepyng so for woo.

---

29. he] om. B¹, Co, C³, Adv.².—ther to mekely] mekely ther to B¹, Co; ther to he mekely Adv². 30. knyfe] kyfe Lg.—made full sharpe of] full sharp as Ch; made of sharpe B¹; made full sharp on Co, H², H⁶; mad sharpe of CC.—stone] a stone Co. 32. The] This C², L.—was] om. H⁸.—all] om. C², L. 33. rede] om. C¹.—gan] can Adv². 34. a boode] aboute J.—saythe] spekith C¹. 35. That] And Ch, C¹, C², C³, Hn¹, H³, H⁴, Ash¹, L, An, H⁶, Ad², C⁵, B⁴, Lg.—that he] he L, H⁶, C⁵. 36. for] for the Hn¹.—the] that C²; om. J, CC. 37. þat pyte] om. Ch. 38. Wherfore] Wherwith H¹, Hn¹. 39. Oute brast] Brest owȝt B¹.—on] of Hu.—and] om. Adv².—her self not] not hir self B¹.—not] no CC. 40. bydewede] be wept H¹; weet C¹.—were] om. H¹. 42. So yonge, so fayre wepyng so for woo, B¹.—so for] for D, H¹.

But he a-noon in all his passion,

For all that he was so yong of age,

In man*e*re he had pyte and compassion,

To se his modyr so wepe in hir rage;

And put his hande vnto hir visage,

On mouthe and eyne, passyngly benyngne,

And as he couthe goodly made a signe

50 Wi*th*outyn speche, to stynt her wepyng   f. 69a

That came to her of motherly pyte.

And she full well conceyved his menyng,

For poynt to poynt, and than a-noon gan she

To loke on hym that was so fayre to see,

And his fetures considret by and by,

And in her Armes, wonder womanly,

---

43. he] om. CC.—all] om. Lg. 44. so] om. C[1]. 45. In man*e*re he] He in maner B[2], J, CC.—pyte and] a Ch, H[1], C[1], C[2], H[3], H[4], H[2], Ash[1], L, An, H[5], H[6], Ad[2], B[3], B[4], Lg; om. B[2], J, CC; ȝyt a Hn[1] 46. To se his modyr so wepe in hir rage, H[7].—se] om. D, 47. put his hande] his hande put H[6].—vnto] to B[1], C[2], H[6], B[4]. 48. On] Of CC.— passyngly] passyng C[3], Adv[2]; so passyng H[8]. 49. made] he made B[1]. 50. Withoutyn] With C[1]. 51. to] on to C[1].—motherly] moder L. 52. conceyved] conceyveth Ch, Co, Hn[1], H[3], H[4], Ash[1], L, An, H[5], H[7], H[8], Ad[2], C[5], B[3], B[4], Lg, Hu; conseyving H[1], Adv[2]. 53. and] om. B[2], J, CC, H[5].—than] om. C[1].—a-noon] om. B[1]. 54. so fayre] fayre H[1]; fayre so Hu; so fayre and free Hn[1].—see] be Adv[2]. 55. considret] considere H[1], H[5]; considereth H[8]; to considre H[2]; conseyvid C[1]. 56. her] om. L.—wonder] wondred Ch; wonderly C[3].

Sche toke hym vp *and* preide him be styll,

As of modris is pleinly the man*e*re,

And he in all obeythe to her wille,

60   Though he wer yong, and gan to chaunge his chere.

And w*ith* hir kerchefe she made his eyne clere,

On his chekes, in all that eu*e*re she may,

Ful modurly the ters sche wypte away.

Howe in iiii man*er*
of wyse criste was
circu*m*cised as Alquyn
saythe Ca° lxi°[1] 2[m]

And lyke as Alquyn wryt, it is devysede

    That criste Ih*esus*, who-so luste to see,

In four man*e*re was truly circumsisede;

Firste of his fader at his Natyvyte,   i

Withe the knyfe of wilfull poverte;

And nowe this day, whiche is not fenyde,   ii

70   Eke w*ith* a knyf bi þe lawe ordeyned;

---

57. Sche toke hym vp *and* preide him be stille, H7.—preide] pray D. 58. As of modris is pleinly the man*e*re, H7.—is pleinly is D. 59. he in all] in all B1; he in all manere B2, J, CC. 60. wer] was H1, J.—and] om. H1, J; he C1.—gan] began B1, H6; om. B4. —to] om. L, B4.—chaunge] down H1; changid B4; geange CC.—his] om. Co, C1, C3, B5, H7, H8, Ad3, Adv2, Hu. 61. made] wypid C1.—his] is B1. 62. On] Ande B1 H7; Of C1; Ande on B3.—in] om. C2.—all] om. L.—eu*e*re] om. B1, C2. 63. Ful modurly the ters sche wypte away, B1.—sche] om. D. 65. so] om. H2; evere B1; that H8.—to see] take hede and see H2. 66. In four man*e*re was truly] In foure maner was B1, C1; Was in foure manere B2, J. CC; In four maner trewly was C2; That four maner wise was truly H2; In foure maner of wise was truly Ash1; In four manerys he was L. 67. Firste] The firste B1, H7, Adv2, Hu.—fader] moder Adv2.—at] and J. 68. the] a H2, H6.—wilfull] om. Adv2. 69. whiche] which that Hn1.—is] it Hu. 70. Eke w*ith* a knyf bi þe lawe ordeyned, H7.—þe] om. D.

---

[1]crossed through

The thred man*e*re, ye may eke considre, iii

How with the knyfe of grete adu*e*rsyte,

That he was kyt firste whan he cam hyddre,

Takyng for vs his humanyte;

And alther laste, w*ith* full grete cruelte, iiii

For vs he suffrede circu*m*cision

Vpon the crosse duryng his passion.

How criste suffred circu*m*cision in his chosin peple Ca° lxii°¹ 3ᵐ

80 A lso in four man*e*re, who-so can take hede,

Criste in his chosen by gode inspection,

Her in this worlde, w*ith*-oute any drede,

Of newe he suffreth circumcision.

The firste is made by fals detraction i

That kytteth away bothe frende and fame,

And the shynyng, of her gode name.

---

71. The] And the B². — ye may eke] eke we may B¹; eke is to B²; ye may H²; is eke to J, CC; ye may also Adv², H², Hu. 72. with] that C¹, CC, H⁸. — knyfe] kynge CC. — grete] om. L, B³. 73. kyt firste] first but C¹; kitte with L. B³. — he] om. Ch, Ad², C⁵, Adv². — hyddre] there H⁶. 74. his] oure Ch, B², H¹, C¹, C², H³, H⁴, Ash¹, An, H⁶, Ad², C⁵, B⁴, Lg; here B¹, H⁸; here his Co, C³, B⁵, H⁷, Ad³, Adv², Hu. 75. alther laste] at the last B¹, Co, C¹, Hn¹, H⁷, Adv², Hu. — w*ith* full] with B¹, H⁷; full of H¹. 76. suffrede] suffreth H⁴, An. 78. And] om. Ch, B¹, B², Co, H¹, C¹, C², C³, B⁵, Hn¹, H³, H⁴, H², Ash¹, L, J, An, CC, H⁵, H⁶, H⁷, H⁸, Ad³, Ad², Adv², C⁵, B³, B⁴, Lg. — eke] also B¹, H⁷, Adv², Hu. — man*e*re] manere wyse B²; maner was CC. 79. Criste] om. H¹, Hn¹, H². — cheson] cheldrin C¹; chosen peple Co. 80. Her in] Or ellis in CC. — oute] om. Adv². — any] om. Ch, B¹. 81. Of] Al B³; Atte L. — he] om. Ch. — suffreth] suffered B¹, B², C¹, C², Hn¹, H², Ash¹, H⁸, Adv², Hu. — circumcision] a circumcision B¹, Co, H¹, B⁵, H⁸, H⁷, Ad³, Adv², Hu. 84. shynyng] shewynge Co, B⁵.

---

¹crossed through.

    ii   The secunde is by fals tyrannye,   f. 69b

               Of suche that haue noo concyence at all,

               But take the aweye by cursyd Robberye,

               Vnrightfully, her godes temporall.

    iii   And the thryde is, sothely most mortall:

90   Of herytykes that falsely disobey

               To holy chirche and to our faythe verrey.

    iiii   The fourt is made by effusion of blode,

               By tyrantes that the body slethe,

               When thay of malice ayayne the faythe be **wode**

               To execute her venyme vp by dethe,

               To make marters yelden vp the brethe;

               Whome criste Ihesu, eternally in **glorye**,

               Ordeyned hath a palme of victorie.

---

85. is] om. CC.—by] the C¹. 86. that haue] as hath B², C², B⁵, CC, H⁶; that hath Co, C¹, H⁷, H⁸, Ad³, Hu; as have H¹. 87. takethe] taken B¹, C³, L, B³.—cursyd] fals C¹. 88. Vnrightfully] Unworthily B¹; Unrightful Ch, CC. 89. is sothely] sothly is Ch, B², C², H³, H⁴, Ash¹, L, J, An, CC, H⁵, H⁶, Ad², C⁵, B⁴, Lg; othis C¹; sothly Hn¹.— mortall] temporall J; of all CC. 90. disobey] doth obey Co, B⁵. 91. holy] foule the C¹.—and to] of C¹; and B⁵; and fro CC.—verrey] verely C¹. 93. slethe] doith sleeth B¹. 94. of] bi H².—faythe] fourth C³.—be] er H¹. 95. vp] upon hem L; upon the CC; up hem B³. 96. make] om. H², Lg.—yelden] to yelden Ch, B¹, B², H¹, C¹, C², Hn¹, H¹, H⁴, Ash¹, J, An, CC, H⁵, H⁶, H⁷, Ad², C⁵, B⁴, Lg; that yelden H².—the] her B², H¹, J. 97. Whome] Whan B², CC.—Ihesu] om. B², CC. 98. Ordeyned hath a palme of victorie, B¹.—of] of his D.

How criste shedde his
blode V tymeȝ in his   100
manhode Caº lxiiiº¹ 4ᵐ

E ke ·V· tymes criste in his manhede
Shed his blodely effusion.

And alther firste, when he dyd blede

   i   Vpon the day of circumcision;

And next, in sothe, to-fore his **passyon,**

   ii   Vpon the hyll for anguysche when he **swette**

The rede blode, whiche all his body wette;

   iii.   The thryde tyme, his blode moste vertuouse

Gan rynne oute by many a cruell wounde,

Whan that he was, this kyng moste **graciouse,**

Of the Iewes to a pyler bounde;

   iiii. 110 The fourt tyme eke, as it is founde,

He spent his blode for our alther goode,

   v.   When he was nayled high vpon the rode;

---

99. Eke] Also Adv²; Also I fynd Hu.—.V. tymes criste] Cryste fyve tymes C¹; fyve tymes
Crist Ihesu Lg. 100. by effusion] by affeccioune C¹; four our redempcioun L, B³; by full
effusion Hu. 101. alther firste] first of alle B¹, Co, C³, B⁵, H⁷, H⁸, Ad³, Adv², Hu; atte
last C¹; aldirlast Ad².—he] that he Hn¹. 102. Vpon] On B¹.—of] of his B¹, Co, C³, B⁵,
H⁴, H⁷, H⁸, Ad³, Adv², Hu; of the C¹. 103. And] And the B¹, C³, B⁵, H⁷, H⁸, Ad³, Hu.—in
sothe] forsoth C¹.—to fore] before Adv². 104. Vpon] For uppon B², J, CC.—for] of H².—
he] om. Lg.—swette] om. H¹; smert C¹. 105. The] With the CC.—whiche] w B²; with C²,
C³, J; om. H², CC.—body wette] we C¹. 107. Gan] Began H⁶; can CC.—oute] ower Ch;
doun H²; om. Ash¹.—a] om. Co, H¹, C², C³, B⁵, H², H⁵, H⁷, H⁸, Ad³, Adv², Lg, Hu, V.
108. that] om. B¹.—this] the B¹, B², Co, C³, B⁵, H⁴, H², J, CC, H⁷, H⁸, Ad³, Adv², Hu.—
kyng] ginge H⁷. 109. to] was to H⁶.—bounde] was bounde Adv²; y-bounde L, B³. 110.
fourt] fryste CC.—eke] om. C², CC; also Hu. 111. his] al his Hn¹.—blode] good C¹.—our
alther] our alles B¹; all oure Ash¹. 112. high] om. B¹, L, Ad³, Adv².—vpon] on B¹, H⁸,
Ad³.—the] the high Ad³.

---

¹crossed through

And alther laste, whan Longeus a-ferre,

Thorugh his hert, playnely as I fynde,

On Caluery hym perced wit*h* a spere,

That blode and water, as bokes maken mynde,

Gan streme dovne to his eyne blynde;

By whose vertu a-noon this paynym knyght,

Only of grace, recouerede hathe his sight.

120   And in bokes, eke as it is tolde,   f. 70a

How the pece of his Incision

Was by an Angell, in an vrne of golde

To Charles brought in a vysyon.

And he a-noon, of grete affection

Of this myracle, for the excellence

Made it be kept for grete reuerence

---

113. alther] at the last H¹, C¹, C². 115. perced] perisshed H², H⁶, B³. 116. That] The B², J.—maken] maketh Ch, Co, C², B⁵, Ash¹, J, Ad², B⁴. 117. Gan] Began H⁶; con Adv².—dovne] adoun CC.—to] tyll CC.—his] om. C¹. 118. whose] hoo ys CC.—vertu] voyce vertu H⁶.—this] the C³.—paynym] paynynge Hu. 119. recouerede hathe] hath recovered L, Adv²; recoverid H¹; recover CC. 120. bokes] his bokes C²; a boke J.—eke] also Hu. 121. the] his Ash¹.—pece] peces Hu.—his] this B², J, CC.—his Incision] Cristis vision H¹; his in seschon CC. 122. by an] by V.— in an vrne] man bren Co; man wyne C¹; in a vessel Hn¹; in an urynal H².— of] and C¹. 124. of] in a C. 125. the] hye H⁶; the grete B², CC. 126. Made] Or had Lg.—be] om. Ch, B¹.—for] with H¹; in L, CC; for the Ch.

At aquys grene, but yf bokes lye,

Full many yere by revolucion,

In a chirche, sothely, of marye.

130　But Clerkes han an oypnyon

That in þe day of resurreccion,—

Whan criste Ihesu roos fro dethe to lyfe,—

The same pece retournede as blyfe

To the place where that it cam froo,

Sythen that it was, sothely as I fynde,

Of his manhede pertenyng therto,

And a partye longyng to his kynde;

Though it so be that bokeȝ maken mynde

That it in Rome is as yet reservede,

140　And yere by yere, whan this fest is seruede,

---

127. At] And H⁷. 128. many] many a B¹, B², Hn¹, H⁴, H², L, An, CC, H⁷, Ad³, Ad², C⁵, B³, Lg. 129. chirche] chayre H⁶. 130. han] have Co, C², C³, B⁵, H², J, CC, H⁶, H⁷, Ad³; yit have H¹; hath C¹.—an] om, C¹. 131. That in þe day of resurreccion, H⁷. —of] of his D, C², H⁶, Ash¹. 132. criste Ihesu] Ihesu Crist Ch. 133. retournede] turned B¹, B².—as also Ch, J, CC, H⁸, Adv², C²; als Co, H³, An, H⁵, H⁷, Ad³, Ad², B⁴, Lg, Hu; as is H¹.—blyfe] blithe H⁷; by lyve Adv². 134. where] om. B⁴.—that] as H¹; om. L.—it] om. C². 135. that] om. B¹, B², H¹, C², J, CC, H⁷, H⁸, Lg.—it] as B². 136. his] thys Adv².—pertenyng] and perteynynge B², CC; apeteynynge H¹. 137. partye] part H¹. 138. so] om. B¹.—bokeȝ] boke Ash¹.—maken] maketh H¹. 139. it in Rome is as yet] in Rome it is as yet Co, B¹, Hn¹, C⁵, H⁷, Ad³, Adv², Hu; in Rome it is yet C², H⁸, C³; it in Rome is yet Ch, H¹, C¹, H³, H⁴, H², J, An, H⁶, Ad², C⁵; it in Rome yit is B², CC; yit in Rome is B⁴; in Rome is as yit Lg.—reservede] preserved Ch, B², C¹, H³, H⁴, Ash¹, L, J, An, CC, H⁵, H⁶, Ad², C⁵, B³, B⁴, Lg. 140. And yere] And there H¹, C³, H², H⁸.—this] the Co, B⁵, Hn¹, J, CC, Lg.

In a chirche, whiche men of custome calle

S*an*cta sanctor*um*, of olde fundacion,

The same day ther, the preste3 all

Solempynly make a stacion,

Whanne alle the peple gon on processioun,

Fully in hope the better for to spede,

Fro yere to yere, ther thay syng and rede.

And ferthermore, the story dothe devyse,

The same day, right furthe-w*ith* a-noon,

150   In the Temple, as they hym circu*m*cise,

He namede was Ih*e*sus of Ichon;

The whiche name, long or that agon,

Was of the Angell tolde and sayde afore

To his modur or that he were bore.

141. whiche] om. H². that L.—of] on B¹. 142. of] by Adv.². 143. ther] om. C¹.—the preste3] prestes B⁴; the lordis B², J, CC. 144. make] made B², Hn¹; there make B⁵.—a] there Ash¹. 145. Whanne alle the peple gon on processioun, B¹.—gon] gothe D, C¹, C³.—on] a D; on a B⁴.—Whanne alle] While CC.—peple] preestes H⁶. 146. the] om. L, Adv².—for to] to B¹. 147. ther] whan CC.—syng] do singe L. 148. devyse] devised H⁶. 149. The same day right furthe-w*ith* a-noon, B¹.—The] This D. 150. the] the the C¹.—as] as as Ad²; when C¹.— hym] hym dyd Adv². 151. namede was] was named H¹.—Ichon] everychon B¹, Adv². 152. or] ere H⁸.—that] om. H⁸.—agon] gon Ash¹. 153. the] an H¹, C³.—afore] before B¹, B², CC; to fore C¹. 154. To his modur or that he were bore, B¹.—were] was D.

Howe the peple of god
that duke Iosue had in
gouernaunce were saved
by the stedefaste by leve
of the name of Ihesus
Ca° lxiv°¹ 5ᵐ

O ne to reherse, the grete worthynesse   f. 70b

Of this name, whiche may nat be discrivede

My wittes been so dull, with rudnesse

160 And in the cheynes of ignoraunce gyvede

That I alas, of conyng, am depryvede

Thorough lak of witte, on eny manere wyse

To vndirfong, so passyng high empryse

For this is the name, who so can discerne

Most excellent, and moste of dignyte

The name of names, sacred from eterne

As saythe Bernarde, who so lust to see

Fygured firste, vnto Iosue

Thorough his knyghthode, whan that he shulde lede

The peple of god, to saue hem in her nede

---

155. the] to B³.—grete] hy H². 156. this] the Lg.—not] om. H⁴.—discrivede] dissevered Ash¹. 157. dull] dulled B⁵, L, B³.—with] of C³, H².—dull with] full of CC. 158. And] om. C³.— gyvede] y-gyved B¹, H², CC, H⁷, Ad³. 159. I] om. B², J, CC.—am] I am B², J, CC; an Co. 160. on] in V.—eny] every B¹, Co, C³, B⁵, Hn¹, Adv²; many L, H⁶. 161. vndirfong] undir- stonde Ch, H¹, Hu.—so] the L, B³.—passyng] wondre H²; om. H⁶.—high] hys Ch; an hye B¹, Co, B⁵, H⁷, Ad³, Adv², Hu; hie an H⁶; and high Hn¹. 162. This and the following stanza have been transposed by the Durham scribe. All other MSS have the order of the text above. MS. H⁶ transposes lines 162 and 169 only. 162. is] om. L.—who so can] who that can B²; who can so H⁸; who so gan Ash¹. 163. and] famous and B², CC. 164. The name] That L.—from] om. C². 165. saythe] seynt B²; seyth sent B¹, CC. 166. vnto] to CC; unto good Hn¹; unto duke H². 167. that] om. B¹, H¹, C², Hn¹, H², Ash¹; the B², Co. 168. hem] he An.—in] at B², J, CC.

---

¹crossed through

Howe the name of
Ihesus is moste   170
souerayne medycyne
ayenst all manere of
maladye Ca° lxvᵗᵒ

For this is the name that herteȝ most **desyre**;

Ther is ther-in so passyngly Swetnesse.

For it may best hem w*ith* grace enspyre,

And wit*h* plentee of all gostly richesse.

It is comforte and socour in sekenesse,

Refute also, reste and remedye

To all thoo that felen maladye;

Ayenste langour the beste medycyne,

In all this worlde that owher may be fou*n*de.

For this name is so hevenly and dyvyne,

That herteȝ seke it dothe w*ith* hele habou*n*de.

180   It curythe sores, it helyth eu*er*y wou*n*de,

And savethe men fro many a swerde and spere,

Wher thay ryde in perel ny or fere.

---

169. is] om. H¹. 170. Ther is ther-in] For ther ynne ys Ch, C², Hn¹, H³, H⁴, H², Ash¹, L, An, H⁵, H⁶, Ad², C⁵, B³, B⁴, Lg; For ther nys B², J, CC; For there inne Co; For this is the name of C¹.—so] no CC.—passyngly] passyng C¹, C², C³, H⁶, H⁸, C⁵.— Swetnesse] a swetnes H⁶. 171. best hem w*ith* grace] best with grace hem B¹, C³, H⁷, H⁸, Ad³, Adv², Hu; best with grace Lg, C¹; best in grace hem B⁵; hem best with grace L. 172. all] om. B¹, Hu. 173. in] of all B¹.—sekeness] swetnesse H¹. 174. Refute] Refuge H¹. 175. thoo] them C¹.—felen] fallen in C².—maladye] melodye C¹. 176. the beste] eke H²; the Lg. 177. worlde] om. CC.—owher] ever H¹; oure L; owere CC; man C¹.—be fou*n*de] fynd C¹. 178. so] om. Ch, B². 179. herteȝ] herte H².—it] om. C³.—hele] helth H¹, B¹, H⁶; help C¹; here H². 180. sores] om. Hn¹.—it helyth] and heleth B², J, CC.—eu*er*y] many a H⁶; every maner Hn¹. 181. men] man Ch, C¹, H³, H⁴, H², Ash¹, An, H⁵, H⁶, Ad², C⁵, B⁴, H¹.—many a] maym of Ch, C¹, H³, H⁴, H², Ash¹, An, H⁵, H⁶, Ad², C⁵, B⁴, H¹; mayne of C³; mayne a H¹.—and] or C¹, H⁵. 182. Wher] Whethir H¹; Where ever Ch, B¹, B², Co, C¹, C², C³, Hn¹, H³, H⁴, Ash¹, L, An, CC, H⁵, H⁶, H⁷, H⁸, Ad³, Ad², C⁵, Adv², B³, B⁴, Lg, Hu; Where every J; Where that H².—ryde] ben H⁶.—in perel ny or fere] on londe fer or nere Ch, C¹, C²; in londe fer or nere B², H³, H⁴, Ash¹, L, An, CC, H⁵, Ad², C⁵, B⁴, Lg; in lond ferre and nere J; in lond fer and or nere B³; in lond fer ne nere H⁶; in perell or in were Hn¹; or go night or ferre H¹; in perill or in fere B¹.

Cap. 6ᵐ 4 lib.
How thys name
Iesus is medycine
for all maladyes¹

It is first wryten in the boke of lyfe,

For worthyest and most of reuerence;

And it is eke best *preseruatyfe*

Ayene the assaut and the violence

Of wykkede eayre, to voyde pestelence.

And from the dethe, hem that plenyn sore,

Of his vertu to helthe it dothe restore.

190   It is also sothefaste saluacion   f. 71a

To all that ben in pou*er*t and in nede;

It is defence, it is *protection*

In yche p*er*ell and in eu*er*y drede.

It is also the guerdoun and the mede

To hem that ben in exile, of outerage,

Repayre fynall of hir pilgrimage.

---

183. is] om. CC.—first] om. H¹, H⁶. 184. For] For the Ch, B¹, B², C¹, Ash¹, J. 185. eke] the C¹; also Hu.—best] highest H⁸. 186. the assaut] the ascent B², J, CC, H⁶; thassaust Co; the saute C².—and the] of C¹; and B², J, CC, H⁶. 187. wykkede] whiche Co.—eayre] awe CC.—to] forto CC. 188. And] om. Ch.—from the] for H¹; from Co. —hem] they C¹, Ash¹. 189. to helthe] it helpis H¹; to helpe B², Hn¹, J, CC.—it dothe] to H¹. 190. It] He H¹.—aslo] all H⁸. 191. all] all thoo B², J, CC; hem also C¹. and in] or in B¹, Ad³; and B², J, CC, C³. 193. and in] and H², J. eu*er*y] eche B¹.—drede] nede H¹. 194. guerdoun] rewarde B¹, Hn¹; gardeyne H⁸.—and the] of every L. 195. exile of] excelle of Co; excell CC; exile and H⁸. 196. Repayre] Repent CC.—hir pilgrimage] all good dede H¹.

¹Marginal gloss in a later hand.

Howe the name of Ihe*s*us
is likenyd to iiij stremys
that refressheth all
Realmys Ca°lxvj^{t°1} 7^m

I

ii

iii

iiii

i

$\begin{array}{ll} & \text{I}t \text{ is the well } with \text{ the foure stremes,}\\ & \quad \text{Wher-of Bernard wrytyth in sentence,} \end{array}$

200   That thorughe the worlde refressheth al Remys,

It is so holsome and of suche excellence.

The firste he calleth the streme of sapyence,

Of whiche the floode most inly is habounde;

And Rightwysnesse he namethe the secounde;

And the thryde he calleth holynesse,

For it excellyth in *p*erfection;

The fourthe also, as I can well expresse,

Is the floode of our Redempcion.

And of the firste, in conclusion,

Of whiche the streme3 bene so fresshe and fyne,

210   Who so loke aright, is holy our doctryne.

---

197. It] this Ch, B², C¹, C², C³, B⁵, Hn¹, Ash¹, H³, H⁴, H², L, J, An, CC, H⁵, H⁶, Ad²,
C⁵, B³, B⁴, Lg.—with] that C¹; of CC.—foure] om. Ash¹. 198. Bernard wrytyth] Writ
Bernard Ch, C¹, C², Ash¹, L, J, An, H⁴, H⁵, H⁶, Ad², C⁵, B³, B⁴, Lg, V; Writ seynt
Bernard B², CC.—in] in his Ch, C², H⁴, H², Ash¹, L, J, An, H⁵, H⁶, Ad², C⁵, B³, B⁴,
Lg, V; his C¹. 199. thorugh] om. Hn¹.—the worlde] om. Ash¹. 200. It] He B².—so] om.
B², C¹, Hn¹. 201. he calleth] is callid C¹. 202. is] om. B¹, CC. 203. namethe] named B²,
C¹, J, CC. 204. he calleth] is callid C¹; he callyd CC.—holynesse] also holynesse Hn¹;
holsomnesse Lg. 206. also as] om. Hn¹; so as CC; also B¹, Co, C¹, C², C³, B⁵, H², H⁷,
H⁸, Ad³, Adv², Hu.—well] om. B², H¹, C¹, C²; now ri3t well Hn¹. 207. Is] To H¹; It
is Ad³, Adv²; Is in B¹; That is B², J, CC; In the C¹; For hit is Hn¹.—flode] flome B²,
J; floure CC.—our] om. C¹. 208. of] om. Hn¹. 209. Of] Of the C².—the] om. H¹; al the
C².—streme3] armys C².—bene so] ben C², J, CC; be as C². 210. so] om. H¹.—holy our]
our holi B¹, H¹; holy Lg.

---

¹crossed through

And of his Right, to make mencion,

The holsome welle ay dothe flowe and flete,

W*ith* mercy medled and remyssion,

Tofore his dome his Ire forto lete.

And of the thryde, the water is so swete,

By gode ensa*m*ple, who so can disserne,

In vertu aye how we shull vs gou*er*ne.

And of the foruthe, to speke in speciall,

Is all our helthe and our saluacion;

220 For ther-in is our remedye fynall

A3enste dethe and full p*r*otection;

Whos floode sprong oute of crist*es* passion.

And who that liste, by water to atame,

He shall it fynde enclosede in this name.

---

211. And] om. C³.—of his] of this H¹; thereof C¹; of the H²; of C³.—Right] aright H¹; om. C¹; ryghtwysnesse C³, Hn¹; secunde H².—to] forto C¹.—mencion] of mencioun C³. 213. With] Whiche H⁷.—and] and eke H¹; in H⁶. 214. forto lete] to lete Ch, C²; forlete C¹. 216. By gode ensa*m*ple who so can disserne, H⁷.—so] that D. 217. vertu] om. C¹.—ay] ever B¹, H⁷, H⁸, Ad³, Adv², Hu, Co; om. B², B⁵, J, CC; woo C¹.—vs] om. H¹. 219. Is] In C¹.— our] om. C¹.—helthe] help H².—our] eke H²; om. Ch, Co, C¹, C², C³, B⁵, Hn¹, H³, H⁴, Ash¹, L, J, An, H⁵, H⁶, H⁷, H⁸, Ad³, Ad², C⁵, Adv², B³, B⁴, Lg, Hu. 220. in] om. C¹, Lg.—fynall] om. H⁶; speciall Ch. 221. and] and a C¹.—full] fall Ch. 222. floode] blood Ch, B¹, B², Co, C¹, C², C³, B⁵, H³, H⁴, Ash¹, J, An, CC, H⁵, H⁶, H⁷, H⁸, Ad³, Ad², C⁵, Adv², B⁴, Lg, Hu.—sprong oute] spring but C². 223. that] so B¹, C¹, C², C³, B⁵, CC.— by] that H¹. 224. enclosede] closed Ch, B¹, B², Co, C², B⁵, H³, H⁴, Ash¹, J, An, H⁶, Ad², C⁵, B⁴, Lg.—this] the Ch, B², C², H³, H⁴, Ash¹, J, An, CC, H⁶, Ad², C⁵, B⁴, Lg; his Co, B⁵, H².

Of perfyte Ryches, it is tresourye,   f. 71b

Whiche may nat wast but iliche abyde.

The fyre it quencheth also of envye,

And repressith the bolyng eke of pryde,

And thorugh mekenesse setteth Ire asyde.

230   And who that hathe this name in Remembraunce,

The spryt of slouthe hym may do no greuaunce.

It is also the myghty pavys fayre

Ayenst wanhope and desperacion;

Cristall schelde of pallas for dispayre,

Ther-of to voyde the foule abusion.

And who that makyth his inuocacion

To this name *with* hert and stablenesse,

It yevethe hym strength, it yeuyth hym sikernesse

---

225. tresourye] the tresoure B², L, J, B³; tresour Ch, C², H³, H⁴, An, H⁵, Ad², C⁵, Adv², B⁴, Lg; tresour sikerly H². 226. iliche] a liche B¹; ay liche B⁵, H², Adv²; ever iliche B², J, CC; ever to H². 227. it] om. C¹; is Ash¹, B⁴.—quencheth] quenchid Ash¹, B⁴.—also] om. B¹.—envye] envie the erroure B², J; envie in the errowre CC. 228. repressith] reprochit CC.—the bolyng eke] eke the bollynge B¹, C², Ash², CC, H⁶; the blowing eke C¹; the bollynges eke B⁵; eke the boluyng eke H³; the boluyng also Hu. 229. setteth] set C¹; putteth H⁸. 230. who] who so C¹, H⁶.—this] his C¹.— Remembraunce] remembrance ave Ch. 231. The spryt of slouthe hym] Hym the spirite of slouthe Ch, B¹, B², H³, H⁴, H², Ash¹, L, J, An, CC, H⁵, H⁶, Ad², C⁵, B³, B⁴, Lg. —no] him no B¹, H⁸; do no maner Hn¹. 232. the myghty] myghty it Adv².—pavys] pathys B¹, Co, C¹, C², B⁵, Hn¹, H², H⁷, H⁸, Ad³, Adv², Hu. 233. Ayenst] And ayenst B², J, CC. 234. for] for to Hn¹; afore H². 235. to voyde] to avoyde Ch, H¹, C², C³, H³, H⁴, H², Ash¹, J, CC, C⁵, B⁴, Lg; tavoide Ash².—abusion] ambusion B¹, B², H⁸; ambicioun Hn¹. 236. makyth] make H¹, Ash².—his] this Ch, H⁷; in his B¹; om. C¹.— inuocacion] convocacion CC. 237. this] hys Ad².—and] om. Ch; of B², C¹, Ash², Hn¹, H³, H⁴, H², Ash¹, L, J, An, CC, H¹, H⁵, H⁶, Ad², C⁵, B³, B⁴, Lg. 238. strength it yeuyth] strength and also H¹, Ash²; strength and eke L, B³; strength and C²; strength and eke H².—sikernesse] sekenesse H¹, Ash², L, B³.

The cruell fyre and brennyng to w*ith*-stande

240 Of lechery and all temptacion.

It is refute to fre and eke to bonde,

That haue ther-in her hole affection;

Whose vertu was to kyng Salamon,

Full long afforn in dyvyne oracle,

As I fynde, shewede by myracle.

How prophete3 and martirs suffrede deth for the name of Ih*esu*s Ca° lxvii° 8ᵐ

This is the name of *prophete3* specifiede

In her writynge ande in her boockes oolde;

Of aposteles most hyly magnyfied,

By whose vertu thay the trouthe tolde.

250 This made also matris to be bolde,

And myghtyly like sterne champyons,

W*ith* stable herte to suffre her passions.

---

239. and] of C¹.—to] om. Adv². 240. and] and of H², Ash¹, Hu; om. B¹, C¹.—all] alle the B¹, C¹; the B², J, CC; om. Ash; all other H⁶. 241. eke] om. B¹, Ash²; also Hu. 242. That] To CC.—her] om. B⁵, H³; there in H⁸.—hole] full Co, C³, B⁵, H⁷, Ad³, Adv², Hu; a full H⁸. 243. was] om. B², J, CC. 244. afforn] om. H¹, Ash².—in] in full CC. 245. I] om. H¹, C¹.—shewede] is wryten C¹.—myracle] meoneracle CC. 246. of] that Ash², C², C³, H⁸.—prophete3] prophecies Ash¹.—specifiede] prophesied B¹, B², CC; speciall Ch, C¹, H³, H⁴, An, H⁶, Ad², C⁵, B⁴. 247. In her writynge ande in her boockes oolde, B¹.—in] om. D. 248. Of aposteles moost hyly magnified, B¹.—hyly] high D; holy H¹, Ash¹. 249. the] that H¹, Ash². 250. This] Thei Lg.—made] name H².—martris] materes Co; vertues C². 251. myghtyly] myghti B², Co, C¹, C², C³, B⁵, Hn¹, H², L, An, H⁸, Adv², B³.

By this name they were victoryouse,

In her torment pacience to haue.

This is the name that ignacious

Had in his hert of golde full depe grave;

Wher of the Tyraunte gretly gan abave,

Whan that he sawe his hert kytte atweyne,

And letters newe depicte in eu*er*y veyne.

260   This is the name that to confessours   f. 72a

Was full repast in her abstynence;

This is the name that in sharpe shoures

Of flesshely luste was holy her defence.

It ȝaf hem myght to make resistence

Ayene synne, and knyghtly to werreye,

And to contynue in vertu tyll thay deye.

---

253. this] his Ash². —they] the C¹. 254. torment] tormentis C¹, H²; turnement B¹, B⁴, Hu. —pacience] passyng penance H². 256.] In gold depe hadde in his hert y-grave Ch. —his] om. H¹, H², Ash². —golde] good gold B², J, CC. —full] om. H³, H⁴, An, H⁶, Ad², C⁵, B⁴. 257. gretly gan] gan hym sore Ch, B², H³, H⁴, Ash¹, L, J, An, H⁵, H⁷, Ad², C⁵, B³, B⁴, Lg; gan hym C²; gan Ash²; soon gan Hn¹; gan sore H²; gan hym self sore CC; began hym sore H⁶; gan gretly H⁸; gretly con Adv². 258. that] om. B¹, C³, B⁵, Hu. —saw his hert] was this H⁸. 259. newe] now H⁸. —in] on H³, H⁶. —veyne] payne Adv². 260. to] so H⁸; the C²; om. B¹, B², H¹, J, CC, Ad²; *inserted above.* 261. Was] With B², J, CC. —repast] replete C². 262. is] om. Ash². —in] in the H¹, Ash², L, B³. 263. Of] Was H²; Fro H⁶. —luste] om. H⁸. 264. It] That Ch, Ash¹. —make] make hem Ch, Ash¹. 265. and] om. H¹, Ash², Adv². —knyghtly] myghtyly B¹, B². —werreye] waradie B², CC. 266. to] om. C¹.

How prophete3 preste3
and kyng*es* and myghty
men were anoynted
Ca° lxviii°²

It is the fest *and* the sugred foode

Of maydenhode and of virgynyte;

The oyle of grace, holsom to all gode,

270 Whiche in the lampes of p*er*fyte chastyte,

Brynnyng so clere w*ith* loue and charyte,

That wordly wyndes, boystous in blowyng,

Ne may nat quenche the light of his shynyng.

This is the name that moste yeveth melodye

Vnto the eere, and the swettest son.

It is the name of hevynly Armonye,

To avoyde synne and all temptacion,

W*ith* full accorde ayenst dyuysyon.

It causeth hertes no langer to debate,

280 That partyde werne thorwe the wrest of hate.

---

267. It is the fest *and* the sugred foode, B¹.—the] om. D, Co, B⁵, H⁸. Ad³. 268. and of]
and Ch. 269. of] and Ch. 269. of] of all CC.—holsom] fulsome H⁶.—to all] to CC. 270.
Whiche] With C².—the] om. L.—chastyte] charite H⁶. 271. and] of Hn¹.—charyte] chastite
H⁶. 272. worldly] worldis H¹.—in] and B², C¹, C³, B⁵, L, J, CC, H⁶, C⁵; om. H². 273.
Ne may] Mowe L, B³.—nat] om. B¹.—his] hire Co, B⁵, Adv². 274. This] It H¹, Ash².—
moste yeveth] most Ch; giveth most C¹, Hn¹, H².—melodye] mekely H⁸. 275. and the] and
B², J, CC; and most C¹.—swettest] swetnes H¹, C¹, Ash².—son] of soun H¹, Ash², CC.
276. of] most C¹. 277. To avoyde] Tavoide Ash²; To voide oute Ch, B², C¹, C², H³, H⁴,
Ash¹, L, J, An, CC, H⁵, H⁶, Ad², C⁵, B³, B⁴, Lg.—all] om. H⁶. 279. It] That B¹.—hertes]
hert H¹.—no langer to] to longer H¹; no more to CC. 280. partyde] perced H¹, C³, Ash².—
werne] ben Ch, B², C¹, C², Hn¹, H³, H⁴, Ash¹, L, J, An, CC, H⁵, H⁶, Ad², C⁵, B³, B⁴,
Lg.—thorwe] with Ch, B², C¹, C², Hn¹, H³, H⁴, Ash¹, L, J, An, CC, H⁵, H⁶, Ad², C⁵,
B³, B⁴, Lg, H¹, C³, H².

---

¹crossed through

This name is Ioye of soroughfull in distresse,

Eternall mede of hem that levyn in blisse,

Salue vnto hem that langour in sekenesse,

Vesture in colde to hem that clothes mysse,

Souerayne repaste, hungry for to wysse,

For to escape the cruell violence

Of nedys swerde, whetted wi*th* Indygence.

Criste is a name of sothefast sacrament,

That first was yeue of holy vnction.

290   And he was callede cryst for this entent.

For he for man shuld make oblacion.

And for he came for our saluacion,

To scour a-waye the rust of all our blame,

He hathe *of* Ih*e*sus worthyly the name.

---

281. is] of B², J, CC.—Ioye] joyeful B¹.—of] to C¹, Adv².—in] om. CC, H⁶. 282. Eternall]
Eterne CC.—mede] made Ch, Hn¹, J, An; medee L.—of] to B¹, B², Ash¹, CC; unto J.—
levyn] ben C², H⁶. 283. Salue] Glad C¹.—vnto] to H¹, Ash², CC.—langour] lyven H⁴, An.
284. in colde to hem] to hem in colde H², Ash¹. 285.] Of the right way that they not mysse L,
B³.—for to] to B¹.—wysse] lysse Ash². 286. For to] And forto B¹, C³, H⁸, Ad³, Adv², Hu;
And to Co, B⁵.—cruell] carnell H². 287. nedys] medys C³; nede is H⁴.—whetted] whiche B²,
J, CC; om. H⁶; whettyng Adv²; swetted Hu.—with] of CC. 288. Criste] And Criste B¹;
Cristis J, CC.—is] om. J, CC.—a] the Ch, C², H³, H⁴, H², Ash¹, An, H⁵, H⁶, Ad², C⁵, B⁴,
Lg; om. B².—of] our B², CC. 289. of] to Ash¹, H⁸; for B²; in B¹. 290. And] As H⁵;
That H⁸.—he] om. B¹, C³.—cryst] first Ch, B², C², H³, H⁴, Ash¹, L, J, An, CC, H⁵, H⁶,
Ad², C⁵, B³, B⁴, Lg; crist first H².—this] the C². 291. For he] That H¹.—he man] man C³.
292. And] For H⁶.—for he] he B¹. 293. all] om. B¹, B², C¹, J, CC. 294. worthyly] ful
worthily Co, B⁵, C³, H⁷, H⁸, Adv², Hu; ful worthi B¹.—the] om. B¹; his H².

I fynde in bokeʒ of olde antiquyte,   f. 72b

In her writinge as clerkis list expresse,

How ther wer foure persones, of degre,

Some tyme a-noynt for her worthynesse:

Some for manhode, som for holynesse,

300   Wiþ obseruaunceʒ and solempnyte,

As was covenable vnto her degre.

Propheteʒ, prestes, and thay that beren crovnes

As worthy kynges, of euery region,

Anoyntede werne, and myghty champions

Withe-in palestre thrugh her high renon,

Or in Champclos, hardy as lyon,

Entre wolde some quarell to darreyne,

Singulerly, by emprise of hem tweyne.

---

295. in] bi C². —bokeʒ] boke Adv². 296. In her writinge as clerkis list expresse, H⁷. —list] list to D. 297. of] yn L, B³; of won Adv². 298. Some tyme] Whilom H¹, Ash². 299. Some for] Some of H⁸. —som] and som B¹, C¹, C³, H², H⁶, H⁷. —holynesse] worthinesse B¹, H²; nobilnesse H⁶. 300. obseraunceʒ] observance Ch, B¹, B², H¹, C¹, H³, H⁴, H², J, An, CC, H⁶, H⁸, Ad², C⁵, Adv², B³, B⁴. 301. covenable] cromycle B². —vnto] to Ch, B¹, B⁵; for H⁶. —her] his B³. 302. prestes] and prestes Co, C¹. —beren] weren B², H³, H⁴, L, J, An, CC. 303. As] And Co, C¹. —of] in Hn¹. 304. Withe in] With won Adv². —palestre] ponestre H⁸. —thrugh] with B², J, CC. —her] om. L. 306. as] as a Ch, B², H¹, C¹, C², C³, Ash², J, CC, H⁶, H⁸, Hu. —lyon] hound Ch. 308. Singulerly by enprise of hem tweyne, B¹. —by] by the D. —hem] om. D.

And crist was all, by reason as I preve,

310 Firste a prophete by holy informacion,

And by his doctryne, most worthy of byleve.

And he was eke the myghty champyon,

That syngulerly for our saluacion

Faught with the fende and had of hym victory,

Mawgre his myght, and wan the palme of glory.

And he was prest, man to reconsile,

That bansshede was oute of his herytage;

Whom a serpent falsely dyd exile,

Of fals malice in a soden rage.

320 And he was borne, only by lynage,

To ben a kyng, and by power eterne,

When he is crownede, his peple to gouerne.

---

309. And] om. C1.—all] om. L; also H6.—as I] and H8.—preve] finde B1, C3, H7; fynde
and preve C1. 310. a] of a L, B3.—holy] om. Ch, B2, H1, C1, C2, Ash1, H3, H4, H2, J, An,
CC, L, H5, H6, Ad2, C5, B3, B4, Lg, V. 311. most worthy] worthyest L.—byleve] byleve
mynde C3; lynede B1; leve B2, J, CC. 312. he] om. C1, CC, Hu.—eke] also Adv2. 314.
fende] fynde Hu.—of hym] the B1, Co, L, B3, Hu; om. C3, H7, Hn1, B5, H8, Ad3, Adv2;
of hym the B2, C1, C2, H4, J, CC, Lg. 315. wan the palme of glory] his tyrranye H2.—wan]
wan of hym Ash1; had Ad3. 317. bansshede] vanysshed Ch.—his] om. B1, Adv2. 318. Whom]
Whan Ch, H1.—falsely] om. B1; fully C3.—exile] by gile B1, L, H6, H7, B3. 319. fals]
falsly Lg.—in a] and of CC. 320. he] om. C1, H8; Criste H1, Ash2.—by] by hys Adv2. 321.
a] om. C2.—and] om. B1.—by] by his B2, J, CC. 322. When] And whan Ch, H3, J.—he is]
he was H1, Ash2; hys CC.—to] for to B1.—to gouerne] om. H3.

How crist Ihesu was
bothe prophete, preste,
kyng, and myghty
Champion
Ca° lxix°¹ x^∎

Nowe criste Ihesu, sothefaste prest and kyng,

And for mankynde most worthy werryour,

Prophete also, ande trewest in leueynge,

Be thou our helpe, be thou our socour,

And like a kyng, be thou our gouernour

And Champyon, to helpe vs in our nede,

And like a prophete, to wyssen vs and rede.

330 O criste Ihesu to the I clepe and cry,   f. 73a

Fro day to day to helpe vs and releve,

And of thy grace, vs wrecches for to gye,

That or that thou thy rightwysnesse preve,

Lat pite firste þe to mercy meue.

And or they swerde of vengeaunce vs manace,

Lat reuthe afore thy rightful dome enbrace.

---

323. Ihesu] om. CC.—prest and kyng] kynge and preste C². 324. most worthy] most worthiest
H⁷.—worthy werryour] wordly werrid C¹. 325. Prophete also ande trewest in leueynge, B¹.—
ande] om. D, B⁵, B³, L, Co. 326. helpe] om. CC. 327. a] as a Adv².—thou] om. C².—our]
a L.—gouernour] werreour governour B¹. 328. And] And a C¹.—in] at CC. 329. a] to a
Ash².—to wyssen] to wisdam CC; thu helpe Adv².—vs] om. CC, B¹, B², J.—and] and to
B¹, C¹, C². 330. O] om. C¹. 331. vs and] and us Hn¹; us and to B¹. 332. vs] thy C¹.—for
to] to C². 333. That or] And or B¹, Co, C³, B⁵, H⁸, Ad³, Hu; or CC.—that thou] thou C¹, C²,
B⁵, Ash².—thy] om. B¹. 334. Lat pite firste þe to mercy meue, H⁷.—þe to] to thy D.—
meue] preve B², J, CC. 335. And] om. B², J, CC.—thy] thow thy L. 336. reuthe] trouthe
Ch, B², Co, C¹, C², H³, H⁴, An, CC, H⁶, Ad², C⁵, B⁴, Lg; rough H¹; ryght H⁸.—thy]
the CC.—rightfull dome] right wisdom Ash², L, B³.

---

¹crossed through

For of our helpe thou art the pyler,

Ayene dispayre holy our sustynaunce;

Our strength, our myght, our refute fer *and* nere,

340   In yche p*er*ell, to save vs, fro myschaunce.

Thou art our store, and our suffysaunce

And in myscheve, whan drede wolde vs assayle,

Thou art our schelde, thou art our supportayle.

Thou art myghty, and thou art meke also,

And thou art Rightfull, and thou art mercyable,

Lambe and lyon, callede bothe twoo,   Agnus leo *et* Rex

And sothefaste kyng, whose Regne is ymmutable;

To repentant, by rygour nat vengeable,

And ay afforne, in punysshyng of thy lawe,

350   Pees to p*re*ferre, or right his swerde may drawe;

---

337. of] om. Co, H¹, C¹, B⁵, H⁸, Ad².—helpe] helthe Hn¹, H⁵; self H⁶. 338. our] thy
B⁵. 339. myght] my C¹. 340. yche] every Co, C³; om. C². 341. our store] our force
Ch, B², H¹, C¹, C², Ash², H⁴, H², Ash¹, L, J, An, CC, H⁵, H⁶, H⁷, Ad², C⁵, B³, B⁴,
Lg; force H³.—and our] and all our L, B³.—suffysaunce] sustynaunce Adv². 342. in]
om. H⁵.—drede] deth C¹.—wolde vs] us wolde Co. 343. schelde] drede CC.—thou art]
and B¹, Co, C³, B⁵, Hn¹, H², H⁷, H⁸, Ad³, Adv², Hu. 344. myghty] meke B¹, B², J,
CC.—and thou art] and Co, H⁸; thou art C¹.—meke] myghti B¹, B², J, CC; meke hert
C¹. 345. And] om. C².—thou art Rightfull] also rightful Hn¹.—and] om. C¹.—thou
art mercyable] eke merciable B¹, Hn¹, H², H⁷, Ad³; merciable C², C³; thou mercyable
H⁵. 346. Lambe] A lambe B², J, CC.—lyon] a lyon CC.—callede] y-called B², J; om.
CC; eke called Ash¹; thu art called Ad². 347. sothefaste] soth C¹. 348. repentant]
repentaunce Ch, Hn¹, H³, H⁴, H⁶, Ad², C⁵, B⁴.—rygour] reynes C¹.—not] and Ash¹;
and not CC; of H⁶.—vengeable] variabill C¹. 349. thy] the H¹, C¹, CC, H⁸, Adv², Lg.
350. p*re*ferre] preserve Ch, B², H³, H², J.—may] om. B¹, C², H⁸.

And to bryng the lost chepe ayene,

Oute of deserte vnto his pastur*e*,

That was erant, ydyll, and in veyne,

O criste Ih*e*su, of thy benyngne cure,

More Redy ay to saven and to cure

All that been sore, and scabbede eke w*ith* synne,

Rather w*ith* pyte than w*ith* reddour wynne.

N owe thou that art the verrey rightful lyne,

All this is crokede, godely to redresse,

360 All maiste of mercy all our myscheves fyne,

O criste Ih*e*su, well of all swettnesse,

Lorde of pyte, lord of Rightwysnesse,

Haue vpon vs this day compassion,

That callede is thy Circumcision.

Howe by the name of I*he*sus Synners be made rightfull Ca° lxx°[1] XI^m

De misericordia

---

353. erant] errynge Ch. 354. criste Ihesu] Ibesu crist Ch. 355. More] Modir Ch, H². —ay to saven] ay to serve H²; to save ever B¹; ever to save B², B⁵, CC, H⁷; to save C¹; to save ay C², B⁴.—and to] and Ch, H².—cure] recure B¹, C¹; lure L, B³; ensure H⁶. 356. been] om. CC.—and] om. H⁸.—eke] om. C².—with] of B⁵. 357. than w*ith* reddour] than with rigoure B¹, H¹, C², C³, B⁵, H², CC, H⁷, H⁸, Ad³, Adv²; that with reddour B²; than thou with rigour Ash²; than thow with reddour H⁶. 358. Nowe] O B³.—thou that] sith thou H¹; thowe C¹, H⁶, Hu.—the] be C¹, Hu. 360. maiste] must C¹.—all] of all CC; om. B¹, C³, B⁵, Hn¹, H⁷, H⁸, Ad³, Adv², Hu. 361. well] o well B¹, H⁷, Hu.—of all] of B¹, B², Co, C², J, CC, H⁸, H⁷, Ad³.—swettnesse] witnesse CC. 362. lord] and lorde Ch, C¹, C², C³, Ash², Hn¹, H³, H⁴, H², Ash¹, L, An, H⁵, H⁶, Ad², C⁵, B³, B⁴, Lg; o lorde B¹; and welle B², J, CC. 363. vs] om. CC. 364. callede is] ys callyd C³.

---

[1]crossed through

And graunt vs grace, withe dew reuerence,   f. 73b

This high feste, so noble and so digne,

Worship and halowe, devoyde of all offence.

And be to vs goodly and benygne,

That wer this day merkyde *with* a signe

370 And the carecte by the laws ordeynede,

And of mekenesse, haste it nat dysdeynede.   De humilitate

And so as thou that neu*er*e dydest trespasse,

Through thy mekenesse and lawly subiection,

Suffre woldeste, this day of thy grace,

For our offence, Circumcision,

So kypt from vs all temptacion

Of worldly lust, and make the flesshe to s*er*ue

To the spyryte tyl the body sterue.

---

366. This] The H³.—so digne] digne C³. 367. halowe] alowe CC.—devoyde] to voyde
Ch. 368. be] to be H⁸.—goodly] godly C². 369. wer] where Co; was B⁵; om. Hu.—
a] the Ch, B¹, Co, H¹, C¹, C³, B⁵, Ash², Hn¹, H³, H⁴, H², Ash¹, L, An, CC, H⁵,
H⁶, H⁷, H⁸, Ad³, Ad², C⁵, Adv², B³, B⁴, Hu; thy B², J, Lg. 370. And the] And
Adv².—by] and Hn¹.—lawe] syngne Adv². 371.] Is verrey soth and nothinge feyned
Ash².—haste it nat] hast not B², J, CC; hast is it not H¹; hast nouȝt it H³; hath it
not Adv². 372. so as thou] so hast thou B², J, CC; also as thou C¹.—that neu*er*e
dydest] dedest never Ch, Adv²; never dide C¹; never didest C², C³, H²; that never dyde B¹,
B², Ash¹, J, CC, B⁴. 373. thy] the Lg.—lawly] thy C¹; lowe Hn¹, Adv²; holy Ad³. 374.
Suffre] Suffrid H⁸, Ad³.—this] thus this H⁷. 375. Circumcision] have circumcisioun Ash²,
H⁶, C⁵. 376. So] To Ch, B¹, B², Co, H¹, C¹, C², B⁵, Ash², Hn¹, H³, H⁴, H², Ash¹, L,
J, An, CC, H⁵, H⁶, H⁷, H⁸, Ad³, Ad², C⁵, Adv², B³, B⁴, Lg, Hu. 377. the flesshe] us the
C¹; the fresche C². 378. To] Till C¹.—spyryte] serpent C¹.—tyl] to C¹, CC, H⁸;
that C³, B⁵, Hn¹, H⁷, Ad³, Hu.

And graunt vs grace to leve chaste and clene,

380 O criste Ihesu, while that we been here,

Þorue preiere of þat heuenly quene

That is a mayde and mothir eke in-fere.

With helpe of hir, graunt vs this newe yere,

So prudently with vertu vs provyde,

Our vices all þat we may circumcide.

And criste Ihesu, we pray vnto the,

Lat thy name, wher we ryde or gone,

In eche perell and aduersite,

Be our defence ayenst our mortall foon,

390 To make hem stonde still as any stone;

And all that cast vs falsely to werry,

Make her malice mekely to obeye

---

379. vs] om. H¹.—and] om. Ch, H¹. 380. that] om. C¹.—we] om. H⁸.—been] lyven Hn¹.
381. Þorue preiere of þat heuenly quene, H⁷.—þat] the D, Co, B⁵.—Þorue] Through the
Ch, B², C¹, C², H³, H⁴, Ash¹, L, J, An, CC, H⁵, H⁶, Ad², C⁵, B³, Lg, Hu; thi B⁴.
382. a mayde] mayde Ch, B², C¹, C², C³, Ash², H¹, H³, H⁴, Ash¹, L, J, An, CC, H⁸,
Ad², C⁵, Adv², B³, B⁴, Lg; bothe mayde B¹, H⁷.—eke] also Hu. 383. vs] us now L.
384. vs] us to B¹, H³, Adv².—provyde] devide B², J, CC. 385. may] mowe H³. 386.
criste Ihesu] Ihesu Criste Hn¹.—vnto] eke unto H¹. 387. wher] whether Ch, B², C²,
Ash², H³, H⁴, Ash¹, L, J, An, CC, H⁵, H⁶, Ad², C⁵, B³, B⁴, Lg.—ryde] rydy Adv².—
or] and H⁸. 388. In eche] In eke H¹.—and] and eche Ch, B², Co, C², B⁵, Ash², Hn¹,
H³, H⁴, J, An, CC, H⁶, H⁵, H⁷, H⁸, Ad², Ad³, C⁵, Adv², Lg, Hu; and in eche B¹;
and in H²; and every C³; and all L, B³; and eke B⁴. 390. hem stonde] stonde hem L;
stonde Lg, C².—any] a H¹. 391. cast vs] cast B⁴; us caste B¹, C³, B⁵, Hn¹, H⁷, H⁸,
Ad³, Adv², Hu.—falsely to] falsly forto B²; ayenst us C¹.—werry] verely C¹. 392. Make]
Lorde make Hn¹.—to] forto C¹.

To thy name, and make hem stonde a-bake,

Or thay haue power to haunte her cruell myght.

And wikkyd sprytes, so horyble and blak*e*,

That besy been to wayte vs day and nyght,

Lat thy name dryve hem oute of sight;

And in our forhede when we Ih*e*sus enp*r*esse,

Make vs of grace her malice to opresse.

400   For to thy name holy we comende   f. 74a

Our lyfe, our dethe, body, hert, and all,

Our soule also, when we hense wende,

O crist Ih*e*su, o lorde ay Imm*i*ortall,

Prayeng to the when thou vs deme shall,

To save all tho fro eternall shame,

That haue ful faythe and hole trust in thy name.

---

393. thy] the H[1].—stonde] to stonde B[1]; alle stand B[4].—a bake] bak H[1]; al backe Ash[2], H[4], An, Ad[2], C[5]. 394. cruell] crewe B[1]. 395. blak*e*] so blak B[1], B[5], L, Adv[2], B[3]. 396. That] They L.—day] bothe day B[1], Lg. 398. in] on C[2].—forhede] forhedys C[3].—enp*r*esse] dresse L. 399. her] his H[8].—opresse] a presse CC. 400. to] we B[2], J, CC; om. H[1], Ash[2], L; in C[1], Adv[2].—holy we] now whe holly B[1]; holy B[2], J, CC; we holy Co, C[3], B[5], Adv[2], H[8], Hu; we holy do C[1]; we holy now Hn[1]. 401. our dethe body] our deth our body Co; our body our deth C[1].—hert] om. C[1]. 402. we] he H[3].—hense] shall hennes B[1]. 403. Ih*e*su] om. CC.—ay] om. Ch, B[1], B[2], C[1], C[2], Ash[2], Hn[1], H[3], H[4], Ash[1], L, J, An, CC, H[5], H[6], H[7], Ad[2], C[5], B[3], B[4], Lg; evere Co, C[3], B[5], H[8], Adv[2], Hu.—Immortall] mori B[1]; of all C[1]. 404. thou vs deme] we depart B[2], J, CC; thou us deyne Hu. 405. all tho] us all H[1]; all B[1]; all tho than B[2], J, CC; all tho that C[2], Lg.—shame] om. B[2]. 406.] And bring us to the blisse all to gedre in same H[1].—haue] han B[1], Adv[2]; hath C[1], CC.—and hole] to C[1]; holy Adv[2].—trust] trowith CC.—name] name. Amen. B[1], B[2], Ash[2], H[7], Adv[2].

BOOK V

Thow lord, whose light discendyth fro so ferre   f. 74a

With-howten whome phebus ne no sterre

Thorowe the roundenesse of the speres nyne,

Vpon heven power hath to shyne,

Let nowe thy light my derkeness enlumyne;

That thorough thy helpe I may my style gye

Some what to sayne of thy Epiphanye.

howe by the prophecys of Balam wacche was made vpon the hyll to asspye the sterre that tolde cristes birthe Ca° lxxj°[1] 12m

And lat my breste, benygne lorde, be dewede

Doun with some drope fro thy maieste

10   That were this day by a sterre shewede

Oute of the Est to worthy kyngeȝ thre,

Whiche on the nyght of thy Natyuyte,

Gan firste asspye the bright bemes clere

Of this sterre on the heven apere—

---

1. Thow lord] now lord C[1].—whose light discendyth] who descendith his lyght Hu.—fro so ferre] fro ferre B[1]; so ferre B[4]; Hu; þe fier H[1]; so fro ferre J, C[5], Ch. 2. the] þy J.—speres] spere B[2], J; spiritis H[8]; spurtis C[1].— nyne] dyuyne B[2], CC, J; none Ash[1]. 3. ne] nor H[1]; ner Hu. 5. thy] þe þi H[7].—light] lyȝhtnesse B[1].—enlumyne] illumine B[1], C[2]. 6. That] om. B[1], H[7].—may] om. Hn[1].—my] om. H[1].—style gye] still gye B[2], H[1]; me guy C[1]; style gre C[2]; liste ge Lg. 8. my] thy Ash[1].—benygne lorde be dewede] ben lorde deuyded B[2]; ben lorde dewede J; lorde be dewede Ash[1], CC. 9. with] from Hu.—fro] of CC. 10. were] was CC, Adv[2].—shewede] y shewede B[2], B[5], Ash[1], H[3], H[5], H[6], CC, J, C[5], Ad[2], Adv[2], Lg, Ch. 12. Whiche on] withoute H[8].—the] þis B[4], Ash[1], H[3], H[4], C[2], C[5], Ad[2], An, Ch.—thy] be Adv[2]. 13. Gan] Began H[6].—asspye] to spy C[1].—bright] om. B[2], CC, J. 14. Of] om. B[1], H[3], H[7].—this] the C[1]; thi H[6].—on] in C[3].—on the] on B[1], C[1]; on to CC.—on the heven] on thenene Hu.—apere] to apere C[1].

---

[1]crossed through

Of whome the spryng was not causell

Of fortune ne soden aventure

For many a day or this thyng befelle,

And many a yere by recorde of scripture,

With a-waytyng and wondre bysy cure,

20   In verrey sothe as I Remembre can.

A certeyne kynryde towarde the Occian,

Whiche of the stok and the lyne cam—

Who so lust loke, in bokes fro a ferre—

And of the blode of olde Balaam,

That som tyme had with his asse werre,

The whiche sayde ther shulde ryse a sterre

Oute of Iacob and from Israell—

Albe ther of no tyme he couthe tell—

15. spryng] spryngyng H², H⁶.—not] nought C°.—causell] causell H¹, H⁶, V. 16. ne] nor H¹.—soden] of sodyn B¹, CC, C³, Adv², L. 17. a] om. Ash¹, H¹.—or] ere H⁸.—thyng] om. C², Adv².—befelle] fell C³, Co. 18. a] om. H¹.—by] as by C¹. 19. and] and a B¹, CC, Adv²; and many a C¹; and many C²—wondre] om. H¹, C¹, C². 21. kynryde] kinde C². 22. of] om. C¹.—the] om. J, C¹.—and] om. C¹; and of B¹, B³, CC, Adv², L.—the] om. H⁶. 23. so] om. B³; þat H⁸.—loke] to loke B¹, C², C³, Adv², Hu.—loke in bokes] in bokes to loke B², CC, J; in bookie look C¹.—bokes] boke B¹, C².—a ferre] fer B¹, 24. of] from H².—the] om. H¹.—olde] om. CC. 25. That som tyme had] That whilom and H¹. 26. ther shuld ryse] rise þer scholde C²; that theer shuld ryse Hu, Co, 27. Oute of] of H², 28. H¹ as D. Albe that he thereof no tyme cowde tell B², B³, B⁴, Ash¹, H³, H⁵, H⁶, J, C⁵, Ad², L, An, Lg, Ch, V; albe ther þat he no tyme could tell H⁵, H⁷ C² Hu; thow he coude ther off no time tell B¹; al be thogh he no thing þerof coude tell H²; all be it that he þer of no tyme coude telle H⁴; al be it he there of no þing coude tell CC; al be that he þer of coud tell C¹; albe therof that he nothyng coude tell C³; all yett þer of he coude cowde not tell Adv²; al be of þat he no tyme coude tell Hn¹.

Vpon whose worde fully in byleve, f. 74b

30 Ther shulde aryse suche a sterre bright.

Worne xij. chose the trouthe for to preve,

With-inne mydwynter eu*er* fro*m* nyʒt to nyght,

Whan in aquarye phebus shed his light;

For to awayte in all her best wyse

Whanne þis sterre on heuene wolde arise.

And these xij. wern of the kynrede

Of balam, as ʒe haue herde me telle,

That yere by yere shulde take hede

Vpon an hill by-syde a lytell well.

40 And ther in fere a certen space dwelle,

A-noynted *and* bathed *and* in clothes whight.

And of custome thay slepen but a lyte,

---

29. worde] wordis C². 30. Ther] Where CC; The C⁵.—aryse] rise Ash¹, C², Adv².—such] liche B¹.—a] om. V.—bright] light B², B⁴, H³, H⁴, H⁵, H⁶, CC, J, C¹, C², C⁵, Adv², An, Lg, Ch, V. 31. xij.] xiij. Lg.—chose] choseid B²; chosen B¹, Ash¹, H¹, H², H³, H⁴, H⁵, H⁶, H⁷, CC, J, C¹, C², C⁵, Ad², Ad³, Adv², L, An, Lg, Hn¹, Co, V.—for] om. B¹, Ash¹, C¹, Adv². 32. With inne mydwynter eu*er* from nyʒt to nyght B¹.—euer] evyn D, H¹, H³, H⁵, C¹.—with] which H¹.—euer from] om. Adv². 33. in] om. Ash¹, H⁵, H⁸,—shed] shewith B¹; shade C¹, Ad², Ad³, An, Lg.—his] is J. 34. awayte] wayte B¹, B⁵, H⁷, H⁸, Hu.—all] om. Adv².—her] þer H¹, C³. 35. Whanne þis sterre on heuene wolde arise H⁷.—this] the D. H⁵, H⁸, Hn¹.—on] in B⁴, H¹, H⁴, H⁶, C³, C⁵, Ad², An, Ch, Co; of Adv².—wolde] schuld Adv².—arise] rise B¹, B², H¹, Adv². 36. these] this H⁸.—the] om. Ash¹, H², C⁵, Ad², An, Ch. 37. Of balam as ʒe haue herde me telle H⁷.—haue] om. D, Ash¹.—me] om. B², H⁸, J.—ʒe] I CC.—herde me] me herde B¹. 38. That] And Adv². 39. an] and H⁵, H⁸; al H⁷. 40. ther in] ther y B³; therefore C³.—in fere] a fer H⁶, C¹.—a certen] certen C¹; a lytell Adv².—space] place C¹.—dwelle] to dwelle B¹, B², B⁵, H², CC, J, C¹. 41. A noynted *and* bathed *and* in clothes whight B.—A noynted] A noynt D, C¹.—bathed and in clothes white] clothid and in bathis white H¹.—and] om. CC, C¹.—in] om. C³. 42. of] ther of B², B³, H⁵, CC, J, L, V; þey of B⁴, Ash¹, H³, H⁴, H⁶, C¹, C², C⁵, Ad², An, Lg, Ch.—thay] there B¹, B⁵, H¹, H², H⁷, H⁸, C³, Ad³, Hu, Hu¹, Co; þere in Adv².—slepen] speke B⁴, H³, H⁴, H⁶, C⁵, Ad², An, Ch.—a lyte] lyght B¹.

But in prayer and certeyne ryteȝ vsede,

Thay muste wake and wayte in speciall—

And none of hem plattely excusede—

Vpon this hill namede Victoriall.

And if one dyed, than his sonne shall

By statute olde his place ocupye,

Or elles one that were next of alye.

50   And this contyneude duryng many yere

By custom vsede of antiquyte—

As phebus went by meovyng circuler—

So thay kept her tymeȝ by decre,

And iche yere wer certeyne dayes thre

By calkyng cast and computacion,

Sowght *and* chosen ouȝt by good eleccioun

---

43. certeyne] in certayn H¹, H³, H⁶, C⁵, Ad², Adv², An, Ch; in a certeyne B⁴. 44. wake] make L.—wake and wayte] wayte and wake B⁵, Ad³.—and wayte] om. B³. 45. hem] þem C².—plattely] pleynly Adv².—excusede] by excused B¹; to be excused B², B³, B⁴, Ash¹, H³, H⁴, H⁵, H⁶, CC, J, C², C⁵, Ad², Adv², Hu, L, An, Lg, Ch, V; be excused] B⁵, H¹, H², H⁷, H⁸, Ad³, Hn, C¹. 46. this] the CC.—namede Victoriall] name Victorially H⁸. 47. dyed] die B¹, H³, H⁵, C², Lg, Ch.—than] om. Co; þat B⁴, B⁵, Ash¹, H⁴, H⁶, C², C⁵, Ad², An, Lg, Ch; as H³.—his sonne] a nother H⁶.—sonne] soule H¹. 48. By] his B⁴, Ch.—olde] holde B⁴, Ch.—his] *and* his B⁴; that B¹.—ocupye] to ocupie B¹, Adv²; occupied Lg. 49. one] thei CC,—next] hys next C³.—of alye] of his alye B², CC, J; his alye Hn¹; aly C³. 50. contynuede] contynually H¹; continwyng CC.—duryng] om. B¹, H², C³; longe and CC.—yere] a yere B¹, B², B³, H⁵, H⁶, H⁷, H⁸, CC, J, C², Ad², Ad³. Adv², L, Ch, Hn¹; a long yere C³. 51. By] The CC.—antiquyte] olde antiquite B¹, B², CC. 52. As] And Co.—went by meovyng] by moving went C¹. 53. So] And so CC.—her] their B², J.—tymeȝ] time B¹, Ash¹.—decre] degre B¹, B⁵, H², H⁶, H⁸, J, C⁵, Adv², Hu; the ȝeer C¹. 54. iche] euery C³, Co.—were] there were C³.—certeyne] om. B¹, H⁸.—thre] þere Lg. 55. calkyng] calling Ad³.—cast] faste caste H⁸.—and] a H⁶. 56. Sowght *and* chosen ouȝt by good eleccicun B¹.—ouȝt] om. D, CC, C¹.—good] om. B⁵, Adv², V.

For to awayte the vp-rist by the morowe,

Of this sterre *with* his bemes glade,

Whiche Balaam sayde sholde avoyde her sorowe.

60   At his vp-riste whose bemeʒ may not fade,

To shede his lyght in eu*ery* shrowde *and* shade

With-oute wrystyng or drawyng to declyne.

Til at the last for the same fine—

To see þis sterre moast famous of rennoun   f. 75a

On the heven whan it wolde apere—

þe worthi kyngis as made is mencioun,

Vpon this hill to-gydre gon in fere.

For cause thay, who so lust to here,

Werne of the stoke of Balaam dou*n* descendyde;

70   Wher-fore of sort the hylle they ben ascendyde,

57. awayte] wayte B⁵, H¹, H², H⁸, Ad³, Adv².   58. this] the H², H⁸, C².—with] which with H⁶.—his] her H².   59. Which] That H⁶.—sayde] om. C¹.—avoyde] voide C². —her] our B⁵, H⁷, H⁸, C³, Adv², Hu, Ch, Hn¹, Co; þere H⁵; his CC; al our B¹. 60. vp rist] uprisyng B²; rising CC.—whose] his CC.—bemeʒ] brightnesse B³, L.—may] ne may C¹.   61. To shede his lyght in eu*ery* shrowde *and* shade B¹.—shrowde] showre D, H⁵, H⁶, C³, Adv², Hn¹; showris C¹.—To] And L.—shede] shewe B², H², H⁴, H⁶, CC, C¹, C², C⁵, Ad², Adv², L, An, Ch.—in] and H¹.—shade] in shade C¹.   62. or] om. B⁵, Co.   63. Til at the last for the same fine B¹.—the last] last D, H², C¹, Ad²; all the last C¹.   64. To see þis sterre moast famous of rennoun H⁷.—see] om. D.—þis] the B¹, H⁶.   65. it] they C¹; om. B¹.   66. þe worthi kyngis as made is mencioun H⁷. —The] Thre B⁵, C¹, C³, Co; three [second "e" added in later hand] D.—made is] is made Adv².—mencioun] the mencioun B¹.   67. this] þe B⁴, H³, H⁶, C¹, C², C⁵, Ad², An, Lg, Ch, V.—to gydre gon] gon to gidir C¹.—gon] þe gon H¹; goo Adv². —in fere] y fere B³, H², H⁴, H⁵, J, C⁵, L, An. Lg; I fere C², Ad², Ch; on fere Co. 68. thay] that H³, CC; om. Ash¹.—who] were who B⁴.—to] om. H¹.   69. of Balaam] om. B⁵, CC, Co.—dou*n*] om. C¹, C².   70. fore] om. H¹, H².—of] for H⁸.—sorte] forse CC.—the hylle they ben] thei byn the hill B¹, C².—ben] haue H¹; om. C¹.

As fell on hem by custome to succede

At a certeyne yere by reuolucion.

And on this hill estewarde thay toke hede,

By gode avyse in her inspeccion,

The same nyght of the Incarnacion,

Whan criste was borne in Bedlem of marye.

The same hour the sterre thay aspye

Of newe aryse in the Oryent;

Full lustyly of whome the beme₃ light

80   Gan enlumyne all the firmament.

Fro Est to West it yafe so clere a light,

That of the stremys eu*ery* man*e*re wight

Astonyde was thay were so bright and shene,

And to the eye so p*er*saunt for to sene.

---

71. fell] fill H⁸, J, C¹; by fell Adv².—on] om. Adv².—hem] hym H¹.—by] of H¹.—to]
om. Adv². 72. At] And B².—a] om. B¹, H¹, H².—yere] of the yere B², B³, B⁴, Ash¹,
H³, H⁴, H⁵, H⁶, CC, J, C¹, C², C⁵, Ad², L, An, Lg, Ch, V.—reuolucion] reuelacioun B¹.
73. on] of B².—hill] his H¹.—toke] take Hn¹. 74. By] Be CC, J.—her] theyre C³. 75.
the] om. Adv². 76. Whan] þat Adv².—was borne] borne was CC. 77. hour] tyme H¹.—
the sterre] om. Adv².—the sterre thay aspye] the dedyn the sterre aspye CC.—thay aspye]
thei dide a spie B¹, B⁵, H², H⁶, H⁷, H⁸, Ad², Hu, Ch, Hn¹, Co, Adv²; deden asspye
B², J; dyd aspy C³.—aspye] aspid Lg. 78. Of newe aryse] How it new rose H¹. 79. of
whome] om. C¹.—light] bright B¹, B², B³, Ash¹, H¹, H⁶, H⁷, H⁸, CC, J, C⁵, Ad³, Adv²,
L, Hn¹, Co, V. 80. Gan] Began H⁶; Gon Adv².—enlumyne] to enlumyne C³.—all] of Ash¹
81. Est to West] the Est C¹.—to West] to þe West B⁵.—a] *carrotted above* line D; om.
B¹, Hn¹. 82. That of the stremys] of þat þe stremes H⁷. 83. Astonyde] a stoded CC.—was
thay were] were thei shoon B¹, H⁷. 84. And] Un CC.—the eye] them B², CC, J.—eye]
eyithe H⁴.—so] ful B⁴, H⁴, C¹, Ad²; for Ash¹, H³, C⁵, An, Ch.—p*er*saunt] plesante B⁵,
H⁸, C¹.—for] om. B¹, CC, C¹; on Ad³.—sene] shyne An.

The whiche sterre drewe his cours full right

Towarde the hill—liche as bokeȝ tell—

Where the kynges the long wynters nyght

It to awayte solitarye dwelle.

And they anone vpon her knees felle

90 And thanked god *with* all her hertes luste

Which hathe not hem defraudyd of her truste.

And all the nyght to-gydre as thay woke

Vp on this sterre that shoon so fayre *and* clere;

And sodenly vpwarde as they gan loke

They sawe a childe above the sterre apere:

So yong, so fayre, in a golden spere,

Full ryally stonde, and above his hede

A large crosse that was of blode all rede.

how iij kyng*es per*-ceyved the sterre that shewede crist*es* birthe Ca° lxxij°[1]

13

---

85. The] om. B³, L.—drewe] thorow B², CC, J.—full] of B⁴, Ash¹, H³, H⁴, H⁶, C¹, C⁵, Ad², An, Lg, Ch; om. C². 86. bokeȝ book H¹; the bookis C¹. 87. Where] *"h" is carrotted above line in another hand*, D.—the kynges] om. C¹; the kyng CC.—the long] þis long C². 88. It to awayte] It for to wayte B¹, H⁷; The kyngis lay and C¹.—solitarye] ful solitarie H².—dwelle] to dwelle B⁴, L; did dwell H¹. 89. they] ther H³, H⁴, H⁶, Ad², Ad³, An, Lg, Ch; these Ash¹.—vpon] on B⁵, H¹, H⁸, C³, Ad³, Adv², Hu, Hn¹, Co.—her] þere H⁵, C⁵.—felle] þey fell Ch. 90. god] om. H⁸.—*with* all her hert*es* luste] *with* hert and wyll entere C³, Hn¹.—her] om. B¹, H⁷; þe H¹.—luste] free B³, L; iuste H¹. 91. Which hathe not hem defraudyd of her truste] That they of her desir defrauded not be B³, L ["not" omitted]; That he to hem shewyd þe sterre bryȝt *and* clere Hn.—hem] him H¹.—hem defraudyd] defrawded he*m* Adv².—truste] lust B¹, B⁵, Ash¹, H¹, H³, H⁵, H⁶, H⁷, H⁸, C⁵, Ad², Ad³, An, Lg, Ch, Co, V. 92. the] that H⁶, C³.—woke] toke H⁴. 93. Vp on this sterre that shoon so fayre *and* clere B¹.—this] the D, B⁵, H², H⁶, C², Adv², L, Hn¹.—that shone] om. C², Hu.—so fayre] so bright H², C¹. 94. sodenly] as thei sodenly B¹, B⁵, H⁷, H⁸, C³, Ad³, Adv², Hu, Hn¹, Co.—as they gan loke] upwarde gan looke B¹; vpward gan to loke B⁵, H⁷, H⁸.—as they] om. H¹.—gan] om. V.—loke] to loke H². 95. sawe] sey Hu.—the] a B¹.—sterre] sterris Co. 96. So yong so fayre] So faire so ȝonge H³.—so fayre] and faire H².—golden] goodely Ash¹. 97. Full ryally] So ryal Hn¹.—stonde] stod H¹, Hu; stondyng Adv².—and] om. B², H², H⁸, CC, J, C¹, C⁵, Adv². 98. A] And a B³, L.—of blode] aboue B², H¹, CC, J.—all] full CC; so Adv²; om. B¹, H².—of blode all rede] al blode rede B⁴.

[1]Crossed through.

The whiche childe spake to hem a-noon   f. 75b

100   Above the hill withe voyse and chere benyng,

And bad hem faste that thay shulde gone

Into Iuda right as any lyne,

And folowe all-waye the sterre for a signe

That shal hem bringe into that regioun;

Where as the kynge moost worthi of renooun,

Was borne that tyme to haue the Regale

Of Iwes lande of verrey dwe right,

Whom the sterre dyd specifie,

Whan he was borne with his clere light.

110   And thay a-noon whan passed was the nyght,

The next morne no lenger lust a-byde

But towards hym cast hem for to Ryde.

---

100. Above] About Ad².—withe voyse and chere benyng] with clere and voys benyngne B¹; with chere *and* vois benigne H⁷; with cler voyce *and* benyng Adv². 101. faste] om. Adv².— thay] the B¹.—gone] fast gone Adv². 103. And folowe all waye] Ande alway folewe B¹.—And folowe all waye the sterre for a signe] And alwey the sterr folow to be your syne C².—for a signe] of a signe H⁸; as for a sygne CC, C²; schene Adv².—a] om. H¹. 104. That shal hem bringe into that regioun B¹.—hem] om. D, C³, C⁵; thanne B²; hym H¹.—into] to D, CC, C³, C⁵; you to B², CC, J.—that] þe H²; om. H¹. 105. Where as the kynge moost worthi of renooun B¹.—as] at D; that B², H⁶, CC, J, C⁵, Adv².—worthi] is worthi CC; om. H¹.—of renooun] arenoun H¹; on renoun H⁷. 106. the] om. H¹, H². 107. Of Iwes lande of verrey dwe right] Of Iewes be lond of dauid verrey ryȝt Adv².—Of] Of the B³, L.—of verrey] by verry H²; be verrey Ch. 108. Whom] To whom B², B³, B⁴, Ash¹, H³, H⁴, H⁵, H⁶, CC, J, C², C⁵, L, An, Lg, Ch, V.—dyd] dide there B³, B⁴, Ash¹, H³, H⁴, H⁵, C⁵, Ad², An, Lg, V; ther did B², CC, J, Ch; to hym dide Hn¹; dud so well H². 109. clere light] cheere liȝt Lg. 110. thay] om. CC. 111. next] om. C².—morne] morewe B¹, B⁴, H³, H⁴, H⁶, H⁸, C², Ad², Ch, Co.—lust] þe luste C².—a byde] to a bide B¹, B⁵, H¹, H⁷, H⁸, CC, C², Ad³, Adv², Hu, Hn¹, Co. 112. hem] to hem B¹; om. H⁸, Adv².—for] om. B¹, C¹, C²; forth C³.

With grete aray and Riall appareyle,

As was sittyng to her worthynesse,

They shope hem furthe and for thay nolde fayle

To do honour to his nobilnesse,

With hem they toke golde and great Richesse,

To spende and yeve and also for thay ment

Withe yefftes grete the childe to present.

120   And furthe thay gone, no lenger wolde thay tarye,

Thorow mani a londe *and* many a diuerse yle,

Eueryche of hem on a dromondarye,

Whiche weren so swifte that full many a myle

Thay passed han *with* in a lytyll while;

That in the space of dayes but xiij^{ne},

By condit only of the sterre shene,

---

113. grete] a grete B4.—appareyle] of parayll CC. 114. her] þer B5, C3. 115. shope] ȝede C2.—hem] hym H1.—nolde fayle] wolde not fayle B1, CC, C5, Adv2; nold not faille B2, H6, J, C5. 116. To do honour to his nobilnesse H7.—do] done D.—to] vnto D; onto C1.—his] this is B1; his high H1; his gret H2; thys hygh C5; þys Ch.—noblenesse] nobles B5, CC, C1, C3; noblesse H1, H6, J, C5, Ad2, Ad3, L, An, Lg, Ch, Hn1, Co, V. 117. gret] om. B2, CC, J; eke H2. 118. thay ment] to ment H1. 119. to present] for to presente B1, H1, H7, Adv2, Hn1. 120. And furthe] Than forth Ad3.—gone] goth Ch; om. B3.—wolde] will H1; om. C2.—thay] om. B1. 121. Thorow mani a londe *and* many a diuerse yle B1.—a] om. B5, H1, H7, Co.—many a] many D, B5, H1 H7, C3, Adv2, Hu, L.—many] om. H2, Co.—yle] hill CC. 122. Eueryche] Ech C1; Euery Co.—of] on Ad3.—on] upon B3, C1, V; in H6; om. CC.—a] om. H1. 123. weren] was Adv2.—so full C3.—full] om. B3, CC, J.—a] om. H1. 124. passed] passen H1; wold pas C1.—han] thanne B2, J; om. Adv2.—*with*] om. B1, B5, H2.—in] om. H1.—a] om. B4.—lytyll] om. CC. 125. That] om. C1.—the] om. B1, B3, B5, H1, C1, Ad3, Adv2, Hu, L, Co.—but] om. B4, J, Adv2, Lg, Ch.—xiij^{ne}] fiftene B4; xviij C1. 126. condit] cownt Adv2.—shene] so schene C2, Hn1.

how the kyng*es* cam to
Iheru*sa*lem and askyde
wher criste was borne
Ca°xxiii°1 14ᵐ

Thay entrede ben into Iher*usa*lem,

    That of Iuda was the cheffe Cyte;

Conveyed eu*ere* wi*th* the bright beame

Of the sterre that was so fayre to see.

130   And whan that thay a-mydde the Cyte be,

Not astonyed, axede in audience:

Ubi est qui natus est   Wher is the kyng grettest of Reuerence,

Rex Judeoru*m*   Of Iwes borne for to bere the crowne,   f. 76a

Whose sterre we seen in the Orient

That from hevyn cast his streme꒱ downe,

Which all the worlde vndir the firmament

Is gladde to see and we of one entent,

Han yftey꒱ brought oute of our contre,

140   Hyme to hono*ur* in his ryall see?

---

127. into] to Adv². 129. eu*ere*] ay H¹. 130. sterre] bryght sterre L.—was] who C¹.—so] om.
Adv².—fayre] bright B², CC. 131. that] om. B¹, B⁴, Ash¹, H⁴, H⁶, C¹, C², C⁵, Ad², Adv²,
An, Lg, Ch.—thay] om. C¹.—the] of the C¹.—be] om. V. 132. Not] Nought Co.—axede] but
axed Hn¹. 133. of] in CC; on C¹. 134. for to bere the crowne] to be kynge and for to bere
the crown B¹.—for] om. Adv².—the] a Adv². 135. sterre] om. Hu.—seen] se B¹, H², CC,
C⁵, Adv², Hu; saw B³, L. 136. That] and C³.—from] om. Hu.—cast] he casht B¹, C³.—
downe] om. H¹. 137. vndir the firmament] y seye verament H². 138. see] om. Co.—one] our
H¹, H⁶; om. B⁵. 139. Han] Whe han H⁸.—our] om. H⁸. 140. Hyme to hono*ur* in his ryall
see] In his riall see hym to hono*ur* H².

---

¹crossed through.

And whan herode of her comyng knewe,

He troubled was and also all the towne,

And gan a-noon to chaunge chere and hewe;

And made in hast, a convocacion

Of all the presteȝ dwellyng environ;

To knowe clerly and be certyfyde,

Of the place that was specifiede

Of prophetis where crist shal be borne.

And thay a-noon the trouthe to hym tolde:

150 In Bedlem, as thay full long afforne

Founden oute in her bokeȝ olde,

And all the manere to hym thay vnfolde,

Fro poynt to poynt, as Mathewe makyth mynde;

Redyth his gospell and ther ye shall it fynde

---

141. And] That B1, H7, H8, C3, Co; Than H1, Ad3, Adv2; om. H2.—herode] the herode
B1; þat herowde Hn1.—her] theyr C3; the Hu. 142. troubled] trouble Co.—was] om. C2.—
all] om. H1, H3. 143. gan] began H6, Adv2.—chere and hewe] hew *and* chere Hu. 144. in
hast] om. H1.—convocacion] conuencion H1. 145. all] om. C2.—the] om. B4.—presteȝ]
prest Adv2.—environ] þerechon H2. 146. be] to be B3, H2, H6, Adv2, Hu, L. 147. the]
that Ash1.—place] space Ash1, H3, C2, C5, Ad2, An, Lg, Ch; speche H6. 148. Of prophetis
where crist shal be borne B1.—of] and of H1.—prophetis] colde prophetis Hn1.—shal] shulde
D, B4, C1, Hn1. 149. thay] ther L; om. C1.—to] om. B1, C2, Hu, Ch.—hym] hem J; om.
H2. 150. full] om. B5, H2.—afforne] to fore C1. 151. oute] om. C1.—in] of CC—her]
theyre C3. 152. to hym] om. CC.—to hym thay] thei to hym Ad3.—thay] þei dyd Adv2.—
vnfolde] told C1. 153. makyth] make B2; makyd Hu. 154. Redyth] Rede C1, Hu, Co.—his]
the B1, C1; as H5.—ther] om. Ash1.—ye] thou Co; om. C1.—it] ye CC; om. B1, H1,
H8, L, Ch.

nd then herde gan the kynges calle,

And of þis mater entretid priueli;

Ande curiously how that it was falle,

Be-gan enquere and axede bysely.

And of the sterre also by and by,

160   He axede hem and in wordes fewe

How and in what wyse it gan firste shewe.

And whan thay had tolde hym eu*er*y dele,

Thay dep*a*rtede oute of his p*re*sence.

But firste he bad hem to enquere well

Of the childe w*it*h all her diligence.

And whan thay hade done hym Reu*er*ence,

He chargede hem vndir wordes fayre,

Hamwarde by hym algates to repayre,

howe kyng heroude
sent fore the iij
kyngeʒ to enquere
of crist*es* birthe
Ca° lxxiiij°[1] 15[m]

---

155. And] om. H[1], C[1].—than] om. C[2].—gan] can B[1], Adv[2]; began H[6].—calle] to call C[1]. 156. And of þis mater entretid priueli H[7].—And] om. C[1].—of] om. D, Ash[1], H[2], H[6].—entretid] treted B[1], B[4]; entrete H[1]. 157. Ande curiously how that it was falle B[1].—curiously] ceriously H[1], H[4], Ch; trewly C[1].—that] om. D, H[6], C[1], C[2], Co.—how that] that how H[3].—it] om. H[1].—was] is H[1], C[1].—falle] be fall C[1], C[2]. 158. Be gan] He gan H[1], C[1], C[3], C[5], Ch; He con Adv[2]; He began H[6].—enquere] to enquere H[8].—and axede] om. CC, Ad[2].—axede] axe B[2], H[1], H[2], H[8], C[3], Ad[2], Hu, Co.—bysely] full bysyly Adv[2], Hn[1]. 159. also] and also B[2]. 160. and] om. B[2], CC, J, C[1], Adv[2], L, Co; eke and Hn[1].—wordes] a wordis Co. 161. How and] om. H[2].—in] om. H[4], Ad[2].—gan] began H[6]; con Adv[2].—shewe] to shew H[6], C[1], Hn[1]. 162. tolde] I told C[1]. 163 departede] parted Adv[2]. 164. hem] om. H[1].—to] for to B[1]; om. H[1], Adv[2], Co. 165. her] ther Ash[1], H[1], C[3], Hn. 166. done] do B[1], C[2], C[3].—hym] her H[6], Hu; om. H[8], Adv[2]. 167. hem] om. L.—fayre] fewe H[4]. 168. Hamwarde by hym algates to repayre] Algatys be hym homward to repayre CC.—algates to] þey schuld Adv[2].—algates] om. H[8].

---

[1]crossed through.

To yeffe hym clerly informacion   f. 76b

170   Of her exployt and of the childe also;

Surely affermyng by fals collusion,

That he hym-self wold aftir goo

Unto the childe and his deuer doo,

To worshipp hym—and all vndir colours,

The worme abit as serpent vndre floures

Daryth full ofte and kepyth hym couertly;

Of kynd malice tyll thay a tyme see

To shede her venym, and than sodenly,

All at ones, when thay vnwarrest be,

180   They styng and hurte and shewe her cruelte,

And her venym vnder floures fayre

Full ofte is hydde tyll thay may appayre.

---

169. hym] om. H¹.—clerly] clere Ash¹, CC. 170. her] ther Hu.—and] om. Lg.—of] om. H¹, H⁵.—the] hire Co. 171. collusion] conclusion H⁸, C³, Adv², Hu, Co. 172. That he hymn self wold aftir goo] After Hym self wuld go B⁵, Co.—wold aftir] after wolde B¹; wolde haue sone aftyr CC.—aftir] sone after B², B³, B⁴, Ash¹, H³, H⁴, H⁵, H⁶, J, C⁵, Ad², L, An, Lg. Ch, V. 173. the] þis C².—his] al his B³, L. 174. and all] ande as B¹, B⁵, H¹, H⁷, C³, Ad³, Hu, Hn¹, Co; as H⁸, Adv².—and] om. H⁴.—colours] coloure Ch. 175. The] As B², B³, B⁴, CC, J, L.—worme] vrtike H¹.—abit] abideþ B⁵, H⁴, H⁶, Adv².—as] or B¹, B², B³, B⁴, H⁶, H⁷, CC, J, C⁵, Ad², Hn¹, Co.—as serpent] om. C².—floures] floure Ch. 176. hym] hym self H⁸; om. Lg.—couertly] ful couertly B¹; couerte H⁸. 177. Of kyng] ful of H².—tyll thay a tyme] tyl a tyme þei B⁵.—a] ay H³. 178. her] þere H⁵.—than] that C³. 179. thay] men B¹, B⁵, H⁷, H⁸, C³, Adv², Hu, Hn¹. Co; þat men H¹, Ad³.—vnwarrest] unwarned H⁸, Adv². 180. and hurte] inherte H⁸, Adv²; full sore C¹; om. C².—and shewe] *and* schede C². 181. her] þere H⁵, C³; he CC.—floures] clouris Hn¹. 182. Full ofte] And often B², CC, J.—ofte] of Ad³.—appayre] repeyre CC, Adv².

As s*erpent* cou*er*eth hym vndir floures to styng and shede his venom whom he may hurt. So fals heroude shewed fals fenyng word*es* to haue dissayved thees kyng*es*. Ca° xvj[1]

Right so thou serpent of Iniquite,

Fals tygre full of doublenesse,

Vndir colour of humylite

Thy venym darithe and also thy falsenesse!

O thou Tyrant! O Rote of cursidnesse!

Thou herodis of malice most mortall,

What wenst thou hym that knowyth all

190   To disceyve w*ith* thy slyghtly wyle,

What can sugur vndur galle faine?

What wenyst thou the kynge₃ to be gyle

And of malice bryng hem in a trayne?

Of whose comyng though þat thou disdeyne,

It may not helpe pleynely ne a-vayle,

For of thy purpose sothely thou shall fayle.

---

183. thou serpent] this fals serpent C[1].—of Iniquite] thorowe thyn Iniquite Ash[1]; ful of iniquite B[1], B[2], B[3], B[4], H[2], H[3], H[4], H[5], H[6], H[7], CC, J, C[1], C[2], C[5], Ad[2], Ad[3], L, An, Lg, Ch, Hn[1], V. 184. full] ri₃t ful Hn[1].—of] of fals C[1]; om. H[5]. 185. Vndir] Loo undir Hn[1].—colour] the colour B[3], L; faire coloure H[6], C[5]. 186. darithe] derkith C[1]. —also] B[1], B[5], H[2], H[7], H[8], C[3], Ad[3], Adv[2], Hu, Hn[1], Co.—thy] om. C[1]. 187. Rote] thu roote B[1], B[2], Ash[1], H[2], J, C,. 188. malice] all malice Ch. 189. What] That CC.— **hym that knowyth all**] þat thou knowest all H[8]; *and* knowist all C[1]; þat þou knowst all Adv[2]. 190. disceyve] disseyve hym C[1].—slyghtly] flesscheli B[1], C[1], Ad[2], Ad[3], Hu; slyly H[2], Ch; slei₃t Lg.—wyle] wise H[2]. 191. What can sugar vndur galle faine B[1].—What] that D, B[3], B[5], H[5], CC, C[3], Ch; Whene Co.—What can sugur vndur galle faine] To bryng so grete undir feyne H[8]; What can sugir wondir fyne C[1]; To bryng sug*re* und*ir* feyn Adv[2].—What can] What gan Ash[1]; Thou cast H[1]. 192. What] om. H[6].—thou] om. C[5]. 193. bryng hem in a trayne] to brynge hem to a treyne B[3], L.—hem] hym H[1], Ch; om. B[1].—a] om. CC. 194. þat] om. B[1], C[1], C[2], Adv[2]. 195. It may not helpe pleynely ne a vayle B[1].—helpe playnely] pleynely helpe H[8], Adv[2].—ne] ner D; nor H[8], Adv[2].— a] om. H[8]. 196. of] om. H[8].—sothely] surely B[1], B[5], H[7], H[8], C[3], Ad[3], Adv[2], Hu, Co; playnli B[2], Ash[1], H[3], H[4], H[5], H[6], CC, J, C[1], C[5], Ad[2], An, Ch, V; certes B[3], L; platly H[1]; uitterly H[2]; trewly Hn[1]; om. C[2].—sothely thou shall fayle] þou shalt pleinly faille Lg.

---

[1]lx is erased.

For by grace thay shull in quyete,

Maugre thy myght, all thy danger passe;

For though that thou *with* wordes hony swete

200   Maliously vpon her dethe compasse,

Thay shall scape dispyte of all thy face,

For all the coniecte of thy prynses wyse,

As the story shall a-noon dyvyse.

And so *with* venym in his herte loke,   f. 77a

He yaffe hem leve passe thorough his Reame

In her Repayre hym castyng to be wroke,

If thay reto*ur*ne by Ier*us*al*e*m.

And so þe sterre hem brouȝte bedlem,

And lyne right the childes hede aboue,

210   Wher as he lay, stille gan to houe.

---

198. thy myght] the myght Ash¹.—all] and B¹; *and* all C¹; om. H⁸, Adv².—thy] the H⁶; om. L.—all thy danger] þi daunger al passe Lg. 199. that] om. C², Adv².—thou] om. B⁴.— with] with þi H⁵.—wordes hony] hony wordis B², CC, C¹. 200. vpon] om. CC.—her] theyr C³. 201. dispyte] in dispite H⁶, C¹, C³; in spite H⁸, Adv²; spyte Ash¹, CC, C².—all] om. B³, H¹, C¹, C², C³, Adv², V. 202. For] of B¹.—the] thi Lg.—wise] vyce An. 203. shall a noon] a noon shal B¹, H⁸, Adv². 204. so] om. B⁵, C¹.—loke] y loke B⁴, Ash¹, H³, H⁴, H⁶, C², C³, C⁵, Ad², An, Lg, Ch, V. 205. He yaffe hem leve] He shal hem lete H².—hem] þam H¹.—passe] to passe B¹, B², B³, H¹, H⁴, H⁷, H⁸, CC, J, C², C³, Ad³, Hu, L.—thorough] out thorow B², CC; thorow out H⁸, Adv². 206. hym castyng] castyng hym B⁵, Co.—hym] om. H⁴, An, V.—castyng] cast Ad². 207. reto*ur*ne] retowrned H⁴, Adv², Hu; turne H⁷, Ad³.—reto*ur*ne by] turned to B¹.—by] ayen by B², B³, B⁴, Ash¹, H³, H⁴, H⁵, H⁶, CC, J, C¹, C⁵, L, An, Lg, Ch; aȝen to C². 208. And so þe sterre hem brouȝte to bedlem H⁷.—þe] *inserted above line,* H⁷; thys L.—hem brouȝte] brought hem D, B¹, H³, CC, C³, Co, V. 209. And] And as V.—childes hede aboue] childe aboue H⁸, Adv². 210. Wher as he lay stille gan to houe Ad³.—as] that H⁷.—he] thay D, B⁴, B⁵, C¹.—gan to] can it B¹; gan for to H¹; gan still C¹; gan H⁶; hyt gan C³; began to Adv²; gan he C².

B ut who the Ioy can tell or endyte

    Or with his mouthe, who can the myrthe expresse,

Or who can playnly with his penne wryte,

The grete blisse or elles the gladnesse

Which thay made in verrey sothefastnesse

Aftir her iourney and her long waye,

Above the house whan thay the sterre sey,

Thatte gan to hem clerly certifie

Withoute more the childeʒ dwellyng place?

220   And thay a-noon faste gan hem hye

With lusty hert and gladde of chere and face,

To worthe doun in a lytyll space.

Thay made hem redy and with reverence;

Thay entrede in and cam to his presence,

Of the Ioya that thees iij kynges had whan thay fovnden criste Ca° xvij°[1]

---

211. can telle] telle can B¹, C³.—can] coude B², B³, B⁴, Ash¹, H³, H⁴, H⁵, H⁶, CC, J, C¹, C², Ad², Adv², L, An, Lg, Ch, V. 212. who] om. B⁴, Ash¹.—can] gan Ash¹. 213. who] om. C².—can] gan Ash¹. 214. or elles the gladnesse] or elles the grete gladnesse B¹; or the grete gladness CC; and þe gladnesse B⁴.—elles] om. B², B³, Ash¹, H³, H⁴, H⁵, H⁶, J, C¹, C², C⁵, Ad², L, An, Lg, Ch, V. 215. in verrey] in her B¹; with verry H².—verrey ferier CC; om. H⁶, C⁵. 216. her] theyre C³.—and] and in B⁵; in C¹.—her] theyre C³; om. B¹, H⁸, Adv², 217. the] þys Ch.—thay the sterre] þe sterr þei H¹.—thay] om. L. 218. gan] can H², Adv².—hem] theym C³.—certifie] specifie H⁶. 219. Withoute] With Adv².—dwellyng] is dwellyng H⁸. 220. faste] full faste H⁸.—gan] began H⁶; con Adv².—hem] om. B¹; to H¹. 221. and gladde of chere and face] glade chere and mylde of face H⁸, Adv².—and] om. H². 222. To worthe] So Worthely B², CC, J; To light Ash¹; and lyʒte H⁸, Adv²; They worth C¹.—in a lytyll space] of her hors in a litel space B¹.—a] so CC; om. B. 223. hem] þem B⁵; than J. 224. entrede] entren B³, B⁴, Ash¹, H², H³, H⁴, H⁶, H⁷, CC, C², C³, C⁵, Ad², Ad³, Hu, L, An, Lg. Ch, Hn¹, Co; in H⁸, Adv².—his] om. B¹, B², B³, B⁴, B⁵, H¹, H², H³, H⁴, H⁶, H⁷, H⁸, CC, J, C³, C⁵, Ad², Ad³, Hu, L, An, Lg, Ch, Hn¹, Co, V; þe H⁵, C¹.

[1]x is crossed out.

Wher as the childe, most worthy of degre,

Was *with* marie in an oxes stalle.

And full humbly the kyngeʒ all thre,

To-fore the childe on her knes gan falle,

And brought her tresour and her yeftys alle

230 As Reuerently as thay can devyse.

And hym *pre*sent in all her best wyse,

Lyche her astateʒ, eu*er*yche aftir othir,

Makyng her *pre*sent *with* all humylyte,

Lyches her age as brothir aftir brothir.

Golde, franke and Myrr thay yaffe hym all thre,   Offerent **Aurum,**

Aftir the custome of perce and Calde,   thus, *et* mirram

For of that lond whanne kyngis *pre*sent make,

The custome is suche yefteʒ for to take.

---

225. as] þat C². —om. H⁵.—most worthy] worthiest H¹. 226. Was *with* marie in an oxes stalle H⁷.—oxes] oxe D, B¹, B³, Ash¹, H¹, H⁶, CC, J, L. 227. full] om. B², B³, B⁴, Ash¹, H¹, H², H³, H⁴, H⁵, H⁶, H⁸, CC, J, C¹, C², C⁵, Ad², Adv², L, An, Lg, Ch, V.—all] om. B⁴, C³. 228. To fore the childe on her knes gan falle B¹.—To fore] Be for Adv².—on] upon Hu.—her] om. B², B⁵, H⁶, H⁸, CC, J, C².—gan] thay D; ganne to B², CC, J; om. H¹, H², C¹, C³, V. 229. her] hem B³; þer B⁵, H²; theyre C³.—and her] *and* it þer B⁵.—her] þere H⁵; om. C². 230. As] Als H⁵, H⁷; and C¹.—can] gan Ash¹; coude H⁶, C², C⁵. 231. And] om. H¹, H⁶, CC.—*pre*sent] presentid B¹, B², B³, B⁵, H⁶, H⁷, H⁸, C³, Ad³, Adv², Hu, L, Hn¹, Co; presenting CC.—in] and in Ash¹; on H⁸, Adv².—all] om. Ash¹, H⁸, C³, Adv².—her] the Ash¹; theyr C³. 232. her] as theire H⁶; as her C⁵.—eu*er*yche] ilche B¹; eche H⁶, C¹, C², C³, Hu; one H⁸; ychon Adv²; euery Co.—othir] another H⁸. 233. her] þer B⁵, C³. 234. her] þer B⁵.—as brothir aftir brothir] euerich after other H⁴.—as] om. B¹.—brothir] other V. 235. franke] frankensence B¹.—and] om. Lg.—yaffe] haue Ash¹; broght H², Hn¹. 236. Aftir] As H⁶.—the] om. B², B⁴, B⁵, H⁵, H⁶, H⁸, CC, C², C³, C⁵, Ad², Adv², Hu, An, Lg, Ch, Co, V; hir C¹.—of] om. C¹.—and] and of B², CC, C³, Ch. 237. For of that londe whanne kyngis *pre*sent make B.—that] those D; þis Hn¹.—londe] londys D, Co.—*pre*sent] present*es* B³, C³.—make] take B³. 238. yefteʒ] present*es* H⁶, CC.—for] om. B¹, H⁸, Adv², L.—take] make B³, Ash¹, Lg.

And this was done w*ith* foyson and plente

240   In verrey sothe and grete haboundau*n*ce;

For in her p*rese*nt was noo scarcete,

For of Riche3 they had all suffisauance.

Wher-fore thay cast with deuoute obeysaunce

Of dewe right w*ith* the childe to parte

Of her tresour or that thay departe.

**Howe the offryng these
iij kyng*es* shall be
vndirstand gostely Ca°
xviij**[1]

A**nd for that golde is payede for tribute,**
      As it is founde of Antiquyte,

Ther-fore these kynges for a man*e*re sewte—

That thay hem aught of verrey deute—

250   Thay brought hym golde oute of her contre,

And yaffe it hym w*ith*outyn Repentaunce,

Holy of hert for a reconysaunce.

---

239. foyson] deuocioun foisoun B[1]. 241. her] herte B[2]; theyr C[3].—*prese*nt] *prese*ntis H[1], H[4].—noo] non B[1]. 242. of] in Ch.—all] gret C[2]; om. C[2]. 243. fore] om. C[2].—deuoute] ful devout Hn[1]. 244. w*ith* the childe] the child with B[1].—with the childe to parte] to do her homage B[3], L.—to] om. C[2]. 245. Of her] and offre B[3], L; Of þer B[5], H[8], C[2], C[3].—or that thay departe] to the child of tendre age B[3], L.—that] om. B[1], CC, C[1], C[2]. 246. for] om. Adv[2].—that] this CC; om. C[5].—for tribute] with tribute B[2], CC, J; to tribute B[5], H[8], C[3], Ad[3], Hu, Co; tribute C[1]. 247. of] in bokes of B[3], L; of olde Ash[1], CC, C[3]; in H[2]; bi C[2]. 248. Ther-fore] Wherefore B[1], B[2], H[7], CC, J.—these] the B[2], B[3], B[4], H[3], H[4], H[5], H[6], CC, J, C[1], C[2], C[5], Ad[2], L, Lg, Ch, V.—sewte] of sute B[1], CC, Adv[2]. 249. hym] to hi*m* B[1], B[5], H[7], H[8], C[3], Ad[3], Adv[2], Hu, Hn[1], Co; om. H[6]; ham Ash[1].—aught] owe B[5], ofte H[8].—of] for C[1], Ad[2].—verrey] a man*e*re C[1]. 251. it] om. Ch. 252. Holy of hert] Holy of al her hert B[5], Adv[2], Hu, Co; Holli of al herte H[7]; Holy with all hare hertes H[8]; W*ith* all theyr hert C[3].—for a] with all C[1].—a] om. B[5], Co.

---

[1]lx is erased.

And franke also, as clerkeȝ can devyse,

Ordenyde is in conclusion,

To God only to make sacryfyce.

W*ith* contryte hert *and* deuocion,

Therfore to hym for oblacion

Thay broughten frank to signyfye thanne,

That he was bothe sothefast god and man.

260   Ande for thei wolde in alle thynge obeie

To his highnesse w*ith* all bysy cure,

In token he shulde for mankynde deye,

Thay brought hym myrre to his sepulture;

For like a man dethe he must endure,

And w*ith* his blode shed in his passion,

Of oure trespas to make redempcioun.

---

253. And] om. B², CC.—also] ensense C³; om. C¹.—as] as so as Ch.—can] gan Ash¹. 254.
in] as in Ash¹, C¹; also in Hn¹; in short B¹. 255. only] aboue H¹. 256. contryte] devoute
B², CC, J.—deuocion] hygh deuosion C³. 257. for] of H⁸; for an C¹.—oblacion] obligacion C¹.
258. frank] ensence C³; om. H⁸, Adv². 259. bothe] om. B¹, B⁵, H⁶, H⁸, C¹, C³, Adv², Hu,
Co. 260. Ande for thei wolde in alle thynge obeie B¹.—thynge] thing*es* D, B⁵, H¹, CC,
C. 261. highnesse] wille H⁸.—all] om. B¹.—bysy] her bysy B¹, Ash¹, H¹, H³, H⁴, H⁶,
H⁷, C², C⁵, Ad², Ad³, An, Hn¹; his busy Hu, Lg, Ch; theyr besy C³; her H⁸, Adv².
262. In token] þat Adv².—he] that he Co. 263. hym] om. B¹, B⁴, H⁷, C¹, Ad³, Lg.—to his]
in Adv². 264. dethe he] he dethe CC. 265. And] om. B¹, H⁶.—shed] schall Adv².—in] om.
C¹. 266. Of oure trespase to make redempcioun B¹.—Of] For B⁴, Ash¹, H², H³, H⁴, H⁵,
H⁶, C¹, C², C⁵, Ad², An, Ch, Co.—to make] make D, H¹, H², C², Adv².

In franke also, who þat can discerne,

Is vndirstonde the highe maieste

Of his power whiche that is et*er*ne;

270   And eke also his high deite.

And golde betokenyth his high dygnyte,

And myrre declareth vnto us at all

Of his manhode that he was mortell.

And golde betokenythe of loue the fervence   f. 78a

That he to man had of affection.

And frank betokenethe the sou*er*eygne excellence,

In holynesse his conu*er*sacion.

And myrre betokenethe the tribulacion

That he suffrede and all the grete penaunce,

280   For vs in erthe by contynuaunce.

---

267. who þat] who so B², B⁴, CC, C¹, Adv², Ch; who can C³.—who] om. C².—can] gan CC.—discerne] disserve C⁵. 268. the] also his CC.—highe] om. Adv². 269. whiche] the weche CC, Adv²; om. H¹, C².—that] om. B¹, H⁸, CC. 270. eke] om. H⁸, C², Adv².—his] of his L, Co.; om. Lg. 271. his] the H⁶, C³; om. H¹—high] worthy C³; om. C². 272. declareth] betokeneth H², H⁸, Adv².—vnto] to B¹, H², Adv².—at] *carrotted above line* D; om. B¹, B³, B⁵, Ash¹, H¹, H², H⁵, H⁶, H⁸, CC, J, C¹, C², C³, L, Ch, Co. 273. Of] þat of C².—that] om. C², Co.—he was] is H⁸. 274. the] *and* the B¹; om. H¹, Adv².—fervence] reuerence CC. 275. of] om. C¹.—to man had of] manhode hath H². 276. souereygne] gret H². 277. his] hir B²; ther CC; and in C¹; of Adv²; of his B³, L; is V.—conu*er*sacion] conversion H⁶. 278. the] his H⁸, Adv²; om. C¹, C². 279. and] in B¹, B⁴, V.—all] om. C¹.—the] his B⁴, B⁵, CC, Co. 280. by] by gret B¹.

In golde he was knowen as a kyng,

In frank a prest, who so can take hede,

Of myrre also this day the offryng

Was longyng only to his manhede.

And thus he was *with*outyn any drede,

Bothe kyng and prest as I discerne can,

And for our sake in erthe a mortall man.

In golde also, metall most gloryouse,

Fygured was his high deite;

290   In franke also—that is so *p*reciouse—

The soule of criste most p*er*fyte of degre;

And Myrre betokeneth thurugh his dignyte,

His flesshe the whiche by disposicion,

May neu*e*re suffre noo corrupcion.

---

281. golde] god Ad², An, Ch.—he was] was he H¹.—a] om. C², Adv². 282. a] as a B², J;
as CC.—who] he H¹.—so] þat B⁵, H¹, Hn¹; om. Hu, Co. 283. Of] In B⁵.—myrre] om.
CC.—also this day the] this day the also B¹.—this] the C¹.—the] of the C¹; of C²; om.
H⁸, Adv². 284. to] un to Adv², Hu, L, Hn¹. 285. thus] þis C². 286. discerne] descrive H⁶,
J, C¹, C⁵, L, An, Lg, Ch; weel Hu. 287. for] om. H¹.—a mortall] by come H⁸, Adv². 288.
metall] mortall H⁵. 289. Fygured was] In franke figured was H¹.—his] in his B¹.—high]
om. C².—deite] degre CC. 290. franke] riche franke H¹.—also] om. B¹, B⁵, H¹, H⁸, C³,
Ad³, Co.—is] was H⁸; he V.—so] so inly B¹, Ad³; also so Hn¹; om. C². 291. the soule
of criste most p*er*fyte of degre] Considrid was the worthy mageste Ash¹.—criste] his humanite
V.—degre] in degre B⁵, H², C¹, Co. 292. thurugh] trouthe J; bi C². 293. His] The B³.—the]
om. B², Ash¹, CC, C², Ad³.—the whiche by] also *and* his H². 294. May] myghte B³. L.—
neu*e*re] om. B¹.—noo] any H¹; om. B³, C³.

And of these yefteȝ passyng Reuerent,
Full of mysterrye and hevenly privete,
Whan thay had made her presente
Vnto the childe ay sittyng on her knee,
With grete avyse thay gan be-holde and se—
300   To fore that thay Remevyde fro that place—
His godely chere and his fayre face.

Considryng his feturs by and by,
With grete insight and humble entencion,
And ay the more thay loke bysyly,
The more thay ioyen in her inspection;
And thought all, as in her reason,
Though kynde and god had sette in ·o· fygure,
The beaute holy of euery creature.

---

295. these] þe B⁵, C³; this CC.—passyng] so passyng Adv²; most C¹. 296. and] and of Co. 297. Whan] And whan B², B⁴, Ash¹, H², H³, H⁴, H⁵, H⁶, CC, J, C¹, C², C⁵, Ad², An, Lg, Ch.—had] om. C².—made] om. C², Lg.—her] theyre H⁶, C³, C⁵.—presente] glorious present Ad³; lowly present Hn¹. 298. Vnto] On to J, C¹; To C².—ay] om. B¹, B⁵, H², H⁷, H⁸, C², C³, Ad³, Adv², Hu, Hn¹, Co.—sittyng] knelynge B¹, C³.—her] þer B⁵, C³.—knee] knes B³. 299. With] And B², Ash¹, H³, H⁴, H⁵, CC, J, Co, C², C⁵, An, Ch; And Ad².—grete] hir B²; there CC.—gan] began B⁴, B⁵, H⁴, H⁵, H⁶, H⁸, CC, C⁵, Adv², An, Lg, Ch; hym H¹; do C²; can Hn¹. 300. To fore that] To fore B³, C³; To fore or C¹; Before or CC; Be for Adv²; or H².—that] om. B¹, B³, B⁵, H⁷, H⁸, Ad³, Co.—Remevyde] remeve B², B⁴, B⁵, H², H³, H⁴, H⁵, H⁶, CC, J, C³, Ad², Ad³, Hu, An, Ch, Hn¹, Co, V; meue B³, L.—that place] þe place B⁵, H⁸, Hu, Co, V. —fro that place] from þat ilke place H⁷, Ad³; out of the place C³, Hn¹. 301. and his fayre face] and faire of face C². 303. grete] besy B³, L. 304. ay] euer B¹, B², B⁵, H⁷, H⁸, CC, C¹, C³, Ad³, Adv², Hu, Hn¹, Co.—the more] om. C².—thay] the B³; that they Hu.—loke] loked B¹, H⁶, Adv²; lokyn H⁷. 305. ioyen] liked B¹, Adv²; like B⁵, H¹, H⁷, H⁸, C³, Ad³, Hu, Hn¹, Co; thynke B², Ash¹, H², H³, H⁴, H⁵, H⁶, CC, J, C², C⁵, Ad², An, Lg, Ch, V; desire B³, L.—in] on Ch.—her] their B², CC, C⁵; om. H⁸, Adv². 306. thought] þei þought H¹.—all] alwaye, B², B³, B⁴, Ash¹, H³, H⁴, H⁵, H⁶, CC, J, C⁵, Ad², L, An, Lg, Ch, V; al so H²; om. H¹.—as] om. B³, H¹, H⁸, C², Adv², L.—her] þer B⁵, H¹, CC, J, C³, V; his H³.—reason] entencioun C¹. 307. Though] Thorugh H¹.—kynde and god] god and kynde B³, H², H⁵, C³, L.—had sette] I sette B², J.— sette] om. C². 308. holy] al B¹, H⁷; only Ch.

It myght not in sothenesse haue be liche   f. 78b

310   To his fayrnesse nor p*e*regall,

For he that is above nature ryche

Hath made this childe fayrest in speciall.

For in his face they byholden all

The hole beaute and fayrnesse eke also,

Of hevyn and erthe to-gydre bothe twoo.

Wherefore no wondre though thay hem delyte

Most passyngly vpon hym to see,

For thay in hert reyoisen hem not a lyte

On hym to loke that thay haue liberte,

320   For ay the more playnely that thay be

In his pr*e*sence, the parfyte hote fyre

Of hertly Ioye hem brent by desyre.

309. not] nought J; om. H². —in sothenesse] soithly B¹, H²; in sothefastnesse H⁶, H⁸, C², Adv², Hu, Co. —haue] a B¹; euen B⁴; heven C⁵; eny C¹. Ad²; to hym H⁶; om. H⁸, C², Ad³, Co. 310. nor] neþthir B¹, H⁷, C¹, C², Hn¹; nouther B³, B⁴, Ash¹, H¹, H³, H⁴, H⁵, J, C⁵, Ad², L, An, Lg, Ch, V; ne B², B⁵, CC, C³, Ad³, Co; or H². 311. is] om. H¹. — ryche] right CC. 312. this] his H¹. —fayrest] farith H¹; om. H⁸, Adv². 313. thay] the B¹. —byholden] behelde B¹, B³, H⁶, H⁷, H⁸, C³, Ad², Ad³, Adv², Hu, L, Ch; holden H². —all] also C². 314. hole] holi CC, C². —eke] om. B¹, H⁸, C¹, Adv², Hu. —also] al C². 316. Wherfore] Therfor H¹, H⁸, Adv². —thay] om. B¹. —hem] þem H⁵; had H⁸; hym C⁵, Hu; om. C². —thay hem] ther be CC. 317. passyngly] passynge H⁸, CC, Adv². —vpon] to up on B¹; on C¹, Adv². —hym] hem H⁵, H⁷. 318. For thay in hert reyoisen hem not a lyte] For of her ioye who can telle or write B³, L. —For thay] om. C². —in hert] om. Ash¹. —reyoisen] reioysed B¹, H⁸, Adv². —hem] om. B¹, B⁵, H¹, H², H⁷, CC, C³, Ad³, Adv², Hu, Hn¹, Co. 319. that] whils C¹. —thay ther Hu. 320. For] And C³. —ay] euer B⁵, H⁷, H⁸, C³, Ad³, Adv², Hu, Hn¹, Co. —ay the more] euermore B¹. —playnely] the playnly H⁶. 321. hote] hool B¹, B⁵, H⁷, C², C³, Ad³, Co, moste Ash¹. —fyre] feer Hu. 322. by] in B², B³, B⁴, Ash¹, H³, H⁴, H⁵, H⁶, CC, J, C¹, C², C⁵, L, An, Lg, Ch, V.

And of ·o· thyngh full gode hede thay toke:

How that the chylde demurely cast his sight

Tawardes hem and godely gan to loke

On her faceȝ with his eyne bryght;

And how that he put his Armeȝ right

Godely to hem makyng a manere signe

To hem of thankyng, with chere full benigne.

330   And of his mothir thay muche thyng enquere,

Touchyng his birthe with humble affeccion;

And she ansewerde, moste femynyne of chere,

Full prudently to euery question

With chere demure and loke ycaste adoune,

With all the porte of womanly clennesse,

Hir-self demenyng and chefly with mekenesse.

---

323. full] om. B1, B4, B5, H3, H4, H6, C1, C5, Ad2, An, Ch.—thay] theer Adv. 324. the chylde demurely] demurly þe childe C2.—demurely] demewre H6; full demurely H8; diuersly C1.—his sight] his loke sight B5; aseght H1. 325. gan] began H6, Adv2.—to] om. C2. 326. her] theyr C3.—his] her C5, Ad2, An, Ch.—eyne] eye Adv2. 327. how] who B1.—that] om. H8, C2, Adv2, Hu.—his] om. Hn1.—Armeȝ] arme B2. 328. makyng] mankynde Ash1.—a manere signe] with chere ful benigne Lg.—manere] om. B1, C2. 329. to hem] And to hem B2; om. B2, H1, C2, L, Hn1.—of] of a H1; of louely thankynge Hn1.—thankyng] thanke CC.—with] of CC, J, V.—chere] om. C1.—full] right H1; om. H6, C2, L. 330. thay] om. C1, Adv2.—muche] might B2, CC, J.—thay much thing enquere] moch þing þei enquere B5, H1; mechynge C2. 331. his] hir H5.—with] om. C1. 332. ansewerde] andwerith B1, B2, B3, H1, H2, H3, H4, H5, H7, C5, Ad2, Ad3, Adv2, Hu, L, An, Ch, Hn, V. 333. euery] eueryiche H1. 334. demure] benynge H6.—and] with B1; her B5, H7, H8, C3, Ad3, Adv2, Hn1, Co.—loke] Ie Ash1.—ycaste] castynge B1; caste B5, Ash1, H1, H6, H7, H8, C2, C3, Ad3, Hu, Hn1, Co.—adoune] doun B1, H2, H6, C2. 336. and] om. B2, B3, B4, Ash1, H3, H4, H5, CC, J, C5, Ad2, An, Lg, Ch, V.—and chefly] and cleerli H1; principally H6; goodly C1; om. C2.

Of vertuose pou*e*rte
and mekenesse of
our lady Ca°lxxiiii°¹
19ᵐ

O she that was of hevyn and erthe quene,
And of hell, lady and eke pryncesse,
O what was he, alas, that may susteyne
340 To be proude considryng her mekenesse!
O pryde, alas, o Rote of our distresse!
Though thy boste above the skyes blowe

No*t*a bene **nota**

Thy bildyng high shall be brought full lowe!

O thou suquydre, alas, whi nylt thou see   f. 79a
Howe she that hathe hevyn in hir demayne,
And souerayne lady is bothe of londe and see,
And of the axtre by-twene the pole3 tweyne
And all the enbrasyng of the golden cheyne,
Yet vnto god, I say in sothefastnesse,
Above all this agrede her mekenesse.

---

337. O] as B³, L; om. C¹, V.—erthe] of erthe H⁷—quene] the quene Ash¹. 338. of hell] all hole CC.—and eke pryncesse] and here eke princesse Co.—eke] om. B², B³, B⁴, Ash¹, H¹, H², H³, H⁴, H⁵, H⁶, CC, J, C¹, C², C⁵, Ad², L, An, Lg, V.—pryncesse] her princesse B¹, B⁵, H⁷, H⁸, C³, Ad³, Hu; emp*e*rasse Ch. 339. what] who Adv².—was] is B¹, B³, H¹, H², H⁷, Ad³, Adv², L, Hn¹.—he] sche An, Hn¹; om. Adv².—that] om. Adv².—may] my3t B⁴, H⁶, H⁸, Ch; woll H². 340. To] For to H¹.—considryng] considrid B¹, B⁵, Ash¹, H⁶, H⁷, Ad², Ad³, Adv², Hu, An, Lg, Ch, Hn¹, Co. V. 341. our] om. B¹. 342. Though thy boste] Thow thu thi bost B¹, H¹, H⁷, H⁸, C³, Ad³, Adv², Hu; Thorow thyne oste B², CC, J.—skyes] skye H², C³. 343. high] om. C².—full] to be ful Lg. 344. thou] om. B², B³, Ash¹, H¹, H², H³, H⁴, H⁵, CC, J, C¹, C⁵, Ad², V.—nylt] *"wilte"* is under-dotted *for erasure and "nylt" appears above it in another hand* D; wilt B², H⁸, CC, C³.—see] not see B², H⁸, CC, J, C³. 345. she that hathe] þat she had B⁴, Ash¹, H⁴, H⁶, C², C⁵, Ad², An, Lg, Ch; she had C¹.—hathe hevyn] heuen hath Hn¹.—in] at C³. 346. souerayne] om. B², B³, B⁴, Ash¹, H¹, H², H³, H⁴, H⁵, H⁶, CC, J, C², C⁵, Ad², Hu, L, An, Lg, Ch, V.—is bothe] as bothe is H⁶.—is] om. H⁸, Adv².—of] on C², Lg, Hn¹; and B².—and] om. H¹. 347. of] om. Adv².—axtre] aix H¹.—by twene] atweyn H¹.—pole3] peples H². 348. all] of B⁴, Ash¹, H⁴, H⁶, C¹, C⁵, Ad², An, Ch; of al B³.—golden] goodly B¹, B⁵, H⁷, H⁸, C³, Ad³, Adv², Hu, Hn¹, Co. 349. vnto] onto C⁵; in to C².—god] hir B², B³, B⁴, Ash¹, H³, H⁴, H⁵, H⁶, CC, C¹, C², C⁵, Ad², L, An, Lg, Ch, V; om. J.—sothefastnesse] sothenesse H⁸, Adv². 350. this] binge H¹.—agrede] grewe C¹.—her] is her B², CC, J, CC, J, Adv²; *with* H⁶.

---

¹Crossed **through.**

O pompe elate, with thy cherez bolde,   Nota bene nota

Remembre and see and loke how that she—

On whom kyngez haue yoye to by-holde—

In her presence to knelen on her knee,

Though she of wemen be highest in degre,

Take hede and see how lowly in a stable

Howe that she satte this lady worshipable.

Wer ther of golde any clothez founde,   Nota bene nota

Of silke damaske or ryche tarteryne?

360   Or was ther arras a-bouȝte hir head vp boonde,

Or was ther any veluet Crymesyne,

Or was ther any samyte or satyne

Or wer ther any tappytez large or wyde.

The nakyd grounde to keuer or to hide?

---

351. pompe] *crossed out in* B⁵.—cherez] sterres Ash¹. 352. and see] om. Hu.—and loke
how that she] how and loke how þat sche H⁸.—and loke] om. C¹.—how] om. Ch. 353.
On] Of B², J, C¹; In Ch.—kyngez] that kyngis B¹.—haue] om. C². 354. on her] on
theire H⁶, C⁵, L.—knee] kneis C². 355. she of wemen] she a woman B⁴, H¹; she
woman Ash¹; of women sche C²; she of womonhede Adv².—in] of B¹, B⁵, Ash¹, H¹,
CC, C³, Adv², Hn¹, Co.—degre] degres B², C². 356. and see] om. B¹.—stable] stall
C¹, C³, L; stall or stabill Ash¹. 357. Howe that she satte, this lady worshippable] How
she sat that ladi worchipable B¹; She sat with hir sone this lady hommble B³; She
sat with hir sone this lady honorable L; She sad þis ladi woundir worshapble H¹;
Thys swete lady most worshypfull of all C³.—Howe] om. Hn¹.—that she] om. C².—
this] þat H⁷.—worshippable] worship of all C¹. 358. any] as any Lg. 359. or ryche]
or of riche B¹, B⁵, Hu, Co.—ryche of H⁸, Adv². 360. Or was ther arras a bouȝte hir
heed vp boounde B¹] Or were þer ony hornes high robis rownde H¹.—Or was ther
arras] Or perrey or aras C².—ther] the Co.—a bouȝte] above D, Co; tostred aboute
B³, L.—heed] om. H⁶.—vp] om. B², B⁴, Ash¹, H³, H⁴, H⁸, CC, J, C¹, C², C³, Ad²,
Adv², An, Lg, Ch, V.—boounde] I hong C¹; om. C².—hir heed vp boounde] al rounde
B³, L. 361. was] were H¹.—veluet] violet H⁸; om. C².—Crymesyne] or Crymesyne B³, H¹,
H², H⁸, C¹, Adv², L. 362. was] were H¹.—was ther] om. C².—samyte] palle B³, An; chamlyt
Adv². 363. wer] was B¹, H², H⁸, C³, Adv².—wer ther] om. C².—or] and H⁶, C²,
L. 364. The nakyd grounde to keuer or to hide B¹.—nakyd] bare C¹.—keuer] curen
H⁵, C⁵, Ad².—or] and D, C³, C⁵.—to] om. C², Adv², Hu.—hide] honge C¹.

Or was her palyce bilt of lyme and stone,   No*t*a bene nota

Or the pillours sette vp of Marble graye,

Or the growne pavede on to gon,

Or fresshe *par*lours gla3ed bright as day,

Or were ther any chaumbre3 of a ray,

370   Or for estate3 was ther any hall

Saue a dongon and an oxe stall?

Or of hir bede was the appareyll   No*t*a *bene* **nota**

Of golde or sylke curteynede large a-boute,

Or were ther shete3 of longe or wyde entayle

Kyt oute of Reynes nay *with*-outyn*n* doute?

Or were there any lade3 for to loute

To hir highnesse *with* bysy obse*r*uance,

Or of maydens any attendaunce?

---

365. was] were H1.—her] ther B1, H1, CC, C1, C2, Co; his Hu; the V.—palyce] any
paleyse C2.—of lyme] with lyme C1, Adv2.—and] or B2, B5, H2, H6, C2, Ad3, Hu, Hn1, Co.
366. sette] I set C2.—up of] up on B1, B2, B3, Ash1, H2, H3, H4, H5, H7, CC, J, C2, C3,
Ad2, Hu, L, Lg, Ch, Hn1, V; on B4, B5, H6, C5, Ad3, An, Co; with H8, Adv2. 367. pavede]
pathed B1, H7, Ad3, Hu.—to] for to B1, B3, L. 368. *par*lours] floures B2, J; wyndowes B3,
L.—bright] or bry3t Adv2.—as] and B3, L. 369. were] was H8. 370. estate3] any astatis
B1, B2, B4, C2; be statis. 371. an] om. H.—oxe] oxes B2, B4, H1, H3, H5, H6, H7, H8, C1,
C2, C5, Ad2, Ad3, Hu, An, Lg, Hn1, Co, V. 372. of hir bede] for hir a beed B1; on hir
bede H8; be bedde C2.—the] þer B4, H6, H8, CC, C3, Adv2.—appareyll] any appareile
H6, H8, C1, Adv2. 373. Of] om. B1.—or] and H3, H4, H6, CC, Ad2, An, Ch; or of L.—
curteynede large] large curtenid B1; conteyned large B5.—large] om. CC. 374. ther] the
B1, B2, B4, Ash1, H1, H2, H3, H4, H5, H6, H7, H8, J, C3, C5, Ad3, Hu, L, An, Lg,
Ch, Hn1 Co, V.—of] om. H8, Adv2.—or wyde entayle] or wyde of entayle Adv2; enteile
C2. 375. oute] om. B3, B5, H8, C2, C3, Ad3, Adv2, Hn1, Co.—nay] not B4.—Kyt oute of
Reynes] Oute of Reynes Kutte Hn1; Curteyne of reynes H8. 376. any lade3] ladies any H2.—
for to loute] to hir for to lou3te B1, B5, H7, C3, Ad3, Hu, Hn1, Co; hir to allowte H8,
C2; hur a lowtt Adv2.—loute] alowte Ch. 377. To hir] To do hir plesance B1, B5, H7, C3,
Ad3, Hu, Hn1, Co.—highnesse] plesaunce H8, C2, Adv2.—bysy] all H8, Adv2; esy Lg.
378. of] of any C2; om. H1, H8, Adv2,—any] of any H1; doyng any Adv2.—attendaunce]
tendance C1.

Nota bene nota

O as me semythe, of verrey dewe right,

380　Ye wemen alJ shulden take hede—

With your perleȝ and *your* stoneȝ bright—

How that your quene, floure of womanhede,

Of no devyse enbroyded hath her wede,

Ne furrede withe Ermyne ne *with* tresty graye,

Nota bene nota　　　　Ne martren ne sable, I trowe in gode faye,

Was noon founden in her garment,

And yet she was the fayrest for to see

That eu*er*e was vndir the firmament.

Wherfore, me semyth, ye shulde haue pyte

390　To se a lady of so high degre,

So semely atyrede, o ye wemen all.

Be-holde howe narowe closede in an oxe stalle.

---

379. O] om. B³, L.—right] *and* riȝt C². 380. þe] Yee C¹, Ch.—wemen] woman H¹; wymen yee C¹. 381. perleȝ and *your* stoneȝ] stonnys and perlys briȝt B⁵, Co; stones and ȝoure perles bryȝt Ch.—stoneȝ] ryche stonȝ Adv²; precious stones B¹. 382. that] om. B², CC, J.—your] þe C².—floure] om. C². 383. embroyded] hathe enbrowdid CC.—her] his Hu. 384. Ne] om. H¹.—ne *with*] nor with H⁸, Adv²; or CC.—*with*] om. H³, C². 385. Ne martren] nor martyn H¹; Martyn ne H².—martren] "-en" *carrotted in another hand to replace "is" crossed out in original "martris"*, D.—ne] *inserted by another hand before "sable"*, D; om. B¹, B⁵, H⁷, H⁸, C³, Ad³, Adv², Co.—I trowe] om. C².—trowe] trust H³. 386. Was] Ther was B¹, B⁵, H⁷, H⁸, C³, Adv², Hu, Hn¹, Co. 387. yet] om. B¹.—for] on B⁵, H⁸, Adv², Co; om. C¹. 389. Wherfore] Thanne B², B³, CC, L, V; þat B⁴, Ash¹, H¹, H², H³, H⁴, H⁵, H⁶, J, C², C⁵, Ad², An, Lg, Ch; Them C¹. 390. of so high degre] so worthy and of heye degre Hu.—degre] degres B². 391. semely] symply B¹, B³, B⁵, Ash¹, H¹, H², H⁵, H⁷, H⁸, C¹, C³, Ad³, Adv², Hu, L, Hn¹, Co, V.—atyrede] araied H¹. 392. Be holde howe narowe closede in an oxe stalle] Beholde hyr paleys was but an ox stall C³.—Be holde how] om. B², B³, B⁴, Ash¹, H¹, H², H³, H⁴, H⁵, H⁶, CC, J, C¹, C², C⁵, Ad², Hu, L, An, Lg, Ch, V.—narowe] So narow B², B⁴, Ash¹, H³, H⁴, H⁵, H⁶, CC, J, C¹, C², C⁵, Ad², L, An, Lg, Ch, V; And so narowe B³, H², L; So pareli H¹; So streyghtly Hu.—closede in] she is closed in B¹; clothid be sid H¹; sche was bi side H⁷; sche closid in H⁸, Adv², closed byside Hu; she she closed was beside Ad³, Hn¹.—closed] om. B⁵, Co.—oxe] oxes B², B⁴, B⁵, H³, H⁵, H⁷, C¹, C⁵, Ad², Ad³, Hu, Hn¹, Co, V.

Late be *your* pryde and *your* affeccion

Of riche aray, and nothyng yov delite

In worldely pompe and suche abusion

Of sundri clothis, reede, bleke *and* white.

And be well ware, or the spere byte

Of cruell dethe and the fell smerte.

Nota bene nota   My councell is to lyfth vp yowre hert

400   To that lady and to that worthy quene,

Þat ȝou may beest helpe in ȝour nede,

And yov releve in eu*er*y woo and tene,

And delyu*er*e from all myscheve and drede.

And þinkeþ pleynly *and* takyth riȝt good hede,

Þat al schal passe, aray *and* eke richesse,

When ye lest wene and all *your* semblynesse.

394. and] om. C². 395. abusion] ambusioun B¹, H⁷. 396. Of sundri clothis reede blake *and* white H⁷.—Of] In D, B², H⁶, C¹, Co.—sundri] dyvarse Adv².—reede] of reede B¹, Ash¹; with rede C¹.—and] or H⁶. 397. well] om. C².—spere] swerde C³. 398. and] or and H¹; and or C³.—the] of V. 399. My councell is to lyfth vp yowre hert B¹.—to lyfth vp] to god lyfte up L.—yowre] thyne D, H⁶. 400. to] om. B¹, H¹, H⁷, H⁸, C³, Adv², Hu, Hn¹—that] om. H. 401. þat ȝou may beest helpe in ȝour nede H⁷.—ȝou] om. B⁴.—ȝou may] ȝew C¹.—beest helpe] helpe best D.—ȝour] al ȝoure B⁴.—nede] worthi nede CC.—all] euery B¹, H⁷, Ad³; om. CC. 402. Woo] word Co. 403. and] To H⁶.—delyuere] you delyuer B³, CC.—all] euery B¹, H⁷, Ad³; om. CC. 404. and þinkeþ pleynly *and* takyth riȝt good hede H⁷.—þinkep] thankythe D, J.—*and* takyth] to take C¹.—riȝt] om. B¹, B², B⁵, H¹, H², H⁸, CC, J, C¹, C², C³, Adv², Hu, Co.—good] fulle Hu. 405. þat al schal passe aray *and* eke richesse H⁷.—schal] suche CC.—eke] also B¹; all D; om. B⁵, H⁸, Co. 406. lest] list H¹.—all] eke Ch.—*your*] þe H².

Lat hem affore be to yov a kalendere: No*t*a be*n*e nota
Isoude, Elyn, and eke polixene,
Hester also and dydo w*ith* her chere,
410 And Riche Candace, of ethyope quene,—
Ligge þei not graue vndre clowris grene?
And yet all this may not yo*ur* pryde atame,
Nought withestondyng þat ye shall do the same.

f. 80a   Eke after dethe a-bydyth no memorye,   No*t*a be*n*e nota
For ay w*ith* dethe comyth for-yetylnesse;
And fare well than arey and all veyneglorye,
Saue only vertu that stant in sikernesse.
I take recorde of the high mekenesse
Of hir that is of holynesse welle,
420 Of whome I thynke sothely for to telle,

407. hem] him C².—affore] be afore B² CC, J; tofore B⁵, Hn¹; be to fore C¹.—be to yov] you B², CC, J, C¹; ȝow be Hu.—] om. H⁸.—a] *carrotted* above line, D; as B⁵; om. B¹, H¹, C³, Co, V. 408. Elyn] Coleyn H⁶.—and] om. C¹.—eke] *and* also Adv²; om. C³, Ch.—polixene] fayre pollicene B¹, B⁵, H⁷, H⁸, C², C³, Ad³, Adv², Hu, Hn¹, Co. 409. also] om. H⁶.—also and] and also B¹.—chere] gudly chere Adv². 410. Riche] om. B³, L.—of] and Co.—quene] the quene C¹, Adv², L. 411. Ligge þei not graue vndre clowris grene H⁷.—Ligge] Ben D.—þei not] not þe H¹, L; dede C².—graue] groiff B²; *in* graue C², C³; graued Hu; now B¹.—clowris] colours D, B³, B⁴, H³, H⁴, H⁵, H⁶, H⁸, C¹, C⁵, Ad², Ad³, Hu, L, An, Lg, Ch; floures B⁵, CC, Co; clottes H², Adv²; turues Ash¹, C³. 412. And] om. H².—yet all] al yit H¹.—may not] ne may C¹. 413. þat] om. B¹, B³, H³, C¹, C², L.—ye] om. Hu.—do] to H⁸, Adv². 414. Eke] And B⁴, Ash¹, H³, H⁴, C¹, C², C⁵, Adv², An, Lg, Ch.—no] om. Hu. 415. ay] eu*er* B¹, B², B⁵, H⁷, CC, Adv², Hu, Hn¹, Co; yeven H⁸.—with] aftyr Hu.—for] forth CC.—for yetylnesse] fornefulnesse H⁸. 416. And] om. H⁶.—fare well than] than farewell Hu.—than] om. Ch.—aray and all veyneglorye] all grete ary and all veyneglorye H⁸; all grett a ray *and* veynglory Adv²; all aray *and* veynglory C¹.—aray and] om. C².—all] om. H², H⁶, Hn¹. 417. that stant] styll þat stond H².—stant] stondith B¹, B⁵, H⁶, H⁸, CC, Adv². 418. the] thy B²; om. B¹, H⁴.—high] om. H².—the high] all H⁸, Adv². 419. Of hir that is] For that is H⁸; of þat þat is C¹; þat is Adv².—welle] the well B¹, B⁵, Ash¹, H², H⁷, H⁸, C¹, C², C³, Ad³, L, Co, V. 420. Of whome] om. H¹.—whome] om. CC.—sothely] shortly H².—for] om. B¹, H⁸, CC, C³, Adv².

How that she satte, for all hir worthynesse,
Holdyng hir childe full lowly on the grounde;
And kyngeȝ knelyng, as ye haue herde expresse,
Be-holdyng hir in vertu most habounde,
Til at þe laste þey haue a leyser founde
To take her leve, and the same day
Thay gon to Ryde homwarde on her waye.

Nota bene nota

And sewyng aftir on the next nyght,
While thay slepte at her logyng place,
430 Came an Angell, a-peryng with grete light,
And warnede hem that thay ne trace
By herodeȝ, but bade þat thay shulde pace
Withe-oute a-bood, in all the haste thay may
To her kyngedom by another way.

howe the Angell
warnede the iij
kyngeȝ not to passe
by heroude but by
an othir way Ca°
lxxix°[1] 20ᵐ

---

421. that] om. H8, Adv2. 422. full] om. B2, B3, B4, Ash1, H1, H2, H3, H4, H6, CC,
J, C1, C2, C5, Ad2, L, An, Lg, Ch, V.—on] in C3. 423. And] om. H1.—ye] om. B4.—haue herde]
han herde B4.—haue] om. C2. 424. Be holdyng] By held H8; Be hold Adv2.—in] om.
Ash1.—most] to C1. 425. Til at þe laste þey haue a leyser founde H7.—Tyll] And B3,
L; That Hu.—þe] om. D.—haue] hadde B1, C3.—leyser] letter Ad3.—founde] I founde
H1.—haue a leyser founde] a leyser they found C1. 426. her] theyr C3.—the] on the B1,
H7, Ad3, 427. Thay] Thanne B2; om. V.—gon] began H6, Adv2, V.—on] in B2, B4, Ash1,
H1, H2, H3, H4, H8, CC, J, C1, C3, C5, Ad2, Hu, An, Lg, Ch, Hn1, Co; by Adv2; om.
B1, C2.—her] þer B5, C3, þe Adv2. 428. aftir] om. Ch.—on] *carrotted above line in another
hand* D; om. B4, C2, Adv2. 429. While] The whiles H8.—slepte] slepe C2.—at] in Ash1.
C2.—her] þer B5, C3.—logyng] longing CC; lyggynge Hu. 430. Came] Ther cam B1, B5,
H7, H8, C3 Ad3, Adv2, Hu, Hn1, Co; Come V. 431. thay] om. An.—ne trace] not ne trace
B2, B4, B5, H7, J, Ad3, Hu, An, Ch, Hn1, Co, V; not trace Ash1, H1, H4, H6, CC,
C2, C3, C5, Lg; ne thei ne trace B1; noȝt take trace H8; tooke not the trace Adv2. 432.
but] om. B4.—bade] om. B2, B3, B4, Ash1, H3, H4, H6, CC, J, C2, C5, Ad2, L, An,
Lg, Ch, V.—þat] om. B1, B5, H1, H2, H7, C2, Ad3, Hu, Hn1, Co.—pace] not pace B4.
433. oute] om. B2, CC, J.—a bood] tariyng H1; abidyng H6.—all] om. B2, CC, J.—the
haste thay may] the hast that they may B2, CC, J, Adv2; haste that þey may B4, B8;
that thei may B1.— may] myȝte C1. 434. To her kyngedom by another way B1.—her]
theyre D, B5, C3.—kyngdome] kyngdomes C3.—by] home by H8, Adv2.—waye] waye to go
tiȝte C1.

---

[1]crossed through.

And in shorte tyme, to her Region

Thay ben repayrede, the gospell tellyth vs.

And of her nameʒ, to make mencion,

The first in Ebrwe was callede Appellius;   Appellius

The next Amerus, the thryde Damathus;   Amerus

440   And in greke, the first Galgatha,   Damathus

And Serachym, the thryde Malgalatha.   Galgalath

Sarachim

And in latyn, as bokeʒ maken mynde,   Malgalatha

The first of hem named was Iasper;   Iasper

And the secounde, playnely as I fynde,   Baltaʒer

Lyche myne Auctour reherseʒ as I dar,   Melchiore

Called was and namede Balthasar;

And the thryde—ye gete of me no more—

As I Rede was callede Melchiore.

435. her] þer B⁵, C³. 436. ben] om. H¹.—tellyth] seiþ C², V.—vs] thus B², B⁴, Ash¹, H⁴, H⁶, CC, J, C¹, C⁵, Ad², Hu, L, Lg, Ch, V. 437. And] om. C¹.—of] om. C².—her] theyre C³, Hu.—to make] to take H¹. 438. callede] slepid H⁷, C³, Hu, Hn¹. 439. next] secunde B⁴, C¹, Hn¹. 441. And] And the secounde B¹, B², CC, J; The secunde B⁴.—And Serachym] The secounde Marachym B³, L.—the] *and* þe C¹; om. Adv². 443. named was] was named B³, B⁴, C¹, Adv², L.—named] I named C².—was] is B¹, CC. 444. playnely as I fynde] as I finde pleinly Lg.—I] we Adv². 445. reherseʒ] rehersyng H⁶, H⁸, C³, Hu.—as] om. H¹, C¹, Ad².—as I dar] can and dare B², CC; as I can or dare H⁶; is I can or dar J. 446. Called was and namede] Calde *and* named was B¹, Adv²; Named was *and* called H¹; Was called and namede H⁶; I namyd was C¹, C². 447. And] om. B², H⁶, C³.— ye gete of me no more] of me ʒe gett no more B⁵. 448. As I rede was] Was as I rede C¹.— As] om. B³.—was callede] called was B¹, H², Co.—callede] i-called Ch.

Of whose repayre, as some bokeȝ sayne,   f. 80b

450   That first of all thay wente to the see,

And retournede to her kyngdome agayne.

Thay shippede hem at Tharce the Cyte,

For whiche heroude, of cursede cruelte.

In *spiritu* vehementi   In Tharce made all the shippeȝ brenne,

conterens naves Tarsis   Wher-of wrytheth Dauid, the sauter if ye kenne.

And vnto yov clerly to specifie,

Towchynge this fest *and* this solempnite,

Wherof is sayde this worde Epyphanye,

Whiche is a worde of grete Auctoryte;

460   And sayde and componede, who so can se,

Of Epi firste, and phanos, sothe to sayne.

And of o worde combynede of these twayne,

---

449. Of] That CC.—bokeȝ] booke H¹. 450. the] om. Co. 451, And] And to B³, L.—
retournede] returnynge B¹, B⁴, B⁵, Ash¹, H², H³, H⁴, H⁷, H⁸, J, C³, C⁵, Ad², Ad³,
Hu, An. Lg, Ch, Hn¹, Co, V; retourne B³, L.—her] þer B⁵, C³, Hu. 452. Thay] The
C¹.—shippede] shippen Ash¹, C².—hem] om. B³, C², C³, L, Hn¹, Co.—at] in CC.—theȝ
that B¹.—Cyte] huge Cyte C³. 453. For whiche] wherfore B³, L.—whiche] þe whech Adv²,
Co.—heroude] the heroude B¹; grounde C².—herode of cursede cruelte] cursed herode
of cruelte.—of] and J. 454. the] om. Hu, Hn¹—brenne] to brenne B³, H⁶, H⁷, CC, J,
Hn¹; be brent C¹. 455. wrytheth] say H¹; om. C².—wrytheth Dauid] david wrytþ
Adv². in the] B¹, B², H¹, H⁶, CC; in his C¹.—if] of H¹; as H².—if ye kenne] ye hit
kenne C¹, Adv²; ȝit I kene C¹. 456. And vnto yov clerly to specifie] Cleerly to you
for to specifie H¹.—to specifie] doith specyfy C¹; for to specyfye L. 457. Towchynge
this fest *and* this solempnite B¹.—this] the D.—this solempnyte] solempnyte H¹, C², Hn¹. 458.
is] y H².—worde] holy fest B², CC; worthi fest H⁶, J; word*es* Adv².—Epyphanye] of Epiphanie H⁸. 460 And] om. H¹, C².—componede] compassed H⁶.—so] that B¹, B⁵, H¹, Ad³, Adv²,
Hn¹, Co; as B²; om. Hu.—who so] þat can H⁷, H⁸; whose that C³. 461. sothe] om. B², Ash¹.
—to] for to B², CC. 462. of] om. B², B³, B⁴, B⁵, Ash¹, H³, H⁴, H⁶, H⁸, CC, J, C², C³, C⁵,
Ad², Adv², Hu, L, An, Lg, Ch, Co, V; so B¹, H⁷, Ad³, Hn¹.—o] om. H².—combynede]
compowned H¹; comprehendid CC; comeþ C²; compilede Co; combyned J, Ad³.—these] hem
H⁶; this H⁸, CC, C³, Ad³.

Comyth this worde of Epyphanye.

And this word Epi, by descripcion

Is sayde of heght, as I can signyfie;

And of a shewyng by demonstracion

Is phanos sayde; and so by gode reason,

Epi and phanos, bothe knyt in fere,

Is a shewyng that dothe a-lofte pere.

470   And for this day, a-lofte was the sterre

Which cristeʒ birthe and Incarnacion

W*ith* his stremeʒ gan shewe fro so ferre,

Fro Est to West in many a Region.

Wherfore this fest, in conclusion,

As ye to-forne haue herde me specifye,

This fest is callede of Epiphanye.

---

463. of] om. B², B³, H⁶, CC, J, L, Co. 464. word] om. B³.—descripcion] discreccion H⁸, Hn¹. 465. Is] I H¹.—heght] heigh H¹, H⁶. 466. And] om. C¹.—of] om. C³.—a] om. H⁸, C².—of a] as H¹.—demonstracion] discripcion H⁶. 467. so] om. B¹. 468. bothe knyt] y knyt H², C¹, C².—knyt] but CC. 469. that] as it H⁶.—dothe a lofte] a lofte doth H¹, H⁸.—a lofte] on loft Adv²; also J; om. H⁶. 471. and] and his H², C², Adv². 472. gan] coun B¹; can C¹.—shewe] shede B⁴, H³, H⁴, C¹, C², C⁵, Ad², Lg, Ch.—fro] om. B¹, B², H⁶, CC, J.—ferre] far H¹. 473. a] om. B⁵, H¹, H², J, Hu, Co, V. 474. Wherfore] b*er*for H¹; Wherof H⁶.—in] by Adv². 475. As] And H¹.—to forne] be for Adv².—herde] om. H⁸. 476. This fest is callede] Is called the feste B³, C³, L.—of Epiphanye] worthili epiphanie B¹, H⁷, Ad³.—of] the Hn¹; om. Hu.

The wheche feste haith a prerogatif

Of myracleȝ notable in speciall,

For thyng*es* foure wrought in crist*es* lyfe

480 Wern on this day by his power Riall.

The first of all most memoryall

Is of the kyngeȝ, as ye haue herde me sayne

Whiche were in ydelle to Reherse agayne.

The secounde is, as it is sothely tolde, .ij.   f. 81a

That criste Ihe*s*u, this day of saint Iohn,

The yere whan he was xxx^{ti} wynter olde,

Baptisede was in the flume Iourdan.

At whiche tyme, thre kyngeȝ vnder one,

Discendeth this day worthy of memorye.

490 The firste was that from the high glorye, .i.

---

477. The wheche feste haith a prerogatif B¹.—wheche] om. H².—fest] om. H⁷.—haith] is D. 478. notable] noble H¹, CC. 479. thyng*es* foure] four thingis C¹, C², Adv².—crist*es*] his B², H⁶, CC, J. 480. day] om. H¹.—by] doon by Hn¹. 481. of all] fest H⁶.—most memoryall] and moste memorial Hn¹; for a memoriall B², B³, B⁴, Ash¹, H¹, H², H³, H⁴, H⁶, CC, J, C¹, C², C⁵, Ad², L, An, Lg, Ch, V. 482. of] om. H¹.—the] these CC.—haue] om. H¹, H², C².—herde me] me harde B¹. 483. in] but B², H⁶, CC, J.—Reherse] here C². 484. The secounde is as] The secunde it is B⁴, Ad².—as it] om. C¹.—as] om. H³, H⁴, C⁵, An, Ch.—sothely] sortly B¹; pleinly H¹; soth y H²; om. H⁸. 485. saint] om. Hu. 486. whan] was L.—wynter] yeres B¹; yere H⁶, C¹. 487. was] he was B⁴, H⁴, C¹, C⁵, Ad², An, Ch.—the] om. H⁸, C¹, C³, Co. 488. whiche] þe which Adv². 489. Discendeth] Descendid B¹, C³, Adv², Hn¹; Fellen H¹; appered B², B³, B⁴, Ash¹, H², H³, H⁴, H⁶, CC, J, C¹, C², C⁵, Ad², L, An, Lg, Ch, V.—this] þat C².—worthy] worþily Lg.—of] in B¹; om. H¹. 490. that] om. C¹, L, V.—the high] þe se of H²; that hye L.

The faders voyce, as clerkeȝ lust endyte,

Came dovne to erthe that men myght here;

And like a dove *with* fayre feders white,

The holy gost also dyd a-pere;

And criste Ih*e*su, the faders son entere   .ij.

This day aperyng in our mortall kynde,

Was of saint Iohn Baptiȝede, as I fynde.   .iij.

And for as moche as thay all thre

This day were sene by sothefaste apparence—

500   Thay beyng one in p*er*fyte vnyte—

Therfore, this day of moste Reuerence,

Named is truly in sentence,

Theophanos, for god in trible wyse

Ther in aperyd, as yo haue herde devyse.

491. endyte] to endite B¹, H², Adv². 492. erthe] the erthe C³. 493. fayre] om. C², Adv².
494. also] did also H¹. 495. entere] et*er*ne B². 496. our] *your* H⁸, L. 497. saint] om. H².
498. And] As B¹.—as] als CC, Adv².—thre] þere Hn¹. 499. sothefaste] soth H¹; om. B¹.
500. Thay] Ther Hu.—in] om. C².—p*er*fyte] om. B², H⁶, CC, J. 501. of moste] moost of
B¹. 502. sentence] his sentence Ash¹; þe sentence C²; this sentence B², B³, B⁴, H³, H⁴, H⁶,
CC, J, C¹, C⁵, Ad², L, An, Ch, V. 503. trible] trowbyll CC; Theble Ad². 504. Ther in]
The C¹.—devyse] me deuyse B¹.

For theos is as moche for to mene

As god in englisshe, yf ye lust to se;

Phanos a shewyng wi*th*outen any wene,

As ye haue herde aforne rehersed of me;

And for in erthe, o god in Trynyte,

510 This day aperede wi*th*outen any lye,

Ye truly may calle it theophane.

Eke whan crist was passede xxx" yere,

This day he turnede water in to wyne

That passyngly was to the eye clere

And of tarage inly gode and fyne,

The whiche he sent to Archideclyne.

And for this myracle Inly vertuouse,

In Galele was shewed in a house.

505. theos] this H8.—for] om. B1, Adv2. 506. yf ye] if that ye] B1, CC; who so Hn1.—
to] for to B2, H1, CC.—se] here V. 507. Phanos] Ande phanos B1, B2, B3, H4, Ash1,
H3, H4, H6, H7, CC, J, C1, C2, C5, Ad2, Adv2, L, An, Lg, Ch, Hn1, V.—a] as H1,
H3, H4, C5, Ad2; ay Ch.—a shewyng] alashewynge B1.—any] om. C2. 508. haue] om.
C1.—aforne] to fore C1; om. H6.—aforne rehersed] rehersed a forne B1, Adv2.—rehersed]
reherce B2, H7, C3, Hu, V; rehersyn Co. 509. And] om. B2, B3, Ash1, H2, H3, H4, H6,
CC, J, C1, C2, L, Lg, V. 510. any] om. B5, C2. 511. ye truly may] Therfore ye may H6;
ʒe trewly mowe yee C1; Ye may truly Adv2.—calle it] it calle B1, B2, B4, Ash1, H3, H4,
H5, H7, H8, C2, C3, C5, Ad2, Ad3, Adv2, Hu, An, Lg, Ch, Hn1, V.—it] þe B4, Ash1,
H8, C3, Adv2; om. B3, L.—theophane] Epiphanye B4, Ash1, H8, C1, C3, Adv2, 512. Eke]
Also H8, Hu.—whan] whan þat H1.—passede] of age Hn1; om. B4, Ash1, H3, H4, C1, C5,
Ad2, An.—yeer of age C1. 513. he] om. H1.—in] om. B1. 514. passyngly] passing CC.—
was] om. B1, C1.—to] i*n* C2; om. CC. 515. tarage] talage B2, H1, H4, CC, Hu, An; cariage
C2. 516. to] unto H8. 517. for] om. Adv2.—myracle] mariage C2.—Inly] in C1. 518. was
shewed] she went H1.—shewed] shewith C1.—in] and in B1.

This same day whiche men dyd espye—

520   As holy chirche maketh mencion—

Therfore it is namede Bethphanye.

For Bethe in Inglisshe by discripcion

Is callede an house or a mancion.

Of whiche myracle, renomed of fame,

Bethphanye this day hathe the name.

Eke in the yere of his passion,

Fer in desert this day also, I rede,

With loves fyve, thorough his grete foyson,

Fyve thousande I fynd that he dyde fede.

530   Of whiche myracle, yf ye take hede,

This day is last namede phagyphanye,

Lyke as it firste was clepid Epiphanye.

519. whiche] þat C². —men] many H¹. 521. Therfore] Wherfore B³, H¹, L; Ther C¹.—
it is] is it H², J, Adv².—it is namede] named it is H¹.—namede] called H⁶; mede CC;
y named Ad³; now named Hn¹. 522. For] *added in margin preceding* "Bethe", D; om.
Ash¹, Ch.—Bethe] om. C². 523. Is callede] Called is B¹, B⁵, H⁷, H⁸, C³, Ad³, Adv²,
Hu, Co.—or] or H².—a] om. B¹. 524. renomed] renoun B²; renewide C².—of] or B².
525. hathe] wordely B⁵, Co; worthili H⁷, C³, Ad³, Adv²; worthi Hu.—the] his V; om. H⁶.
526. Eke] Also H⁸, C², Adv², Hu.—of] a forne B¹, B⁵, H¹, H⁷, H⁸, C³, Ad³, Adv², Hu,
Co. 527. Fer] For H², J, Hu, Co; om. Hn¹.—this day] om. H²; also þis day H⁸.—I rede]
as I rede B⁵, H⁶. 528. With] of H⁸.—loves fyve] v. loves B⁵.—grete] om. H². 529. that]
om. H¹.—dyde] hadde B²; om. B⁵. 530. Of] Of þe Adv². 531. last] om. B⁴, C², Adv².—
last namede] named last Co. 532. Lyke as it firste was clepid Epiphanye H⁷] *entire line
omitted in D.*—it] the B⁴, C¹, C³, Hn¹; om. H³, H⁴, Ad², An, Ch.—as it] om. B¹.—
firste was clepid] cleped was first H²; was fyrst called Adv².—clepid] called B².

For this worde phagi vnto our entent

Is sayde of fedyng or refeccion;

For whiche myracle passyng excellent,

That is so famous and of so high renou*n*—

Like as the gospell maketh mencion—

Þerfore þis dai amonge þe oþyr alle,

Ye Iustely maye phagyphanye it call.

A notable declar-   540
acion of these iij
gyfteȝ of the iij
kyng*es* Ca°[1]

N owe criste Ihe*su*, this day this high feste,

We the beseche w*ith* hert, will and thought,

Only of mercy to here our Requeste:

For the myracles that thou therin hast wrought,

For loue of hem that the so ferre hau sought,

The worthy kyngeȝ that came oute of Calde

The for to honour in Bedlem the Cetye.

---

533. For] And B[3], L.—vnto] to B[1], H[6], Ch. 534. of] a C[1].—or] eyther B[1], B[5], H[7], H[8], C[3], Ad[3], Hu; or a C[1]; or ells Adv[2].—refeccion] of refectioun B[1]. 536. so famous] famous Adv[2].—of so high] so hye of B[5], C[1], C[2], Co.—so] om. Hn[1].—high] grete B[2], H[5], J. 537. maketh] makid B[1]. 538. þerfore þis dai amonge þe oþyr alle H[7].—day] om. B[1].—þe] that D, B[2], H[4], H[8], CC, Hn[1]. 539. Iustely may] may Iustly B[2], H[6], J, C[1], Adv[2].—iustely] om. C[2].—may] may it B[4], C[5], Ad[2], An, Ch.—it] om. Ash[1], H[2], C[1], Hu. 540. day] hee day Adv[2].—this high feste] in this hye fest H[6]; of this hiȝe fest H[6]; of this hiȝe feeste C[1]; the high feste C[3]; and fest Adv[2]. 541. the] to C[1]; om. C[2].—will] om. C[2]. 542. our] there CC. 543. myracles] miracle B[1], H[2], Co.—thou] om. B[1].—therin] ther J.—hast] hatly H[1]. 544. of] om. H[8].—of hem] om. Adv[2].—the] om. B[2], H[6], CC, J.—so] from Hu. 545. came] come H[1], C[1], C[2], Adv[2], An.—oute] om. C[2]. 546. for] to B[4], Ash[1], H[5], H[4]; om. C[1], C[2], C[5], Ad[2], Adv[2], An, Lg, Ch, V.—the] thi B[1], B[2], B[5], H[7], J, Ad[3], Hu; om. Adv[2].

---

[1]lxxx° is crossed out and no number substituted.

And thourgh prayer of these kyngeȝ thre,

That for thy loue token her viage,

Ihesu defende vs fro all aduersite;

550　And make vs stronge and sure in our passage

In this exile and parlous pylgrymage,

Whiche our fomen of malice and of pryde

Hath in this lyfe by-sett vs on euerysyde.

The whiche our golde of perfyte charite　　　Nota bene nota　　f. 82a

Wolde vs by-Ryve by persecucion,

That we shulde offre of fervence vnto the

Of hertly loue and high deuocion.

And eke our franke of contemplacion,

Wher-with we shulde make our sacryfyce

560　Of high disdeyne and malice they dispyce.

---

547. And] And so H8.—prayer] the praier B2, B3, B4, Ash1, H3, H4, H5, H6, CC, J, C5, Ad2, L, An, Lg, Ch, V; þe praieris C2; þy grace and preyer C1.—these] this H8, CC, Ad3, Lg; the C1, C2, Hn1.—kyngeȝ] om. Adv2. 548. her] there CC, C3.—viage] voyage Hu. 549. all] om. Adv2. 550. vs] om. H8, Adv2.—stronge and sure] sure and strong B2, CC.—and sure] om. C2, C3.—passage] Iourne C1. 551. In] om. B1.—this] that H6; om. Adv2. 552. Whiche] In whiche B3, L; With B2, B4, Ash1, H2, H3, H4, H6, J, C1, Ad2; Which with H1.—of pryde] pryde C2, Co. 553. Hath] Euer H1.—in] om. Adv2.—Hath in this lyfe] In þis lif haþ C2.—by sett vs] us besette B2, B3, B4, H3, H4, H5, H6, J, C1, C2, Ad2, L, An, Lg; viset us H8; vs sette CC; so biset C5.—vs] om. B5, Hn1.—on] om. Ash1; in H2, H5, H8, C1, C2, C3, Co.—euerysyde] eueriche aside Ash1, H3, H4, H5, C5, Ad2, An, Lg. 554. of] and H1. 555. by Ryve] birede C2. 556. offre] om. B2, H6, CC, J.—fervence vnto the] seruie to þe C2. 557. high] of hie B1. 558. eke] also Hu. 559. we] he B4, H3, H4, Ad2, Ch. 560. they] ther L.—dispyce] dispite H8.

For golde of trouthe is falsely nowe alayede

By feyned loue and Symylacioun,   Nota bene nota

And fayth w*ith* fraude is corrupte and affrayed

With double tunges *and* detraccioun;

Our franke also of high p*er*fection

That shulde brenne clere above the skye,

Is w*ith* the Coode medelede of envye.

That it alas yeve may no light

In the sensure of trwe affeccion;   Nota bene nota

570   For day of trouthe is turnede vnto nyght

Thorough wrong reporte and false suspecion.

And þus good feith is rollid up soo doun,

And trwe menyng darkyd with a skye

That we in Englisshe calle flaterye.

---

561. of] *and* H², H⁶; now of C².—falsely nowe] now falseli H¹, L; om. C².—alayede]
alied B³; delaide C². 562. By feyned loue and Symylacioun H⁷.—Symylacioun] dis-
symulacion D, C², Co. 563. fraude] franke H⁸.—is] om. H¹. 564. With double tunges
and detraccioun B¹.—detraccioun] foule detraction D, Ch, Hn¹. 565. Our] Of our H¹.
566. That] om. C².—clere] hye cleer Hu.—aboue] aboute H⁸. 567. w*ith* the] om. C².—
the] om. B¹, H¹, H², H⁷, H⁸, C³, Ad³, Adv², Hu.—with the Coode medelede] goode
medelide C²; medlyd w*ith* cood C³.—Coode] gum B³, L; cold B⁵, H², Co; clowde H⁵;
hoode CC.—of] and of B¹; of foule C³. 568. it alas] alas it H¹; is allas H⁴.—yeve may]
may yeve B¹, Ash¹, H¹, H³, CC, C¹, C², Hu, Ch; may leve H². 570. day] the day
H⁶, C¹, C², Adv².—vnto] to B¹, C²; into þe C¹. 571. reporte] reports Ch.—false] om.
H⁶, C². 572. And þus feith is rollid up soo doun H⁵.—soo] om. B², H⁸, CC, C², C³,
V.—rollid up soo doun] turnede vp syde dovne D; trobled up *and* doun B¹; troubled up
so down H⁶, H⁷, Ad³; passed up so doun H². 573. darkyd] darkeþ Adv².—a] the H⁵;
om. B¹. 574. calle] callen hit H⁸.

And thus our offryng gothe all moste all wronge, No*ta* be*ne* nota

Of gold and franke for ought I can aspye

And our myrre hathe be byhynde longe.

Vs to p*r*eserue from all suche trecherye,

For nowe is turnede to ypocrysye

580 Our holynesse, and that is grete routhe,

And cause whie, for fraude hathe banysshede trouthe. No*ta* be*ne* nota

But crist Ih*es*u, that all this maist amende,

And that is mysse in eche estate redresse,

This hie fest suche grace to vs sende,

That we the golde of faythe and stablonesse

And eke the franke of p*er*fyte holynesse,

May on this day p*r*esent vnto the

Withe all trwe hert as dyd the kyng*es* thre.

---

575. And thus our offryng gothe all moste all wronge] And thus almoste oure offeryng goyth wronge CC.—thus] this H8, C2, C3; om. H2.—our] om. H1, H2.—moste all] om. C2.—all] om. B4, Ash1, H1, H3, H4, H6, C1, C5, Ad2, Adv2, Hu, An, Hn1.—all wronge] to wronge H8, C3, V. 576. Of] Or B2; Our B3, L; For CC, Ch.—and] of B1, B4, B5, Ash1, H3, H4, H5, H7, H8, J, C3, C5, Ad3, Adv2, Hu, An, Lg, Hn1, Co; or B2, CC, Ch; our B3, L.—ought] naught H6; ouȝt þat B4, H2, Ch.—ought I can] I can ouȝt C2. 577. hathe be byhynde longe] hath ben behynde ful long B2, B3, B4, H3, H5, H6, CC, J, Ad2, L, Lg, Ch, V; hathe behid fullonge Ash1, H4; haþ behynd full long An.—long] so long C2. 578. suche] om. B1, H7, H8, C2, C3, Ad3, Adv2, Hu, Co. 579. is] it is C1.—to] into B2, B3, B4, Ash1, H3, H4, H6, CC, J, C1, C3, C5, Ad2, L, An, Lg, Ch, V; the H2. 580. Our] All our Adv2.—grete] om. H1. C2, Adv2. 581. for] om. Co.—fraude] franke H8.—banysshede] vanysshid C1, Ch. 582. crist Ihesu] Ihesu criste C1.—all this maist] maist al this H3, C2; this moste CC.—this] om. H8. 583. And] om. C2.—eche] euery C2. 584. This hie fest suche grace to vs sende B1.—This] In this C1.—to] vnto D; on to C1; om. H3, H8, C2. 585. we] wiþ H5, C1.—the] om. Hn1.—the golde of faythe and stablonesse] the faith and gold of stablenesse B2, CC. 596. eke] also Hu. 587. May] We may H1.—on] om. B2, H6, CC, J; in C2.—p*r*esent vnto the] as dide þe kynges þre C2.—vnto] onto B4, Ash1, Hu, Lg. 588. all] as C3.—as dyd the kyng*es* thre] p*r*esent un to þe C2.—the] these B2, B4, Ash1, H3, H4, H5, H6, CC, J, C3, Ad2, L, An, Lg, Ch, Hn1, V.

Nota bene nota

And grau*n*t also, bothe to high and lowe,   f. 82b

590 To haue suche myrre in her adu*e*rtence,

That eu*e*ry wight his owne faute3 knowe,

And that no man be hasty of sentence

To deme lightly byfore or in absence;

For sodem dom meynt w*ith* ignoraunce,

Hathe a long tayle sewyng of repentaunce.

Nota bene nota

For in sothenesse, if that eu*e*ry man

Wolde make amyrrour of his awne mynde,

To deme hym-selffe of thyng that he well can,

And open his yen that hau be longe blynde

600 To se his faute3 that he shulde well fynde,

I trow in soithe, for any haste or rape,

Harmele3 fro dome his felowe shulde ascape.

---

589. to] vnto C². 590. myrre] myrthe H⁸.—her] ther CC, C³.—aduertence] aduersite B², B⁴, H⁴, H⁵, C⁵, Ad², An, Lg, Ch, Hn¹; costience H². 591. his] her C².—knowe] may knowe B¹. 592. sentence] his sentence Hn¹. 593. byfore] tofore H⁸, C¹, C³.—absence] any absence H⁶. 594. sodan] sodeyid H¹.—meynt] medelid B¹, H⁶. 595. Hathe] With CC.—sewyng] shewing C¹, C⁵.—of] a B¹; wiþ B⁵. Co; or C¹. 596. sothenesse] sothfastnesse B², H¹, CC.—if that] and B¹; 3it that C¹. 597. Wolde] om. B², H⁶, CC, J.—of] in H¹.—awne] youre Ash¹. 598. of thing that] as Ch.—well] wil B¹. 599. Ande open his yen that hau be longe blynde B¹.—open] vpon D, B³, H², H³, C¹, Ad³.—long] so long D.—hau be longe] hath so longe be Hn¹. 600. faute3] defautes B¹, C³; the fawtes; own fautes B³, L.—shulde well fynde] coude fynde B², B³, B⁴, Ash¹, H¹, H², H³, H⁴, H⁵, H⁶, CC, J, C¹, C⁵, Ad², An, Lg, Ch, Hn¹, V.—shulde] schall H⁸.—well] wil B¹; om. C². 601. I trowe in soith fro any haste or rape H⁷.—I trowe in soith] Now C².—or] om. B⁴, Ash¹, H³, H⁴, C⁵, Ad², An, Ch.—rape] Iape D; smert C¹. 602. fro] for B⁴, Ad².—dome] deth Hu.—felowe] neghbur B³, L.

Howe we shulde pray
to god to do this
offryng gostely.
Ca° lxxxj°[1] 22[m]

N owe crist Ihesu—that knowest euery herte

And no thyng may be hyd fro thy presence,

Ne fro thyn eye declyne ne asterte—

Graunt vs this day of thy magnyfycence

The golde of loue, the franke of Innocence,

And the chast myrre of clene entencion,

So to presente in our oblacion

610 To thyne highnesse þat it be acceptable;

While þat we lyue eure from ȝeere to ȝeere,

As was the offryng in Bedlem in a stable,

Made vnto the and to thy mothir dere

Of the kynges, that with the stremes clere

Of a sterre conveyde werc by grace,

Wher thou lay to come to the place.

---

603. crist] om. C[1]. 604. presence] hyȝe presence Hn[1]. 605. Ne fro] That from B[2], CC,
J.—eye] eyȝen B[4], B[5], H[8].—ne] may ne B[2], H[6], CC, J. 606. day] om. C[3].—of] for
C[2]. 608. the] om. Co.—clene] cleer H[1]. 609. in] the in Hn[1]. —our] thyn Hu. 610. þat
it] that we may H[6]; to C[1].—it] om. L. 611. While þat we lyue euere from ȝeere to ȝeere
H[7].—While] Which D. þat] om. B[1], Ash[1], C[1], Ad[2], Ad[3], Lg, Ch, Hn[1].—lyue] haue
D.—euere] om. B[2], C[1]. 612. was] we C[3].—in] at B[3], H[1], L.—a] þe H[2].—stable] stalle
Lg. 613. vnto] onto C[1].—to] om. H[1]. 614. with the] we whith B[2], CC, J.—the] om.
H[6]. 615. a] the H[6].—conveyde were] were conveyid C[1], C[2].—were] thei weren B[1]. 616.
thi H[6], C[2], Ch; that C[1].

[1]crossed through.

And vnto the this day we clepe and call—

Þou blissful quene of kingis emperesse,

That yaf thy sonne, soukyng in a stalle,

620 That chast mylke of virgynall clennesse—

That thou this fest, o sterre of holynesse,

Conueye oure offringe to þat sterri see

Wher next thy son thou hast the souereynte.

And gode lady in this sorowefull vale

Of trouble and wo and of hevynesse—

Sithe thou of Iacob art the right scale,

The weye of lyffe the ledder of holynesse—

Towarde that courte the evyn way vs dresse,

And make thy men thedir to assende

630 Wher euere is blisse, and Ioye hath non ende.

---

617. vnto] on to C1.—the] om. B2, B4, H6, H8, CC, J, C1. 618. þou blissful quene of kingis emperesse H7.—blissful] blissede D, B1, H3, H8, C1, C2, Hn1.—kyngis] kyngis all C1. 619. yaf.] haue H6.—thy] ye H1.—soukyng] souke Ash1, CC, C1, Hu. 621. That thou this fest o sterre of holynesse] That sat the Sterr of all our distres C1.—thou] in H6.—this fest o sterre of holynesse] this sterre o feest of holynesse Hu.—o sterre of holynesse] offerre of holynesse H8.—o] of H2. 622. Conueye oure offringe to þat sterri see H7] So kepe with all from unsikirnes C1.—þat] the D, B5, An; þi Adv2. 623. the] thy B2, H5, C1; om. B1, H8, Adv2. 624. vale] world and vale Ash1. 625. and] of B1, H6, C3, Adv3, Adv2, Hu, Hn1, Co; om. C2, Ch. 626. of] om. H8.—right] high H1. 627. lyffe] love Adv2.—ledder] water B5.—holynesse] heuenlynesse L. 628. that] þe B5, H4, H6, Adv2, An, Co.—courte] contrey C2, L.—the evyn] of euen H6.—evyn] hy H2; om. C2. vs] þu C2; to Adv2; om. B1, B2, B4, Ash1, H1, H2, H3, H4, H5, H7, CC, J, C1, C5, Ad2, Ad3, An, Lg, Ch. 629. men] meyne L.—assende] descende C2. 630. euere] ay H1.—is] his H8.—is blisse and Ioye] is ioy and blisse H2.— hath non] with outen B2, B3, Ash1, H6, CC, J, L, V; þat hath no H1, H2.—non ende] none in eende Ad2.

For certeȝ lady, in this lyfe we lakke

Of sothefast yoye, all the suffysaunce

Save amonge we knele afore the Rakke:

Where *with* thy sonne was some tyme thy pleasaunce,

And vs reyoysyng, as by Remembraunce,

Only by lykenesse to loke on thyne ymage

And on thy sonne *with* his fayre visage.

But, o, alas, ther is but a lykenesse

Of portrature that dothe vs grete offence,

640   For we may not haue full the blissednesse

Of thy vysage ne of thy *p*resence;

And so to vs grete harme dothe aparence,

Whan that we sene of our desyre we fayle,

We may well pleyne but it may not avayle.

631. lady] modur Adv^2; om. CC. 632. all] and all Ash^1, Co.—the] oure Adv^2. 633. amonge] euere amonge Hn^1.—afore] tofore H^7, C^1; among Adv^2; before Hu. 634. *with*] ynne B^2, CC; þat H^2; om. H^6, Hn^1.—thy sonne] þe sonne Adv^2.—was some tyme] whilom H^1.—was] had C^1.—some tyme] om. H^6.—thy pleasaunce] þe pleasaunce H^2; pleasaunce C^1. 635. reyoysyng] reyoysen L.—as] and H^1.—by] by a Adv^2. 636 lykenesse] sekenesse H^1.—to loke] om. C^1.—thyne] þis Hn^1. 637. visage] viage V. 638. But, o, alas] But o ladi H^1; Owte alas CC, J.—o] om. B^2, H^6, Co.—a] om. C^3. 639. portrature] a picture H^6. 640. For] But C^3.—haue] se H^6.—haue full] ful haue B^5.—full the] þe full Hn^1.—full] fully B^2, Ash^1, H^2, H^6, H^8, C^3; om. CC. 641. thy] þis C^2.—ne] nother B^2, B^3, B^4, Ash^1, H^3, H^4, H^5, H^6, CC, J, C^2, C^5, Ad^2, L, An, Lg, Ch, C^1; nor B^5, H^1, H^2, Adv^2. Hu. V.—of] al V; om. H^2.—*p*resence] hyȝe presence H^7. 642. so] om. B^2.—to] om. H^8.—grete harme dothe] doth gret harm H^2, C^1. 643. we] to B^5, Co; þat we Adv^2; om. H^6, CC. 644. We] As we C^2.—well] wil B^1; pleynly C^2; om. B^1, B^2, B^3, B^4, Ash^1, H^1, H^2, H^4, H^6, CC, J, C^1, C^5, Ad^2, An, Lg, Ch, Hn^1, V.—may] wil B^1, B^5, H^1, H^7, H^8, C^3, Ad^3, Adv^2, L, Co.

Yet day by day of trwe affection,

We gon of newe thy likenesse for to see,

Wher-of o thyng we haue compassion:

To see þe beestis þat so humble be

To stonde my atwene thy sonne and the,

650   The rude Asse and the oxe also.

And then we sayne, compleynying in our woo,

With all our hert: o what thyng may this be,   Nota bene nota

To se that lorde in a Rakke lye

That hath the hevyn vndir his powste,

And all this worlde power hath to gye!

O how it is that the Regalye

Of heven and erthe is brought dovne so lowe

That noman luste vnethes his power knowe!

645. Yet] And yet B1, H7, Ad3; Rit H1; Ye H4. 646. gon of] gon on B1, C1, Lg.—likenesse] hiʒenes C2. 648. To see þe beestis þat so humble be H7.—þe] thy D; thoo B1. 649. To] om. B3, C3, L.—ny] so ny B1, B2, B3, B4, Ash1, H3, H4, H5, H6, H7, CC, J, C1, C2, C3, C5, Ad2, An, Lg, Ch, V; in Adv2; om. H8.—atwene] om. C3. 650. The] Thou H3. 651. then] whanne B2, Hu.—in our woo] morn *and* woo C1; om. Ash1. 652. o] om. B1, B5, H2, H7, H8, C3, Ad3, Adv2, Hn1, Co.—thyng] om. H2. 653. that] a H1.—lye] so lye Hn1. 654. hath the hevyn] holdeth heven V.—the] om. H6, C2, Adv2.—vnder] in B4, H2, H3, H4, C1, C5, Ad2, An, Ch.—powste] power Hu. 655. worlde] wolde B2.—power] om. H6. 656. it is] is it B1, B2, B3, B5, H5, H6, H7, H8, CC, J, Ad3, Adv2, Hu, L, Hn1, Co.—that] so nowe þat Hn1.—the] the hie B3, L. 657. is] om. H1.—dovne] om. Ch.—so lowe] alowe B2. 658. noman] no Co.—vnethes] an erþe C2; om. Lg.—vnethes his power] hys power unneþes Adv2.—knowe] to knowe B1, H8, C1, C3; for to knowe Hn1.

And sodenly our herteȝ gynnythe colde,   f. 83b

660   Sore a-stonyed *and* is for woo niȝ mate,

So grete a quene whan that we be-holde

Alone syttyng all disconsolate

So fayre, so gode, and of so hygh estate,

Most womanly and benygne of chere,

Thy sonne and thou, to-gydre bothe in fere,

In the boundeȝ of so narowe a dongeon,

Wher-of all erthe tremble sholde and quake,

And eu*er*y wight by lamentacion

Wepe and pleyne, sighe and sorowe make;

670   O blisfull quene, only for thy sake,

To see on the none other awaytyng,

But besteȝ rude w*ith* hay hem-selffe fedyng.

659. herteȝ] hert H¹.—colde] to coolde B¹, B³, H⁶, L, Hn¹. 660. Sore a stonyed *and* is for woo niȝ mate H⁷.—Sore] For B², B³, B⁴, Ash¹, H¹, H², H³, H⁴, H⁵, CC, J, C¹, C², C⁵, Ad², L, An, Lg, Ch, Hn¹, V; all for H⁶; so fore Hu.—is] om. C³, V.—Sore astonyede and is for woo] Sore for wo is astonyed and B¹.—niȝ] ne D, H⁵, Adv², V; right H².—mate] in a hate H¹; made H. 661. that] om. B¹, B⁵, C², Co. 662. all] and alle B¹, H⁷, C¹, C³; and B⁴, H⁸, Adv², Hu; of H⁵; om. Co.—disconsolate] desolate B¹, CC, C¹. 663. of so hygh] so hiȝe of a C¹.—of] om. H¹, CC. 664. and benygne of] in benyng and C¹; and ryght benygne of C³. 665. to gydre bothe] bothe to gedre B², H⁶, CC, J, C²; om. B¹. 666. In] With B³, C³, L.—narowe] foule B¹.—a] of oo B²; om. H⁴.—dongeon] dominoun B², B³, L; domynacion CC, J. 667. erthe] hert H¹, C¹; þe erth H⁵.—tremble sholde] shuld both trembill C¹. tremble] treble B².—sholde] shall CC, C². 669. Wepe and] We may L.—and] om. B¹.—sighe] syke Adv². 670. blisfull] blessid B¹, Hn¹.—quene] oonly quene C¹. 672. besteȝ] best H¹.—rude] B⁴, Ash¹, H³, H⁴, H⁶, C¹, C⁵, Ad², An, Ch.—w*ith* om. B.—hay hem selffe] hem selfe hey Lg.—hem selffe] them Hu.

But in o thyng comforte yet we fele,

O goode lady sothely while we see,

Thre worthy kyngeȝ a-fore thy face knele,

Bryngyng her yefteȝ with all humylyte

And hem gou*er*ne like to thy degre,

With meke attendaunce and full besy cure;—

But all this thyng we se but in picture.

680   Alas the while and yet it dothe vs ease,

And in p*ar*tye aswagethe our grevaunce,

For no thyng may our sorowe so appese

As eu*er* of the to haue a remembraunce.

For in the is our hole suffisaunce,

And though we leve in lango*ur* for absence,

Yet gode lady for thy magnyficence,

---

673. in] of H2.—comforte yet] ȝit comfort C2, Ad2.—yet] om. C1, 674. goode] goodly
B2, CC, Ad3.—sothely] om. B2.—while] while that B2; whanne B1, B5, H1, H7, H8
C3, Ad3, Adv2, Hu, Co; ȝif B4, H3, H4, C1, C5, Ad2, An, Ch.—see] sothly see Ch.
675. Thre] The B2, B3, H2, H3, H6, CC, J, Hu, L.—worthy kyngeȝ] kynges, worthi
B1.—a fore] to fore H8, C1. 676. Bryngyng] Bryng B5; And bryng C1.—her] theyr C3;
om. B3, C3, L. 677. hem] hym H1; theym C3.—to] om. C1.—thy] here H1.—degre]
degres B2; gre C2. 678. full] full of Co; om. C2.—besy] be Ch. 679. this] om. C1.—
thyng] om. C2.—se] se not H2. 680. while] om. C1.—and] om. H6, Adv2, Hu.—yet
it] in this B2. 681. And] om. H6, J.—in] a B5, Co.—aswagethe] savith C1. 682.
sorowe] socour B1.—so] om. H8, C2, Ch. 683. As eu*er* of the to haue a remembraunce
B1.—As] But H8.—eu*er*] ay H1.—of] on D, Adv2.—a] om. D, B3, H8, CC, C1, C2, C3,
L, V. 684. For] and CC.—the] the lady B2, B3, B4, Ash1, H3, H4, H5, H6, CC, J,
C1, C2, C5, Ad2, L, An, Lg, Ch, V; om. Hn1.—is] þis Hn1.—our] al B4.—hole] om.
H8.—our hole] hole our B2, B3, Ash1, H3, H4, H5, H6, CC, J, C1, C2, C5, Ad2, L,
Ch, V; holy all our H2.—suffisaunce] sustenaunce B3, B4, Ash1, H3, H4, H5, CC, J,
C1, C2, C5, Ad2, L. Lg, Ch, V. 685. in langour for absence] *and* langour for they sake
C1.—absence] thyne absence B2, B3, B4, Ash1, H3, H4, H5, H6, CC, J, C5, Ad2, L,
An, Lg, Ch, V.—for absence] fro þi p*re*sence C2.

To thy *serva*unteȝ, of thy grace nowe see,

And to thy sonne, be for vs a mene.

This high feste, which longyth vnto the—

690   In whiche thou were honourede like a quene

With myrre and frank and golde that shone so shene—

Nowe for the honoure this day was to the,

And for the loue of the kyngeȝ thre,

Whan we shall parte oute of this woofull lyffe   f. 84a

And make an ende of this captivyte

Of herodeȝ thourght his mortall stryffe,

The fende betrappe vs thurgh his cruelte;

That tyme lady of thy benygnyte,

A-yentse the snares of this dredfull werre,

700   To lyfe et*er*ne be thou our lode sterre.

---

687. thy grace] grace Adv². —nowe] om. B², B³, B⁴, Ash¹, H², H³, H⁴, H⁵, H⁶, CC, J, C¹, C², C⁵, Ad², L, An, Lg, Ch, V. 688. to] unto H⁶.—thy] om. C².—be for vs] for us be H³.—for vs] to vs H², Hn¹. 689. whiche] that B², H⁶, CC, J, C³.—vnto] to B¹. 691. With myrre and frank and golde] w*ith* gold mirre and frank H⁶.—and frank] frank C², L.—and golde that shone so shene] and gold þat schyne þe so schene Adv².—that shone] H²; om. B¹, B⁴, C².—so] full C³; om. H³, CC, V. 692. the] om. C².—thi] that B², H⁶, CC, J.—was] that was B³, L.—was to the] was do to the B¹, B⁵, C³, Hn¹. 693. the loue] loue B¹.—the kyngeȝ] kyngeȝ H¹; these kyngeȝ C³. 694. Whan] Than H¹.—parte] dep*ar*te H², C³. 696. Of] Or B³, B⁴, H², H⁶, An, Lg, Ch. Hn¹. V.—herodeȝ] fals herodes H².—thourght] w*ith* H⁶.—his] this B¹, B⁵, H⁷, C³, Ad³, Adv², Hu, Co.—stryffe] liyf B. 697. us] om. Ash¹, H⁸. 698. That] Now that B², B⁴, Ash¹, H³, H⁴, H⁵, H⁶, CC, J, C⁵, An, Lg, Ch; Now or that V.—lady] om. V.—benygnyte] dignite H⁸. 699. This] his H¹, H⁶; þe CC, Lg.—dredfull] mortall B³, L. 700. sterre] sterre, Amen B², H⁵, H⁷, H⁸, J, An.

BOOK VI

Glorye and pryes, laude and high hon*our*,
O blisfull quene, be yeve vnto the
That were of god the cheve chaste toure,
Surely foundede vpon humylyte,
Schitte *with* þe keie of clene virginite;
Fro all synne fully to be assurede,
Of the holy goste rounde aboute ymurede.

That neu*ere* brennyng of no flesshely hete
Asayle myght thyn holy tabernacle,
10 Withe dewe of grace thy closet was so swete,
Fulfilled with vertu oonly by myracle.
God chese thy wombe for this habitacle
And halowede it so clene in eu*ery* coste,
To make it sacrary for his awne goste.

Howe our lady
was puryfiede.
Ca° lxxxij°[1] 22

---

1. and] in H[1]; om. B[1], H[6].—pryes] preisyng B[2], CC; pes Ash[1], Ch. 2. blisfull] blessid B[1]. 3. That were of god] With verri god B[2], H[6], CC, J.—cheve] chose B[2], B[4], Ash[1], H[2], H[3], H[4], H[5], H[6], CC, J, C[2], C[3], C[5], Adv[2], Hu, L, An, Lg, Ch, Hn[1], V; close C[1]. —cheve chaste] chaff chosen B[1]; chaste chosen B[5], H[1], H[7], H[8], Ad[3]. 4. foundede] groundid B[1], B[5], H[2], H[8], Ad[3], Adv[2], Hu.—Surely foundede] Foundid surely Hn[1].—vpon] on C[2]. 5. Schitte *with* þe keie of clene virginite H[7].—Schitte] and shytte Hn[1].—the] om. H[1]. —clene] pure C[3], Hu; om. D. 6. Fro] and fro H[1], Hn[1].—fully] suerly H[3]; sothly C[1]. —fully to be] to be fully C[2].—to be] om. Adv[2]. 7. Of] And of B[2], B[4], Ash[1], H, CC, J, C[1], C[2], C[5], An, Hn[1], V; And with B[3], L; with C[3].—rounde aboute] al abouȝt B[5]; rounde to be C[3].—aboute] om. H[5]. 8. That neu*ere*] þat non Adv.—brennyng] no brennynge B[1], B[2], B[3], B[4], Ash[1], H[3], H[4], H[5], H[6], H[7], CC, J, C[1], C[5], Ad[3], L, An, Lg, Ch; in no brennyng C[2].—no] om. B[1], B[4]. 9. Assayle myght thyn holy tabernacle B[1].—thyn] the D, Ash[1]. 10. dewe] the dew C[3]. 11. Fulfilled with vertu oonly by myracle B[1].—with] by D, H[6]; of C[3]; of all Hn[1].—by] *with* H[8]. 12. for] only for H[2].—habitacle] tabernacle B[1], B[5], H[1], H[7], H[8], Ad[3], Adv[2], Hu, Co. 14. To make it sacrary] For to make secret Co.— for] to Co.

---

[1]crossed through.

Not wi*th*stonding þat þou were so clene

Above all othir by election,

Of mekenesse oonly, oo thu heuenely quene,

Thou list to haue non indignacioun.

The dayes passede of thy purgacion

20 To fulfille the pr*e*cept of the lawe

In eu*er*y thyng and not o poynt wi*th* drawe.

But euer lyke, as it is specifiede,

Leuitici, who so can vndirstonde,

To the temple to be puryfyede

Thou mekely came thyn offryng in thyne hande,

Al-be þe lawe sette on þee no bonde.

For it is there makede mencion,

Touchyng the lawe of purgacion,

---

15. Not wi*th*stonding þat þou were so clene H⁷.—Not] Nought D, B³, B⁴, B⁵, Ash¹, Co.—that] om. B¹.—so clene] a maide clene V. 16. election holy eleccioun B¹; pure election C³. 17. Of mekenesse oonly oo thu heuenely quene B¹.—oonly] also H¹.—heuenely] hevyn D, Adv²; holi H¹; art heuenely L. 18. Thou list to haue non indignacioun H⁷.—Thou] To D.—to] not to C¹. 19. dayes] day B², B³, B⁴, Ash¹, H², H³, H⁴, H⁵, H⁶, H⁸, CC, J, C¹, C², C⁵, L, An, Ch, Hn¹, V.—passede] to passe B², B³, B⁴, Ash¹, H³, H⁴, H⁵, H⁶, CC, J, C¹, C², C⁵, L, An, Lg, Ch, Hn¹, V; is passed H², H⁸.—thy] þe Hn¹.—purgacion] Purificatioun. Hn¹. 20. To] But to B², B³, B⁴, Ash¹, H³, H⁴, H⁵, H⁶, CC, J, C¹, C², C⁵, L, An, Lg, Ch, V; But liste to Hn¹. 21. not o] on no C²; no B¹; nouȝt Hn¹, Co. 22. euer] euyn B², B³, B⁴, H², H⁴, H⁵, H⁶, CC, J, C¹, C³, Lg, Ch, Hn¹, Co, V. 23. Leuitici who so can vndirstonde B¹.—Leuitici] In leuitici H².—who so] who D, H¹, Hn¹. 24. to be] for to be L. 25. Thou mekely] Mekely þou B⁴.—came] come B¹, B³, B⁴, H¹, H², H³, H⁴, H⁵, H⁷, H⁸, C², C³, Ad³, Adv². 26. Al be þe lawe sette on þee no bonde H⁷.—Albe] Thoughe B², CC.—þe lawe] that lawe D.—no] om. D. 27. it is] om. B¹; her is C²; hit H⁸, C³, Adv², Co.—there] om. C².—makede] made B², B³, B⁴, H⁴, H⁵, H⁶, CC, J, C¹, C², C⁵, L, An, Lg, Ch, V; y maked H¹; y made H²; pleynly maketh C³. 28. of] and C¹.—purification H⁶, Hn¹.

If a woman conceyve by a man

30 And haue a childe by medelyng hem betwene,

Þat be a male, þe lawe techith þan

Fourty dayes that she shulde be vnclene,

And kepe her close that no man shulde hir seen;

And aftir that she sholde hir offryng,

In lawe expressed, to the temple brynge.

But taketh hede, in conclusion,

How this lawe like, as ye shall fynde,

Ne was not put but by condicion

Only to hem that corrupt wer by kynde,

40 Thorugh touche of man, of suche it made mynde.

The days noumbrede of her purgacion,

To come and make her oblacion

---

29. If] That yf B³, L.—a] om. B², H⁶, CC, J.—conceyve] be conceyvid C¹; conceiued Lg. 30. And] To H⁴.—by] om. B⁴, C¹.—medelyng] medill C¹. 31. þat be a male þe lawe techith þan H⁷.—þat] If it B¹, B², CC; That if it H²; And it H⁶; Yf he Adv².—male] man B², CC.—techith] touchyth D, B³, B⁵, H⁶, J, C². 32. that] om. H¹.—she] om. B¹.—shulde] shal B¹, H⁷, H⁸, Ad³.—vnclene] all clene H⁶. 33. shulde her] her schuld B⁵.—shulde] shal B¹, H⁷, Ad³; om. C². 34. she] om. B¹.—offryng] offryng brynge C¹. 35. In lawe expressed to the temple brynge B¹.—In] In þe H¹, C²; By C¹; The B³.—expressed] expresse D, B⁴, H⁶, H⁸, CC, C², Ch.—to] on to Co. 36. hede] þe hede H⁴.—in] now in B⁵, H⁸, C³, Ad³, Adv², Co. 37. like] om. H¹.—ye] om. H⁵.—shall] shul B¹, B², H⁵, C⁵, Hu, Lg, Hn¹. 38. Ne] om. B³, H¹, L.—put] om. B⁴, H⁶.—but] om. C¹. 39. hem] þem B⁵.—corrupt were] were corupte H⁸, C¹.—by] of B¹. 40. touche] touchinge B⁴.—of suche] of which H¹, H⁶; so C².—it] om. C¹.—made] maket B¹, H², H⁷, Ad³, Adv². 41. noumbrede] were fyllyd Hn¹.—purgacion] purgacions B⁴, Ash¹, H³, H⁴, H⁵, L, An, Lg, Ch; Purification Hn¹. 42. To come and make] She mekely made B¹, H⁷; The dayes nombred of B⁵, H⁸, Ad³, Adv², Co.—oblacion] oblacions B⁴, B⁵, Ash¹, H³, H⁴, H⁵, L, An, Lg, Ch.

And bryng a lamb, the whiche in sacrifice

Shulde all be brent in the holy place;

And a pygeon, as lawe dothe devyse,

She shuld eke offre as for her trespase.

And all fylthe fro hir to enchace,

She of the prest, halowede and sanctifiede,

Returned hom al fulli purified.

50   And if she had in her possession

Redely no lambe only for pouerte,

Then shulde she take for her oblacion

Two turtle doves and ther-*with*-all go fre;

Or two pegyons, like as ye may se,

Levitici, wher by distynccion,

Of þis offringe is made discripcion.

43. the] om. B¹, Co. 44. all be] be all H⁶.—brent] brouȝt H³, H⁴, C¹, C⁵, Ch.—the] to B⁴. 45. lawe] the lawe Ash¹, H², H⁴, H⁸, Co. V. 46. shuld] schal C².—eke] also Hu.—as] om. B¹, B⁴, Hn¹. 47. And than all fylthe fro hir] All filthe from her than H⁶, Ad³.—all] of B⁵; the C³.—to] om. B¹, B⁴. 48. sanctifiede] sacrified H³, H⁴, C⁵, Hu, An, Ch. 49. Returned hom al fulli purified B¹.—Returned] Retourne D, B², B⁵, CC, J, C¹, C³, C⁵,—hom] hem B³, C³.—fully] ful V. 50. if] om. B¹.—she] þat she H¹.—possession] power possession H⁶. 51. Redely no lambe only for pouerte] No lombe redili for poverti B¹; Oonly for pouerte redy no lambe C¹.—Redely] Redy B³, H¹, H⁷, CC.—only] om. H². 52. shulde she] she shulde B¹, B⁵, H⁷, H⁸, C², C³, Ad³, Co. 53. Two] The H⁸, C².—ther] þat H¹.—all] om. B⁴. 54. pegyons] doves H². 55. Levitici] in leuitici H², C³; Late se CC.—wher] wher as Adv². 56. Of þis offringe is made discripcion H⁷.—þis] his D, H³,—made] om. B¹.—discripcion] a descripcion C³.

But this mayde, who so can take hede,

Excludet was for condicion

That bare her childe wi*th*oute manys seede,—

60 Beyng eu*er*e clene from all corrupcion—

Wher thorugh, she was fro suche oblacion

By lawe exempt, and was vnder no charge

For hir clennes stondyng at hir large.

For of her wombe, the cloyster virgynall,

f. 85a

Was eu*er*e liche, bothe firste and laste,

Closed and shette as castell principall;

For the holy goste devysede it and cast

And at bothe tymes shet iliche faste,—

In hir childyng no more thorugh grace broke

70 At hir conceyvyng than it was vnloke.

57. can] will H⁶. 58. for] from B², H¹, H⁶, CC, J; by B³, Ash¹, L; for þis H¹, C³.
59. That] She C³.—her] a B⁴, Ash¹, H³, H⁴, C⁵, Ad², An, V.—childe] gylt C².—
wi*th*oute] wi*th* H⁸.—manys] man H¹. 60. eu*er*e] ai H¹.—from all] with owte CC.—
all] om. Ch. 61. Wher thorugh] Wher for H¹, C².—fro] from all H². 62. exempt] exempted
Ch. 63. For] From H⁶.—stondyng] but stondyng H², Hn¹.—hir] om. C², Adv². 64. of]
of the B¹; in CC; al C².—cloyster] closet B¹. 65. Was eu*er*e] Eu*er* was Adv².—eu*er*e]
every Ch.—liche] I liche B¹, B², B⁴, B⁵, Ash¹, H¹, H², H³, H⁴, H⁵, H⁷, J, C¹, C², C³,
C⁵, Ad², Hu, L, An, Lg, Co, V.—bothe firste and laste] first and last B².—and] *and*
þe H⁵. 66. Closed] Was closed B², H⁶, CC, J.—and] as Ch.—as] as a B², H⁸, C¹, C²,
Ch. 67. it] om. H¹, H³, Co. 68. at] om. Ash¹, H¹, H⁸.—tymes] tyme Ash¹.—shet] loke
B³, L; y shet H¹; shitte it H⁴, C¹; shit is C⁵, An, Ch; I schute C².—iliche] liche
B³, H³, H⁴, C², C⁵, L, An, Ch. 69. In] At H²; And in V.—broke] I broke B², B³, B⁴,
Ash¹, H³, H⁴, H⁵, H⁶, H⁷, CC, J, C², Ad², Ad³, Adv², L, An, Ch, Hn¹, V. 70. At]
And Ash¹.—than] that H⁸.

For nature wi*th*outyn any stryfe,

Of Repuugnaunce or any recistence,

Yaffe this mayde a speciall p*r*erogatyffe:

As mother parede to haue experience

Only of childyng and fele non offence,

Neyther of sekenesse ner of suche man*e*re woo

In traveylyng as othir wymen doo.

She was exempt from all suche passion

For hir clennes and so was noon but she,

80   And yet her tyme of puryficacion

Sche dide a-byde of hir humilite.

And like as lawe ordeynyth by decre,

Aftir all this, of custome as she aught,

To the temple she hir offryng brought,

---

71. any] om. CC.—stryfe] man*e*re stryfe B³, L. 72. Of] om. B¹, B², B³, B⁴, Ash¹, H¹, H³, H⁴, H⁵, H⁶, CC, J, C¹, C², C⁵, Ad², L, An, Lg, Ch, Hn¹.—or any] gructhynge or B³, L. 73. this] unto this B³, L; his Ash¹.—mayde] moder *and* maide Ash¹.—speciall] om. B¹, B², B⁴, H¹, H², H³, H⁴, H⁵, H⁶, H⁷, CC, J, C¹, C², C⁵, Ad², Ad³, An, Lg, Hn¹, V. 74. As] As a B², B³, H¹, H⁵, H⁶, CC, J, C¹, C², L, V; And as Ash¹.—parede] pure B¹; pured B⁵, H⁷, H⁸, C³, Ad³, Adv², Hu, Co; om. B², B³, B⁴, Ash¹, H², H³, H⁴, H⁵, H⁶, CC, J, C¹, C², C⁵, Ad², L, An, Lg, Ch, Hn¹, V. 76. and fele] felte H⁶, CC; and felt J. 76. ner] nor B¹, Adv²; neither Co; ne B², B³, B⁵, Ash¹, H², H³, H⁴, H⁵, II⁶, H⁷, H⁸, CC, C¹, C², C³, C⁵, Ad², Ad³, L, An, Lg, Ch, Hn¹, V.—suche] non siche CC; othir C¹.—man*e*re] o*þ*er C².—suche man*e*re] no Adv². 77. traveylyng] traueile C².—othir wymen] al o*þ*er C². 78. She was exempt] Ther sche exempte was C².—all] all manner B², H⁶, H⁸, CC, J. 80. yet] right H⁶.—her] om. H¹.—puryficacion] purgacioun Lg. 81. Sche dide a byde of hir humilite H⁷.—a blde] obeye D; obeie, *and* bide B¹; om. H¹. 82. And] om. C³.—like] *ʒ*it Lg.—as] a H⁸; as the C¹.—ordeynyth] ordeined B¹, H¹, H⁷, H⁸, J, C¹, C³, Ad³.—by] in hir C¹.—decre] degree B¹, H¹, H², H⁸, CC, C¹, C², C³. 83. of] by B¹; om. CC, C¹. 84. she] om. B¹.—hir] *þ*e H⁵.

To yeffe ensample only of mekenesse,

To þe lawe sche mekely wolde obeye

Fro poynt to poynt—the gospell saythe expresse—

And on noo syde wold it not with-seye.

And þouȝ þat sche bar of golde no keye,

90   To by a lambe for pouert constreynyng,

Yet she full mekely to make hir offryng

Brought two turtleȝ—as it is sayde afforne—

That was the offryng of pore folke ichone,

Whiche to the temple whan that she hath borne,

As custome was, she offrede hem a-noon.

And aftir that olde Symeon,

With humble herte and full bysy payne,

The childe enbrasyng in his Armeȝ twayne,

---

85. only] for C¹. 86. To þe lawe sche mekely wolde obeye H⁷.—sche mekely] mekely she D, B², B⁴; humbly she B³, L; she lowli H¹; she only mekely B¹.—sche mekely wolde] she wold mekely C¹.—wolde] dide H¹, H⁴, H⁶, C². 87. saythe] seyd B⁵ Co; dothe H⁸, C¹. 88. on] in B¹, B⁵, H⁷, C³, Ad³, Adv², Hu, Co; om. H⁶.—syde] maner B¹, B⁵, H⁷, C³, Ad³, Adv², Hu, Co.—wold] sholde B³; she wolde Hn¹; om. H¹.—not] ones B³, L; right not H¹; nouȝt An, Hn¹; om. B¹, C².—wold it not with seye] bar of gold no keye H⁵. 89. And þouȝ þat sche bar of golde no keye H⁷.— þouȝ] om. H⁵.—þat] om. B³, C¹, L.—bar of golde] of gold bar B¹, B², B⁴, H⁵, H⁶, CC, J, C².—no] the D, B⁵, Hn¹, Co; not þe C², CC. 90. by] bere B⁵.—for] om. B¹. 91. Yet] And yet B¹, H⁷.—she] om. B¹, B⁵, H⁸, Ad³, Adv², Hu.—make] makyng H¹. 92. Brought] She brouȝt B¹, H⁷, Ad³, Hu, Lg.—it is] I H¹.—it is sayde] ye haue herd H⁶.—afforne] to forn B⁵, H⁸; om. Lg. 93. the] om. C¹. 94. to] in C¹.—that] om. H².—hath] hadde Ash¹, H⁵; was V. 96. olde Symeon] sone come old Symeon H². 97. full] a ful B⁴, Ash¹, H³, H⁴, Ad², Lg; with full H⁸, Co; with H⁶; ful of C¹; om. CC, L.—bysy] om. B⁴, Ash¹, H¹, H³, H⁴, C¹, C⁵, Ad², An, Ch.—payne] beyn H¹ 98. enbrassyng] enbrasid C¹.—in] with H⁶.

Howe Symeon re-
ceyved criste of 　　100
our lady in the
Temple Ca° xxiij°[1]

O f hir modur goodly gan hi*m* take.
　Of lovyng hert and grete deuocion,

And suche a ioye of hym gan to make

Withe-in hym-self of high affection,

That he ne couthe, neythir by worde ne sou*n*,

Oute warde declare, neythir w*ith* chere ne face,

The passyng Ioye that gan his hert enbrace.

And he was rightfull holy and vertuouse,

This olde man, this blissede Symeon,

Dredeful also and passyngly famous

Amonge the preeste**ȝ** to Recken hem eu*e*rychone

110　　That was expectant of full long a-goon,

On the comfort and consolacion

Of Iserael in his entencion

---

99. Of his modur goodly gan hi*m* take B[1].—goodly] mekely V; om. Lg.—gan] he gan
D, J; he can H[1]; began H[6]; can Adv[2].—goodly gan him take] gan hym take goodly C[1].
100. Of] with B[3].—lovyng] longynge Lg. 101. And suche a ioye of hym gan to make
H[7].—a ioye] Ioye D, H[2].—gan] he began B[1]; began H[6]; can Adv[2].—to] om. C[2]. 102.
of] with B[1], CC.—affection] deuocioun H[1]; aspeciowne C[3]. 103. ne] not H[1]; om. CC.
—neythir by worde ne son] bi word nor bi reason H[1].—neythir] om. C[2].—ne son] ne
by sonn B[1]; neither by son B[2]. 104. Oute warde] outwardly B[2], H[6], CC, J.—neythir w*ith*
chere ne face] w*ith* chere ne w*ith* face H[1].—with] by B[2], H[2], H[6], CC, J; om. H[2].—ne]
nor Hu. 105. gan] began H[6]; can B[1], H[4], An, Hn[1].—enbrace] to enbrace H[6]. 106. he]
om H[5].—vertuouse] *"r" carrotted above line* D.—rightfull holy and vertuouse] right holy
and inly vertuous H[6]; *and* hooly vertuous Adv[2]. 107. This] This blessyd B[1].—blissede]
om. Hu. 108. Dredeful also and passyngly famous H[7].—Dredeful] Dredyng Hu.—also]
and also B[1]; om. C.—passyngly] passyng D, H[1], H[8], CC, C[1], C[2], Co. 109. to] as to
Hn[1]; om. B[1].—Recken] reckened B[1]; reede Adv[2].—hem] om. B[1], B[5].—eu*e*rychone]
ichon Ash[1], C[1]. 110. That] And B[3], L.—was] were B[2], CC, C[2].—of full long a goon]
folowing anon C[1].—full] om. Hn[1]. 111. On] Of B[1], B[4], Ash[1], H[1], H[3], H[4], H[7], C[1],
C[5], Ad[2], An, Lg, Ch, V; O B[2], H[6], J; om. B[3], L; Astre H[5].—and] *and* the B[1], B[3], B[5],
CC, L. 112. in] of H[2].

---

[1]x is crossed out.

For he had answewer of the holy goste

In his prayer that he shulde see,

The byrthe of cryste that is of power moste

And eke fro deeth þat he schal goo free

To the tyme of his Natyvyte;—

And to the day that *with* his eyne olde,

The birthe of hym that he may be-holde—

120 The whiche day is by grace come.

And for þat he bi reuelacioun

The tyme knewe, he hath the waye nome

To the temple *with* hygh deuocion,

To se of criste the *p*resentacion;

Howe that Marye and Ioseph eke also,

The childe presente *and* her offerynge do.

---

116. And eke fro deeth þat he schal goo free H7.—eke] also Hu; he Hn1; om. C1.—fro] of Ash1, C2.—schal] shulde D, B1, B3, H1, L, Ch, Hn1. 118. And to the day that] And un to the tyme that he CC; And see the day H8.—that] om. B1, B5, H7, C3, Adv2, Hu, Co.—with] he w*ith* B2, J.—his] om. H2, L. 119. that] the Hu.—may] might B2, H6, CC, J. 120. grace] the grace C1.—come] y come B4, H2, C1, C2, Hn1. 121. And for þat he bi reuelacioun H7.—that he] þe Hn1.—reuelacioun] reuolucion D, B3, B4, Ash1, H1, C3. 122. he] *and* C2; om. Lg.—the way] his waye B5.— nome] y nome B1, H2, H7, CC, Hn1. 123. To the temple] þe temple to H1.—hygh] om. B1, H7. 124. *p*resentacion] redemcion H8. 125. eke] om. B1, B5, H7, H8, C2, C3, Ad3, Adv2, Hu, Co. 126. The childe presente *and* her offerynge do B1.—presente] *p*resentede D.—and] in and Ash1.—her] theyr C3.—doo] om. H1.

Life of Our Lady

And for that criste was the first born,

Afftir the lawe in his tendre age—

Not of levi as ye haue herde to forn,

130 But of Iuda comyng by lynage—

Therfore his mothir, most holy of visage,

Hir offringe made list not for to striue,

For hym ayeyne to pay shillyng*es* fyfe—

Liche as the custome of the lawe was— f. 86a

She mekely made his redempcion.

And Symeon, beholdyng all this case

Full stilly in his inspeccion,

For love brennyng be affeccion,

Of verrey hert sodenly abrayede,

140 Holdyng the childe evyn thus he sayde:

127, And] All CC.—the] om. B¹, B², Ash¹, H¹, H⁶, CC, J, C². 129. Not of] Put on H¹.—
haue herde] herde haue H⁴,—to] be B¹, H². 130. But] and H¹. 131. of] the V. 132.
Hir offringe made list not for to striue H⁷.—Hir] His B³, H¹, L.—made] made me C².
—list] *and* list B¹, B³.—for] om. C².—to] om. C³.—striue] stryfe D, B⁴, B⁵, H¹, H⁵,
H⁶, C², C³. 133. hym] om. C².—shillyng*es*] cicles H¹. 135. She] So L.—his] her H¹,
CC. 136. all] om. C¹. 137. stilly] stabull *and* stille Ash¹; stille, H⁶; stylly stood C³.—in]
þanne in Hn¹. 139. Of] By C¹.—hert] hete B⁴, H⁵, H⁶, CC, J. 140. evyn] euere B¹; riȝt
C¹.—thus] this H⁴, H⁸.

O blisfull lorde, of thy high grace

    If that thou lust now thou maiste me lete

Oute of this life in pees and rest pace;

And suffre me to dey in quyete.

For nowe to me dethe is wondir swete;

Nowe haue I seen thy helthe and thy socour,—

And of mankynde lorde and savyour—

Whiche thou hast dight affore the faceȝ all,

Of yche peple to make hem glad and light—

150 To lete thy grace so to erthe falle,

Thorugh all the worlde to shewe his bemeȝ bryght,

That may be callede for comforte of his light,—

Of foreyne folke the reuelacion,

The glorye also and the savacion

Howe where and
whan Symeon made
Nunc dimittis ca°
xxiiij°[1]
Nunc dimittis *servum
tuum domine, etc.*
Quia viderunt
oculi mei
salutare, *etc.*
Quod parasti
ante faciem, *etc.*

Lumen ad
reuelacionem *etc.*

---

141. O] om. H², C¹.—blisfull] blessed B². 142. that] om. H¹, C¹.—now] om. H⁴, An.—lete] lede C¹; lyght Hu. 143. Oute] And B², H⁶, CC, J.—pees and rest] rest and pese C¹.—pace] to pace B¹, B⁴, H², C¹; passe H⁸. 145. nowe to me dethe is] nowe is deth to me C¹.—nowe] that B³.—dethe is] chere B³. 146. haue I seen] I have seen H¹.—seen] sey H⁸, C¹.—helthe] helpe B², H², H⁶, H⁸, CC, J.—thy socour] socour H¹, H². 147. And] om. C¹, Ad².—of] of all L.—lorde and savyour] my helpe and savioure Ash¹.—lorde] loue H⁴. 148. thou] om. C¹, Ad².—affore the faceȝ] to fore thy facis C¹.—faceȝ] face Hu. 149. Of] To Hn¹.—yche] euery Co; thy V.—hem] om. B¹. 150. To lete thy grace so to erthe falle B¹.—to erthe] to the erthe D, H⁸, C², C³, Adv²; on þe B⁵.—so] om. C¹. 151. all the] þis C².—his] þin Hu.—bryght] lyȝte C¹. 152. may be callede] callid mai be H¹.—for] om. H¹, H⁶.—his] the B³, L.—light] sight B³, L; myght H⁶, J. 153. foreyne] floreyn B², CC, J; thy C¹.—of foreyne] A forn C³.—reuelacion] revolucion H⁶. 154. The glorye] Of glory C¹.—also and] *and* also B¹.—also] om. Ch.

---

[1]lx is erased.

Of Israel thy peple in speciall,

To voyde hem oute of all derkenesse.

And Marye full mekely listenyth all,

And gan merveyle *with* grete avysenesse

Of the wordes that he gan expresse;

160　And Iosephe eke gan to wondir also.

And Symeon he*m* blessynge bothe two,

Spake to Marye and seyde in audience:　　Et benedixit

By-holde and se in thyn inspection,　　illis Symeon

　　　　　　　　　　　　　　　　　　　Ecce positus

How he is put in ruyne and offence　　est hic In

　　　　　　　　　　　　　　　　　　　Ruinam *et*

Of many one here in his region;　　resurrectio-

　　　　　　　　　　　　　　　　　　　nem

And to some in resurexion　　Et tuam

That shall releve, thorugh his myghty grace.　　ip*s*ius a*ni*mam

　　　　　　　　　　　　　　　　　　　pe*r*transibit

And thorugh thy sawle shall a sharpe swerde pace,　　gladius

---

155. thy] the B¹, B³, H¹, H⁴, H⁷, H⁸, CC, Adv². L. 156. voyde] bryng Adv².—of] clene of H².—all] om. B¹, H⁸. 157. listenyth] listened B⁵. 158. And gan] And can H¹; And began H⁶; Gan to C².—merveyle] to m*er*veile B⁴.—with] þan with Ch.—avysenesse] avisement H⁶. 159. Of the wordes that he gan expre*s*se B¹.—the] these D.—that] om. CC, C², Hu.—gan] began H⁶; can Adv². 160. Iosephe eke] eke Iosephe B¹.—eke] om. C².—gan to] began to H⁶; dyd Adv². 161. And Symeon he*m* blessynge bothe two B¹. —he*m* blessynge] blessyng hem D; hem blessede B³, H¹, H⁸, CC, C¹, C³; blessed hem B⁵.— bothe] also bothe B², H⁶, CC, J. 162. Spake] And spake B³, H⁸. 164. is] om. H¹.— and] *and* in C¹.—offence] defence Hn¹. 165. his] þys Ch. 166. to] of L.—in] into B³, L; om. H¹. 167. shall] om. H¹, C², Adv².—grace] and grace B², H⁶, CC, J, V, 168. sharpe] om. B², H⁶, CC, J.

Of hertely woo to as his passion— f. 86b

170 That passyngly shall bit*ter* be and fell—

To opyn herteʒ by confession

Her synfull thoughteʒ opynly to tell.

And Anna than, the doughter of phanuell,—

Born of the trybe and of the kynrede

Called Aser, sothely as I rede,

Of the Ioye that
Anna the doughter
of Phanuel made
whan crist was
offrede in to
the Temple
caº xxvº[1]

That was that day Ronne fer in age,—

Whiche in the temple by contynuaunce,

Sole by her self oute of maryage,

180 Lay niʒt *and* day in fastynge *and* penau*n*ce,

In wyddowe abyte sad of conten*a*unce.

And in prayer was hir bysy cure,

Which in that hour of grace or aventure,—

---

169. hertely] erthli CC. 170. passyngly] passinge C². —shall bit*ter*] bitter schal C². —shall] om. B¹. —bitter be] be bitter C¹. —be] om. C⁵. 171. herteʒ] hir hertis C¹; his herte C². —confession] trewe confessioun B¹. 172. Her] Theyr C³. —synfull] sorowfull B², B³, B⁴, Ash¹, H², H³, H⁴, H⁵, H⁶, CC, J, C¹, C², C⁵, Ad², L, An, Ch, Hn¹, V. —thoughteʒ] hertis B², CC. 173. than] om. H⁶, H⁸, C³, Adv², Hu, Ch, Hn¹, V. —the] om. B², B³, B⁵, Ash¹, H², H³, H⁴, H⁵, H⁷, J, C⁵, Ad², Hu, L, An, Co. —of] om. B¹. —phanuell] samuelle H⁸. 174. the] om. Ad³. —and of] and B⁴, Ash¹, H³, H⁴, C², C⁵, Ad², An, Ch; om. Hn¹. 175. Aser] Asie H¹. —sothely] sodenly C¹; soþly to þe C². 176. That] om. B¹, H⁷, Ad³; What CC. —that day] the day C¹; than H⁶. —day] om. H⁶. —fer] om. B², CC, J, H⁶. 177. Whiche] With B², B⁴, H¹, H³, H⁴, H⁵, CC, J, C², Ad², An, V. —in] om. V. —the temple] om. B², H⁶, CC, J. 178. by] om. Ash. 179. Lay niʒt *and* day in fastynge *and* penaunce H⁷. —nyght and day] soule by hir selff C¹. —in fastynge] fastyng D, B⁵, C², V. —and penau*n*ce] in penaunce D, B⁵, C², V; and in penaunce B¹, C¹, Ch. 180. In wyddowe abyte] and evir abood C¹. —wyddowe] wedewhode B³; wedowes C³. —of] and H⁴; in C². —conten*a*unce] gou*er*naunce B², H⁵, H⁶, CC, J. 181. And] om. Hu. —in] hir B³, L. —prayer] preyers H¹. —hir] al hyr Hu. 182. Which] With B², H⁶, CC, J. —of] by B³. —or] and B¹, H⁸; or of H¹, Ch.

---

[1]x is erased.

Whan criste was ther *with* his mother dere

In the tyme of his oblacioun—

This Anna cam, demure and sad of chere,

And vnto hym *with* grete deuocion,

Whan she hym sawe, fel on knees dou*n*,

Recomfortede of all her olde smerte,

Hym honouryng *with* all hir hole herte.

190   Sayde opynly that all myghten here;

Bethe myrry and light in yo*ur* entencion,

And eu*er*y man be glad and of goode chere,

For nowe is borne for our savacion,

He that shall make our Redempcion.

This yonge childe, blissed mot he be,

That me hathe grauntede his face for to se.

183. Whan criste was ther] Was crist þere Hn¹.—*with*] within C¹. 184. In the tyme of his oblacioun B¹.—the] this D, C². 185. cam] come H², H³, H⁵; om. B², H⁶, CC, J. 186. And] om. H⁶, C¹. 187. she] om. B³, L.—fel on knes] on knees fell down Adv², Hu.—fel] falle CC.—knes] her knees H².—doun] a doun B¹, B², H⁶, J, Ad³, Hu. 188. Recomfortede] Recomfort B², H, CC, J.—of] hir of B¹.—her] oure Ch, Co.—olde smerte] smerte olde B²; hool smerte Hu. 189. honouryng] honoride C².—hole] om. C². 190. Sayde] And sayde B¹, B⁵, H⁸, C³, Ad³, Adv², Hu, Co; Sey L.—all] all men B⁵, H², Co.—myghteȝ] myght it H⁶. 191. myrry] lygh *and* m*er*ie B¹.—your] euery C¹. 192. of goode] good H⁷, H⁸, C¹, Ad³, Hn¹.—of] in H². 193. For] om. H².—for our] our for our B¹. 194. shall make] make schall Adv².—our] all our C¹. 196. That] And B².—me] he B², CC, J; om. H⁶.—for] om. B¹, C², C³.

And then in sothe whan eu*er*y thyng was dou*n*

Aftir the lawe w*ith*outen excepcion,

And that Anna and holy Symeon

200 Had of this childe made declaracion—

As ye haue herde in conclusion—

The childe and Ioseph and this mayde free,

Reto*ur*nede home into galelee.

N owe as me semythe in this high ferre

That named is the puryficacioun,

Eu*er*y man aught to be myrry;

And withe gode hert and hole entencion,

Deuoutely bryng his oblacion.

And offre a turtil, firste of Innocence,

210 And a dove next for his offence;

f. 87a

A pr*o*fitable declar-
acion of the pr*o*pre-
tees of the Turtle
Ca° xxvj°[1]

---

197. then] om. Hu, Hn¹. 198. excepcion] any excepcioun B¹. 199. that] þanne B⁴, Ash¹, H³, C¹, C², C⁵, Ad², Ch.—and holy Symeon] hir selfe *and* holy Simeon Ash¹; and old symeon H¹. 200. made] om. B⁵, H⁸, C³, Adv², Co. 201. in] om. H¹. 202. The] This B⁴, B⁵, Ash¹, H³, H⁴, H⁵, C¹, C², C⁵, Ch.—and Ioseph and this mayde free] ande the mayden and ioseph fre B¹.—this mayde] his modyr H⁸, Adv².—this] þe C², Ad³, Hn¹. 203. home] homward B¹; theym C³; ben home H¹.—into] to H¹. 204. as] *carrotted above line* D; om. B⁵, H², H⁸, C³, Hu, Hn¹. 205. That named is the puryficacioun B¹] That is so hye of pius Deuocion Ash².—the] om. D, Hu, Co. 206. Euery] Eu*er*yche B³, L.—myrry] glad *and* merie B¹, B², B³, B⁴, Ash¹, Ash², H², H³, H⁴, H⁵, H⁷, CC, J, C¹, C², C⁵, Ad², L, An, Ch, Hn¹, V; glad merye H⁶; ryght mery C³. 207. gode] om. C¹. 208. Deuoutely] Devoue C¹.—bryng] bryngynge B¹; bryng vp Hn¹. 209. And offre a turtil firste of Innocence H⁷.—offre] of D.—a] the B³, L; om. B⁴, Ash¹, H³, H⁴, C¹, Ad², An, Ch, V.—a turtil firste] first a turtul B¹; I first the turtle Ash²; firste þe turtile C⁵.—turtil] turtillis C¹.

---

[1]x is erased.

For grete mysterye is in bothe tweyne:

The tone commendyde for his chastite,   Nota bene nota

And that othir, if I shall not feyne,

Is symple and meke withoute cruelte;

The turtle prysede of trouthe and honeste,

And the dove hathe kyndely excellence

Of mekenesse and hertely pacience.

And who that wol his offryng make a-right,   Nota bene nota

He may not fayle noon of bothe twoo:

220   Fyrste shyne in clennes with his chaste light

As the Turtle, and ther with also,

Liche the dove, bothe in wele and woo,

His hert daunt so by a-temperaunce

To voyde rancour and plant in sufferaunce.

211. For] And for H³; And CC.—is] om. Hu.—in] om. C². 212. The tone] That oon B⁵, H¹, H², H⁴, H⁸, C², C³, Ch, Co.—commendyde] commendith C¹, Co.—his] hye B¹; hir H⁷.—chastite] charite C¹. 213. And] om. C².—that] the B¹, B³, B⁴, Ash¹, H², H³, H⁵, H⁷, CC, J, C¹, C³, Ad², Ad³, Adv², Hu, L, An, V.—if] for B¹. 214. and meke] *and* clene *and* meke B¹.—withoute] and without H⁸, C³, Adv². 215. prysede] preysith C¹.—of trouthe and honeste] and ther with alsoo B². 217. mekenesse] verry mekenesse B², B³, B⁴, Ash¹, Ash², H², H³, H⁴, H⁵, H⁶, CC, J, C¹, C², C⁵, Ad², L, An, Ch, V.—and] of B¹; and of H¹. 218. who] he Adv².—his] this Co.—make] do C², C³.—aright] om. L. 219. not] om. B³.—noon] om. B⁴; one H⁶; of non CC. 220. clennes] mekenesse B¹, B⁵, H⁷, C³, Ad³, Adv², Hu, Co.—his] a B¹. 222. the] as the C¹.—woo] in wo H⁶, L. 223. hert] om. CC—daunt] to daunte H⁶.—so] om. Ch.—a] om. B¹, B², B³, Ash², CC, Adv², L. 224. To voyde rancour] The plant rancour C¹.—in] om. C¹.—sufferaunce] suffisaunce H⁸.

And as the Turtle by contemplatyffe

For synne soroweth *with* waymentyng,—

Only for loue of thilke ete*r*nall lyfe

That lastythe aye and may haue no endyng—

And as the birde sheweth the com*m*yng

230   Of grene ver *with* fresshe budde3 newe,

Ryght so of vertu with floures fayre of hewe.

He muste ensample of the Turtle take,

And be well ware that he not varye

But life sool whan he hathe lost his make;

And in prayer be also solytarye,

And loke all waye that he not ne tarye

On noo caren of no flesshely hede.

And withe all this to take also hede,

---

225. by] to be CC; full C³.—contemplatyffe] contemplacion H⁵. 226. For] And for B³, H¹, L; That for C³.—soroweth] sorowe B³, L.—with] sore wit*he* B¹, H⁷, Ad³; eu*er* with H²; in H⁸.—waymentyng] *under-dotted as if for deletion and followed by another, "morninge", in another hand* D; grete weymentyng B², B³, Ash¹, Ash², H³, H⁵, H⁶, CC, J, C¹, C⁵, Ad², An, Ch, Hn¹, V. 227. for] of Hn¹.—of] for H⁶.—thilke] that B², H⁶, CC, C². C³; þys Adv²; om. H¹.—lyfe] division Ash². 228. aye] euer B¹, B⁵, H⁷, H⁸, C², C³, Ad³, Adv², Hu, Co.—and may haue no] wit*h*outen C³; and has none Ash²; and may not C¹.—haue] om. H⁴, C⁵, Ad², Ch.—endyng] endiff C¹. 229. And] om. H³, C³.—as] ri3te as C¹.—the] þis H¹; om. B³, L.—the com*m*yng] fressh buddis newe C¹. 230. ver wit*h*] wherewith C⁵.—fresshe] his fresshe B¹. 231. Ryght so of vertu with floures fayre of hewe B¹.—of vertu] vertu D, CC, C².—fayre] fresshe H⁶, H⁸, C².—of hewe] and hewe Ch; and newe H⁸. 233. well] om. B², H², H⁶.—not] ne B¹; om. H⁶.—varye] ne varie B², B⁵, Ash¹, Ash², H⁵, H⁷, J, C⁵, Ad², Ad³, Adv², An, Ch, Hn¹, Co, V. 234. he] that he Ash¹.—hathe] om. C².—lost] lesiþ C². 235. also] eke Hn¹.—solytarye] in solatrie B¹. 236. And] To C¹.—all waye] awaye B¹; also H⁴.—he] sche H⁷; ye CC.— not] nought Co.—ne] om. B¹, B³, H⁴, CC, C¹, C², C³, Hu, L.—tarye] vary CC. 237. On] Of B⁴, Ash¹, H³, H⁴, CC, C⁵, Ad², Ad³, Ch; In H².—of] *"ne" and "on" carrotted in another hand before and after "of"* D; ne of no Ash¹; for C², C³,—hede] hete B⁴; dede C². 238. all] om. C².—to take also] also to take H¹; also take C²; to make CC. —also hede] good hede B³, B⁵, CC, C¹.

That he his lyfe lede not in veyne,   f. 87b

240   But like a dove, bysely espye

Where he of vertu gedre may the greyne;

And þat he fle not oute of companye—

Wantynge also the galle of enuye—

And that he haue ay indignacion

Of synfull luste full of corrupcion,

On eny caryne to fostre hym or fede.

And euermore with all his besy payne,

Eschewyng, synne, loue god and drede;

And with the dove sighen and compleyne

250   For his offence, *and* with wynges tweyne,

Take his flight as fer-furthe as he can,

Thorugh perfyte loue bothe to god and man.

---

239. he] yee C¹; om. CC.—his] your C¹; om. H¹.—lede] lyve CC. 241. he] om. CC.—he
of vertu] of vertu he B⁵.—of] in C¹. gedre] gendre B², CC, J. 242. fle] fly C¹.—not]
nouȝt C⁵, Ad², An, Hn¹, Co.—oute] om. Ad².—of] of good H¹; the H³. 243. Wantynge
also the galle of enuye B¹.—of] of all D, H¹. 244. that he haue ay] he þat ay haue C².—
he] om. B¹.—ay] euer B¹, B⁵, H⁷, H⁸, C³, Ad³, Adv², Hu, Co; eke ay Hn¹. 245. Of]
Thorow B¹, B⁵, H⁷, H⁸, C³, Ad³, Adv², Hu, Hn¹; To Co; om. H².—full] oute B⁴,
H³, H⁴, C¹, C⁵, Ad², An, Ch; om. CC. 246. On] And B², CC, J; Of Ash², H²; In H¹;
or Ch; And on H⁶.—eny] no H⁶.—to fostre hym or fede] her for to fede H⁶.—fostre]
suffre B², J.—hym] and hym H⁸.—fede] on feede B², CC, J; to fede B¹, H⁸; and
feede B⁴, Ash¹, Ash², H², H³, H⁴, H⁵, C¹, C², C³, C⁵, Ad², Adv², An, Ch, Hn¹, V.
247. And] For and Co.—all] om B¹, Ash¹, CC.—his] her H⁶, C². 248. loue] louyng Hn¹.
249. dove] turtill Ash¹. 250. For his offence *and* with wynges tweyne B¹.—his] her
C².—*and*] om. C².—wynges] his wyngeȝ D, B², H¹, H². 251. Take] To Take H¹.
252. bothe] om. B⁵, H⁸, C³, Co.—man] eke to man C³.

And as the dove touchithe eke her make

Nota bene nota

Only w*ith* kyssyng whan thay to-gydre gone,

So muste he, whe*þ*er he slepe or wake,

Thorughe charyte set his hert in one;

And like a dove, make his nest of stone.

This is to say, among all his pleasaunce

He muste his flesshe dau*n*te w*ith* pen*a*unce.

Nota *bene* nota   260   And as a dove w*ith* hir eyne meke,—

Of kynde espyeth a-myddes the Ryu*e*re

Occuli eius caput

columbe super Riuos

aquar*um*

The haukes shadowe when he dothe her seke,

And flieth away or he come eny nere—

Right so must he, w*ith* p*er*fyte eyne clere,

A-myd the waters full of woo and stryfe,

In the wawes of this mortall lyfe

---

253. as the] a H¹.—the] om. Hn¹.—touchithe] all soo towcheth Hu.—eke] hie eke H¹; om. C², Adv², Hu. 254. with] by B¹, B⁵, H⁷, H⁸, CC, C³, Adv², Hu, Hn¹, Co.—gydre] odyr CC. 255. So muste he whe*ʒ*er he slepe or wake H⁷.—muste he] muste CC.—whe*ʒ*er] wher D.— he] ye CC, C¹. 256. his] your C¹.—in one] a non B², H⁶, CC, J; on oon H⁷. 257. make] maketh C⁵.—his] her B⁵, C²; your C¹.—of] on B⁴, Ash¹, H³, H⁴, H⁶, CC, J, C⁵, Ad², An; in C¹, C², Adv², Ch.—stone] lym and ston B², H⁶, CC, J; a ston C². 258. This] That Ash², H¹.—all] om. H⁷, Ad³; the B¹.—his] hie B¹; your C¹; her C². 259. He] you C¹.— his] your C¹. 260. And] om. C¹.—a] the B¹, B³, B⁴, B⁵, Ash², H⁵, H⁷, C¹, Ad³, L, Co.—with] withynne H⁸.—hir] om. CC.—meke] make B². 261. espyeth] assaieth aspieth B², J.—the] of the H⁶. 262. shadowe] shade B³, L; shades V.—her] om. B¹. 263. And flieth away or he come eny nere] Sechinge his repaste bothe ferre *and* nere Ash².—flieth] flee C¹; fleeth C³.—or] ere H⁸.—he] om. CC.—come] om. C²; comyth Hu.—eny] hir H¹, C¹. 264. he] yee C¹.—perfyte] bri*ʒ*t C². 265. waters] watyr CC, C².—full] om. C². 266. this] his B⁴, Ash², H³, H⁴, H⁸, C¹, C⁵, Ad², An.—lyfe] stryfe L.

Nota bene nota

The dedely shade of the fynde eschewe—

That waytyth hym with snares large and huge

And to þe deeth euere doith him purswe

270 To trappe hym here in this deluge—

And like a dove fle to his refuge,

By grace only if he may escape,

Or dethe be-tray hym with his soden Rape.

And who by clennesse with the Turtle fleethe— f. 88a

As I to forne haue made mencion— Nota bene nota

And like the dove, affore his parell seeth,

Of dethe to eschewe the persecucion,

And can he meke in tribulacion,

I dar Recorde and wryte it for a sothe,

280 Truly to god he is offryng dothe.

267. shade] shades B1, B5, H8, Ad3, Hu; shadewe B2, Ash2, CC, J, C3, Adv2.—fynde] fendis H8. 268. waytyth] wacheth C3.—hym] ȝewe C1. 269. And to ȝe deeth euere doith him purswe H7.—to] om. B1.—suere] doith euere B1; doith ȝewe ay C1; ay B2, B3, B4, Ash1, Ash2, H1, H2, H3, H4, H5, CC, J, C2, C5, Ad2, L, An, Ch, D.—doith] om. D. V.—doith him] hym doth H1; doth to hym Hn1. 270. trappe] by trappe H2, V.—hym] ȝewe C1.—here] euere B1; om. C2.—in] now in C3.—this] his B1, B4, Ash2, H3, H4, C5, Ad2, L, An, Ch, Co; the Adv. 271. fle] om. C1. 272. By grace only] Onli bi grace H1.—he] yee C1. 273. be tray] by trappe B1, H1, H2, H7, CC, C1, C2, Hn1; betrace B2, B3, B5, Ash1, H3, H8, J, C5, Ad3, Ad2, Adv, Hu, An, C1.—hym] ȝewe C1.—soden] om. B1. 274. who] who so B2, B3, B4, Ash1, Ash2, H3, H4, H5, CC, J, C1, C2, C5, Ad2, An, Ch, V; om. H1.—by] with CC, C1, Ad2; om. B2, CC, J.—clennesse with the Turtle fleethe] canne and with the turtle wull flee B2, CC, J. 275. made] of C3. 276. the] a B2, B3, B4, Ash1, Ash2, H3, H4, H5, CC, J, C1, C5, Ad2, L, An, Ch, Hn1, V.—affore] beffore H2. 277. Of] or B1, B7,—to eschewe the] come to eschewe B1, H7, Ad3; to pursue may Ash2. 278. can] om. B1, B5, Ash1, H7, H8, C3, Ad3, Adv2, Hu, Co.—be] to be C3, Adv2.—in] in al B1, B5, H7, H8, C3, Adv2, Hu, Co. 279 dar] thar Ash1.—Recorde] recorde it B2, B4, H3, H4, H5, CC, J, C1, C5.—wryte] telle Ch.—it] om. B3, L.—a] om. B1, B5, H3, H8, C3, Adv2, Co. 280. Truly to god he is offryng dothe] þe trew offeringe he doþe C2; Truly hys offryng vnto god he doth C3.

But who that eu*e*re lyfe in chastite

And hathe envye enclosede in his thought,

He mai wel offre, what so þat he be,

To god a turtle but the dove nought.

Wherfore, they muste be to-gydre brought,

That clennesse by sothefaste vnyte

W*i*th*o*utyn partyng be knytte w*ith* charyte.

And sothely thanne, ther is no more to seyne,

Whan his offryng and oblacion

290   Is iustely made to god of bothe tweyne,

It is acceptede of more deuocion.

And for to make a shorte discripcion

Of the Turtle and the doveʒ kynde,

Reed here these verses and ye shall it fynde:

---

281. But] And B⁴, H⁴, C¹, C⁵ Ch.—that] so C¹, Hu.—eu*e*re] om. C¹.—eu*e*re] leuyth eu*e*r H⁸. 282. hathe] euyr haue CC.—envye] no envye C²; om. CC.—enclosede] closed B¹, B³, B⁴, B⁵, H², C², Ad³, Ch, Hn¹, V.—in his thought] in hert and thoght V; in his herte *and* þought Ash¹.—thought] herte B², B⁴, H⁴, H⁵, C⁵, An. 283. He mai wel offre what so þat he be H⁷.—wel] eke Hn¹.—what] where D; who J, L.—that] euere B¹, CC; om. B⁴, H¹. 284. a] the H².—the] a B⁵, H⁸, C², C³, L, Co. 285. Wherfore] And þerfore H¹.—be] om. B¹. 287. Be] om. C².—with] in Adv². 288. ther is] is þer Adv².—is] om. B³. 289. his] þis H¹.—and] and his B¹, CC, C¹, C², Adv², CC.—oblacion] obligation C¹. 290. of] om. C¹.—bothe] om. H¹. 291. It] þat B⁵.—acceptede] accepte B¹, B⁵ C², C³, Ad³, Co.—of] to H⁸, Adv²; Co.—accepted of more] more accepted of B³. 293. Turtle] turtles B², J.—the] of þe Adv². 294. here] occurs only in D and Ash¹. —these] this H², H⁴, CC, Ad³, Ch, Hn¹.—verses] vers B¹, B², H², H⁷, CC, J, Ad³, Hu, Ch, Hn¹. Co.—and] *and* ther B¹, H², H⁷.—ye] om. C².—it] he*m* B¹; om. B², H¹, J, C².

Alta petit Turtur cantando gemit veniens ver

Nunciat et caste viuit solusq*ue* moratur

Pullos nocte fouet morticinium quoq*ue* fugit

Grana legat volitat sociata cadaucra vitat

Felle caret plangit socium q*ue per* oscula tangit

300 Petra dat huic nidu*m* fugit hostem in flumine visu*m*

Rostro non ledit geminos pullos bene nutrit.

This fest also—bothe of more and lesse

Thorugh oute the worlde in euery Region—

Called is the fest of candilmasse.

For sondrye skylles in conclusion—

As olde boke3 maken mencion—

And howe that firste this feste toke his name,

So as I can to yov I will atame.

---

295. Alta] letter erased between t and a, D.—veniens] om. H¹. 297. quoq*ue*] quo Ash¹; que Ash², H⁵, C⁵. 298. Grana legat volitat sociata cadaucra vitat B¹.—volitat] volutat D.—legat] legit B³; ledit Adv².—cadaucra vitat] canto vera vita H¹. 299. q*ue*] qui Ash². 300. nidu*m*] nitidum Ash².—hostem] om. H¹.—in] om. B⁵, Ash², H⁸, Ad³. 301. pullos] pulles Ash².—bene] om. H².—pullos bene] b*ene* pullos bene C². 302. of] om. C¹, Hu. 303. oute] all C¹; om. C².—in] of CC. 305. skylles] causis C². 307. And] om. C¹.—howe that firste this feste toke] how this fest first toke B², B³, Ash¹, H³, H⁴, H⁵, CC, J, C⁵, Hu, L, An, V; how þis feeste toke first B⁴, C², Ch; hou3 of þat furste þis feste toke B⁵, H⁸, C³, how þat his feeste first tooke H⁷, Ad³; who that this fest first took B¹; How this feest first toke C¹; how of that first the feste tooke Co. 308. to yov I will] I will to you H¹; I woll 3ewe C¹.—will] gynne B², CC, J.

How Candilmas
firste toke the name   310
Ca° xxvij°[1]

Some tyme, when Rome thorough his high Renou*n*,
  Was most flouryng in power and in myght,
Eu*ery* fifte ȝeere bi reuolucyoun,
In februarie vpon the first nyght,
Eche man and childe *with* a tapre light,
Went in the Cyte tweyne and tweyne a paas
Vn to a temple whiche þat sacrid was

To februa of olde fundacion—
Þat modir was to mars omnipotent—
In whose honoure this p*ro*cession
Ordenede was by greate avysement.

No*ta* quid lustrum   320
At eche lustre wenyng in her entent,
That hir power and greate worthynesse
Preferryde was, thorough helpe of this godesse,

---

309. Some tyme] Whilom H[1].—when] in B[2], CC, J.—thorough] was C[2].—his] of C[2];
om. H[2], C[2], Ch.—high] om. B[2], B[4], H[2], CC, J. 310. Was most flouryng] Most flourynge
was Hn[1].—flouryng in power and in] of power flouring on his C.—in power] thorow
power CC.—in myght] myght B[2], H[2], H[8], C[1], C[2], Ch. 311. Eu*ery* fifte ȝeere bi reuolucyoun
H[7].—fifte] fyfty D, B[1], Ash[1]; fyftethe H[2]; fiftene H[4], An; *five* B[5], H[1] H[8], C[2], Hn[1];
om. B, L. 312. vpon] on B[1], B[3], B[5], H[1], H[2], H[7], H[8], C[3], Ad[3], L, Hn[1], Co; in C[1], C[2].
313. Eche] Euery Co.—man] a man B[1].—tapre] tabir B[3]. 314. in] into B[4], C[2], C[3].—tweyne
and tweyne] two and two B[1], B[2], H[1], H[2], H[3], H[4], H[7], CC, J, C[1], C[2], C[5], Ad[3], An, Ch,
Hn[1], V. 315. Vn to a temple whiche þat sacrid was H[7].—Vn] om. B[1].—a] the D, B[1],
B[3], B[4], H[1], H[4], H[8], CC, C[2], C[3], An, Hn[1].—whiche þat] the whiche D, B[1]; that þat
H[8]; where CC.—sacrid] tyme H[8]; I sacride C[2]. 316. To] Of Hn[1]. 317. þat modir was
to mars omnipotent H[7].—to] of B[1]; and H[8].—omnipotent] Armypotent D, C[3]. 319. by]
in B[1]. 320. At] And B[2], B[5], Ash[1], H[1], CC; That B[3], H[8], L; In Hn[1].—eche lustre]
eu*ery* plesure H[6]; ichon CC.—lustre] lust B[3]; loueȝ H[8]; om. C[2].—her] his B[2], H[8];
þer B[5]. 321. That] þer C[2].—and] *and* her B[1], H[7], Ad[3].—grete] om. B[1]. 322. Preferryde]
Prefervid B[3], B[5]; Preserved Ch.—thorough] bi þe B[5].—this] þi H[5]; the CC; his Hn[1].

---

[1]x is erased.

From all assaute of eu*er*y aduersarie—

Supposyng fully in her opynyon,

That she fortune made debonayre

For to susteyne the honour of her towne,

And thorough her helpe and mediacion,

That myghty mars to encrece her glorye,

In all conquest yeff to hem victorye.

330   For whiche cause thorugh oute the Cyte,

As ye haue harde of high and lowe estate,

Was first ordeynede this solempnyte

In the Temple that was consecrate

To februa, the goddesse fortunate,

Thorough helpe of whome they wer victoryous.

And so this custume supersticious,

323. From all assaute of eu*er*y aduersarie H5.—From] For D, H6, J, V.—assaute] assawtes B1, B3, H7, C1, Ad3; the assautys C3.—of euery] and all H2; and eu*er*y V.— aduersarie] aduersite H1, H2, H8, C2; ver sery CC. 324. fully] om. H8.—her] theyr C3. 325. made] a februs made H8.—debonayre] of her bowntie H1; hur to obbey H6. 326. For] om. C2.— susteyne] schowe H6.—her] ther H4, C3; owre CC; om. B1. 327. her] om. B5.—and mediacion] a*nd* hir mediacioun B1.—mediacion] meditacion H6. 328. That] And C2.—to] om. H6, C3.—encrece] encreased H6.—her] þer B5, C3.—glorye] gey H6. 329. In] And in H6.—conquest] conquestis B2.—yeff to hem] to hem yeaue H2.—to] om. B1, H6, CC.— victorye] the victorie B2, H6, CC, C1. 330. oute] om. H8. 331. of high and lowe] of lowe and hyʒ Ch. 332. first ordeynede] made first V.—this] wit*h* H8. 333. In] in to CC. 334. To februa the goddesse fortunate B.—To] For C2.—februa] februarye D.—the] om. Hn1. 335. whome] hem CC.—victoryous] ful glad H6. 336. this] the CC.—supersticious] euer was had H6.

In Rome twone, as myn auct*ou*r seythe,

Observede was long and many a day.

Yet aftir that they turnede to the faythe,

340 But eu*e*re in one this Ryte thay kept alway—

For olde custome is harde to putte away,

And vsage grevythe folke3 full sore

To do a-way that thei haue kepte of yore.

But at the laste Pope Sergius,   f. 89a

Of the peple seyng this erroure,

And that the custome was full p*e*rilous,

Dyd his devo*u*r and also his laboure,

This ryte to chaunge into the honoure

Of our lady, so that this high feste,

350 Fro the highest dou*n* to the leste,

---

337. Rome twone] neþ Rome C². 339. Yet] and C¹.—that om. C².—to] into B³, H⁵, L. 340. But] om. H¹.—eu*e*re] om. B³, B⁵, H⁸, Hn¹, Co.—in one] om. C¹.—this Ryte thay kept] thcy kept this ri3t C¹.—Ryte] cultu*s* H⁶.— thay] om. C².—kept] kepe H⁸. 341. olde] om. C¹.—is] om. C³.—to] om. Ch. 342. And] And also B², B⁴, Ash¹, H³, H⁴, H⁵, H⁶, CC, J, C¹, C², C⁵, An, Ch, V; also H².—folke3] also folke B¹, H⁷, Ad².—full] om. CC. 343. To do a way that thei haue kepte of yore B¹.—do] done D, B², H¹, J.—a] akei C².—haue] om. H¹.—kept] used CC.—of] full D, B⁵, H⁸, C³, L, Hn¹, Co; to C¹; afor of H¹; om. B³, H², CC, C², Ch.—yore] afore CC; fore C¹. 344. But] But all H².—Pope] bys [*carrotted*] Pope B², H⁵; *crossed out in* H⁶, Co; the pope H¹, C¹; om. Hn¹. 345. this] the B³, B⁵, H², CC, Hn¹, Co. 346. full] so H⁸, C³; om. H³, C². 347. also] eke H². 348. This] The Ash¹, C¹, Ch.—ryte] cultu*s* H⁶.—into] *"to" is carrotted above the line* D; vnto H², Ch. 349. lady] ioy H⁸.—so that] at H⁸.—this] the B², H⁶, CC, J. 350. the] all the Ash¹.—dou*n* to] unto B³, H², H⁸; yn to L.—leste] lowest H¹.

Euery man and woman in her honde

To the Temple shulde a tapre bryng,

Þoruʒ out þe worlde in euery manere londe;

And ther with all make her offryng,

Aftir the gospell the presteʒ hand kyssyng,—

With light solempne that all myghten sene,—

In honour oonly of þe heuenly quene

That best may be our mediatrice

To hir son that is with-oute fayle,

360   Bothe lorde and kyng, and she Emperatrice

Of londe, of see, of pees *and* of batayle,

Withouten whome no conquest may avayle,

For she hath power more in sothefastnesse,

Then februa of Rome the goddesse.

---

351. her] theyr C³. 352. shulde a tapre] a taper shulde H³.—shulde] thei shulde B¹; shall CC. 353. þoruʒ out þe worlde in euery manere londe H⁷.—out] all D, B⁴, H¹, H².—manere] cristen H¹; om. B¹, H², C². 354. all] om. C².—her] þer B⁵, C³. 355. the] and the B¹.— kyssyng] to kis C¹. 356. all] *carrotted above line* D; all thei H⁶; all men CC, C¹.— myghten] myght it B¹, B², B⁴, B⁵, Ash¹, H³, H⁴, H⁵, H⁷, H⁸, J, C³, C⁵, Ad³, An, Ch, Hn¹, Co, V; may C¹. 357. In honour oonly of þe heuenly quene H⁷.—honour] the honour C³.—of] om. B¹.—þe] our D; "*the*" *crossed out and* "*oure*" *carrotted* L.—heuenly] heuen D, B², CC, J, Ad³, L, V. 358. our] euer oure B², H⁵, CC, J, V.—mediatrice] good mediatrice Ad³. 361. Of londe of see of pees *and* of batayle H⁷.—of see] and see D, B³, B⁴, H¹, H², H⁶, H⁸, CC, C¹, C², L; and of se Ch.—and] om. B¹.—of batayle] batayle D, B³, H⁴, C², L. 362. Withouten] With B³, B⁵, H⁸, L, Co. 363. she hath power more] her power is more H⁶.—sothefastnesse] sothnesse B¹, B⁵, H¹, H⁴, H⁸, C³, Ad³, L, Hn¹, C. 364. Then] þer C².—februa] had februa H¹; Februari Ch.—the] om. H⁸.

And thus this ryte was vtterly Refusede

By Sergius, as ye haue herde devyse,—

That was afforne of hem of Rome vsede

Full many a day in her paynym wyse

Whom to sue al oristen must dispise—

370   And of candeles whan this ryte gan passe,

Came the name first of Candelmasse.

This feste also of full long a-gone,

The name toke of the procession—

Made of Anna and holy Symeon,

When thay hym mette with grete deuocion,

Brought to the Temple to his oblacion

As was the lawe custom *and* vsaunnce

Of holy chirche for a remembraunce—

365. thus] om. B⁵, H⁷, C¹, C³, Ad³, L.—thus this ryte] in this Citee B³; this Cite H⁸, Hn¹, Co.—this] om. B⁵.—ryte] cultus H⁶. 366. haue] om. H¹. 367. afforne] to fore C¹.—of hem of Rome] of Rome of hem H¹; in Room of hem C¹; in Rome C², Ch.—of hem] by hem H⁶, C³.—of Rome] in Rome Hn¹, Co. 368. a] om. H¹—in] of B¹.—her] theyre C³; om. C². 369. Whom to sue al cristen must dispise B¹.—to] for to C³.—sue] shewe B³, H⁶, C²; serue B⁴; eschewe H⁸.—al] om. C².—cristen] cristene men Hn¹, Ad³, Co.—must] most D, B³, Ash¹, C¹, C², Ch, Hn¹, Co; mote H¹, H², H⁷, C³; om. Ad³. 370. candeles] candell B², H⁵; candelmasse B³, B⁵, H⁸, Hn¹, Co.— this] the B³, H⁴, C¹, L, An.—ryte] light B³; Ire H⁸.—gan] can B¹; dide H³; began H⁶. 371. Came] Come B², J, Hn¹, Co, V; cam B⁴.—the] to the B², B⁴. 372. long a gone] yere agon H¹.—a] om. Co. 373. the procession] holy procession Ch. 374. and] and of B², B³, H¹, H⁸, CC, J, C¹, L. 375. hym] om. H⁶. 376. to the] on to the C¹.— to his] for his B¹; to here B³; of his H¹, C³; his H⁶. 377. As was the lawe custom *and* vsaunnce B¹.—As] And as D, H⁸, L.—was] om. H⁸.—custom] of custom B³, L. 378. Of holy chirche for a remembraunce B¹.—Of] With D, B², B⁵, H¹, H⁸, C³, Hn¹, Co, V.— for] of Ch.

Observede furthe yet fro yere to yere   f. 89b

380 Of februarye on the first day,

Withe sacrede light vpon tapers clere—

Shynyng as bright as phebus dothe in may—

Whan the peple in what thay can or may,

Full Redy ben of on entencion

To make in fygure a presentacion

Of criste Ihesu with all her full myght,

Syngnyfyede, who so can take hede,

Withe the tapre that we offre light:

For firste the wax betokenyth his manhede,

390 The weyke his soule, the fyre his godhede;

And as the wax is made and wrought of newe,—

Thorough small bees of floures fresshe of hewe,

---

379. Observede] Obserueth H⁶; And so seruethe B¹.—furthe yet] ȝit forth C¹.—furthe] om. H¹, C².—yet] om. B¹, B², H⁶, H⁸, CC, J, C¹. 380. Of] On B¹; As C².—februarye] februa B³, L.—on] un to H⁸.—first] second H⁶, C³. 381. Withe] The B³.—vpon] vppon þe B⁴, H⁸, C³. 382. as bright] bright H¹.—bright] clere Ash¹.—phebus] flourys B³, L.—dothe] om. B¹, H¹, C². 383. Whan] Withyn Ad³.—what] that B¹, H⁶, V.—in what thay] that C¹.—can] gan Ash¹. 384. Redy] redely H².—of] in C¹. 385. a] the C¹; and L; of a Hn¹, Co. 386. Of] To H⁶.—her] theyr C³.—full] om. C¹. 387. Sygnyfyede] Signefyeng B², B³, H⁸, CC, L. 388. With] By B², B⁴, Ash¹, H¹, H², H³, H⁴, H⁵, H⁶, CC, J, C¹, C², C³, C⁵, Ch.—the] om. B¹.—tapre] taple Ad³.—that] whyche C³.—we] wer C².—offre] of B¹. 389. the] þat H¹; in H².—betokenyth] betokenyd B¹; tokenyth H¹.—his] in his H⁷. 391. And] For B², Ash¹, H³, H⁴, H⁵, H⁶, CC, J, C¹, C², C⁵, An, Ch, V.—the] om. V.—and wrought] om. B², Ash¹, H³, H⁴, H⁵, H⁶, CC, J, C², C⁵, V.—made and wrought] wrought and made C³.—wrought] brought H¹, H². 392. Thorough] Of B², H⁶, CC, J; Bi C².—Of] *and* B¹.

Thorughe clennesse only and diligent labo*ur*

Of blossomes gedrede and to the hyve brought—

So c*r*istes manhode grewe oute of a floure,

Whose fresshe beaute of coloure fadyth nought;

For of a mayde clene in will and thought—

Like as wax of floures soote and glade

Is tried out *and* doith hem not to fade—

400 So criste Ih*esu*, conservyng her clennesse,

His manhode toke of a mayden free,

She standyng hole flouryng in fayrenesse

Withe all the fresshenesse of virgynyte.

And as a tapre is one to gyder and three,

So thilke lorde, that is bothe thre and one,

Toke flesshe and blode to save vs eu*er*ycheone,

393. clennesse only and] om. H⁶.—only] om. C³.—diligent] of dilygent L.—labour]
labour of the bee B², H⁶, CC, J. 394. Of] Or B; On Ash¹, H³, H⁵, H⁶, J; Onto Ch.—
the] om. Ash¹, H², H³, C², C⁵. 395. So c*r*istes manhode grewe oute of a floure Ad³.—
So] Of B¹, H⁷.—grewe] growe D, B³, C³, Hn¹, Co; take B², H⁶, CC, J.—oute of a
floure] of a maiden free B², H⁶, CC, J.—oute] om. B⁴. 396. beaute of coloure] colour
of beaute B³, H⁴, L; coloure brent H⁸.—of] *and* C². 397. For] Of C¹.—of] om. B²,
CC, J.—in] of H¹.—and] *and* in B¹, C¹. 398. wax of floures] the waxe on floures H⁶.
399. Is tried out *and* doith hem not to fade H⁷.—tried] turnede D, B³, B⁵, H⁸, L, Hn¹,
Co.—hem] hym B³, H¹.—hem not] neu*er* a C².—to] a CC; om. D, B¹, B³, L. 400. So]
As H⁶.—conservyng] concernyng B², H¹, CC, J, C², C⁵, L, An.—her] his H¹, H².
401. of] in C². 402. hole] a loon C¹.—in] her Ch. 403. of] of pure C³. 404. a] the
B¹, H¹.—one] *carrotted above line* D.—to gyer and three] and theron thre C³.—and three]
on three B¹, Ash¹, H³, H⁴, C¹, C⁵, Ad³, An, Hn¹, Co, V; in three B², B³, B⁴, H⁶, H⁸,
CC, J, C², L, Ch; of three B⁵, H¹, H², H⁷. 405. thilke] that B², B⁵, H⁶, CC, C², C³.
406. eu*er*ycheone] echeon CC.

Of a mayde whiche this day fro Bedlem,

Mekely went to be puryfyede

To the temple in Iherusalem,—

410 As here-to-forne it is specifiede,—

In whose honoure this feste is magnyfyede

Of all cristen w*ith* fresshe tapers shene,

To signyfye, who that will be clene,

Moste offre a tapre to-gyder made of thre: f. 90a

Faythe and werke and trwe entencion;

For sothefastely but thay coniunede be

W*ith*-oute partyng or dyvysion,

Neythir his offryng ne oblacion—

How fayre outewarde playnely that it seme—

420 To god above it may neu*ere* cueme.

---

407. whiche] þe which H². —day] om. H¹. 409. in] of B¹; vn to B³, L [*scratched out and replaced by "in"*]. 410. it is] is B³, B⁵, H², L, Hn¹, Co. 411. In whose honoure] In honour of her H⁶.—feste] day B¹, H².—magnyfyede] honourid C¹. 412. cristen] cristen me*n* C⁵.—with] of B³, L [*scratched out and replaced by "with"*].—tapers] om. B², CC, J. 413. that] so B², B⁴, Ash¹, H³, H⁴, H⁵, H⁶, CC, J, C¹, C³, C⁵, An, Ch, V; ho so C². 414. Moste] muste B², H⁷, CC, J, C¹.—to gyder] om. B¹, H¹. 415. Faythe] Of feith B³, B⁴, Ash¹, H³, H⁴, H⁵, H⁶, CC, J, C¹, C², C⁵, L, An, Ch, V.—and werke] werke B¹, B³, B⁵, H⁷, H⁸, C², C³, Ad³, L, Hn¹, Co, V. 417. partyng] any partyng C¹.—dyvysion] any dyuysion C³; diminucioun B¹. 418. his] of H⁸.—ne] nor B¹, H²; neither B², CC.—oblacion] his oblacioun B¹, B², C³; of oblacion Ch. 419. playnely] om. B¹, H¹, C².—it seme] is to seme B³. 420. To god aboue it may neu*er* cueme H⁵.—it may] may it D, B⁵, H⁷, C³, Ad³, L, Hn¹, Co.—cueme] quemeth B¹.

For þouȝ his tapre brene briȝte as day

And environ make his light to shede,

If werke fro faythe proloynede be away

And trwe entent folowe not the dede,

Fare well his gwerdon, his meryte and his mede,

For whan these thre be not knytte in one

He is not able to offryng for to gone.

For if these thre to-gyder be not meynt—

Feith, werke *and* hool entencioun—

430   His offryng farythe but as a tapre queynt

That yefethe no light ne bryghtnesse envyron,

Full derke and dede fro all deuocion.

His offryng is but if these ilke thre

Ben knytte in one thorough perfyte vnyte.

421. For þouȝ his tapre brene briȝte as dai H⁷.—For] And Ash¹, H⁴, H⁵, H⁶, J, An, Ch; All C¹.—his] this B², Ash¹, H³, H⁵, H⁶, CC, J, C¹, An, Ch.—þriȝte] liȝt C².—dai] any day D, Ash¹, L [*carrotted*]; nyght and day H⁶. 422. shede] schewe C². 423. If] His B³.—fro] of B⁴, H³, H⁴, H⁶, C⁵, An, Ch; *and* C¹.—werke fro faythe] feiþ fro werke C².—proloynede] be prolongid B¹. 425. his] þis H¹.—gwerdon] rewarde B¹.—his gwerdon] om. C².—gwerdon his meryte] merite his guerdon C¹; merite H⁶. 426. these] this H⁸, CC; the V.—be] buth Hn¹, Co.—not] nouȝt Hn¹, Co; om. B¹, C². 427. he] Hit C².—is] nys H³, H⁴, Ch.—to offryng for to gone] unto offring gone H¹. 428. not] om. B².—meynt] mette B¹; menged H⁶. 429. Feith werke *and* hool intencioun B¹.—werke] and werke, D, H¹, Ad³.—hole] holy B³. 430. but] om. H¹.—but as] as dothe CC.—as] om. B⁴.—a] om. Ch.— queynt] quenched H⁶. 431. no] om. C².—ne] but B⁴, Ash¹, H³, H⁴, C¹, C⁵, An, Ch; non CC; nor V; om. C².—bryghtnesse] om. C². 432. Full] For B¹, B⁴, H³, H⁴, H⁶, H⁷, H⁸, CC, J, C¹, C², C³, C⁵; From H¹, Ch.—derke] derked B², CC.—all] al that H². 433. His] þis C².—if] of Ash¹, H¹, H⁴, H⁵, C⁵, An; om. B³, B⁵, H², H⁷, H⁸, CC, J, C², C³, Ad³, L ["yff" *in margin*], Hn¹, Co.—these] þis H¹, CC.—ilke] om. B¹, B², B⁴, Ash¹, H¹, H³, H⁴, H⁵, H⁶, CC, J, C¹, C², C⁵, An, Ch, V. 434. thorough] by B³, H², L; of bi H¹; in C¹.

Now criste that art the sothefast holy light,

The hert of man graciously enlumyne;

Vpon vs wrecches, fro thy see so bryght,

So lat the sonne of thy mercy shyne

For loue of hir that is a pure virgyne—

440   Whiche on this day to the temple went

Of mekenesse onely the for to *present*—

Thorough whose prayer, lorde of thy grete myght,

Graunt vs grace in thy high holde

Whan we deye to holde our tapreȝ light

To-for thy see—where as it is tolde,

Seuene chaundeleris alle of pure golde,

Fresshely *with* light stand affore thy face—

Thyder to come of mercy graunt vs grace.

435. criste] criste ihesu B¹.—the] om. H¹.—sothefast] sothfastly H¹.—holy] om. B¹, B⁴, H⁶, C².—light] nyght B². 436. hert] hertis C².—graciously] gracious B³; to B⁴; for to B², Ash¹, H¹, H², H³, H⁴, H⁵, H⁶, H⁸, CC, J, C¹, C², C⁵, An, Ch, V.—enlumyne] to enlumine B¹; enlyȝth H⁶; lumine H⁸. 437. vs] his Hn¹, Co; the L; om. H¹.—fro] for B¹, B³, H⁵, Ad³, L, Hn¹. Co.—thy] the B², CC.—thy see] to se B³, L; the eye CC; these J.—see] om. B².—so] om. V. 438. So] om. B¹, B², B⁴, Ash¹, H¹, H², H³, H⁴, H⁵, H⁶, H⁸, CC, J, C¹, C², C⁵, An, Ch, V.—lat] that B³, L; Leue Ash¹; Lytc H¹.—the] thi H⁸, C³.—thy] om. C. 439. hir] þe C².—a] om. B², CC. 440. on] om. C¹. 441. the] ther B², J; om. B³, H⁸, CC.—for] om. H¹, H⁶, C¹, C². 442. whose] om. H¹.—grete] om. B¹, H⁷. 443. grace] om. CC.—high] free B², CC, J. 444. deye] shull passe L. 445. where] there B², CC, C³.—as] that B³, B⁴, B⁵, Ash¹, H², H³, H⁴, H⁷, C¹, C², Ad³, L, An, Ch, Hn¹, Co; om. B¹.—as it] at CC. 446. Seuene chaundeleris alle of pure golde H⁷.—Seuene] By H⁸.—chaundeleris] candellstycks Ch.—alle] biþ C²; om. B¹.—alle of] of all Ash¹, H⁵, H⁶.—pure] pured D, C¹, C², C³, Hn¹; brent H⁸. 447. *with*] with the B², J.—light] lightes B³, L.—stand] standyng B⁴; stondith C¹; to stonde V.—affore] to fore C¹. 448. Thyder] Whyder C³.—of mercy] of thy mercy L; lorde C².—graunt] to graunt B², CC, J.—grace] thi grace B¹.

And in this exile, where as we soiourne,

450   Graunt vs lorde while that we ben here

In februarye—as phebus dothe retourne

The circuyt of his golden spere—

Vpon this day, ay fro yere to yere,

With tapres fresshe and bryght torches shene

To kepe and halowe in honour of that quene,

To whome this feste is in speciall

Dedicate, bothe of more and lesse—

Whiche bare hir childe in a lityll stall

Bitwene an ox and a sely asse.

460   And blissede quene, this fest of Candelmasse,

To thy seruanteʒ shelde and socoure be,

To kepe and save from all aduersyte.

Amen.

---

449. where] there CC.—as] þat H². om. C². 450. vs] also B¹.—while] þe while H¹.
—that] om. C².—ben] lyue C². 451. retourne] turne B², CC. 452. The] In the H¹,
CC.—circuyt] circuit hoole C³.—his] this B². 453. ay] euere B¹, B³, B⁵, H⁷, C³, Ad³, L,
Hn¹, Co; om. H¹.—to] unto H¹. 454. bryght torches] light right H¹. 455. To kepe and
halowe] Toke and halowid H⁴.—in] om. CC.—honour] worship H¹.—that] þe C². 456.
is] om. B², H⁶, CC, C³.—speciall] principall B², CC. 457. Dedicat] Ys dedicate C³.
—bothe] is bothe H⁶. 458. bare] leide H¹.—hir] a B⁵.—in] but in J.—stall] space H⁸.
459. Bitwene an ox and a sely asse Ad³.—Bitwene] By twyxe D, B⁵, Ash¹, H¹, H²,
C³.—sely] om. CC. 461. thy] þe H¹. 462. save] save hem H¹; save vs [*carrotted*] H⁶.
—Amen] om. H⁴, H⁵, H⁸, Ad³.

7. NOTES

BOOK I

1–63. Lydgate places Our Lady above the stars. See *Wisdom,* VII, 29: "Est enim haec speciosior sole, et super omnem dispositionem stellarum: luci comparata, invenitur prior." (Since Lydgate would have known only the Vulgate, all Biblical references in these notes are taken from *Biblia Sacra Juxta Vulgatae Exemplaria et Collectoria Romana,* ed. A. C. Fillion, Paris, 1894). This comparison of Our Lady to a star, fairest of all stars, is found frequently in Lydgate's works. See Ernst Sieper, *Reson and Sensuallyte* (1901-3; *EETSES,* 84, 89), note for ll. 417ff. and J. Schick, *Temple of Glas* (1891; *EETSES,* 60), note for ll. 251-2.

1. *thoughtful*   "Thought" is a common word in the love poetry of Lydgate's time, meaning heavy thought, sorrowful meditation, or trouble. See Axel Erdmann and Eilert Ekwall, *Siege of Thebes* (1911-30; *EETSES,* 108, 125), note for line 3414; see also Schick, *Temple of Glas,* note for line 1. Cf. line I, 276 below.

2. The reference here implies that Lydgate is beginning his work during the winter months. Judging from lines II, 1609-12, when the poet ends Book II some time before the kalends of April or May, the work was begun around January, or early February.

2. *slombre of slouthe*   Lydgate likes to join these two alliterates. See O. Glauning, *Two Nightingale Poems* (1900; *EETSES,* 80, note to l. 57.

22. *passethe*   Meaning "to surpass" or "excell". See Erdmann, *Siege of Thebes,* note to ll. 895 and 469.

22–28. *Constellations and stars*   See Schick, *Temple of Glas,* note to ll. 1348-9. He cites Lydgate's fondness for mentioning the heavenly bodies.

24. *Boetes Arthour*   Arcturus is the brightest star of the constellation Boötes. Cf. *Court of Sapience,* ed. R. Spindler (Leipzig, 1927), ll. 2132, 3135; see also Chaucer, *Boece,* IV, Meter 5, 2-5.

25. Hesper, the evening-star, king of the western land, star of the sunset.

27. *mydenyght and at morwe*   This phrase, meaning the whole day or always, is common in Lydgate. See Erdmann, *Siege of Thebes,* note for l. 2509.

31. *Iacob*   See *Numbers,* XXIV, 17: "Orietur stella ex Jacob, et consurget virga de Israel." See also *Apocalypse* II, 28; XXII, 16.

37. *Of Aurora, aftir the mourwen gray*   See Glauning, *Two Nightingale Poems,* note to l. 71, for Lydgate's use of this expression. See also "Letabundus", line 137: "After Aurora in the morowe gray," (H. N. MacCracken, *The Minor Poems of John Lydgate* (1911-34; *EETSES,* 107 and *EETS,* 192), I. 53); also "Ave Jesse Virgula," ll. 49-52 (MacCracken, *Minor Poems,* I, 300); and "To Mary, Queen of Heaven," ll. 25-27 (MacCracken, *Minor Poems,* I, 285).

41. *golde wayne, bournede*   See E. Krausser, *The Complaint of the Black Knight* (Halle, 1896), note to l. 31. See also *House of Fame,* 1384, "As burned gold hyt shoon to see"; *Franklyn's Tale,* 511; *Confessio Amantis,* II, 272; *Troy Book,* III, 4801, 5624.

43–46. See *Isaias,* XI, 1. "Et egredietur virga de radice Jesse, et flos de radice ascendet." The "Tree of Jesse" abounds in medieval art as a symbol of the genealogy of Christ. It is pictured in MS H^1.

48–49. *Estwarde to vs in the orient*   See also line I, 134. See F. J. Furnivall and K. B. Locock, *Pilgrimage of the Life of Man* (*EETSES,* 77, 83, 92), note to l. 12330. Bartholmaeus Anglicus, *De Prop. Rerum,* Lib. XIX, cap. 22: "All the planets move by double moving; by their own kind of moving out of the west into the east, against the moving of the firmament; and by either moving out of the east into the west, and that by ravishing the firmament. By violence of the firmament they are ravished every day out of the east into the west. And by their kindly moving, by which they labor to move against the firmament, some of them fulfill their course in shorter time and some in longer time."

73. *garden*   For the metaphor likening Mary to a garden, see the Seventh Responsory of the Divine Office for December 8: "Hortus conclusus soror mea sponsa, hortus conclusus, fons signatus." (*In Conceptione Immaculata B. Mariae Virginis*).

88–90. *Scypyon, Sesar, Fabion.* See "Misericordias Domini," l. 52 (MacCracken, *Minor Poems,* I, 73). Lydgate frequently refers to historical characters as examples.

97–105. *hooly Isaye*   See *Isaias,* XI, 1-3. "Egredietur virga de radice Jesse, et flos de radice ejus ascendet; et requiescet super eum Spiritus

Domini, spiritus sapientiae, et intellectus, spiritus concilii et fortitu-
dinis, spiritus scientiae et pietatis, et replevit eum spiritu timoris
Domini." See also "Whan the Holygost in thy brest light, Bilded of
XII stones, civitas murata," in "Ave Jesse Virgula," ll. 54-56 (Mac-
Cracken, *Minor Poems*, I, 301).

120–121.   *And whanne the Angell, at the gate of golde*   This is the beautiful
gate of *Acts* III, 2, to which, according to Josephus, there was an
ascent by many steps from the valley of Kedron. Cf. Alex. Roberts
and James Donaldson, *The Ante-Nicene Fathers* (Buffalo, 1886),
VIII, 370n.

130.   *venym, callet serpentyne*   Lydgate was fond of this expression. See
Glauning, *Two Nightingdale Poems,* note to 1.315 (II).

133.   *dyd appere*   In this use, "dyd" is an auxiliary, not a causative in the
sense of "make". See Glauning, *Two Nightingdale Poems,* note for
1.38 (II).

138–158.   *Genesis* XXXII, 24-32.

169–175.   *Albumazar*   An Arabian astronomer of the ninth century (d. 886).
His real name was Abu-Maaschar, and he lived in Khorasan, Persia.
His principal works were translated into Latin, *De Magnis Con-
junctionibus* (Augsburg, 1489); *Introductorium in Astronomiam*
(Venice, 1506) and *Flores Astrologici* (Augsburg, 1488). Albumazar
is cited three times in Gower's *Confessio Amantis,* VII, 283, 989,
1239; in the *Fall of Princes,* II, 2489; and in *Siege of Thebes,* 2973,
for which see Erdmann's note. Albumazar's notes on the signs of
the zodiac are given by Vincent of Beauvais in *Speculum Naturale*
(1494 ed.), XV, 36: "Virgo inutili & inepto: ut sint agri steriles: &
id genus."

178.   *fadirs sapience*   See also II, 524; Glauning, *Two Nightingale
Poems,* note to 1. 183. See Chaucer, *Canterbury Tales,* B, 1660-1662:
"Thurgh thyn [Mary's] humblesse, the Goost that in th'alighte,
Of whos vertu, whan he thyn herte lighte,
Conceyved was the Fadres sapience."

193–5.   *The fifteen steps*   These steps correspond to the fifteen Songs of
Degrees, see *Psalms* CXX-CXXXIV. For a description of these steps
see A. Roberts and J. Donaldson, *op. cit.,* VIII, 37n.

216.   *purviaunce*   Providence (the learned doublet). Cf. *Troilus and
Criseyde,* II, 527; also Schick, *Temple of Glas,* note to 1. 1331.

246–259. On the Virgin's daily life in the Temple, see also St. Jerome, "Letter to Chromatius and Heliodorus," Letter XLIX, Migne, *PL,* XXX, 302-303.

286. *sterres seven*   Usually means the planets; occasionally the stars of the Ursa Major, or the Pleiades. The symbol of the Virgin Mary is common in Middle English literature. See Sieper, *Reson and Sensuallyte,* note to ll. 1276-7. See also lines I, 579 and II, 122, below.

302–308. Lydgate's comparison of the Most Blessed Virgin to mythological beauties is typical. See Schick, *Temple of Glas,* cxxi n. For direct reference, see Schick, *Temple of Glas,* for Dido, note to ll. 55-61; for Lucrece, note to ll. 100-101; for Helen, ll. 92-93; for Polyxena, ll. 97-99. See also "A Valentine," ll. 22-54 (MacCracken, *Minor Poems,* I, 305-306).

309–315. As an example of Lydgate's listing of Biblical heroines, see "A Valentine," ll. 29-53 (MacCracken, *Minor Poems,* I. 305-306).

319–320. *the Rubye*   Lydgate was fond of this comparison. See Schick, *Temple of Glas,* note to lines 257-261; also Furnivall-Locock, *Pilgrimage,* note to line 7105. Henry V wore in his helmet at Agincourt the famous ruby of the Black Prince to whom it is said to have been given by Dom Pedro, King of Castille, after the battle of Najira, near Vittoria, 1327 A. D. Cf. *PMLA,* XXIV (1909). 599n.

323–336. *Salamon*   See *Wisdom* VII, 7-30.

328–9. *lylieȝ meynt and fresshe Rosys*   The lily and the rose as symbols of purity and martyrdom are common in the writings of the Fathers. Chaucer uses these same symbols in the *Second Nun's Tale,* 230 ff.; see F. N. Robinson, *The Poetical Works of Geoffrey Chaucer* (Cambridge, 1933), p. 865. See also Schick, *Temple of Glas,* note to line 276; also "To St. Edmond", line 65, and "To St. Ursula" (MacCracken, Minor Poems, I, 126 and 144).

332. *ennuede*   This word is found frequently in Lydgate. See Schick, *Temple of Glas,* note to line 275.

335–336. *phebus platly or lucyne*   Phebus, for the sun, and Lucina, for the moon, are common in Lydgate. See Glauning, *Two Nightingale Poems,* note for l. 26; see also Erdmann, *Siege of Thebes,* note to ll. 1051-3; and Schick, *Temple of Glas,* note to ll. 4-7.

344.   *tryacle*   A medieval compound of various ingredients formerly believed to be capable of curing or preventing the effects of poison. Chaucer uses the term in l. 381, *Man of Law's Tale.* See Glauning, *Two Nightingale Poems,* extensive note to l. 224 (II) ; Sieper, *Reson and Sensuallyte,* note for l. 3414. Cf. Lydgate's "Invocation to Seynte Anne", line 53 (MacCracken, *Minor Poems,* I, 130-3).

337–359.   *saint Ancelme*   See "Oratio LV ad Eamdem Sanctam Virginem Mariam," Migne, *PL,* CLVIII, 961-962. The same praises and tributes are found in "Hymni et Psalterium De Sancta Virgine Maria," *ibid.,* 1035-1040.

354–7.   *One of the fyve*   See St. Matthew XXV, 1-13. See also "The Legend of St. Petronilla", ll. 27-30 (MacCracken, *Minor Poems,* I, 155).

364–378.   *vii ● gyftes of the holy goste*   For an extensive treatment of the seven gifts and their accompanying virtues see *The Book of Vices and Virtues,* ed. by W. Nelson Francis (EETS, 217), pp. 116-290.

379–385.   *the trone*   See *Exodus* XXV, 17-40; also *Zacharias,* IV, 2.

387–413.   *vii ● vertues*   Lydgate's source for these seven virtues is vague. They are contained at the end of *The Court of Sapience.* See Robert Spindler, *The Court of Sapience* (Leipzig, 1927), pp. 215-6.

407–413.   *As saythe Ambrose*   This reference is found in St. Ambrose, "De Virginibus", II, Chapter 2: "Virginibus exemplum Mariae proponitur, cujus variae virtutes enumerantur, castitas, humilitas, vitae asperitas, secessus amor; quae quidem virtus ubi testimonio evangelico probata est, inde etiam ejus pietas erga propinquas, descendi sedulitas, atque adeundi templi studium commendatur. Narratur denique quemadmodum illa tot muneribus exornata, innumeris virginibus obviam ventura sit, nec sine magnifico triumpho ad thalamum Sponsi, & caelestia altaria quibus ob castitatem similes fuere, deductura." *Sancti Ambrosii Mediolanensis Episcopi Opera* (Paris, 1690), ll. 165-166.

430–431.   *in Isaye*   See *Isaias,* VII, 14: "Propter hoc dabit Dominus ipse vobis signum: Ecce virgo concipiet, et pariet filium, et vocabitur nomen ejus Emmanuel."

435–532.   *hir petycions*   See "3. The Sources, Books I and II," pp. 90-91. These seven petitions occur also in *Ludus Coventriae,* 220-224, except that the fifth petition here is placed last. See Miss K. Black, *Ludus Coventriae (EETSES,* 120), p. 79. See also *The Mirrour of the Blessed Lyf of Jesu Christ,* ed. by Lawrence F. Powell (Oxford, 1908), pp. 20-21, the English translation of "Meditationes Vitae Christi," *Sancti Bonaventurae Opera* (Venice, 1751-1756), XII, 384; L. Oliger, "Revelationes B. Elizabeth," *Antonianum,* I (1926), 24-83, esp. 54-56; and C. Horstmann, *Richard Rolle,* I, 158-161.

468.   *queme and serue*   See Glauning, *Two Nightingale Poems,* note to l. 231, and Schick, *Temple of Glas,* note to l. 1312.

526–530.   These lines are reminiscent of two prayers in the *Litany of Saints*: "Ut ecclesiam tuam sanctam regere et conservare digneris, te rogamus, audi nos;" and "Ut nosmetipsos in tuo sancto servitio confortare et conservare digneris, te rogamus audi nos."

557.   *sugrede tonge*   A frequent expression in Lydgate. See Sieper, *Reson and Sensuallyte,* note for ll. 1765, 5213, 6398.

565–7.   *holy writte   See Leviticus,* XV, 1-17.

574.   *Abell*   The virginity of Abel was maintained by many writers, among them Bede, Bonaventura, Bernard, and Albertus Magnus.

592.   *slepe or wake*   An absurd use of a common formula. See Schick, *Temple of Glas,* note to line 1163.

708–712.   There are some discrepancies in the various accounts of this legend. In the earliest records a dove arises or alights on the rod, as in Protevangelium and Pseudo-Matthew; in later versions, influenced no doubt by a recollection of Aaron's rod, flowers were added, as in *Evangelium De Nativitate Mariae.* The last named prefixes its account of the miracle with Isaias' prophecy about the rod arising out of the root of Jesse *(Isaias,* XI, 1-2) after which it continues: "Secundum hanc ergo prophetiam cunctas de domo et familia David nuptui habiles non conjugatos virgae suas allaturos ad altare praedixit, et cujuscumque post allationem virgula florem germinasset, et in ejus cacumine spiritus Domini in specie columbae consedisset, ipsum esse cui virgo commendari et desponsari deberet."

722–762.   *Marriage of Mary*   Lydgate refers to this marriage with Joseph as a sorrow of Mary in "The Fifteen Joys and Sorrows of Mary," ll. 183-187 (MacCracken, *Minor Poems,* I, 275).

748–749.   *Dathan Abyron*   See *Numbers* XVI, 1-34.

768–771.   *fyve maydens*   Lydgate's source for the names of the maidens is the Gospel of Pseudo-Matthew. Mention of the maidens who dwelt with Our Lady after the Betrothal to Joseph is found also in the *Legendae Catholicae,* W. B. Turnbull, Edinburgh, 1840. This volume, edited from the Auchinleck MS, Advocates Library, 19.2.1., contains a poem, "Joachim and Anne," pp. 125-164. This poem, based on the Gospel of Pseudo-Matthew, relates the life of Our Lady from her birth to Joseph's return, his chagrin at finding Mary great with child, and his subsequent belief in her. (See Wells' *Manual,* pp. 300, 321, 323.) The only parallel between the *Life of Our Lady* and "Joachim and Anne" is their mutual dependence in part on the Gospel of Pseudo-Matthew. The number of the maidens and their names in "Joachim and Anne" and Life of Our Lady are identical. St. Jerome in "Letter to Chromatius and Heliodorus" says: "Virgo autem Domini Maria, cum aliis septem virginibus coaevis et collectaneis, quas a sacerdote acceperat, ad domum parentum suorum in Galilaeam reversa est." (Migne, *PL,* XXX, col. 303). The *Cursor Mundi* records: "With hir she ledde maydenes seven, her names herde I never neven," ll. 10819-20, (*Cursor Mundi,* ed. R. Morris, *EETS,* 57, pp. 622-3). Wace, in "La Conception Nostre Dame", says: "Set puceles o soi mena Qui li evesques li livra, Qui erent de son parente Et toutes VII de son ae." (*L'Établissement de la Fête de la Conception Notre-Dame,* edd. Mancel et Trebutien, Caen, 1842, p. 37). Wace's source, *Evangelium de Nativitate S. Mariae,* Ch. VII, is verbatim with St. Jerome. (Cf. *ibid.,* Appendix, 105). Towneley Play X, "The Annuciation", mentions only the "maydens that kyngys doghters were" (*Towneley Plays,* edd. G. England and A. W. Pollard, *EETSES,* 71, p. 94). York Play XIII, "Joseph's Trouble about Mary," refers to the maidens only as "prima puella" and "secunda puella". (See *York Plays,* ed. L. T. Smith, Oxford, 1885, pp. 105 ff.) The *Ludus Coventriae,* "Betrothal of Mary," lines 352-355 reads: "I shal these iii here take Susanna the fyrst shal be Rebecca the secunde shal go with the Sephore the thrydde loke that ye thre This mayden nevyr ye forsake." (Ed. K. S. Block, *EETSES,* 120, p. 93). C. Horstmann, *Richard Rolle of Hampole,* I, 375: MS Thornton f. 176: "With oure lady and hir X Maydenys." This same reference is found in Wright and Halliwell, *Reliquiae . Antiquae* (London, 1841), I, 126. The *Legenda Aurea* gives seven maidens, no names. (ed. Graesse, 1846, p. 589).

778. *as made is mencion*   For the frequency of this phrase in Lydgate see Erdmann, *Siege of Thebes,* note to l. 2577.

810. *baner sprede*   See Glauning, *Two Nightingale Poems,* note for ll. 289 (II) and 316 (II). See also "Vexilla Regis Prodeunt," ll. 1-4 (MacCracken, *Minor Poems,* I, 25).

869. *I am to Rude*   Lydgate frequently asserts that he has no "kunnyng to descryve" whatever he is about to write upon. See Sieper, *Reson and Sensuallyte,* note for l. 317.

876–880. *Besechyng all*   Begging the reader to correct his work is a common practice of Lydgate, as of other poets. It is found also in French originals of his other works. See Schick, *Temple of Glas,* note for line 1400.

BOOK II

1–350. *The Four Daughters of God*   See the discussion of this allegory in the source chapter ("3. Sources, Books I and II," p. 84 ff.). Lydgate's placing the dispute of the four virtues, Mercy, Truth, Peace and Justice, before the Annunciation is in keeping with tradition. Samuel C. Chew, *The Virtues Reconciled* (Toronto, 1947), p. 47, points out that St. Bernard's sermon, the *Meditationes Vitae Christi,* the *Ludus Coventriae,* and many Books of Hours place this point in sacred history immediately before the Annunciation.

MS Trinity College, Dublin 423, *The Life of the Virgin Mary and of Christ,* a fifteenth-century text, based on the Gospel of Pseudo-Matthew and the *Meditationes Vitae Christi,* inserts the dispute before the Annunciation. See Thomas K. Abbott, *Catalogue of the MSS in the Library of Trinity College, Dublin* (London, 1900), p. 65. Though the Four Daughters of God allegory is told or pictured in connection with other occasions such as the Visit of Mary to her cousin Elizabeth, the Crucifixion, the Agony in the Garden and the Judgment, it is found most often before the Annunciation. Lydgate refers to this allegory in his poem, "On the Prospect of Peace." See Political *Poems and Songs,* ed. by Thomas Wright (London, 1861), II. 209-215. He refers to the allegory again in lines III, 1608-1617 below.

1. *feterde in prison*   This is found frequently in Lydgate. See Schick, *Temple of Glas,* note to l. 648.

88. *olde serpent*   Lydgate frequently calls the devil, "the olde serpent". See Erdmann, *Siege of Thebes,* note to ll. 4660-4667.

120. *Is not thy mercy, grete*   Cf. *Psalm* CIII, 11; see also "Misericordias Domini," 19-32 (MacCracken, *Minor Poems,* I, 72).

120-1. Cf. *Psalm* CVIII, 4.

122-5. Cf. *Psalm* XXXVI, 5.

126-7. Cf. *Psalm* CXXXVI, 1-26.

131-132. Cf. *Psalm* LXIII, 3.

137-140. Cf. *Psalms* CXLV, 1-21 and CXLIX, 3.

141-4. See also II, 1056-7 below. Lydgate here refers to the necessity of God's mercy, or grace, in man's salvation. After original sin, Christ's redemptive sacrifice was necessary because man did not have adequate dignity to repair the harm done, or rather to make reparation to the offended divine majesty. The Psalmist notes: "Domine in coelo misericordia tua, et veritas tua usque ad nubes. Et circuit orbem terrarum." (*Psalm* XXXV, 6.) St. Bonaventure: "Coeli non indigent misericordia, qua in eis nulla miseria. Secundum hunc modum misericordia solummodo est in terra." (*Bonaventura Opera,* Maguntiae, VII, 703).

158-9. *prynce, of pees*   See *Isaias* IX, 6; "Parvulus enim natus est nobis, et filius datus est nobis; et factus est principatus super humerum ejus; et vocabitur nomen ejus, Admirabilis, Consiliarius, Deus, Fortis, Pater futuri saeculi, Princeps pacis."

162-3. *Iob Recordith*   See *Job* V, 24-25: "Et acies quod pacem habeat tabernaculum tuum, et visitans speciem tuam, non peccabis. Scies quoque quoniam multiplex erit semen tuum, et progenies tua quasi herba terrae."

183. *next of alye*   See Erdmann, *Siege of Thebes,* note to l. 2081.

195. *touchyng this matier*   This is common in Lydgate; it is in Lydgate the equivalent of the French "quant à". See Sieper, *Reson and Sensuallyte,* note to l. 315. The expression is also found in II, 1173 and II, 1345 below.

264. *halte or lame*   See Sieper, *Reson and Sensuallyte,* note to l. 275a. See also Schick, *Temple of Glas,* note to l. 323.

274–8. C. F. Bühler, *The Sources of the Court of Sapience* (Leipzig, 1932), p. 26, notes the similarity of St. Bernard (*PL*, CLXXXIII, 389) and Lydgate in the appeal to Solomon or Wisdom in the dispute.

330–350. For a discussion of the rôle of Mary as "mediatrix inter nos et Deum" in the literature of the Middle Ages, see C. F. Bühler, *op. cit.,* pp. 37-40. With the growth of the monastic life there was a corresponding increase in the literature of the Virgin.

339–347. *the vnycorne* The Physiologus and medieval books on natural history relate how the unicorn in the presence of a virgin loses its ferocity and is easily captured. See Sieper, *Reson and Sensuallyte,* note to ll. 6691-95, and Furnivall-Locock, *Pilgrimage,* note for l. 14720. Miss Hope Traver comments on this tradition from the bestiaries and notes that its application to Mary is found in early French and German art, where also it is allied to the Four Daughters of God allegory. (See *The Four Daughters of God,* pp. 24-25). Odell Shepard describes this same legend of the unicorn and its taming by Mary. However, he seems unaware of the Four Daughters of God relationship in the naming of the hounds of the hunter. He says: "Veritas, Justitia, Pax, and Misericordia—strange names indeed, considering the purpose the animals serve." (*The Lure of the Unicorn,* New York, 1930, pp. 58-59). John Mirk cites St. Augustine in likening St. Paul to a unicorn tamed by a clean maiden. See *Mirk's Festial* (*EETSES, 96*), p. 55.

351–518. Lydgate's source for the story of the Annunciation is the *Gospel of St. Luke,* Chapter I, 26-38. See source references ("3. The Sources, Books I and II," p. 95).

372 ff. *Bernarde* See "De Laudibus Virginis Matris," Homilia III: "Ut autem nunc a propheticis verbis incipiam: Vae mihi, non quidem, sicut Prophetae, quia tacui, sed quia locutus sum, quoniam vir pollutus labiis ego sum. Heu quot vana, quot false, quot turpia per hoc ipsum spurcissimum os meum evomuisse me recolo, in quo nunc caelestia revolvere verba praesumo! Vehementer timeo, ne jam jam audiam ad me dictum: Quare tu (Psal. 49, 16) enarras justitias meas, & assumis testamentum meum per os tuum? Utinam & mihi de superno altari, non quidem carbo unus, sed ingens globus igneus afferatur, qui videlicet multam & inveteratam prurientis oris mei rubiginem ad plenum excoquere sufficiat! quatenus Angeli ad Virginem & Virginis ad ipsum grata invicem ac casta colloquia dignus habear meo qualicumque replicare sermone." *Sancti Bernardi Opera,* edd. Horstium and Mabillon (4v, Paris, 1719), I. 75.

425.   *mercy passith Right*   See Chaucer's *Knight's Tale,* 3059, where the Christian doctrine of grace is referred to in much the same terms.

430–434.   *Isaye*   See *Isaias,* VI, 5, 6, 7: "Et dixi: Vae mihi, quia tacui, quia pollutus labiis ego sum, et in medio populi polluta labia habentis ego habito! et regem Dominum exercituum vidi oculis meis. Et volavit ad me unus de Seraphim, et in manu ejus calculus, quem forcipe tulerat de altari, et tetigit os meum, et dixit: Ecce tetigit hoc labia tua, et auferetur iniquitas tua, et peccatum tuum mundabitur."

507.   *transitorye fame*   A frequent expostulation of Lydgate's. See Sieper, *Reson and Sensuallyte,* note for ll. 680-2.

514–18.   On Christ's becoming man by the humility of Mary, see Sieper, *Reson and Sensuallyte,* note to ll. 6546-9. He traces the idea to St. Bernard's "Beata Maria, ex virginitate placuit Deo, sed ex humilitate concepit deum."

521–526.   *sonne persheth thorugh the glas*   This comparison of the conception of Christ with the passing of the sun through glass is in the theological tradition of the time. The expression is found frequently in Latin and vernacular literature. One mention of the symbol is found in the writings of St. Ildephonsus of Spain: "Solis radius specular penetrat, et soliditatem ejus insensibili subtilitate pertrajicit; et talis videtur intrinsecus, qualis et extrinsecus. Itaque, fratres, nec cum ingreditur volatur nec cum egreditur dissipat, quia in ingressu et egressu ejus specular integrum perseverat. Specular ergo non rumpit radius solis; integritatem Virginis ingressus aut regressus vitiare paterat Deitatis." (Migne, *PL,* XCVI, col. 282).

527.   *in party or in all*   This phrase is of common occurrence in Lydgate. See Schick, *Temple of Glas,* note for ll. 431 and 1155.

528ff.   It was common practice in medieval literature to liken Mary to the fleece of Gedeon, the gate of Ezechiel, and the rod of Aaron. These same symbols of Our Lady are found in *The Miroure of Mans Saluacionne,* a fifteenth century translation of the *Speculum Humanae Salvationis.* See *The Miroure of Mans Saluacionne* (Roxburghe Club, London, 1888). Chapters III-XI of *The Miroure* are concerned with Our Lady's life; however, aside from the mutual citation of these symbols, there is no relationship whatever between *The Miroure* and the *Life of Our Lady.*

531ff. *vii pilers* Proverbs, IX, 1: "Sapientia aedificavit sibi domum, excedit columnas septem."

547–550. *castell* For a discussion of the allegory of the castle as applied to **1663–1664.** the Most Blessed Virgin in medieval literature, see Roberta D. Cornelius, *The Figurative Castle* (Bryn Mawr diss., 1930), esp. Chapter IV, pp. 37-48, "The Blessed Virgin as a Castle."

561–63. *Cocle* See Lydgate's "Ballade at the Reverence of Our Lady", ll. 127-8 (MacCracken, *Minor Poems,* I, 259):

"O precyous perle, with-outyn ony pere,
Cokyl with gold dew from above yreyned."

See also Bartholomew Anglicus, *De Proprietatibus Rerum, in Medieval Lore,* ed. R. Steele (London, 1924), p. 25: "For by night in spring time oysters open themselves against dew, and receive dew that cometh in between the two shells, and hold and keep it; and that dew so holden and kept feedeth the flesh, and maketh it fat; and by its incorporation with the inner parts of the fish breedeth a full precious gem, a stone that is called Margarita." See also St. Isidore, *Etymologiarum,* Lib. XVI, Chap. X, No. 1, *PL, LXXXII,* 575. The same figure is found in the *Liber Festivalis:* "Thus may I liken our lady reasonably to a precious stone that is called onex, and is as clere as cristalle, and shall of kynde, whan the sonne shyneth hote on hym, opene and receyve a drope of the dewe of heven in to hym, and thenne closeth his ageyn tyl IX monethes after, and than hit openeth and falleth out a stone of the same kynde, and so closeth ageyn as close as ever hit was wythouten wemme, and never openeth after. Thus our lady, that was as clere as ony cristalle . . ." Caxton's edition of 1483, quoted by H. J. Todd in *The Works of Edmund Spenser, Variorum Edition* (Baltimore, 1934), III, 250.

568–574. *the gate* See *Ezechiel,* XLIV, 1, 2, 3, 4. This passage from very earliest times was interpreted as mysteriously foreshadowing the unstained virginity of Mary, to whose womb the Holy Ghost only was to have access. The reference is found frequently in the literature of the time. See Sext of the Divine Office for December 8 for this comparison of Mary with the gate of Ezechiel: "Porta haec clausa erit, non aperietur, et vir non intrabit per eam, quoniam Dominus Deus Israel ingressus est per eam: eritque clausa Principi. Princeps ipse sedebit in ea." *(In Conceptione Immaculata B. Mariae Virginis).*

576–579.   *flees, of Gedon*   See *Book of Judges,* VI, 36-40; also "A Valentine", ll. 80-81, (MacCracken, *Minor Poems,* I, 308); "Letabundus", ll. 110-112 (MacCracken, *Minor Poems,* I, 52).

589-590.   *Riche ourne*   See *Exodus,* XVI, 33-34. "Dixitque Moyses ad Aaron: Sume vas unum, et mitte ibi Man, quantum potest capere gomor, et repone coram Domino ad servandum in generationes vestras sicut praecepit Dominus Moysi. Posuitque illud Aaron in tabernaculo reservandum."

594–595.   *yerde of Aron*   See *Numbers,* XVII, 6-11. See also "A Valentine", 82-83 (MacCracken, *Minor Poems,* I, 308).

606.   *the sterres, in the frosty nyght*   See Chaucer, *Canterbury Tales,* Prologue, 268, for this same line in the description of Friar Hubert!

610–616.   *the trone*   See *II Paralipomenon* IX, 17, 18, 19: "Fecit quoque rex solium eburneum grande, et vestivit illud auro mundissimo. Sex quoque gradus quibus ascendebatur ad solium, et scabellum aureum, et brachiola duo, altrinsecus, et duos leones stantes super sex gradus ex utraque parte; non fuit tale solium in universis regnis."

624–646.   *the woman, that saint Iohn*   See *Apocalypse* XII, 1: "Et signum magnum apparuit in caelo: mulier amicta sole, et luna sub pedibus ejus, et in capite ejus corona stellarum duodecim;" Lydgate also refers to this vision in "Ave Jesse Virgula," ll. 81-110 (MacCracken, *Minor Poems,* I, 302); in "A Valentine", ll. 87-89 (*Minor Poems,* I, 308) and in "To Mary, Queen of Heaven," ll. 43-48 (*Minor Poems,* I, 286).

652–931.   The practice of assembling examples of marvels in nature as symbols of the miracle of the Virgin Birth seems to have been a common one in medieval times. G. R. Owst treats this subject at great length (see *Literature and Pulpit in Medieval England,* Cambridge, 1933, pp. 149-209). An example of collections of this nature is the *Defensiorum inviolatae perpetuaeque virginitatis castissimae Dei genetricis Mariae,* Franciscus de Retza, 1470. This work consists of sixteen folios, with 54 pictures and accompanying texts, presenting arguments from the Fathers to prove that Mary retained her virginity even in giving birth to Christ. There are examples given from St. Ambrose, St. Jerome, St. Gregory, St. Augustine, and others. There are other enlarged editions of this work dated 1471, 1480, and 1490. (See *Catalogue of Printed Books in the British Museum,* Ann Arbor, 1946, XXXV. 18.)

The *Cursor Mundi,* lines 11213-26, contains a short passage recounting that God, who made the dry rod bear blossoms and fruit without its being covered with soil, could also cause a child to be born of a virgin at the end of the ninth month. It adds that He who wrought all things in a little time, made the dumb ass to speak, and clave the sea to destroy his enemies, could cause a virgin to give birth to a child. Here, *Cursor Mundi* is paraphrasing its source, Wace's *L'Établissement de la Fête de la Conception Notre-Dame* (edited by G. Mancel et G. S. Trebutien, Caen, 1842), pp. 48-49.

654–658.   See *St. John,* XX, 19-31.

667–670.   See *Acts* XII, 5-19.

680.   *Hildefons*   St. Ildephonsus of Spain. See Migne, *PL,* XCVI, 53-110.

687–690.   *vultures*   See St. Ambrose, *Hexameron,* V, 20, 64-65 : "Diximus de viduitate avium eamque ab illis primum exortan esse virtutem ; nunc de integritate dicamus, quae in pluribus quidem avibus inesse adseveratur, ut possit etiam in vulturibus deprehendi negantur enim vultures indulgere concubitu et conjugali quodam usu nuptialisque copulae sorte misceri atque ita sine ullo masculorum concipere semine et sine conjunctione generare natosque ex his in multam aetatem longaevitate procedere, ut usque ad centum annos vitae eorum series producatur nec facile eos angusti aevi finis excipiat. Quid aiunt qui sollent nostra ridere mysteria, cum audiunt quod virgo generavit et inpossibilem innuptae, cujus pudorem nulla viri consuetudo temerasset, aestimant partum? inpossibile putatur in dei matre quod in vulturibus possible non negatur? avis sine masculo parit et nullus refellit ; et quia desponsata Maria peperit, pudori ejus faciunt quaestionem, nonne advertimus quod dominus ex ipsa natura plurima exempla ante praemisit, quibus susceptae incarnationis decorem probaret, astrueret veritatem?" *Sancti Ambrosii Opera,* ed. Schenkl (Prague, 1896), I, 188-9.

694–698.   *Plunius*   This reference is to Pliny, *Natural History,* Book II, Chapter 98, "Juxta Harpasa, oppidum Asiae, cautes stat horrende,

uno digito mobilis; eadem, si toto corpore impellatur, resistens."
Historia Naturalis, ed. C. Alexandre (11v. Paris, 1827), I, 424.

708–711. This reference is to Pliny, Book II, Chapter 98. "In Taurorum paeninsula in civitate Parasino terra est, qua sanantur omnia vulnera." *Historia Naturalis,* I, 424.

722–726. This reference is to Pliny, Book II, Chapter 106: "In Dodone Jovis fons quum sit gelidus et inmersas faces extinguat, si extinctae admoveantur accendit." *Historia Naturalis,* I, 442-443.

736–739. This reference is to Pliny: "In Falisco omnis aqua pota candidos boves facit." *Historia Naturalis,* I, 445.

775–6.   These lines seem a negation of free will in man's salvation or loss. However, we are led to consider three things here: God was free to choose His creation; God was free to choose any sequence of events; i.e., any possible universe; God was free to make man free. But in realizing (i.e., making real, actualizing) any one of these possible universes, He of necessity knew its sequence of events, else He were not *infinite.* If the sequence of events He actualized were to involve men who were free to "save or lese" themselves, His actualizing would not be the cause, but rather the occasion of their choice. Again, Lydgate's reference to God's free choice in saving or damning men might be centered about the free gift of grace with which man can be saved, without which he cannot. I am inclined to think this interpretation, which is more in keeping with the Augustinian theology Lydgate seems to have studied, is the correct one. St. Augustine argued this point of doctrine in his discourses against the Pelagians. See also lines 141-144, and 1056-1057 below.

792–798. *graved*   See *Exodus* XXIV, 12: "Dixit autem Dominus ad Moysen: Ascende ad me in montem, et esto ibi; daboque tibi tabulas lapideas, et legem ac mandata quae scripsi, ut doceas eos." See also *Exodus,* XXXI, 18: "Deditque Dominus Moysi, completis hujuscemodi sermonibus in monte Sinai, duas tabulas testimonii lapideas, scriptas digito Dei."

799–802. *busche*   See *Exodus,* III, 2 ff. For an excellent treatment of the use of the burning bush as a symbol of the spotless virginity of the Virgin Mary, see Miss G. L. Morrill, *Speculum Gy de Warewyke* (*EETSES,* 75), pp. cxxi-cxxiv. See also F. J. E. Raby, *History of Christian-*

Latin Poetry (Oxford, 1927), p. 369. Cf. also "To Mary, the Queen of Heaven" (MacCracken, *Minor Poems,* I, 286) :

> "O bush unbrent, shewed to Moyses
> Judith the secounde, that saved all Israel,
> Assenek off Egipt, of beute pereles,
> Sovereyn Sara of refut cheeff Rachel
> For our Savaciour salued bi Gabriel
> Reclinatorye throne of Kyng Salamoun."

806–809. *yerde of Moysez*   See *Exodus* VII, 8-12.

810–812. *the Byble*   See *Exodus* XVII, 1-7.

813–816. *Sampson*   See *Book of Judges,* XV, 18-19 : "Sitiensque valde, clamavit ad Dominum, et ait : Tu dedisti in manu servi tui salutem hanc maximam atque victoriam ; en siti morior, incidamque in manus incircumcisorum. Aperuit itaque Dominus molarem dentem in maxilla asini ; et egressae sunt ex eo aquae ; quibus haustis, refocillavit spiritum, et vires recepit. Idcirco appellatum est nomen loci illius : Fons invocantis de maxilla, usque in praesentem diem."

817–821. *flodeʒ of Iordon*   See *Book of Josue* III, 14-17.

822–823. *the Asse*   See *Numbers* XXII, 22-35.

825. *yrne*   See *IV Kings* VI, 2-6, in which the prophet Eliseus made iron swim in the water.

827–837. *Abacuk*   See *Daniel,* XIV, 32-38. This entire story is recounted here. See also James Hastings, *A Dictionary of the Bible* (5v, New York, 1899), II, 272. Lydgate refers to the story in "On De Profundis", ll. 35-37 (MacCracken, *Minor Poems,* I, 79) and Misericordias Domini," ll. 161-164, (*Ibid.,* 76).

841–846. *the sonne, at Gabaon*   See the *Book of Josua* X, 12-14 : "Tunc locutus est Josue Domino, in die qua tradidit Amorrhaeum in conspectu filiorum Israel, dixitque coram eis : 'Sol, contra Gabaon ne movearis, Et luna contra vallem Aialon. Steteruntque sol et luna, Donec ulcisceretur se gens de inimicis suis. Nonne scriptum est hoc in libro Justorum? Stetit itaque sol in medio caeli, et non festinavit occumbere spatio unius diei. Non fuit antea nec postea tam longa dies, obediente Domino voci hominis, et pugnante pro Israel."

848–851.   *the shade to Retourne*   See *Isaias,* XXXVIII, 4-8.

862–864.   *the Be*   See St. Ambrose, "De Virginibus," I, 8, 40: "Favum itaque mellis tua opera componant; digna enim virginitas quae apibus comparetur; sic laboriosa, sic pudica, sic continens. Rore pascitur apis, nescit concubitus, mella componit. Ros quoque virginis est sermo divinus; quia sicut ros Dei verba descendunt. Pudor virginis est intemerata natura. Partus virginis foetus est labiorum, expers amaritudinis, fertilis suavitatis In commune labor, communis est fructus." See *Sancti Ambrosii Opera* (Paris, 1690), II, 156.

877–878.   *the Barnacle*   See G. R. Owst, *Literature and Pulpit in Medieval England* (Cambridge University Press, 1933), p. 203: "Bromyard mentions the bird called Bernac, which is nourished and born of timber, as they say, and finally adheres to the timber by its beak alone. When that has been removed, it plunges itself into the water." See also *NED,* s.v. "Barnacle", 1: "This bird (Barnak) of which the breeding-place was long unknown, was formerly believed to be produced out of the fruit of a tree growing by the seashore, or itself to grow upon the tree attached by its bill (whence called also Tree Goose) or to be produced out of a shell which grew upon this tree or was engendered as a kind of 'mushroom' or spume from the corruption or rotting of timber in the water."

903.   *Inow suffice*   This redundant expression was common in Lydgate's and Chaucer's work. See Schick, *Temple of Glas,* note to 1. 1026 and Sieper, *Reson and Sensuallyte,* note to lines 2316 and 2983.

906–910.   *saint Gregory*   See "XL Homiliarum in Evangelia," Lib. II, Hom. 26, Migne *PL,* LXXVI (Paris, 1857), 1197: "Prima lectionis hujus evangelicae quaestio animum pulsat, quomodo post resurrectionem corpus dominicum verum fuit, quod clausis januis ad discipulos ingredi potuit. Sed sciendum nobis est quod divina operatio si ratione comprehenditur, non est admirabilis; nec fides habet meritum, cui humana ratio praebet experimentum. Sed haec ipsa nostri Redemptoris opera, quae ex semetipsis comprehendi nequaquam possunt, ex alia ejus operatione pensanda sunt, ut rebus mirabilius fidem praebeant facta mirabiliora. Illud enim corpus Domini intravit ad discipulos januis clausis quod videlicet ad humanos oculos, per nativitatem suam clauso exiit utero Virginis. Quid ergo mirum si clausis januis post resurrectionem suam in aeternum jam victurus intravit, qui moriturus veniens non aperto utero Virginis exivit."

956. *the gospell* This is an indication of Lydgate's use of the Gospel as his source for his account of the Visitation. See also line II, 1065 below.

981–1060. *Paraphrase of Magnificat* See *St. Luke* I, 46-56. The popularity of these lines of Lydgate is seen by the three extant MSS of this portion alone of the *Life of Our Lady,* C⁴, Ad¹, and Adv¹. Ms Adv¹ has been printed in two editions of the Bannatyne Manuscript. See *The Bannatyne Manuscript,* Hunterian Club (3v, Glasgow, 1873), "Song of the Virgin Mary," I, 64-67; and *The Bannatyne Manuscript,* ed. by N. Tod Ritchie (Edinburgh and London, 1928), pp. 60-63.

1025. *the wheell* This is Fortune of the Middle Ages. Boethius gave her form and figure in the second book of *De Consolatione Philosophiae.* Dante placed her in the Fourth Circle of Hell as mistress of "vain goods". See *Roman de la Rose* (II, 4863-4892) in reference to Fortune's wheel. See the extensive discussion of Fortune in Howard R. Patch, *The Goddess Fortuna in Mediaeval Literature* (Cambridge, Mass., 1927), and in W. E. Mead, *The Pastime of Pleasure* (*EETS,* 173), note to lines 3109 ff. See also Erdmann, *Siege of Thebes,* note to l. 1755; *Troy Book,* III, 4084; "God is Myn Helpere", ll. 41-48 (MacCracken, *Minor Poems,* I, 28). For the Wheel of Fortune see Lydgate's *Pilgrimage of the Life of Man,* ll. 19423-19676.

1193. *daliaunce* Speech, conversation; see Sieper, *Reson and Sensuallyte,* note for ll. 2232, 6576, and 7024; and especially Schick, *Temple of Glas,* note to l. 291.

1241. *purposede uppe and downe* See Schick, *Temple of Glas,* note to l. 606 and Sieper, *Reson and Sensuallyte,* note to l. 2256.

1257–77. *Crysostomus* See St. Chrysostom: "Eruditi Commentarii in Evangelium Matthai Incerto Auctore, Homil. I": "Propter tres ergo causas apparuit ei. Primum ne justus homo ignorans faceret rem injustam ex proposito justo; deinde propter honorem matris ipsius. Nam si dimissa fuisset, etsi non apud fideles, tamen apud infideles turpi suspicione carere non poterat. Tertio, ut intelligens Joseph sanctam conceptionem diligentius se in futurum custodiret ab illa, quam prius." (Migne, *PG.,* LVI, 633.)

1312. *Tyten* See Sieper, *Reson and Sensuallyte,* note to ll. 449-54.

1411ff.   *Trial by Drink*   See *Book of Numbers,* V, 11-31. Lydgate's narration of the trial of Joseph and Mary parallels closely the account in
the Gospel of Pseudo-Matthew. For further reference see J. G.
Frazer, *Folklore in the Old Testament* (3 v, London, 1918), III,
304-6; Stith Thompson, *Motif-Index of Folk-Literature,* III, 312.
Lydgate refers to this trial as one of the sorrows of Mary, then cites
her triumph in the trial as one of her joys. See "The Fifteen Joys
and Sorrows of Mary," ll. 192-195 and 71-75 (MacCracken, *Minor
Poems,* I, 275; 270-271).

1474-5.   *Hornes shrynke in*   Truth is pictured as having figuratively the
horns of a snail, which shame causes to shrink, a phrase meaning to
lower one's pretentions. See Henry Bergen, *Troy Book* (4v,
EETSES, 97, 103, 106, 126), note to line I, 2199; see also Henry
Bergen, *The Fall of Princes* (4v, *EETSES,* 121-4), note to line I,
6724.

1483-4.   *siluer, is fynyde be assay*   See *Psalm,* XI, 7: "Eloquia Domini,
eloquia casta; argentum igne examinatum, probatum terrae, purgatum
septuplum." See Schick, *Temple of Glas,* note for lines 1191-92.

1527.   *fresshe of hewe*   Lydgate uses this term frequently in reference to
the complexion. See Erdmann, *Siege of Thebes,* note to l. 3956. See
also II, 1564 below.

1620-1.   *phebus*   These lines imply the first day of spring, since "phebus" is
the sun god and Aries, the constellation which the sun enters on the
first day of spring. This is March 20 or 21 nowadays. On the Julian
calendar of Lydgate's era it would have been about March 12. See
Chaucer, *Astrolabe,* II, 1, ll. 7-17.

1628ff.   Lydgate is fond of introducing the name of his great "master" into
his writings. See Schick, *Temple of Glas,* pp. xci-xcii and his extensive note for l. 110. This commendation of Chaucer is well known;
it parallels the *Troy Book,* I, 4677-4735; and *The Fall of Princes,*
I, 274-357.

1649.   *traceȝ*   See Glauning, *Two Nightingale Poems,* note for l. 195.

1658.   *my penne, be quakyng ay for drede*   This is a favorite expression of
Lydgate. See Schick, *Temple of Glas,* note to l. 947. See also "The
Legend of Seynt Margarete," l. 57 (MacCracken, *Minor Poems,* I,
175).

1659.   *Cleo, ne Caliope*   Lydgate frequently says that he is not under
patronage to Clio or Calliope. See *Troy Book,* III, 5445. See also
Schick, *Temple of Glas,* note to l. 1303.

BOOK III

1. *Whanne al was hust* *Wisdom* xviii, 14-15. This text, by way of accommodation, came to be applied to the Christmas feast. See the Antiphon to the Magnificat in Vespers of the Sunday within the Octave of the Nativity. Cf. also Peter Comestor's *Sermo in Nativitate Domini,* Migne, *PL,* CXCVIII, 1758; and Peter Cellensis' *Sermo,* Migne, *PL,* CCII, 658.

4. *Lucyne* For Lydgate's frequent use of Luciana and Phebus for the moon and sun respectively, see O. Glauning, ed., *The Two Nightinggale Poems* (1900; *EETSES,* 80), note to l. 26; and A. Erdmann, ed., *The Siege of Thebes* (1911-20; *EETSES,* 108, 125), note to ll. 1051-3. The practice is discussed also by J. Schick, ed., *Temple of Glas* (1891; *EETSES,* 60), note to ll. 4-7.

10. *or maies dai the ferthe* Apparently indicating that Book III was begun on May 4. For a discussion of the dating of the entire work, see R. Klinefelter, (" The Date," p. 4. ff.).

12–20. There appears to be some confusion here. Although Bede is quoted in line 15 as the source of this information, he gives the date as the third year of the hundred ninety-fourth Olympiad. Bede's material is to be found in two different places: *De Temporibus Liber,* Migne, *PL,* XC, 290; and *De Temporum Ratione,* Migne, *PL,* XC, 545.

19. *withoutyn werre* The coming of the Prince of Peace in the midst of a universal *Pax Romana* is often referred to in patristic writings which base themselves on *Psalm* LXXXV, 3 and *Isaias* IX, 6. Less redundantly, of course, the phrase could be taken as meaning "without doubt", a common usage in Lydgate. Cf. Schick, *Temple of Glas,* note to l. 651.

19. *of Olympyades* In the Greek calendar, the four-year period between Olympic games. Cf. Peter Comestor, *Historia Scholastica,* Migne, *PL,* CXCVIII, 1285.

21. *And by cronycle* In this instance, the *Legenda Aurea,* (ed. Th. Graess Leipzig, 1881), although Peter Comestor's *Historia* may be what Lydgate had in mind.

22–87. *Luke* II, 1-5 is the basis for this, but the *Legenda Aurea,* ed. Graesse, p. 41; the *Liber de Ortu Beatae Mariae et Infantia Salvatoris a Beato Matthaeo* (referred to as the *Evangelium Pseudo-Matthaei*) in *Evangelia Apocrypha,* ed. Constantinus Tischendorf (Leipzig, 1876), p. 76; the *Historia Scholastica,* Migne, *PL,* CXCVIII, 1539; have all embellished the Evangelist's account.

47. *swere for swete or sowre*   This oath is presumably based on the contents of the two vats of Jupiter, one sweet and the other bitter. See Ernest Sieper, *Reson and Sensuallyte* (1903); *EETSES,* 89), note to line 47; and Schick's *Temple of Glas* in the note to line 198 of the "Compleynt" appended to his text.

50. *To tempre hym*   If this be the correct reading (the MSS have a number of variants) it is probably a borrowing from the Latin *obtemperare,* to obey.

56. *I fynde ferthermore*   Lydgate is still using the same source. This type of phrase has the two-fold purpose of providing a rhyme-tag and displaying his erudition. It occurs again at line 60 and elsewhere throughout the poem. His other works are replete with similar instances too numerous to catalogue here.

68. The Roman calendar was based on the founding of the city, i.e., *ab urbe condita.* This date can be found in Bede. See the note to lines 12-20 above.

69. *VIIᵉ and fiftene*   To be read: "seven hundred and fiftene".

71. *Phebus*   The sun. See note to line 4 above.

72. *Of Capricorne*   An astronomical indication of the season. The sun was in its lowest position in relation to the constellation Capricorn.

75. For the use of the golden number in construing calendar dates, see the introduction to any edition of the *Roman Martyrology.*

85. Both *Matthew* I, 3, 6; and *Luke* II, 4, 31, 33; trace the geneology of Christ from David and Juda.

88–151. This section can be found in the aprcryphal gospels, cf. *Evangelium Pseudo-Matthaei,* ed. Tischendorf, pp. 76 sqq., and the Greek version in the *Proto-Evangelium Jacobi,* ed. Tischendorf, p. 32.

89. *dyd her brydill lede*   A graphic touch represented nowhere in the sources.

128. *drawe to declyne*   Lydgate uses this phrase also in the *Siege of Thebes,* l. 2904.

144. *hastyd it*   Used reflexively. Compare the French *se depcher.*

145. *To Abraham and Isaak*   In Genesis XXVI, 4, 24.

146. *And to Iacob*   In *Genesis* XXVIII, 14.

156. *mate sumdel*   Somewhat fatigued. Cf. German *Matt.*

157. For the Gospel reference to the overcrowded inn, see *Luke* II, 7.

161. The diverse traditions of the stable and the cave are treated by Reinhard Frauenfelder, *Die Geburt des Herrn* (Leipzig, 1939), pp. 19, 32.

168. *a newe soden light*   This miraculous light is emphasized in the *Legenda,* ed. Graesse, p. 41, and in the *Evangelium Pseudo-Matthaei,* where the scene occurs in a subterranean cavern; see Tischendorf, p. 77.

175. *sonne of myght*   Refers to Christ. The usual phrase is "sun of justice" from *Malachias* IV, 2 but Lydgate's rhyme-scheme would not have been served thereby.

179. *Whan all was huste*   Once again, *Wisdom,* XVIII, 14. See the note to line 1 above.

185. *Withoutyn helpe of any mydwyfe*   Despite the later introduction of Sephora and Salome, Lydgate here keeps to the tradition that no one was present when Mary was delivered. Vincent de Beauvais, *Laudes Virginis Mariae* (Vincentius Bellovacensis, *Opuscula,* Basel, 1481, fol. 220ʳ) quotes Saint Jerome on the point: *"Ergo in partu Virginis obstetrix nulla fuit, nulla muliercularum sedulitas intercessit."*

201. *As I fynde*   In the *Evangelium Pseudo-Matthaei,* Tischendorf, pp. 77 sqq. For a cryptic account of this whole section, see the *Evangelium Infantiae Salvatoris,* in the same volume, p. 182.

215. *sonne of grace*   Refers to Christ. See note to l. 175 above.

231–6. The practice of anointing new-born infants with the mother's first milk (colostrum) may have been usual in the Middle Ages. It is still done in some parts of Europe. I have been unable to trace it in the sources beyond a passing mention in the *Meditationes Vitae Christi.* Cf. *Sancti Bonaventurae Opera Omnia* (13v, Paris, 1868), XII, 518.

301.   These lines referring to the star have as their source the *Evangelium Pseudo-Matthaei,* p. 80.

316–333.   *Balam the sonne of Beor*   Reference is here made to the prophecy of Balaam that a star should rise out of Jacob. Cf. *Num.* XXIV, 17. The *Historia Scholastica* specifically applies this prophecy to Mary: *"Orietur stella ex Jacob et consurget virga, id est Maria, ex Israel . . ."* Cf. Migne, *PL,* CXCVIII, 1239. See also Lydgate's "Ave Jesse Virgula" in H. N. MacCracken, *The Minor Poems of John Lydgate* (1911) ; *EETSES,* 70), I, 300.

342.   *was there by loke*   Literally, was there locked in.

346.   *hangeth as a ball*   This concept of the world as a toy in the Christ Child's hand is common in early Christian poetry. In the *Breviary,* the hymn at Matins for the Common of the Blessed Virgin contains this idea as well as others touched on in this part of the *Life of Our Lady:*

> Quem terra, pontus, sidera
> Colunt, adorant, praedicant,
> Trinam regentem machinam
> Claustrum Mariae bajulat.
>
> Cui luna, sol, et omnia
> Deserviunt per tempora,
> Perfusa caeli gratia
> Gestant puellas viscera.
>
> Beata Mater munere
> Cujus, supernus Artifex,
> *Mundum pugillo continens,* [italics mine]
> Ventris sub arca clausus est.

It occurs again in the Responsory to the eighth lesson of Matins for the Sunday after Christmas: ". . . *stabulo ponitur qui continet mundum."* It is interesting to note that Francis Thompson revived the figure in the nineteenth century.

355.   *Scephora*   None of Lydgate's sources give this name to the believing midwife. The *Legenda Aurea* calls her Zebel (Cf. Graesse, p. 41) and the *Evangelium Pseudo-Matthaei* names her Zelomi (Cf. Tischen-

dorf, p. 77). In *The Blessed Virgin Mary in the Medieval Drama of England* (Holland, 1928), p. 98, J. Vriend notes that there is great variation in the appellations accorded one of the midwives. The incredulous one is always called Salome, But the other, although she usually bears the name of Zebel or Tebel, sometimes becomes Zelomi, Rachel, or even (as in our present text) Sephora. The *Proto-Evangelium Jacobi* continually refers to her as simply ημαια, the midwife. Cf. Tischendorf, p. 33. This variety and anonymity of the first midwife may be due to the fact that an ancient inscription on a fresco in the Cemetery of Saint Valentine on the Via Flaminia in Rome gives only Salome's name. This inscription dates from the eighth century. (Cf. Frauenfelder, p. 21)

In the Old Testament there was a midwife called Sephora (*Exodus* I, 15) and the *Historica Scholastica* speaks of her (Cf. Migne, *PL,* CXCVIII, 1142). Then too, the wife of Moses (*Exodus* II, 21) is briefly referred to in the gloss of the *Legenda* text which deals with the Circumcision (Cf. Graesse, p. 83): "Tollit illico Sephora acutissimam petram et circumcidit carnem praeputii filii sui circumcisione . . ." (The text of this gloss is from *Exodus* III, 27. Lydgate may have appropriated her name for the anonymous midwife.

371. See Graesse, p. 42: "A saeculo non est auditum . . ."

390. *as hir aughte*   As she should. An impersonal verb with the dative "hir".

409. *the hem of his vestement*   Not as such in the sources. It is obviously the *fimbria vestimenti* of Matt. IX, 20.

414. *pleyne hem*   As in French, used reflexively here.

425. *as she dyd enbrace*   Has the meaning of "unbrace" here. That is, she prepared to, made ready to.

427. *with-oute more*   A direct translation of the Latin phrase *sine mora,* without delay.

448. For the occurrence of the Nativity on a Sunday night and at midnight, see *Legenda Aurea* ed. Graesse, p. 41, and *Historia Scholastica,* Migne, *PL* CXCVIII, 1540.

451. *The viij kalendes . . . of Ianuarie*   This is the Roman calendar's (and the Roman Martyrology's) way of referring to December 25;

that is, eight days before the calends of January, which in that month occur on the first day.

454.   Lydgate says that this information is from the *Vision of Elizabeth*. Neither Elizabeth of Hungary nor Elizabeth of Schönau agrees with him. Sources generally hold to the age of fifteen. Cf. *Meditationes,* p. 518; the *Gospel of Joseph,* ed. Tischendorf, p. 128; and R. Klinefelter ("3, The Sources, Books I and II", p. 91).

459.   *Luke* II, 8-20, gives the story of the shepherds.

485.   *Glory and honour*   A "liberal" translation of the Gloria of the Mass.

532.   Cf. *Luke* II, 19. *"Maria autem conservabat omnia verba haec, conferens in corde suo."* This was also hinted at in l. 348.

539.   *Bonaventure*   The *Meditationes Vitae Christi* were erroneously attributed to Saint Bonaventure. (See "3. The Sources, Books III and IV", p. 102 n). Lydgate is here quoting from the meditation for Monday, pp. 518-525. Cf. *Sancti Bonaventurae Opera Omnia,* XII, 518-525.

560.   *Othir thynges tweyne*   The two marvels are: the maternity of a virgin and the appearance of divinity in human form. Cf. *Meditationes, Sancti Bonaventurae Opera Omnia,* XII, 520.

578.   *Isaias* XVI, 1. The attribution to David in the text is faulty. Cf. also the First Lesson of Christmas Matins: *"Populus qui ambulabat in tenebris, vidit lucem magnam: hatbitantibus in regione umbrae mortis, lux orta est eis." Isaias* IX, 2.

596.   *Dauid*   There is probably confusion here with *Ecclus.* XXXVI, 1-18. *Psalm* XXX, 17, although not so close, might conceivably save the attribution.

612.   The Advent cry of the liturgy: *"Veni Domine et noli tardare, relaxa facinora plebis tuae . . ."*

614.   *Zacharias* IX, 9-10.

624.   *Baruch* IV, 36.

631.   *Isaias* XLV, 8.

648.   *Jeremias* XXXIII, 15-18.

657.   *Malachias* IV 2. Cf. also *Mal.* III, 17.

663.   *Micheas* V, 2.

670.   *Daniel* II, 34-35. Saint Epiphanius, among others, applied this text to Our Lady: *"Mons nullatenus incisus, praeruptam habens petram Christum, de qua sapientissimus Daniel: 'Abscissus est lapis de monte sine manibus,' hoc est absque viro solidam petram Christum Virgo peperit." Biblia Mariana,* ed. Sebastianus Uccello (Turin, 1924), p. 90.

678.   *the grete ymage*   The idol set up by Nabuchodonosor. Cf. *Daniel* III, 1-11.

691.   *Psalm* CXXXII, 3. Vincent de Beauvais in his *De Laudibus Virginis Mariae* (*Opuscula,* Basel, 1481, fol. 97ᵛ) quotes Saint Bernard on this point: *"Cui utique distillantibus caelis tota se infudit plenitudo divinitatibus adeo ut de hac plenitudine omnes acciperemus qui vere sine ipsa nihil aliud quam arida terra sumus."*

698.   The cloud seen by the servant of Elias. Cf. III *Kings* XVIII, 42-44.

705.   Cf. Chaucer's *Canterbury Tales,* Prol. 2.

707.   *the felde flouryng*   A reference to Isaac's blessing given to Jacob in *Genesis* XXVII, 27.

730.   *the floure delys*   The fleur-de-lis, the lily. Ucello, *Biblia Mariana* p. 304, quotes a large number of texts in which Mary is referred to as a lily.

732.   *in canticis*   A possible reference to the text: *"Ego flos campi et lilium convallium." Cant.* II, 1 or VII, 11. In neither instance, however, is Solomon primarily concerned with a field. *Cant.* III, 13-14, a text frequently applied to the Blessed Virgin in the liturgy, emphasizes the abundance of the "tempre eyre": *"Emissiones tuae paradisus malorum punicorum fructibus. Cypro cum nardo, Nardus et crocus, fistula et cinnamomum cum universis lignis, Libani, myrrha et aloe cum omnibus primis unguentis."* Saint Jerome, in a quotation included by Vincent de Beauvais in *De Laudibus Virginis Mariae* (fol. 210ᵛ), covers the idea of Lydgate's lines at this point: *"Emissiones tuae paradisus. Vere hortus delitiarum in quo consita sunt universa genera florum et odoramenta virtutum. Sicque conclusus ut nesciat violari nec corrumpi ullis insidiarum fraudibus. Fons itaque sigillo totius trinitatis signatus ex quo fons vitae manat, in cujus lumine omnes videmus. . . . Cujus profecto uteri emissio supernorum omnium*

civium est paradisus. De isto namque ventris agro patriarca Isaac longe odorans aiebat: Ecce odor filii mei sicut odor agri pleni quam benedixit dominus'."

741.   *The garnet apull*   In comparing Mary with the pomegranate, Lydgate is emphasizing what was thought to be the medicinal value of that fruit. Cf. *The Herbal of Rufinus,* ed. Lynn Thorndyke (Chicago, 1946), p. 182. In Lydgate's "A Commendation of Our Lady" (in Skeat's Supplement to *The Complete Works of Geoffrey Chaucer,* Oxford, 1897, p. 279) we read in line 21: "O punical pome ayens al pestilens." Cf. also Pliny's *Natural History* XII, 19.

748.   *accesse*   An attack, as of fever. Cf. Schick, *Temple of Glas,* note to l. 358.

763.   *the Olyfe*   The olive-tree. The application of this figure to Our Lady is frequent, but the beauty of the plant is usually commended, not denied as is the case here. Cf. *Biblia Mariana,* pp. 336-7.

773.   *the coote polymete*   An allusion to Joseph's varicolored robe; the *tunica polymita* of the Vulgate. Cf. *Genesis* XXXVII, 3.

777.   *Alysaundre*   Presumably, Alexander Neckham, whose *Commentarium Super Cantica* was contained in the monastic library at Bury. Cf. M. R. James, *The Abbey of Saint Edmund at Bury* (Cambridge, 1895), p. 16.

785.   *gauell*   Other MSS show different readings, but the context clearly indicates that Lydgate is here referring to the sheaf in Joseph's dream. Cf. *Genesis* XXXVII, 7.

797.   *Sonne and mone*   The second of Joseph's dreams. *Genesis* XXXVII, 9.

800.   The identity of this Guydo is somewhat difficult to determine. Richard of Saint Laurence and Albertus Magnus both speak of Mary as *"Horreum repositorium frumenti"* in the same manner as Lydgate does in these lines. Cf. *Biblia Mariana,* p. 289.

803.   The seven years of plenty which Joseph gathered into the barns of Egypt. Cf. *Genesis* XLI, 47.

826.   *the signes twelfe*   The twelve signs of the Zodiac.

829.   *troni and dominacion*   Two of the nine choirs of angels.

833.   *in the sauter*   *Psalm* CXLVIII. See also *Psalm* CXVII, 24.

845. *Angels and virtutes*   Two more of the nine choirs. Seraphim are mentioned in l. 837 above, but no attempt is made to complete the enumeration. Note the Latin form of Virtues.

856. *in hys fadres thought*   Cf. *John* I and XVII, 5.

862. *Iacob*   The marginal gloss has "*Iacob in libro de Testamentis XII* [Patriarcharum]." See the edition of that work printed by the Stationers Company (London, 1619), pp. B₂b-B₃a. However, *Genesis* XLIX, 8-12 is closer to our text.

863. *attropos . . . cloto . . . lachasis*   A display of Lydgate's erudition in the field of mythology. These are the three Fates ("*tres sunt fatales quae fila ducunt sorores*"). Clotho held the distaff, Lachesis turned the spindle, and Atropos cut the thread with her shears. Cf. C. M. Gayley, *The Classical Myths in English Literature* (Boston, 1898), p. 72; Schick, *Temple of Glas,* note to l. 782; Erdmann, *Siege of Thebes,* note to l. 734; and Henry Bergen, *Lydgate's Troy Book* (1906-10; *EETSES,* 97, 103, 106), II, 880.

879. *Maugre echone that the reuers mene*   That is, in spite of everyone who tries to oppose you.

888. *a duke*   Keeps the literal meaning of the Latin *dux,* a leader.

910. A reference to the *Testament of Joseph* contained in Robert Grosseteste's *Testaments of the twelve Patriarches* (London, 1619), p. K₄b.

920. *Lincolne*   Robert Grosseteste, Bishop of Lincoln.

930. *by sheltroun in batayle*   In this way, Lydgate indicates the unanimous opposition among the beasts to the lamb. *Psalm* II, 2, which is sung at the beginning of Christmas Matins has the same thought: "*Astiterunt reges terrae et principes convenerunt in unum, adversus Dominum et adversus Christum ejus.*"

942. *clad in oure armoure*   That is, assuming our humanity.

946. *myghty bretherne two*   Juda and Levi. The lines that follow show the kingship and priesthood of Christ through his descent from the two sons of Jacob who were respectively the bearers of these prerogatives. Saint Augustine says: "*Matthaeus suscepisse intelligitur incarnationem Domini circa stirpem regiam . . . venit ipse unus utramque personam in se portans, sacerdotis et regis.*" *Opera Sancti Augustini* (Venice, 1720), III. 483. See also Max Degenhart, *Lydgate's Horse, Goose and Sheep* (Erlangen, 1900), note to l. 308.

953.   This picture of the branches on the tree of Jesse entwining till they met in Mary was a common medieval illustration. It may have been hinted at in the retable designs behind Our Lady's altar at Bury Cf. James, *The Abbey of Saint Edmund,* pp. 142-3. It forms one of the illuminations of MS. H[1].

970.   This allusion to a cave shows the influence of the Pseudo-Matthew account.

971.   *kynde and a mayde*   Nature and the Blessed Virgin are conceived as entering into controversy over the simultaneous virginity and maternity involved here.

981.   *champartye*   A contest, rivalry. This meaning arises out of Lydgate's erroneous interpretation of Chaucer's *Knight's Tale,* l. 1091, where it has the accepted meaning of prowess, lordship. Cf. Erdmann, *Siege of Thebes,* note to l. 2244; F. J. Furnivall and K. B. Locock, *The Pilgrimage of the Life of Man* (1904; *EETSES,* 92), note to l. 6148; and Sieper, *Reson and Sensuallyte,* note to l. 1950.

1010.   *and holy chirche*   The espousal of Christ and the Church is a traditional concept. Cf. *Meditationes,* p. 520 for a close parallel. The same thought is expressed above in l. 539. For an allusion to this tradition, the reader's attention is called to Alcuin's *Compendium in Canticum Canticorum,* Migne, *PL,* C. 659: *"In tempore incarnationis illius, quo ad copulandam sibi ecclesiam sponsam ex virginali utero processit . . ."* The Antiphon for the Magnificat in the First Vespers of the Christmas Office says: *"Cum ortus fuerit sol de coelo videbitis regem regum procedentem a patre tamquam sponsam de thalamo suo."*

1020.   *by recorde of patriarkes*   This description of the ornate chamber is based on Solomon's *Canticle* with the usual patristic application to Our Lady, Christ, and the Church.

1028.   For the gems of moral virtue, see Saint Bernard's Homily on the text *Missus est Angelus,* where he says: *"His nimirum Virgo regia gemmis ornata virtutum . . ."* Cf. Migne, PL, CLXXXIII, 62.

1032–6.   The violets, roses, and lilies symbolizing holiness (or virginity), martyrdom and chastity, are favorite figures with Lydgate. See Schick, *Temple of Glas,* note to l. 276; and MacCracken, *Minor Poems,* I, 126, 144.

1040–6. These lines are from the *Meditationes,* p. 520. Vincent de Beauvais quotes Saint Jerome *Super Psalmum XVIII* as saying: *"Hinc itaque scriptum est: In circuitu ejus tabernaculum ejus—Christus enim in Maria velut in thalamo sponsus et quasi tabernaculum ejus fuit Mariae corpus."* (*Laudes Virginis Mariae,* fol. 210ᵛ).

1049. King David is thought to have exalted the day of the Nativity in *Psalm* LXXX and *Psalm* II, 7. David's playing of musical instruments is described in II *Kings* VI, 5.

1060. That all creation joined in adoration of the new-born Babe is the the tenor of the *Legenda Aurea,* Graesse, pp. 43-46, where we find Anselm's theory that inorganic, organic, sensitive, rational, and purely spiritual beings all participated in one grand act of homage to the Creator. The famous Christmas hymn of the *Breviary,* *"Jesu Redemptor",* expresses this thought in the fifth stanza:

> *Hunc astra, tellus, aequora,*
> *Hunc omne quod coelo subest,*
> *Salutis auctorem novae*
> *Novo salutat cantico.*

1069. The Roman temple's destruction has been discussed ("3. The Sources, Book III," p. 116). Cf. also Alexander Neckham's *De Naturis Rerum* (Rolls Series, 74), p. 310.

1116. *stellifiede* Set among the stars, deified. See Schick, *Temple of Glas,* note to 1. 136; and Furnivall-Locock, *Pilgrimage,* note to 1. 18835.

1123–7. A curious instance of Lydgate's cumbersome style. It causes him to leave the sentence uncompleted.

1128. *the skyes donne* Commonly used by the monk. Cf. Schick, *Temple of Glas,* note to 1. 30. The original text is that of the *Legenda Aurea,* Graesse, p. 43: ".... *obscuritas noctis in claritatem diei versa est."* For prophecies of this phenomenon, see *Psalm* CXXXVIII, 12 and *Isaias* XXX, 26. It is interesting to note that this scene is the reverse of that which took place at the crucifixion.

1135. *as bokes telle* Another display of Lydgate's scholarship. This time the source is *Legenda Aurea,* Graesse, p. 43.

1252. · Cf. Chaucer's *Canterbury Tales,* Prol. 2. This whole section is highly reminiscent of Lydgate's "maistre". In fact, the Chaucerian lines seem so to distract our poet that he becomes involved in another impossible sentence.

1259. Bacchus, the god of vineyards and of wine. Cf. II, 879 of the present poem, where practically the same wording is used. See also Bergen, *Troy Book,* II, 5789-90.

1280. *the prophete Ieremyee* Lydgate here turns back a few pages in the *Legenda Aurea* for the story of the Egyptian statue. See Graesse, p. 43. Reference to this legend is made in the *Historia Scholastica,* Migne, *PL,* CXCVII, 1440.

1299. For comparable references to Ptolemy, see Erdmann, *Siege of Thebes,* note to l. 2973; Furnivall-Locock, *Pilgrimage,* note to l. 20040; and Bergen, *Troy Book,* I, 1702. Lydgate apparently does not distinguish between the various personages bearing this name.

1306. *by holy prophecye* That is, of Jeremias, as indicated in the text above.

1316. *Mawmetre* During and after the Crusades, Christian Europe regarded all forms of heathenism as "mawmetry". Cf. Furnivall-Locock, *Pilgrimage,* note to l. 17243.

1317. *Carnotence* An allusion to John of Salisbury. Lydgate refers to him in the same manner in the *Fall of Princes* ed. Henry Bergen (1918-27; *EETSES,* 121, 122, 123, 124), VII, 1650. The name arises from the diocese: *episcopus Carnotensis.*

1318. *In his boke Policraticon.* English versions may be found in *The Statesman's Book of John of Salisbury,* ed. John Dickinson (London, 1927), and *The Frivolities of Courtiers and Footprints of Philosophers,* ed. Joseph Pike (London, 1938).

1333. *compace* For Lydgate's other uses of this word, see Schick, *Temple of Glas,* note to l. 37; and Sieper, *Reson and Sensuallyte,* note to l. 3773.

1388. I have been unable to trace the story of the nine suns. There is, of course, some relation to *Daniel* II, 36 and VII, 17.

1430. *In grete Austyne* This is the famous sermon attributed to Saint Augustine (Migne, *PL,* XLII, 1117) and treating the prophecies relating to Christ. It gained wide currency during the Middle Ages. See Karl Young, *The Drama of the Medieval Church* (2v, Oxford, 1933), II, 125sqq. The name of Jesus may be seen in the acrostic formed by the Sibylline verses which Pseudo-Augustine quotes. It spells out the Greek inscription of the early Christian church: Ἰησοῦς Χριστὸς Θεοῦ Υἱὸς Σωτήρ, Jesus Christ, son of God,

Saviour. (Cf. Migne, *PL*. XLIII, 1126). The first letters of these words in turn form another: ἰχϑυς (fish) which was one of the first liturgical symbols employed by the Church in the catacombs.

1443.　*skye*　In the sense of clouds, fog. For this use, see Sieper, *Reson and Sensuallyte,* note to l. 1007.

1454.　*And tolde hem eke playnely*　The allusion here is to the prophecy considered to be in the Sibylline tradition and embodied in the famous Eclogue of Virgil, iv, 4-10:

> *Ultima Cumaei venit jam carmina aetas;*
> *Magnus ab integro saeculorum nascitur ordo:*
> *Jam redit et Virgo, redeunt Saturnia regna;*
> *Jam nova progenies coelo dimittitur alto.*
> *Tu modo nascenti puero, quo ferrea primum*
> *Desinet, ac toto surget gens aurea mundo,*
> *Casta, fave, Lucina.*

1460.　*the golden worlde . . . the kyngdom of Satourne*　See Virgil's Eclogue above. The Pseudo-Augustinian sermon even quotes the line: *"coelo dimittitur alto."* Cf. Sieper, *Reson and Sensuallyte,* note to l. 1299.

1462.　Proba was an early Christian poet whose piety exceeded her literary abilities. Cf. M. Manitius, *Geschichte der Christliche-Lateinischen Poesie bis zur Mitte der 8 Jahrhunderts* (Stuttgart, 1891), p. 123; and A. Heider, *The Blessed Virgin in Early Christian Latin Poetry* (Washington, 1918), pp. 19-24. In Migne, *PL,* LXXXIII, 1094, we are told that *"Proba . . . in laude Christi versata est, componens centonem de Christo, Virgilianis coaptum versiculis."*

1467.　*Abdia* I, 17-21.

1478.　*Naum* I, 15—II, 1.

1485.　*Habacuc* III, 4-7.

1487.　*of grene box*　The only Biblical reference to "grene box" is in *Isaias* XXX, 8: *"Nunc ergo ingressus scribe ei super buxum . . ."* and it seems to have no relevance here.

1499.　*Baruch* IV, 36. The remainder of the lines find their source in *Jeremias* XXIII, 5.

1506.　*Sophonias* III, 8-11.

1522.   *Daniel* VII, 13-14.

1532.   *Ezechiel* XXXIV, 23 and XXXVII, 22-23.

1546.   *Aggeus* II, 7-8.

1553.   *Zacharias* I, 11. See also *Psalm* LXXI, 7-9.

1564.   *Malachias* I, 11. This seems to be indicated by the *"ab ortu solis usque ad occasum"* in the marginal gloss.

1575.   *Amos* IX, 11.

1580.   *Isaias* LII, 15.

1583.   *as in Esdre*   For a discussion of this "Book of Esdras" see "3. The Sources, Book III", pp. 129-30. The *Historia Scholastica* also contains this story of Zorobabel and his decision in favor of truth. Cf. Migne, *PL,* CXCVIII, 1481.

1590.   *While they were at travers*   While they were arguing. Lydgate uses the word "travers" elsewhere (*Pilgrimage* 1. 6999: *Fall of Princes* II, 4387, V, 1567) but not in this dialectic sense.

1603.   The reference here is to John XIV, 6: *"Ego sum . . . veritas."*

1610.   The ensuing lines allude to the allegory of the Four Daughters of God. Lydgate gives a full account of it earlier in Book II, 1-350. Cf. R. Klinefelter "3. The Sources, Book II", p. 84.

1620.   The defeat and capture of Sedecias are related in IV *Kings* XXV, 4sqq. and *Jeremias* XXXIX, 5.

1626.   Christ will rebuild Jerusalem better than Nehemias. Cf. Books I and II of *Esdras,* where the reconstruction of the city and Nehemia's part in it are described.

1636.   *donion*   With the meaning of dwelling, habitation. Cf. Glauning, *The Two Nightingale Poems,* note to 1. 33 of the second poem.

1539.   Here begins a very creditable prayer which appears to be substantially Lydgate's own.

1643.   *the hilles of golde Deuteronomy I,* 1.

1653.   Cf. Migne, *PL,* XXXIX, 1984, and "3. The Sources, Book III", p. 130.

1658.   *welle of our welfare*   A common patristic phrase: *fons salutis.* For this use of "well" see Schick, *Temple of Glas* note to 1. 292.

1667. An instance of the separable use of the verb "vouchsafe".

1673. *Euere among* Used adverbially: often, now and again. Cf. Glauning, *The Two Nightingale Poems,* note to l. 61 of the second poem.

1698. *malyce serpentyne* For Lydgate's fondness of this way of referring to the devil, see Glauning, *The Two Nightingale Poems,* note to l. 315 of the second poem; and Erdmann, *Siege of Thebes,* note to l. 4660-67.

1703. That is, an antidote against sin. For this also, see Glauning, *The Two Nightingale Poems,* where it is treated at length in a note to l. 224 of the second poem; Sieper, *Reson and Sensuallyte,* note to l. 3414; and Furnivall-Locock, *Pilgrimage,* note to l. 15338.

1723. *the manne* A reference to the manna which fed the Israelites in the desert. Cf. *Exodus* XVI, 31.

1746. Speaking of Mary as "of mercy the ryuere" is an allusion to the Church's doctrine that, through her free cooperation in the Redemption, she became the Mediatrix of all graces. For the influence of this teaching on the thought of the Middle Ages, see Curt Bühler, *The Sources of the Court of Sapience* (Leipzig, 1932), pp. 37-40. The doctrine on the subject is well presented by Anselm Stolz in *Katholische Marienkunde: Maria in der Glaubenswissenschaft,* ed. Paul Strater (2v, Paderborn, 1947), II. 241-259.

1748. The star that brought forth the sun is a phrase out of Saint Augustine's *Sermo X ad Fratres in Eremo:* "Stella proferens solem." Cf. Migne, *PL* XL, 1252.

1752. *was bothe two* That is, both maid and mother.

1758. *Withoute eclipsyng* This figure is often used in patristic literature dealing with the Blessed Virgin. The following quotation is typical: *"Luna plena quae nunquam minuta fuit aut deficit, aut private fuit essentiali lumine, nempe sua virginitate."* Cf. Uccello, *Biblia Mariana,* p. 306.

1761. The Rose of Jericho is another figure of Our Lady. Cf. Uccello, *Biblia Mariana,* p. 90, where Richard of Saint Laurence's *De Laudibus Virginis Liber IX* is quoted: *"Rosa capitis confortativa; per caput mentem intellige; confortavit enim formidantem et desperantem quando locuta est ad cor ejus. Ideo dicitur rosa in Jericho, quod interpretatur defectus, quia saepe, nisi confortaret peccatores, deficerent."*

1765. This line is from *Ecclus.* XXIV, 17.

1767. *Psalm* XVIII, 6.

1768. *Cant.* II, 1.

1770. The story of Naaman the Syrian and his being cured of leprosy is told in IV *Kings* V, 1-19. However, the water of the Old Testament account is that of Jordan, not Siloe. Obviously, Lydgate had *John* IX, 7, in mind at the same time.

1772. *Tu gloria Jerusalem, tu laetitia Israel. Judith* XV, 10.

1774. See II *Kings* XXIII, 15-16: *"Desideravit ergo David, et ait: O si quis mihi daret potum aquae cisterna quae est in Bethleham juxta portam!"* A prayer of Saint Methodius applies this to Our Lady: *"Cisterna Bethlehemitica vitae refocillatrix a Davide desiderata, ex qua immortalitatis poculum cunctis emanavit."* Uccello, *Biblia Mariana*, p. 242.

1777. Physon was one of the four rivers of Paradise. Cf. *Genesis* II, 10-11 and *Historia Scholastica*, Migne, *PL*, CXCVIII, 1068. It is used as a figure of the Blessed Virgin as follows: *"Flumen Phison quia sicut flumen Phison habet ortum a Paradiso, et in arenis ejus gemmae pretiosae inveniuntur, sic sacratissima virgo ortum habuit ab eo, qui est Paradisus deliciarum . . ."* Uccello, *Biblia Mariana*, p 278.

1779. The promised land flowing with milk and honey is spoken of in *Exodus* III, 17.

1788. This and subsequent lines are reminiscent of the *Salve Regina* antiphon: *". . . Eia ergo, advocata nostra, illos tuos misericordes oculos ad nos converte."*

1801. *Now this mydwynter etc.* An allusion that seems to place the composition of this part of the poem in the Christmas season.

BOOK IV

1.   *Ianus Bifrons* The two-faced god of the Roman household.

1–11.   This passage is cited by Schick, *Temple of Glas,* p. cviii as proof for a 1409-11 date of composition. R. Klinefelter in his edition of Books I and II ("The Date," pp. 410), takes issue with him. These introductory lines of Book IV are reminiscent of *The Troy Book,* IV, 6974.

18.   Luke's brevity compresses the story into one verse: *"Et postquam consummati sunt dies octo ut circumcideretur puer, vocatum est nomen ejus Jesus, quod vocatum est ab angelo priusquam in utero conciperetur." Luke* II, 21. The fourth Book of our poem is little more than a protracted expansion of this text.

30.   Lydgate now turns to the *Meditationes* for his information. Despite MS variations regarding the "knyf", there seems to be no question of MS. D's correctness: the Latin text has *"cum cultello lapideo."* Cf. *Meditationes,* p. 522. See also *Legenda Aurea,* Graesse, p. 83.

34.   *Bonaventure* As noted above, the *Meditationes* were falsely attributed to Saint Bonaventure and may still be found among his works.

58.   *As of modris* A deft Lydgatean touch that is not in the Latin, French, or English texts of the *Meditationes.*

64.   *Alquyn* I have been unable to locate this material in the works of Alcuin. Professor Schick's remark about Lydgate's occasional inaccuracy in quoting authorities is reassuring.

99–119.   The source of these lines is *Legenda Aurea,* Graesse, p. 82.

113.   Longinus is the traditional name given the Roman centurion who opened the side of Christ with his spear. This item is not represented in the *Legenda Aurea* text presently being quoted, but later on in that same work we read that, " . . . *cum ex infirmitate vel senectute oculi ejus caligassent, de sanguine Christi per lanceam currente fortuito oculos suos tetigit et protinus clare vidit."* Graesse, p. 202. For other instances of Lydgate's use of this story, see Furnivall-Locock, *Pilgrimage,* l. 19953 and note; as well as Glauning, *The Two Nightingale Poems,* I, 385 and note. This latter editor reads *Longens* in place of our Longeus.

120.   *In bokes eke*   That is, in *Legenda Aurea,* Graesse, p. 86; in Peter Comestor's *Historia Scholastica,* Migne, *PL,* CXCVIII, 1541; and in *The Stacions of Rome* ed. F. J. Furnivall (1867; *EETSES,* 25), lines 337-8. For a quite different version of the legend, see the *Evangelium Infantiae Salvatoris,* Tischendorf, p. 183.

127.   *aquys grene*   That is, Aix-la-Chapelle (Aachen). The Latin form is Aquis Granae.

133.   *as blyfe*   The frequency of this phrase and its pleonastic use of "as" is discussed by Glauning, *The Two Nightingale Poems,* notes to II, 186 and I, 219.

148.   *The story dothe devyse*   Both *Luke* II, 21 and *Legenda Aurea,* Graesse, p. 80sqq.

157.   For a discussion of Lydgate's excessive modesty, see Sieper, *Reson and Sensuallyte,* note to l. 317; and Schick, *Temple of Glas,* pp. cxl-cxlii.

165.   It is unlikely that Lydgate went directly to Bernard since the *Meditationes* quotes the saint at length. Cf. *Meditationes,* pp. 628-630.

166.   *Fygured first unto Iosue*   See *Josue* V, 2sqq.

197–244.   *Legenda Aurea,* Graesse, p. 81 is the source of these lines, despite another reference to Bernard in l. 198. The text, of course, can be traced to Bernard in Migne, *PL,* CLXXXIII. 846. This sermon forms the Lessons of the Second Nocturne of Matins on the Feast of the Holy Name, January 2.

210.   An obscure line, the meaning of which I cannot determine with any degree of security. If "holy our doctryne" is read as "our holy doctryne" an acceptable meaning can be arrived at.

211.   *of his Right*   "Righteousness" is apparently the intended meaning. MSS. C³ and Hn¹ actually read "ryghtwysnesse".

222–224.   Another passage that does not lend itself to facile interpretation. However, if *flood* is taken in the sense of *flowing,* with *whos* referring to our salvation, the meaning is clear.

232.   The *pavys* was an elongated shield that had been developed at Pavia in Italy. Cf. *NED,* s. v., "pavys".

234.   Lydgate frequently mentions the shield of Pallas. Cf. Sieper, *Reson and Sensuallyte,* note to 1. 1188 and 11. 1194-1206; Schick, *Temple of Glas,* note to 1. 248; and Bergen, *Troy Book*, Introd. p. cxxvii.

243.   How the virtue of the Holy Name was miraculously shown by divine oracle to Solomon is difficult to determine. The reference may be to *Prov.* VIII, 22-31, a sequence of lines that is included in the psalter of the Breviary and is regarded as Messianic in character.

255.   The story of Saint Ignatius Martyr is found later on in *Legenda Aurea,* Graesse, p. 157: *"Legitur autem quod beatus Ignatius inter tot tormentorum genera nunquam ab invocatione nominis Jesu Christi cessabat. Quem cum tortores inquirerent, cur hoc nomen toties replicaret, ait: hoc nomen cordi meo inscriptum habeo et ideo ab ejus invocatione cessare non valeo. Post mortem igitur ejus illi qui audierant, volentes curiosius expereri, cor ejus ab ejus corpore avellunt et illud scindentes per medium totum cor ejus inscriptum hoc nomine, Jesus Christus, litteris aureis inveniunt."*

285.   *wysse*   Teach and advise us. For Lydgate's use of this word, see Schick, *Temple of Glas,* note to 1. 637.

289.   That is, the "anointed one", from the Greek χριστός, one who was anointed with χρισμα.

291.   The name Jesus comes from the Hebrew word for saviour. Cf. *Matt.* I, 21.

295.   *bokeȝ of olde antiquyte*   The *Legenda Aurea,* Graesse, pp. 80-81.

308.   *the emprise of hem tweyne*   The contest between two participants.

318.   See the third chapter of *Genesis.*

334.   The meaning is: let pity move thee to mercy before thy justice (righteousness) intervene with the sword of vengeance.

351.   *the lost chepe*   A reference to *Luke* XV, 4sqq.

357.   From IV, 246 to this point, the many and varied invocations suggest the litany of the Holy Name:

       246. specified by prophets—*Jesu rex prophetarum*

       248. magnified by apostles—*Jesu doctor apostolorum*

250. strength of martyrs—*Jesu fortitudo martyrum*

258. food of confessors and guardian of their virtue—*Jesu lumen confessorum*

267. food of virgins and oil for their lamps—*Jesu puritas virginum*

274. sweetest sound in the ear—*Jesu amabilis* (literally, of course, it is St. Bernard's *dulcis in aure*)

279. source of peace—*Jesu Deus pacis*

281. joy of the sorrowful—*Jesu refugium nostrum*

282. reward of the blessed—*Jesu corona sanctorum omnium*

283. salve of the sick—*salus infirmorum* (from the litany of the Blessed Virgin)

284. clothing for the naked⎫
285. food for the hungry ⎬ *Jesu pater pauperum*

359. *Luke* III, 5 quoting *Isaias* XL, 4.

370. A reference, perhaps, to the character imprinted by the Sacrament of Baptism which replaced the ceremony of circumcision.

390. *stille as any stone* Used frequently by Lydgate. Cf. Schick, *Temple of Glas,* note to 1. 689.

383. Another indication that Lydgate was writing this at the beginning of a new year.

398. An allusion, presumably, to the custom of making a small sign of the cross on the forehead. This is part of the ceremonies of Baptism also.

BOOK V

2. *Thorowe the roundenesse of the speres nyne* "Since it was deemed impossible in ancient times, that the planets could move freely in space, the theory arose of a system of planets of which each was fixed to a sphere. These spheres were concentric and fitted into one another like a series of round boxes. Each planet was fastened to its own sphere, and it followed that there should be the same number of spheres as there were heavenly bodies having different motions and periods of revolution. Plato considered the earth as resting and motionless on its axis in the centre of the universe. Then followed, in seven circles, the seven planets (the sun and moon being included). The utmost sphere, enclosing all the others, held the fixed stars." Ernest Sieper, Lydgate's *Reson and Sensuallyte* (EETSES, LXXIX, London, 1903), p. 82, for the line 276, "mevyng of the speres nyne". See also l. 551 of *Secrees of old Philosoffres;* l. 449 of *Henry VI's Triumphal Entry into London;* l. 9, *A Song of Just Mesure,* l. 85, *Exposition of the Pater Noster;* l. 102, *The Legend of St. Austin at Compton.* (Reference to Lydgate's minor poems in the notes for Book V are from H. N. MacCracken, *The Minor Poems of John Lydgate* [1911-34; EETSES, 107 and EETS, 192]).

5. *my derkenesse enlymnye* Also, *A Procession of Corpus Christi,* l. 5: *"For now þis day al derkenesse tenlymyne."*

7. *Epiphanye* See Book V, ll. 460-476 for Lydgate's explanation of the name.

8. *And lat my breste, benygne lorde, be dewede / Doun with some drope fro thy maieste* In the Prologue to the *Troy Book,* Lydgate makes a similar appeal to Calliope, mother of Orpheus: *"And of thy golde dewe lat the lycour wete / My dulled brest, that wyth thyn hony swete / Sugrest tongis of rethoricyens / And maistresse art to Musicyens"* (ll. 55-58).

11. *Oute of the Est* "Quod vero dicitur 'in Oriente,' duobus modis intelligi potest: id est: positi nos in orientali parte, vidimus stellam supra Judaeam, et intelleximus regem ibi natum; sive positi nos in quacunque regione nostra vidimus stellam in orientali parte, et intelleximus regem natum in Judaea." Remegius, *Miscellanea.* Homilia VII. Migne, *PL,* CXXXI, c. 902. And further, "Sed si nepotes Balaam fuerunt, quaerendum est quare dicat sanctus evangelista illos

venisse ab Oriente. Et sciendum quia quicunque ab illa regione venit, quae in orientali parte posita est, bene ab Oriente venire dicitur. Et ob hoc magis credendum est quod nepotes fuissent Balaam, quia regio Ammonitarum vicina erat terrae Judaeorum . . ." *ibid.* c. 901.

15.   *not causell*   The sighting of the star was not accidental or by chance.

18.   *by recorde of scripture*   Reference is to the Apocryphal Gospel of Seth from which the story of the origin of the Magi in the following lines is taken, probably by way of the *Opus Imperfectum* of Chrysostom. Joannes Chrysostomus, *Opus Imperfectum,* Migne, *PG,* LVI, 637 ff.

19.   *besy cure* (see also *Book V,* 678; *Book VI,* 181). Common Lydgate phrase: *Troy-Book,* Book V, 1. 183; *Reson and Sensualyte,* ll. 955, 2236.

      Lydgate used the word *"besy"* often as an adjective or adverb. *"bysy payne:" Book VI,* ll. 97, 247; *Troy-Book,* Book IV, 1. 201; *Reson and Sensuallyte,* ll. 177, 511; *bysely: Book V,* 1. 158.

24.   *olde Balaam*   ". . . Balaam the son of Beor, a soothsayer, who dwelt by the river of the land of the children of Ammon . . ." *Numbers* 22:5, *The Holy Bible* (Vulgate).

25.   *with his asse werre*   The angel moves the tongue of the ass to utter words of rebuke against the brutal fury and folly of Balaam. *Numbers* 22:28-30. The ass, who saw the angel on the road, refused to walk over him and Balaam, who did not see the angel, had been angered.

26–27.   *ther shulde ryse a sterre*   "A star shall rise out of Jacob and a sceptre shall spring up from Israel . . ." *Numbers* 24:17.

28.   *no tyme he couthe tell*   The time of the coming of the star was not revealed to Balaam.

31–51.   *Werne xij. chose*   "Itaque elegerunt seipso duodecim quidam ex ipsis studiosiores, & amatores mysteriorum caelestium, & posuerunt seipsos ad exspectationem stellas illius. Et si quis moriebatur ex eis, filius ejus, aut aliquis propinquorum, qui ejusdem voluntatis inveniebatur, in loco constituebatur defuncti." *Opus Imperfectum,* c. 637.

52.   *As phebus went by meovyng circuler*   See note to line 2.

54.   *certeyne dayes thre*   I have not been able to discover the source of this statement. The *Opus Imperfectum* simply says the Magi went to the mountain every year "post messem trituratoriam", that is, after the

harvesting of the grain. I must admit the same for lines 55-56: *By calkyng cast and computacion / Sowght and chosen ougt by good eleccioun.*

59.   *Whiche Balaam sayde sholde avoyde her sorrowe*   Probably refers to the remainder of Balaam's prophecy of the star: "A star shall rise out of Jacob and a sceptre shall spring up from Israel. . . . and he shall possess Idumea: the inheritance of Seir shall come to their enemies, but Israel shall do manfully." *Numbers* 24:17-18, *The Holy Bible* (Vulgate).

86.   *Towarde the hill liche as bokeg tell*   Lydgate's source: the *Opus Imperfectum,* most likely.

102.   *right as any lyne*   A very common expression in Lydgate. See Sieper, *op. cit.,* p. 67.

168.   See also *Cristes Passion,* 1.107: *"A swerd of sorwe sholde perce to the herte."*

175f.   *The worme abit as serpent vndre floures / Daryth full ofte and kepyth hym couertly.* Here Lydgate uses one of his favorite figures of speech. See Professor Sieper's note, *op. cit.,* p. 119.

183.   *Right so thou serpent of Iniquite*   J. Schick, *Lydgate's Temple of Glas* (London, 1891, EETSES, LX), p. 82, points out that Lydgate frequently uses the term "serpent" when speaking of the vices. I give his list and others: serpent of Ielousie *(Temple of Glas, Reson and Sensualyte, Fall of Princes);* a fals serpent, callyd Ignoraunce, The olde serpent hadde at hym enuye, *(St. Edmund);* The olde serpent, which is called in Sathan *(St. Margaret)*; The olde Serpent, he levyathan *(The Siege of Thebes)*; serpent of doubleness *(Fall of Princes)*; serpent of discorde, þe olde serpent, þat is lowe felle, þe vile serpent, he Leuysthan *(Troy-Book)*; serpent of foryethfulnesse *(Troy-Book)*; serpent of newfanglenes, the false serpent of discencion, serpent of high presumpcion, serpent of enuy *(Fall of Princes). Serpent of Division,* is the title of one of Lydgate's works.

184.   *Fals tygre full of doublenesse*   Sieper, *op. cit.,* p. 132, gives the origin of the story of the deception practiced on tigresses to lure away their young by use of mirrors. The story of the tiger also appears in *The Siege of Thebes,* ll. 3839-3846. See also *Troy-Book,* Book I, l. 217. The use of the adjective "fals" appears to be another Lydgate favorite: fals lust, false serpent of discencion *(Fall of*

Princes); fals serpent, callyd Ignoraunce (*St. Edmund*); false hatrede, false treason, falsly of malice (*Fall of Princes*).

191.   *What can sugur vndur galle faine?* "The sweetness of false delight ending in bitterness is a favourite theme of Lydgate and contemporaneous writers," writes Sieper, *op. cit.*, p. 112. See *Reson and Sensuallyte,* ll. 3363-69, *Troy-Book,* Prologue, l. 277, *The Pilgrimage of the Life of Man,* l. 14387, *Secrees,* l. 677, *The Order of Fools,* l. 30.

222.   *To worthe doun in a lytyll space*   Possibly Venerable Bede's "et cadentes in pavimento terrae", *Chronicon Antiquissimum* Migne, *PL,* XLIV, c. 1166.

237–238.   *For of that land whanne kyngis present make/The custome is suche yeftez for to take*   The *Legenda Aurea* (ed. Th. Graesse 2 ed. Leipzig, 1876), p. 93: "Prime, quoniam traditio antiquorum fuit, ut dicit Remigius, ut nullus ad Deum vel ad regem vacans introierit Persae autem et Chaldei talia munera consueverant offere." But Remegius in the source cited actually had an added concept: "quia isti verum regem et verum Dominum existimaverunt, ideo non vacui venerunt," *op. cit.,* c. 906.

337–338.   One of Lydgate's favorite salutations to Our Lady. Also in *A Prayer to Mary in whom is Affiaunce,* l. 2: "*Lady of this world, of helle eeke emperesse*"; *The Fyfftene Ioyes of Oure Lady,* l. 29: "*O qwene of heven, of helle eke Emparesse!*"; *To Mary, Queen of Heaven,* l. 1: "*Queen of heuene, of helle eeke emperesse.*"

342–343.   Like phraseology in *Fabula Duorum Mercatorum,* l. 548f.: "*Wher is the clarioun of thy cry and boost/That to (the) skyes my fame did beede*"; *Misericordias Domini,* l. 38: "*With boosty blowe in charys cleer*"; *The Legend of St. Austin at Compton,* l. 191: "*What maner boost that ony man list blowe.*"

347.   *axtre*   The earth's axis. Also "axeltre", as in Book II, 759. In the Troy-Book, Book IV, l. 627ff., Lydgate makes a tongue-in-cheek observation about the axetree which is a rare instance of humor in his writings (Chaucer makes the same joke in *Franklin's Tale* V. 1018 and *Troilus and Criseyde* ii, 904-905):

> *Til Phebus char lowe gan declyne*
> *His golden axtre, þat so cler doth shyne,*
> *—þis is to seyne, þe sonne wente doun—*

348.   *golden cheyne*   Because of his familiarity with Homer, it may be presumed that the reference here is to the *Iliad,* Book VIII, 19:

"Fasten ye a rope of gold from heaven, and all ye gods lay hold thereof and all goddesses." [S. H. Butcher and Andrew Lang, *The Complete Works of Homer.* (Modern Library Edition) p. 130] "The so-called 'aurea catena Homerii' was frequently employed in the emanistic system of late Antiquity and their descendents" (Ernst Robert Curtius, *European Literature and the Latin Middle Ages.* Translated from the German by Willard R. Track, N. Y. 1953, p. 110). See also l. 14 of *Gloucester's Approaching Marriage* and l. 116 of *Henry VI's Triumphal Entry into London.* (See also Chaucer, *Knight's Tale,* 2987-2992).

351. *O pompe elate* "A favorite combination of Lydgate's" (Erdman, Axel, and Ekwall, Eilert, *Lydgate's Siege of Thebes* (London, 1930, EETSES, CXXV), p. 109. The authors refer to *The Siege of Thebes,* l. 3530, *St. Giles,* l. 172, and *Troy-Book,* I, 3110.

358–362. See also *Troy-Book,* Book II, 713-716: *"Wevers also of wolne & of lyne / Of cloth of gold, damaske, and satyn, / Of welwet, cendel, & double samyt eke / And euery clothe þat men list to seke".*

363. *tappyteȝ* Professor Sieper, *op. cit.,* p. 110, says "the word is not frequent". He cites lines 2766 of *Reson and Sensualyte* and I, 1 A iv b. of *Fall of Princes.* In the *Fabula Duorum Mercatorum,* l. 194, is the line: *"Her ioiful somer is tapited al in greene."* Also, *The Complaint of the Black Knight,* l. 51.

369. *any chaumbreȝ of a ray* Probably should read "array", which would mean a richly furnished room. "Ray" as a single word means "Striped cloth". See Locock, Katherine, *The Pilgrimage of the Life of Man* (London, 1904, EETS, XCII), p. 678, for a discussion of the latter meaning of this word.

408–410. *Isoude, Elyn, and eke polixene / Hester also and dydo with her chere / And Riche Candace, of ethyope quene* Lydgate lists several outstanding beauties of the past to illustrate the passing of fine raiment and vanity: Iseult, the Celtic beauty, Helen of Troy, Polyxena of Troy, Esther, the Jewish queen, Dido of Carthage and Candace, the queen of Ethiopia. Professor Schick, *op. cit.,* p. 82, is reminded of Candace, the queen of Ethiopians, whose eunuch Philip baptized (see *Acts of the Apostles,* 8:27). In Book II, 302ff., see a longer listing. For further examples of this favorite device of Lydgate's, see the accounts of beauties in: *A Ballade of her that hath all virtues,* ll. 8-28; *The Floure of Curtesye,* ll. 190-217; *A Valentine,* ll. 22-68; *Temple of Glas,* ll. 64-128; *A Lover's New Year's Gift,* ll. 33-42;

On Gloucester's Approaching Marriage, ll. 71-84; *Horns Away,* ll. 25-29; *That now is Hay some-tyme was Grase,* ll. 49-51; *Timor Mortis Conturbat Me,* ll. 81-88; *A Wicked Tunge wille Sey Amys,* ll. 106-119. Lydgate's model probably is Chaucer's 'Balade' in the Prologue to the *Legend of Good Women.*

411. *Ligge þei not graue vndre clowris grene?* Webster's *New International Dictionary* lists *clowre,* n., grassy ground; sod. *Obs.* NED lists *clowre.* Obs. Also *clour, clower.* Surface of the ground, grassy ground, sward, turf.

The entire line is the H⁷ substitution for D. The substitution was made because D alone has "Ben" and all other mss. have variant spellings for the first word of the line, i.e. *lie.* The mss. which have some form of "colors" number 17 and are as follows; D, B³, B⁴, H³, H⁴, H⁵, H⁶, H⁸, C¹, C⁵, Ad², Ad³, Hu, L, An, Lg, Ch. The following have "floures": B⁵, CC, C², Co. The following have "clotes": H², Adv². The following have "turfs": Ash¹, C³. The following have "clowris": B¹, B², H¹, H⁷, J, Hu, V. The variants number 15. This lack of a clear majority for "colors" and the use of the word in *The Order of Fools,* l. 52: *"For a goselyng that greseth bareyn clours,"* and *Secrees of old Philosoffres,* l. 1341: *"hath spred his bawme on bankys & on clours,"* prompted the retention of the entire H⁷ line.

436. *. . . the gospell tellyth vs*   Matthew 2 :12.

493. *And like a dove with fayre feders white*   Probably the symbol most frequently used of the Third Person of the Trinity.

515. *And of tarage inly gode and fyne*   Professor Sieper, *op. cit.,* pp. 117-118, writes that the word is Old French *terrage, tarrage, tarage* and is found in *Reson* and *Sensualyte, Secress, Pilgrimage of the Life of Man, Chorle and Bird, Tretis of the Kynges Coronacion, Troy-Book* and *Fall of Princes,* and gives its meaning as "kind or quality and in some instances, flavor."

516. *archideclyne Master of the feast.*   From the Greek word αρχι, chief, and τρικλίνος, a dining-room. The Greek word was carried over into the Latin translation of St. John's gospel. The word also occurs in l. 3589 of Lydgate's *The Pilgrimage of the Life of Man;* l. 312 of *Henry VI's Triumphal Entry into London;* l. 128 of *The Fyfftene Ioyes of Oure Lady* and ll. 107, 120 of *The Fifteen Joys and Sorrows of Mary.*

552.   *fomen*   Literally, foes in war, here, the vices of malice and pride.

573.   *darkyd with a skye*   Same figure used in Letabundus, l. 168: *"Of worldly trouble voyde every troubly skye."*

574.   *That we in Englisshe calle flatereye*   The word Lydgate has translated may be the French *papelardie,* a flattering parasite, a sycophant; hypocrite. Also *attrib.* or as *adj.,* hypocritical (*Oxford English Dictionary,* Oxford, 1933). Lydgate seems to use the word to mean flattery, hypocrisy and treachery interchangeably (see *Book V,* ll. 575-581). It appears in *The Pilgrimage of the Life of Man,* l. 13921f.: *"The forthe corde callyd 'Papyllardie' / Wych ys a maner of ypocrysie,"* and the interchangeability of terms seems clear in *Exposition of the Pater Noster,* l. 262f.: *"Ipocrysie, fraude, compassed guyle / Symylacioun, and flattery put in press."*

588.   *trwe hert*   Lydgate commonly used "hert" with an adjective: *"hole hert:"* Book VI, l. 198; *Reson and Sensuallyte,* l. 178.

   "hert hole and entere:" *Legend of Seynt Margarete,* l. 446, *Reson and Sensuallyte,* l. 873.

   "devout hert:" *Legend of Seynt Margarete,* l. 531; *The Legend of St. Austin at Compton,* l. 399.

   "glad herte": *The Legend of St. Austin at Compton,* l. 62; *"feythful herte:"* *Troy-Book,* Book V, l. 3461.

   "heuy hertes:" *The Testament,* l. 12.

594–595.   *For soden dom meynt with ignorance / Hathe a long tayle sewyng of repentaunce.* From the preceding lines, I gathered that this involved sentence was intended to mean that quick decisions made without knowledge are repented for a long time afterwards.

622.   *sterri see*   Literally, a "see" is a seat, especially a throne. The reference here is to the Catholic doctrine that Our Lady is Queen of Heaven. Lydgate used a like terminology in speaking of Christ's Ascension into heaven in *Gloriosa Dicta Sunt De Te,* l. 206: *"After ascende to his hevenly see".* See also *Benedictus Deus,* l. 46: *"Iesabell prowd was cast down from hir see"; Reson and Sensuallyte,* ll. 1294ff: *". . . Satourne / . . . / Out of his myghty Royal Se."*

625.   *Sithe thou of Iacob art the right scale.* The reference is to Jacob's ladder (scale): "And he (Jacob) saw in his sleep a ladder standing upon the earth, and the top thereof touching heaven: the angels also of God ascending and descending by it." (*Genesis* 28:12, Vulgate).

645. *trwe affection* "Affection", preceded by an adjective is very common in Lydgate:

"*trwe affection:*" *The Virtues of the Mass,* 1. 428; *The Legend of St. Gyle,* 1. 263; *A Seying of the Nightingale,* 1. 30.

"*hole affection:*" *The Virtues of the Mass,* ll. 10, 252, 316, 394; *Exposition of the Pater Noster,* 1. 326; *The Fifteen Ooes of Christ,* 1. 68, 204; *A Prayer to St. Leonard,* 1. 7; *To Ositha,* 1. 10; *Troy-Book,* Book IV, ll. 272, 298; *Reson and Sensualyte,* 1. 4842.

"*humble affecyoun:*" *A Prayer upon the Cross,* 1. 34; *The Fifteen Joys and Sorrows of Mary,* 1. 303; *To St. Thomas* (II), 1. 117; *The Legend of Seynt Margarete,* ll. 442, 494.

"*gret affecioun:*" *A Valentine,* 1. 4; *The Legend of St. Gyle,* 1. 274; *The Legend of St. Austin at Compton,* 1. 373.

666. *so narowe a dongeon.* A room, dwelling place. See also Lydgate's *A Sayenge of the Nightingale,* 1. 33; "*On dyamaundes sette is* the Dungeoun."

700. *lode sterre* A star that leads, guiding star. See also *The Pilgrimage of the Life of Man,* 16679, 16956; *To Mary, the Queen of Heaven,* 1. 2; *Stella Celi Extirpuit,* 1. 1; *The Testament,* 1. 93.

BOOK VI

1. Common Lydgate combination: the "Lenvoie" to the *Troy-Book,* 1. 18: "*And euermore with laude, honor & glorie*"; *The Legend of Dan Joos,* 1. 92: "*Lawde, honour, pryce and hygh reuerence*"; *An Epistle to Sibille,* 1. 110: "*She gat hir price, lawde and gret honour.*" (References to Lydgate's minor poems in the notes for Book VI are from H. N. MacCracken, *The Minor Poems of John Lydgate* [1911-34; EETSES, 107 and EETS, 192]).

2. *blisful* (also Book V, 618, 670). Professor Schick, *op. cit.,* p. 94, writes that the word "blisful" is a common epithet for Venus. However, Lydgate also uses it of Our Lady in 1. 65, *A Commendation of Our Lady,* 1. 33 of *Stella Celi Apparuit,* and four times in his adaptation of St. Bernard's prayer in *The Pilgrimage of the Life of Man,* ll. 16285-16361. Chaucer also used it in his *ABC Prayer to the Virgin,* 1. 24. In Book VI. 141, Lydgate also addresses the word to God: "*O blisfull lorde.*" In *To St. Anne,* 1. 65, is found "*O blissful sugre-canne!*"

3. *the cheve chaste toure* In the Litany of the Blessed Virgin Mary, two of the invocations addressed to Our Lady are "tower of David"

and "tower of ivory". The first has its origin in the *Canticle of Canticles* 4:4, "Thy neck is as the tower of David, which is built with bulwarks; a thousand bucklers hang upon it, all the armor of valiant men." The second is also from the *Canticle,* "Thy neck as a tower of ivory" (7:4). The original tower of David symbolized strength and survived even the destruction of Jerusalem. Although there was no material prototype for the tower of ivory, the ancients held ivory as a symbol of purity. Remegius in commenting on the phrase "a domibus eburneis" of *Psalm* 44:9, wrote, "Nam in eis habitat etiam Dominus et dicuntur eburneae domus propter castitatem et sermonis nitorem. Nam elephas cujus ossa ebur sunt castissimum animal dicitur", *op. cit.,* p. 380.

8. *That neuere brennyng of no flesshely hete*   Our Lady was free from all temptations of the flesh.

28. *Touchyng*   "The word touching occurs very frequently in Lydgate's translations; it is, of course, the equivalent of the French *quant à*; as an easy way of getting started it is often to be found at the beginning of a chapter", Sieper, *op. cit.,* p. 86.

30. *And haue a childe by medelyng hem betwene*   To conceive by sexual intercourse.

59. *That bare her childe wtihoute manys seede*   Our Lady's child was not conceived through the agency of a man but by the power of the Holy Ghost.

69–70. *In hir childyng no more thorugh grace broke/At hir conceyvyng than it was vnloke.* Our Lady's virginity was kept perfectly preserved both in the conception and the birth of her Child.

71. *For nature withoutyn any stryfe*   Our Lady experienced no pains of childbirth. See Lydgate's *Gaude Virgo Mater Christi,* l. 9ff.: *"whiche has chylded with-outen soore or peyne/With þe lylye of mooste pure chastytee/Of all mankynde þe trouble to restreyne."*

75. *prerogatyffe* In *The Pilgrimage of the Life of Man* l. 16405, Lydgate uses the word again of Our Lady: *"thow art devoyde by a singuler prerogatyff, from alle unclennesse off synne"* and l. 102 of *Ave, Jesse Virgula!: "To-forn alle women plus preuilegiata."*

129–130. *Not of levi as ye haue herde to forn/But of Iuda comyng by lynage* An example of Lydgate's involved syntax in which he intends to say that Simeon had a revelation that Our Lady, because of the Virgin Birth, is not literally bound to the law of Leviticus for first-born males and at the same time that the holy man had also been told that the Child was of the line of Juda.

215–217.   In *A Commendacion of Our Lady,* ll. 78-79, Lydgate expresses the identical sentiment of Our Lady:

> *O trusty turtle, trewest of al trewe,*
> *O curtesye columbe, replete of al mekenesse*

223–308.   The patristic and medieval writers made wide use of natural history to illustrate theological principles and "in patristic circles the knowledge of the animal kingdom came to be represented by the curious book called the 'Physiologus'" [Taylor, Henry Osborn, *The Medieval Mind.* 2v. (N. Y. 1927), vol. 1, p. 76].

Lydgate made use of the habits of the turtle and the dove to compose a homily for his description of the feast of the Purification. The Latin stanza, ll. 295-301, which seems to be the poet's basis for the treatment of the turtle and the dove was part of a song known familiarly in the Middle Ages. The author of the *Speculum Naturale Vincentii* (microfilm of Incunabula No. 59 (1494), Library of Catholic University of America), C. LIII, c. 199, after quoting from Isodore's *Etymologia,* refers to lines 299ff: "Glos(s)a super cantica primo capitulo: Columba felle varet: rostro non ledit: in cavernia petrarum nidificat: alienos pullos nutrit iuxta fluenta manet. Meliora grana elegit: per cantu gemitum reddit: gregatim volat: alis se defendit: visum recuperat."

In *An Old English Miscellany* (EETS, 49, ed. Rev. Richard Morris, LL.D., the Arundel MS. 292), "A Bestiary", contains the "Natura turturis" and Natura columbe et significatio", as well as the Harleian MS. 3093 "Incipit Liber Fisiologus a Thetabaldo Italico Compositus" from which the Old English bestiary is translated and further illustrates the antiquity of the allegory in English literature.

229–231.   *And as the birde sheweth the commyng / Of grene ver* . . . See the Latin lines 295-6: Alta petit Turtur cantando gemit veniens ver / Nunciat . . .

211–301.   The twelfth-century Alexander Neckam in his *De Naturis Rerum* (London, 1863), edited by Thomas Wright, evidently knew the Latin stanza used in the *Life of Our Lady* (Book VI, 295-301) for he quotes whole phrases from it. In *Cap.* LVI, (page 106), he writes:

De columba

Columbae proprietates Sacra Scriptura variis in locis latissime prosequitur. Unde et tanto brevius eas tangere libet, quanto diffusius ab aliis explicantur. Columba siquidem gemitum habet pro cantu, sanctae ecclesiae vel etiam cujuscunque fidelis animae typum gerens. In hac namque valle lacrimarum gemere debemus, ut ad locum exultationis veniamus. Non vesitur cadavere, sed purissimum granum eligit. Sic et sancta ecclesia grano illo vescitur de quo scriptum est, "Nisi granum frumenti cadens in terra mortuum fuerit, ipsum solum manet," Nec cadaveribus voluptatum foetentium sacrosancta allicitur ecclesia, sed reficitur deliciis spiritualibus. Felle carere dicitur; sic et amaritudinis fraterni odii ignara est ecclesiae caritas. In grege volat, unde per eam designatur grex fidelium in societate spirituali degentium, sicut per turtures nonnunquam solitarii designantur. Super aquarum fluenta residet, et acciptris effugiat insidias. Sic et fidelis anima Sacra Scriptura quasi speculo utitur, ut tuta sit a circuitu hostis antiqui. Sicut etiam columba in vulneribus Jesu Christi meditatur et quiescit . . .

Sed quid est quod columbae felle carere perhibentur, cum inter se dira usque ad sanguinis effusionem ineant certamina? Placet nonnullis non mediocriter in naturis rerum instructis, fel per corpus ipsarum diffundi adeo ut caro ipsa amaritudine quadam respersa sit, aut certe delicioso sapore destituta . . .

Cap. LIX (page 108)

De turture.

Etiam vulgo notum est turturem et amoris veri praerogativa nobilitari et castitatis tutulis donari. Mortuo igitur compare suo, viroris aspernatur delicias. Quasi ergo unum par turturum sunt anima casta et hospes ejus, corpus loquor. Cum itaque corpus mundo est mortuum, adeo ut idem habitus religionis susceptae protestetur, non interest animae curiositatibus mundanae gloriae capi seu delectari.

234. *But life sool whan he hathe lost his make.* The resemblance to 1. 835 of Chaucer's "Merchant's Tale" is startling: *"Soul as the turtil that lost hath hir make."* The Latin line in Lydgate is 296: *". . . et caste viuit solusque moratur."* The turtle's widowhood was celebrated

in earlier literature. St. Gregory Nazianzen, *Carmen Liber I Theologica* (Migne, Paris, 1862), *PG*, XXXVIII, p. 619, wrote:

> *Audio quod alata turtur, turture dilecto*
> *Viduata, conjugem suum casta lugens*
> *Non admittit alium maritum suum supra nidum*

Lauchert, F., *Geschichte des Physiologus* (Strassburg, 1889), p. 259 (translated from the Greek): "I have heard and learned this of turtledoves and pigeons. The physiologus said that the turtle dove is very talkative but when it loses its mate, it recalls and pines away for it and does not lie with another." Alanus de Insultis, *De Planctu Naturae, Migne, PL,* CCX, c. 436: "turtur suo viduata consorte, amorum epilogare dedignans, bigamiae refutabat solatia." See Professor Sieper, *op. cit.,* p. 131-132, for additional literary analogues. See also the quotations from Fulgentius and Bede in the section on the sources of Book V, p. 173.

In *Reson and Sensuallyte,* Lydgate uses the same material to celebrate perpetual conjugal fidelity:

> *And as a turtil from her make*
> *Departeth by no maner weye*
> *In-to the tyme that he deye,*
> *Far wel al Ioy and lustyhede.*
> *Fare wel myrthe and al solace,*
> *For solytary in euery place*
> *The turtul playneth euer in woo*
> *That hir make ys thus agoo,*
> *And lyst nat for his peynes kene*
> *To resten in weyes grene,*
> *Nor on trees but bareyn*
> *For the constreynt of hir peyn:*
>
> (ll. 6860-6872)

237. *On noo caren of no flesshely hede* This line refers to the Turtle in the Latin, line 297: *morticinium quoque fugit.* The line (246): *On eny caryne to fostre hym or fede* refers to the dove which Lydgate make clear enough in his homily but which he omitted to distinguish in making the Latin quotation.

242-243. *And þat he fle not oute of companye / Wantinge also the galle of enuye* See the Latin line 299: *Felle caret plangit socium.*

249–251. *And with the dove sighen and compleyne / For his offence, and with wynges tweyne, / Take his flight as fer-furthe as he can*   These lines may be based on *Ezechiel* 7:16, ". . . and they shall be in the mountains like doves of the valleys, all of them trembling, every one for his iniquity."

253–254. *And as the dove touchithe eke her make / Only with kyssyng whan thay to gydre gone*   The Latin line is 299, *per oscula tangit*, but Lydgate must have had a fuller source. *The Speculum Naturale Vincentii, op. cit.*, c. 199, has "eo quod nidos suos frequentent et osculo amorem concipiant". See also St. Isidore, *Etymologia* (Migne, Paris, 1850), *PL*, LXXXII, c. 467; "Columbae . . . osculo amorem concipiant."

257. *And like a dove make his nest of stone*   Although the basis for this line is undoubtedly line 300; *Petra dat huic nidum,* the ultimate sources may be biblical: *Jeremias* 48:28: "Leave the cities, and dwell in the rock, you that dwell in Moab; and be ye like the dove that maketh her nest in the mouth of the hole in the highest place", and *Canticles* 2:14: "My dove in the clefts of the rock, in the hollow places in the wall . . ."

261–263. *Of kynde espyeth a-myddes the Ryuere,* etc.   The Latin line 300: *fugit hostem in flumine visum.*

310. See also *Guy of Warwick,* l. 14: *"But he, allas! flouryng in hys myght."*

316. *To februa of olde fundacion*   An interesting sidelight is the similarity of the description of the temple of Februa in lines 316-338 and the description of the temple of Venus in Lydgate's *Troy-Book,* Book II, 3435ff.

320. *at eche lustre*   A purification of the people at the quinquennial census; a period of five years.

344. *But at the laste Pope Sergius*   "Pope Sergius I (687-701) introduced a procession for this day. The Gregorianum (tradition of the eighth century) does not speak of this procession, which fact proves that the procession of Sergius was the ordinary "station", not the liturgical act of the day. The feast was certainly not introduced by Pope Gelasius to suppress the excesses of the Lupercalia . . . The blessing of the candles did not enter into common use before the eleventh century; it has nothing in common with the procession of the Lupercalia". *The Catholic Encyclopedia.* (New York, 1908), III, 246.

425.   *Fare well his gwerdon, his meryte and his mede*   Compare *The Temple of Glas*: *"And siþ ʒe haue þe guerdon & þe mede"* (1. 806).

446.   *Seuene chaundeleris alle of pure golde* "And I turned to see the voice that spoke with me. And being turned, I saw seven golden candlesticks: and in the midst of the seven golden candlesticks, one like to the Son of Man, clothed with a garment down to the feet, and girt about the paps with a golden girdle." *Apocalypse* 1:12-13 (Vulgate).

450.   *while that we ben here*   Also in *The Virtues of the Mass,* 1. 529: *"whyle we byn here."*

451–452.   Phebus, the sun, was thought to circle the earth once a day.

> *Which also fer as Phebus in compas*
> *A natural day goth is cercle aboute.*
>   (*Troy-Book,* Book II, 1. 238f.)

Lydgate frequently speaks of the course of Phebus and in a variety of ways. *"His chare of golde his course so swiftly ran",* The Complaint of the Black Knight, 1. 595; *"The goldene chaar of Phebus in the hayr",* A Mydsomer Rose, 1. 49; *"Goldyne Phebus feyre in chare shyninge",* A Freond at Neode, 1. 4; *"And Phebus was ascendyng in his spere",* Troy-Book, Book I, 1. 3911; *"which also fer as Phebus in compas / A natural day goth is cercle about,"* Troy-Book Book II, 238f; *The hour whan he* (Phebus) *made his stedis drawe / His rosen chariet lowe vnder the wawes",* Troy-Book, Prologue, 127f.

459.   *a sely asse*   Unfortunate, pitiful. Lydgate used the word in this sense also in the first Nightingale poem, 1. 151: *"Oo sely appell, so eten of a tre!",* and in *The Pain and Sorrow of Evil Marriage,* 1. 84.

461.   *To thy seruantez shelde and socoure be / To kepe and save from all aduersyte*   A favorite Lydgate invocation: *"To save thy servauntis from all aduersite",* 1. 82, *The Fifteen Joys and Sorrows of Mary; "Of folk þat languissh in tribulacioun / Preserue and keep from al aduersitee";* 1. 23, *To Mary, the Queen of Heaven.*

8. Glossary

(**Abbreviations**: *a.,* adjective; *adv.,* adverb; *adv. phr.,* adverbial phrase; *conj.,* conjunction; *fig.,* in a figurative sense; *impers.,* impersonal; *NED,* New English Dictionary; *pers.,* personal; *pl.,* plural; *ppl.,* participle; *ppl. a.,* participial adjective; *prep.,* preposition; *pr. ppl.,* present participle; *pt. ppl.,* past participle; *sb.,* substantive; *sb. pl.,* substantive plural; *s. v.,* sub voce, 'under the word'; *transf.,* in a transferred sense; *v. intr.,* intransitive verb; *v. refl.,* reflexive verb; *vbl. sb.,* verbal substantive; *v. tr.,* transitive verb)

a-bake, *adv.,* aback, back, in retreat, IV 393

abave, *v. refl.,* to be disconcerted, disturbed, apprehensive, IV 257

abit, abyde, *v. intr.,* 3rd pres. and pret., wait for, V 111, 175; VI 81

abode, *sb.,* delay, III 1207; "**witheoute a-bood:**" *prep.,* without and abode, without delay, immediately, V 433

abrayde, breyde, *v. intr.,* to break forth abruptly into speech, or simply to begin to speak, to start, to awaken out of unconsciousness, I 139; II 1116, 1278; III 182, 1442; VI 139

abroche, *v. tr.,* to pierce, to let the contents out, "abroche a tonne", to pierce the cask, to make (as of the truth) to flow, II 1471; *adv.,* in the phrase, "**to set abroche**", to tap, to make flow, III 1694

abusion, *adv.,* injustice, outrage, injury, wrong, IV 235

abyte, *sb.,* habit, dress, VI 180

acesse, *sb.,* attack of fever, III 748, 755, 763

acomptyng, *vbl.,* calculation, computation, IV 13

adaweth, *v. tr.,* to abate, clear up, brighten, I 28

adewe, *v. tr.,* to moisten, bedewe, II 632, 1778

adu(v)ertence, *sb.,* observation, notice, attention, consideration, III 389; V 590

affrayed, *pt. ppl.,* disturbed, frightened, V 563

agrysyde, *pt. ppl.,* to be full of horror, greatly afraid, shudder, tremble with fear, II 379

alayede, *ppl. a.,* mixed, debased, modified, V 561

algates, *adv.,* at all events, at any rate, in any case, V 168

allegede, *ppl. a.,* cited, quoted, III 1429

alleggeaunce, *sb.,* (from "allegen," v., to relieve), alleviation, lightening, relief, II 4

alth(þ)er, *gen. pl.* of all (O. E. *ealra*) of all. Used in combination (usually prefixed with superlatives, II 782; III 548, 637, 704, 767; IV 75, 101, 111, 113

alye, *sb.,* kinship, lineage, II 183; III 726; V 49

ambiguyte, *sb.,* uncertainty, doubt, hesitation, II 912, 1412

ameen (Ameyn), *sb.* one who acts as mediator, "go between", an ambassador, intercesor, II 38, 271, 336

ancyll, *sb.,* a maid-servant or handmaid (L. *ancilla;* O. Fr. *ancelle, ancele*), I 345

a-noon, *adv.,* at once, quickly, anon, V 99, 110, 143, 149, 203, 220; VI 95

aparence, *sb.,* manifestation, disclosure, semblance, V 642

apeche, *v. tr.,* to cast a slur upon, to inform against, II 1138

aquarye, *sb.,* one of the zodiacal constellations, giving its name to the eleventh sign of the zodiac, which the sun enters on the 21st of January, V 33

aquys grene, *sb.,* Aachen, Aix-la-Chapelle; from the Latin *Aquis Granae,* IV 127

archideclyne, *sb.,* the president or ruler of a feast, V 516

armonye, *sb.,* music, tuneful sound, harmony, II 980, 1003

aryse, *pt. ppl.,* having risen above the horizon; *transf.,* of the day, morning, V 78

a-sault, (assaut,), *sb.,* attack, assault, III 1085; IV 186; VI 323

as(s)pye, *v. tr.,* espy, observe, V 13, 576

assurede, *ppl. a.,* made safe, secured; safe, secure, VI 6

astert(e), *v. tr.,* to escape (an uncontrolled word from the lips, a gesture, etc.), I 424; II 1010; *v. intr.,* escape, V. 605

astonyed, *pt. ppl.* and *ppl. a.,* amazed, astonished, III 211; V 83, 132, 660

aswagethe, *v. tr.,* softens, calms, allays (excited feelings), V 681

asyse, *sb.,* mode, manner, quality, III 1082

atame, *v. tr.,* undertake, venture, meddle with, III 45, 112, 1433; IV 223; V 412; VI 308

at ones (at-onys), *adv.,* at once, immediately, III 529, 610, 794, 1391, 1677; V 179

Attropos, *sb.,* one of the three Fates (see note to line III 863, p. 697).

auctor, *sb.,* altar, III 1210. Otherwise the word has the usual meaning of "author".

auctorysede, *ppl. a.,* confirmed, vouched for, authorized, III 1464

in audience, *adv. phr.,* so that all may hear, publicly, VI 162

ava(y)le, avalede, *v. tr.,* to put down, put away, abase, humble; *v. intr.,* to be of benefit, have effect; II 1030; III 234, 755, 932, 1117, 1214, 1349, 1665

avaunce, *v. tr.,* to further, promote, help, I 377

aventure, *sb.,* event, fortune, prodigy, III 438, 1085; V 16; VI 182

averred, *sb.,* see "verre".

avoyde, *v. tr.,* to get rid of, clear away, do away with, V 59

avyse, *sb.,* consideration, reflection, deliberation, V 299

avysement, *sb.,* thought, thinking, consideration, reflection, VI 319

avysenesse, *sb.,* advisedness, prudent consideration, caution, I 403; VI 158

awaytyng, *pr. ppl.,* waiting upon (as a servant or attendant), V 671

axeltre, *sb.,* the axis of the earth; *fig.,* the golden axtree of the sun, II 759

axtre, *sb.,* axis, V 347

ayre, *sb.,* heir, III 1009. Otherwise the usual meaning is "air".

bandon, *sb.,* jurisdiction, authority, control, dominion, II 59

barme, *sb.,* bosom, lap, III 846

barnacle, *sb.,* (O. F. *bernaque;* med. L., *bernaca, berneka*). A species of wild goose, II 876

bav(w)me, *sb.,* balm, soothing liquid, sap of the vines of Engaddi, III 234, 736, 1250, 1276

behotyth (behothest), behight, *v. tr.* and *intr.,* to vow, promise, I 552; II 160

bet, *adv.,* better, III 1626

betyde, *v. intr.,* to happen, occur, III 289

bewrye, *v. tr.,* to reveal, betray, divulge, II 1134

blyf(v)e, *adv.,* with speed, with haste, eagerly, quickly, immedately II 1250; III 762; IV 113

bolyng, *vbl. sb.,* boiling; *fig.,* passion, IV 228

bonche, *v. tr.,* to strike, beat, thump, II 1577

bonde, *sb.,* slave, bondsman, IV 241. Otherwise it has the usual meaning of "bond".

boote, *sb.,* remedy, relief, welfare, III 704

bornede, *ppl. a.,* burnished, polished, shining, III 1022

boste, *sb.,* proud, or vain-glorious speech; vaunt, brag; V 342

boteler, *sb.,* steward, cellarer, butler, III 1711

bourne, *sb.,* bower, chamber, III 789

boyled, *pt. pl.,* inflamed; said of passions, persons under the influence of the passions, II 416

brede, *sb.,* breadth; in the phrase **"all aboute in brede"**: in every direction, III 1664

burgh, *sb.,* borough, small municipality, III 25

burgeon (burion), *sb.,* a bud, sprout, III 947, 964, 998, 1502

buryovne, (burioun), *v. tr.* and *intr.,* to bud forth, germinate, III 637, 1101

byfrons, *a.,* two-fronted, two-faced, (Lat. *bifrons*), said of the god Janus, IV 1

byleve, *sb.,* credibility, faith, belief, IV 311; V 29

by loke, *ppl. a.,* locked in, incarcerated, III 342

byrafte, *ppl. a.,* snatched away, bereft, III 1620

byrell, *sb.,* crystal, glass, III 1019

by-ryve, *v. tr.,* tear, rend, lacerate, V 555

caas, *sb.,* case, instance, situation, III 1350

calkyng, *vbl. sb.,* calculation, V 55

cancre, *v. tr.,* to eat into as a cancer (O. E. *cancer, cancor;* Nor. F. *cancre*), II 923

cancred, *pt. pl.,* cankered, ulcerated, gangrened, II 400

in canticis, *sb.,* (Latin, "in Canticles", i.e., Solomon's poem in the Old Testament), III 732

capcious, *a.,* apt to understand, able to comprehend, III 563

carecte, *sb.,* mark, sign, character, IV 370

caren (caryne), *sb.,* dead, putrefying flesh of man or beast, VI 237, 246

cast(e), *v. tr.* and *intr.,* calculated astrologically, V 55; molded, formed, determined to do something, II 1243; VI 67

castyng, *a.,* resolving, contriving, planning, V 206

causell, *a.,* of the nature of cause and effect, V 15

champartye, *sb.,* originally, sharing of power or leadership; but here, due to Lydgate's misreading of Chaucer's *Knight's Tale,* 1.1091, it must be taken as meaning contest, rivalry, striving, III 981

champclos, *sb.,* a combat field, ground set aside for jousting, IV 306

chare, *sb.,* chariot; *fig.,* of the sun, III 1572; IV 3

chaundeleris, *sb. pl.,* stands or supports for a candle; a candelstick, a chandelier, VI 446

chere, *sb.,* disposition, frame of mind, mood, especially as showing itself by external demeanour, V 143, 221, 301, 329, 334, 409, 664; VI 104, 185, 192

chese (chees), *v. tr.,* to choose, select, III 275, 1603

chevalre, *sb.,* band, host, army, chivalry, III 482

cheyne, *sb.,* a chain; *fig.,* a binding or restraining force, II 774; V 348

childe, *v. intr.,* to bear a child, give birth, III 567, 1091

childyng, *vbl. sb.,* child-bearing, parturition, delivery, VI 68, 75

chose, *ppl. a.,* chosen, selected, III 1767

circumcide, *ppl.,* circumcisede, *v. tr.,* to circumcise; *fig.,* to free oneself from vice, IV 28, 66, 150, 385

clennesse, *sb.,* purity, chastity, cleanness, III 187, 240, 363, 781, 787

clepe and call, *v. tr.,* summon, cite (Scotch Law, NED), V 617

clepid, *pt. ppl.,* called by the name of, called, named, V 532

clipsyng, *vb. sb.,* overshadowing, eclipsing, III 884, 1030, 1246, 1758

Cloto, *sb.,* one of the three Fates, III 864 (see note, p. 697).

clowris, *sb., pl.,* grassy ground, sward, turf, V 411

clyptyke lyne (eclyptic line), *sb.,* the great circle of the celestial sphere which is the apparent orbit of the sun. So called because eclipses can occur only when the moon is on or near this line. Also, the great circle or terrestrial sphere which at any moment lies in the plane of the celestial ecliptic, I 33

collusion, *sb.,* underhand, scheming, fraud, a trick or ambiguity in words or reasoning. II 1366; V 171

compace, *v. tr.,* to encircle, surround, enwrap, III 851; *sb.,* the compass, the four directions, III 1333

compendious, *a.,* concise, brief, IV 20

concerne, *v. tr.,* ponder, consider, III 348

coniecte, *sb.,* device, contrivance, V 202

coniunede, *pt. ppl.,* joined together, connected, united, VI 416

consecrate, *ppl. a.,* devoted to, consecrated to, III 1073

conseyte, *sb.,* opinion, idea, judgment, III 1126

consistorye, *sb.,* gathering, assembly, III 1173

conuersacion, *sb.,* mode or course of life; the action of living or having one's being in a place or among persons, V 277

coode, *sb.,* pitch, cobbler's wax, V 567

co(o)ste, *sb.,* country, coast, II 944

copeȝ, *sb. pl.,* copes, cloak, canopy of night, I 160

corage, *sb.,* heart, spirit, mind, III 711, 742

corden (accorde), *v. intr.,* to reconcile, II 154

corteyne, *v. tr.,* to shrowd, cover as with a curtain, III 1129

corven, *ppl. a.,* cut, carved, III 668, 675, 686, 696; IV 32

coste, *sb.,* side (French *côtè*), III 233, 686, 1377, 1419; VI 13

couerte, *sb.,* shelter; in the phrase **"in couerte"**: secretely, III 887

counterpayse, *v. tr.,* to weight against, put in the balance against, II 1645

covenable, *a.,* suitable, becoming, fitting, IV 301

croppe, *sb.,* terminal bud of an herb or flower, top of a branch, head of a tree, III 1255

crovne, *sb.,* top of the head, vertex, pate, III 677, 1214, 1618

crymesyne, *a.,* crimson, V 361

cueme (queme), *v. tr.,* please, gratify, be acceptable, VI 420

cure, *sb.,* care, heed, concern, providence, (Lat: *cura*), III 376, 538, 1340; IV 354; V 261, 678; VI 181. Otherwise it has the usual meaning of "cure".

customable, a., customary, usual, regular, III 1324

dar, *v. tr.* and *intr.,* to dare, be bold, III 854

darith(e), *v. intr.,* lies hid, lurks, V 176, 186

darreyne, *v. tr.,* to settle, arbitrate, IV 307

daungerles, *a.,* without danger, free from danger (earliest use according to NED), II 337

daunte, *v. tr.,* vanquish, subdue, control, quell, III 1407; VI 223, 259

dawe, *v. intr.,* to dawn, grow light, III 602, 1569

debonayre, *a.,* gracious, kindly, gentle, III 251, 267, 690; VI 325

declyne, *v. intr.,* turn or bend aside, deviate, turn away, V 605; *sb.,* of the sun or day: the action of sinking towards its setting or close, V 62

defaced, *pt. pl.,* defaced, destroyed the reputation or credit of, discredited, defamed, II 199

degre, *sb.,* a stage or position in the scale of dignity or rank; relative social or official rank, grade, order, estate, station, V 225, 355, 390, 677

dele, *sb.,* part, portion, deal, III 156, 520, 787; V 162

demayne, *sb., trans.* and *fig.,* possession, dominion, power, V 345

deme, *v. tr.,* to sit in judgment upon, to think, be of the opinion, decree, ordain, III 1524; IV 404; V 593, 598

demenyng, *v. refl.,* conduct oneself, V 336

depure(y)d(e), *ppl. a.,* freed from impurity, cleansed, purified, II 1484; III 1025, 1770

derne, *a.,* intimate, confidential, trustworthy, III 500

desert, *sb.,* worthiness of reward, deserving, worth, II 1433

deuer, *sb.,* a dutiful act of civility or respect, V 173

devour, *sb.,* that which one ought to do or has to do; duty, business, appointed task, VI 347

devoyde, *v. tr.,* to do away with, get rid of, III 126, 718

devyse, dyvyse, *v. intr.,* set forth in detail, recount, describe; *v. tr.,* order, appoint, divide, separate, part, distribute; *sb.,* something artistically devised or framed, V 203, 230, 253, 383, 504; VI 45, 67, 366

dewe (dwe), *a.,* that is owing or payable, V 107, 244, 379

deynous, *a.,* deignous, disdainful, haughty, II 46

deyuere, *sb.,* duty, obligation; cf. NED, *s.v.,* under the French form *devoir,* III 1063

dight, *v. tr.,* order, keep in order, manage, govern, VI 148

digne, *a.,* worthy, fitting becoming, IV 366

discripcion, *sb.,* enrollment, listing; of. cf. Lat. *descriptio,* III 53, 67, 79

discryvyng, *vbl. sb.,* registration, enrollment, III 59

discured, *ppl.* **discure;** *v. tr.,* to discover, make known, reveal, perceive, divulge, II 1482

disease, *sb.,* discomfort, misery, trouble, III 468

disioynt, *sb.,* state of emotional excitement, perplexity, distress, II 1406

disporte, *sb.,* diversion, recreation, source of pleasure, III 270

distyllyng, *v. intr.,* trickling down (as tears), III 123

do, *v. causal* with *obj.* and *inf.,* to cause to be done, to make (someone or something) act, III 706

dom(e), *sb.,* judgment, decision, sentence, III 1505; IV 214, 336; V 594, 602

dominacion, *sb.,* Dominations, one of the nine choirs of angels, III 829, 1382

donion, *sb.,* dwelling-place, habitation, III 1636

donne, *a.,* dark, beclouded, dun, III 1128, 1399

dool, *sb.,* sorrow, grief, III 591

doubleness, *sb.,* duplicity, deceitfulness, treachery, V 184

dresse, *v. intr.,* and *refl.,* advance, proceed, set oneself to, III 140, 166, 416, 585; *v. tr.,* direct, guide, turn I 397; V 628

duete, *sb.,* homage, submission, due respect, reverence, V 249

duryng, *ppl. a.,* lasting, persisting, enduring, III 486

edyfye, *v. tr.,* to build, construct, III 1628

eere, *sb.,* head of grain, ear of corn, IV 275

elate, *a.,* lofty, proud, V 351

empryse (enprise), *sb.,* undertaking, event, plan, enterprise, II 413, 1101; IV 161, 308

empysperye, *sb.,* hemisphere, I 7

enbrasyng, *vbl. sb.,* wrapping, circling about, V 348

enbroyded, *pt. ppl.,* embroidered, V 383

enchac(s)e, *v. tr.,* drive, banish, disperse, scatter, II 1276; III 576, 1519; VI 47

enchasede, *ppl. a.,* brightened, beautified, III 1131

endelong, *prep.* and *adv.,* along, lengthwise, at full length, III 1106

endi(y)te, *v. intr.,* put into words, relate, describe, tell, express, III 910, 1104; IV 18; V 211, 491

engendrure, *sb.,* given existence to, being produced, II 884

engyne, *sb.,* cunning, trickery; ingenuity, skill; in a bad sense, snare, wile, II 1535; III 1351, 1698

enlumyne (enlumen), *v. tr.,* to light up, illumen, III 169, 583, 1029

ennoysed, *ppl. a.,* confused, bewildered, as by darkness, II 178, 1125. See NED, s. v. "enoyse", where it is noted that this use of the word is peculiar to Lydgate.

ennuede, *pt. ppl.,* shaded, blended in colors, I 332

entayle, *sb.,* pattern, form design, plan, III 1333, 1346; V 374

entendement (intendment), *sb.,* the faculty or action of understanding, II 75

entente, *sb.,* manner, method, intention, III 39, 407, 625, 913, 1033, 1081; IV 290

entere, *a.,* whole, entire, intense, sincere, satisfying, II 717, 761; V 495

entermellyde, *ppl. a.,* fused, intertwined, intermingled, III 951

entretid, *v. intr.,* entered into negotiations, V 156

envi(y)ron, *adv.,* nearby, round about, close by, in the area; cf. French *environ,* III 104, 169, 867, 1197; V 145; VI 422, 431

erbor (harbour), *sb.,* shelter, place of sojourn, lodging, resting-place, II 804

erecte, *a.,* lifted up, elevated, raised, III 252

espye, *v. tr.,* discern, discover, catch sight of, V 519; VI 240, 261

estate3, *sb. pl.,* outward displays of one's condition; grandeur, pomp; *sb. sg.,* status, standing, position, degree of rank, V 370, 583

euer among, *adv. phr.,* from time to time, occasionally, III 1673

every dele, *adv.,* in every way or part, completely, III 1434

execute, *v. tr.,* carry into effect, follow out, IV 95

exployt, *sb.,* an enterprise, project, V 170

exployte, *v. tr.,* to cause to succeed, prosper, II 435

face, *sb.,* phase, position, III 71; impudence, effrontery; countenance, V 201, 221, 301; VI 104

fage, *v. intr.,* to fage from the truth (NED, to coax, flatter), II 1537

faine, feyne, *v. tr.,* put a false appearance upon; disguise, dissemble, conceal, II 1537; V 191, 562; VI 213

falle, *v. intr.,* to happen occur, befall, III 474, 1713

fane, *sb.,* (Lat., *fanum,* temple) a temple. See NED, *s.v.,* "fane", in which Lydgate's use of this word in the *Life of Our Lady* is noted. III 1082, 1228

faute3, *sb.,* defect, imperfection, V 591, 600

faye, *sb.,* faith, V 385

fayne, feyne, *v. tr.,* to pretend, simulate, indulge in fiction, II 1537; III 430, 559, 1545

feffed, *pt. ppl.,* given legal possession, allowed to use, II 1050

fel (fele, felle), *a.,* cruel, savage, fierce, III 324, 341, 360, 535, 724, 931; IV 175

fere (feer), *sb.,* company, crowd; **in fere,** together, in common, all together, I 601; II 47, 508, 867; V 40, 67, 468, 665

ferre (fer), *a.,* far, distant, III 216, 300, 909, 953, 1186; IV 113, 182, 339; V 527

ferre, ferye, *sb.,* a week-day according to the Roman calendar, (Lat., *feria*), IV 10; VI 204

ferforth, fer furthe, *adv.,* as long as (in reference to degree and extent), II 705; VI 251

fervence, *sb.,* warmth of the emotions, intensity of feeling or desire, fervency, V 556

fette, *ppl. a.,* brought, fetched, III 235

fine, *sb.,* aim, purpose, object, V 63

flete, *v. intr.,* to float, III 803

Flora, *sb.,* goddess of Spring, III 1269

floure delys, *sb.,* the fleur-de-lis, lily, III 730

flowre, *sb.,* "bear the flour", to gain victory, to have preeminence (NED 6b), II 749

flume, *sb.,* a stream, a river, V 487

folde, *sb.,* time(s), III 906

fomen, *sb. pl.,* foes in war; here, the vices of malice and pride, V 552

fone, *sb. pl.,* enemies, foes, III 871, 1493; IV 389

foyson, *sb.,* plenty abundance, II 858; V 239, 528

foryetylnesse, *sb.,* oblivion, forgetfulness, III 1246; V 415

frele, *a.,* frail, weak, III 784, 997

frowarde, *a.,* obstinate, perverse, wicked, III 125

fulsomnesse, *sb.,* abundance, plenty, III 1661

furthe, *adv., prep.,* and *sb.,* of movement or direction: forwards; of extent in time: onwards, immediately afterwards and continuously, V 115, 120; VI 379

fygured, *ppl. a.,* allegorical, mystical, symbolical, III 166; IV 267

fyne, *a.,* clear, pure, of good quality, III 865, 1265

fyne, *sb.,* the end, finish, III 1195

fyne, *v. tr.,* to put an end to, stop, arrest, I 30; III 131, 865, 969, 1384, 1420; IV 360

gadre, *v. tr.,* assemble, gather, III 1508

garnement, *sb.,* clothing, garment, III 784

garner, *sb.,* storage-place, storehouse, III 799

garnet apull, *sb.,* pomegranate, III 754, 760

gavel, *sb.,* a quantity of grain cut and made ready for the sheaf, III 785, 790

gedrede, *pt. ppl.,* gathered, VI 394

glade, *v. tr.,* to gladden, make joyful, III 177, 727, 1169

glede, *sb.,* a gleed, live coal, II 735

gostly, *a.,* spiritual, pertaining to the soul, IV 172

govndy, *a.,* bleared, cloudy, II 936

graffe, *sb.,* a graft, scion, bud, III 1001, 1615

graue, *sb.,* buried, V 411

gray, *quasi-sb.,* an old man, III 868

graye, *sb.,* gray fur; usually understood to be of badger-skin, V 384

grayne (greyn), *sb.,* section of fruit, III 754, 757. Otherwise has usual meaning of "corn".

gre, *sb.,* gree, one of a flight of steps, I 193

grevaunce, *sb.,* distress, injury, harm, III 739; IV 231

grevous, *sb.,* hardships, sufferings, troubles, II 558

grocche, *v. intr.,* to complain, murmur, III 1437

grochyng, *pr. ppl.* of **grocche,** *q.v.,* III 51

gye, *v. tr.,* govern, rule, direct one's course, II 537; III 432, 1652, 1799; IV 332; V 655

gyse, guyse, *sb.,* fashion, style, I 665

gyvede, *ppl. a.,* bound, chained, constrained, IV 158

halfendele, *adv.,* partly, half, halfway, III 1366

halowe, *v. tr.,* to make holy, consecrate, hallow, III 1479; IV 367

happe, *sb.,* fortune, luck, chance, III 1345

hardy, *a.,* rash, heedless, III 33, 1232

harmeleȝ, *a.,* free from guilt, innocent, V 602

hast, *sb.,* rashness, V 601

hatte, *v. intr.,* to be called, to bear the name of, I 119

haunce, *v. tr.,* exalt, raise, celebrate, III 1051

hele, *sb.,* well-being, health, prosperity, III 722, 1737; IV 179

helyth, *v. tr.,* heals, cures, IV 180

herarchy (hierarchy), *sb.,* each of the three divisions of angels, every one compromising three orders, in the system of Dionysius the Areopogite, II 123

herbe, *sb.,* vegetation, foliage, grass, III 1274

herbygage, *sb.,* shelter, accommodation, III 159

herodis, herodeȝ, *sb.,* Herod, V 188, 696

heste, *sb.,* bidding, command, promise, III 674, 1308

hight, *v. tr.,* is called, named, bears the name of, III 1427; in the sense of tell: bid, command, III 681, 1478

hole, *a.,* free from damage, defect; untainted, VI 402

holde, *sb.,* house, dwelling-place, temporary abode, I 360; VI 443

holy, *adv.,* wholly, completely, III 602, 830, 979, 1652; IV 210, 263, 338, 400

hool, *a.,* of will, intention, affection: full, complete, VI 429

houe, *v. intr.,* to hover over, V 210

huyste (huste), *ppl. a.,* hushed, quiet, III 1, 179

hydre, *adv.,* hither, toward this place, IV 73

indiction, *sb.,* a special year used in determining dates in the Roman calendar. See note for l. 75, III, p. 690.

in fere (infere), *a.,* in company, together, IV 382

iloke, *pt. ppl.,* locked up, secured, II 518

inly, *adv.,* inwardly, internally, III 735; IV 202

intoxicate, *a.,* poisonous, full of venom, III 1700

ioyne (yoyne), *v. tr.,* command, charge, impose an obligation on, III 1477, 1796

issewe, *sb.,* product, end-result, lineal descendants, III 1409

kalendes, *sb. pl.,* the first (sometimes the third) day of the Roman month, the calends, II 1612; III 451

kenne, *v. tr.,* know, make known, direct, guide, teach, III 1651; V 455

kever, *v. tr.,* to cover, V 364

kynde, *a.,* innate, inherent; *sb.,* nature; a natural group of animals; "of kynde", *adv. phr.,* naturally; III 213, 563, 569, 746, 771, 777, 784, 790, 986, 998, 1046, 1248, 1403, 1721; IV 137; V 177, 307; VI 261, 293

kyndely, *a.,* acceptable, agreeable, pleasant, genial VI 216

kynrde, *sb.,* race, family, or stock, from which one springs, V 21, 36; VI 174

kyt (kytte), *v. tr.,* to cut, sever, cut away, IV 73, 83, 258, 376; V 375

Lachasis, *sb.,* one of the three Fates, Lachesis, III 865 (see note, p. 697).

lak, *v. tr.,* to blame, censure; want, need, III 1371; IV 160

laude, *sb.,* praise, high commendation, VI 1

laudes, *sb.,* (Latin plural), praises; Lauds, the second unit of the Roman Breviary, III 832

lees, *sb.,* falsehood, lying, II 689

leesyng, *vbl. sb.,* diminution, lessening, losing, III 1758

lese (lee), *sb.,* falsehood, lie, III 16, 551

lesith, _v. tr.,_ diminishes, loses, weakens, lessens, III 1245

lete, _v. tr.,_ stop, hinder, IV 218

leve, _v. intr.,_ continue in life; live out, survive, V 685

leven, (levyn), _sb.,_ levin, flash of lightning, bright flame, I 860; II 608; III 1211

leyser, _sb.,_ leisure, V 425

liggen (liggest), _v. intr.,_ to lie, to rest, to be in a prostrate position, III 274, 281; V 411

light, _a., joyful,_ light-hearted, III 447, 465, 615, 1378, 1489, 1555, 1668

list, _v. tr.,_ desire of wish for something, VI 132

lode sterre, _sb., fig._ a "guiding star"; that on which one's attention or hopes are fixed, V 700

loute (lowte), _v. intr.,_ and _tr.,_ to bend to, bow before, submit to, III 333, 872, 1358; V 376

lucyne, _sb.,_ the moon, goddess of the moon, III 4; IV 6

lust (luste), _v. impers._ with _dat.,_ it pleases; _pers._ to desire, be pleased to, III 11, 147, 257, 275, 290, 372, 450, 565, 621, 910, 959, 1304, 1547, 1604, 1667, 1671, 1687; IV 65, 165, 296; V 90, 111, 506, 658; VI 142

lustely, _ad.,_ with spirit, vigorously, joyously, III 919, 1156

lustre, _sb.,_ a period of five years, VI 320

lusty, _a.,_ joyful merry, jocund, V 221

lye, _sb.,_ falsehood; in _adv. phr.,_ **"withouten any lye"**: truly, without fable, V 510

lyen right, _adv. phr.,_ straight, direct, III 945, 1160; V 209

lyte, _adv.,_ a little bit, a small degree, IV 19; V 318

maieste, _sb.,_ majesty; greatness and glory of God; also, an image in religious art (from OF. _maysté_) ; see NED, _s.v.,_ "Majesty", 7a. III 493, 1335

mali(ci)ously, _adv.,_ in a spirit of ill-will; wickedly V 200

mancion (mansion), _sb.,_ dwelling-place, shelter, temporary abode, III 171, 302, 403

manere, _sb.,_ the state of the case with respect to a person, thing or event; the character, disposition, or nature of, V 82, 152, 248, 328; VI 76

manne, _sb.,_ manna, food showered from heaven, III 1723, 1737

martren, _sb.,_ the skins or fur of the animal now called marten, V 385

mate, _a.,_ Ger. _matt,_ weary, exhausted, faint, III 156; V 660

maugre, _prep.,_ French _malgré,_ in spite of, III 874, 879, 1448; IV 315; V 198

mawmetrye, _sb.,_ idolatry, paganism, heathen worship, III 1316

mede, _sb.,_ reward, compensation, IV 282; VI 425

mede (medyth), _v. tr._ and _intr.,_ to reward, compensate, III 1783

medelede, *pt. ppl.,* mixed, mingled; combined, blended V 567

medelyng, *pr. ppl.,* having sexual intercourse, VI 30

mene, *sb.,* a mediator between God (or Christ) and man, V 688

merye, *a.,* happy, joyful, bright, I 6

meynt, *pt. ppl.* of **meng,** mingled, mixed; constr. "with", I 328; V 594; VI 428

more, *sb.,* delay; cf. Lat. *mora;* II 427

mote (moot), *v. modal,* expresses not only possibility but permission, and even obligation, III 977

mow, *v. intr.,* to be able to, possess ability, II 337

myscheve, *sb.,* misfortune, trouble, woe, III 724, 580, 1712; IV 342, 360

mysse, *v. tr.,* to lack, be without, IV 284; V 583

ne, *conj.* nor, III 398, 887, 606, 993, 999, 1061, 1245, 1238; as a negative particle, III 214, 398, 612, 764, 765, 1245, 1554; IV 273

neyghen (neyeth), *v. intr.,* draw near, approach, IV 3

norchyng, *vbl. sb.,* food, sustenance, III 1688

occian, *sb.,* the ocean, V 21

Olympiades, *sb. pl.,* a period of four years between the Olympic games, III 19

or, *conj., adv.,* before, ere, III 429, 655, 865, 932, 1113, 1144, 1520, 1562

orlage, *sb.,* an instrument for telling the hours, a time-piece, a dial, hour-glass, clock, II 849

orytorye (oratorye), *sb.,* shrine, chapel, I 865; II 1596

othir, *conj.,* either; used correlatively with "or", III 1096

ournede, *ppl. a.,* horned, having horns, IV 8

outerage, *sb.,* arrogance, presumption, injustice, III 679; IV 195

owher, *adv.,* anywhere, IV 177

paas, *sb.,* gait, step, walk, way of walking or progression, VI 314

palestre, *sb.,* arena, a wrestling place, IV 305

pall, *sb.,* scarf, cloak, III 900

paragall, *a.,* fully equal, I 82; **peregall (peragall),** III 1188, 1237; V 310

parede, *pt. ppl.,* ready, prepared, formed, shaped, VI 74

parell, *sb.,* danger, peril, VI 276

partye, *sb.,* part, section, portion, III 1155; IV 137; **"in partye",** *adv. phr.,* partly, V 681

passyng, *ppl. a.,* surpassing, preeminent, III 730

pavys, *sb.,* large convex shield, said to have been developed in Pavia, IV 232

pawmes, *sb. pl.,* palms of the hands, III 1682

pay, *sb.,* pleasure, liking, satisfaction, so as to please (God), I 458

payage, *sb.,* payment, as of a tribute, III 1323

paynym(e), *a.,* pagan, heathen, III 1294; IV 118; VI 368

persaunt, *a.,* penetrative, keen, piercing, V 84

phares, *sb. pl.* See NED, *s. v.,* "phare", a lighthouse or beacon for mariners (Fr. *phare,* Lat. *pharus*). According to NED, this must be the first use in English. III 129

plant, *v. tr.,* to bewail, deplore, mourn, VI 224

plattely (platly), *adv.,* flatly, plainly, without quibbling, I 335; II 42; III 1217; V 45

pleyne, *v. intr.* and *refl.,* to murmur, complain (Fr. *se plaindre*), III 404; IV 178, 188; V 644, 669

pollute, *a.,* polluted, defiled, III 1544

polymete, *a.,* vari-colored, III 773

poole, *sb.,* the North Pole, I 10

porte, *sb.,* dignified carriage, stately bearing, V 335

possede, *v. tr.,* to own, possess, III 1640

powste, *sb.,* power, authority, II 584; V 654

poyntell, *sb.,* a stylus, pen, II 793, 1661

prees, *sb.,* crowd, throng, multitude, I 701; II 808; III 163

preve, *sb.,* proof, demonstration, III 366

prime, *sb.,* Prime, the first of the Little Hours of the Roman Breviary, the time at which it is said in choir; six o'clock in the morning, II 1189; III 1113

proloynede, *pt. ppl.,* put far away; removed, VI 423

pryse, *sb.,* reward, cost, price, prize, III 697; praise, VI 1

purviaunce, *sb.,* direction, government, providence of God (see note for l. 216, I, p. 672), I 216, 653, 818

pyment, *sb.,* a drink composed of wine sweetened with honey and flavored with spices (see NED, *s. v.,* "Piment", 1 a), III 237, 1662

pypens, *sb., pl.,* pepin, seed of a fleshy fruit, III 747

queme (quemen), *v. tr.,* to please, gratify, to be acceptable (to a person), I 468; II 237; III 962

quere, *sb.,* choir, chorus, III 832

queynt, *a.,* beautiful, pretty, fine, dainty, VI 430

quyte, *v. refl.,* with "of": to clear oneself; prove one's innocence, do one's part, III 34, 190

rakke, *sb.,* cloud formation; a rack; a frame made with upright bars of wood or metal to hold fodder for horses or cattle, III 135; V 633, 653

raught, *pt. ppl.,* of **reche,** *v. tr.,* to lay hold of, seize, extend to, III 965; *v. intr.,* reached, came into contact with, extended to (of inanimate objects), II 609

rawes, *sb.,* rays or beams (of the sun, etc.), I 159

reame, *sb.,* a kingdom, sphere, domain, province, V 205

reccles, *a.,* heedless, imprudent, III 98

receyte, *sb.,* a place or reception or accommodation for persons, a place of refuge, I 360

recone(y)saunce, *sb.,* acknowledgment, recognition of obligation, III 35; V 252

reddour, *sb.,* severity, strictness, rigor, IV 357

redresse, *v. tr.,* set aright, do away with, atone, III 591

reedyfye, *v. tr.,* rebuild, reconstruct, III 1577

refute, *sb.,* shelter, protection, one who gives aid and protection, succour, I 204; III 752, 1696, 1740, 1745

regal(y)e, *sb.,* government, rule, away, III 1315, 1526, 1579; V 106, 656

releve, *v. intr.,* rise again, VI 167

remys, *sb.,* realms, kingdoms, IV 199

repayre, *sb.,* resort, dwelling-place, goal; the art of making one's way to a place; *v. intr.,* go, betake oneself to or from a place or person, III 1627; V 206, 436, 449

resorte, *sb.,* refuge, source of comfort or assistance, III 271

reuthe, *sb.,* pity, compassion, mercy III 336

revers, *sb.,* opposition, antagonism, III 879

reynes, *sb.,* a kind of fine linen or lawn made at Rennes in Brittainy, V 375

by revolucion, *adv. phr.,* in due course of time (in reference to return or recurrence of a point or period of time); the lapse of certain time, V 72; VI 311

reyse, *v. tr.,* to exalt, magnify, extol, III 1644

right, *a.,* straight, direct, III 100

rought (recche), *v. intr., pr. sing.* **recche;** *pt. sing.,* **rouȝte;** *pt. ppl.* **rouȝt;** to reck, to be troubled thereby, to be anxious about, to take heed to, I 236

routhe, *sb.,* mischief, calamity, ruin, V 580

rudeness, *sb.,* ignorance, lack of education, III 157

rust, *sb., fig.,* moral decay, corruption, IV 293

sacrary, *sb., fig.,* a temple, shrine, sanctuary, VI 14

saluede, *v. tr.,* saluted, greeted, III 948

samyte, *sb.,* a rich silk fabric worn in the middle ages, sometimes interwoven with gold, V 362

sapience, *sb.,* wisdom, understanding, II 278, 525, 540, 1538

sat. *v. impers.,* in phr.: "**hit sat ryȝt well**": it was fitting, proper, III 188, 197

sauf . . . vouche, *v. tr.,* vouchsafe, grant; used as a separable verb, III 1667

sau(w)ter, *sb.,* psalter, the psalms of David, II 132; III 597, 833; V 455

sawes, *sb. pl.,* sayings, proverbs, prophecies, III 1053

scale, *sb.,* a ladder; in figurative and allusive uses, freq. with references to Jacob's ladder (*Gen.* XXVIII, 12), V 626

scarste, *sb.,* scarcity, dearth, famine, III 1716

see, *sb., transf.* and *fig.,* one's place of abode; esp. the dwelling place of a monarch, a god or the like, V 622; VI 437, 445

seler, *sb.,* a storage-room, cellar, III 1689, 1714

sely, *a.,* artless, simple, "silly", I 724; VI 459

semblynesse, *sb.,* beauty of face or figure, V 406

sencere, sensure, *sb.,* thurible, incense-pot, censer, III 1222; V 569

in sentence, *prep. phr.,* in substance. "Very common in Lydgate, often as a mere expletive", (NED). V 502

sentens, *sb.,* significance, meaning, intelligence, sound judgment, I 413

servage, *sb.,* servitude, bondage, III 1222

serve, *v. tr.,* to keep, observe; Lat. *servare,* IV 141

sewte, *sb.,* suit royal, suit of court. In the phrase "**for a manere sewte**", attending at court, V 248

sewyng. *pr. ppl.,* following, V 428, 595

sheltroun, *sb.,* close-ranked body of armed men, phalanx, III 930

shene, *a.* and *adv.,* bright, resplendent, beautiful, attractive; by analogy, shining, I 48; III 303, 337, 1568, 1756, 1760; V 691; VI 454

shope, *v. tr.,* prepared, V 115

shrowde, *sb.,* clothing, vesture; *transf.* and *fig.,* esp. the vesture in which the world or the things of nature are clothed, V 61

sikernesse, sidernes, *sb.,* the state of being secure, freedom from danger, assurance, security, I 396; IV 238; V 417

sittyng, *ppl.* a., becoming, befitting, proper, suitable, V 114

skalis, *sb. pl.,* shells, outer coverings, husks, III 747, 756, 760

skye, *sb.,* clouds, fog, III 1443, 1525; V 573

skylle, *sb.,* reason, III 256, 1226, 1239; VI 305

slyghtly, *a.,* marked or characterized by, displaying or indicating artifice, craft or cunning; of an insidious or wily nature, V 190

smert(e), *sb.,* mental pain or suffering; grief, sorrow, affliction, V 398; VI 188; *v. intr.,* to ache, cause distress, be painful, III 770

socour, *sb.,* help, succor, III 408, 895, 1475; IV 173, 326; *v. tr.,* to help, assist, III 420, 1064

solempne, *a.,* performed with due ceremony and reverence; having a religious character; sacred, VI 356

sool, *a.,* alone, III 221

sort, *sb.,* the choice resulting from a casting of lots, V 70

sother, *adv.,* more truly, with more truth, III 1372

sothefastely, *adv.,* truthfully, truly, veritably, VI 416

sothefastnesse, *sb.,* truth; truthfulness or veracity; "in sothefastnesse" in sooth, truly, V 215, 349; VI 363

sothely, *adv.,* truly, verily, assuredly, certainly, really, indeed, V 196, 420, 484, 674; VI 175, 288

in sotheness, *adv. phr.,* in truth, reality, V 309, 596

sothfast(e), *a.,* truly or actually that which the name implies; true, real, veritable, very; said esp. of God or of the persons of the Trinity, V 259, 499, 632; VI 286, 435

sotyll, *a.,* able, clever, skillful, III 1347

soukyng, *pr. ppl.,* (of an infant) nursing at the breast, V 619

spere, *sb.,* the orbit of a planet, V 96; VI 452; the sting of a reptile or insect, V 397

spousayle, *sb.,* espousal, marital engagement, III 1008

stablenesse, *sb.,* the quality or condition of being stable, V 585

stacion, *sb.,* station, one of the churches in Rome to which the faithful go in procession on certain days of the year; also, position, astronomical location, III 72

stellefied, *ppl. a.,* deified, regarded as a celestial being, set among the stars, III 1116

stere, *v. refl.,* to control oneself, restrain one's emotions, IV 39

sterne, *a.,* fierce, severe, harsh, III 102; IV 251

sterue, *v. intr.,* to die, IV 378

stoke, *sb.,* wood; trunk or stem of a living tree, III 947

stole, *sb.,* neck-band, scarf, shawl, stole, III 899

stondyng at hir large, *adv. phr.,* standing at liberty, VI 63

stounde, *sb.,* a time, awhile, moment; cf. Germ. *stund,* III 1548

stound mele, *adv.,* from time to time, at intervals (see NED, *s. v.,* "stoundmeal"), II 1384

stye, *v. intr.,* to rise, ascend, III 151

stynte, *v. tr.,* to stop, put an end to, cause to cease, III 190, 768, 1134; IV 50

sue, *v. tr.,* follow, as a disciple or imitator, VI 369

sufferaunce, *sb.,* patient endurance, forebearance, VI 224

suffisaunce, *sb.,* plenty, sufficiency, III 737

supportayle, *sb.* support, source of security, IV 343

suquydre (surquydre), *sb.,* pride, presumption, arrogance, II 508; V 344

synke, *v. tr.,* to penetrate into, enter or be impressed in the mind or hear, II 1078

tapitis, *sb.,* tapestry, V 363

tarage, *sb.,* taste, flavor, V 515

tarteryne, *sb.,* a rich stuff, apparently of silk, imported from the East, probably from China through Tartary, V 359

tempre, *v. refl.,* to control oneself, govern oneself, III 50

tene, *sb.,* rage, malice, ill-will, grief, woe, III 502, 877, 1361; V 402

trace, *v. tr.* and *intr.,* take one's course, proceed, traverse, III 976; V 431

transmygracion, *sb.,* the Babylonian captivity of the Jews, III 1622

travers, *adv.,* across, in opposition to (cf. French *a travers*), III 1590

trayne, *sb.,* trap, snare, stratagem, trick, artifice, II 90

tresty, *a.,* variant of "trusty", V 384

troni, *pl.,* Lat. form of Thrones, one of the nine choirs of angels, III 829

tryacle, *sb.,* remedy against poison, medicine, I 344; III 1703

trystesse, *sb.,* sorrow, woe, I 205

tune, *sb.,* cask, barrel, tun, III 1690

twynne, *v. intr.,* to depart, go away, I 62

twynnyth, *v. intr.,* depart from, separate from, leave, III 264

uiage, *sb.,* journey, V 548

unconnyng, *sb.,* ignorance, lack of cunning or wit, III 401

underpight, *pt. ppl.,* supported, upheld, II 530

undirfong, *v. tr.,* to receive, accept, undertake, III 1619; IV 161

unethes, *adv.,* not easily, scarcely, hardly, V 658

unwarly, *adv.,* without warning, unexpectedly, III 101

unwrye, *ppl. a.,* revealed, laid bare, uncovered, III 137

upriste, *sb.,* the rising up (as of the sun), II 1570

usaunnce, *sb.,* habit, custom, wont, VI 377

vengeable, *a.,* bent on vengeance, vindictive, IV 348

ver (wer), *sb.,* springtime, I 65; VI 230

verre, *sb.,* glass, III 1018

virtutes, *sb., pl.,* Lat. form of Virtues, one of the nine choirs of angels, III 841

volunte, *sb.,* will, III 990

v(u)oyde (voide), *v. tr.,* to void, clear away, do away with, empty, I 49, 145, 150, 379; III 1168; VI 156, 224

vre (eure, ewre, ewere), *sb.,* destiny, fate, fortune, I 788; II 1444

wakir (waker), *a.,* unsleeping, vigilant, careful, I 415

wanhope, *sb.,* despair, hopelessness, IV 233

wantruste, *sb.,* lack of faith or confidence, doubt, III 382

waymentyng, *vbl. sb.,* lamentation, wailing, bitter sorrow, VI 226

wayte, *v. tr.,* to ambush, lie in wait for, IV 396

welden, *v. tr.,* to join together closely, bind, III 851

welfull, *a.,* wealful, gracious, favorable, I 848

wem, *sb.,* injury, harm, III 365

wemme, *sb.,* moral defilement, stain of sin, chiefly in phrase **"withouten wem"** (immaculate), II 526

wene, *ppl. a.,* supposed, believed, II 489; **wenyng,** *pr. ppl.,* supposing, imagining, expecting, hoping, VI 320

wene, *v. intr.,* diminish, decrease, become faint, want, III 1567; V 406, 507; to think, realize, be aware of, III 1372

wen(y)st, *v. tr.,* expect, anticipate, surmise, suspect, think possible or likely, V 189, 192

wer (werre), *sb.,* doubt, perplexity, uncertainty, I 626; II 733, 1601; III 971, 1136; war, III 19; **werre,** *a.,* cautious, wary, V 25

werkeman, *sb.,* in sense of skilled artisan, craftsman, III 1118, 1125

werreye, *v. intr.,* to make or declare war; *v. tr.,* to assault, attack, I 230; II 426; IV 265, 391

wexe, *v. intr.,* to grow, wax, to increase in size, II 780

whete, *sb.,* corn, grain, wheat, III 802

whette, *ppl. a.,* sharpened, whetted, III 655; IV 287

wight, *sb.,* person, III 202, 282, 421, 725, 743

wonne, *v. intr.,* to dwell, III 845, 1749

worthe, *v. tr.,* to pay divine honors to; to worship, V 222

wrest, *sb.,* twist, wrench, violent pull, IV 280

wroke, *v. tr.,* to punish or chastise (a person) : to visit with retributive punishment, V 206

wrysting, *ppl. a.,* that declines, from the meridian towards the west (said chiefly of the sun when it is nearing the western horizon, NED), V 62

wynde (wende), *v. intr.,* to go, travel, wend, IV 403

wyssen, *v. tr.,* to direct, lead, guide, instruct, IV 285, 329

wyte, *v. tr.,* to be in fault, to be blamed, II 1395

yfynede, *ppl. a.,* refined, purified, III 907

yerde, *sb.,* a rod, stick, I 658, 660, 667, 679

ymouled, *pt. ppl.* (moul), grown mouldy, made mouldy, II 308

ympne, *sb.,* hymn, song, III 547

yore, *adv.,* long since, long ago, in phr. "yore agon": since long ago, II 1626

yschrouded (shrouded), *ppl. a.,* concealed, veiled, enveloped in a shroud, II 480, 1466